HOLT
PSYCHOLOGY:
Principles In Practice

CONTENTS

...he Author

...pencer A. Rathus, Ph.D.

...r. Spencer A. Rathus obtained his Ph.D. fro...
...t Albany. He has experience as a clinical ps...
...rofessor, researcher, and author. As a clinic...
...vorked at a community mental health cent...
...ractice, and with college students. He is cu...
...aculty at New York University. As a research...
...shed some 30 articles in professional journ...
...he widely used Rathus Assertiveness Sched...
...merous college textbooks in a number of a...
...uctory psychology textbook, *Psychology: C*...
...n edition.
...he American Psychological Association, serv...
...ociation Task Force on Diversity Issues at th...
...of Education in Psychology, and speaks at a...

...a Dionisi

...ration Source

...nston

11 12 13 14 15 16 - 1678 - 15 14 13
4500230741

Psychology and Your World

CAREERS IN PSYCHOLOGY

EXPLORING DIVERSITY

PSYCHOLOGY IN THE WORLD TODAY

Case Studies

CASE STUDIES AND OTHER TRUE STORIES

READINGS IN PSYCHOLOGY

ANALYZING PRIMARY SOURCES " "

Technology Activities

internet connect

Skill-Building Activities

SKILLS HANDBOOK

BUILDING SOCIAL STUDIES SKILLS

PSYCHOLOGY IN ACTION UNIT SIMULATIONS

CHARTS AND GRAPHS

Multifactorial Model of Schizophrenia

Genetic Factors

Complications during pregnancy and birth

Stress

SCHIZOPHRENIA

Viral infections

Family environment

How to Use Your Textbook

Use the chapter opener to get an overview of what you will learn.

A Day in the Life appears at the beginning of each chapter. This feature illustrates psychological concepts by following the experiences of teens in everyday life.

Key Terms lists important concepts you will encounter as you read the chapter. The terms will be defined in context.

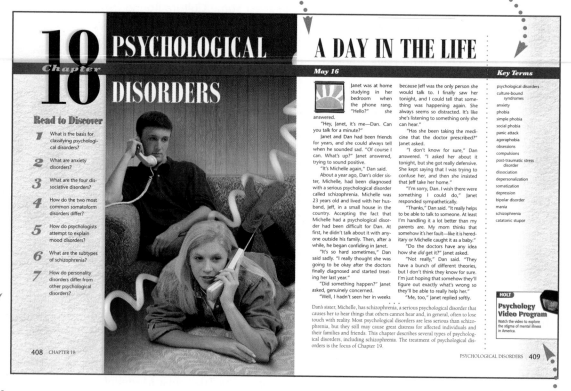

Read to Discover questions begin each chapter of *Holt Psychology: Principles in Practice.* These questions serve as your guide as you read the chapter. Keep them in mind as you explore the chapter content.

Psychology Video Program helps students connect topics in psychology to events in the current world (available on VHS and on DVD).

Use these built-in tools to read for understanding.

TRUTH OR fiction?

Read the following statements about psychology. Do you think they are true or false? You will learn whether each statement is true or false as you read the chapter.

- Very few people are actually affected by psychological disorders.
- People sometimes forget a very traumatic event as a way of coping with the psychological stress of the trauma.
- People whose illnesses are "all in their heads" do not really have symptoms of disease.
- Depression is the most common type of psychological disorder.
- Some people never feel guilty, even when they commit serious crimes.

Truth or Fiction? questions, which are woven throughout the chapters, provide an engaging way to explore many interesting facets of psychology.

Estimates suggest that about one out of every three people in the United States will experience a psychological disorder at some point in life.

SECTION 7
What Are Psychological Disorders?

Psychology is the scientific study of behavior and mental processes. **Psychological disorders** are behavior patterns or mental processes that cause serious personal suffering or interfere with a person's ability to cope with everyday life.

Many people believe that psychological disorders are uncommon, affecting relatively few individuals. It is true that the great majority of people are never admitted to mental hospitals, and most people never seek the help of psychologists or psychiatrists. And although many people have relatives they consider eccentric, few people have family members they consider to be truly abnormal.

Estimates suggest, however, that almost one third of the adults in the United States have experienced some type of psychological disorder (Goldstein et al., 1986). In addition to the many people with substance abuse problems, 23 percent of people in the United States experience some type of psychological disorder in their lifetime. In any given month, the figure is approximately 13 percent (Regier, 1993). As Dan's family discovered, psychological disorders can affect almost anyone.

A DAY IN THE LIFE

410 CHAPTER 18

TRUTH OR fiction? • REVISITED •

It is not true that very few people are actually affected by psychological disorders. Millions of people are affected by psychological disorders during their lifetimes.

Identifying Psychological Disorders

Deciding whether particular behaviors, thoughts, or feelings are "normal" or "abnormal" can be difficult. What is normal is often equated with what is average for the majority of people. Using this definition of normality, deviation from the majority becomes the primary criterion for abnormality.

People with psychological disorders usually do not differ much from "normal" people. In fact, the primary difference is the simple exaggeration of certain behaviors or mental processes. For example, laughing is a normal and healthy response to humorous situations. However, someone who laughs all the time, even in very inappropriate situations, might be considered abnormal.

Symptoms of Psychological Disorders

Several behavior patterns and mental processes may suggest that an individual has a psychological

Charts, graphs and other visuals illustrate the concepts discussed in the chapter.

Questions help ensure that you understand the information in the visual.

Typical Subtests from the Wechsler Scales

VERBAL SUBTESTS

General Information
1. How many wings does a bird have?
2. How many nickels make a dime?
3. What is steam made of?
4. Who wrote *Tom Sawyer*?
5. What is pepper?

General Comprehension
1. What should you do if you see someone forget his book when he leaves a restaurant?
2. What is the advantage of keeping money in a bank?
3. Why is copper often used in electrical wires?

Vocabulary
This test consists simply of asking, "What is a _____?" or "What does _____ mean?" The words cover a wide range of difficulty.

Similarities
1. In what way are a lion and a tiger alike?
2. In what way are a saw and a hammer alike?
3. In what way are an hour and a week alike?
4. In what way are a circle and a triangle alike?

Arithmetic
1. Sam had three pieces of candy and Joe gave him four more. How many pieces of candy did Sam have altogether?
2. Three women divided 18 golf balls equally among themselves. How many golf balls did each person receive?
3. If two buttons cost 15¢, what will be the cost of a dozen buttons?

PERFORMANCE SUBTESTS

Digit Symbol
The test taker is asked to learn to associate meaningless figures with numbers.

Block Design
The test taker is asked to copy pictures of geometric designs using multicolored blocks.

Picture Completion
The test taker is asked to identify what is missing from a picture such as this one.

Picture Arrangement
The test taker is asked to arrange pictures such as these in a sequence so that they tell a story.

FIGURE 9.3 These items are similar to those on the revised *Wechsler Adult Intelligence Scale (WAIS-R)*. The WAIS-R contains several subtests; some measure verbal ability, and others measure performance. The WAIS-R is now more widely used than the classic Stanford-Binet Intelligence Scale. Because the Wechsler tests place more emphasis on performance than does the Stanford-Binet, they are not as likely to put less verbally oriented people at a disadvantage.

INTELLIGENCE 213

Use these tools to pull together all of the information you have learned.

SECTION 3 REVIEW

Homework Practice Online
Keyword: SY7 HP18

1. Explain how dissociative fugue differs from dissociative amnesia.
2. **Critical Thinking** *Evaluating* In some cultures, people are encouraged to go into trancelike states. Should this type of dissociation be considered a sign of a psychological disorder? Why or why not?

Homework Practice Online lets you log on to the HRW Go site to complete an interactive self-check of the material covered in the section.

Critical Thinking helps you explore the section objectives and gain a strong understanding of the section content.

Thinking Critically questions ask you to use the information you have learned in the chapter to extend your knowledge.

Building Social Studies Skills is a way for you to build your skills at analyzing information and gain practice in answering standardized-test questions.

Writing About Psychology activities let you practice your writing skills to explore in more detail topics you have studied in the chapter.

Graphic Organizers will help you pull together and organize important information for your writing assignments.

Psychology Projects is an exciting and creative way to demonstrate your understanding of psychology.

Use these online tools to review and complete online activities.

Homework Practice Online lets you log on for review anytime.

Internet Connect activities are just one part of the world of online learning experiences that awaits you on the HRW Go site. By exploring these online activities, you will take a journey through some of the most interesting psychological materials available on the World Wide Web. You can then use these resources to create real-world projects, such as newspapers, brochures, and reports.

Why Psychology Matters

Have you ever wondered. . .

Why do people dream? How does stress affect health? Why are some memories so vivid? Maybe you are curious about the ways people learn.

Every day, psychologists study a fascinating topic—people. Psychologists study the reasons we wake up in the morning and go to sleep at night. They study why we eat and why we stop eating.

Psychology and Your World

When you think of psychology, what comes to mind? Perhaps you picture a person on a couch talking to a therapist. Maybe you picture a scientist in a laboratory carrying out research. These things are important, but the study of psychology includes much more. Psychology involves asking questions and solving problems.

Psychologists study how people perceive the world. You may take the brilliance of a sunset for granted, but psychologists do not. They study the ways in which colors stimulate cells in our eyes, how messages from those cells are transmitted to the brain, and how we piece those messages together into a sunset.

Psychology and People

Psychologists study people, how they think, how they see themselves, and why they behave the way they do. For example, each day at school, you learn new things. Psychologists want to know how people learn and remember information. How much do you think you can remember? Believe it or not, psychologists have discovered that there is no known limit to how much you can learn and know.

Psychologists are interested in how we see ourselves.

Psychologists are also interested in why certain things can go wrong with people. Why do some people become anxious, depressed, or lose touch with reality? Psychologists work to develop ways to help people with problems such as these.

Psychology and You

Over the years, you have grown and become more able and independent. Psychologists study development and how life is different at various stages, such as adolescence. For example, psychologists examine why teenagers strive for independence, why they often have an intense need for privacy, and why so many of them will take risks they would not take as children or adults.

Psychology is the study of behavior and mental processes. By learning about psychology, you will gain fresh insights into your understanding of yourself and others.

Skills Handbook

CRITICAL THINKING
AND THE STUDY OF PSYCHOLOGY

The study of psychology involves more than simply memorizing a series of names and terms. You will need to develop a variety of critical thinking skills to fully grasp the range of concepts and methods used in the study of psychology. Critical thinking is the reasoned judgment of information and ideas. People who think critically study information to determine its accuracy. They evaluate arguments and analyze conclusions before accepting their validity. Critical thinkers are able to recognize and define problems and develop strategies for resolving them.

The development of critical thinking skills is essential to understanding how psychology applies to you and your world. For example, critical thinking skills enable you to evaluate statistical information you hear in news stories.

Helping you develop critical thinking skills is an important part of Holt Psychology: Principles in Practice. Using the following critical thinking skills will help you better understand the concepts involved in psychology.

■ **Analyzing Information** is the process of breaking something down into its parts and examining the relationships among them. An *analysis* of something's parts enables you to better understand the whole. For example, to analyze the relationship between biology and behavior, you might study the nervous system, the brain, and the role of heredity in shaping personality.

■ **Sequencing** is the process of placing events in correct chronological order to better understand the relationships among these events. You can sequence events in two basic ways: according to *absolute* or *relative* chronology. Absolute chronology means that you pay close attention to the actual dates events took place. Placing events on a time line would be an example of absolute chronology. Relative chronology refers to the way events relate to one another. To put events in relative order, you need to know which one happened first, which came next, and so forth.

■ **Categorizing** is the process by which you group things together by the characteristics they have in common. By putting things or events into categories, it is easier to make comparisons and see differences among them.

■ **Comparing and Contrasting** involves examining events, situations, or points of view for their similarities and differences. *Comparing* focuses on both the similarities and the differences. *Contrasting* focuses only on the differences. For example, by comparing gender roles in different cultures you might note that although women have traditionally been primarily responsible for raising children, men and women increasingly share that responsibility. By contrasting, on the other hand, you might note that in many cultures women are still primarily responsible for raising children.

■ **Summarizing** is the process of taking a large amount of information and boiling it down into a short and clear statement. Summarizing is particularly useful when you need to give a brief account of a longer story or event. For example, it might be more useful to summarize the history of psychology than to take time away from your study of current research in the field.

■ **Drawing Inferences and Conclusions** is forming possible explanations for an event, a situation, or a problem. When you make an *inference,* you take the information you know to be true and come up with an educated guess about what else you think is true about that situation. A *conclusion* is a prediction about the outcome of a situation based on what you already know.

■ **Evaluating** is assessing the significance or overall importance of something. When evaluating conclusions you should base your judgment on standards that others will understand and are likely to think important.

■ **Supporting a Point of View** involves identifying an issue, deciding what you think about the issue, and persuasively expressing your position on it. Your stand should be based on specific information. In taking a stand, state your position clearly and give reasons to support it.

■ **Making Generalizations and Predictions** is the process of interpreting information to form more general statements and guess about what will happen next. A *generalization* is a broad statement that holds true for many types of behaviors or situations. Making generalizations can help you see the "big picture" of events. It is very important, however, that you avoid including situations that do not fit the statement. When this occurs, you run the risk of creating a stereotype, or overgeneralization. A *prediction* is an educated guess about an outcome. When you read about psychology, you should always be asking yourself questions like, "What will happen next? If this person does this, what will that mean for . . .?" , and so on. These types of questions help you draw on information you already know to see patterns in psychology.

■ **Identifying Bias** is the process of identifying a writer's strong feelings. Many people have strong opinions that appear in their writings. Remember that just because you hear something in a source, be it a research study, statistics given in a news story, or a television program, you do not have to agree with what is said. When looking for bias, examine the sources of information the author uses. How reliable are those sources? Consider why the writer supported one view over another. Be sure to distinguish between provable facts and someone's opinions.

■ **Finding the Main Idea** The ability to identify and understand the main idea is crucial to understanding any complex subject. This is particularly true of the study of psychology because the significant theories and methods may sometimes get lost among numerous detailed examples.

Psychology: Principles in Practice is designed to help you focus on the main ideas in psychology. The Read to Discover questions, along with the "Truth or Fiction?" statements that introduce each chapter are intended to guide your reading. The Section Review questions that close each section are intended to help you gauge whether or not you have grasped the main ideas of the section. You will still need to focus your reading, however. Applying these basic guidelines will help you identify the main ideas in whatever subject you read.

How to Find the Main Idea

1. **Read introductory material.** Read the title and the introduction, if there is one. They often indicate the main ideas to be covered.

2. **Have questions in mind.** As you read, formulate questions about the subject that you think may be answered by the material. Having such questions in mind will help you focus your reading.

3. **Note the outline of ideas.** Pay attention to any headings or subheadings. They will provide a basic outline of the major ideas. You may also want to write down this outline and use it to guide your reading.

4. **Distinguish supporting details.** As you read, distinguish sentences providing supporting details from the general statements they support. A series of examples may lead to a conclusion that restates or reinforces a main idea.

Cause: Phineas Gage experiences severe physical trauma to the underside of the frontal lobes of his cerebral cortex.

Effect: Gage's personality changes. He becomes ill-mannered, foul-mouthed, and undependable.

Cause: A person experiences a very depressing situation.

Effect/Cause: The depressing situation may reduce the activity of noradrenaline in the brain.

Effect: The chemical changes in the brain may worsen the depression.

■ Identifying Cause and Effect

Identifying and understanding cause-and-effect relationships is one essential concept in the study of psychology. It is necessary to investigate not only what caused a certain behavior or feeling to occur, but also what emotions, thoughts, and behaviors may happen as a result. To help determine the answers, psychologists ask such questions as: What is the individual's or group's background? Is this an isolated incident or does the behavior indicate a pattern? What external events may contribute to this type of feeling or pattern of behavior? Could biological processes be involved in producing this type of behavior?

CLUE WORDS AND PHRASES

CAUSE	EFFECT
as a result of	aftermath
because	as a consequence
brought about	depended on
inspired	gave rise to
led to	originated from
produced	outcome
provoked	outgrowth
spurred	proceeded from
the reason	resulting in

How to Identify Cause and Effect

1. **Look for clues.** Certain words and phrases are immediate clues to the existence of a cause-and-effect relationship. Examples of such clue words and phrases are listed here.

2. **Identify the relationship.** Read carefully to identify how concepts are related. Writers do not always clearly state the link between cause and effect.

3. **Check for complex connections.** Beyond the immediate cause-and-effect relationship, check for other, more complex connections. Note, for instance, whether (1) there were additional causes of a given effect, (2) a cause had multiple effects, and (3) these effects themselves caused further events.

Applying Your Skill

Review the example in the diagram above, taken from the case study on page 65. The diagram demonstrates an important cause-and-effect relationship. Also keep in mind that in some instances an effect may also become a cause.

Practicing Your Skill

From your knowledge of psychology, choose a sequence of feelings, thoughts, and behaviors that may share a cause-and-effect relationship. Draw a simple cause-and-effect chart that could be used as part of a visual presentation. Be sure that the chart shows the relationship between these feelings, thoughts, and behaviors. Then write a paragraph that explains the connections.

■ Problem solving is the process of finding an effective solution to a problem. Listed below are guidelines for the problem-solving process.

1. **Identify the problem.** Identify just what the problem or difficulty is that you are facing. Sometimes you face a difficult situation made up of several different problems. Each problem may require a different solution.

2. **Gather information.** Conduct research on any important issues related to the problem. Try to find the answers to questions like the following: What caused this problem? Who or what does it affect? When did it start?

3. **List and consider options.** Look at the problem and the answers to the questions you asked in Step 2. List and then think about all the possible ways in which the problem could be solved. These are your options—possible solutions to the problem.

4. **Consider advantages and disadvantages.** Consider the advantages and disadvantages of all the options that you have listed. Make sure that you consider the possible long-term effects of each possible solution. You should also determine what steps you will need to take to achieve each possible solution. Some suggestions may sound good at first but may turn out to be impractical or hard to achieve.

5. **Choose and implement a solution.** Select the best solution from your list and take the steps to achieve it.

6. **Evaluate the effectiveness** of the solution. When you have completed the steps needed to put your plan into action, evaluate its effectiveness. Is the problem solved? Were the results worth the effort required? Has the solution created any other problems that now need to be addressed?

Practicing Your Skill

The feature on page 412 discusses the challenges mental-health professionals face in dealing with criminal defendants who may or may not have a psychological disorder severe enough to justify avoiding punishment for the crime. Imagine that you are a psychologist who has been asked by a court to evaluate whether a person is legally sane and can thus be put on trial for a crime. Use the problem-solving guidelines above to help you decide how best to approach the issue.

■ Decision Making Psychologists face many difficult decisions in their practices and during research. With the use of decision-making skills you will be better able to make a decision on important issues. The following activities will help you develop and practice these skills. Decision making involves choosing between two or more options. Listed below are guidelines that will help you with making decisions.

1. **Identify a situation that requires a decision.** Think about your current situation. What issue are you faced with that requires you to take some sort of action?

2. **Gather information.** Think about the issue. Examine the causes of the issue or problem and consider how it affects you and others.

3. **Identify options.** Consider the actions that you could take to address the issue. List these options so that you can compare them.

4. **Predict Consequences.** Predict the consequences of taking the actions listed for each of your options. Compare these possible consequences. Some options might be easier or seem more satisfying. But do they produce the results that you want?

5. **Take action to implement a decision.** Choose a course of action from your available options and put it into effect.

Practicing Your Skill

Chapter 19 describes different methods of therapy. Imagine that you are a psychologist who has been asked to help a person develop a more positive outlook and higher self-esteem. Use the decision-making guidelines above to help you decide which method would best help the person.

■ **Conflict Resolution** Every year, psychologists help many people learn how to resolve conflicts. The following guidelines can be useful in resolving conflicts.

1. **Consider Persuasion.** Try to persuade the person you have a conflict with to come around to your point of view. You might want to come up with persuasive arguments for your position, then rank each reason in order of persuasiveness. Finally, present the most persuasive reasons to the other person in an effort to sway his or her point of view.

2. **Compromise.** Realize that sometimes compromise is necessary to resolve a conflict. Consider giving up something to reach an agreement. Decide what you would be willing to give up to resolve the disagreement. Then encourage the person you are having a disagreement with to meet and discuss what he or she would be willing to give up to reach an agreement.

3. **Debate the Issue.** Suggest to the person you are having a disagreement with that you and he or she hold a debate. Gather information about the advantages and disadvantages of your position. Then consider preparing flash cards outlining your best arguments. Finally, recommend that you and the other person debate your disagreement.

4. **Consider Negotiation.** Begin negotiations about the conflict. Suggest to the person you

have a disagreement with that you and he or she meet to discuss your positions and what they would be willing to agree upon. Perhaps by working together to resolve the conflict, you will arrive at a solution that neither of you had considered before.

Practicing Your Skill

Chapter 14 discusses theories of personality. Imagine that you are a psychologist, and that a colleague of yours strongly disagrees with you about which theory of personality best explains a particular client's behavior. Use the conflict resolution guidelines above to help you and your colleague resolve your disagreement about the best way to help the client.

Kohlberg's Stages of Moral Development

Stage	Moral Reasoning Goal	What Is Right?
preconventional level		
1	Avoiding punishment	Doing what is necessary to avoid punishment
2	Satisfying needs	Doing what is necessary to satisfy one's needs
conventional level		
3	Winning approval	Seeking and maintaining the approval of others using conventional standards of right and wrong
4	Law and order	Moral judgments based on maintaining social order High regard for authority
postconventional level		
5	Social order	Obedience to accepted laws Judgments based on personal values
6	Universal ethics	Morality of individual conscience, not necessarily in agreement with others

According to Lawrence Kohlberg, people's moral development follows a specific sequence. Not every person reaches the highest stage.

Using Primary and Secondary Sources

There are many sources of firsthand psychological information, including self-reports, recorded interviews, diaries, letters, photographs, laboratory data, and other documented research results. These are examples of *primary sources*. Primary sources are considered valuable tools for studying psychology because they offer a close-up view of clinical experiences and research results.

Secondary sources are descriptions or interpretations of events written after the events have occurred by persons who did not participate in the actual events. Textbooks, such as *Holt Psychology: Principles in Practice*, biographies, encyclopedias, and other reference works are secondary sources.

How to Study Primary and Secondary Sources

1. **Study the material carefully.** Consider the nature of the material. Is it anecdotal (telling a story) or scientific? Is the material upon which the conclusion was made based on firsthand information or on the accounts of others? Note the main ideas and supporting details. They are often important clues about the source of the material.

2. **Consider the audience.** Ask yourself: For whom was this information meant originally? For example, case history that was written for and published in a professional journal would probably differ in style and perhaps also in content from a case history relayed orally by a professor during a class lecture.

3. **Check for bias.** Watch for words or phrases that signal the author's one-sided view of a person, event, or concept.

4 **When possible, compare sources.** Study more than one source on a topic, if available. Comparing sources gives you a more complete, balanced account of a subject.

Practicing Your Skill

1. What distinguishes secondary sources from primary sources?

2. Why is it important to consider the origin of a source?

Building Vocabulary

As you read *Holt Psychology: Principles in Practice* you will encounter new and unfamiliar words. With regular effort, however, you can master these new terms and turn the study of psychology into an opportunity to enlarge and improve your vocabulary. The steps listed below will help you accomplish this.

How to Build Vocabulary

1. **Identify unusual words.** As you read the chapters, list any words that you cannot immediately define or pronounce.

2. **Study context clues.** Study the sentence and paragraph in which you find the new term. The setting in which the word appears, or the *context*, may give you clues to the word's meaning by providing examples or definitions of more familiar words that have the same meanings.

3. **Use the dictionary.** Use a dictionary to learn the definitions of words on your list.

4. **Review new vocabulary.** Be on the lookout for ways to use the new words in homework assignments, classroom discussions, or in ordinary conversation.

Practicing Your Skill

1. Define *context*. How can a word's context provide clues to its meaning?

2. As you read the rest of this Skill's Handbook, list any unfamiliar words that you encounter. Write down what you think that word means, then check your guesses against a dictionary's definition or this book's Glossary.

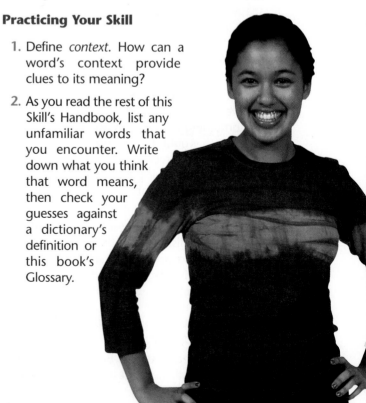

Creating an Outline

An outline is a tool for organizing information. It is a logical summary that presents the main points of what you plan to communicate. Creating an outline is an important part of writing a paper. An outline enables you to highlight the main ideas you intend to express in your paper and list the supporting details you want to cover. The writing process itself becomes much easier when the outline on which an essay is based is thorough and well organized.

How to Create an Outline

1. **Order your material.** Decide what information you want to emphasize. Then order or classify your research material with that focus in mind. Determine what information belongs in the introduction, what should be in the body of your paper, and what to reserve for the conclusion.

2. **Identify main ideas.** After organizing your material, identify the main ideas you plan to highlight in each section. These topics will be the main headings of your outline.

3. **List supporting details.** Determine the important details or facts that support each main idea. Rank and list them as subheadings, using additional levels of subheadings as necessary. Subheadings must come in pairs, at the least. That is, no *As* without *Bs*, no *1s* without *2s*, and so forth.

4. **Put your outline to use.** Structure your paper according to your outline. Each main heading, for instance, might form the basis of a paragraph's topic sentence. Subheadings would then make up the content of the paragraph.

Practicing Your Skill

Read Section 1 in Chapter 3. Create an outline to organize the complex biological concepts described in the section. Then use the outline to write a brief essay about the nervous system.

Conducting Library Research

To complete research papers or special projects related to the field of psychology, you may need

Using PQ4R

I. What is classical conditioning?
  A. Who is Ivan Pavlov?
  B. What do US, UR, CR, and CS mean?
  C. How is adaptation to the environment related to conditioning?
    1. What is a taste aversion?
    2. What is extinction?
    3. What is spontaneous recovery?
    4. How do generalization and discrimination relate to classical conditioning?
  D. What are some applications of classical conditioning?
    1. What are flooding and systematic desensitization?
    2. What is counterconditioning?
    3. How does the bell-and-pad method for bed-wetting work?

to use resources other than this textbook. Conducting thorough research generally requires using the resources available in a library.

Finding Information

To locate a particular book in a library, you need to know how libraries organize their materials. Books of fiction are alphabetized according to the last name of the author. To classify nonfiction and reference books, libraries use the Dewey decimal system and the Library of Congress system. Both systems assign each book a *call number* that tells you its classification.

To find the book's call number, look in the library's card catalog or online catalog. These sources list books by author, by title, and by subject. Finding a particular book is simple if you know the author's name or the book's title. If you do not have this information, however, or if you just want to find some books about a general subject, you can look up that subject heading.

Using Resources

In a library's reference section, you will find encyclopedias, indexes to magazines and newspapers, specialized dictionaries, atlases, and abstracts. Early in your research, encyclopedias will often be an effective resource. Encyclopedias include articles explaining basic psychological concepts and methods, historical information, and biographical sketches of important figures in the field of psychology.

Libraries also house specialized dictionaries of psychological terms and concepts. These dictionaries define and describe the more important terms, people, and theories.

Periodical indexes can also be extremely useful. They are especially helpful if you are looking for relevant, up-to-date articles containing facts and statistics about a particular subject. *The Readers' Guide to Periodical Literature,* which lists articles published in magazines, can be extremely useful. Additionally, the *New York Times Index* catalogs all news stories published in the the *New York Times,* the U.S. daily newspaper with perhaps the most extensive coverage of current events and issues.

Practicing Your Skill

1. What kinds of references contain information about terms used in psychology?
2. Where would you look to find recent coverage of a controversial new theory?

■ Writing About Psychology

Holt Psychology: Principles in Practice provides you with numerous writing opportunities using psychology-related terminology correctly. Chapter reviews contain exercises that give you the chance to focus your writing on a particular aspect of psychology.

How to Write with a Purpose

Always keep your basic purpose for writing in mind. This purpose may be to analyze, to evaluate, to synthesize, to inform, to persuade, or to hypothesize. Every purpose for writing suggests its own form, tone, and content. The point of view you adopt will shape what you write, as will your intended audience.

Each writing opportunity provided in this textbook will have specific directions about what and how to write. Regardless of your subject matter, you should follow certain basic steps in the writing process. The following guidelines can help you improve your writing.

How to Write a Paper

1. **Identify your purpose in writing.** Read the directions carefully to identify the purpose for your writing. Keep that purpose in mind as you plan and write your paper.

2. **Consider your audience.** When writing for a specific audience, choose the tone and style that will best communicate your message.

3. **Create an outline.** Plan before you begin writing. Organize themes, main ideas, and supporting details into an outline.

4. **Collect information.** Conduct research, if necessary. Your writing will be more effective if you have many details at hand.

5. **Write a first draft.** Remember to use your outline as a guide when you attempt the first draft. Each paragraph should express a single main idea, or a set of related ideas, with details for support. Be careful to clearly demonstrate the relationships between ideas, and to use proper transitions—sentences that build connections between paragraphs. Be sure to use standard grammar, spelling, sentence structure, and punctuation.

6. **Review and edit.** Revise your draft as needed to make your points clearly. Improve your sentences by varying their length and structure, by omitting clichés and substituting more precise language, and by adding appropriate adjectives and adverbs. Then check for correct spelling, punctuation, and grammar.

7. **Write your final version.** Prepare a neat, clean final version. Appearance is important; while it may not boost the quality of the writing, it can affect the way your effort is perceived.

Practicing Your Skill

1. What factor, more than any other, should affect how and what you write? Why?

2. Why is it important to consider the audience for whom you are writing?

3. What steps should you take to edit a first draft? Why is this important?

■ Using the Internet

The Internet is a vast, world-wide collection of linked computers that convey and receive data. Millions of information sources are found on the Internet, in no order and with no one person or organization in control of the content. Government agencies, universities, libraries, non-profit and for-profit organizations, businesses, and individuals put the information "out there" for anyone's use—often for free. In the United States alone, more than 174 million people use the Internet. Millions of students in the United States and around the world have learned to use the Internet as a rich source of information. By learning the fundamentals of on-line research, you will obtain access to this enormously helpful source.

Data on almost every conceivable subject is available to anyone who has access to a computer, an Internet provider, a telephone jack and cable access or a modem. A *modem* is an internal or external device connected to your computer that enables your computer to transmit and receive information electronically via telephone lines.

The World Wide Web

Several attempts have been made to organize the vast amounts of information available on the Internet. One such effort is the World Wide Web. The Web was designed to make all online information part of one matrix of interconnected documents and services. Almost every resource available on the Internet can be accessed via the World Wide Web.

Information on the Web is organized according to category and is stored in a particular, unique location. The location is known as an address, or *URL*—short for Universal Resource Locator—on the Internet. Software programs called *Web browsers* enable a computer to locate addresses and to search subject categories anywhere on the Internet, including the World Wide Web.

Web Pages

Web URLs share certain basic characteristics because most Web documents are created using the same computer language, HyperText Markup Language, or HTML. A Web URL always begins with the four letters *http,* which simply states that the address was created in HTML. Your Web browser can go directly to any URL that you type into its locator box.

All Internet addresses indicate the domain, or the nature of the information's source. These sources are indicated by suffixes on the address. The suffixes include the following: *gov* for government agencies; *com* for a business or commercial enterprises; *org* for nonprofit organizations; and *edu* for educational institutions.

Your browser is like a taxi that does not recognize landmarks, but finds its way only by specific addresses. If you know the address you need, getting there is a snap. Just be sure to type the address exactly as you have seen it, including strange-looking symbols, spaces, and upper- and lower-case letters. This is critical because if you give it an incorrect address— even a "dot" out of place—you will receive a message on your screen that the Web site cannot be retrieved.

Once you have typed in the correct address, your browser will take you to a Web homepage, the opening page of a Web document. Think of it as a table of contents. Web pages contain underlined or highlighted words and images called hyperlinks. Clicking on a hyperlink will take you to a related or "linked" Web page, either within this site or in another location on the Internet. Hyperlinks function in a nonlinear fashion. By clicking on hyperlinks, you can "surf the Net," traveling to a seemingly unlimited number of Web sites.

Navigating the Web

You can navigate your way around the Web in three ways:

- by clicking on the hyperlinks that interest you, and exploring the Web.
- by using search tools, primarily keyword searches, that identify your subject category.

- by commanding the browser to go directly to a specific Internet resource that may be in another collection of organized data.

It is important to write down any potential sources of information in a log. This will enable you to easily find the URL again and command your browser to take you there.

The best way to familiarize yourself with the Internet is to spend some time exploring the Web—clicking on hyperlinks, and finding your way back. If your time on the Internet is limited, however, and you need to conduct research on a specific topic, you will need to focus your search.

The Internet offers many sources for research. Many of the world's libraries and archives can be searched from any computer with online access. Be aware that search tools are constantly changing. Get to know the strengths and weaknesses of your search tool choice. Some large Web sites—such as American Online, CNN, MSN, Netscape, and Yahoo!—offer links to a broad range of information. Sites such as CNNfyi.com allow you to access a wealth of current information. These sites are also useful when transferring information from written to visual form.

A broad search of the Web will give you a sense of just how many documents are related to your subject, but it will not tell you whether these documents will be useful or relevant to your particular research project. Rather than scanning an overwhelming amount of data, you can limit your initial search by these two methods:

- Lists of lists, or menus. Use a keyword search (or the URL, if you have it) to go directly to an on-line reference library, such as the Library of Congress, which lists Web sites by subject and gives their URLs.
- Clearinghouse lists. These are roughly equivalent to on-line encyclopedias merged with directories.

A Trial Run

Let's say you want to research a paper on the following topic: "The Effect of Weather on People's Moods." A hunch told you that the rainy day was putting you and your friends in bad moods. The following steps provide an example of how you might successfully navigate the Web and complete your research.

1. **Decide on your topic:** moods and weather.

2. **Determine your research needs.** Gather no more and no less information than is necessary to complete your project.

3. **Create a list of possible keywords,** for example, climate, rain, depression, happiness, and even rainy-weather cities, such as Seattle and London.

You may find a promising Web site containing hyperlinks that lead you to a Web page in the "health" category. Here you may find a description of "seasonal affective disorder." This sounds like your topic, only it is more about seasons (winter) than rain. Still, it's too close to ignore. So you can go "surfing."

Clicking on one hyperlink may not reveal anything relevant. Another hyperlink on the next "page," however, may tell you about light therapy treatment, and refer you to a hospital research program using light therapy in London.

At this point, you may need to stop and evaluate your approach. Ask yourself: Am I now on a fascinating but completely irrelevant side alley? If you answer yes, which, at some point in time, will happen, you will need to reassess your topic.

Ask yourself whether your topic has changed, and if so, do you want to get it back on your original track or follow this somewhat different and, it seems, more focused direction? Often, the process of researching reveals that a selected topic was too vague at the start.

Sometimes, however, you do not have the option of altering or narrowing your topic, either because it was assigned or because you committed yourself to it. What can you do? Don't get frustrated, there are still several options.

- Try other approaches. University psychology departments, research facilities, and professional psychological associations worldwide usually have Web sites.

- Try using another Web browser. All software packages are not identical. Some are more powerful than others and will retrieve more data, or more specific data.

Above all, be patient with yourself. You are developing a new and complex skill. It takes practice, experience, and faith in your own intuition to develop truly efficient on-line research skills that will help you as you study about psychology.

Becoming a Strategic Reader

by Dr. Judith Irvin

Everywhere you look, print is all around us. In fact, you would have a hard time stopping yourself from reading. In a normal day, you might read cereal boxes, movie posters, notes from friends, t-shirts, instructions for video games, song lyrics, catalogs, billboards, information on the Internet, magazines, the newspaper, and much, much more. Each form of print is read differently depending on your purpose for reading. You read a menu differently from poetry, and a motorcycle magazine is read differently than a letter from a friend. Good readers switch easily from one type of text to another. In fact, they probably do not even think about it, they just do it.

When you read, it is helpful to use a strategy to remember the most important ideas. You can use a strategy before you read to help connect information you already know to the new information you will encounter. Before you read, you can also predict what a text will be about by using a previewing strategy. During the reading you can use a strategy to help you focus on main ideas, and after reading you can use a strategy to help you organize what you learned so that you can remember it later. Holt Psychology: Principles In Practice was designed to help you more easily understand the ideas you read. Important reading strategies employed in Holt Psychology: Principles In Practice include:

A Methods to help you **anticipate** what is to come

B Tools to help you **preview and predict** what the text will be about

C Ways to help you **use and analyze visual information**

D Ideas to help you **organize the information** you have learned

A. Anticipate Information

How can I use information I already know to help me understand what a new chapter will be about?

Anticipating what a new chapter will be about helps you connect the upcoming information to what you already know. By drawing on your background knowledge, you can build a bridge to the new material.

1 Each chapter of *Holt Psychology: Principles In Practice* asks you to explore the chapter before you start reading by forming opinions based on your current knowledge.

> **TRUTH OR fiction ?**
>
> Read the following statements about psychology. Do you think they are true or false? You will learn whether each statement is true or false as you read the chapter.
>
> ■ Psychologists never guess about the answers to the questions they ask.
> ■ You have to do a study more than once to be sure its results are valid.

2 / **4**

A Before Reading Agree/Disagree	B After Reading Agree/Disagree
Psychologists never guess about the answers to the questions they ask.	
You have to do a study more than once to be sure its results are valid.	

3 Read the text and discuss with classmates.

5 You can also refine your knowledge by reviewing the **Truth or Fiction Revisited** boxes.

Anticipating Information

step 1 Identify the major concepts of the chapter. In *Holt Psychology: Principles in Practice,* these are presented in the **Truth or Fiction** feature at the beginning of each chapter.
▼
step 2 Agree or disagree with each of the statements.
▼
step 3 Read the text and discuss your responses with your classmates.
▼
step 4 After reading the material that deals with the **Truth or Fiction** statement, revisit the statements and respond to them again based on what you have learned.
▼
step 5 Go back and check your knowlege by reviewing the **Truth or Fiction Revisited** boxes.

> **TRUTH OR fiction ■ R E V I S I T E D ■**
>
> *It is not true that psychologists never guess about the answers to the questions they ask.* After psychologists ask a research question, they form a hypothesis, or an educated guess, about the answer.

B. Previewing and Predicting

How can I figure out what the text is about before I even start reading a section?

Previewing and predicting are good methods to help you understand the text. If you take the time to preview and predict before you read, the text will make more sense to you during your reading.

1 Usually, your teacher will set the purpose for reading. After reading some new information, you may be asked to write a summary, take a test, or complete some other type of activity.

Previewing and Predicting

step 1
Identify your purpose for reading. Ask yourself what you will do with this information once you have finished reading.

▼

step 2
Ask yourself what is the main idea of the text and what are the key vocabulary words you need to know.

▼

step 3
Use signal words to help identify the structure of the text.

▼

step 4
Connect the information to what you already know.

"After reading about self-esteem, you will work with a partner to create a poster and . . ."

2 As you preview the text, use *graphic signals* such as headings, subheadings, and boldface type to help you determine what is important in the text. Each chapter of *Holt Psychology: Principles in Practice* opens by giving you important clues to help you preview the material.

Looking at the chapter's title, main heading, and subheadings can give you an idea of what is to come.

Read to Discover questions give you clues as to the chapter's main ideas.

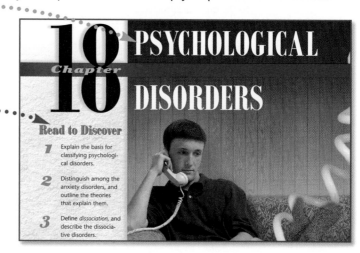

Chapter 18 PSYCHOLOGICAL DISORDERS

Read to Discover

1 Explain the basis for classifying psychological disorders.

2 Distinguish among the anxiety disorders, and outline the theories that explain them.

3 Define *dissociation*, and describe the dissociative disorders.

3 Other tools that can help you in previewing are **signal words**. These words prepare you to think in a certain way. For example, when you see words such as *similar to, same as,* or *different from,* you know that the text will probably compare and contrast two or more ideas. Signal words indicate how the ideas in the text relate to each other. Look at the list below for some of the most common signal words grouped by the type of text structures they include.

SIGNAL
words

Cause and Effect	Compare and Contrast	Description	Problem and Solution	Sequence or Chronological Order
because	different from	for instance	the question is	not long after
since	same as	for example	a solution	next
consequently	similar to	such as	one answer is	then
this led to...so	as opposed to	to illustrate		initially
if...then	instead of	in addition		before
nevertheless	although	most importantly		after
accordingly	however	another		finally
because of	compared with	furthermore		preceding
as a result of	as well as	first,		following
in order to	either...or	second ...		on (date)
may be due to	but			over the years
for this reason	on the other hand			today
not only...but	unless			when

4 Learning something new requires that you connect it in some way with something you already know. This means you have to think before you read and while you read. You may want to use a chart like this one to remind yourself of the information already familiar to you and to come up with questions you want answered in your reading. The chart will also help you organize your ideas after you have finished reading.

What I know	*What I want to know*	*What I learned*

C. Use and Analyze Visual Information

How can all the pictures, graphs, and cartoons help me be a stronger reader?

Using **visual information** can help you understand and remember the information presented in *Holt Psychology: Principles in Practice*. Good readers make a picture in their mind when they read. The pictures, charts, graphs, time lines, and diagrams that occur throughout *Holt Psychology: Principles in Practice* are placed strategically to increase your understanding.

Analyzing Visual Information

step 1 As you preview the text, ask yourself how the visual information relates to the text.

step 2 Generate questions based on the visual information.

step 3 After reading the text, go back and review the visual information again.

step 4 Connect the information to what you already know.

1 You might ask yourself questions like these:

Why did the writer include this image with the text? What details about this image are mentioned in the text?

2 After you have read the text, see if you can answer your own questions.

What are the people in this picture doing?

Why are they sitting in a circle?

What does this picture tell me about psychology?

3 After reading, take another look at the visual information.

4 Try to make connections to what you already know.

D. Organize Information

Once I learn new information, how do I keep it all straight so that I will remember it?

To help you remember what you have read, you need to find a way of **organizing information**. Two good ways of doing this are by using graphic organizers and concept maps. **Graphic organizers** help you understand important relationships—such as cause-and-effect, compare/contrast, sequence of events, and problem/solution—within the text. **Concept maps** provide a useful tool to help you focus on the text's main ideas and organize supporting details.

Identifying Relationships

Using graphic organizers will help you recall important ideas from the section and give you a study tool you can use to prepare for a quiz or test or to help with a writing assignment. Some of the most common types of graphic organizers are shown below.

▶ Cause and Effect

Psychological events cause people to react in a certain way. Cause-and-effect patterns show the relationship between results and the ideas or events that made the results occur. You may want to represent cause-and-effect relationships as one cause leading to multiple effects,

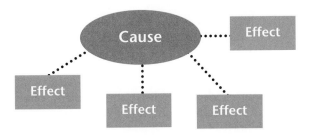

or as a chain of cause-and-effect relationships.

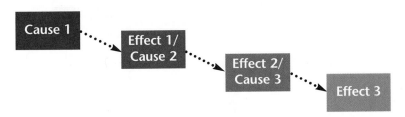

Constructing Graphic Organizers

step 1 Preview the text, looking for signal words and the main idea.

▼

step 2 Form a hypothesis as to which type of graphic organizer would work best to display the information presented.

▼

step 3 Work individually or with your classmates to create a visual representation of what you read.

▶ ### Comparing and Contrasting

Graphic Organizers are often useful when you are comparing or contrasting information. Compare-and-contrast diagrams point out similarities and differences between two concepts or ideas.

Characteristics   Shared Characteristics   Characteristics

▶ ### Sequencing

Keeping track of dates and the order in which events took place is essential to understanding end results. Sequence or chronological-order diagrams show events or ideas in the order in which they happened.

First Event

Next Event

Next Event

Last Event

▶ ### Problem and Solution

Problem-solution patterns identify at least one problem, offer one or more solutions to the problem, and explain or predict outcomes of the solutions.

Problem

Solution #1

Solution #2

Solution #3

Solution #4

Identifying Main Ideas and Supporting Details

One special type of graphic organizer is the concept map. A concept map, sometimes called a semantic map, allows you to zero in on the most important points of the text. The map is made up of lines, boxes, circles, and/or arrows. It can be as simple or as complex as you need it to be to accurately represent the text.

Here are a few examples of concept maps you might use.

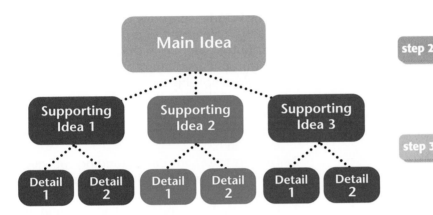

Constructing Concept Maps

step 1 Preview the text, looking at what type of structure might be appropriate to display on a concept map.

step 2 Taking note of the headings, bold-faced type, and text structure, sketch a concept map you think could best illustrate the text.

step 3 Using boxes, lines, arrows, circles, or any shapes you like, display the ideas of the text in the concept map.

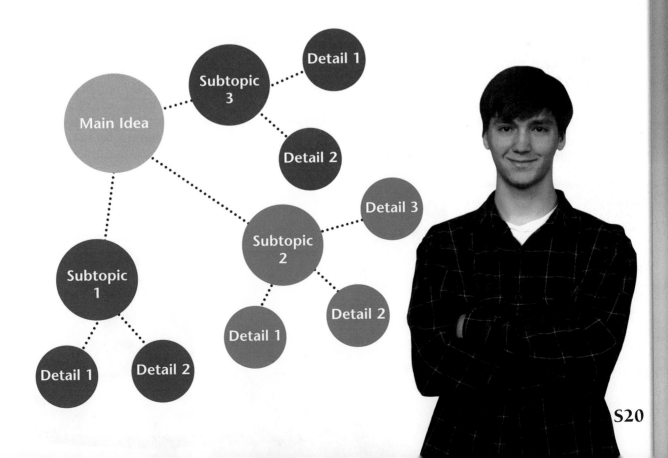

Standardized Test-Taking Strategies

A number of times throughout your school career, you may be asked to take standardized tests. These tests are designed to demonstrate the content and skills you have learned. It is important to keep in mind that in most cases the best way to prepare for these tests is to pay close attention in class and take every opportunity to improve your general social studies, reading, writing, and mathematical skills.

Tips for Taking the Test

1. Be sure that you are well rested.
2. Be on time, and be sure that you have the necessary materials.
3. Listen to the teacher's instructions.
4. Read directions and questions carefully.
5. DON'T STRESS! Just remember what you have learned in class, and you should do well.

Practice the strategies at go.hrw.com

STANDARDIZED TEST PREP ONLINE
keyword: SY7 STP TOC

Tackling Social Studies

The social studies portions of many standardized tests are designed to test your knowledge of the content and skills that you have been studying in one or more of your social studies classes. Specific objectives for the test vary, but some of the most common include the following:

1. Demonstrate an understanding of issues and events in history.
2. Demonstrate an understanding of geographic influences on historical issues and events.
3. Demonstrate an understanding of economic and social influences on historical issues and events.
4. Demonstrate an understanding of political influences on historical issues and events.
5. Use critical thinking skills to analyze social studies information.

Standardized tests usually contain multiple-choice and, sometimes, open-ended questions. The multiple-choice items will often be based on maps, tables, charts, graphs, pictures, cartoons, and/or reading passages and documents.

Tips for Answering Multiple-Choice Questions

1. If there is a written or visual piece accompanying the multiple-choice question, pay careful attention to the title, author, and date.
2. Then read through or glance over the content of the written or visual piece accompanying the question to familiarize yourself with it.
3. Next, read the multiple-choice question first for its general intent. Then reread it carefully, looking for words that give clues or can limit possible answers to the question. For example, words such as *most* or *best* tell you that there may be several correct answers to a question, but you should look for the most appropriate answer.
4. Read through the answer choices. Always read all of the possible answer choices even if the first one seems like the correct answer. There may be a better choice farther down in the list.
5. Reread the accompanying information (if any is included) carefully to determine the answer to the question. Again, note the title, author, and date of primary-source selections. The answer will rarely be stated exactly as it appears in the primary source, so you will need to use your critical thinking skills to read between the lines.
6. Think of what you already know about the time in history or person involved and use that to help limit the answer choices.
7. Finally, reread the question and selected answer to be sure that you made the best choice and that you marked it correctly on the answer sheet.

Strategies for Success

There are a variety of strategies you can prepare ahead of time to help you feel more confident about answering questions on social studies standardized tests. Here are a few suggestions:

1. Adopt an acronym—a word formed from the first letters of other words—that you will use for analyzing a document or visual piece that accompanies a question.

Helpful Acronyms

For a document, use SOAPS, which stands for

S Subject
O Overview
A Audience
P Purpose
S Speaker/author

For a picture, cartoon, map, or other visual piece of information, use OPTIC, which stands for

O Occasion (or time)
P Parts (labels or details of the visual)
T Title
I Interrelations (how the different parts of the visual work together)
C Conclusion (what the visual means)

2. Form visual images of maps and try to draw them from memory. Standardized tests will most likely include maps showing many features, such as states, countries, continents, and oceans. Those maps may also show patterns in settlement and the size and distribution of cities. For example, in studying the United States, be able to see in your mind's eye such things as where the states and major cities are located. Know major physical features, such as the Mississippi River, the Appalachian and Rocky Mountains, the Great Plains, and the various regions of the United States, and be able to place them on a map. Such features may help you understand patterns in the distribution of population and the size of settlements.
3. When you have finished studying a geographic region or period in history, try to think of who or what might be important enough for a standardized test. You may want to keep your ideas in a notebook to refer to when it is almost time for the test.

4. Standardized tests will likely test your understanding of the political, economic, and social processes that shape a region's history, culture, and geography. Questions may also ask you to understand the impact of geographic factors on major events. For example, some may ask about the effects of migration and immigration on various societies and population change. In addition, questions may test your understanding of the ways humans interact with their environment.

5. For the skills area of the tests, practice putting major events and personalities in order in your mind. Sequencing people and events by dates can become a game you play with a friend who also has to take the test. Always ask yourself "why" this event is important.

6. Follow the tips under "Ready for Reading" below when you encounter a reading passage in social studies, but remember that what you have learned about history can help you in answering reading-comprehension questions.

Ready for Reading

The main goal of the reading sections of most standardized tests is to determine your understanding of different aspects of a piece of writing. Basically, if you can grasp the main idea and the writer's purpose and then pay attention to the details and vocabulary so that you are able to draw inferences and conclusions, you will do well on the test.

Tips for Answering Multiple-Choice Questions

1. Read the passage as if you were not taking a test.
2. Look at the big picture. Ask yourself questions like, "What is the title?", "What do the illustrations or pictures tell me?", and "What is the writer's purpose?"
3. Read the questions. This will help you know what information to look for.
4. Reread the passage, underlining information related to the questions.

5. Go back to the questions and try to answer each one in your mind before looking at the answers.
6. Read all the answer choices and eliminate the ones that are obviously incorrect.

Types of Multiple-Choice Questions

1. **Main Idea** This is the most important point of the passage. After reading the passage, locate and underline the main idea.
2. **Significant Details** You will often be asked to recall details from the passage. Read the question and underline the details as you read, but remember that the correct answers do not always match the wording of the passage precisely.
3. **Vocabulary** You will often need to define a word within the context of the passage. Read the answer choices and plug them into the sentence to see what fits best.
4. **Conclusion and Inference** There are often important ideas in the passage that the writer does not state directly. Sometimes you must consider multiple parts of the passage to answer the question. If answers refer to only one or two sentences or details in the passage, they are probably incorrect.

Tips for Answering Short-Answer Questions

1. Read the passage in its entirety, paying close attention to the main events and characters. Jot down information you think is important.
2. If you cannot answer a question, skip it and come back later.
3. Words such as *compare, contrast, interpret, discuss,* and *summarize* appear often in short-answer questions. Be sure you have a complete understanding of each of these words.
4. To help support your answer, return to the passage and skim the parts you underlined.

5. Organize your thoughts on a separate sheet of paper. Write a general statement with which to begin. This will be your topic statement.
6. When writing your answer, be precise but brief. Be sure to refer to details in the passage in your answer.

Targeting Writing

On many standardized tests, you will occasionally be asked to write an essay. In order to write a concise essay, you must learn to organize your thoughts before you begin writing the actual composition. This keeps you from straying too far from the essay's topic.

Tips for Answering Composition Questions

1. Read the question carefully.
2. Decide what kind of essay you are being asked to write. Essays usually fall into one of the following types: persuasive, classificatory, compare/contrast, or "how to." To determine the type of essay, ask yourself questions like, "Am I trying to persuade my audience?", "Am I comparing or contrasting ideas?", or "Am I trying to show the reader how to do something?"
3. Pay attention to keywords, such as *compare, contrast, describe, advantages, disadvantages, classify,* or *speculate.* They will give you clues as to the structure that your essay should follow.
4. Organize your thoughts on a separate sheet of paper. You will want to come up with a general topic sentence that expresses your main idea. Make sure this sentence addresses the question. You should then create an outline or some type of graphic organizer to help you organize the points that support your topic sentence.
5. Write your composition using complete sentences. Also, be sure to use correct grammar, spelling, punctuation, and sentence structure.
6. Be sure to proofread your essay once you have finished writing.

Gearing Up for Math

On most standardized tests you will be asked to solve a variety of mathematical problems that draw on the skills and information you have learned in class. If math problems sometimes give you difficulty, have a look at the tips below to help you work through the problems.

Tips for Solving Math Problems

1. Decide what is the goal of the question. Read or study the problem carefully and determine what information must be found.
2. Locate the factual information. Decide what information represents key facts—the ones you must have to solve the problem. You may also find facts you do not need to reach your solution. In some cases, you may determine that more information is needed to solve the problem. If so, ask yourself, "What assumptions can I make about this problem?" or "Do I need a formula to help solve this problem?"
3. Decide what strategies you might use to solve the problem, how you might use them, and what form your solution will be in. For example, will you need to create a graph or chart? Will you need to solve an equation? Will your answer be in words or numbers? By knowing what type of solution you should reach, you may be able to eliminate some of the choices.
4. Apply your strategy to solve the problem and compare your answer to the choices.
5. If the answer is still not clear, read the problem again. If you had to make calculations to reach your answer, use estimation to see if your answer makes sense.

Statistics

The Steps of Scientific Research

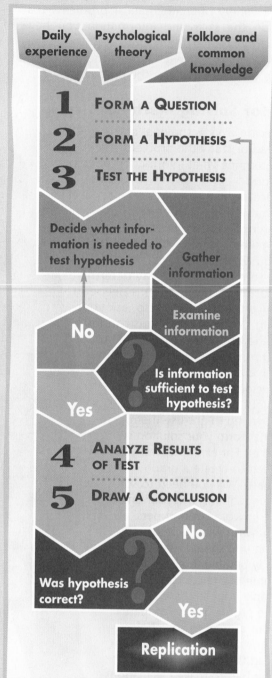

Daily experience · Psychological theory · Folklore and common knowledge

1 FORM A QUESTION

2 FORM A HYPOTHESIS

3 TEST THE HYPOTHESIS

Decide what information is needed to test hypothesis

Gather information

Examine information

No

Is information sufficient to test hypothesis?

Yes

4 ANALYZE RESULTS OF TEST

5 DRAW A CONCLUSION

No

Was hypothesis correct?

Yes

Replication

A flowchart is used to illustrate a sequence of events or the steps in a process. This flowchart demonstrates the steps a researcher generally follows.

Reading Charts and Graphs

Charts and graphs are used to organize and present information visually. They categorize and display data in a variety of ways, depending on the type of chart or graph being used and the subject matter of the data.

Using Charts

There are several type of charts. This textbook uses the following types of charts to illustrate various concepts: flowcharts, Venn diagrams, organization charts, and tables.

A *flowchart* illustrates a sequence of events or the steps in a process. "The Steps of Scientific Research," shown to the left, is an example of a flowchart. Cause-and-effect relationships are also frequently depicted in flowcharts.

Venn diagrams use circles to represent simple relationships among sets. Overlapping regions in the Venn diagram represent the intersection of information. The Venn diagram shown on page S26, for example, demonstrates that Seoul is located within South Korea and South Korea is in Asia. Therefore, it follows that Seoul is located in Asia.

An organization chart, such as the one on page S26 titled "Divisions of the Nervous System," displays the structure of a particular organization or concept. It illustrates the ranking or function of the organization's internal parts and the relationship between those parts.

A *table* is generally a multi-column chart that presents data in categories that are easy to understand and compare. This textbook frequently uses tables to organize data and concepts. For an example, see page 430.

Using Graphs

There are also several types of graphs used in this textbook. Each has certain advantages in displaying data for a particular emphasis.

A *line graph,* for example, plots changes in quantities over time. It consists of a horizontal and a vertical axis. One axis generally lists numbers or percentages, while the other axis usually marks off periods of time. A line is created by plotting data on the grid formed by the intersecting axes and then connecting the dots. "Average Growth Rates for Boys and Girls from Childhood Through Adolescence" is an example of a line graph.

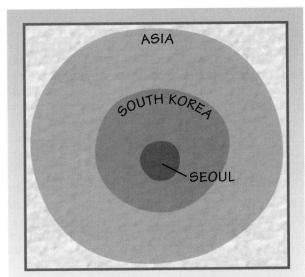

Venn diagrams represent the intersection of information. For example, Seoul is in South Korea, which is in Asia. Therefore, Seoul is in Asia.

ber of pain receptors and sensitivity to pain and pressure in different parts of the human body.

A *pie graph*, or *circle graph*, displays proportions at a glance by showing sections of a whole, like slices of a pie, with the whole equaling 100 percent. "United States Population by Group" is an example of a pie graph.

How to Read Charts and Graphs

1. **Read the title.** Read the title to identify the focus of the chart or graph, remembering what each kind is designed to emphasize.
2. **Study the parts.** To identify the type of information presented, read the headings, subheadings, and labels that define each axis, bar, or section of the graph. Study the categories used and the specific data given for each category in a chart.
3. **Analyze the details.** Note increases or decreases in quantities. When reading dates, note intervals of time. When viewing a flowchart, follow directional arrows or lines. When reading graphs, look for trends, relationships, and changes in the data.
4. **Put the data to use.** Formulate generalizations or draw conclusions based on the data presented.

A *bar graph* can also be used to display changes in quantities over time. More often, however, bar graphs are used to compare quantities within the same category, and to summarize the differences succinctly. For example, the bar graph on page S27, "Distribution of Pain Receptors" compares the number

In an organization chart, the structure of a particular concept or organization is illustrated graphically. This organization chart, for example, shows the divisions of the human nervous system, the parts of those divisions, and the relationship between each of those parts.

Average Growth Rate for Boys and Girls from Childhood Through Adolescence

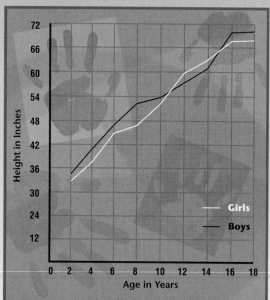

Line graphs are effective tools for illustrating the changes of a particular quantity over time. For example, this line graph demonstrates the change in height of boys and girls throughout the years of adolescence.

Source: Tanner, J.M. (1978). *Fetus into man: Physical growth from conception to maturity.* Cambridge, MA: Harvard University Press. (p. 118)

Practicing Your Skills

Use the flowchart, "The Steps of Scientific Research," on page S25 to answer questions 1 and 2. Then complete questions 3 and 4 using the bar graph on this page.

1. Write a detailed description of the steps illustrated in the chart, but do not use numbers or refer to the chart.
2. Decide whether the information is more easily understood in chart form or in a prose description. Give reasons for your opinion.
3. Which part of the body has the most pain receptors? The fewest?
4. Assuming that the information presented in this graph is valid, do you believe that individuals differ in their sensitivities to pain? How could you account for someone claiming to have a "high pain threshold"?

Analyzing Observations

Conducting a research study is actually only a small part of the research process. Imagine that you decide to conduct a survey about the amount of television teenagers watch daily. After you conducted interviews and received dozens of completed questionnaires you would probably feel overwelmed by the amount of data you had collected. What is the next step?

When faced with this situation, psychologists use mathematical procedures, called *statistics*, to organize, analyze, and interpret the data. Psychologists then use the statistical analyses to construct charts and graphs. In short, statistics help psychologists make sense of their research findings.

Distribution of Pain Receptors

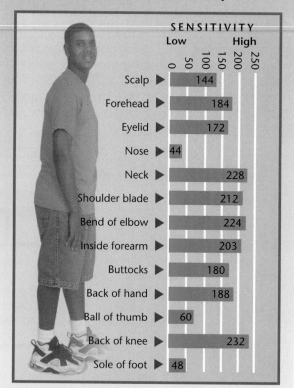

Bar graphs are a common method of comparing quantities within the same category. This bar graph compares the levels of sensitivity to pain in the various parts of the human body.

Source: Strughold, H. (1924). On the density and thresholds in the areas of pain on the epidermis in the various regions of the body. 7 Biol, 80, 367-380 (in German)

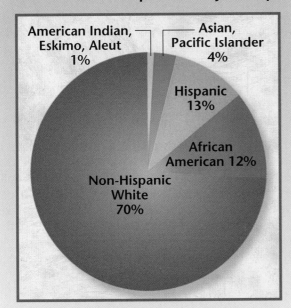

United States Population by Group

American Indian, Eskimo, Aleut 1%

Asian, Pacific Islander 4%

Hispanic 13%

African American 12%

Non-Hispanic White 70%

Pie graphs are effective tools for illustrating the proportional divisions of a central concept. This pie graph, for example, demonstrates the proportions of the various ethnic groups as a percentage of the U.S. population as a whole. Hypothetically, if the U.S. population was one million, how many African Americans would you expect there to be?

Source: Statistical Abstract of the United States 1995. Figures have been rounded.

Understanding Frequency Distributions

One of the most common forms of statistical analysis researchers use to organize their data is the *frequency distribution.* A frequency distribution is a way of arranging data to determine how often a certain piece of data—such as a score, salary, or age—occurs. In setting up a frequency distribution, researchers arrange the data from highest to lowest, and enter a mark when a piece of data occurs. The sum of each group's marks determines the frequency.

If there are too many different pieces of data to list individually, as is sometimes true for class scores, a researcher may substitute specific numerical spans, called *class intervals,* for individual scores. Again, the data are arranged from highest to lowest. A frequency distribution would allow a teacher to see at a glance how well a group of students did on a test, for instance, but it does not provide any information about individual performance.

Understanding Bell Curves

One of the most useful statistical concepts for psychologists is the *bell curve,* or *normal curve.* The bell curve is an ideal, a hypothetical standard against which actual categories of people or things (such as scores) can be measured and compared.

Usually, bell curves are used to categorize characteristics of people in large groups. The closer the group comes to the center of the curve, where the most "normal" traits congregate, the more validity the study appears to have.

For example, the bell curve, "Distribution of IQ Scores," shown on page S29, illustrates a hypothetical standard against which actual IQ scores can be compared. This curve is a model of an ideal. It shows what would happen if the largest number of scores fell exactly in the middle of a range of scores. A comparison of the actual scores against this bell curve tells psychologists how representative the IQ test really is.

A bell curve is a normal frequency distribution. This means that after counting the occurrence, or *frequency,* of specific data (scores for instance), researchers can create an arrangement, or *distribution,* that is concentrated on or near the curve's center, which represents the norm. The fewest entries of data should appear at the far ends of the distribution—away form the highly concentrated norm.

It follows then, that when the graphed results of an experiment come close to matching a bell curve, the results are assumed to be highly representative of that experiment. If most scores or data cluster towards the ends of the curve, however, the experiment or test is assumed to be unrepresentative of the group.

Bell curves and frequency distributions seem very complicated. However, they are simply ways to condense information and put it in a visual form. Within moments of glancing at a real plotted curve and the bell curve beside it, researchers can judge approximately how far from the norm their experimental group was, and how closely their results conform to what is "perfectly" normal.

Practicing Your Skills

1. Define *Frequency distribution,* and identify a situation in which you have applied this concept.
2. Look at the bell curve on page S29. What percentage of students would be expected to score between 90 and 110? Between 70 and 130?
3. What problems can you identify with basing assumptions on a bell curve?

Distribution of IQ Scores

Bell curves, or normal curves, represent a hypothetical standard against which actual categories of people or things can be measured and compared. This bell curve illustrates a hypothetical standard against which actual IQ scores could be compared. If the actual scores closely represent this standard, the IQ test is considered to be valid.

Mean, Median, and Mode: Measures of Central Tendency

Three other measures are used to compare data that fall within the central points of a distribution: the *mode*, the *mean*, and the *median*.

Mode

Simply, the *mode* is the piece of data (or the score) that occurs most often in a given set of numbers. To find the mode, examine any frequency distribution and choose the number that appears most often. The mode is of limited use to researchers because "occurring most often" in a distribution may mean,

for instance, that this number occurred only twice among fifty different test scores.

Mean

The *mean* is an average. The mean is found by adding all the scores or data together and then dividing that sum by the number of scores. The formula for finding the mean is:

$$\text{mean} = \frac{\text{sum of the scores}}{\text{number of scores}}$$

A significant disadvantage of using the mean is that any extreme score, whether high or low, distorts a researcher's results. For instance, if five waiters earn $300, $350, $325, $390, and $600 per week respectively, the mean—or average—weekly salary for this group would be $393. Yet three of the five waiters earn less than the average amount. In this circumstance, using the mean would not necessarily be representative of the waiters' wages.

Median

The *median* is the score or piece of data that falls precisely in the middle of all the scores when they are arranged in descending order. Exactly half of the students score above the median, and exactly half score below it. In the previous example of waiters' salaries, the median would be $350, because two waiters earned more and two earned less than $350.

The median, unlike the mean, is usually an actual number or score. To find the median of an even number of scores, you would find the median of the two numbers that fall in the middle, and then take the mean of those two central numbers in the distribution.

One major advantage of the median is that extreme scores, high or low, will not affect it. For example, examine the following two distributions:

> **Group X:** 4, 10, 16, 18, 22
> **Group Y:** 4, 10, 16, 18, 97

The median for each group is 15, because that number falls precisely in the middle of all the scores. However, the mean for Group X is 14 (4 + 10 + 16 + 18 + 22 = 70; 70 ÷ 5 = 14), while the mean for Group Y is 29 (4 + 10 + 16 + 18 + 97 = 145; 145 ÷ 5 = 29). The mean changes dramatically simply by introducing one extreme score. The median, however, remains the same.

The kind of central point that researchers choose to use in any given situation depends on what they are trying to find out. The median is not the best choice in all instances. Actually, in a bell curve—the idealized norm—the mode, the mean, and the median are identical.

Variability

Knowing what the mode, the mean, and the median are tells a researcher a great deal but not everything about the data. Researchers also need to know how much *variability* there is among the scores in a group of numbers. That is, researchers must discover how far apart the numbers or scores are in relation to the mean. For this purpose, psychologists use two measures: the range and the standard deviation.

Range
The *range* is the mathematical difference between the highest and lowest scores in a frequency distribution. If the highest grade in a class is 100 and the lowest is 60, the range is 40 (100 – 60 = 40).

Two groups of numbers may have the same mean but different ranges. For example, consider the batting averages of two baseball teams:

> **Team A:** 210 250 285 300 340
> **Team B:** 270 270 275 285 285

The mean for each team is 277. However, the range for Team A is 130 points, whereas the range for Team B is 15 points. This would tell a researcher that Team B is more alike in its batting abilities than is Team A.

The range tells psychologists how similar the subjects in each group are to one another in terms of what is being measured. This information could not be obtained from the mode, the mean, or the median alone, since each is just one number and not a comparison.

The disadvantage of the range, though, is that it takes only the lowest and highest scores of a frequency distribution into account. The middle numbers may be substantially different in two groups that have the same range. For example, here are two distributions:

> **Group A:** 5, 8, 12, 14, 15
> **Group B:** 5, 6, 7, 8, 15

Each group has the same range of 10. But the scores in Group A differ greatly from the scores in Group B.

For this reason, psychologists often use the standard deviation.

Standard Deviation
Psychologists sometimes want to know how much any particular score is likely to vary from the mean, or how spread out the scores are around the mean. To derive these measures, researchers calculate the standard deviation. The closer the standard deviation is to zero, the more reliable that data tends to be.

Let's say that the standard deviation of Team A's batting average is about 44.2, and the standard deviation of Team B's batting average is 6.8. From this information we know that the typical score of Team A will fall within 44.2 points of the mean, and the typical score of Team B will be within 6.8 points of the mean. This tells us that the quality of batting is more consistent on Team B than on Team A.

Two bell curves can have the same mode, mean, and median, but different standard deviations. If you were plotting two bell curves on a line graph, and one curve had a much larger standard deviation than the other, the curve with the larger standard deviation would show a more pronounced bell shape on the graph.

Correlation

Correlation is a measure of the relationship between two variables. A *variable* is any behavior or condition that can change in quantity or quality. Examples of variables that people frequently encounter are age, hair color, weight, and height.

Correlation and causation are two types of relationships between variables that have great importance for psychologists.

When two variables are related, they are said to have a *correlation*. Changes in variables often occur together. Sometimes, an increase or decrease in one is accompanied by a corresponding increase or decrease in the other. For example, a decrease in someone's caloric intake is accompanied by a decrease in that person's weight. Such variables are said to be *positively correlated.*

Sometimes, when one variable increases, the other decreases, or vice-versa. These variables are said to be *negatively correlated.* Examples of positive and negative correlations are illustrated in the chart on page S31.

Correlation coefficient

The *correlation coefficient* describes the degree of relationship between variables. The concept of correlation allows researchers to predict the value of one variable if they know the value of the other and the way that the variables are correlated. A perfect correlation would have a coefficient of +1.00; a perfect negative correlation has a coefficient of –1.00. A correlation coefficient of zero indicates that there is no correlation between two variables.

Perfect positive correlations (+ 1.00 coefficient), when graphed, form a straight line that leans to the right; a perfect negative correlation (–1.00 coefficient), shown on a line graph, would form a straight line to the left. In reality, few correlations are perfect. While one variable may increase or decrease in relation to the other, both variables probably will not change to the same degree.

The following is an example of a strong negative correlation with predictive potential: The more hours Tracy spends commuting to work, the less she enjoys driving. We can predict that if Tracy shortens her commute, her enjoyment of driving will increase.

Causation

Although correlation is an important concept in statistics, it does not explain everything about relationships between variables. For one thing, correlation does not speak to the concept of causation. No correlation, of any degree, in itself proves that one variable causes another.

It is difficult to determine whether one variable actually causes another. Researchers determine causal relationships scientifically rather than relying on the intuitive sense of causality that may be implied in a correlation. They compare the differences between an experimental group—the group that displays the condition that is being studied—and a control group, in which this condition is not present. The *independent variable* is the variable being manipulated by the researcher.

If Group A is exposed to a virus and gets sick, and Group B is exposed to the same virus but has been vaccinated and does not become ill, there appears to be a causal relationship at work. It seems that the vaccine protected Group B from the virus, and therefore from illness. But researchers probably would want to examine how the vaccine actually worked—if it did. It may have been coincidental that Group B remained well.

Positive and Negative Correlations

Positive Correlation

Generally speaking, people who have a higher need for achievement achieve higher salaries.

Need for achievement (High / Low) vs. Salaries (Low / High)

Negative Correlation

Generally speaking, the immune systems of people who are under high amounts of stress tend to function more poorly than the immune systems of people who are under less stress.

Stress measured by life changes (High / Low) vs. Immune system functioning (Low / High)

Correlations represent the relationship between two variables. When two variables show a positive correlation, one rises as the other rises. If the two variables are negatively correlated, one of the variables rises as the other falls.

UNIT 1

INTRODUCTION TO
PSYCHOLOGY

CHAPTERS

1   *What Is Psychology?*

2   *Psychological Methods*

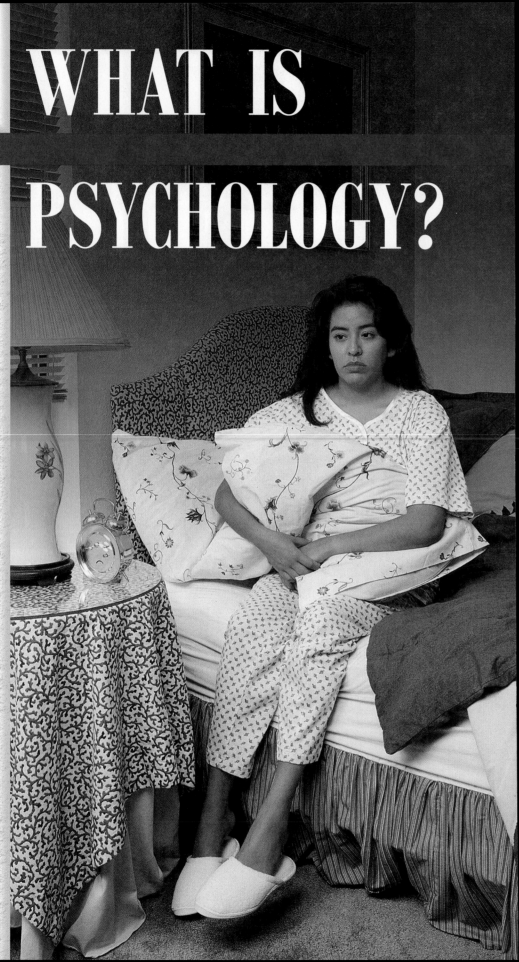

WHAT IS PSYCHOLOGY?

Read to Discover

1 What are the goals of psychology, and how is psychology a science?

2 What do psychologists do, and what are their areas of specialization?

3 How has the study of psychology developed over time?

4 What are the seven main contemporary perspectives in psychology?

A DAY IN THE LIFE

The alarm shook Linda out of a dream. Shafts of light pierced the window blinds in her room. She shut off the alarm, rose, and raised the blinds. A world of color splashed in. As she stifled a morning sneeze, Linda recalled that yesterday in psychology class her teacher had challenged the students to touch their noses with their eyes closed. Linda had succeeded, but Todd had jokingly poked himself in the eye. She remembered the incident and laughed. Her laughter stopped when she remembered that she was going to have a math test today. Then she relaxed. "No sweat; I'm really good at math," she thought. And after school, she had plans to meet some friends. "I wonder if Marc will be there," she pondered. (Linda thought Marc was very attractive.) She reflected sadly that Nick would not be there. Nick had a drug problem, and his parents had convinced him to go to a treatment center for help. Linda sighed to herself, then turned away from the window and went to the kitchen for breakfast. She was hungry.

Sleeping and waking, our perceptions of the worlds within and around us, memory, emotion, attractions between people—these are some of the topics of interest to psychologists. The kinds of questions that psychologists might ask about Linda's thoughts and behavior on this morning include the following:

- How did the alarm wake Linda? What happened inside her brain that woke her?
- Linda raised the blinds, and her morning became alive with color. How are we able to sense the world outside? Why do most of us see colors while some of us cannot?
- Linda was able to touch her nose with her eyes closed. What body senses enable us to know where our body parts are, and what we are doing when our eyes are closed?
- Linda is good at math. Why do students do well in some high school subjects such as math but struggle in others? How are factors such as motivation and intelligence involved?
- Linda was looking forward to meeting her friends. Why do most of us seek friendship? How is our behavior influenced by other people?
- Linda thought Marc was attractive. What is attraction? What is love? Why do we find some people attractive and others less so?
- Nick was involved with drugs. How do drugs affect people psychologically? In what ways are drugs harmful?
- Linda was hungry for breakfast. What makes us hungry? Why are some people overweight and others dangerously thin?

Psychologists are so intrigued by these types of questions that they make the attempt to answer them their life's work.

Key Terms

- psychology
- behavior
- cognitive activities
- psychological constructs
- theory
- principle
- basic research
- introspection
- associationism
- structuralism
- functionalism
- behaviorism
- Gestalt psychology
- psychoanalysis
- psychodynamic thinking
- biological perspective
- evolutionary perspective
- cognitive perspective
- humanistic perspective
- psychoanalytic perspective
- learning perspective
- social-learning theory
- sociocultural perspective
- ethnic group

HOLT

Psychology Video Program

Watch the video to explore the world of psychology.

TRUTH OR fiction?

Read the following statements about psychology. Do you think they are true or false? You will learn whether each statement is true or false as you read the chapter.

- Psychologists have very little interest in studying people's emotions.
- A book on psychology, with content similar to that found in this textbook, was written by Aristotle more than 2,000 years ago.
- In the Middle Ages, some innocent people were allowed to drown as a way of proving that they were not possessed by demons.
- Some psychologists view our strategies for solving problems as mental programs operated by our very own personal computers—our brains.
- Sigmund Freud's theories continue to influence psychology today.

SECTION 1

Why Study Psychology?

What do you hope to learn from the study of psychology? Perhaps you hope to gain a better understanding of why people act as they do or, more specifically, why *you* act as you do. Or perhaps you want to learn more about your thoughts and feelings; in doing so, you might discover more-effective ways to handle, or help others handle, the stresses of daily life. Whether your reason is general or specific, the study of psychology will give you new ways to look at and interpret the world and the people who inhabit it.

Behavior and Mental Processes

Psychology is the scientific study of behavior and

mental processes. **Behavior** is any action that other people can observe or measure. For example, Linda awakened, rose from her bed, raised the blinds, and laughed. All of these activities are behaviors. All are observable by other people.

Behavior also includes activities such as walking and talking, pressing a switch, turning left or right, sleeping, eating, and drinking. Behavior even

includes automatic body functions such as heart rate, blood pressure, digestion, and brain activity. Behavior can be measured by simple observation or by laboratory instruments. For example, brain activity can be measured by scientific instruments such as the electroencephalograph (EEG).

Linda also engaged in mental processes, or **cognitive activities**. These activities include dreams, perceptions, thoughts, and memories. For example, Linda was dreaming when her alarm rang. Brain waves that indicate dreaming can be measured, but dreaming itself is a private mental process—dreams are known only to the dreamer. Linda also perceived a world of color. Activity of the cells in a person's eyes can be measured as they respond to color, but only Linda could see her own mental image of the world. Linda laughed as she remembered the nose-touching psychology lesson. Memories, too, are private mental processes.

Psychologists are also interested in studying people's emotions, or feelings. Emotions can affect both behavior and mental processes. For example, Linda experienced a moment of anxiety when she remembered her math test, and she felt happiness at the thought of seeing Marc. Perhaps Linda's heart raced a bit when she thought about the test or about Marc. Her heart activity was an example of behavior, but her thoughts about the math test and about Marc were private mental processes. We would be unable to observe or measure Linda's thoughts directly. But if she told us about them, we would be observing a behavior—Linda *telling* us about her thoughts. Researchers often use **psychological constructs** to learn more about human behavior. These constructs are used to talk about something we cannot see, touch, or measure directly.

TRUTH OR fiction

■ REVISITED ■

It is not true that psychologists have very little interest in studying people's emotions. Psychologists know that emotions are important because they can influence both behavior and mental processes.

The Goals of Psychology

In general, scientists seek to observe, describe, explain, predict, and control the events they study. Psychologists have the same goals. They observe and describe behavior and mental processes to better understand them. A better understanding of behavior enables psychologists to explain, predict, and control behavior.

An example of how psychologists apply the goals of psychology can be seen in the case of Buffalo Bills placekicker Scott Norwood. Norwood had toiled for many years perfecting his techniques and preparing for the day when he might play in a Super Bowl. For several hours a day, he practiced and improved his form on the field. He kicked field goals from various distances and in all extremes of weather. Then he got his chance—the Bills and the New York Giants met in Super Bowl XXV. But when Norwood had the opportunity to win the game with a field goal, he missed, handing the victory to the Giants in the final seconds of the game. Norwood had lost his composure, which left him unable to perform under pressure.

Losing one's "cool" and failing to perform effectively in a crucial situation—such as during an important game or while taking a major test—can be very hard on a person. It can hurt an individual's self-esteem and self-confidence.

Sports psychologists help athletes such as Scott Norwood handle performance problems by applying the goals of psychology. First, they observe and describe the behavior. By measuring athletes' heart rates and other body processes, psychologists know that problems may occur when athletes are highly excited. Interviews with athletes reveal that they often feel anxious during big games. They may become distracted by the cheers or jeers of the crowd and lose their concentration. They cannot focus on the jobs they are supposed to be doing.

Psychologists then explain the behavior in terms of the feelings of anxiety and the distractions that hinder the athletes' performance. The relationship between anxiety and performance is somewhat complex. A little anxiety is often a good thing. It motivates us to practice for a game or to study for a test. It makes us alert and ready. On the other hand, too much anxiety is harmful. It may make us shaky and distract us from the task at hand.

Psychologists next predict that athletes will do best when anxiety is moderate and will falter when anxiety becomes too intense. Finally, they help athletes change, and thus control, their behavior and mental processes by teaching them ways of keeping their anxiety at a tolerable level. Psychologists also teach athletes how to filter out the sounds of the fans so they can focus on their task—helping the team win the game.

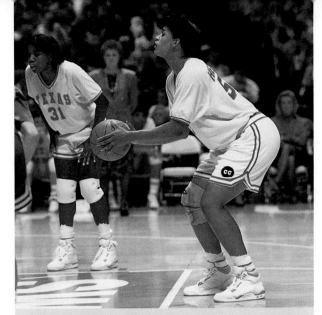

Some athletes use positive visualization to help them perform successfully in high-pressure situations such as close games.

One method that sports psychologists recommend to help athletes perform more effectively under pressure is called positive visualization. In this method, athletes imagine themselves going through the motions in a critical game situation. For example, a basketball player might imagine taking a free throw in overtime during a close game. She concentrates on blocking the noise of the crowd from her mind and focuses on the rim. She sees herself raising the ball with one hand as she guides it with the other. She then imagines releasing the ball and watching it glide through the net.

The goal of "controlling" behavior and mental processes is often misunderstood. Some people mistakenly think that psychologists seek ways to make people behave as the psychologists want them to—like puppets on strings. This is not so. Psychologists know that people should be free to make their own decisions. Psychologists know much about the factors that influence human behavior, and they use this knowledge to help people accomplish their own goals.

Psychology as a Science

Psychology is a social science, but it has foundations in the natural sciences. The social sciences, which also include history, anthropology, economics, political science, and sociology, deal with the structure of human society and the nature and interactions of the individuals who make up society. These individuals and their behavior and mental processes are the focus of psychology.

The natural sciences, which include biology, chemistry, and physics, are concerned with the nature of the physical world. Some areas that psychologists study, such as the functioning of the brain, are closely related to the natural sciences, particularly biology. Like natural scientists, psychologists seek to answer questions by following the steps involved in scientific research. These steps include conducting surveys and experiments, collecting and analyzing data, and drawing conclusions.

Research   As a science, psychology tests ideas through various research methods. Two widely used methods are surveys and experimentation. A survey is a method of collecting data that usually involves asking questions of people in a particular group.

Although most psychologists are interested mainly in human behavior, some choose to focus on animal behavior, such as that of sea snails, pigeons, rats, and gorillas. Some psychologists believe that research findings with certain animals can be applied to human beings. Others argue that humans are so distinct that we can only learn about them by studying people. The truth probably lies somewhere in between. For example, by studying the nerve cells of squid, psychologists have been able to learn about the workings of human nerve

cells. However, only by studying people can psychologists learn about uniquely human qualities such as morality, values, and love.

Psychologists rely on research to learn whether certain methods will work before they use them with clients. When the research is conducted with people, psychologists make every effort to protect the research participants. You will read more about research methods in Chapter 2.

Psychological Theories   Psychologists organize their research about behavior and mental processes into theories. A **theory** is a statement that attempts to explain why things are the way they are and happen the way they do. Psychological theories discuss principles that govern behavior and mental processes. A **principle** is a rule or law, such as the principle that you will probably get better grades if you study more. Psychological theories may include statements about behavior (such as sleeping or aggression), mental processes (such as memories and mental images), and biological processes (such as the effect of chemicals in the brain).

A useful psychological theory allows psychologists to predict behavior and mental processes. For example, if a theory about fatigue is useful, psychologists can apply it to predict when people will or will not sleep. If a theory does not accurately predict behavior or mental processes, psychologists consider revising or replacing the theory.

In psychology, as in other sciences, many theories have been found inadequate for accurately explaining or predicting the things with which they are concerned. As a result, these theories have been discarded or revised. For example, many psychologists once believed that stomach contractions were the cause of hunger. But then it was observed that many people feel hungry even when they do not have stomach contractions. As a result, psychologists now believe that stomach contractions are only one of many factors affecting appetite.

Psychologists often conduct surveys to learn about people's behavior and mental processes.

SECTION 1 REVIEW

go.hrw.com
Homework Practice Online
Keyword: SY7 HP1

1. What defining characteristics of psychology differentiate it from other related social sciences?
2. Define *theory* and *principle*.
3. **Critical Thinking**   *Summarizing* What is psychology, and what are the five goals of psychology?

CASE STUDIES
AND OTHER TRUE STORIES
Thinking Critically About Astrology

This chapter explores the scientific approaches and methods of psychologists. Psychologists are critical thinkers, which means that they are skeptical. They insist on seeing the evidence before they will accept people's claims and arguments about what is truth and what is fiction. As scientists, psychologists know that beliefs about the behavior of cosmic rays, chemical compounds, cells, or people must be supported by evidence. Persuasive arguments and reference to authority figures are *not* scientific evidence.

False sciences do not rely on verifiable evidence. Even so, false science is widespread. Think of the claims made by tabloid newspapers—each week, they announce 10 new sightings of Elvis Presley and 10 new encounters with extraterrestrials.

By examining one false science—astrology—we can learn why false science cannot be relied upon. Astrology is based on the idea that the positions of the stars, Moon, and planets affect human personality and destiny. One can also supposedly foretell the future by studying the positions of these bodies. Astrologers prepare forecasts called horoscopes, which are based on people's birth dates and indicate what is safe for them to do. Read the following description of personality. Would it be on target if you read it in your horoscope?

You have the inner potential for change. You have unused potential that you have not yet turned to your advantage. There are parts of your personality known to you alone. You have the ability to handle conflicting demands. You also have a strong potential for improvement.

This horoscope would actually apply to many different kinds of people. The tendency to believe such a general personality report is called the Barnum effect, after circus promoter P. T. Barnum, who once declared that a good circus had to "have something for everyone." General personality

Thinking critically is an important skill.

reports "have something for everyone," which allows palm readers and fortune-tellers to sound as if they are right on target.

Supporters of astrology might offer the following arguments:

- Astrology has been practiced for many centuries and is part of human tradition.
- Astrology seems to provide a path to meaning in life and, for a fortunate few, a road to riches.
- People in high positions have followed the advice of astrologers.
- If one heavenly body, the Moon, is powerful enough to sway the tides of the seas, why should the pulls of the stars and planets not affect people's destinies?
- Astrology is a special art and not a science. Therefore, we should not subject astrology to scientific testing.

Think critically about the claims of astrologers. For example, does the fact that astrology has a lengthy tradition mean that it is true? Are the tides similar to human personality and destiny?

Astrological predictions routinely fail. But does it matter? Will believers in astrology be persuaded by facts? Probably not. Even in our age of scientific enlightenment, millions of people will continue to consult their horoscopes. Psychology, however, is grounded in facts. Psychological findings are of value because they are routinely subjected to careful scrutiny.

THINKING CRITICALLY

1. **Drawing Inferences and Conclusions** What are false sciences, and why do you think they are so widespread?
2. **Comparing and Contrasting** How does psychology differ from false sciences?

What Psychologists Do

All psychologists share a keen interest in behavior and believe in the value of scientific research. They also share the belief that theories about behavior and mental processes should be supported by scientific evidence. They accept something as true only if the evidence shows it is so.

Some psychologists are interested mainly in research. They investigate the factors that give rise to behaviors and that explain certain mental processes. They form theories about why people and animals do the things they do. Then they test their theories by predicting when specific behaviors will occur.

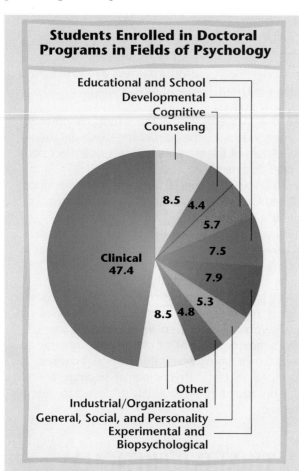

FIGURE 1.1 *Nearly half (47%) of the doctoral students who enroll in doctoral programs in psychology enroll in clinical programs. The next most popular field is counseling psychology. The figure combines students enrolled in public and private institutions.*

Source: Kyle, T. M. & Williams, S. (2000 May); 1998–1999 APA Survey of Graduate Department of Psychology, Tables 13A &13B

Other psychologists consult. That is, they apply psychological knowledge in the form of therapy to help people change their behavior so that they can better meet their own goals. Still other psychologists teach, sharing their knowledge of psychology in classrooms and workshops.

Clinical Psychologists

Clinical psychologists make up the largest group of psychologists. Clinical psychologists are the people most of us think of when we hear the term "psychologist."

Clinical psychologists help people with psychological problems, such as anxiety or depression, or severe psychological disorders, such as schizophrenia. Clinical psychologists help their clients overcome problems and adjust to the demands of their lives. They also help people who have problems with relationships, drug abuse, or weight control. Most likely, a clinical psychologist was helping Linda's friend Nick overcome his drug problem.

Clinical psychologists are trained to evaluate psychological problems through the use of interviews and psychological tests. Then these psychologists help clients understand and resolve their problems by changing ineffective or harmful behavior. (See Chapter 19.)

Clinical psychologists work in hospitals, in prisons, in college and university clinics, and in private practices. Some clinical psychologists divide their time among clinical practice, teaching, and research.

Clinical psychologists should not be confused with psychiatrists. A psychiatrist is a medical doctor who specializes in the treatment of psychological problems and who can prescribe medication for clients. Psychologists also specialize in the treatment of psychological problems, but because they are not medical doctors, they may not prescribe medication for their clients.

Counseling Psychologists

Like clinical psychologists, counseling psychologists use interviews and tests to identify their clients' problems. Counseling psychologists typically treat people who have adjustment problems rather than serious psychological disorders. For example, a counseling psychologist's clients may have difficulty making decisions about their careers, or they may find it hard to make friends. They may be experiencing conflicts with family members, teachers, employers, or colleagues. Counseling psychologists help their clients clarify their goals, overcome their adjustment problems, and meet challenges. Counseling psychologists are often employed in businesses and in college and university counseling and testing centers.

School Psychologists

Your school district may employ one or more school psychologists. School psychologists identify and help students who have problems that interfere with learning. Typical problems that school psychologists deal with include peer group and family problems, psychological problems, and learning disorders, which are problems in learning to read, write, or do math.

School psychologists identify students with problems by talking with teachers, parents, and the students themselves. School psychologists may also administer tests, such as intelligence tests and achievement tests. These tests, which are usually given to large groups of students, help identify students with special abilities as well as students who need assistance. For example, the psychologist at Linda's school noticed her exceptional results on the math section of an achievement test and recommended placing Linda in an advanced math class.

School psychologists also observe students in the classroom to see how they interact with their teachers and peers. After gathering the information they need, school psychologists advise teachers, school officials, and parents about how to help certain students reach their potential or overcome their learning difficulties.

In addition, school psychologists make recommendations regarding the placement of students in special classes and programs. In some school districts, student placement is the major responsibility of the school psychologist.

Educational Psychologists

Like school psychologists, educational psychologists are concerned with helping students learn. But they generally focus on course planning and instructional methods for an entire school system rather than on designing a program of study for an individual student.

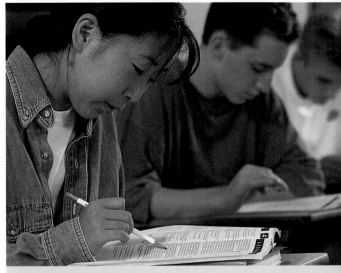

School psychologists may administer various types of tests to find out about students' abilities. Educational psychologists may help construct such tests.

Educational psychologists are concerned with theoretical issues that relate to measurement of abilities, learning, and child and adolescent development. Their research interests include the ways in which learning is affected by the following:

- psychological factors, such as motivation, emotions, creativity, and intelligence
- cultural factors, such as beliefs
- economic factors, such as the level of income earned by a person's family
- instructional methods used in the classroom

Some educational psychologists help prepare standardized tests, such as the Scholastic Aptitude Test (SAT). They study various tests to determine the type of test that can most effectively predict success in college. They may also examine individual test items to determine whether these items make a useful contribution to the test as a whole.

Developmental Psychologists

Developmental psychologists study the changes that occur throughout a person's life span. These changes can be of the following types:

- physical (including changes in height and weight, adolescent growth, sexual maturity, and the physical aspects of aging)
- emotional (for example, development of self-concept and self-esteem)

- cognitive (such as changes from childhood to adulthood in mental images of the world outside or how children learn right from wrong)
- social (such as formation of bonds between parents and children, relationships with peers, or intimate relationships between adults)

Developmental psychologists also attempt to sort out the relative influences of heredity and the environment on development. (See Chapters 3 and 10.)

Some developmental psychologists are especially interested in the challenges of adolescence. For example, how do adolescents handle the competing, and often contradictory, messages of peers (who pressure them to act in one way) and parents (who want them to act in another way)? How can psychologists help parents and school officials encourage adolescents to avoid activities that may be harmful to their physical and psychological well-being? What are the causes of depression and suicide among teens? How can people help prevent these painful situations from occurring?

Personality Psychologists

Personality psychologists identify characteristics, or traits. Shyness and friendliness are examples of traits. Personality psychologists look for the many different traits people have, and they study the development of these traits. Personality psychologists share with clinical psychologists an interest in the origins of psychological problems and disorders. These psychologists are also concerned with issues such as anxiety, aggression, and gender roles. Gender roles are the behavior patterns expected of women and men in a given culture.

Social Psychologists

Social psychologists are concerned with people's behavior in social situations. For example, they would be interested in studying the reasons for Linda's attraction to Marc. Whereas personality psychologists tend to look within people for explanations of behavior, social psychologists generally focus on external influences. Social psychologists study the following issues:

- the ways in which women and men typically behave in a given setting
- the physical and psychological factors that attract people to one another

- the reasons people tend to conform to group standards and expectations
- how people's behavior changes when they are members of a group
- the reasons for and the effects of prejudice and discrimination within various groups and from one group to another
- the situations in which people act aggressively and those in which they help others

Experimental Psychologists

Psychologists in all specialties may conduct experimental research. However, experimental psychologists conduct research into basic processes such as the functions of the nervous system. Other basic processes include sensation and perception, learning and memory, and thinking and motivation.

Experimental psychologists would be interested in exploring the biological reasons why Linda's alarm clock woke her. They would want to know what triggered her memory of the psychology class's nose-touching demonstration. In addition, experimental psychologists would be interested in the biological and psychological factors that contributed to Linda's feeling of hunger.

Some experimental psychologists focus on the relationships between biological changes (such as the release of hormones into the bloodstream) and psychological events (such as feelings of anxiety or depression). These experimental psychologists are called biological psychologists.

Experimental psychologists are more likely than other psychologists to engage in basic research. **Basic research** is research that has no immediate application and is done for its own sake. The findings of experimental psychologists are often put into practice by other psychological specialists. For example, basic research into motivation has helped clinical and counseling psychologists develop ways of helping people control their eating habits. Basic research into learning and memory has helped educational psychologists enhance learning conditions in schools.

Other Specialists

You have already read about sports psychologists and how they can help athletes. There are several other specialties in psychology.

Industrial and Organizational Psychologists

Industrial psychologists focus on people and work. Organizational psychologists study the behavior of people in organizations, such as business firms. Industrial psychology and organizational psychology are closely related. Psychologists in these fields are often trained in both areas.

Industrial and organizational psychologists are employed by business firms to improve working conditions and increase worker output. They may assist in hiring, training, and promoting employees. They may also devise psychological tests for job applicants and conduct research into the factors that contribute to job satisfaction. In addition, some industrial and organizational psychologists have counseling skills and help employees who have problems on the job.

Environmental Psychologists   Does crowding in cities make people irritable? Does smog have an effect on people's ability to learn? Environmental psychologists ask these types of questions. They focus on the ways in which people influence and are influenced by their physical environment. Environmental psychologists are concerned with the ways in which buildings and cities serve or fail to serve human needs. They investigate the psychological effects of extremes in temperature, noise, and air pollution.

Consumer Psychologists   Consumer psychologists study the behavior of shoppers to explain and predict their behavior. They also assist others in applying the findings of such studies. For example, they work with advertisers to create effective newspaper ads and television commercials. They advise store managers about window displays and shelf arrangement to attract customers. Have you ever noticed that in many supermarkets, milk is shelved far away from the store entrance? That is because milk is an item that many people buy frequently. Its placement at the rear of the store ensures that shoppers will pass—and hopefully buy—other items on the way to the milk shelf.

Forensic Psychologists   When an attorney wants an expert witness to testify whether a person accused of a crime is or is not competent to stand trial, the attorney might call on a forensic psychologist. These psychologists work within the criminal justice system. In addition to testifying about the psychological competence of defendants, they may explain how certain kinds of psychological prob-

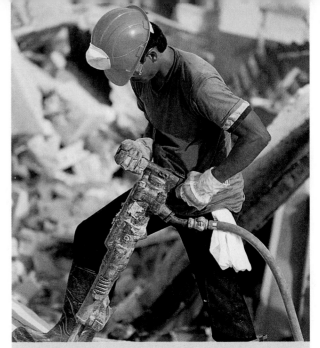

*A worker clears rubble from the site of a collapsed building. **What types of psychologists might be interested in studying the effects of such work?***

lems give rise to criminal behavior. Police departments employ psychologists to do the following jobs:

- assist in the selection of police officers
- help police officers cope with job stress
- train police officers in the handling of dangerous situations such as suicide threats, hostage crises, and family violence

Health Psychologists   Health psychologists examine the ways in which behavior and mental processes are related to physical health. They study the effects of stress on health problems such as headaches and heart disease. Health psychologists try to explain why some people follow their doctor's advice and other people do not. Health psychologists also help people adopt healthful behaviors such as exercising.

SECTION 2 REVIEW

go. hrw .com **Homework Practice Online**

Keyword: SY7 HP1

1. In what way are psychiatrists and psychologists different?

2. List three subspecialties of psychology and describe the work of each.

3. **Critical Thinking**   *Analyzing Information* If you decided to become a psychologist, which subspecialty of psychology would you prefer and why?

A History of Psychology

People have always been interested in the behaviors of other people. Thus psychology is as old as human history. Interest in the actions, motives, and thoughts of human beings can be traced as far back as the philosophers and scientists of ancient times.

Roots from Ancient Greece

More than 2,000 years ago, Plato (428–348 or 347 B.C.), a student of Socrates in ancient Greece, recorded his teacher's advice: "Know thyself." This phrase has remained a motto of psychological study ever since. Socrates suggested that we can learn much about ourselves by carefully examining our thoughts and feelings. Psychologists call this method of learning **introspection**, which means "looking within."

One of Plato's students, Greek philosopher Aristotle (384–322 B.C.), raised many questions about human behavior that are still discussed. Aristotle outlined the laws of **associationism**, which are still at the heart of learning theory more than 2,000 years later. He showed how experiences often remind us of similar experiences in the past, how the face of a loved one makes us feel secure, and how thought leads to ideas as we dream and as we daydream. One of Aristotle's works is called *Peri Psyches,* which means "about the mind." Aristotle's approach was scientific. He argued that human behavior, like the movements of the stars and the seas, is subject to certain rules and laws. He believed one such universal law was that people are motivated to seek pleasure and to avoid pain—a view still found in some modern psychological theories. *Peri Psyches* also explores topics such as sensation and perception, thought, intelligence, needs and motives, feelings and emotions, and memory.

Socrates encouraged people to examine their thoughts and feelings—to know themselves.

TRUTH
OR
fiction
■ R E V I S I T E D ■

It is true that a book with content similar to that found in this textbook was written by Aristotle more than 2,000 years ago. The name of that book is *Peri Psyches.*

The ancient Greeks also theorized about various psychological problems, such as confusion and bizarre behavior. Throughout human history, many people have attributed such disorders to supernatural forces. The ancient Greeks generally believed that the gods punished people for wrongdoing by causing them confusion and madness. However, the Greek physician Hippocrates (c. 460–c. 377 B.C.) was an exception. He suggested that such problems are caused by abnormalities in the brain. But this idea that biological factors can affect our thoughts, feelings, and behavior influenced thinking about psychology for more than 2,000 years.

The Middle Ages

During the Middle Ages, most Europeans believed that problems such as agitation and confusion were signs of possession by demons. A popular belief of the time was that possession was punishment for sins or the result of deals made with the devil.

Certain "tests" were used to determine whether a person was possessed. One of the most infamous tests, the water-float test, was based on the principle that pure metals sink to the bottom during the smelting process whereas impure metals float to the surface. Individuals who were suspected of being possessed were thrown into deep water. Suspects who managed to keep their heads above water were assumed to be impure and in league with the devil. They were then executed for associating with the devil. Those who sank to the bottom, on the other hand, were judged to be pure. Unfortunately, some of those enjoyed no better fate—they drowned.

TRUTH OR **fiction** ■ REVISITED ■

It is true that in the Middle Ages some innocent people were allowed to drown as a way of proving that they were not possessed by the devil. The method was based on a water-float test used for judging the purity of metals.

The Birth of Modern Science

People of the 1500s, 1600s, and 1700s witnessed great scientific and intellectual advances. In the 1500s, for example, Polish astronomer Nicolaus Copernicus challenged the view that the sun revolved around Earth, suggesting instead that Earth revolves around the sun. In the 1600s English scientist Sir Isaac Newton formulated the laws of gravity and motion. English Philosopher John Locke, building on principles of associationism, theorized that knowledge is not inborn but is learned from experience. In the late 1700s French scientist Antoine Lavoisier founded the science of chemistry and explained how animals and plants use oxygen in respiration.

The scientific approach also led to the birth of modern psychology in the 1800s. Psychologists argued that ideas about human behavior and mental processes should be supported by evidence. In the late 1800s psychological laboratories were established in Europe and the United States. In these laboratories, psychologists studied behavior and mental processes using methods similar to those Lavoisier had used to study chemistry. Most historians of psychology point to the year 1879 as the beginning of psychology as a modern laboratory science. In that year, German psychologist Wilhelm Wundt established his laboratory in Leipzig.

Wilhelm Wundt and Structuralism

Wilhelm Wundt (1832–1920) and his students founded a field of experimental psychology that came to be known as **structuralism**. Structuralists were concerned with discovering the basic elements of consciousness. Wundt broke down the content of consciousness into two categories: objective sensations and subjec-

Wilhelm Wundt

tive feelings. Objective sensations, such as sight and taste, were assumed to accurately reflect the outside world. Subjective feelings were thought to include emotional responses and mental images.

Structuralists believed that the human mind functioned by combining these basic elements of experience. For example, a person can experience an apple objectively by observing its shape, color, texture, and taste. The person can also experience the apple subjectively by remembering how good it feels to bite into one. Using the method of introspection, Wundt and his students carefully examined and reported their experiences.

William James and Functionalism

A decade after Wundt established his laboratory, introspection convinced Harvard University professor William James (1842–1910) that conscious experience cannot be broken down as structuralists believed. James maintained that experience is a continuous "stream of consciousness."

William James

He focused on the relationships between experience and behavior and described his views in *The Principles of Psychology*. Many consider this book, published in 1890, to be the first modern psychology textbook.

James was one of the founders of the school of **functionalism**. Functionalists were concerned with how mental processes help organisms adapt to their environment. They stressed the application of their findings to everyday situations.

Calvin and Hobbes

by Bill Watterson

Functionalism differed from structuralism in several ways. Whereas structuralism relied only on introspection, the methods of functionalism included behavioral observation in the laboratory as well as introspection. The structuralists tended to ask, What are the elements (structures) of psychological processes? The functionalists, on the other hand, tended to ask, What are the purposes (functions) of behavior and mental processes? What do certain behaviors and mental processes accomplish for the person (or animal)?

Functionalists proposed that adaptive behavior patterns are learned and maintained because they are successful. For example, some students study diligently because they have learned that studying leads to good grades. Less-adaptive behavior patterns are dropped or are discontinued. For example, if you ask someone for a date repeatedly and are refused each time, eventually you will probably stop asking the person out.

Adaptive (successful) actions are repeated and eventually become habits. The formation of habits is seen in such acts as turning doorknobs or riding a bicycle. At first, these acts require our full attention. But through repetition—and success—they become automatic. The multiple tasks involved in learning to type on a keyboard or to write in longhand also become routine through successful repetition. We then perform them without much attention. Habit allows us to take the mechanics of typing or writing for granted and to concentrate instead on *what* we are typing or writing.

John B. Watson and Behaviorism

Picture a hungry rat in a maze. It moves along until it reaches a place where it must turn left or right. If the rat is consistently rewarded with food for turning right at that place, it will learn to turn right when it arrives there the next time—at least, when it is hungry. But what does the rat *think* when it is learning to turn right at that place in the maze?

Does it seem absurd to try to place yourself in the mind of a rat? It did to John B. Watson (1878–1958), when he was asked by examiners to consider this question as a requirement for his doctoral degree in psychology.

John B. Watson

He was asked this question because functionalism was the dominant school of psychology at the time. Functionalists were concerned with the stream of consciousness as well as with behavior. Although Watson agreed with the functionalist focus on the importance of learning, he believed that it was unscientific to study a construct like consciousness—particularly the consciousness of animals. He saw consciousness as a private event that is known only to the individual. He asserted that if psychology was to be a natural science, like physics or chemistry, it must be limited to observable, measurable events—that is, to behavior. As the founder of the school of **behaviorism**, Watson defined psychology as the scientific study of observable behavior.

B. F. Skinner and Reinforcement

Harvard University psychologist B. F. Skinner (1904–1990) added to the behaviorist tradition by introducing the concept of reinforcement. Skinner

EXPLORING
DIVERSITY

Bringing Diversity into Psychology

In the past, psychology—like many other academic fields—was dominated by white men. Not only were the psychologists themselves mostly white men, but most of their research used white male participants and tended to explore issues that were relevant primarily to white men. However, in recent decades that has changed. Today many psychologists are women and members of traditionally underrepresented ethnic groups. In fact, white men now obtain fewer than half of the doctoral degrees in psychology.

Not only are psychologists as a group more diverse now than they used to be—so is their research. A great deal of current psychological research deals with questions of gender, culture, prejudice, and stereotypes. The work of African American psychologist Kenneth Bancroft Clark exemplifies such research.

Clark was born in the Panama Canal Zone in 1914, the son of West Indian parents. Miriam Clark, his mother, brought her children to the United States for their education. They settled in the Harlem section of New York City.

Although most African American children at the time were advised to attend vocational high schools, where they could learn specific job skills, Kenneth Clark attended an academic high school. He went on to Howard University in Washington, D.C., where he majored in psychology and married Mamie Phipps. The Clarks then attended Columbia University, where they both earned Ph.D. degrees in psychology.

In 1946 the Clarks founded the Northside Center for Child Development. Kenneth and Mamie Clark's clinical work led to several studies showing the negative effect of segregation on the self-esteem of African American children. In one

Kenneth B. Clark

well-known study (Clark & Clark, 1947), African American children were asked to choose between white and black dolls after being given instructions such as "Give me the pretty doll" or "Give me the doll that looks bad." The Clarks reported that most children preferred the white dolls over the black ones and concluded that the children were demonstrating their feelings that society as a whole preferred white people.

In the early 1950s Kenneth Clark began working with the National Association for the Advancement of Colored People (NAACP) to end school segregation. In 1954, when the Supreme Court overturned the "separate but equal" doctrine, it cited Clark's work on the effects of discrimination on the personality development of both African American and white children. In his book *Prejudice and Your Child,* published in 1955, Clark described the effects of segregation on white children as well as on African American children.

Clark's later work examined the quality of education and the problems of juvenile delinquency and crime. He was among the first experts to recommend preschool classes, after-school programs, and community participation.

Think About It

Analyzing Information Kenneth Clark is only one of the many people who have contributed to psychology's diversity. Select one of the following psychologists and prepare an oral report on his or her life and work: J. Henry Alston, Mary Whiton Calkins, Lillian Comas-Diaz, Beverly Greene, Gilbert Haven Jones, Christine Ladd Franklin, Jorge Sanchez, Stanley Sue, Margaret Floy Washburn.

B. F. Skinner

showed that when an animal is reinforced, or rewarded, for performing an action, it is more likely to perform that action again in the future. He demonstrated that laboratory animals, such as rats and pigeons, are capable of learning complex behavior patterns if they are reinforced in the right ways. Behaviorists have taught animals to push buttons, turn in circles, climb ladders, push toys across the floor, and even shoot baskets by rewarding the animals for performing the desired behavior.

According to Skinner, people learn in the same way animals do. Like animals, people learn to behave in certain ways because they have been reinforced for doing so.

The Gestalt School

Look at the two drawings in Figure 1.2 and answer the questions posed in the caption. These drawings demonstrate the idea that the perception of something is affected by the context in which it occurs. For example, in Drawing A, the circles in the centers of the two sets are the same size. However, we may think they are different sizes because of the differing contexts in which they appear. That is, one circle is surrounded by larger circles and the other is surrounded by smaller circles.

In Drawing B, the second symbols in the two rows are identical. The symbol in the top row may look like the letter B because it is with the letters A, C, and D. However, when the identical symbol is with the numbers 12, 14, and 15, it may look more like the number 13. Even though the two symbols are identical, the context in which each one appears influences what we perceive it to be.

German psychologists Max Wertheimer, Kurt Koffka, and Wolfgang Köhler were fascinated by the ways in which context influences people's interpretation of information. In the 1920s they founded the school of **Gestalt psychology**. The psychology of *Gestalt,* which means "shape" or "form" in German, is based on the idea that perceptions are more than the sums of their parts. Rather, they are wholes that give shape, or meaning, to the parts. As such, Gestalt psychology rejects the structuralist idea that experience can be broken down into individual parts or elements.

Gestalt psychologists also reject the behaviorist notion that psychologists should concentrate only on observable behavior. In addition, Gestalt psychologists believe that learning is active and purposeful. They disagree with the behaviorist view that learning is mechanical.

These circus lions probably learned how to do their tricks by being reinforced, or rewarded, for each behavior that contributed to the overall effect the trainers were trying to achieve.

FIGURE 1.2 *Look at Drawing A. Are the circles in the centers of the two sets of circles the same size? In Drawing B, what is the second symbol in each line? We perceive images in terms of the contexts in which they occur, so two images that are identical may appear to be different if their surroundings are different.*

Köhler and the other founders of Gestalt psychology demonstrated that much learning, particularly problem solving, is accomplished by insight, not by mechanical repetition. Insight is the reorganization of perceptions that enables an individual to solve a problem. In other words, insight is the sudden appearance of the Gestalt, or form, that enables the individual to see the solution.

Sigmund Freud and the School of Psychoanalysis

Sigmund Freud

Sigmund Freud (1856–1939), a Viennese physician, was perhaps the most famous of the early psychologists. The school of thought that he founded, called **psychoanalysis**, emphasizes the importance of unconscious motives and internal conflicts in determining human behavior.

Freud's theory, more than the others, has become a part of popular culture. You may be familiar with several Freudian concepts. For example, have you ever tried to interpret a slip of the tongue, or have you ever tried to figure out the meaning of a dream you had? The ideas that people are driven by hidden impulses and that verbal slips and dreams represent unconscious wishes largely reflect Freud's influence on popular culture.

Structuralists, functionalists, behaviorists, and Gestalt psychologists all conducted their research in the laboratory. However, Freud gained his understanding of human behavior through consultations with patients. Freud was astounded at how little insight these patients had into their own ideas and feelings. He came to believe that unconscious processes, particularly sexual and aggressive urges, are more important than conscious experience in governing people's behavior and feelings.

Freud's theory which is sometimes called **psychodynamic thinking**, assumed that most of what exists in an individual's mind is unconscious and consists of conflicting impulses, urges, and wishes. According to Freud's theories, human behavior is aimed at satisfying these desires, even though some of them seem socially inappropriate or even unacceptable. But at the same time, people want to see themselves as good and decent human beings. Thus, they often are consciously unaware of the real motivations for their behavior. Freud attempted to help people gain insight into their unconscious conflicts and find socially acceptable ways of expressing their wishes and meeting their needs.

SECTION 3 REVIEW

Homework Practice Online
Keyword: SY7 HP1

1. Describe the main differences between structuralism and functionalism.

2. How did the field of psychology develop?

3. **Critical Thinking** *Drawing Inferences and Conclusions* Identify one example of the influence that Sigmund Freud's psychoanalytic theory has had on popular culture.

Contemporary Perspectives

Today few psychologists describe themselves as structuralists or functionalists. Few would consider themselves Gestalt psychologists although the school of Gestalt psychology has inspired current research in perception and problem solving. The numbers of traditional behaviorists and psychoanalysts also have been declining. Many current psychologists in the behaviorist tradition have modified the theories of Watson and Skinner. Similarly, many contemporary psychoanalysts do not use the methods Freud did.

Nevertheless, the historical traditions of psychology find expression in contemporary perspectives on psychology. The most important of these are the biological, evolutionary, cognitive, humanistic, psychoanalytic, learning, and sociocultural perspectives. Each perspective emphasizes different topics of investigation and has different approaches.

The Biological Perspective

The **biological perspective** emphasizes the influence of biology on our behavior. This perspective has roots in associationism. Psychologists assume that our mental processes—our thoughts, fantasies, and dreams—are made possible by the nervous system. They point particularly to its key component, the brain. Biologically oriented psychologists look for the connections between events in the brain, such as the activity of brain cells, and behavior and mental processes. They use several techniques, such as CAT scans and PET scans, to show which parts of the brain are involved in various mental processes. (See Chapter 3.) Biological psychology has shown that certain parts of the brain are highly active when we listen to music, other parts are active when we solve math problems, and still other parts are involved with certain psychological disorders. Biological psychologists have also learned that certain chemicals in the brain are connected with the storage of information—that is, the formation of memories.

Moreover, biological psychologists are interested in the influences of hormones and genes. Hormones are chemicals that glands release into the bloodstream to set in motion various body functions, such as growth or digestion. Genes are the basic units of heredity. Biological psychologists study the influences of genes on personality traits, psychological health, and various behavior patterns.

The Evolutionary Perspective

The **evolutionary perspective** focuses on the evolution of behavior and mental processes. British scientist Charles Darwin theorized that in the struggle for survival, the most-adaptive organisms have a greater chance of surviving to maturity, when they can reproduce. For example, people who are naturally resistant to certain diseases are more likely to transmit their genes to future generations. Evolutionary psychologists suggest that many kinds of behavior patterns, such as aggressive behavior, also have a hereditary basis. These psychologists believe that inherited tendencies influence people to act in certain ways.

The Cognitive Perspective

The **cognitive perspective** emphasizes the role that thoughts play in determining behavior. Cognitive psychologists study mental processes to understand human nature. They investigate the ways in which people perceive information and make mental images of the world, solve problems, and dream and daydream. Cognitive psychologists, in short, study what we refer to as the mind.

The cognitive tradition has roots in Socrates' maxim "Know thyself" and in his method of introspection for learning about the self. Cognitive psychology also has roots in structuralism, functionalism, and Gestalt psychology. Each of these schools of thought has addressed issues that are of interest to cognitive psychologists.

Another aspect of the cognitive perspective involves information processing. Many cognitive psychologists have been influenced by computer science. Computers process information to solve problems. Information is first fed into the computer. The information is then placed in the working memory while it is being worked on. After being processed, the information is stored more or less permanently on the computer's hard drive, a compact disk, or another storage device.

Many psychologists speak of people as having working memories and storage facilities (or long-term memories). If information has been placed in computer storage or in a person's long-term memory, it must first be retrieved before it can be worked on again. To retrieve information from computer storage, people must know the name for the data file and the process for retrieving data files. Similarly, cognitive psychologists believe people need certain cues to retrieve information from their long-term memories. Otherwise, it is lost to them.

Cognitive psychologists sometimes refer to our strategies for solving problems as our "mental programs" or "software." In this computer metaphor, our brains are the "hardware" that runs our mental programs. In other words, our brains are our own *very* personal computers.

TRUTH OR **fiction** ■ REVISITED ■

It is true that some psychologists view our strategies for solving problems as mental programs operated by our own very personal computers—our brains. These psychologists are called cognitive psychologists, and they study how we process information.

Cognitive psychologists believe that people's behavior is influenced by their values, their perceptions, and their choices. For example, an individual who interprets a casual remark as an insult may react with hostility. But the same remark directed at another person might be perceived very differently by that person and thus may meet with a different reaction.

The Humanistic Perspective

The **humanistic perspective** stresses the human capacity for self-fulfillment and the importance of consciousness, self-awareness, and the capacity to make choices. Consciousness is seen as the force that shapes human personality.

Humanistic psychology considers people's personal experiences to be the most important aspect of psychology. Humanistic psychologists believe that self-awareness, experience, and choice permit us to "invent ourselves." In other words, they enable us to fashion our growth and our ways of relating to the world as we go through life. Unlike the behaviorists, who assume that behavior is caused largely by the stimuli that act upon us, humanistic psychologists believe that we are free to choose our own behavior.

The humanistic perspective views people as basically good and desiring to be helpful to others. Humanistic psychologists help people explore their

Some cognitive psychologists are interested in the ways in which children view the world.

feelings, manage their negative impulses, and realize their potential.

Critics of the humanistic perspective, particularly behaviorists, insist that psychology should be scientific and address only observable events. They argue that people's inner experiences are unsuited to scientific observation and measurement. However, humanistic psychologists insist that inner experience is vital to the understanding of human nature.

The Psychoanalytic Perspective

The **psychoanalytic perspective** stresses the influence of unconscious forces on human behavior. In the 1940s and 1950s, psychoanalytic theory dominated the practice of psychotherapy and greatly influenced psychology and the arts. Although psychoanalytic thought no longer dominates psychology, its influence continues to be felt. Psychologists who follow Sigmund Freud's approach today focus less on the roles of unconscious sexual and aggressive impulses and more on conscious choice and self-direction.

TRUTH OR **fiction** ■ REVISITED ■

It is true that Sigmund Freud's theories continue to influence psychology today. However, psychoanalytic theory no longer dominates the field, and contemporary psychologists who follow Freud's approach focus on different factors than Freud did.

Contemporary Psychological Perspectives

Perspective	Subject Matter	Key Assumption
Biological	Nervous system, glands and hormones, genetic factors	Biological processes influence behavior and mental processes.
Evolutionary	Physical traits, social behavior	Adaptive organisms survive and transmit their genes to future generations.
Cognitive	Interpretation of mental images, thinking, language	Perceptions and thoughts influence behavior.
Humanistic	Self-concept	People make free and conscious choices based on their unique experiences.
Psychoanalytic	Unconscious processes, early childhood experiences	Unconscious motives influence behavior.
Learning	Environmental influences, learning, observational learning	Personal experience and reinforcement guide individual development.
Sociocultural	Ethnicity, gender, culture, socioeconomic status	Sociocultural, biological, and psychological factors create individual differences.

FIGURE 1.3 *Contemporary psychologists differ in their approaches to psychological thought. These seven broad perspectives are the most common ways that psychologists view behavior today.*

Freud believed that aggressive impulses are common reactions to the frustrations of daily life and that we seek to vent these impulses on other people. Because we fear rejection or retaliation, we put most aggressive impulses out of our minds. But by holding aggression in, we set the stage for future explosions. Pent-up aggressive impulses demand outlets. Partial outlets can be provided by physical activity—for example, sports—but we may also direct hostile impulses toward strangers. (That guy who intentionally bumped into you in the hallway, according to Freud, might be venting unconscious anger toward his parents.)

The Learning Perspective

The **learning perspective** emphasizes the effects of experience on behavior. In the views of many psychologists, learning is the essential factor in observing, describing, explaining, predicting, and controlling behavior. However, the term *learning* has different meanings to different psychologists. For example, traditional behaviorists and social-learning theorists have different attitudes toward the role of consciousness in learning.

John B. Watson and other behaviorists found no role for consciousness. They believed that people act and react because of their learning histories and the influence of their situations, not because of conscious choice. Behaviorists are not concerned with what an organism *knows*. They are concerned with what the organism *does*. Behaviorists emphasize the importance of environmental influences and focus on the learning of habits through repetition and reinforcement.

In contrast, **social-learning theory** suggests that people can change their environments or create new ones. Furthermore, social-learning theory holds that people can learn intentionally by observing others. Social-learning theorists believe that conscious observational learning provides people with a storehouse of responses to life's situations. However, people's expectations and values influence whether they *choose* to do what they have learned how to do.

Psychologists who take the learning perspective believe that behavior is learned either from direct experience or by observing other people. For example, people will behave a certain way when they expect to be rewarded for that behavior. Social-learning theorists have a cognitive leaning. Like cognitive theorists, social-learning theorists believe that people act in a particular way only when they recognize that the circumstances call for that behavior. For example, we act with hostility when we have been provoked, or we act with friendliness when we have been treated well.

The Sociocultural Perspective

The **sociocultural perspective** studies the influences of ethnicity, gender, culture, and socioeconomic status on behavior and mental processes. By taking these factors into account, psychologists can better understand how people act and think. The science of psychology is enriched by awareness of these factors and by taking them into account when conducting research (Denmark, 1998).

One kind of diversity involves ethnicity. Members of an **ethnic group** are united by their cultural heritage, race, language, or common history. The sociocultural perspective helps people appreciate the cultural heritages and historical issues of various ethnic groups. The following items are among the psychological issues related to ethnicity:

- inclusion of people from various ethnic minority groups in psychological research studies
- bilingualism
- ethnic differences in intelligence test scores
- ethnic differences in vulnerability to health problems ranging from obesity to high blood pressure and certain forms of cancer
- prejudice

Sociocultural theorists also study gender, which is the state of being male or being female. Gender is not simply a matter of anatomy. It involves a complex web of cultural expectations and social roles that affect people's self-concepts and aspirations as well as their behavior. One reason for the importance of gender studies is that such studies address issues concerning similarities and differences between males and females.

In the past, much of the scientific research on gender roles and gender differences assumed that male behavior represents the norm (Ader &

One topic explored by followers of the sociocultural perspective is how people of different ethnicities and genders interact with each other.

Johnson, 1994). Such assumptions have changed in recent years. Women, who have entered higher education in great numbers, had traditionally been channeled into domestic pursuits. In the United States, women have attended college only since 1833, when Oberlin College opened its doors to women. Yet today more than half of American college students are women. Two thirds of the doctoral degrees in psychology are awarded to women (Kohout & Williams, 1999).

Following the pattern of American society in general, the field of psychology is becoming more diverse. African Americans make up 6 percent to 7 percent of the first-year students in doctoral departments in psychology, and Hispanics make up 5 percent (APA Research Office, 2000). However, these percentages are far below these groups' representation in the general population.

go.hrw.com **Homework Practice Online** Keyword: SY7 HP1

SECTION 4 REVIEW

1. How do cognitive psychologists compare people's mental processes to the working of computers?

2. How would a psychoanalyst explain aggression?

3. List the seven leading contemporary perspectives in psychology.

4. **Critical Thinking** *Evaluating* How does knowledge of cultural differences enrich the study of psychology?

Chapter 1 REVIEW

Writing a Summary

Using standard grammar, spelling, sentence structure, and punctuation, summarize the information in this chapter. Consider:
- the goals of psychology and psychologists' areas of specialization
- the history of psychology and the seven main contemporary perspectives in psychology

Identifying People and Ideas

Identify the following terms or people and use them in appropriate sentences.

1. psychology
2. cognitive activities
3. theory
4. Aristotle
5. structuralism
6. functionalism
7. B. F. Skinner
8. psychoanalysis
9. humanistic perspective
10. social-learning theory

Understanding Main Ideas

SECTION 1 (pp. 4–6)
1. How do the concepts of theory and principle differ?

SECTION 2 (pp. 8–11)
2. Describe what clinical and counseling psychologists do.

SECTION 3 (pp. 12–17)
3. What view held by the ancient Greek physician Hippocrates was ahead of its time?

SECTION 4 (pp. 18–21)
4. What are the seven main contemporary perspectives in psychology?

Thinking Critically

1. **Analyzing Information** Trace the impact of psychodynamic thinking on current thinking in psychology.

2. **Making Generalizations and Predictions** Sports psychology is an example of a relatively new area of psychological specialization. What do you think might be important areas for psychology in the years ahead? Explain your choices.

3. **Analyzing Information** Trace the impact of associationism on current thinking in psychology.

4. **Evaluating** Describe a commonly held belief about gender differences that sociocultural psychologists might want to research. How might they go about proving or disproving this belief?

5. **Drawing Inferences and Conclusions** Describe the relationship between earlier and later theories related to a given psychological construct.

Writing About Psychology

1. **Summarizing** Find three newspaper or magazine articles that discuss the work done by different psychologists. Write a summary of the articles, describing what type of psychologist is featured in each article.

2. **Analyzing Information** A tip line is a telephone service people can call to hear a recording of helpful information. Write a three-minute script for a tip line on the services different psychologists provide. Consider the kinds of concerns people might want to discuss with each type of psychologist. Use the graphic organizer below to help you write your script.

People's Concerns

Interpreting Graphs

Study the bar graph below. Then use the information in the graph to help you answer the questions that follow.

Employment in Psychology in the United States

300,000
250,000
200,000
150,000
100,000
50,000
0

135,000
42.9%
57.1%
1983

230,000
39.7%
60.3%
1991

266,000
35.1%
64.9%
1999

Years

■ Female Employees □ Male Employees

Source: U.S. Census Bureau

1. How many more psychologists were employed in 1999 than in 1983?
   a. 131,000
   b. 135,000
   c. 266,000
   d. 401,000

2. What conclusions can you draw about the field of psychology in the United States from the years 1983 to 1991?

Analyzing Primary Sources

Read the following excerpt, in which Stephen Poland describes his work as a school psychologist. Then answer the questions that follow.

❝Another benefit you have as a school psychologist is the opportunity to work in a multitude of settings with learners of all ages and backgrounds. . . . School settings allow you to intervene with children who would never come through the doors of a mental health clinic because their families lack the financial resources, motivation, or the knowledge to access these services. Most schools are 'zero reject' service centers that are mandated [required] to serve whoever comes in the door. The impact of your intervention is magnified in a school because you can work with children and their teachers, other school staff, and their parents.❞

3. Which of the following statements best describes Poland's point of view?
   a. Teachers and other school staff interfere with the work of school psychologists.
   b. School psychologists are able to work with people who might otherwise not receive professional assistance.
   c. Because schools do not reject students, school psychologists have a very difficult job.
   d. Many parents do not want their child to meet with the school psychologist.

4. According to this excerpt, why do school psychologists assist a variety of people and problems?

PSYCHOLOGY PROJECTS

Cooperative Learning

Using Your Observation Skills As a class, agree to watch the same program on television. The next day, organize small groups of students to discuss the program's characters. What behaviors did you observe? How did you find out about the characters' thoughts (cognitive activities) and feelings (emotions)? Choose one person in your group to record the group's ideas on the role of observation in understanding differences among people. Share your group's ideas with the class.

🖥 internet connect

Internet Activity: go.hrw.com
KEYWORD: SY7 CH7

Choose an activity on psychology:
- write a profile about a historical psychologist.
- create a pamphlet that discusses the ways in which contemporary perspectives have changed traditional theories and practice in psychology.
- write a short story illustrating a typical day in the life of a psychologist.

2 Chapter

PSYCHOLOGICAL METHODS

Read to Discover

1 What steps do scientists follow in conducting scientific research?

2 Why are proper sampling techniques important?

3 What are the various methods of observation, and how is correlation used in analyzing results?

4 What are the purposes and elements of experiments?

5 How are ethical issues involved in psychological research?

A DAY IN THE LIFE

Dan and Marc were at Todd's, and Dan noticed a new fish tank in Todd's room. "Hey, Todd, when did you get this?"

"Last week," explained Todd. "I finally made enough money at the restaurant to be able to buy a fish tank and some fish. I've wanted fish since I was little."

"Cool! What do you have to do to take care of them?" Marc asked.

"You know, feed them, monitor the water temperature, generally watch over the fish and make sure they're doing okay. Like last week, I noticed that they seemed to be acting a little sluggish. They were eating less than usual, so I figured it was because they didn't like the food I was feeding them. I switched to a different kind of fish food."

"Did it help?"

"It seemed to, although it took a couple of days."

"What kind of fish are in here?" Dan asked.

"Some tetras and a Siamese fighting fish. I wanted to get more than one of the fighting fish, but the salesperson at the pet store said that probably wasn't a good idea."

"Why? What would they do to each other?" Dan wanted to know.

"I'm not sure. Attack each other, I think," Todd speculated.

"Too bad the fish can't tell us!" Dan joked.

Marc was quiet as he watched the fish swim around. "Do you have a mirror?" he asked suddenly.

Todd got a small hand mirror, wondering what Marc was up to. Then Marc held up the mirror so the fighting fish could see its reflection. The fish fanned out its fins menacingly, puffed up its cheeks, and started to dart toward its reflection. Marc moved the mirror away.

"I bet that was its attack reaction! It didn't realize that the other fish was only a reflection of itself," Todd exclaimed excitedly. "It thought it was a rival fish, and it prepared itself to fight!"

"I guess fighting fish really do fight each other," concluded Dan.

"Or maybe Todd just has a weird fish," teased Marc.

- - -

Todd, Marc, and Dan were having fun. They did not realize that they were actually conducting scientific research. By creating the right conditions, Todd and his friends were able to observe the fish and how it reacted to changes in the environment. Similarly, psychologists sometimes bring animals or people into laboratory environments where they can observe them under carefully controlled conditions. At other times, psychologists study the behavior of organisms in the field—that is, where the organisms live naturally. In addition, psychologists sometimes get information by conducting experiments, much as the boys did with the fighting fish. There are many different approaches to research. This chapter explores several of them.

Key Terms

- construct
- hypothesis
- replicated
- survey
- target population
- sample
- random sample
- stratified sample
- bias
- volunteer bias
- case study
- longitudinal method
- cross-sectional method
- naturalistic observation
- laboratory observation
- correlation
- positive correlation
- negative correlation
- experiment
- variables
- independent variable
- dependent variable
- experimental group
- control group
- controlled experiment
- placebo
- single-blind study
- double-blind study
- standard deviation
- ethics
- informed consent

HOLT

Psychology Video Program

Watch the video to see psychological research in action.

PSYCHOLOGICAL METHODS **25**

- Psychologists never guess about the answers to the questions they ask.
- You have to do a study more than once to be sure its results are valid.
- Asking the students in your psychology class for their opinions on a topic is a good way to figure out how people in the larger community feel about that topic.
- Some psychological studies take years or even decades to complete.
- Taking a pill that does not contain any medicine might have the same effects as taking one that does.
- Psychologists sometimes have to deceive participants in a study.

A DAY IN THE LIFE

psychological **construct**. It can be assumed that it is present, but it cannot be seen or measured directly. Therefore, research questions are best directed toward behavior. This is why Todd, Marc, and Dan asked: What do fighting fish do to each other when they are placed together?

Other research questions arise out of psychological theory. According to social-learning theorists, for example, people learn by observing others. Thus, these theorists might ask, what effects (if any) does watching television violence have on viewers?

Research questions also arise from folklore and common knowledge. For example, questions might arise from such well-known—and often-repeated—statements as "Two heads are better than one," "Opposites attract," and "Beauty is in the eye of the beholder." Psychologists ask, is it true that pairs or groups of people solve problems more effectively than people working alone? Are people with opposite personality traits really attracted to each other? Is beauty a matter of individual preference, or are there common standards for beauty?

SECTION 1

Conducting Research

Psychology, like chemistry and biology, is an experimental science. In an experimental science, assumptions (such as about the behavior of chemical compounds, cells, or people) must be supported by evidence. It is not enough to argue that something is true just because someone says it is. Psychologists and other scientists make it their business to be skeptical of claims that lack actual scientific evidence.

Psychologists use a variety of research methods to study behavior and mental processes. These methods differ in a number of ways, but psychologists tend to follow the same general procedure when conducting their research. This procedure consists of five steps: forming a research question, forming a hypothesis, testing the hypothesis, analyzing the results, and drawing conclusions.

Forming a Research Question

Psychologists begin a study by forming a research question. Many research questions arise from daily experience. For example, Todd, Marc, and Dan were wondering about the aggressiveness of Siamese fighting fish. But aggressiveness, like anxiety, is a

Forming a Hypothesis

After psychologists ask a research question, they form a hypothesis about the answer. A **hypothesis** is an educated guess. The accuracy of a hypothesis can be tested by research.

Psychologists may word a hypothesis in the form of an if-then statement. If-then reasoning is an example of social scientific reasoning. Todd engaged in if-then reasoning. *If* Siamese fighting fish are aggressive, he reasoned, *then* they will attack one another. Todd did not realize that he was engaging in social scientific reasoning, but he was. Todd was also making an educated guess. His guess was based on the fact that the fish were called "fighting fish." It was also based on the pet shop salesperson's advice not to put more than one fighting fish in the same tank. Because it is only an educated guess, a hypothesis must be tested.

Testing the Hypothesis

Because psychology is a science, psychological knowledge rests on carefully examined human experience. No matter how good a hypothesis sounds and no matter how many people believe it, a hypothesis cannot be considered to be correct until it has been scientifically tested and proved to be right. Psychologists do not rely on people's opinions. Instead, they examine the evidence and draw their own conclusions.

Psychologists answer research questions or test hypotheses through a variety of methods. To test the hypothesis that two fighting fish would attack each other, the best method would probably be to put two real fish in the same tank. But Todd did not have another fighting fish, so this was not possible. Marc suggested using a mirror to create the illusion of another fighting fish. He hoped that Todd's fish would react to its reflection in the same way it would react to a real fish. In that way he, Todd, and Dan would be able to find out whether it is true that fighting fish do attack each other. Thus, holding a mirror in front of the fish was the method Marc chose to test the boys' hypothesis.

A DAY IN THE LIFE

Analyzing the Results

After psychologists have tested their hypotheses, they analyze their results. In other words, they ask what their findings mean. After Todd, Marc, and Dan saw the fighting fish fan out its fins and puff up its cheeks apparently in reaction to seeing the image of another fish, they had to figure out how to interpret that reaction. Todd interpreted the fish's actions as going into attack position.

In most psychological studies, psychologists collect a great deal more information, or data, than Marc, Dan, and Todd did with the fish. For example, psychologists would test their hypothesis on more than one fish. They might spend weeks, months, or even years gathering data. The more information collected, the more complex task it is to analyze it. Often, psychologists look for patterns and relationships in the data. They must decide which data support their hypothesis and which data do not.

Drawing Conclusions

Once psychologists have analyzed their research observations, they draw conclusions about their

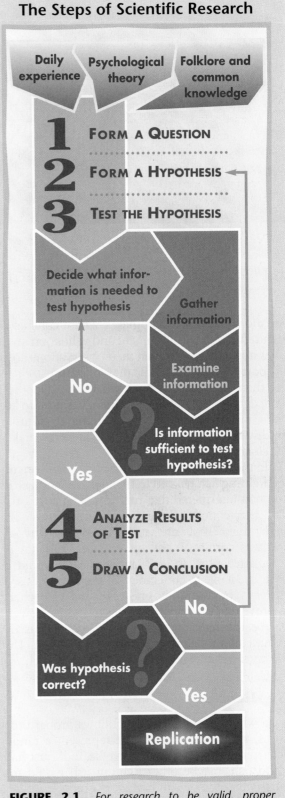

The Steps of Scientific Research

Daily experience · Psychological theory · Folklore and common knowledge

1 FORM A QUESTION

2 FORM A HYPOTHESIS

3 TEST THE HYPOTHESIS

Decide what information is needed to test hypothesis

Gather information

Examine information

No

Yes

Is information sufficient to test hypothesis?

4 ANALYZE RESULTS OF TEST

5 DRAW A CONCLUSION

No

Yes

Was hypothesis correct?

Replication

FIGURE 2.1 *For research to be valid, proper scientific procedures must be used. These are the steps that researchers generally follow.*

Despite the claims of fortune-tellers, little if any scientific evidence supports the existence of precognition or other forms of ESP. Studies that seem to support ESP usually cannot be replicated.

When scientists replicate a study but obtain different results than were obtained the first time, the findings of the first study are questioned. This is one reason that most psychologists do not believe that extrasensory perception (ESP) is a valid scientific phenomenon, even though some isolated studies have supported the existence of ESP. These studies have not yielded the same results when replicated.

TRUTH OR fiction
■ R E V I S I T E D ■

It is true that you have to do a study more than once to be sure its results are valid. The repeating of an experiment is called replication. If a study does not produce the same results more than once, the results may not have been accurate.

Sometimes scientists repeat a study under slightly different circumstances than those in the original study. In the fish example, to confirm the hypothesis that fighting fish attack each other, it would probably be best to replicate the experiment by using two or more real fish rather than one fish and its reflection.

Sometimes researchers repeat a study using a different set of participants. Todd, Marc, and Dan could have tried the same experiment with a few other fighting fish. If these fish acted differently than Todd's did, this would indicate that Todd's fish was somehow unusual. The boys might even try the experiment with different *types* of fighting fish to see if all the fish have the same reaction. They might also try the experiment with both male and female fighting fish. In many animal species, males have different behavior patterns than females. Thus, it is important to study both males and females if the goal is to make generalizations about all members of the species.

In a study in which people are the participants, researchers might want to replicate the study using participants who differ not only in gender but also in such characteristics as age, ethnicity, social and economic background, level of education, and geographic setting. For example, if a study was done for the first time only with teenagers, the researchers might include participants from other age groups the next time. That way, the researchers could be sure that the findings were consistent among a variety of age groups.

questions and their hypotheses. These conclusions are useful in the development and validation of theories in psychology. When their observations do not support their hypotheses, they often must change the theories or beliefs from which the hypotheses were derived. Therefore, psychologists need to keep open minds. They must be willing to adjust or modify their hypotheses if their findings make it necessary to do so.

In the fish example, once the boys had seen how the fighting fish reacted to the image of another fish and had interpreted that reaction as an attack reaction, they concluded that, yes, fighting fish do fight each other. They were satisfied that Todd's hypothesis was correct. If the fighting fish had not had such a reaction, Todd, Marc, and Dan would not have been able to conclude that the hypothesis was correct. They would not necessarily have been able to prove that the hypothesis was *incorrect*, however. Maybe the fighting fish realized that it was only looking at a reflection and not at a real fish. Thus, the boys would have had to do more research.

Replication

Even when a study carefully follows proper procedures, its findings might just represent a random occurrence. As Marc put it, maybe Todd just had a weird fish; maybe other fighting fish would react differently. For the findings of a study to be confirmed, the study must be **replicated**. That is, the study must be repeated—and it must produce the same results as before.

New Questions

Whether the findings of a research study support or contradict the hypothesis of that study, they are likely to lead to new research questions. Once Todd, Marc, and Dan had performed their fish experiment, they might have asked any number of other questions. For example, *why* do fighting fish attack each other? Does it have to do with mating, with turf, or with something else entirely? Is it a reaction they have instinctively from birth, or do they learn it as they mature? Are there any circumstances under which fighting fish do *not* attack each other? Do any other animals have similar attack reactions? Do people ever act like that?

Even if Todd's fish had totally ignored its reflection, that too would have raised new questions. Would it also ignore a real fish? And if so, why is it called a fighting fish? Under what circumstances does it fight?

Once new questions have been asked, the process begins all over again. The researchers must propose a new hypothesis about the answer to the new question. And once again, the hypothesis must be tested.

The rest of this chapter explores the different types of research methods that psychologists use to test hypotheses. These methods include the survey method, various observational methods, and the experimental method. Each of these methods has advantages and disadvantages, and some methods are better suited to certain kinds of research studies than are other methods. It would be convenient if there were one perfect method that could be used in all circumstances. But human beings are complex, and the human experience has many dimensions. Thus, several different research methods are needed to study it.

SECTION 1 REVIEW

Homework Practice Online
Keyword: SY7 HP2

1. List and describe the five steps that scientists follow when conducting research.

2. Why is replication of a research study important?

3. **Critical Thinking** *Analyzing Information* Locate a newspaper or magazine article that discusses the findings of a recent research study. Summarize the study, and then list two new questions that might be asked based on the findings of the study.

Surveys, Samples, and Populations

When Todd, Marc, and Dan wanted to know what fighting fish would do to each other, it would have been convenient (as Dan pointed out) if they could have just asked the fish. But, of course, fish cannot talk. People, on the other hand, *can* talk. Thus, when psychologists want to find out about people's attitudes and behaviors, one possible way to gather information is to ask people directly.

The Survey Method

Gathering information by asking people directly is usually accomplished by means of a survey. In a **survey**, people are asked to respond to a series of questions about a particular subject.

Psychologists D. L. DuBois and B. J. Hirsch (1990), for example, used the survey method to examine mixed-race friendships among high school students. (See Figure 2.2.) The survey asked high school students to identify the races of their friends. More than 80 percent of white and African American students reported having a friend of the other race in school. However, far fewer students

Friendship Patterns Among High School Students

Students	White	African American
Have a friend of another race in school	87%	82%
Have a friend of another race outside of school	23%	42%

FIGURE 2.2 *Research indicates that although many students have friends of a different race, fewer students see those friends outside of school.*

Source: "School and Neighborhood Friendship Patterns of Blacks and Whites in Adolescence" by D. L. DuBois and B. J. Hirsch, 1990, *Child Development*, 61, pp. 524–536.

Calvin and Hobbes

by Bill Watterson

reported seeing these friends outside of school. DuBois and Hirsch concluded that the reason may be that even though many of the respondents attended integrated schools, the neighborhoods they lived in may have been segregated.

Psychologists conduct surveys by asking people to fill out written questionnaires or by interviewing people orally. By distributing questionnaires or by conducting interviews over the telephone or in person, researchers can rapidly survey thousands of people. Computers often aid in the analysis of the information collected.

The findings of interviews and questionnaires are not necessarily completely accurate. People may not be honest, for whatever reasons, about their attitudes or behavior. Some people may fear that their responses will not be kept confidential. Thus, they answer only what they are willing to reveal to the world at large. Other respondents may try to please the interviewers by saying what they think the interviewers want to hear.

The significant risk of obtaining inaccurate data through interviews and questionnaires became clear from the results of a 1960s survey about tooth-brushing habits. If people had brushed their teeth as often as they claimed, and used the amount of toothpaste they said they used, three times as much toothpaste would have been sold in the United States as was actually sold at that time (Barringer, 1993). The survey respondents might not have wanted the interviewers to know that they did not brush their teeth as often as their dentists advised.

Populations and Samples

When researchers conduct any type of study, they must consider what group or groups of people they wish to examine and how respondents will be selected. This is particularly true with surveys.

Imagine that your town or city is about to hold a referendum on whether to institute a 10:00 P.M. curfew for people under the age of 18. How might you most accurately predict the outcome of the referendum? You might conduct a poll by asking people how they are planning to vote. But whom would you select to be in the poll?

Researchers who conduct studies in densely populated areas have a large pool of possible participants from which to draw.

Suppose you only polled the students in your psychology class. Do you think you would be able to make an accurate prediction? Probably not. Many of the people in your psychology class are probably under the age of 18 and thus might be particularly likely to oppose the curfew because they believe it would restrict their freedom. However, these students are too young to vote. The voters in the actual referendum would all be at least 18. Since the curfew would not restrict them, they might be more inclined to vote for it. Thus, a poll of your psychology class would probably not be very useful for predicting the outcome of this particular referendum.

To accurately predict an outcome, it is necessary to study a group that represents the target population. A **target population** is the whole group you want to study or describe. In the curfew example, the target population consists of all possible voters on the referendum. It does not consist of nonvoters. The question is not whom the referendum will affect if passed, but whether the referendum will be passed or not. Thus, only voters are relevant to the survey.

It would be costly and difficult—if not impossible—to interview or question every member of a target population (in this case, all voters in the area). Instead, researchers study a **sample**, which is only part of the target population.

Selecting Samples

Psychologists and other scientists select samples scientifically to ensure that the samples accurately represent the populations they are supposed to represent. In other words, a sample should be as similar as possible to the target population. Otherwise, researchers will be unable to use the sample to make accurate predictions about the population from which the sample is drawn.

A high school class does not represent all the people in the town or city where a school is located, particularly in terms of opinions on an issue that pertains to age (such as a curfew for people under 18). Thus, the answers of people in a high school class might be biased (and, of course, most high school students are not old enough to vote). In this case, they would probably be biased against the curfew. On the other hand, researchers probably could predict the outcome of the referendum by interviewing as a sample a large number of people who represent all voters in the town or city.

One way that scientists obtain a sample that they hope represents the target population is by using a random sample. In a **random sample**, individuals are selected by chance from the target population. Each member of the population has an equal chance of being chosen. If the random sample is big enough, chances are that it will accurately represent the whole population.

Researchers can also use a stratified sample. In a **stratified sample**, subgroups in the population are represented proportionally in the sample. For instance, about 12 percent of the American population is African American. A stratified sample of the American population would thus be about 12 percent African American. (See Figure 2.3.)

A large random sample is likely to be accurately stratified even if researchers take no special steps to ensure that it is. A random sample of 1,000 to 1,500 people will usually represent the general American population reasonably well. A sample of 5 million motorcycle owners, however, would not. A large sample size by itself does not necessarily guarantee that a sample represents a target population, particularly if the sample is not a random sample. Motorcycle owners probably do not represent all people in the United States.

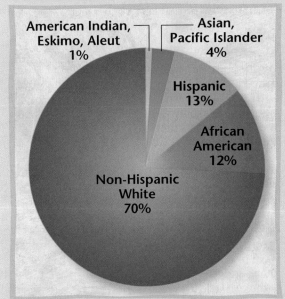

FIGURE 2.3 *In a stratified sample of the U.S. population, various groups should be represented in the same proportions as they are present in the whole population.* **Based on this chart, in a stratified sample consisting of 100 people, how many African Americans would you expect to find in the sample?**

Source: U.S. Census. Figures have been rounded.

EXPLORING
DIVERSITY

Representing Human Diversity in Research

Most psychologists today appreciate the need to allow for the wide diversity of members of society in their research. This has not always been the case. For example, throughout the history of psychology, men have been included as research participants more often than women. A key reason for this stems from the pool of available research subjects. Many research participants have traditionally been drawn from the armed services and universities. The majority of people in the armed services are male. And only in recent years has the number of women in colleges and universities grown equal to (and exceeded) that of men.

Many research studies draw their participants from college campuses, which have grown increasingly diverse in recent years.

The relatively small research pools led psychologists to mistakenly generalize their findings beyond men. Researchers tended to conclude that what was true for white men was true for all of society. When this sort of overgeneralization occurred, important distinctions between groups tended to be ignored.

Health, for example, has been an area where cultural, ethnic, and gender differences have not always been taken into account. Some surprising results have been obtained as studies have broadened their scope beyond white men. For example, researchers have discovered significant differences between how men and women are affected by heart disease. Although women receive less treatment for heart disease than men, they are at greater risk of dying from the condition. Researchers are studying whether this increased risk exists because of differences in the types of treatment women receive from health-care providers.

Ethnic differences in research results have also arisen as the pool of study participants has broadened. Researchers have learned that African Americans of both genders are more likely to suffer from heart disease than members of the white population. This higher risk arises, in part, from correspondingly higher rates of hypertension and diabetes in the African American population.

Domestic violence is another area of study that has benefited from studies with more diversified groups of participants. Much research has been performed on the prevalence of violence against women. But more recent research has revealed that men, too, are victims of domestic violence. Psychologists have also studied the repercussions that domestic violence has beyond the victim of the physical assault. Children in particular suffer emotionally in a household where violence occurs.

Recent research has also focused on issues significant to members of the older population. Studies have shed light on a variety of topics of concern to the elderly, such as the way older people cope with the changes in their health and in social relationships.

The American Psychological Association (1994b) recommends that the write-up of a study's results include a clear description of the research sample in terms of ethnicity, gender, and any other potentially relevant characteristics. For example, if a sample uses only male participants, the report should include this information. When such descriptions are included, the reader is less likely to assume that a study's findings apply equally to all groups.

THINK ABOUT IT

Analyzing Information What might be some ways to increase the number of participants from traditionally underrepresented groups in psychological studies?

TRUTH OR **fiction**
▪ R E V I S I T E D ▪

It is not true that asking the students in your psychology class for their opinions on a topic is a good way to figure out how people in the larger community feel about that topic. To find out how community members feel about a topic, you would need to select a sample that represents the community. Your psychology class probably does not.

Generalizing Results

Sometimes, for one reason or another, researchers do not use a sample that represents an entire population. In some cases, the researchers want to know about only one group within the population and thus have no reason to study other groups. In other cases, it may be impractical or impossible to obtain a random or stratified sample.

In such cases, researchers are cautious about generalizing their findings to groups other than those from which their samples were drawn. Similarly, because their sample used only one fish, Todd, Marc, and Dan could not conclude that *all* fish would fight each other or even that all Siamese fighting fish would. Todd's one fish could not be assumed to represent all fish. Thus, the boys could not know for sure whether they would get the same results if they used other types of fish.

The same is true with people. Researchers cannot learn about the preferences of all people by studying only one group of people, such as men. In a study about car preferences, for example, psychologists would avoid generalizing from a sample that was made up only of men because men's preferences for cars might not be the same as women's. In other words, if researchers found that men prefer certain types of cars, the researchers could not conclude that women prefer those same types of cars if the study did not include women.

The gender of the individuals in the sample is not the only characteristic that researchers must take into account. For instance, researchers cannot learn about the attitudes of Americans in general if they limit their observations to people who live in one part of the country (for example, the Midwest) or to people from one socioeconomic background (for example, wealthy people).

Men and women might tend to prefer different types of cars, so a study of people's car preferences would need to have both male and female participants.

Volunteer Bias

Researchers often have little control over who responds to surveys or participates in research studies. Although the researchers may choose to whom they give a questionnaire, they usually cannot force people to complete the questionnaire. Another factor that psychologists must take into account is **bias**, or a predisposition to a certain point of view. People who volunteer to participate in studies often bring with them a **volunteer bias**—that is, they often have a different outlook from people who do not volunteer for research studies.

For one thing, volunteers are usually more willing than other people to disclose personal information. Volunteers may also be more interested in research than people who do not volunteer. Furthermore, they may have more spare time to participate in research studies than other people. Depending on what the study is about, any or all of these factors—as well as others—could skew the results. That is, these factors could slant the results in a particular direction.

Have you ever filled out and returned a questionnaire printed in a magazine? Popular magazines such as *Glamour, Seventeen,* and *Psychology Today* often survey readers' attitudes about various topics

The Survey Method

Research Method	Description	Advantages	Disadvantages
Survey Method	People respond to a series of questions about a particular subject.	It enables the researcher to gather information about large numbers of people.	People may not be entirely honest in answering questions. Survey samples are not always representative of the target population.

FIGURE 2.4 *One way to learn about people's behaviors and attitudes is simply to ask them. Psychologists often do just that by conducting surveys. Surveys, however, have some disadvantages.*

and behaviors in certain circumstances. Such a questionnaire might, for instance, ask readers how they like to spend their leisure time. Do they prefer to go to the movies, visit with friends, read magazines, or listen to music?

Thousands of readers complete these types of questionnaires and send them in. However, do the respondents represent the general population of the United States? Probably not. In a magazine survey, a disproportionate number of responses to the question posed above would probably be "read magazines." After all, the questionnaire itself comes from a magazine. People who do not like to read magazines probably would not fill out the questionnaire. They would not have seen it in the first place. Such magazine surveys are affected by volunteer bias. For example, readers who have enough time to fill out the questionnaire may tend to have different leisure preferences than people who are too busy to fill out the questionnaire. This volunteer bias might affect the findings.

SECTION 2 REVIEW

go.hrw.com **Homework Practice Online** Keyword: SY7 HP2

1. What are two different ways by which surveys are conducted?

2. Explain the importance of random and stratified sampling.

3. **Critical Thinking** *Contrasting* Give an example of a survey that might produce different results depending on whether participants volunteered or were selected randomly. How might the results differ, and what would account for the difference?

Methods of Observation

Almost everyone, at one time or another, observes other people. We observe people as they talk, eat, work, play, and interact with others and with us. Based on our observations of other people (and also of ourselves), we tend to make generalizations about human behavior and human nature.

Our observations and generalizations usually serve us fairly well in our daily lives. But no matter how many experiences we have had, most of our personal observations are fleeting and haphazard. We sift through experience for things that interest us, but we often ignore the obvious because it does not fit our ideas about how things ought to be. Thus, we cannot draw scientific conclusions based only on our own unstructured observations.

Even the most respected psychologists may use their personal observations as a starting point for their research and as the basis for their hypotheses. Once they have begun their investigations, however, psychologists use more careful methods of observation. The survey method, discussed above, is one such method of observation. Other methods of observation include the testing, case-study, longitudinal, cross-sectional, naturalistic-observation, and laboratory-observation methods.

The Testing Method

Psychologists sometimes use psychological tests to learn about human behavior. There are several types of psychological tests. Intelligence tests measure general learning ability. Aptitude tests measure specific abilities and special talents, such as musical ability and mechanical skills. Still other tests measure vocational interests.

Personality tests are another type of psychological test psychologists use. Personality tests measure people's character traits and temperament. For example, personality tests might be used to assess whether people are socially outgoing or aggressive. Personality tests might also be used to diagnose psychological problems such as anxiety and depression. (See Chapter 15.)

The Case-Study Method

Another research method psychologists use is the case-study method. A **case study** is an in-depth investigation of an individual or a small group. To learn about the people who are being studied, researchers may observe or speak with them, interview others who know them, and find out more about their backgrounds and personal histories. Psychologists use what they learn in a case study to generalize broader principles that apply to the larger population.

Sigmund Freud developed psychoanalytic theory largely on the basis of case studies. Freud carefully studied the people who sought his help. He interviewed some of them for many years, developing as complete a record of their childhoods as he could. He also looked for the factors that seemed to contribute to their current problems.

Some case studies focus on rare circumstances or events. One such case study involved a girl named Genie. When she was only 20 months old, her father locked her in a small room. She was kept there until she was rescued at the age of 13 (Rymer, 1993). Her social contacts were limited to her mother, who fed her, and her father, who often beat her. No one spoke to her. And in all those years, she herself did not say a word.

After her rescue, Genie's language development followed the normal sequence of language development. (See Chapter 8.) Genie never learned to use language as well as most people, however. This case study suggests that there is a special period in early childhood when it is easiest for people to learn language.

Although case studies sometimes offer great insights, psychologists are cautious about generalizing from case studies. This is particularly true of case studies that cannot be replicated, such as

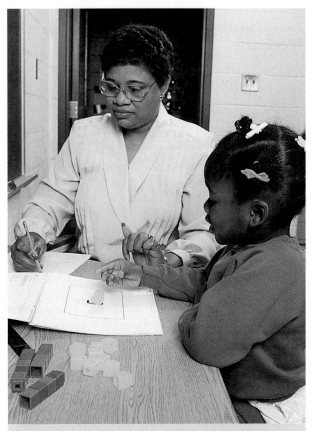

Some aptitude tests measure the test taker's physical or perceptual abilities.

Genie's. Because of the rarity and cruelty of Genie's experience, scientists would never repeat this study. Thus they cannot know for sure, on the basis of Genie's experience alone, whether the theory about a special language-learning period in childhood is correct. Perhaps other unknown factors were responsible for Genie's apparent inability to achieve full language competence.

Furthermore, case studies lend themselves to some of the same pitfalls that surveys do, particularly when the case studies are based on interviews with people about their past experiences. Most people's memories are filled with gaps and inaccuracies (Loftus, 2004). Some of these inaccuracies occur because people tend not to remember the details of events. Some people even intentionally distort their pasts to impress the researcher. And sometimes without meaning to, researchers encourage people to answer in certain ways to fulfill the researchers' expectations. For example, some psychoanalysts have been criticized for encouraging people to interpret their behavior according to Freud's psychoanalytic theory (Hergenhahn, 2005).

Longitudinal and Cross-Sectional Methods

Just as Freud studied some of his patients over a matter of years, so too do some psychological studies observe participants over a long period of time. Some research topics, such as those concerned with development throughout the life span, deal with how people or other organisms change over time.

To study such topics, psychologists often use the **longitudinal method**. In this method, researchers select a group of participants and then observe those participants over a period of time, often years or even decades. By using this method, psychologists can observe the ways in which individuals change over time.

Usually the observations are conducted at intervals, perhaps once a year. For example, if psychologists wanted to find out more about how people learn language, they might select a group of six-month-olds who are not yet using language. Then once a month, the researchers might observe the children to find out how their language skills are changing over time. By the time the children are three or four years old, they are no longer learning language at such a rapid pace. The psychologists might then observe them only once or twice a year.

TRUTH
OR
fiction
■ R E V I S I T E D ■

It is true that some psychological studies take years or even decades to complete. These studies may be longitudinal studies, which examine the ways in which individuals change by observing them over a long period of time.

Needless to say, longitudinal studies are extremely time-consuming. Imagine how much patience you would need knowing that even if you started a study right now, you would not get conclusive results for another 5, 10, or 15 years. Moreover, longitudinal studies tend to be expensive, and they are risky. There is often no guarantee that participants will remain available over the long time period that they are to be studied.

To avoid some of the problems with longitudinal studies, psychologists may use the cross-sectional method to find out about changes over time. In the **cross-sectional method**, instead of following a set of individuals over a number of years, researchers select a sample that includes people of different ages. The researchers then compare the behavior of the participants in the different age groups. For example, in a language-learning study, psychologists might select 12-month-olds, 14-month-olds, and 16-month-olds. They would then observe the language skills of members of each age group and compare the groups with one another in order to make generalizations about how children learn language over time.

Information gained in cross-sectional studies is less reliable than information from longitudinal studies. When psychologists study one individual over a period of time, as in a longitudinal study, they know that any changes they observe in that individual are due to her or his experiences or development. But when they compare groups of people of different ages at the same time, as in a cross-sectional study, psychologists cannot be certain what factors are responsible for differences among the participants. Perhaps the differences are due to developmental changes, but perhaps the participants were simply different from the beginning.

The Naturalistic-Observation Method

One way that psychologists sometimes find out about children's language skills is to observe children as they use language naturally, such as while they interact with other children and adults in play groups. This is called **naturalistic observation**, or field study. People often use naturalistic observation in their daily lives without even knowing it. That is, they observe other people or animals in the "field"—in their natural habitats. In the case of people, field settings include homes, schools, office buildings, restaurants—any place where people spend time.

A DAY IN THE LIFE

If Todd had wanted to use naturalistic observation to observe fish, he would have had to go to a river, a lake, or an ocean—someplace where fish exist naturally. But without realizing it, Todd used naturalistic observation all the time to watch people. In his job at the restaurant, Todd could not avoid noticing the different ways that customers ate their food. Some people gobbled down their meals quickly, almost without pausing. Others ate delicately, carefully chewing each bite. He wondered what accounted for these differences in people's eating habits.

Psychologists also wonder about such questions. They have, like Todd, used naturalistic observation to study how people eat. They have watched people in restaurants to learn, for example, whether slender people and heavy people eat their food differently. Such field research has shown that heavy people tend to eat somewhat more rapidly than slender people. Heavy people also chew less often and leave less food on their plates.

This type of study has led to suggestions about how heavy people might diet more effectively. For example, they might eat more slowly and take less food to begin with so that when they clean their plates, they have eaten less. (See Chapter 13.)

In naturalistic observation, psychologists try not to interfere with the organisms they are observing. In the restaurant example, psychologists would not ask the diners questions or encourage them to eat a particular food. They would simply observe the people eating.

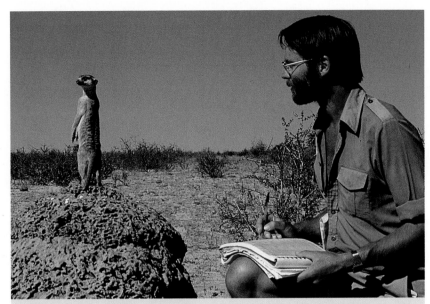

This researcher is using naturalistic observation to study a meerkat, a small mammal native to Africa.

The Laboratory-Observation Method

Some matters simply cannot be studied in a naturalistic setting. For example, Todd could not realistically have observed his tropical fish in their natural habitat.

Sometimes it is more useful for a psychologist to observe behavior in a laboratory rather than in the field. This method is called **laboratory observation**. Laboratories are not necessarily sterile rooms tended by people in white coats; a laboratory is any place that provides the opportunity for observation or experimentation. As such, many laboratories are quite informal.

In fact, Todd's fish tank was a type of laboratory, a small artificial lake. To make the environment suitable for the fish, Todd had to do many things, such as monitor the temperature and acid content of the water. Once he had set up his laboratory, he was able to observe the behavior of the fish. He watched the fish dart under the protecting leaves. He saw how they created and defended their turf.

He observed their mating behavior and watched them breed. Sometimes their behavior amazed him—such as when they immediately swam to the surface of the water when he turned on the light. In just a few days after Todd had brought the fish home, they had learned that they would be fed when the light went on.

Like Todd, psychologists often study animals by using the laboratory-observation method. B. F. Skinner created special enclosed environments, which became known as Skinner boxes, to study the behavior of animals such as rats. In one of these miniature laboratories, a food pellet drops into the box when the rat in the box presses a lever. Rats learn quickly to press the levers, especially when they are hungry. Other psychologists have built mazes to see how effectively rats learn routes through the mazes. (See Chapter 6.) Both the Skinner box and the maze are examples of laboratories.

Psychologists sometimes use a laboratory to control the environment of a study. For example, if they wanted to see whether the amount of light in a room affects how much people eat, they would need to be able to control the lighting in the room where people were eating. Similarly, Todd's fish tank was a place where he could observe the behavior of the fish while he controlled what happened in the environment. He could, for instance, observe how the fish responded if he changed the temperature of the water or the type of food he fed them.

Six Methods of Observation

Research Method	Description	Advantages	Disadvantages
Testing Method	Several types of tests measure various elements of human behavior such as abilities, interests, and personality.	Convenient method for researchers to gain insight to certain aspects of an individual's abilities or behavior.	Does not always provide a complete representation of an individual's true abilities or personality.
Case-Study Method	Researchers conduct in-depth investigations of individuals or small groups.	Provides insight into specific cases.	May focus on isolated circumstances or events that cannot be replicated. People interviewed in case studies may distort their past experiences. Researchers may unintentionally encourage people to answer questions a certain way.
Longitudinal Method	A group of participants are observed at intervals over an extended period of time.	Enables researchers to see how individuals change over time.	Time-consuming and expensive. Participants may not be available for the duration of the study.
Cross-Sectional Method	Researchers compare the differences and similarities among people in different age groups at a given time.	Less time-consuming than the longitudinal method for studying changes over time.	Differences between the members of the sample cannot necessarily be attributed to age or development.
Naturalistic-Observation Method	Researchers observe the behavior of people or animals in their natural habitats.	Enables researchers to witness the behavior of people or animals in settings that are not artificial.	Researchers have no control over the setting or the events that occur.
Laboratory-Observation Method	Participants are observed in a laboratory setting.	Enables researchers to precisely control certain aspects of the study.	Laboratories cannot duplicate real-life environments.

FIGURE 2.5 *Psychologists employ several types of observation methods to conduct research.*

Analyzing Observations

Once psychologists have made their observations, they must analyze and interpret them. One method they use is **correlation**, which is a measure of how closely one thing is related to another. The stronger the correlation between two things, the more closely those two things are related. For example, there is a strong correlation between height and ability to reach items that are located on the top shelf of a cabinet. The taller the person, the greater that person's ability to reach the top shelf.

In psychology, researchers often look for correlations between various characteristics or traits. For instance, are people with a stronger felt need than others for achievement more likely to advance in their jobs? What is the relationship between stress and health? Between grades earned by students and extracurricular involvement?

Positive and Negative Correlation   To determine whether there is a correlation between achievement and occupational success, a researcher might compare need for achievement as measured by a personality test with the salaries of the test takers. There is, in fact, a correlation between the need for achievement and salaries, and it is a **positive correlation**. (See Figure 2.6.) That is, as one goes up, so does the other. Generally speaking, people who feel a greater need to achieve earn more money (Ginsburg & Bronstein, 1993; Gottfried et al., 1994).

There are, of course, some exceptions. Some people are highly motivated to achieve, but they do not have high-paying jobs. Others are average in their need for achievement but earn very high incomes. Therefore, factors other than a need for achievement also contribute to high salaries. One such factor is the type of job one has; people in some kinds of jobs earn more than people in other kinds of jobs. In addition, for people to succeed, they also have to know how to interact with others, how to manage people, and how to manage multiple tasks at one time (Collier, 1994; Sternberg et al., 1995). Thus, there is a positive correlation between success and a variety of factors.

In contrast, there is a **negative correlation** between stress and health. As one goes up, the other goes down. (See Figure 2.6.) As the amount of stress on people increases, their immune systems become less capable of fighting off illness—thus, the greater the stress, the poorer the health. This is why students under stress are more likely than other students to get colds (Cohen et al., 1993).

Positive and Negative Correlations

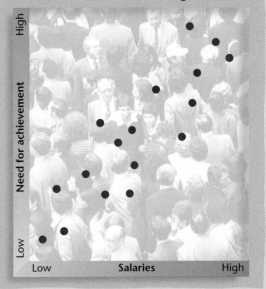

Positive Correlation

Generally speaking, people who have a higher need for achievement achieve higher salaries.

Negative Correlation

Generally speaking, the immune systems of people who are under high amounts of stress tend to function more poorly than the immune systems of people who are under less stress.

FIGURE 2.6   *Each dot represents an observation of one person. When two factors show a positive correlation, one rises as the other rises. When two factors show a negative correlation, one of the factors rises as the other one falls.*

Correlation Versus Cause and Effect

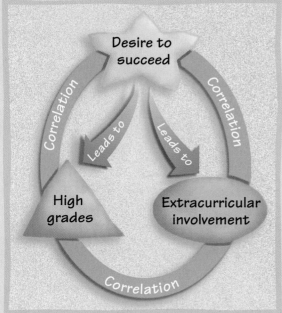

FIGURE 2.7 *Although a correlation may exist between high grades and extracurricular involvement, this does not mean that one causes the other.*

Limits of Correlation Correlation describes relationships. It does not, however, reveal cause and effect. Just because two things are related does not necessarily mean that one causes the other.

For example, suppose you were conducting a study in your school and discovered a positive correlation between students' grades and their level of involvement in extracurricular activities. In other words, suppose you found that students who earn high grades in their classes also participate heavily in extracurricular activities. Does this mean that earning high grades *causes* students to become involved in extracurricular activities or that involvement in extracurricular activities *causes* students to earn high grades? Not necessarily. It might be that there are other factors—such as a general desire to succeed—that encourage or cause *both* high grades and extracurricular involvement. (See Figure 2.7.) Thus, we cannot conclude on the basis of the correlation alone that one causes the other.

Recall that Todd noticed a correlation between the amount of food his fish were eating and the way they were behaving—they were eating less and were acting sluggish. Todd assumed that the fish were sluggish because

they were not eating enough. In other words, he assumed that one factor (decreased amount of food eaten) was causing the other (sluggish behavior). On the basis of this assumption, Todd changed the type of food he was feeding the fish.

But Todd's assumption may have been mistaken. Perhaps, the fish were sick and their illness was causing both the odd behavior and the lack of appetite. There could have been a hidden factor at work that was acting on both of the other factors to create a correlation between them. As you will see, experiments allow us to draw conclusions about cause and effect.

SECTION 3 REVIEW

go. hrw .com **Homework Practice Online**
Keyword: SY7 HP2

1. What is a case study? Name one drawback of the case-study method.

2. What is the difference between the naturalistic-observation method and the laboratory-observation method?

3. **Critical Thinking** *Analyzing Information* Suppose you want to find out if there is a correlation between age and preferred volume level for listening to music for people between the ages of 15 and 55. Which observational methods might you use to study this?

SECTION 4
The Experimental Method

The method researchers use to answer questions about cause and effect is the experiment. In an **experiment**, participants receive what is called a treatment, such as a change in room temperature or a new drug. Researchers then carefully observe the participants to determine how the treatment influences their behavior (if at all).

When Todd switched fish foods to see if the new food would make the fish eat more and stop acting sluggish, he was conducting an experiment. Changing the food was the treatment. Similarly, when Marc used a mirror to see how the fighting fish would react, that too was an experiment. Holding up the mirror was the treatment.

As with other research methods, the experimental method has some limitations. For example, the conditions created in an experiment may not accurately reflect conditions in real life. Almost by their very nature, experiments must simplify things somewhat in order to yield useful information about cause and effect. Nevertheless, experiments do yield useful information much of the time, and for that reason, psychologists frequently turn to the experimental method in their research.

Independent and Dependent Variables

Experiments contain **variables**, which are factors that can vary, or change. In an experiment, the **independent variable** is the factor that researchers manipulate so that they can determine its effect. Suppose researchers are testing the hypothesis that warm temperatures cause aggression in humans. In that experiment, temperature is the independent variable because that is what researchers are manipulating to observe its effect.

In the same experiment, level of aggression is the dependent variable. As you might guess from its name, a **dependent variable** depends on something—the independent variable. The researchers want to find out whether level of aggression depends on temperature.

In Todd's experiment with the fish food, the type of food he was using was the independent variable. The extent to which the fish acted sluggish and the amount they ate were dependent variables.

Experimental and Control Groups

Ideal experiments use experimental and control groups. Members of an **experimental group** receive the treatment. Members of a **control group** do not. Every effort is made to ensure that all other conditions are held constant for both the experimental group and the control group. This method makes it possible for researchers to conclude that the experiments results are caused by the treatment, not by something else.

Researchers randomly assign participants to one group or the other. For example, in an experiment about students' grades and extracurricular involvement, some students would be randomly assigned to participate in extracurricular activities. These students would make up the experimental group. Others would be randomly assigned *not* to participate in extracurricular activities. These students would be the control group. Once researchers ensured that all other factors—such as educational background—were the same for the two groups,

they could then compare the groups to see whether involvement in extracurricular activities makes a difference in the grades participants earn.

A DAY IN THE LIFE

When an experiment uses control groups as well as experimental groups, it is called a **controlled experiment**. When Todd switched foods to see if a different food would change the behavior of the fish, he was *not* conducting a controlled experiment. Because the fish acted less sluggish after he switched their food, he assumed that the new food was responsible. But what if another factor caused the change in their behavior? Perhaps they had been sick and had recovered naturally. Or perhaps the temperature of the water had changed without Todd's realizing it.

To know for sure whether the food was responsible for the changed behavior of the fish, Todd would have to do a controlled experiment. First, he would have to randomly organize the fish into two groups. He would give the experimental group the new food. The control group would receive the usual food. If he separated the groups with a piece of glass in the tank, he could keep all other factors —such as water temperature and acidity—the same for both groups of fish. (See Figure 2.8 on page 42.) If after a period of time the fish that received the new food were no longer acting sluggish, but the fish that received the old food still were, he could conclude that the new fish food had made the difference. But if all of the fish continued to act sluggish, or if they all started to become more active again, something other than the new food was the cause.

Another example of a study in which it is useful to have a control group concerns a key question for psychologists: Does psychotherapy work? In other words, do people who undergo therapy feel better, or feel better faster, than people who do not?

Millions of people seek help from psychologists. Many patients believe their therapists have helped them. For example, a former patient might say, "I was in terrible shape before therapy, but I feel much better now." Yet we do not know what would have happened if this person had not sought help. Many people feel better about their problems as time goes on, with or without therapy. In other words, an individual's involvement in therapy is not part of a controlled experiment. There is no control group— an identical person who has *not* gone to a therapist. Of course, we could never find such a person because no two people are exactly the same.

However, researchers can make up for this by conducting an experiment on the effects of therapy

FIGURE 2.8 *In an experiment to test the hypothesis that a different food changes the behavior of fish, the fish might be divided at random into two groups. The groups are separated by a piece of glass. Except for the type of food received, all other factors, such as water temperature, are kept the same for both groups.*

using a large number of people. In such an experiment, some people would be randomly assigned to an experimental group and would receive therapy. Others with the same problems as those in the first group would be assigned to a control group and would not receive therapy. Even though the people in the experimental group would not be identical to the people in the control group, individual differences would probably average out as long as the

People undergoing therapy might find it helpful not only because of the therapy itself but also because of the expectation that it will help.

groups were large enough. Thus, researchers could determine whether people who receive therapy fare better than those who do not. It would be a controlled experiment.

The Placebo Effect

The question of whether psychotherapy works is further complicated by the fact that people who seek psychotherapy usually expect it to work. Imagine that a person who has a problem is about to see a therapist about it. Chances are, the person is expecting that the visit will be helpful. Otherwise, why would he or she be going?

In research studies and in our daily lives, our expectations affect what happens to us. Feeling better simply because we expect to feel better—and for no other reason—is an example of the placebo (pluh-SEE-boh) effect. A **placebo** is a substance or treatment that has no effect apart from a person's belief in it. For example, one type of placebo is a tablet that appears to contain a real drug but actually has no medicinal value. Someone who has a headache and takes the tablet to feel better might start to feel better even though the tablet does not contain any medicine—as long as the person *thinks* it contains medicine.

Single-Blind Studies

Expectations can create bias toward certain points of view. If a person expects that a drug may have certain effects, he or she will be biased toward paying close attention to any sensations that are similar to those effects.

How, then, can researchers deal with the effects of expectations? How can they learn whether the participants' preconceptions about a new drug are biasing their perceptions of its effects?

One way that researchers can avoid the influence of expectations is by keeping participants unaware of, or blind to, the treatment they are receiving. In a **single-blind study**, participants do not know whether they are in the experimental group or the control group.

Figure 2.9 shows experimental conditions in which some people are given a real drug and others are given a placebo. In this example, half of those given the real drug are deceived. They are told they are taking the placebo. Half of those given the placebo also are deceived. They are told they are taking the drug. The rest of the participants are told the truth about what they are taking.

What does it mean if the people taking the new drug improve faster, regardless of what they have been told, but people who take the placebo do not? It means the drug is effective. What does it mean if all the people who are told they are taking the drug get better faster, regardless of whether they are taking the drug or the placebo? It means that they improve because of their expectations—because of a belief that they are taking a helpful drug—and not because of the drug itself. Thus, the drug in and of itself has few if any benefits.

Double-Blind Studies

Participants may not be the only people involved in an experiment who have expectations. Researchers themselves may also have expectations, such as a belief about the effectiveness of a particular treatment. It is therefore useful if the researchers are also unaware of who has had the treatment and who has had the placebo. A study in which both participants and experimenters are unaware of who receives the treatment is called a **double-blind study**.

Double-blind studies are required by the Food and Drug Administration before new drugs can be put on the market (Carroll et al., 1994). People in these studies are assigned at random to take the real drug or the placebo. Neither the participants nor the people who measure the results know who is taking what. Thus, the people who measure the effects can remain unbiased. After the final measurements are

FIGURE 2.9 *In a single-blind drug study participants are divided into four groups. People in one group receive the drug and are told that they are receiving the drug. Members of the second group receive the drug and are told that they are receiving a placebo. The third group receives a placebo but is told that it is receiving the drug. People in the fourth group receive a placebo and are told that they are receiving a placebo.*

made, an impartial panel (made up of people who *do* know who had the real drug and who did not) determines, on the basis of the measurements of the unbiased observers, whether the effects of the drug differed from those of the placebo.

Central Tendency and Dispersion

Researchers organize data to generalize about the information. Teachers do this every time they analyze test scores. A common technique is to measure or determine central tendency. When the teacher adds all scores and divides the sum by the number of students who took the test, he or she finds the mean, or average score. The mean is most often used as the central tendency. Other methods of arriving at the central tendency include finding the median and the mode. If scores are organized from the lowest to the highest, or the highest to the lowest, the median score is the middle score. Half of the grades are below this score and half are above. The mode is the most frequent score.

To understand the distribution or dispersion of data, researchers must document the range of scores, or how variable the scores are. The two most frequently used measures of variability are range and **standard deviation**. To find the range, the lowest score in the data is subtracted from the highest. This is a simple technique and gives a crude measure of variability. Standard deviation is a measure of distance of every score to the mean. The larger the standard deviation the more spread out the scores are. If five students got 7 out of 10 questions correct on a test, two students got 10 correct, and one got 5 correct, the mode is 7, the median is 7, and the mean is 7.5. To compute the standard deviation, subtract the mean from each score. 10 minus 7.5 equals 2.5. This is a positive deviation because the score is above the mean. Seven minus 7.5 is negative .2, and 5 minus 7.5 is negative 2.5. Test scores that have a large range have a relatively higher standard deviation while test scores bunched together, as in this case, have a relatively small standard deviation.

SECTION 4 REVIEW

Homework Practice Online
go.hrw.com
Keyword: SY7 HP2

1. Define *independent variable* and *dependent variable*. Give an example of each.

2. What is a controlled experiment? What is the difference between an experimental group and a control group?

3. **Critical Thinking** *Evaluating* Why might a double-blind study yield more reliable results than a single-blind study?

Ethical Issues

Ethics are standards for proper and responsible behavior. Psychologists follow ethical standards to promote the dignity of the individual, foster human welfare, and maintain scientific integrity. An important aspect of psychologists' work is to lessen human suffering. Along these lines, ethical standards prevent scientists from undertaking research or treatments that will be harmful to human participants. Specific ethical guidelines have been established by the American Psychological Association (APA). Psychologists are required to be familiar with these guidelines. The APA is a scientific and professional organization of psychologists.

Research with People

Ethical standards limit the type of research that psychologists may conduct. Imagine trying to study whether early separation of children from their mothers impairs the children's social development. Scientifically, such a study might collect important psychological data. But it would be unethical to purposefully separate infants from their mothers to study the effects of such a separation. Such a separation would violate the ethical principle that study participants must not be harmed. Thus, psychologists would not seriously consider running an experiment that involves intentional separation.

One alternative research approach to such a study might be to observe the development of children who have already been separated from their mothers since an early age. However, it could be difficult to draw specific conclusions from this type of research. The same factors that led to the separation—such as the death of the parents—may have influenced a child's development as much as (or perhaps more than) the separation itself. Even if there was a positive correlation between separation from the mother and the child's impaired social development, psychologists could not prove cause and effect—that one was caused by the other.

What are the ethical standards researchers adhere to? The APA guidelines provide a number of provisions that detail what is needed to make a study ethical (APA, 1994a). These guidelines include two important principles: confidentiality and informed consent.

CASE STUDIES

AND OTHER TRUE STORIES

The Hawthorne Plant Study: A Flawed Experiment

In 1927, researchers began a study in the Hawthorne plant of the Western Electric Company in Cicero, Illinois. They had been called in by the factory's managers to find out what conditions in the factory might be changed to boost productivity. The researchers designed a study in which productivity was the dependent variable and length of rest periods, workdays, and workweeks were the independent variables.

The researchers selected five women as participants in the study. The women were to work as a team in a room where they could be observed. The researchers introduced rest pauses of varying lengths throughout the workday. They observed the women to see how their productivity was affected. The researchers then began to shorten the workday and, later, the workweek. Again, they observed the changes in productivity.

At first, the researchers observed that as they increased rest periods and shortened the workday and workweek, the women's overall output increased. It appeared that, with more rest, workers returned to their jobs refreshed and therefore were able to produce more. To check their findings, the researchers slowly returned to the original schedule—with shorter rest periods, a longer workday, and a longer workweek.

To the surprise of the researchers, the women's output remained higher than it had been at the beginning of the study. How could that be? The research team concluded that the increase in output was caused not by the independent variables (length of rest pauses, workday, and workweek) but by another variable—the women's awareness that they were being observed. They felt special because of the unusual attention they were receiving; thus, they worked harder.

This phenomenon came to be known as the "Hawthorne effect." It was a valuable finding, and led to the theory that one effective way to increase worker productivity was simply to pay more attention to the workers. However, the finding was a result of a flawed study design.

To test the variables they wanted to test, the researchers could have conducted a blind study. In such a study, at least some of the participants would not have known they were being observed. Alternatively, the researchers could have established a control group—a group of participants who knew they were being observed but did not receive any of the treatments that the members of the experimental group received.

The design of the Hawthorne study had some other flaws as well. For one thing, the experimental group was exceedingly small. A sample size of five is really not large enough to be able to generalize conclusions about the larger population. Furthermore, the sample did not remain constant over the course of the whole experiment. Two of the women in the group were replaced in the middle of the study because they talked too much, their productivity was low, and they were considered a negative influence on the others. Their removal may have biased the results in favor of increased productivity.

Moreover, the researchers may have misinterpreted the results of the study. The conclusion that productivity remained high even after the women returned to the original schedule was not completely correct. Total output stayed about the same, but it was achieved in more hours. In other words, hourly productivity actually *dropped*. In addition, the researchers never considered that the longer one does a job, the more skilled one becomes. That in itself may increase productivity.

Because of these flaws, the existence of the Hawthorne effect has been called into question (Jones, 1992). The Hawthorne effect remains only a hypothesis.

THINKING CRITICALLY

1. **Summarizing** What flaws did the Hawthorne study have, and how did these flaws affect the study's outcome?

2. **Finding the Main Idea** What is the Hawthorne effect, and why do some people question its existence?

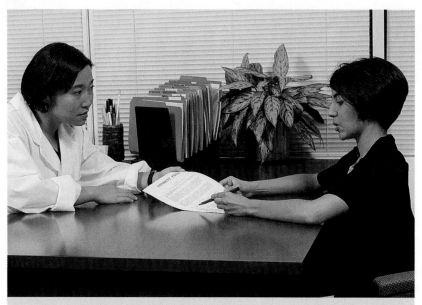

Participants in psychological studies sign consent forms to indicate that they understand the research.

given a general overview of the research and have been given the choice of whether or not to participate. The provision of information and the opportunity to choose give people some degree of control and make participation less stressful (Dill et al., 1982).

Deception   On the other hand, some psychological experiments cannot be run without deceiving people. For instance, new drug experiments and other blind studies cannot be conducted without keeping participants unaware of the treatment they are receiving or of the nature of the study. In order for the study to be valid, some participants must be deceived. In drug experiments, many participants might be told they are taking a real drug when they are actually taking a placebo, or vice versa.

Psychologists have debated the ethics of deceiving participants in research (Fisher & Fyrberg, 1994). According to the APA's statement of ethical principles, psychologists may use deception only under specified conditions:

- when they believe that the benefits of the research outweigh its potential harm
- when they believe that the individuals would have been willing to participate if they had understood the benefits of the research
- when participants receive an explanation of the study after it has occurred

Explaining what happened in the study once it is over helps avoid misunderstandings about the research. Explanations also reduce participants' anxieties and let the participants maintain their dignity (Blanck et al., 1992).

Confidentiality   Psychologists treat the records of research participants and clients as confidential. In other words, the records are private. This is because psychologists respect people's right to privacy. In addition, people are more likely to disclose true information and feelings when they know that what they say will remain confidential (Blanck et al., 1992).

In certain very rare circumstances, such as when a client reveals plans to harm someone, a psychologist may disregard confidentiality in order to protect the well-being of the client or of other people. Such situations, however, are definitely the exception rather than the rule. Even when they do arise, psychologists must think long and hard about whether breaking confidentiality is the appropriate thing to do.

Informed Consent   The APA has distinct restrictions against research studies that could pose a serious threat to the physical or psychological health of participants or that might have long-term, irreversible effects on them. However, the APA acknowledges that some worthwhile studies may cause participants to experience some discomfort or other short-term negative effects.

To help avoid situations in which people volunteer to participate in research without knowing that such effects are possible, the APA generally requires that the participants provide informed consent. **Informed consent** means that people agree, or consent, to participate in a research study only after they have been

TRUTH OR fiction
■ R E V I S I T E D ■

It is true that psychologists sometimes have to deceive participants in a study. Deception may be needed to prevent participants from purposefully or accidentally distorting the outcome of the research. But there are strict rules about deception in research.

Research with Animals

Needless to say, the experiments Todd, Marc, and Dan conducted were done with animals—Todd's fish. Most studies that use animals (such as those in which researchers have rats run through mazes to find out how they learn) do not harm the animals at all. Even the boys' fish experiments did not harm the fish. Marc's idea of using a mirror to find out about the fighting fish was a much more ethical method than using another real fighting fish. Marc was able to move the mirror, but if he had used another real fish, the two fish might have fought to the death.

Sometimes, however, psychologists and other scientists conduct research that may be harmful to animals. Such research studies often use animals because they cannot be carried out with people for ethical reasons. Experiments on the effects of early separation of children from their mothers are an example. These experiments could not be done with people, but they have been done with monkeys and other animals (e.g., Harlow, 1959). Such research has helped psychologists investigate the formation of bonds of attachment between parents and children. (See Chapter 10.)

There are other examples of psychological studies that rely on animals in order to avoid harming humans. Psychologists and biologists who study the brain sometimes destroy parts of the brains of laboratory animals to learn how those parts influence the animals' behavior. This and other types of research on animals have benefited humans. Advances in the treatment of mental disorders, neuromuscular disorders, strokes, visual and memory defects, headaches, and high blood pressure, among others, can be traced to animal research.

Psychologists use animals only when there is no alternative and when they believe that the potential benefits outweigh the harm. Only a small percentage of all psychological studies involve animals. Some researchers argue that many advances in medicine and psychology could not have taken place without harming animals (Bekoff, 2002). Yet many people believe that it is no more ethical to harm animals than it is to harm humans. Although the APA has rules of ethics for how animals used in research should be treated, controversy continues to surround the use of animals in scientific research.

In many studies that use animals, researchers are careful to treat the animals kindly.

Ethics in Using Data

Another area in which psychologists follow strict rules about ethics is in how they produce, store, and present their data. When researchers conduct a study, they need to be as objective as possible in planning their study, in collecting their data, and in analyzing their data. Without this objectivity, the researchers may bias their study, perhaps unintentionally, in favor of their hypothesis.

Even more importantly, when information collected by researchers contradicts their hypothesis, they must be willing to discard their hypothesis in light of the evidence. It might be tempting to toss out all the evidence that contradicts the hypothesis and present to others only the evidence that supports the hypothesis. But this would be misleading and thus unethical. It might also become an obstacle to others' attempts to study psychology.

SECTION 5 REVIEW

go.hrw.com **Homework Practice Online** Keyword: SY7 HP2

1. Explain the purpose of ethical standards in the profession of psychology.

2. Why are confidentiality and informed consent important to psychological research?

3. **Critical Thinking** *Supporting a Point of View* Do you believe that it is ethical or unethical to deceive people about the purposes of research studies? Explain your answer.

Writing a Summary

Using standard grammar, spelling, sentence structure, and punctuation, summarize the information in this chapter. Consider:
- the steps of scientific research and various research methods
- the purpose of experiments and ethical considerations in carrying out experiments

Identifying People and Ideas

Identify the following terms or people and use them in appropriate sentences.

1. hypothesis
2. target population
3. bias
4. case study
5. correlation
6. variables
7. control group
8. single-blind study
9. double-blind study
10. informed consent

Understanding Main Ideas

SECTION 1 (pp. 26–29)
1. Identify and describe the basic methods of social scientific reasoning.

SECTION 2 (pp. 29–34)
2. What are some of the advantages and disadvantages of the survey method?

SECTION 3 (pp. 34–40)
3. Explain the difference between positive correlation and negative correlation.

SECTION 4 (pp. 40–44)
4. Define *mean, median, mode, range,* and *standard deviation.*

SECTION 5 (pp. 44–47)
5. What purposes do ethical standards serve in psychological research?

Thinking Critically

1. **Making Generalizations and Predictions** Surveys are often used to help predict future events, such as election outcomes. How might these surveys affect the outcome of the events?

2. **Drawing Inferences and Conclusions** If correlations do not explain cause and effect, why are they useful?

3. **Summarizing** What are some potential sources for error in conducting research?

4. **Evaluating** Under what circumstances might a psychologist break the promise of confidentiality?

Writing About Psychology

1. **Summarizing** Go to the library and locate a psychological study that includes measures of central tendency and dispersion. Check the research by computing the mean, median, mode, range, and standard deviation. Write a report summarizing your findings.

2. **Supporting a Point of View** Write an essay in which you defend or argue against the use of animal subjects in psychological research. Do some background reading so that you can support your position with facts. Read your essay to the class as part of a class discussion about the ethics of research with animals. Use the graphic organizer below to help you write your report.

Reasons to Support Animal Research	Reasons to Oppose Animal Research

Interpreting Graphs

Study the bar graph below. Then use the information in the graph to help you answer the questions that follow.

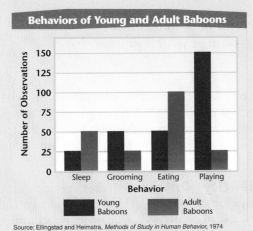

Behaviors of Young and Adult Baboons

Source: Ellingstad and Heimstra, *Methods of Study in Human Behavior*, 1974

1. Which behaviors did young baboons exhibit more frequently than adult baboons?
   a. sleeping and eating
   b. grooming and playing
   c. playing and sleeping
   d. grooming and eating

2. Can you tell which method of observation researchers used to create this chart? If so, which method was used? If not, what methods may have been used?

Analyzing Primary Sources

Read the following excerpt, which is taken from the Ethics Code of the American Psychological Association. Then answer the questions that follow.

"Psychologists strive to benefit those with whom they work and take care to do no harm. In their professional actions, psychologists seek to safeguard the welfare and rights of those with whom they interact professionally and other affected persons, and the welfare of animal subjects of research. When conflicts occur among psychologists' obligations or concerns, they attempt to resolve these conflicts in a responsible fashion that avoids or minimizes harm. Because psychologists' scientific and professional judgments and actions may affect the lives of others, they are alert to and guard against personal, financial, social, organizational, or political factors that might lead to misuse of their influence."

3. Which of the following statements best reflects the ethical values found in the excerpt above?
   a. Psychologists should follow their instincts.
   b. Psychologists may mislead patients, but only under extraordinary circumstances.
   c. When not at work, psychologists may behave however they please.
   d. When conflicts occur, psychologists must work to minimize any harm that may result.

4. According to the excerpt, why must psychologists consider the welfare and rights of their patients?

PSYCHOLOGY PROJECTS

Cooperative Learning

Using Surveys Working in small groups, design a survey of the students in your school. You might find out about their views on a particular issue or their buying habits. Decide on a format and give everyone in the group a role in preparing the questionnaires or in conducting the interviews. Write a summary of the project applying the APA's ethical standards for the collection, storage, and use of the data.

internet connect

Internet Activity: go.hrw.com
KEYWORD: SY7 CH2

Choose an activity on psychological methods to:
- design a hypothetical research program.
- create a 3-D model illustrating cause and effect and correlation.
- apply the APA standards for ethical decision making to historic experiments.

PSYCHOLOGY IN ACTION

YOU MAKE THE DECISION . . .

What type of research method would best determine how many hours of television your classmates watch per week?

Complete the following activity in small cooperative groups. Your group wants to learn how much television your classmates watch per week. But first you need to prepare a presentation in which you explain what type of research method would be the best way to learn about your classmates' viewing habits. Your group has formed the hypothesis that, on average, your classmates watch between 10 and 15 hours per week.

1. Gather Information. Use your textbook and other resources to find information that might help you decide what type of research method would be best to help you learn how much

television your classmates watch per week. What types of research would be reliable for this type of research question? What types of research would be feasible in the time frame you have to complete your work? You may want to divide up different parts of the research among group members.

2. Identify Options. After reviewing the information that you have gathered, consider which research methods you might recommend. Your final decision may be easier to reach if you consider as many options as possible. Be sure to record your options for the preparation of your presentation.

3. Predict Consequences. Now take each option you and the members of your group came up with and consider how each type of research might lend itself to what you need to find out. Ask yourself questions such as,

- Will our group be able to actually observe our classmates as they watch television?
- Will my classmates respond accurately to questions about how much television they watch?

Once you have predicted the consequences, record them as notes for your presentation.

4. Take Action to Implement Your Decision. After you have considered your options, you should create your presentation. Be sure that you are very clear regarding your decision about what research method to use. You will need to support your decision by including information you gathered and by explaining why you rejected other options. You may want to create cluster diagrams or charts to support your decision. When you are ready, decide who in your group will make which part of the presentation. Then make your presentation to the class. Good luck!

UNIT 2

BODY AND MIND

3 BIOLOGY AND BEHAVIOR

Chapter

Read to Discover

1 How are messages transmitted by neurons, and what are the functions of the peripheral nervous system?

2 What are the major structures of the brain, and what is the function of each structure?

3 How do hormones secreted by the major glands of the endocrine system affect the body?

4 What is the role of chromosomes and genes in heredity, and how do psychologists study the role of heredity in determining traits?

A DAY IN THE LIFE

Marc was rushing through the halls to reach class on time. As he ran, thoughts of Linda floated through his mind. He was in some classes with her, and he was beginning to think that she was very attractive. Distracted by these images of Linda, Marc rounded a corner and bumped into Todd, who stepped down hard on Marc's big toe. Marc grabbed his sneakered foot in his hands, then started to rub his toe, which throbbed with pain. In addition, he felt his heart begin to race. Todd cringed and said, "Oh, sorry. I didn't even see you." Still holding his foot, Marc grunted, "Hey, don't worry. It's no big deal."

• • •

No big deal? At first glance, this incident between Marc and Todd seems very simple, but much more actually occurred than meets the eye. The way in which Marc's body responded to having his foot stepped on is of great interest to psychologists. This may seem surprising—after all, what does biology have to do with psychology? In fact, biological functioning has much to do with psychology.

The ways in which our bodies and minds work in relation to each other are quite remarkable. Biological psychologists (sometimes called biopsychologists) study the ways in which our behavior and psychological processes are linked to biological structures and processes. For example, sensation, perception, memory, and thinking are all psychological processes that have at least a partly biological basis. (You will read about these topics in greater depth in later chapters.)

A major area of study for biological psychologists concerns the workings of the nervous system. The nervous system, which includes the brain, is involved in psychological processes such as thought and emotion, movement and sensation, and much more. Based on our knowledge of the nervous system, we can explain how messages were sent from Marc's toe to his brain and back to his foot, causing him to grab his foot and begin to massage his injured toe.

In addition to the nervous system, biological psychologists study the endocrine system. This system is responsible for the secretion of hormones. Hormones serve a wide variety of functions, such as influencing emotions. Marc's emotional response to having his foot stepped on was due in part to the endocrine system.

Biological psychologists are also interested in heredity and how it affects us both physically and psychologically. Heredity influences not only how we look but also how we act. Biological psychologists study the interactions between our heredity and the environments in which we live.

Key Terms

central nervous system
peripheral nervous system
neurons
cell body
dendrites
axon
myelin
axon terminals
synapse
neurotransmitters
spinal cord
somatic nervous system
autonomic nervous system
medulla
pons
cerebellum
reticular activating system
thalamus
hypothalamus
limbic system
cerebrum
cerebral cortex
corpus callosum
association areas
endocrine system
hormones
heredity
genes
chromosomes

HOLT

Psychology Video Program

Watch the video to explore ways in which we learn about the brain and how it functions.

Read the following statements about psychology. Do you think they are true or false? You will learn whether each statement is true or false as you read the chapter.

- Individual cells in the human body can be several feet long.
- Anxiety can give you indigestion.
- A person with brain damage may be able to report that he or she has seen a face but may not be able to identify that it was the face of a close friend.
- Some people are "left-brained" and others are "right-brained."
- The father's genetic contribution—not the mother's—determines the sex of the offspring.

SECTION 1

The Nervous System

The human nervous system is involved in thinking, dreaming, feeling, moving, and much more. It is working when we are active or still, awake or asleep. The nervous system regulates our internal functions. It is also involved in how we react to the external world. Even learning and memory are made possible by the nervous system. When we learn a new behavior or acquire new information, the nervous system registers that experience and changes to accommodate its storage.

The nervous system has two main parts: the central nervous system and the peripheral nervous system. The **central nervous system** consists of the brain and the spinal cord. The **peripheral nervous system** is made up of nerve cells that send messages between the central nervous system and all the parts of the body. In order to understand how the central and the peripheral nervous systems work, we must first understand how nerve cells communicate with one another and how their messages travel through the body.

Neurons

Nerve cells, called **neurons**, run through our entire bodies and communicate with each other. Neurons send and receive messages from other structures in the body, such as muscles and glands. These messages can affect events ranging from the sensation of a pinprick to the first steps of a child, from the writing of a poem to the memory of a past event. Each of us has more than 100 billion neurons, most of which are found in the brain.

Components of a Neuron Neurons are somewhat like trees in structure. Parts of neurons resemble the branches, trunk, and roots of a tree.

The Anatomy of Two Neurons

Dendrites

Cell body

Nucleus

Synapse

Myelin sheath

Axon terminals

Axon

FIGURE 3.1 *"Messages" enter neurons through the dendrites. These messages are transmitted along the trunklike axon to other neurons, glands, and muscles. On many neurons, the myelin sheath protects the axon.*

And, as in forests, many nerve cells lie alongside one another like a thicket of trees. Unlike trees, however, neurons can also lie end to end. Their "roots" are intertwined with the "branches" of neurons that lie below. (See Figure 3.1.)

Every neuron consists of a cell body, dendrites, and an axon. The **cell body** produces energy that fuels the activity of the cell. Branching out from the cell body are thin fibers called **dendrites**. The dendrites receive information from other neurons and pass the message through the cell body.

While the dendrites carry information *to* the cell body, the **axon** carries messages *away*. A neuron has many dendrites but usually only one axon. Axons vary greatly in length. Some are just a tiny fraction of an inch, while others stretch to several feet. Because of the length of their axons, some neurons in your legs are several feet long.

TRUTH OR fiction REVISITED

It is true that individual cells in the body can be several feet long. These cells are nerve cells, or neurons, that are long because they have long axons. Some neurons in the leg stretch from the lower spine to the toes.

Many axons are covered with **myelin**, a white fatty substance that insulates and protects the axon. This myelin sheath, or casing, also helps to speed up the transmission of the message. At the end of the axon, smaller fibers branch out. These fibers are called **axon terminals**.

The Communication Process Messages are sent from the axon terminals of one neuron to the dendrites of other neurons. In order for a message to be sent from one neuron to another neuron, it must cross the **synapse**. The synapse is a junction between the axon terminals of one neuron and the dendrites of another neuron. Messages travel in only one direction. Thus, messages are received by the dendrites and travel through the cell body and the axon to the axon terminals. From there, they cross synapses to the dendrites of other neurons. (See Figure 3.2.) New synapses can develop between neurons that were not previously connected, as when we learn something new.

The information that is sent and the place to which it goes depend on a number of factors. These factors include the locations of the neuron in the

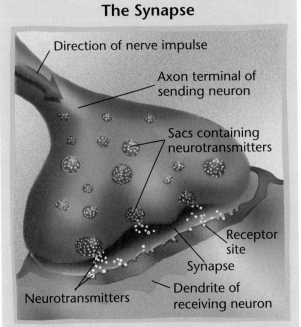

The Synapse

- Direction of nerve impulse
- Axon terminal of sending neuron
- Sacs containing neurotransmitters
- Receptor site
- Synapse
- Neurotransmitters
- Dendrite of receiving neuron

FIGURE 3.2 *There is no physical connection between neurons. A neuron relays its message across a junction called a synapse by releasing chemicals called neurotransmitters. They are received by the next neuron.*

A DAY IN THE LIFE

body and the events that produced the message. For example, the pain in Marc's toe was transmitted to his brain through sensory neurons. Sensory neurons are nerve cells that carry information received by the senses *to* the central nervous system. Motor neurons, on the other hand, are nerve cells that carry information *from* the central nervous system to the muscles and the glands and influence their functioning. Motor neurons took the message to Marc's foot so that he pulled up on it and began to rub it. Other motor neurons stimulated Marc's glands, making his heart beat faster. Still other neurons in his brain enabled him to think over the matter and to decide that Todd should be forgiven.

Occasionally, something happens to disrupt the message-sending process. For example, a hard blow to the head from a car accident or a sports injury can cause a concussion—an injury in which the soft tissue of the brain hits against the skull. Sometimes, the person is affected for only a few seconds. Other times, the person may experience effects for a much longer time. In 1993, Dallas Cowboys quarterback Troy Aikman suffered a concussion during a game in the National Football League playoffs. He

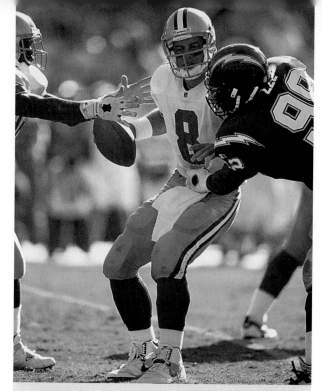

Troy Aikman's concussion in the 1993 football play-offs interfered with his memory of the event.

orders may also be caused by the presence of too much or too little of various neurotransmitters.

Researchers have identified dozens of neuro-transmitters and their functions. For example, acetylcholine is a common neurotransmitter that is involved in the control of muscles. It is used by the motor neurons of the spinal cord and stimulates skeletal muscles. The release of acetylcholine was what led Marc to grab his foot. When the amount of acetylcholine available to the brain decreases, the formation of memories is impaired.

Dopamine is another neurotransmitter. It is involved primarily in motor behavior. A deficiency in dopamine levels plays a role in Parkinson's disease, which is characterized by tremors and unco-ordinated, rigid movements. An excess of dopamine may contribute to the psychological disorder schizophrenia. (See Chapter 18.) Other neurotransmitters include noradrenaline, which is primarily involved in preparing the body for action, and serotonin, which is involved in emotional arousal and sleep.

Although we are often unaware of the processes in our bodies, we can be sure that our bodies are hard at work whether we are running or sitting still.

remembers being at the game, but he cannot remember what happened during the game. Such experiences show that memory is in large part a biological process. (See Chapter 7.)

Neurotransmitters: Chemical Messengers

Neurons send messages across synapses through the release of **neurotransmitters**. Neurotransmitters are chemicals that are stored in sacs in the axon terminals. A neuron fires, or sends its message, by releasing neurotransmitters—much like droplets of water shooting out of a spray bottle. Neurons can fire hundreds of times every second.

There are several types of neurotransmitters. Each has its own structure and fits into a receptor site on the next neuron, similar to the way in which a key fits into a lock. The message is converted into an electrical impulse that travels the length of the neuron. The message is then transmitted to the next neuron by neurotransmitters. The process continues until the message arrives at its destination. This whole process takes only a fraction of a second.

Neurotransmitters are involved in everything people do. Whenever a person waves a hand, yawns, or thinks about a friend, neurotransmitters are involved. Some diseases and psychological dis-

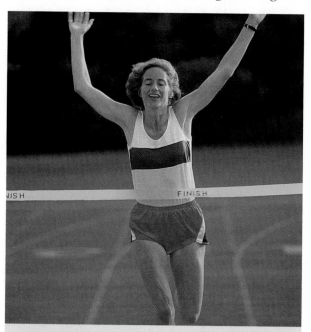

Long-distance runners experience a "runner's high," which may be connected with the release of endorphins. Endorphins are neurotransmitters similar in function to the drug morphine. They have a tranquilizing and painkilling effect on the body.

At any given moment, millions of neurons are shooting neurotransmitters across synapses and sending complicated messages to various parts of the body. These messages are carried via the spinal cord and the peripheral nervous system.

The Central Nervous System

Figure 3.3 shows the central nervous system, which consists of the neurons of the spinal cord and the brain. (The brain is discussed in Section 2.) The **spinal cord** extends from the brain down the back. It is a column of nerves about as thick as a thumb, and it is protected by the bones of the spine. It transmits messages between the brain and the muscles and the glands throughout the body.

The spinal cord is also involved in spinal reflexes. A spinal reflex is a simple, automatic response to something. For example, if a person touches a hot stove, a message goes immediately from his or her hand to the spinal cord. A message to remove the hand is then sent back to motor neurons in the hand. The removal of the hand is a spinal reflex. (The person may also register pain in his or her brain. But the pain is not what causes the reflex. In fact, the pain may not even be felt until after the hand has been removed.)

Many of our simple actions are reflexive. Have you ever wondered why you blink when you get a speck of dust in your eye? Or why some people sneeze when they sniff pepper? Physicians sometimes test people's reflexes to learn whether their nervous systems are functioning properly. When a doctor taps just below the knee to see if you kick, the purpose is to check your knee-jerk reflex to make sure your neurons are responding the way they are supposed to.

The Peripheral Nervous System

The peripheral nervous system lies outside the central nervous system and is responsible for transmitting messages between the central nervous system and all parts of the body. The two main divisions of the peripheral nervous system are the somatic nervous system and the autonomic nervous system. (See Figure 3.4 on page 58.)

The Somatic Nervous System The **somatic nervous system** transmits sensory messages to the central nervous system. It is activated by touch, pain, changes in temperature, and changes in body position. The somatic nervous system enables us to

The Central Nervous System

Brain

Spinal cord

Peripheral nerves

FIGURE 3.3 *Your spinal cord is protected by a column of bones called vertebrae. Similarly, your brain is protected by the skull.*

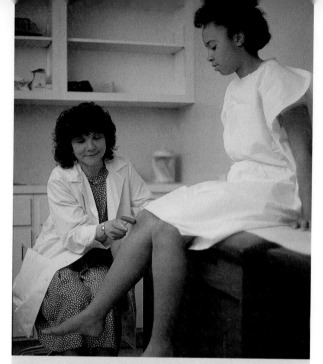

When a doctor hits the knee joint, sensory neurons carry the message from the muscles to the spinal cord. This excites motor neurons, which causes leg muscles to contract, making the leg move.

moved or changed position. It sends messages to the muscles and the glands and helps us maintain posture and balance.

The Autonomic Nervous System The word *autonomic* means "occurring involuntarily," or automatically. The **autonomic nervous system** regulates the body's vital functions, such as heartbeat, breathing, digestion, and blood pressure. We generally do not have to think about these activities—they occur automatically and are essential for keeping us alive.

Psychologists are interested in the autonomic nervous system because of its involvement in the experience of emotion. The response of the autonomic nervous system is particularly important when a person experiences something stressful in the environment.

The autonomic nervous system has two divisions: the sympathetic and the parasympathetic nervous systems. (See Figure 3.4.) These systems generally have opposing functions. The sympathetic system is activated when a person is going into action, perhaps because of some stressful event. It prepares the body either to confront the situation or to run away. This is sometimes called the "fight-or-flight" response. For example, when a person is suddenly attacked by a large angry dog, the sympathetic nervous system is aroused.

The sympathetic nervous system prepares the body by suppressing digestion, increasing the heart

experience the sensations of hot and cold and to feel pain and pressure. For example, we can feel the softness of a cat's fur, warmth if the cat is sitting on our lap, and pain if the cat scratches us. The somatic system also alerts us that parts of the body have

Divisions of the Nervous System

- Nervous system
  - Central nervous system
    - Brain
    - Spinal cord
  - Peripheral nervous system
    - Autonomic system (involuntary muscles and internal organs)
      - Parasympathetic system (calms body after emergencies)
      - Sympathetic system (prepares body for action)
    - Somatic system (voluntary muscles and sense organs)

FIGURE 3.4 *This chart shows the major divisions of the nervous system. The central nervous system consists of the brain and the spinal cord. The peripheral nervous system transmits messages from the central nervous system to all parts of the body.*

and respiration rates, and elevating the blood pressure. Do you ever feel queasy when you are in a stressful situation—such as when your teacher springs a surprise quiz on you? This is because your sympathetic nervous system has kicked into action and has suppressed your digestive processes. And when Todd stepped on Marc's toe, Marc felt his heart start to race—another result of the activation of the sympathetic nervous system.

A DAY IN THE LIFE

TRUTH OR **fiction** ∎ R E V I S I T E D ∎

It is true that anxiety can give you indigestion. Anxiety may cause indigestion by inducing activity of the sympathetic nervous system, which suppresses digestion.

In contrast to the sympathetic system, the parasympathetic nervous system restores the body's reserves of energy after an action has occurred. Heart rate and blood pressure are normalized, breathing is slowed, and digestion returns to normal. If you are having trouble remembering which system is which, perhaps it will help to keep in mind that "sympathetic" and "stress" both start with the letter *s*, while "parasympathetic" and "peace" both begin with *p*. The sympathetic system reacts to stress; the parasympathetic system restores peace.

SECTION 1 REVIEW

go.hrw.com **Homework Practice Online** Keyword: SY7 HP3

1. How do messages travel from one neuron to another?
2. Identify the systems that make up the peripheral nervous system.
3. **Critical Thinking** *Summarizing* In what way do the parasympathetic and the sympathetic nervous systems work together?

S E C T I O N 2

The Brain: Our Control Center

Every person is unique in part because of the capacities for learning and thought made possible by the human brain. In ancient times, hundreds of years before scientists had learned much about how the brain functions, people did not attribute human psychological processes such as thinking to the working of the brain. People thought that what was inside a person's body was not very different from what was inside an animal's body. Therefore, they reasoned, the abilities that make people different from animals—such as creative thought, art, and analytical abilities—could not be explained in biological terms. Instead, it was widely believed that the body was inhabited by souls or demons.

The ancient Egyptians believed that a little person dwelled within the skull and regulated behavior. Greek philosopher Aristotle thought that the soul resided in the heart. Psychologist B. F. Skinner noted that the English language still reflects the belief in the heart as the seat of will, thought, hunger, and joy. We use expressions such as "deep in one's heart," "to know something by heart," and "to have a change of heart."

Today, however, we recognize that the mind, or consciousness, dwells within the brain (Baldo et al., 2004; Buchanan et al., 2004). We know that when

A DAY IN THE LIFE

thoughts of Linda ran through Marc's mind, something was happening in his brain. We now have greater understanding of the brain and the links between biological processes and psychological phenomena.

Parts of the Brain

The human brain is composed of many parts that work together to organize our movements, create our thoughts, form our emotions, and produce our behaviors. Scientists have identified the localized functions of different parts of the brain. The brain is divided into three sections: the hindbrain, the midbrain, and the forebrain. (See Figure 3.5 on page 60.) The hindbrain is the lower portion of the brain and is involved in many vital functions such as heart rate, respiration, and balance. The midbrain includes areas that are involved in vision and hearing. The forebrain, the front area of the brain, is involved in complex functions such as thought and emotion.

The Hindbrain The medulla, the pons, and the cerebellum are important structures of the hindbrain. The **medulla** is involved in vital functions such as heart rate, blood pressure, and breathing. The **pons** is located in front of the medulla and is involved in regulating body movement, attention, sleep, and alertness.

Parts of the Human Brain

MIDBRAIN

⬤ Reticular
activating
system
*(middle
part)*

HINDBRAIN

◼ Reticular
activating system
(lower part)

◻ Medulla

◼ Cerebellum

◼ Pons

FOREBRAIN

△ Reticular
activating
system
(upper part)

△ Thalamus

△ Hypothalamus

△ Cerebrum

△ Cerebral cortex
*(surface of
cerebrum)*

△ Corpus
callosum

Spinal cord

FIGURE 3.5 *The average human adult brain weighs about three pounds and has more than 10 billion cells, many of which are neurons. Although the brain makes up about 2 to 3 percent of a person's body weight, it requires about 20 percent of the blood's oxygen supply.*

Cerebellum is the Latin word for "little brain." The **cerebellum** looks like the larger part of the brain (the cerebrum), under which it rests, but it is much smaller. It is involved in balance and coordination. A person whose cerebellum is injured may have trouble with coordination. The person may walk unsteadily and even occasionally fall down.

The Midbrain   The midbrain is located between the hindbrain and the forebrain. Areas within the midbrain are involved in vision and hearing. Eye movement, for example, is controlled by an area in the midbrain. In addition, the midbrain contains part of the **reticular activating system**. The reticular activating system begins in the hindbrain and rises through the midbrain into the lower part of the forebrain. This system is important for attention,

sleep, and arousal. Stimulation of the reticular activating system makes us alert. It affects arousal by increasing heart rate and blood pressure, and it increases brain activity. Some drugs, such as alcohol, reduce the activity of the reticular activating system, thus affecting alertness and reaction time.

Sudden, loud noises stimulate the reticular activating system and can awaken a sleeping person. However, the reticular activating system can screen out some noises. A person who lives in the city may not be awakened by the sounds of traffic roaring by. This same person may, however, awaken to sounds that are more out of the ordinary, such as a bird singing, even if these sounds are fairly soft.

The Forebrain   Four key areas of the forebrain are the thalamus, the hypothalamus, the limbic system, and the cerebrum. Certain parts of the forebrain are very well developed in human beings. The forebrain is the part of the brain that makes it possible for humans to engage in complex thinking processes.

Thalamus is a Latin word meaning "inner chamber." The **thalamus** is a critical structure of the brain because it serves as a relay station for sensory stimulation. Most of the messages coming from the sense organs go through the thalamus on the way to the higher levels of the brain (those areas responsible for mental processes such as thinking and reasoning). The thalamus transmits sensory information, such as the pain from Marc's big toe, to the areas of the brain that interpret and respond to the information. The thalamus also relays sensory input from the eyes and the ears to the appropriate parts of the brain for interpretation of the input.

Hypo- is a Greek prefix meaning "under." Thus, the **hypothalamus** lies below the thalamus. The hypothalamus is tiny, but it is extremely important because it is involved in many aspects of behavior and physiological functions. It is vital to the regulation of body temperature, the storage of nutrients, and various aspects of motivation and emotion. It is also involved in hunger, thirst, sexual behavior, caring for offspring, and aggression. Disturbances within the hypothalamus can lead to unusual drinking and eating behaviors.

Among lower animals, stimulation of parts of the hypothalamus triggers behaviors such as fighting, mating, or nest building. Although the hypothalamus is also important to people, our behavior is less mechanical and tends to be influenced by cognitive functions such as thought, choice, and value systems.

The **limbic system** forms a fringe along the inner edge of the cerebrum. It is involved in learning and memory, emotion, hunger, sex, and aggression. If a particular part of the limbic system is damaged, people can recall old memories but do not create new memories. For example, a person with damage to that area may have vivid childhood memories of playing with his or her sister but may not be able to remember that this same sister visited earlier that day. Researchers have also found that destruction of another specific area of the limbic system can lead animals to show passive behavior. Destruction of a different area of the limbic system causes some animals to behave aggressively, even when there seems little reason to do so.

The **cerebrum** (Latin for "brain") is the crowning glory of the brain. Only in human beings does the cerebrum make up such a large part of the brain. The cerebrum accounts for about 70 percent of the weight of the brain. The surface of the cerebrum is wrinkled with ridges and valleys. This surface is the **cerebral cortex**. The cerebral cortex is the outer layer of the brain, just as bark is the outer layer of a tree. (*Cortex* is the Latin word for "bark of a tree.")

The cerebral cortex is the part of the brain that we tend to think of when we talk about the brain. It is the part that makes us uniquely human—the part that thinks. In addition to thinking, the cerebral cortex also deals with memory, language, emotions, complex motor functions, perception, and much more.

The Cerebral Cortex: What Makes Us Unique

The cerebral cortex is composed of two sides—a left side and a right side. Each side is called a hemisphere. (The Greek *hemi-* means "half." Thus, each half of the brain is half a sphere, just as each half of planet Earth is a hemisphere.) To visualize the cerebral cortex, think of a walnut. The shell of the walnut is like the skull. Just as the walnut has two sides that are connected, so does the brain. In the brain, the structure that connects the two hemispheres is called the **corpus callosum**.

Interestingly, information received by one side of the body is transmitted to the *opposite* hemisphere of the brain. For example, if you touch something with your left hand, that information is sent to the right side of your brain. Conversely, if you touch something with your right hand, the left hemisphere of your brain receives the information. The corpus callosum aids in getting information from one side of the brain to the other.

Each hemisphere of the cerebral cortex is divided into four parts, or lobes. The frontal lobe lies behind the forehead, and the parietal lobe lies to the top and rear of the head. The temporal lobe lies to the side, just below the ears. The occipital lobe is at the back of the head. (See Figure 3.6 on page 62.)

Some sensations, such as visual sensations, are received primarily in one lobe. However, each lobe does not necessarily act independently from the others. Some functions require the interplay of several lobes. The involvement of the cerebral cortex in the senses and motor behavior is a good illustration of this interaction.

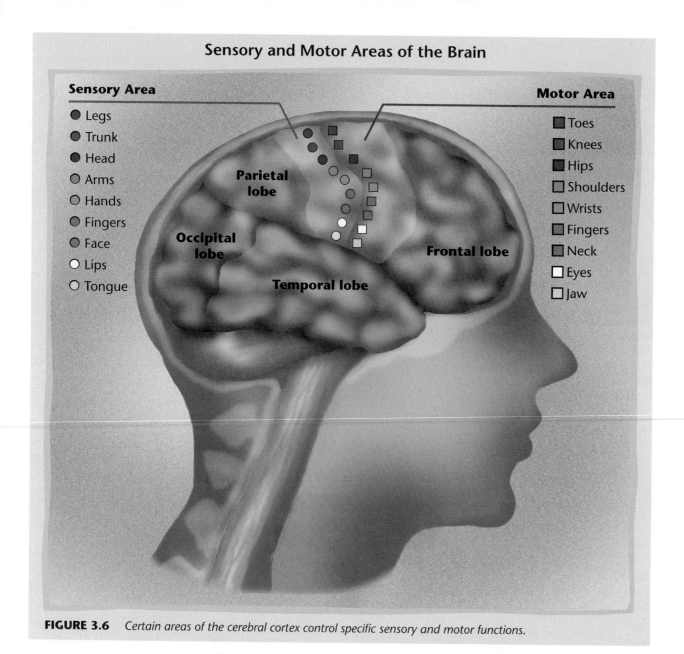

Sensory and Motor Areas of the Brain

Sensory Area
- Legs
- Trunk
- Head
- Arms
- Hands
- Fingers
- Face
- Lips
- Tongue

Motor Area
- Toes
- Knees
- Hips
- Shoulders
- Wrists
- Fingers
- Neck
- Eyes
- Jaw

Parietal lobe

Occipital lobe

Temporal lobe

Frontal lobe

FIGURE 3.6   *Certain areas of the cerebral cortex control specific sensory and motor functions.*

Senses and Motor Behavior   The occipital lobe contains the primary visual area of the cerebral cortex. When light strikes the eyes, neurons in the occipital lobe fire, enabling us to see. We also "see" flashes of light if neurons in the occipital lobe are stimulated by electricity.

Damage to different parts of the occipital lobe can create unusual conditions. People with damage to one area may be able to recognize an object, but they may be unable to differentiate it from another object that is similar. For example, if shown a key, they may know that what they see is a key, but they may not be able to tell it apart from another key that looks different. People with damage to another area may be able to report that they have seen a face, but they may not be able to identify that it is the face of a close friend.

It is true that a person with brain damage may be able to report that he or she has seen a face but may not be able to identify that it was the face of a close friend. Damage to a particular area in the occipital lobe of the cerebral cortex can create this condition.

The hearing, or auditory, area of the cortex lies in the temporal lobe. Sounds are relayed from the ears to the thalamus to the auditory area. When this occurs, we hear sounds. If a specific area of the temporal cortex is damaged, a person may not be able to recognize very common sounds.

Messages received from the skin senses (see Chapter 4) are projected to the sensory cortex in the parietal lobe. These sensations include warmth, cold, touch, and pain. Different neurons fire, depending on whether you have scratched your nose, touched a hot stove, or been stung by a bee. When Todd stepped on Marc's toe, the pain message was relayed from the toe to the parietal lobe of Marc's brain.

The motor cortex in the frontal lobe, was involved when Marc grabbed his foot and started rubbing it. Neurons in the motor cortex fire when we move certain parts of our body.

Association Areas   Much of the cerebral cortex is composed of areas that involve sensory and motor functions. Other areas, called **association areas**, shape information into something meaningful. For example, certain neurons in the visual area of the occipital lobe fire when we see vertical lines. Others fire in response to horizontal lines. Although one group of cells may respond to vertical lines and another group of cells to horizontal lines, association areas put it all together. As a result, we see a box or an automobile or a road map instead of a confusing display of verticals and horizontals.

The association areas in the frontal lobes, near the forehead, could be called the brain's executive center. It appears to be where we solve problems and make plans and decisions (Chafee & Goldman-Rakic, 2000; Duncan et al., 2000; Levy & Goldman-Rakic, 1999).

Executive functions also require memory, like the memory in your computer. Association areas also provide the core of your working memory (Chafee & Goldman-Rakic, 2000; Levy & Goldman-Rakic, 1999). They are connected with sensory areas in the brain and can tap whatever sensory information is needed or desired. The frontal region of the brain thus retrieves visual, auditory, and other kinds of memories and manipulates them—similar to the way in which a computer retrieves information from files in storage and manipulates it in working memory. Other association areas make possible the complex psychological functions of language.

Language Abilities   Although the left and the right hemispheres of the brain have many of the same functions, they differ in a number of ways. For example, for nearly all right-handed people, language functions are based in the left hemisphere. Language functions are also based in the left hemisphere of about two out of three left-handed people.

Within the hemisphere containing the language functions, two key language areas are Broca's area and Wernicke's area. Damage to either area is likely to cause an aphasia, a difficulty with specific aspects of understanding or producing language.

Wernicke's area, which is located in the temporal lobe, pieces together sounds and sights. People with damage to this area may find it difficult to understand speech, and their speech often is meaningless. For example, when asked to describe a picture of two boys stealing cookies behind a woman's back, one person responded: "Mother is away her working her work to get her better, but when she's looking the two boys looking the other part. She's working another time" (Geschwind, 1979).

Broca's area is located in the frontal lobe near the section of the motor cortex that controls the areas of the face used for speaking. When Broca's area is damaged, people speak slowly and laboriously, using simple sentences.

Left Versus Right Hemispheres   The same hemisphere that contains most language functions is usually more involved in logic, problem solving, and mathematical computation than is the other hemisphere (Corballis et al., 2002; Shenal & Harrison, 2003). The right hemisphere is relatively more concerned with the imagination, art, feelings, and spatial relations. People often speak of certain abilities as belonging to the right brain or to the left brain. Thus, people who are very logical are said to be "left-brained," while people who are creative are called "right-brained." This idea, however, has become exaggerated. Although some differences do exist, the hemispheres do not act independently of each other (Colvin et al., 2005).

It is not true that some people are "left-brained" and others are "right-brained." Both hemispheres of the brain are involved in most human activities and abilities.

A common belief is that people who are very logical (such as judges) are "left-brained" whereas people who are more creative (such as artists) are "right-brained." This belief, however, has little scientific validity.

Much of what psychologists have learned about left- and right-hemisphere functioning comes from people who have had split-brain operations. In a split-brain operation, the corpus callosum, which connects the two hemispheres, is cut. This procedure, although performed only rarely, is sometimes used to help people with serious neural disorders such as severe cases of epilepsy. People with epilepsy experience seizures, which are bursts of abnormal neuron firings that generally occur in one hemisphere and then spread to the other. Cutting the corpus callosum can reduce the severity of the seizures by preventing them from spreading. After the surgery, patients usually function quite effectively despite their hemispheres' inability to communicate with each other.

However, the surgery does have some subtle effects on functioning. For example, people may be able to describe verbally the objects they hold in their right hand but not what they hold in their left hand (Gazzaniga, 1992). This is because if an object is held in the right hand, the information is sent to the left hemisphere, which (in most people) contains language abilities. However, if the same object is held in the left hand, this information is projected to the right hemisphere, which has very little language ability. It is important to remember that for people with intact corpus callosums, the hemispheres usually work together. Thus, most people can describe objects held in either hand.

Methods of Studying the Brain

Much of our earlier understanding of the brain came from studies of people with head injuries. Today, researchers increase their knowledge of the brain and its functions by using a variety of techniques to study damaged and intact brains.

Accidents One way that researchers have been able to see how the brain is related to psychological functions is through the study of accidents and brain damage. Brain damage from head injuries can result in loss of vision and hearing, confusion, or loss of memory. In some cases, the loss of large portions of the brain may result in relatively little loss of function. Yet the loss of vital, smaller parts can result in language problems, memory loss, or death. In other words, which particular area is damaged may have a greater effect than the amount of the damage.

Electrical Stimulation of the Brain Electrical stimulation of the brain has shown that specific areas are associated with specific types of sensations (such as seeing light or feeling a tap on the arm) or motor activities (such as walking). In a classic experiment, José Delgado (1969) used electrical stimulation of the brain to show how an animal could be made to change behavioral patterns. The researchers implanted an electrode into a bull's

CASE STUDIES
AND OTHER TRUE STORIES

Is Phineas Gage Still the Same Man?

The ability of the brain to withstand some accidents is nothing less than remarkable. In some instances, people have not only survived severe injuries to the brain, but they have continued to live fairly normal lives. Sometimes, though, the victim is not quite the same as before the accident. Consider the case of Phineas Gage.

Young Mr. Gage was a promising railroad worker. His character was outstanding and he was well liked. But all that changed one day in 1848. While he was tamping down the blasting powder for a dynamite charge, Gage accidentally set the powder off. An inch-thick metal rod shot upward through his brain and out the top of his head.

The rod landed many yards away. Gage fell back in a heap, but he was not dead. His coworkers watched in shock as he stood up a few moments later and spoke. They drove him by oxcart to a local doctor, John Harlow. As the doctor marveled at the hole through Gage's head, Gage asked when the doctor thought he'd be able to return to work.

Everyone, including the doctor, was surprised that Phineas Gage even survived the accident. Two months later, the physical effects of Gage's wounds had healed. He walked about, spoke normally enough, and was aware of his surroundings. However, Gage had changed. He no longer was a dependable worker. He had also become foul-mouthed and ill-mannered. It had become clear that the accident had had some serious psychological consequences.

Gage died 13 years later during an epileptic seizure. Dr. Harlow persuaded Gage's family to donate his skull to the Warren Medical Museum at Harvard University. Generations of biologists and

Phineas Gage's skull

psychologists have studied the skull and wondered how Gage's changes in personality might have been caused by damage to his brain.

According to biologists Hanna and Antonio Damasio (1992), the way in which the rod had entered the brain had spared the parts of the frontal lobes that were involved in language and motor behavior. Thus, Gage was able to speak normally and move about easily. However, the rod had severely damaged a part of the underside of the frontal lobes, causing the disturbance in personality. The Damasios note that people who suffer damage to the same part of the brain today experience similar changes in personality. These individuals are often unable to censor their thoughts before speaking. As a result, they may blurt out thoughts that they would have kept to themselves before their brains were injured.

Other researchers also have found changes in patients' personalities after brain injuries. In general, damage to right frontal areas can produce impulsive and rule-breaking behaviors, such as interrupting conversations (Kolb & Taylor, 1981). People with frontal-lobe injuries are also less likely to make spontaneous facial expressions. The combination of excessive talking and lack of facial expressions may make these individuals seem like different people than they were before.

THINKING CRITICALLY

1. **Comparing and Contrasting** How did Phineas Gage's personality after his accident differ from his personality before his accident?
2. **Summarizing** What changes can frontal-lobe brain damage cause?

brain. When the brain was stimulated, the bull dramatically stopped his charge and circled to the right.

In another classic study, James Olds and Peter Milner (Olds, 1969) used rats who had electrodes implanted in their brains to learn about the functions of the hypothalamus. When the rats pressed a lever, the electrodes stimulated the portion of the hypothalamus where they were implanted. As it turned out, the rats found this stimulation pleasurable—so pleasurable that the rats would press the lever up to 100 times a minute just to receive the stimulation. In some cases, hungry rats chose electrical stimulation over food. The part of the hypothalamus where the electrodes were implanted thus became known as a "pleasure center."

Electrical stimulation of the brain is not always reliable as a research tool. Stimulation in the same place can produce different effects at different times. On one occasion, a rat may eat when a portion of the brain is stimulated, but on another occasion it may drink. The areas that produce pleasant and unpleasant sensations in people may also vary from person to person and from day to day.

The Electroencephalogram   The electroencephalogram (EEG) is a device that records the electrical activity of the brain. Electrodes attached to the scalp with tape or paste detect small amounts of electrical activity called brain waves. Researchers have learned that certain brain wave patterns are associated with feelings of relaxation and with

sleep. (See Chapter 5.) Researchers and physicians can use electroencephalogram readings to help diagnose some kinds of psychological disorders and to help locate tumors.

Scans   In recent years, scientists have designed new techniques for examining the brain. These techniques use computers to generate images of the brain from various sources of information (Goleman, 1995; Posner & Raichle, 1994). Images of the brain can provide information about brain damage and other abnormalities. Imaging techniques can also be used for early diagnoses of cancers and other problems. In addition, physicians can use imaging to aid them during difficult and intricate surgeries.

In computerized axial tomography (CAT) scans, a moving ring passes X-ray beams around and through the head. The density of the brain tissue determines how much radiation is absorbed. Computers measure the amounts of radiation and piece together a three-dimensional view of the brain that can be displayed on a video monitor.

In magnetic resonance imaging (MRI), a person lies in a very powerful magnetic field. Radio waves then cause parts of the brain to give off extra energy. This energy is measured from multiple angles and is translated by computer into a visual image of the brain's anatomy. MRI is more powerful than a CAT scan and can show details more clearly. For example, MRI is more effective at revealing small injuries and abnormalities in hard-to-see areas.

The photograph at left shows an image obtained by a CAT scan. By producing a three-dimensional view of the brain, a CAT scan can reveal hidden brain damage. The photograph on the right shows a person entering MRI apparatus. For people who fear enclosed spaces, the time spent lying in the MRI field can be uncomfortable.

While CAT scans and MRIs can show a snapshot of the brain, positron emissional tomography (PET) scans and a fast kind of MRI called the functional MRI (fMRI) enable researchers to catch the brain at work. In a PET scan, a person is injected with radioactive sugar. As the sugar reaches the brain, more of it is used in the locations where brain activity is greater. A computer then uses the sugar levels to create an image showing the amount of activity in different areas of the brain, as shown at right. The fMRI can show which parts of the brain are most active when we perform different activities, such as listening to music, playing chess, using language, or working out a math problem (Dogil et al., 2002; Rickard et al., 2000). If you raise your hand, the image will show activity in one part of the brain. If you start to sing a song, other parts of the brain will light up. Research with the PET scan and fMRI supports the view that we do much of our problem solving in the frontal lobes of the brain. (Duncan, 2000).

Using these research techniques, psychologists have learned that the mind is a product of the brain. Today it is generally agreed that for every mental event there are accompanying, underlying biological events. Imaging techniques have allowed us to explore more deeply how the nervous system, particularly the brain, functions while we are thinking, feeling, and moving. The study of brain abnormalities has also revealed that when parts of the brain have undergone damage, other areas of the brain can sometimes take over the functions of the damaged areas.

A PET scan shows brain activity as it occurs.

SECTION 2 REVIEW

go.hrw.com

Homework Practice Online

Keyword: SY7 HP3

1. Why is the cerebral cortex important?

2. Describe two differences between the left hemisphere and the right hemisphere of the cerebral cortex.

3. List three different imaging techniques used to study the brain.

4. **Critical Thinking** *Evaluating* Why do you think it benefits people to have brains that are flexible? What would happen if brains were not flexible?

SECTION 3
The Endocrine System

The **endocrine system** consists of glands that secrete substances, called **hormones**, into the bloodstream. The word *hormone* is derived from the Greek *horman,* meaning "to stimulate" or "to excite." Hormones stimulate growth and many kinds of reactions, such as changes in activity levels and moods. Because hormones affect behavior and emotional reactions, psychologists who study the biology of behavior are also interested in the endocrine system.

Like neurotransmitters, hormones have specific receptor sites. Although the various hormones circulate throughout the body, they act only on hormone receptors in certain places. Hormones are produced by several different glands. These glands include the pituitary gland, the thyroid gland, the adrenal glands, and the testes and the ovaries. (See Figure 3.7 on page 68.)

The Pituitary Gland

The pituitary gland lies just below the hypothalamus. It is about the size of a pea, but it is so important that it has been referred to as the "master gland." The pituitary gland, which is stimulated by the hypothalamus, is responsible for the secretion of many different hormones that affect various aspects of behavior.

Growth hormone, for example, regulates the growth of muscles, bones, and glands. Children whose growth patterns seem abnormally slow often catch up to others the same age when doctors give them growth hormone.

Some hormones affect females in relation to pregnancy and mothering. Prolactin stimulates production of milk in nursing women. Oxytocin is responsible for stimulating labor in pregnant women. Sometimes when a pregnant woman is overdue, an obstetrician may induce labor by injecting the woman with oxytocin.

The Endocrine System

Pituitary gland

Thyroid gland

Adrenal glands

Ovaries (female)

Testes (male)

FIGURE 3.7 *The glands of the endocrine system secrete hormones that stimulate various body functions.* **Why do you think psychologists are interested in the endocrine system?**

Oxytocin and prolactin have been shown in some lower mammals to be connected to maternal behaviors such as caring for young (Insel, T. R., 2000). The role of these hormones, if any, in human maternal behaviors remains unclear, however.

The Thyroid Gland

The thyroid gland produces thyroxin. Thyroxin affects the body's metabolism—its rate of converting food to energy. The production of too little thyroxin can lead to a condition called hypothyroidism. People with hypothyroidism often are overweight. For children, too little thyroxin can cause a condition called cretinism, which is characterized by stunted growth and mental retardation.

People who produce too much thyroxin may develop hyperthyroidism. Hyperthyroidism is characterized by excitability, inability to sleep, and weight loss.

The Adrenal Glands

The adrenal glands are located above the kidneys. The Latin prefix *ad-* means "toward" or "at," and *renal* derives from the Latin *renes,* meaning "kidneys."

The outer layer, or cortex, of the adrenal glands secretes cortical steroids. Cortical steroids increase resistance to stress and promote muscle development. They also cause the liver to release stored sugar, making energy available for emergencies.

The adrenal glands also produce adrenaline and noradrenaline. When a person faces a stressful situation, the sympathetic nervous system causes the adrenal glands to release a mixture of adrenaline and noradrenaline. These hormones help arouse the body, enabling the person to cope with the stressful situation. When Todd stepped on Marc's toe, for example, Marc's adrenal glands produced the adrenaline-noradrenaline mixture to help Marc deal with the situation.

Adrenaline also plays a role in the emotions people experience. It can intensify emotions such as fear and anxiety. Another function of noradrenaline is to raise blood pressure. In the nervous system, it also acts as a neurotransmitter.

The Testes and the Ovaries

Other glands are the testes (in males) and the ovaries (in females). These glands produce the hormones testosterone, estrogen, and progesterone.

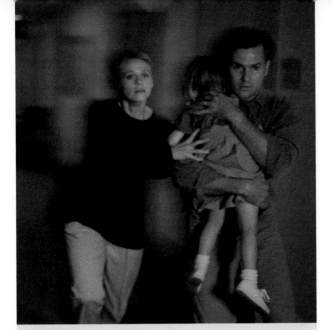

Adrenaline and noradrenaline help people deal with emergencies, such as when parents must rush a child to the hospital.

Testosterone   Testosterone is a male sex hormone, although females have small amounts of this hormone as well. Testosterone is produced by the testes in males. Small amounts of it are also secreted by the ovaries in females. Testosterone plays an important role in development.

In the prenatal period, testosterone influences development of the sex organs. About eight weeks after fertilization, if testosterone is secreted, it stimulates development of male sex organs. If testosterone is not secreted, female sex organs develop.

In adolescence, testosterone aids the growth of muscle and bone as well as the development of primary and secondary sex characteristics. Primary sex characteristics are directly involved in reproduction. Secondary sex characteristics, such as beard growth, distinguish males and females but are not directly involved in reproduction.

Testosterone is a kind of steroid. A small number of athletes use steroids to enhance their athletic ability. Steroids affect muscle mass, heighten resistance to stress, and increase the body's energy supply. Steroids also stimulate the sex drive and raise self-esteem. Because our society is highly competitive, some people are tempted to use steroids, but their use has serious medical and ethical implications. Links have been reported between steroid use and sleep disturbances, liver damage, heart disease, and other medical problems. Ethically, most people believe that the use of steroids is unnatural and unfair to athletes who do not use them.

Estrogen and Progesterone   Estrogen and progesterone are female sex hormones, although low levels are found in males. The ovaries in females produce estrogen and progesterone. Estrogen is also produced in smaller amounts by the testes in males.

Estrogen fosters the development of primary and secondary sex characteristics, such as breast enlargement. Progesterone has multiple functions. It stimulates growth of the female reproductive organs and helps prepare the body for pregnancy. Together, estrogen and progesterone regulate the menstrual cycle and vary greatly during that cycle. Changes in levels of estrogen have been linked to premenstrual syndrome (PMS) in some women. PMS is a collection of symptoms (such as irritability, depression, and fatigue) that some women experience before menstruating.

Estrogen has psychological effects as well as biological effects. Higher levels of estrogen seem to be connected with optimal cognitive functioning and feelings of well-being among women (Ross et al., 2000; Yaffe et al., 2000). Women are also more interested in sexual activity when estrogen levels are high—particularly during ovulation, when they are fertile.

SECTION 3 REVIEW

go.hrw.com   **Homework Practice Online**
Keyword: SY7 HP3

1. Explain the effects of the endocrine system on development.
2. **Critical Thinking**   *Analyzing Information* How does the endocrine system affect behavior?

S E C T I O N **4**

Heredity: Our Genetic Background

Heredity is the transmission of characteristics from parents to offspring. Psychologists are interested in studying heredity, along with the brain and hormones, as a means of understanding why people behave as they do. Heredity plays a key role in the development of traits both in people and in animals. The traits we inherit help shape our behavior.

Heredity is vital in the transmission of physical traits such as height, hair texture, and eye color. Heredity is also related, to some extent, to some psychological traits (Bouchard & Loehlin, 2001;

DNA: The Genetic Code

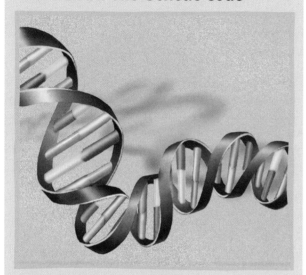

FIGURE 3.8 *The threadlike molecules of DNA that make up chromosomes contain the codes for the development of particular traits.*

Knafo et al., 2005). Researchers have found that some psychological traits such as shyness, leadership ability, aggressiveness, and even an interest in arts and crafts are influenced by heredity. It is important, though, to keep in mind that the environment also plays a role in shaping these traits. Heredity has been shown to be one factor involved in many psychological disorders, including anxiety and depression, schizophrenia, bipolar disorder, and alcoholism (Gregory, 2004; Plomin & McGuffin, 2003; Sansone & Levitt, 2005). (See Chapter 18.)

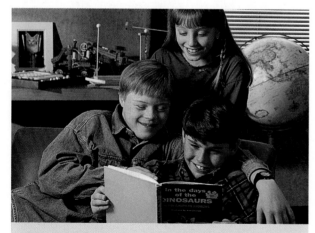

Despite their disability, children with Down syndrome enjoy many of the same activities that other children do.

Genes and Chromosomes

Genes are the basic building blocks of heredity. Traits are determined by pairs of genes, with one gene in each pair inherited from each parent. Some traits, such as blood type, are controlled by a single pair of genes. Complex psychological traits, such as intelligence, involve combinations of genes, as well as environmental factors.

Genes are found in threadlike structures called **chromosomes**, which are composed of deoxyribonucleic acid (DNA). DNA takes the form of a double helix. (See Figure 3.8.) Most normal human cells contain 46 chromosomes that are organized into 23 pairs. In each of the 23 pairs, one chromosome comes from the father and the other chromosome comes from the mother. Each chromosome contains instructions for the development of particular traits in the individual.

Researchers have learned that 22 of the 23 pairs of chromosomes are similar in males and females. The 23rd pair, the sex chromosomes, determines whether we are female or male. In males, the 23rd pair consists of an X chromosome (so called because of its X shape) and a Y chromosome (because of its Y shape). Females have two X chromosomes, so they always pass an X chromosome on to their offspring. The chromosome that comes from the father, therefore, determines the sex of the offspring. If the father contributes an X chromosome, then the offspring is female. If the father contributes a Y chromosome, then the offspring is male.

TRUTH OR fiction
■ REVISITED ■
It is true that the father's genetic contribution—not the mother's—determines the sex of the offspring. The mother always contributes an X chromosome. Thus, it is the X or the Y chromosome from the father that determines the sex of the child.

When a child is born without 46 chromosomes in each cell, physical and behavioral disorders may result. One of the most common disabilities of this type occurs when there is an extra, or third, chromosome on the 21st pair. When this happens, a baby will be born with Down syndrome. People with Down syndrome usually have some level of mental retardation and may have heart and respiratory problems.

The Nature-Nurture Debate

Throughout history, philosophers and scientists have debated the role of biology in determining who we are, as people. This discussion is often called the "nature-nurture debate." *Nature* refers to what people inherit—the biological groundwork that prepares a person to develop in certain ways. *Nurture* refers to environmental factors—what a person is exposed to in life. Nurture includes a variety of factors such as family, education, culture, living conditions, everyday individual experiences, and other factors that make up people's environment.

People who support the "nature" side of the debate argue that people's traits and personality are primarily determined by their biological makeup. The argument is that our inherited characteristics determine the kind of people we are. Supporters of the "nurture" side, argue that the environment we live in and our everyday experiences—not our biological inheritance—determine how we behave and think.

Both of these views are extreme. Today most psychologists agree that the influences of both nature and nurture determine our psychological traits. Biology influences us to act in certain ways, but our environment—along with personal factors such as values and decision making—can modify these plans. It is the interaction of heredity and environment that determines who we are. A person who has the genetic potential to write a brilliant novel will never write that novel if he or she is never taught to read or write. An athlete who has the genetic potential to win a gold medal in figure skating will never win the medal if he or she has never been to a skating rink (or a solidly frozen pond).

Although most psychologists agree that genes and the environment interact, the extent of the role that heredity plays is still a controversial topic. Some psychologists believe that many of our traits, including intelligence, are determined largely by genetics. Others have criticized this view and are concerned about its implications. The heredity view can be interpreted to suggest that we cannot control our destiny because it is determined by our biology. Taken to the extreme, the heredity view might suggest, for example, that we should not try to change something about ourselves with which we are not satisfied. However, most psychologists are careful to note that heredity is not destiny. They emphasize that the environment does play a role in determining how a person develops.

Kinship Studies

The most common way to sort out the roles that heredity and environment play in determining a trait is to do kinship studies. Kinship refers to the degree to which people are related, based on the genes they have in common. Identical twins share 100 percent of their genes. A parent and his or her child share 50 percent of their genes, as do full brothers and sisters, on average. Aunts and uncles related by blood share an average of 25 percent of their genes with nieces and nephews, and first cousins share an average of 12.5 percent.

Psychologists use this information to determine how much a trait is influenced by genetics and how much by environment. They study certain traits or behavioral patterns in individuals and then compare them to those of relatives. If genes are involved in a certain trait, then people who are more closely related, and who share more genes, should be more likely to exhibit the same trait than people who have less overlap in genes or who are not related. Two common types of kinship studies are twin studies and adoptee studies.

Identical twins share the same genetic makeup.

Twin Studies   The study of identical and fraternal twins is a useful way to learn about the relative influences of nature and nurture. Because identical twins share the same genetic makeup, differences between identical twins must be the result of the environment. For example, if one of the identical twins loves jazz, but the other twin prefers rock, that difference must be due to the twins' different experiences in the environment—not their heredity.

In contrast, fraternal twins, like other brothers and sisters, share an average of 50 percent of their genes. Thus, differences between fraternal twins might stem from heredity or the environment. The premise behind twin studies is that if identical twins are more similar on a certain trait than are fraternal twins, then that trait is influenced by genetics.

Researchers have found that identical twins resemble one another more strongly than fraternal twins in certain traits, including shyness and activity levels, irritability, sociability, even happiness (McCourt et al., 1999; McCrae & Costa, 2000; Lykken & Tellegen, 1996). Thus, these traits appear to be influenced by heredity.

Identical twins are also more likely than fraternal twins to share psychological disorders such as autism, substance dependence, and schizophrenia (DiLalla & Carey, 1996). In one study on autism, a disorder characterized by limited social and communication abilities, both twins were likely to be autistic in 96 percent of the identical twin pairs. In contrast, both twins were likely to be autistic in only 24 percent of the fraternal twin pairs (Ritvo et al., 1985). This evidence strongly suggests a role for heredity in autism.

Adoptee Studies   One problem with twin studies is that identical twins tend to be treated similarly and are exposed to similar environments (Coon et al., 1990; Segal, 1993). Because they share the same environment as well as the same heredity, it is sometimes difficult to determine whether their similarities are due to nature or nurture.

One way to try to eliminate the effects of common backgrounds is to study children who have been adopted. Children who have been separated from their parents at an early age and then raised elsewhere provide special opportunities for sorting out the effects of nature and nurture. Psychologists look for the relative similarities between children and their adoptive and biological families. If the children act more like their biological families—with whom they share genes—than their adoptive families—with whom they share the environment—then their behavior may be largely influenced by heredity.

Twins Reared Apart   One of the most useful types of kinship studies examines twins who have been reared apart. Twins reared apart are less likely than twins reared together to share common experiences. Thus, similarities are probably due to genetic factors. In a major study that began in 1979, Thomas Bouchard and his colleagues (1990) examined twins who were reared apart. They found that many psychological and personality traits—including intelligence, traditionalism (following rules), risk avoidance, aggression, and leadership—are influenced by heredity.

Twins reared apart even share many of the same mannerisms, such as how they sit or stand. In one study, one pair of twins each wore seven rings, two bracelets on one wrist, and a bracelet and watch on the other wrist (Holden, 1980). Most researchers, however, acknowledge that the environment also has an important effect on the development of traits and mannerisms.

SECTION 4 REVIEW

Homework Practice Online

Keyword: SY7 HP3

1. Define *gene* and *chromosome*.

2. Describe two methods used to study the role of heredity in determining traits.

3. **Critical Thinking**   *Finding the Main Idea* Why are psychologists interested in heredity?

PSYCHOLOGY

DOES HEREDITY DETERMINE OUR PERSONALITIES?

In 1979 Thomas Bouchard and several colleagues began conducting the Minnesota Study of Twins Reared Apart (Bouchard et al., 1990). The purpose of the study was to discover the extent to which heredity and environment were each involved in determining various psychological and personality traits. More than 100 pairs of identical and fraternal twins who were separated in infancy and reared apart participated in the study. The researchers examined similarities and differences in numerous traits such as intelligence, leadership abilities, and reaction to stress. They also studied social attitudes such as religious beliefs and the tendency to follow tradition.

In the report, Bouchard emphasized the importance of studying twins reared apart:

Monozygotic [identical] and dizygotic [fraternal] twins who were separated early in life and reared apart are a fascinating experiment of nature. They also provide the simplest and most powerful method for disentangling the influence of environmental and genetic factors on human characteristics.

Bouchard and his colleagues drew several conclusions from their research:

The study of these reared-apart twins led to two general and seemingly remarkable conclusions concerning the sources of the psychological differences—behavioral variation— between people: (i) genetic factors exert a pronounced and pervasive influence on behavioral variability, and (ii) the effect of being reared in the same home is negligible for many psychological traits. . . . For almost every behavioral trait so far investigated, from reaction time to religiosity, an important fraction of the variation among people turns out to be associated with genetic variation.

In other words, the results of the study suggested that heredity plays a greater role than environment in determining personality traits and behavior. Bouchard and his colleagues also noted, however, that the strong influence of heredity on psychological traits does not necessarily mean that environmental factors in general—and parenting in particular—play no role whatsoever. Commenting on the role parents play in determining personality traits in their children, the researchers stated:

Psychologists have been surprised by the evidence that being reared by the same parents in the same physical environment does not, on average, make siblings more alike as adults than they would have been if reared separately in adoptive homes. It is obvious that parents can produce shared effects if they grossly deprive or mistreat all their children. It seems reasonable that charismatic, dedicated parents, determined to make all their children share certain personal qualities, interests, or values, may sometimes succeed. Our findings, and those of others, do not imply that parenting is without lasting effects. The remarkable similarity in [identical twins reared apart] in social attitudes (for example, traditionalism and religiosity) does not show that parents cannot influence those traits, but simply that this does not tend to happen in most families.

The study, which lasted more than a decade, indicated that identical twins reared apart are as similar as identical twins reared together, and that identical twins are more similar than fraternal twins. Based on these results, Bouchard and many other psychologists believe that personality, intelligence, and social attitudes are largely determined by heredity, rather than environment.

Think About It

Drawing Inferences and Conclusions One of the findings of the Bouchard study was that children raised in the same family do not necessarily have similar social attitudes or personalities. Why might differences occur?

Writing a Summary

Using standard grammar, spelling, sentence structure, and punctuation, summarize the information in this chapter. Consider:
- the anatomy and functions of given brain areas and the nervous system
- the effects of the endocrine system on development and behavior, and the role of chromosomes and genes in heredity

Identifying People and Ideas

Identify the following terms or people and use them in appropriate sentences.

1. central nervous system
2. neurons
3. myelin
4. synapse
5. autonomic nervous system
6. reticular activating system
7. endocrine system
8. heredity
9. genes
10. chromosomes

Understanding Main Ideas

SECTION 1 (pp. 54–59)
1. Why is the nervous system referred to as a communication system?
2. Give an example of spinal reflex, and explain how the nervous system functions in this reflexive action.

SECTION 2 (pp. 59–67)
3. Which brain structures might be called "little brain" and "big brain"? Why? Besides their size, how are these structures different?
4. List the four lobes of the cerebral cortex and one function of each.

SECTION 3 (pp. 67–69)
5. How are the nervous system and the endocrine system related?

SECTION 4 (pp. 69–72)
6. What is meant by the "nature-nurture debate"?

Thinking Critically

1. **Analyzing Information** Messages travel in only one direction from neuron to neuron. What happens if the message-sending process is disrupted?
2. **Contrasting** How do the functions of the sympathetic and parasympathetic systems differ?
3. **Making Generalizations and Predictions** Imagine that you have to give an oral report in class. Describe how you might feel and act before and after the report. How does your knowledge of the nervous system help you understand your reactions?
4. **Identifying a Point of View** Why do you think some observers think it would be dangerous to adhere to an extreme heredity view of psychological traits?
5. **Drawing Inferences and Conclusions** Which type of kinship study probably yields the most reliable results? Why? What might be some drawbacks of this type of study?

Writing About Psychology

1. **Analyzing Information** Write a two-page paper describing the localized functions of the major brain areas.
2. **Summarizing** The role of parenting is an important issue for those who support the nurture side of the nature-nurture debate. Locate books or journals in the library that deal with parenting. Prepare a one-page summary of the arguments of each side of this debate. Use the graphic organizer below to help you write your summary.

Nature	Nurture

Interpreting Graphs

Study the bar graph below. Then use the information in the graph to help you answer the questions that follow.

Emotional Responses of Fraternal and Identical Twins Raised Apart After Meeting

Source: Segal, *Entwined Lives*, 1999

1. Which of the following statements can be concluded from the information on the chart?

   a. Identical twins feel a greater sense of bonding than do fraternal twins.

   b. There are no differences between identical and fraternal twins.

   c. Twins feel closer than siblings who are not twins.

   d. Identical twins have a less strong sense of bonding than do fraternal twins.

2. What additional information would make this chart more useful?

Analyzing Primary Sources

Read the following Aesop's fable, which raises an important issue in the study of psychology. Then answer the questions that follow.

"The gods were once disputing whether it was possible for a living being to change its nature. Jupiter said "yes," but Venus said "no." So to try the question, Jupiter turned a cat into a maiden and gave her to a young man for a wife. The wedding was duly performed and the young couple sat down to the wedding feast. "See," said Jupiter to Venus, "how becomingly she behaves. Who could tell that yesterday she was but a cat? Surely her nature is changed.

"Wait a minute," replied Venus, and let loose a mouse in the room. No sooner did the bride see this than she jumped up from her seat and tried to pounce upon the mouse. "Ah, you see," said Venus, "nature will out."

3. Which of the following statements best describes the meaning of the fable?

   a. Heredity plays a more important role than environment in determining personality traits.

   b. Environment plays a more important role than heredity in determining personality traits.

   c. Heredity and environment are of equal importance in determining personality traits.

   d. Heredity plays no role in shaping personality traits.

4. In the fable, what method of observation do Jupiter and Venus use to resolve the nature-nurture debate?

PSYCHOLOGY PROJECTS

Cooperative Learning

Reading About Psychology With two or three of your classmates, look for magazine and newspaper articles that deal with biology and behavior. For example, you might find an article describing research that indicates schizophrenia is caused by a chemical imbalance in a person's body, or you might see an article describing a surgical procedure that relieves the tremors of Parkinson's disease. Present a summary of the article to the class. Then place the article in a class file on biology and behavior.

☑ internet connect

Internet Activity: go.hrw.com
KEYWORD: SY7 CH3

Choose a topic on biology and behavior to:
- create a symbol reflecting the functions of the parts of the brain.
- make a chart of the human endocrine system.
- write a report on the influence that heredity and environment have on psychological traits.

Chapter 4

SENSATION AND PERCEPTION

Read to Discover

1 In what way do sensation and perception contribute to an understanding of our environment?

2 How does the eye enable vision?

3 How does the ear perceive sound?

4 What are the chemical, skin, and body senses?

5 What are the laws of sensory perception?

A DAY IN THE LIFE

Linda and Marc were on their first date. They were getting settled in their seats at the movie theater. The movie was about to start, and voices buzzed all around them. Still, Marc did not really hear any of them. He was paying attention to what Linda was saying, and it seemed as if no one else was there at all. The other moviegoers were just gray, colorless shapes in the dim light. Marc hardly even noticed that the popcorn was a little too salty and that the gummy spot under his feet made the soles of his shoes stick to the floor. Instead, he was thinking about how much he liked the smell of Linda's perfume and the touch of her hand, although even these sensations faded into the recesses of Marc's mind as he listened to her speak.

Suddenly a darkened shape said, "Excuse me," and squeezed in front of them to find a seat. A moment later, Marc's toe throbbed with pain, and for the second time in less than a week, Todd was saying, "Oh gee, I'm sorry!" Once again, Todd had accidentally stepped on Marc's foot.

Although Marc was annoyed, he grunted, "It's okay. It's dark in here. I guess you couldn't see." Yet that did not really help his toe, which was still throbbing. However, when Linda asked, "Are you all right, Marc?" her concerned voice practically made the pain in his toe disappear. All of a sudden, he was almost glad the whole accident had happened.

• • •

Like Marc in the movie theater, we all experience the world with our senses. A common belief is that people have five senses: vision, hearing, smell, taste, and touch. But you will learn that people actually have more than five senses. Touch, for example, includes several skin senses—pressure, warmth, cold, and pain. Still other senses tell us the position our body is in without our having to look.

Once we take in information through our senses, we do something with that information to interpret it. What we do depends on many factors—the circumstances, our mood, even our cultural background. Marc, for example, tuned out the background noise in the theater because the only thing he was interested in hearing was Linda's voice. Then, when Todd stepped on his toe, he was both surprised and annoyed. These intense feelings heightened his perception of pain. But just a few seconds later, Linda's concern seemed to drive away the pain.

Psychologists call these two different processes sensation (the feeling) and perception (the interpretation of the feeling). As you read this chapter, you will learn more about these two concepts.

Key Terms

- sensation
- perception
- absolute threshold
- difference threshold
- signal-detection theory
- sensory adaptation
- pupil
- lens
- retina
- photoreceptors
- blind spot
- visual acuity
- complementary
- afterimage
- cochlea
- auditory nerve
- conductive deafness
- sensorineural deafness
- olfactory nerve
- gate theory
- vestibular sense
- kinesthesis
- closure
- proximity
- similarity
- continuity
- common fate
- stroboscopic motion
- monocular cues
- binocular cues
- retinal disparity

HOLT

Psychology Video Program

Watch the video to learn about methods of helping the blind to see.

SECTION 1

Sensation and Perception: The Basics

A DAY IN THE LIFE

When Todd stepped on Marc's toe, the sensation of pain was registered by sensory neurons in Marc's skin. **Sensation** is the stimulation of sensory receptors and the transmission of sensory information to the central nervous system (the spinal cord and brain). Sensory receptors are located in sensory organs such as the eyes and ears and elsewhere in the body. The stimulation of the senses is automatic. It results from sources of energy like light and sound or from the presence of chemicals, as in smell and taste.

Marc perceived the pain in his brain. **Perception** is the psychological process through which we interpret sensory stimulation. Imagine that you are standing at one end zone of a football field while a play is going on. Some of the players are close and rushing toward you; other players are at the other end of the field. Those players who are far away look very small compared to those players who are barreling down on you. Still, you know that the quarterback, who has just thrown a pass from the other end of the field, is not actually tiny. How do you know? The answer is that you know through experience. Perception reflects learning, expectations, and attitudes.

Stimulation of the senses and the ways in which people interpret that stimulation are affected by several concepts. These concepts include absolute threshold, difference threshold, signal-detection theory, and sensory adaptation.

Absolute Threshold

Have you ever had your hearing tested? If so, try to remember the experience. There you were, sitting in a booth or quiet room with earphones on your head. At first, you heard nothing, and perhaps you began to wonder what was going on. Then suddenly, a beep. You had just discovered your absolute threshold for hearing that kind of sound. **Absolute threshold** is the weakest amount of a stimulus that can be sensed. Even before you heard that first beep, the person testing you was trying different beeps, but you simply could not hear them. The first one you heard was the weakest one you were capable of hearing.

Did you know that dogs can hear certain whistles that people cannot? This is because a dog's absolute threshold for certain sounds is different from that of a human being.

Absolute thresholds for humans have been determined for the senses of vision, hearing, smell, taste, and touch. (See Figure 4.1.) However, the absolute threshold for a particular stimulus can differ from person to person. Some people are more sensitive to certain sensory stimuli than others are. These differences stem from psychological and biological factors.

If absolute thresholds differed much from what they are, we might sense the world very differently. For example, if our ears were more sensitive, we might hear collisions among molecules of air. If our sense of smell was as sensitive as a dog's, we might be able to track down someone just by sniffing a piece of his or her clothing.

Difference Threshold

For us to function well in the world, we need absolute thresholds low enough to see, hear, smell, taste, and feel what is going on around us—but not so low that our senses are overloaded with information we cannot use. We also need to be able to detect small differences between stimuli—what makes one stimulus different from another stimulus. The minimum amount of difference that can be detected between two stimuli is known as the **difference threshold**.

Absolute Thresholds for Humans

SENSE	STIMULUS	RECEPTORS	THRESHOLD
Vision	Electromagnetic energy	Rods and cones in the retina	A candle flame viewed from a distance of about 30 miles on a dark night
Hearing	Sound waves	Hair cells of the inner ear	The ticking of a watch from about 20 feet away in a quiet room
Smell	Chemical substances in the air	Receptor cells in the nose	About one drop of perfume diffused throughout a small house
Taste	Chemical substances in saliva	Taste buds on the tongue	About 1 teaspoon of sugar dissolved in 2 gallons of water
Touch	Pressure on the skin	Nerve endings in the skin	The wing of a fly falling on a cheek from a distance of about 0.4 inch

FIGURE 4.1 *This table shows humans' absolute thresholds for various stimuli and five senses.*

Source: Adapted from "Contemporary Psychophysics," by E. Galanter, 1962, in R. Brown et al. (Eds.), *New Directions in Psychology,* New York: Holt, Rinehart and Winston.

For example, imagine that someone shows you two dark blue paint chips. You may think they are the same color, even if they are slightly different. But now imagine that one of the paint chips is removed and replaced with another chip that is just a bit lighter or darker. Do the two paint chips still seem the same color? No. The smallest amount of difference you can see in order to distinguish between the two shades of blue is your difference threshold. Just as with absolute threshold, people's individual difference thresholds vary slightly.

Signal-Detection Theory

As you might imagine, it is easier to hear a friend talking in a quiet room than in a room where other people are laughing loudly. And when your nose is stuffy from a cold, your dinner may seem to have little flavor. In the first case, the setting has made a difference in your sensation and perception. In the second case, your physical condition has made the difference. **Signal-detection theory** is a method of distinguishing sensory stimuli that takes into account not only their strengths but also such elements as the setting, your physical state, your mood, and your attitudes.

Signal-detection theory also considers psychological factors such as motivations, expectations, and learning. For example, even if the place where you are now reading is buzzing with distracting signals such as a breeze against your face, the shadow of passing clouds, or the voices of passersby, you will be able to ignore those influences as long as you are motivated to keep reading. Similarly, people who smell perfumes for a living have learned through years of experience how to detect subtle differences others would not be able to smell.

We focus on whatever we consider important. Marc's toe hurt a great deal when Todd stepped on it, but when Linda asked him if he was in pain, her voice was all that interested him. As another example, suppose that you attend a recital at school. A student you do not know plays the piano. Your mind may wander as you listen. But do you think the student's parents let their minds wander? You can be pretty sure that they do not—the performance is much more important to them than it is to other members of the audience.

The Electromagnetic Spectrum

Wavelength in nanometers*

500   600   700

Cosmic rays ◀ Ultraviolet   **Visible spectrum**   Infrared ▶ Radio waves

White light (source of light)

Visible light

Prism

*1 nanometer = 1 billionth of a meter

FIGURE 4.2 *The electromagnetic spectrum is made up of light that is visible to humans and light that is not* *visible to humans. The light that is not visible includes infrared and ultraviolet light.*

Sensory Adaptation

A DAY IN THE LIFE

When Marc and Linda first walked into the darkened movie theater, they could see little except the colorless shapes of the other moviegoers. As time passed, they became able to see the faces of people around them and the features of the theater. And if Todd had waited a few minutes before trying to find a seat, his eyes would have adapted to the darkness and he might not have stepped on Marc's toe.

Our sensory systems adapt to a changing environment. **Sensory adaptation** is the process by which we become more sensitive to weak stimuli and less sensitive to unchanging stimuli. As time went on, Marc, Linda, and Todd could see the people around them better—the people were weak stimuli. On the other hand, as we adapt to lying on the beach, we become less aware of the unchanging stimulus of the lapping of the waves. Similarly, city dwellers adapt to the sounds of traffic (unchanging stimuli) except for the occasional car backfire or fire engine siren.

SECTION 1 REVIEW

go.hrw.com
Homework Practice Online
Keyword: SY7 HP4

1. Define *absolute threshold.*

2. Give two examples of sensory adaptation.

3. **Critical Thinking** *Drawing Inferences and Conclusions* How do sensation and perception affect people's understanding of their environment?

Vision

Those of us fortunate enough to have good vision usually consider information from vision to be more essential than that from our other senses. No other sense allows us to gather so much information from nearby and distant sources. To understand vision, it is important to know how light works and how our eyes function.

Light

Light is electromagnetic energy. It is described in wavelengths. Not all light is visible to humans. In fact, the light that humans can see makes up only a small part of the spectrum of electromagnetic energy. The wavelengths of cosmic rays are only a fraction of an inch long. The wavelengths of some radio waves extend for miles. The wavelengths of visible light are in between. (See Figure 4.2.)

You have probably seen sunlight broken down into colors as it filters through water vapor—this is what makes a rainbow. Sunlight can also be broken down into colors by means of a glass structure called a prism. The main colors of the spectrum, from longest to shortest wavelengths, are red, orange, yellow, green, blue, indigo, and violet. For generations, people have remembered the order by using the made-up name *Roy G. Biv,* which comes from using the first letter of each of the colors.

It is true that when you look at a rainbow, the wavelength of light determines the colors you see. The wavelength for red is longer than that for orange, and so on through the spectrum of visible light to violet, which has the shortest wavelength.

The Eye

When you take a picture with a camera, light enters through an opening and is focused onto a sensitive surface—the film. Chemicals on the film are changed by the light and create a lasting impression of the image that entered the camera.

Your eye is very similar. (See Figure 4.3.) As in a camera, light enters the eye and then is projected onto a surface. The amount of light that enters is determined by the size of the opening in the colored part of the eye. This opening is called the **pupil**. When you look into someone's eyes, the black circles you see in the middle are the pupils. They may look solid to you, but actually they are openings.

The size of the pupil adjusts automatically to the amount of light entering the eye. Try the following experiment. With a friend, go into bright light, stay there for a few minutes, then go into a much darker area. Notice how the size of your friend's pupils changes. In the bright light, the pupils become very small. This is because the light is bright enough that the eyes need only a bit of it. In the dark, however, the pupils become very large because they need to let in as much light as possible. Pupil size is also sensitive to our emotions. We can be literally

The Human Eye

FIGURE 4.3 *In the human eye, light travels through the pupil to the lens and is then reflected onto the retina. The optic nerve sends the visual information to the brain.*

"wide-eyed with fear," meaning that the pupils open widely when we are afraid.

Once light has entered the eye, it encounters the lens. The **lens** adjusts to the distance of objects by changing its thickness. Hold a finger at arm's length and then bring it slowly toward your nose. You will feel tension in the eye as the thickness of the lens adjusts to keep the finger in focus. When people squint to look at something, they are adjusting the thickness of the lenses in their eyes.

These changes project a clear image of the object onto the retina. The **retina** is the sensitive surface in the eye that acts like the film in a camera. However, the retina consists of neurons—not film. Neurons

IN THE WORLD TODAY

How Did Animals Know a Tsunami Was Coming?

In December 2004, a tsunami from a massive earthquake in the Indian Ocean struck dozens of Asian and African countries. By the year's end, the death toll was estimated at more than 150,000. The devastating tsunami caught the people off guard—but not the animals.

Along the western coast of Thailand, elephants giving rides to tourists began to trumpet agitatedly hours before the tsunami hit. About that time the massive earthquake that would send the big waves rushing toward shore was fracturing the ocean floor. An hour before the waves slammed into the area, the elephants began wailing. Just before the waves struck, the elephants trooped off to higher ground.

Other reports stated that dogs refused to go outside. In one Sri Lankan town, a man said his dogs, who usually enjoyed a run on the beach, probably saved his life. "They are usually excited to go on this outing," the man said (Mott, 2005). But on the day of the tsunami, the dogs refused to go out. A survivor in Thailand said, "Dogs are smarter than all of us . . . [They] started running away up to the hilltops long before we even realized what was coming" (Oldenburg, 2005).

Flamingos usually breed in low-lying areas during December. On the day of the tsunami, however, flamingos on the coast of India abandoned their sanctuary and headed into safer forests before the waves hit shore (Oldenburg, 2005).

In Sri Lanka, a large wave smashed into the Yala National Park. Yet, wildlife officials were surprised to find that hundreds of elephants, tigers, leopards, deer, and other animals had escaped unharmed.

People have reported over the centuries that animals appear to have a sixth sense for detecting earthquakes, hurricanes, volcanic eruptions, and tsunamis before Earth starts shaking. Rats, for example, evacuate buildings. Flocks of sparrows take flight. Dogs howl. Some animals are apparently supersensitive to sound; others to temperature, touch, or vibration. This sensitivity gives them advance warning of natural disasters.

Alan Rabinowitz of the Wildlife Conservation Society in New York says that many animals can detect subtle or abrupt changes in the environment. "Some animals have acute sense of hearing and smell that allow them to determine something coming towards them long before humans," Rabinowitz says (Mott, 2005).

Research shows that elephants are particularly sensitive to ground vibrations. Some birds, dogs, tigers, and elephants can detect sound waves whose frequencies are too low for humans to hear, known as infrasound. Dogs' sense of smell is so superior to humans' that they can sometimes detect subtle chemical changes in the air that warn them of disaster.

Michelle Heupel of the Mote Marine Laboratory in Florida concludes, "I think these animals are more attuned to their environment than we give them credit for. When things change, they may not understand why it's happening, but the change itself may trigger some instinct to move to an area that is safer" (Oldenburg, 2005).

An elephant helps with the cleanup in Indonesia after the 2004 tsunami.

THINK ABOUT IT

Contrasting In what ways do animals' senses differ from those of humans?

that are sensitive to light are called **photoreceptors**. Once the light hits the photoreceptors, a nerve carries the visual input to the brain. In the brain, the information is relayed to the visual area of the occipital lobe. (See Chapter 3.)

The Blind Spot Look again at Figure 4.3 and find the point where the optic nerve leaves the eye. When light hits that point, the eye registers nothing because that area lacks photoreceptors. Thus it is called the **blind spot**. We all have one. If we did not, we would never be able to "see" anything—no visual input would reach the brain through the optic nerve for interpretation.

Rods and Cones Remember how Marc saw only the gray outlines of the other people in the dimly lit movie theater? This was because of the way the photoreceptors in the retina work. There are two kinds of photoreceptors: rods and cones. Rods are sensitive only to the brightness of light. They allow us to see in black and white. Cones provide color vision.

If you are a camera buff, you know that when lighting is low, you get a clearer image with black-and-white film than with color film. In the same way, rods are more sensitive to light than are cones. Therefore, as the lighting grows dim, as in a movie theater when the lights go down, objects lose their color before their outlines fade from view.

Dark and Light Adaptation When you first enter a movie theater, it may be too dark for you to find a seat. As time passes, however, you come to see the seats and the other people more clearly. This adjustment to lower lighting is called dark adaptation. Your ability to see in low light continues to improve for up to 45 minutes.

But what happens when you first move from the dark into the light? Imagine turning on the lamp next to your bed in the middle of the night. At first, you blink, and it almost hurts, but within only a minute or two, you have adapted. Adaptation to bright light happens much more quickly than adaptation to the dark.

Visual Acuity The sharpness of vision is called **visual acuity**. Visual acuity is determined by the ability to see visual details (in normal light). When people have their eyes examined, they have to read the letters on a chart like the one shown above. This is the Snellen Vision Chart. It is used to measure

T E 10
P V L 7
H C O E 5
H P D N L 4
D V H T L U 3
E V O U C T Y 2
P C Y L H N D V 1

If you have ever had your eyes examined, you probably looked at the Snellen Vision Chart, which is used to measure visual acuity.

visual acuity. If you were to stand 20 feet from the Snellen Chart and could only read the T or the E, we would say that your vision is 20/100. This means that what a person with normal vision could see from a distance of 100 feet away, you could see from no more than 20 feet away. In such a case, you would be nearsighted—you would have to be particularly close to an object to make out its details. A person who is farsighted, on the other hand, needs to be farther away from an object than a person with normal vision to see it clearly.

You may have noticed that older people often hold newspapers or books at more of a distance from their eyes than younger people. As people reach middle age, their lenses become relatively brittle. Therefore, it is more difficult for them to focus, especially on nearby objects. As a result, many older people are farsighted.

Color Vision

The world is a place of brilliant colors—the blue of the sky, the reds and yellows of autumn leaves, the vivid greens of spring. The wavelength of light determines the color. People with normal color vision see any color in the spectrum of visible light.

The Color Circle

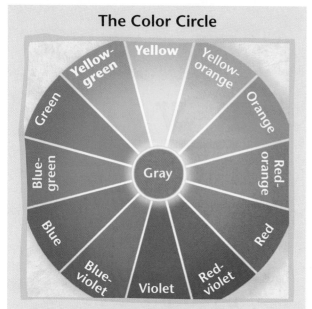

FIGURE 4.4 *The colors across from each other on the color circle are called complementary colors. What is the complement of green?*

enable us to perceive color. Some cones are sensitive to blue, some to green, and some to red. When more than one kind of cone is stimulated at the same time, we perceive other colors of the spectrum, such as yellow and violet.

This is similar to the way color television sets convey colors to the viewer. Although you may not be aware of it, the images you see on a television screen actually consist of thousands of very small dots, called pixels. Each of these dots is either blue, green, or red—the same colors that are perceived by the different types of cones in the eye. There are no yellow, purple, or even black or white dots in the television images. These and other colors are created only through various combinations of blue, green, and red dots.

Afterimages   Look at the strangely colored flag in Figure 4.5 for at least half a minute. Then look at a sheet of white paper. What do you see? If your color vision is working properly and if you looked at the flag long enough, you should see a flag composed of the familiar red, white, and blue. The flag you perceive on the white sheet of paper is an afterimage of the first flag. The **afterimage** of a color is its complementary color. You perceive an afterimage when you have viewed a color for a while and then the color is removed. The same holds true for black and white. Staring at one will create an afterimage of the other.

Color Blindness

If you can see the colors of the visible spectrum, you have normal color vision. People who do not have normal color vision are said to be "color blind."

But what about animals? You may be surprised to find out that dogs and cats see far fewer colors than you do but that insects, birds, fish, and reptiles experience a wide variety of colors.

The Color Circle   Look at Figure 4.4. What you see is called the color circle. It is the colors of the spectrum bent into a circle. The colors across from each other are called **complementary**. For example, red and green are a complementary pair. If we mix complementary colors together, they form gray. You may have learned in art class that mixing blue and yellow creates green, not gray. But this is true only with *pigments,* or substances such as crayons or paints. Here we are talking about *light,* not about pigments.

TRUTH OR fiction
■ R E V I S I T E D ■

It is not true that you get green light by mixing blue light and yellow light. You do get a green pigment when you mix pigments of blue and yellow, but pigments are substances, not light. Mixing blue light and yellow light forms gray.

Cones and Color Vision   Cones, one of the two types of photoreceptors in the retina of the eye,

FIGURE 4.5 *Stare at the center of this flag for 30 seconds, then look at a white piece of paper. You should see a more familiar image—the red, white, and blue American flag. The afterimage of a color is that color's complement.*

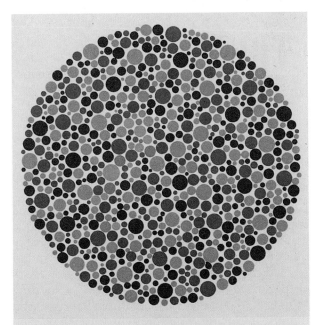

FIGURE 4.6 *This image resembles a test for color blindness. In the actual test, which would be conducted by a trained professional, a person with normal color vision would see an 8, a person with red-green color blindness would see a 3, and a person with total color blindness would see no number.*

These people are partially or totally unable to distinguish color due to an absence of, or malfunction in, the cones. People who are totally color blind are sensitive only to light and dark and see the world as most people do on a black-and-white television set. Total color blindness is rare.

Partial color blindness, on the other hand, is fairly common. People who are partially color blind see some colors but not others. Particularly common is red-green color blindness, in which a person has difficulty seeing shades of red and green. Figure 4.6 shows one of the types of tests that are used to check for color blindness.

SECTION 2 REVIEW

Homework Practice Online
Keyword: SY7 HP4

1. What is visible light?

2. What is the retina, and what is its function?

3. Explain how humans are able to see color.

4. **Critical Thinking** *Making Generalizations and Predictions* Imagine that you became completely color blind. How might your life be different from the way it is now? How would you have to adjust? What occupations or hobbies might become difficult for you?

Hearing

Do you know how you are able to hear your phone ringing? a baby crying? leaves rustling? Sound travels through the air in waves. It is caused by changes in air pressure that result from vibration. Anything that makes a sound—the whisper of your voice, the hum of a tuning fork, the strumming of a guitar—causes vibrations. Each of these vibrations is called a cycle or a sound wave. Every sound has its own pitch and loudness.

Pitch

Sound waves can be very fast, occurring many times per second. The pitch of a sound—how high or low the sound is—depends on its frequency, or the number of cycles per second. The more cycles per second, the higher the pitch of a sound.

Try this experiment. Cut a rubber band into two segments—one long, one short—then stretch each one out and twang it. The shorter one has a higher sound, right? In the same way, women's voices usually have a higher pitch than those of men because women's vocal cords tend to be shorter and therefore vibrate at a greater frequency. Similarly, the strings of a violin are shorter and vibrate at a higher frequency than the strings of a cello. Therefore, the violin's sound is higher in pitch than the sound made by the cello.

The human ear can hear sound waves that vary from 20 to 20,000 cycles per second. Many animals, including dogs and dolphins, hear sounds well beyond 20,000 cycles per second. Although we cannot hear them, the sounds emitted by dolphins help them locate objects. The sound pulses echo back from fish and other objects.

Loudness

What is the softest sound you can hear? What is the loudest? The loudness of a sound is determined by the height, or amplitude, of sound waves. The higher the amplitude of the wave, the louder the sound. The loudness of a sound is measured in decibels, a unit that is abbreviated *dB*. Zero dB is considered the threshold of hearing. Zero dB is about as loud as the ticking of a watch 20 feet away in a very quiet room. (See Figure 4.7 on page 86.)

SENSATION AND PERCEPTION **85**

The Ear

Just as the eye is the human instrument for seeing, the ear is the instrument for sensing all the sounds around us. In fact, the ear is shaped to capture sound waves, to vibrate with them, and to transmit sound to the brain. What we normally think of as the ear is actually the outer ear. We also have a middle ear and an inner ear. (See Figure 4.8.)

The eardrum is the gateway from the outer ear to the middle ear. It is a thin membrane that vibrates when sound waves strike it. As it vibrates, it transmits the sound to three small bones in the middle ear: the hammer, the anvil, and the stirrup. (The stirrup is the smallest bone in the human body.) These bones then also begin to vibrate and transmit sound to the inner ear.

The inner ear consists of the cochlea (KOH-klee-uh). The word *cochlea* comes from the Greek word for "snail." Look at Figure 4.8 again, and you will see why—it is shaped just like the shell of a snail. The **cochlea** is a bony tube that contains fluids as well as neurons that move in response to the vibrations of the fluids. The movement generates neural impulses that are transmitted to the brain via the **auditory nerve**. Within the brain, auditory input is projected onto the hearing areas of the cerebral cortex. (See Chapter 3.)

It is true that the smallest bone in your body is in your ear. It is the stirrup in your middle ear. The stirrup (along with the hammer and the anvil) vibrates and transmits sound to the inner ear.

Locating Sounds

Did you ever sit in front of a stereo, and for some reason, all the sound seemed to come from one side instead of from straight ahead? What you probably did was adjust the balance knob until the sound seemed equally loud in each ear.

Balancing a stereo set is similar to locating sounds. If a sound seems louder from the right, you think it is coming from the right because you are used to a sound from the right side reaching the right ear first.

But what if a sound comes from directly in front of you, from behind, or from above? All such sounds are equally loud and distant from each ear. So what do you do? Simple—you usually turn your head just a little to determine in which ear the sound increases. If you turn to your right and the

Decibel Ratings for Some Familiar Sounds

dB	Sound	Category
150 / 140	Jet engine (close) / Shotgun blast	Severe Pain
120 / 110	Rock concert / Thunder	Pain Threshold
90 / 80	Subway train / Average car	Loud
60 / 40	Conversation at 3 feet / Leaves rustling	Moderate
20 / 0	2 people whispering / Watch ticking	Hearing Threshold

FIGURE 4.7 *Zero dB is the threshold for hearing. Prolonged exposure to sounds greater than 85 dB will cause some hearing loss. Sounds of 130 dB can cause immediate hearing loss.*

The Human Ear

Hammer Anvil Stirrup

Auditory nerve

Cochlea

Ear canal Eardrum

Eustachian tube

FIGURE 4.8 *Sound enters the outer ear and is funneled to the eardrum. Inside the middle ear, the hammer, anvil, and stirrup vibrate, transmitting the sound to the inner ear.*

loudness increases in your left ear, the sound must be in front of you. Of course, you also use information from vision and other cues in locating the source of sounds. If you hear the roar of jet engines, most of the time you can be fairly certain that the airplane is overhead.

Deafness

Not everyone perceives sound. About 2 million Americans are deaf. Deafness may be inherited or caused by disease, injury, or old age.

Conductive Deafness If we see an older person with a hearing aid, we can assume that he or she is probably suffering from conductive deafness. **Conductive deafness** occurs because of damage to the middle ear. Since this part of the ear amplifies sounds, damage to it prevents people from hearing sounds that are not loud enough. Fortunately, people with conductive deafness are often helped by hearing aids. These aids provide the amplification that the middle ear does not.

Sensorineural Deafness Many people do not perceive sounds of certain frequencies. This is a sign of sensorineural deafness. **Sensorineural deafness** is usually caused by damage to the inner ear. Most often, the neurons in the cochlea are destroyed. Sometimes sensorineural deafness is due to damage to the auditory nerve, either through disease or through prolonged exposure to very loud sounds.

Have you ever attended a high-volume rock concert and left with a ringing sensation in your

ears? This may have meant that neurons had been destroyed in your ears. The same thing can happen to workers who operate certain drilling equipment or drive loud vehicles. The next time you are exposed to loud sounds, remember to cover your ears.

Devices called experimental cochlear implants, or "artificial ears," contain microphones that sense sounds and electronic equipment that stimulates the auditory nerve directly. However, if the auditory nerve itself is damaged, a cochlear implant cannot help.

Deafness in the World Today In recent years, people who are deaf have been able to come more into the mainstream of sensory experience as a result of their own efforts, the efforts of others, and new technology. For example, Heather Whitestone, who lost most of her hearing in infancy, became

Heather Whitestone, Miss America of 1995, lost most of her hearing as an infant.

These students at a school for deaf children make the sign for *friends* as part of a school performance. More and more people are becoming familiar with the signs of American Sign Language.

Miss America of 1995. Whitestone is a dancer of classical ballet. She uses the vibrations of the music to dance in rhythm.

Interpreters are often on hand to translate speeches into languages (such as American Sign Language) used by members of the audience who are hearing impaired. More and more schools are offering courses in American Sign Language. Many television shows are now "closed captioned," which means that special decoders make captions of dialogue visible on the screen. And, as you have just read, scientists are always trying to find new ways to counteract damage inside the ear.

SECTION 3 REVIEW

go.hrw.com
Homework Practice Online
Keyword: SY7 HP4

1. What determines the loudness of a sound? How is loudness measured?

2. Define *eardrum* and explain its function.

3. Describe the two kinds of deafness.

4. **Critical Thinking** *Contrasting* How do the causes of conductive and sensorineural deafness differ?

Other Senses

Vision and hearing are just two of many human senses. Others are smell, taste, and the skin and body senses. Smell and taste are called the chemical senses. With vision and hearing, physical energy in the form of light and sound waves stimulates our sensory receptors. With smell and taste, however, we sense molecules of substances. The skin detects touch through pressure, temperature, and pain. Body senses alert us to our posture and movement.

Smell

People do not have as strong a sense of smell as many animals. Dogs use seven times as much of the cerebral cortex for smell as people do. Some dogs are used to sniff out drugs or explosives in suitcases or to track lost children or objects.

But smell is important to people too. Without smell, you would not be able to taste as much as you do. For example, if your sense of smell were not working, an onion and an apple would taste very much alike to you.

Odors of substances are detected by receptor neurons high in each nostril. Receptor neurons react when molecules of the substance in the form of a gas come into contact with them. The receptors send information about the odors to the brain via the **olfactory nerve**.

Our sense of smell adapts quickly. In the movie theater, Marc soon lost awareness of Linda's perfume. We adapt rapidly even to annoying odors. This may be fortunate if we are in a locker room. It may not be fortunate if harmful fumes, such as from cars, are present—we may lose awareness of the smoke or fumes even though danger remains. One odor can also be masked by another, which is how air fresheners work.

Taste

Why would your dog gobble up a piece of a candy bar, but your cat turn up its nose at it? Dogs can taste sweetness, but cats cannot.

Most researchers agree on at least four basic taste qualities—sweet, sour, salty, and bitter. Some argue for a fifth basic taste called umami (ah-MAH-mee). A Japanese word, *umami* means "meaty" or "savory." Other researchers suggest there are even more basic tastes (Schiffman, 2000; Schiffman et al., 2003). Regardless of the number of basic tastes, the flavor of a food is more complex than taste alone. Flavor depends on odor, texture, and temperature as well as taste. For example, apples and onions taste similar, but their flavors differ greatly. If it were not for odor, heated tenderized shoe leather might pass for steak.

TRUTH OR **fiction** ■ REVISITED ■

It is true that raw apples and onions are similar in taste. However, their odors are very different, which gives them different flavors.

Taste is sensed through receptor neurons located on taste buds on the tongue. Some people have low sensitivity for sweetness and may have to use twice as much sugar to sweeten their food as others who are more sensitive to sweetness. People who claim to enjoy very bitter foods may actually be "taste blind" to them. Sensitivities to different tastes can be inherited (Bartoshuk, 2000; Duffy et al., 2004).

By eating hot foods and scraping your tongue, you regularly kill off many taste cells. But you need not be alarmed. Taste cells reproduce rapidly enough to completely renew themselves in a week. The taste system is thus one of the most resilient of all the body's sensory systems. It is very rare for anyone to suffer a complete permanent taste loss.

The Skin Senses

What we normally call touch is better called the skin senses because touch is a combination of pressure, temperature, and pain. Humans have distinct sensory receptors for pressure, temperature, and pain, but some nerve endings may receive more than one type of sensory input. Our skin senses are vitally important to us. Studies have shown that premature infants grow more quickly and stay healthier if they are touched (Field et al., 1986). And older people seem to do better if they have a dog or cat to stroke and cuddle (Pearlman, 1994).

Pressure Your body is covered with hairs, some of them very tiny. Sensory receptors located around the roots of hair cells fire where the skin is touched. Other structures beneath the skin are also sensitive

Raw apples and onions are quite similar in taste. Their odors affect their flavors, however, which are different.

CASE STUDIES
AND OTHER TRUE STORIES

Compensating for Lost Senses: Helen Keller's Story

Most, if not all, of our knowledge of the world comes to us through our senses. What happens, then, if we lose one or more of those senses? Perception may not be lost if other senses can be used to compensate for the missing sense or senses. The life of Helen Keller serves as an excellent example.

Helen Keller was born in Tuscumbia, Alabama, in 1880. She was walking and had just started to learn a few words when suddenly she became very ill. Despite the doctor's prediction that she would die, Keller survived, but she had become both deaf and blind.

It is hard to imagine what it must be like to wake up one day and find nothing but silence and darkness where once you heard sounds and saw objects and people. Not surprisingly, the young Keller became difficult to manage. Fearful, she clung to her mother's apron, and at times she had violent temper tantrums.

When Keller was almost seven, her life changed dramatically. Anne Sullivan arrived in Tuscumbia to teach Keller. Sullivan, who was partially blind herself, had attended the Perkins Institution for the Blind in Boston. Although two operations had restored her eyesight, she understood what it was like to be blind, and she was eager to teach her new pupil.

The situation did not look promising at first. Keller was rude to her new teacher, and she would not sit still to have Sullivan use the manual alphabet. In the manual alphabet, which is still used with people who are deaf and blind, the "speaker" makes the signs right into the hand of the "listener," using the sense of touch to communicate. At first, Sullivan tried the word *doll* when she gave the child a doll as a gift. Keller simply took the present and ran off. Eventually, however, she began to imitate Sullivan. Within days, she signed several words, although she still had some difficulty connecting the words spelled in her hand with the actual objects.

One day, while Sullivan put her pupil's hand under running water, she spelled the word *w-a-t-e-r* into Keller's palm over and over. Suddenly Keller realized that w-a-t-e-r was the "cool something" that was running over her hand, and a breakthrough had occurred. Within one hour, she learned 30 new words.

From that beginning came a long life of both learning and teaching. The easiest words to learn were those that described objects or things Keller could taste or smell. It was harder for the young girl to understand that her feelings—such as anger and love—also had names.

For the first few years, Sullivan was Keller's only teacher. Keller was soon eager to learn more. At the age of 10, Keller decided that she needed to learn to speak. To do so, she took lessons from a teacher of people who were deaf. Eventually, Keller learned to speak by "hearing" the vibrations made when she placed her fingers on Sullivan's larynx. Keller also learned to "listen" to others speak by putting her middle finger on the speaker's nose, her forefinger on the speaker's lips, and her thumb on the speaker's larynx.

Keller wanted to attend Radcliffe College, but to do so she had to complete regular high school. Sullivan accompanied her to class and signed the lectures into Keller's hand. Keller passed her exams and was admitted to Radcliffe. Later, Keller and Sullivan traveled and lectured around the world. They never rested in their efforts to improve the lives of people with deafness and blindness. Most people who are deaf and blind today agree that Helen Keller, who died in 1968, is a powerful role model.

THINKING CRITICALLY

1. **Explaining** How do people compensate for lost senses?
2. **Summarizing** What methods did Helen Keller use to communicate with others?

to pressure. Different parts of the body are more sensitive to pressure than others. The fingertips, lips, nose, and cheeks are more sensitive than the shoulders, thighs, and calves.

The sense of pressure undergoes rapid adaptation. In the movie theater, Marc and Linda held hands, but after a little while they became so used to the feelings of their fingers in each other's hands that they hardly noticed. They had adapted.

Temperature Sensations of temperature are relative. When your body temperature is at a normal 98.6°F, you might perceive another person's skin as being warm. When you are feverish, though, the other person's skin might seem cool.

The receptors for temperature are neurons just beneath the skin. When skin temperature increases because you touch something warm, receptors for warmth fire. Decreases in skin temperature, such as those that occur when you put a cool, moist cloth on your forehead, cause receptors for cold to fire.

We adapt to differences in temperature. Have you ever walked out of an air-conditioned building into the hot sunshine? At first, the heat really hit you, but soon the sensation faded as you adapted to the warmth. In the same way, when you first jump into a swimming pool, the water may seem cold. Yet, after a few moments, the water feels warmer as your body adjusts to it.

Pain When Marc's toe was stepped on, he knew it. Pain told him that something was wrong. Pain is also adaptive—it motivates us to do something to stop it. That is why Marc pulled back his leg.

Headaches, backaches, toothaches—these are only a few of the types of pain most of us experience from time to time. More serious health problems—such as arthritis, cancer, or wounds—also cause pain. Not all areas of the body are equally sensitive to pain. The more pain receptors located in a particular area of our skin, the more sensitive that area is. (See Figure 4.9.)

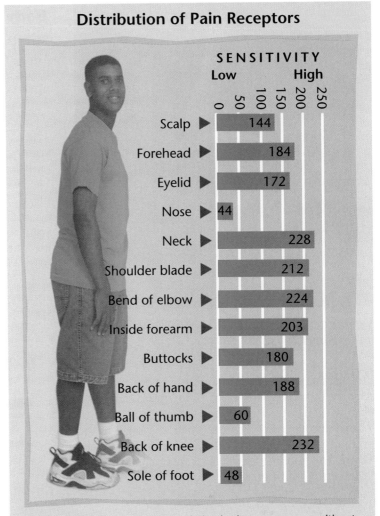

FIGURE 4.9 *Some parts of the body are more sensitive to pressure and pain than others.* **Which part of the body has the fewest pain receptors?**

Source: Strughold, H. (1924). On the density and thresholds in the areas of pain on the epidermis in the various regions of the body. *Z. Biol.*, 80, 367–380. (In German.)

Once a person gets hurt, everything happens very quickly. Pain originates at the point of contact, as with Marc's toe. The pain message is sent from the point of contact to the spinal cord to the thalamus in the brain. Then it is projected to the cerebral cortex, where the person registers the location and severity of the pain. Chemicals called prostaglandins help the body transmit pain messages to the brain. Aspirin and ibuprofen are common pain-fighting drugs that work by curbing production of prostaglandins.

Simple remedies like rubbing and scratching an injured area sometimes help relieve pain. Marc rubbed his toe. Why? One possible answer lies in the gate theory of pain. **Gate theory** suggests that only a certain amount of information can be processed by

Gymnasts rely heavily on their vestibular sense, particularly on the balance beam.

Body Senses

Body senses are the senses that people are least aware of. But do not let that fool you. Without them, you would have to pay attention just to stay upright, to lift your legs to go downstairs, or even to put food in your mouth.

The Vestibular Sense Stand up. Now close your eyes. Do you have to look in a mirror to be certain that you are still upright? No, of course not. Your **vestibular sense** tells you whether you are physically upright without your having to use your eyes. Sensory organs located in the ears monitor your body's motion and position in relation to gravity. Your vestibular sense enables you to keep your balance. It tells you whether you are upside down or not and lets you know when you are falling. It also informs you of whether your body is changing speeds, such as in an accelerating automobile.

It is true that you have a sense that keeps you upright. It is the vestibular sense. Sensory organs in the ears monitor the body's position in relation to gravity.

the nervous system at a time. Rubbing or scratching the area transmits sensations to the brain that compete with the pain messages for attention. Thus, many neurons cannot get their pain messages to the brain. It is as if too many calls are flooding a switchboard. The flooding prevents many or all of the calls from getting through.

TRUTH **or** **fiction** ■ REVISITED ■

It is true that pinching your arm can help relieve the pain in your toe. According to the gate theory of pain, the pinching may flood the nervous system with messages so that the news of the pain in your toe does not get through to the brain.

A fascinating fact in psychology is that many people experience pain in limbs that are no longer there. More than half of combat veterans with amputated limbs report feeling pain in the missing, or "phantom," limbs (Horgan & MacLachlan, 2004; Kooijman et al., 2000). In such cases, there is no current tissue damage, but the pain is real. The pain appears to involve activation of nerves in the stump of the missing limb, along with activation of neural circuits that have memories connected with the limb (Mackert et al., 2003).

Kinesthesis Ask some friends to close their eyes. Then ask them to touch their noses with their index fingers. How close to their noses did they come? Many of them were probably right on the mark, while others could only come close.

How did they locate their noses? Their eyes were closed, so they could not see their hands. They touched their noses through kinesthesis. **Kinesthesis** is the sense that informs people about the position and motion of their bodies. The word *kinesthesis* comes from the Greek words "to move" (*kinein*) and "perception" (*aisthēsis*). In kinesthesis, sensory information is fed to the brain from sensory organs in the joints, tendons, and muscles.

SECTION 4 REVIEW

Homework Practice Online
Keyword: SY7 HP4

1. How does the sense of smell work?
2. What is the vestibular sense?
3. **Critical Thinking** *Summarizing* Identify the chemical, skin, and body senses.

Perception

Every minute of every day, countless impressions are made on our various senses. Imagine the confusion if we did not find ways to organize all that information. Perception is the way in which we organize or make sense of our sensory impressions.

Rules of Perceptual Organization

Gestalt psychologists applied the principle that "the whole is more than the sum of its parts" to the study of perception. Using this principle, they noted many different ways in which people make sense of sensory information. These ways are called the rules of perceptual organization and include closure, figure-ground perception, proximity, similarity, continuity, and common fate.

Closure   Study Figure 4.10. Do you see random blotches of ink or a dog sniffing the ground? If you perceive the dog, it is not just because of the visual sensations provided by the drawing. Those are actually quite confusing. The pattern is not very clear. Despite the lack of clarity, however, you can still see a dog. Why? The answer is that you are familiar with dogs and that you try to fit the pieces of information into a familiar pattern.

What you are doing with this picture is filling in the blanks. Gestalt psychologists refer to this as the

FIGURE 4.11   *Do you see a vase or the profiles of two faces looking at each other? This figure illustrates the Gestalt principle of figure-ground perception.*

principle of closure. **Closure** is the tendency to perceive a complete or whole figure even when there are gaps in what your senses tell you.

Figure-Ground Perception   Now take a look at Figure 4.11. What do you see? In the center of the drawing, you probably see a vase. If you look again, though, you may see more than a vase. Can you see the two profiles that form the sides of the vase?

This drawing is one of psychologists' favorite illustrations of figure-ground relationships. Figure-ground perception is the perception of figures against a background. When you saw a vase, it was a light-colored figure against a dark background. The profiles, on the other hand, were dark figures against a light background.

We experience figure-ground perception every day. If we look out a window, we may see people, buildings, cars, and streets or perhaps grass, trees, birds, and clouds. We see these objects as figures against a background, such as white clouds against a blue sky or a car in front of a brick building. What we perceive as the figure and what we perceive as the background influence our perception.

Other Rules of Organization   Without reading further, describe Part A of Figure 4.12 on page 94. Did you say that Part A consisted of six lines, or did you say that it was three pairs of lines? If you said three pairs of lines, you were influenced by the **proximity**, or nearness, of some of the lines to each

FIGURE 4.10   *Do you see meaningless ink blotches or a dog sniffing? Although the pattern is unclear, you will probably see a dog because dogs are familiar to you and you fill in the blanks.*

other. There is no other reason to perceive them in pairs since all of the lines are the same in every other respect.

Now describe Part B of the figure. Did you perceive it as a six-by-six grid or as three columns of *x*'s and three columns of *o*'s? If you said three columns, then you were grouping according to the law of **similarity**, which says that people think of similar objects as belonging together.

What about Part C? Is this a series of half-circles, every other one turned down? Or did you see a wavy line and a straight line? If you saw the wavy line and the straight line, you were probably organizing your perceptions according to the rule of **continuity**. People usually prefer to see smooth, continuous patterns (like lines and waves), not disrupted ones (like the alternating half-circles).

Finally, there is the law of **common fate**. Have you ever noticed how when you see things moving together, you perceive them as *belonging together*? For example, a group of people running in the same direction would appear to have the same purpose. You assume that they are part of the same group and that they are all running to the same place—that they have a common fate.

Perception of Movement

The next time you are in a car or a bus that is stopped at a traffic light, pay attention to what happens when the vehicle in the next lane begins to move forward. Do you think at first that your vehicle, not the other one, is moving? Is it unclear whether your car or bus is moving backward or the other one is moving forward?

To be able to sense movement, humans need to see an object change its position relative to other objects. We all know that Earth is moving, but do we really feel it? To early scientists, whose only instrument for visual observation was the naked eye, it seemed logical that the sun circled Earth. After all, that is what they seemed to be seeing. To observe that it is Earth that moves around the sun, we would have to be somewhere in outer space. We cannot observe it while standing on Earth itself.

So how do you decide which vehicle is moving at the traffic light? One way is to look for objects that you know are stable, like structures on the side of the road—buildings, signs, or trees. If you are steady in relation to them, then your vehicle is not moving. This also sheds light on how participants in events perceive the action from different points of view, physically and psychologically. Those favoring one side over another tend to be biased in their reporting of events. For example, the viewpoint of someone driving a car that runs a red light may differ from that of someone driving a car in another direction.

Stroboscopic Motion

We have been talking about perception of real movement—movement that actually occurs.

A. Proximity   B. Similarity   C. Continuity

FIGURE 4.12   *How do these drawings illustrate the Gestalt laws of proximity, similarity, and continuity?*

Psychologists have also studied *illusions* of movement. One such illusion of movement is called stroboscopic motion. In **stroboscopic motion**, the illusion of movement is produced by showing the rapid progression of images or objects that are not moving at all. Have you ever seen one of those little books designed to be flipped through quickly so that the figures on the pages appear to move? These books work because of stroboscopic motion.

Movies work in a similar way. Despite the name *movie*, movies do not consist of images that move. Instead, the audience is shown 16 to 22 pictures, or frames, per second.

In a motion picture, frames of stationary images pass at the rate of about 16 to 22 per second, giving the illusion of motion.

Each frame is just slightly different from the previous one. Showing the frames in rapid succession creates the illusion of movement. Why? Because of the law of continuity, humans prefer to see things as one continuous image. Perception smoothes over the interruptions and fills in the gaps.

Depth Perception

Imagine trying to go through life without being able to judge depth or distance. Like Todd in the theater, you might bump into other people or step on their toes. You would have trouble going up or down stairs without stumbling. Depth, in this case, has little to do with the way people sometimes use the word *deep*. It is not, for instance, the depth of a lake or a hole. Depth here means "distance away." For example, without really thinking about it, you decide how far away a glass of juice is from you. Can you just reach out and pick it up, or do you have to get out of your chair? You perceive the depth of objects through both monocular and binocular cues.

Monocular Cues for Depth
Monocular cues need only one eye to be perceived. Artists use monocular cues to create an illusion of depth. These cues create the illusion of three dimensions, or depth, on two-dimensional, or flat, surfaces. Monocular cues cause certain objects to appear more distant from the viewer than others. These cues include perspective, clearness, overlapping, shadow, and texture gradient.

If you take two objects that are exactly the same size and place one of them far away from you and the other nearby, the object that is farther away will stimulate a smaller area of your retina than the one that is near. Even though the objects are the same size, the amount of sensory input from the more distant object is smaller because it is farther away. The distances between far-off objects also appear to be smaller than the same distances between nearby objects. For this reason, the phenomenon known as perspective occurs. Perspective is the tendency to see parallel lines as coming closer together, or converging, as they move away from us. However, experience teaches us that objects that look small when they are far away will seem larger when they are close, even though their size does not actually change. In this way, our perception of a familiar object's size also becomes a cue to its distance from us.

The clearness of an object also helps in telling us how far away it might be. Nearby objects appear to be clearer, and we see more details. Faraway objects seem less clear and less detailed. Thus, the clearer a familiar object seems to be, the closer it is to us.

Overlapping is another monocular cue that tells us which objects are far away and which ones are near. Overlapping is the perceiving of one object as being in front of another. Nearby objects can block our view of more-distant objects. Experience teaches us to perceive partly covered objects as

FIGURE 4.13 *Which circles—the complete circles or those that are partially covered—seem closer to you? Why?*

being farther away than the objects that block them from view. (See Figure 4.13.)

Shadows and highlights also give us information about objects' three-dimensional shapes and where they are placed in relation to the source of light. Look at Figure 4.14. What do you see on the left compared to the right? Your answer probably is that you see a two-dimensional circle on the left and a three-dimensional sphere on the right. What is the difference between the two? The right part of the figure shows a circle with a highlight on its surface and a shadow underneath. Because of these cues, you perceive the highlighted central area to be closest to you.

Still another monocular cue is texture gradient. Texture, of course, is the surface quality and appearance of an object. A gradient is a progressive change. Texture that is farther away from us appears to be denser than texture that is closer, and we see less detail. Therefore, closer objects are perceived as having a more varied texture than objects that are farther away.

The most complex of monocular cues of depth is called motion parallax. It is more complex because, as you have probably guessed by the name, it involves not a stationary picture but the image of something as the viewer moves. Motion parallax is the tendency of objects to seem to move forward or backward depending on how far away they are from the viewer.

If you have the opportunity to take a drive in the countryside, pay attention to what happens to various objects as you move past them. You will notice that distant objects, such as mountains, the Moon,

and stars, appear to move forward with you. Objects at an intermediate distance seem to stand still. Nearby objects, such as roadside markers, rocks, and trees, go by quite rapidly. If you did not know better, you might think that they were moving backward. Through experience, we realize that objects that appear to move with us are at a greater distance than those that pass quickly.

Binocular Cues for Depth Whereas monocular cues can be perceived with just one eye, both eyes are required to perceive **binocular cues** for depth. Two binocular cues for depth are retinal disparity and convergence.

Hold a finger at arm's length. Now slowly bring it closer until it almost touches your nose. If you keep your eyes relaxed as you do this, you will seem to see two fingers. An image of the finger will be projected onto the retina of each eye. Each image will be slightly different because the finger will be seen at different angles. This difference is referred to as **retinal disparity**. The closer your finger comes, the farther apart the "two fingers" appear to be. Thus, the amount of retinal disparity we detect gives us a cue about the depth of an object. However, retinal disparity serves as a cue to depth only for objects that are within a few feet of us, not for objects that are farther away.

The other binocular cue we use is called convergence. Convergence is associated with feelings of tension in the eye muscle. When we try to maintain a single image of the approaching finger, our eyes must turn inward, or converge on it, giving us a cross-eyed look. The closer we feel our eyes moving

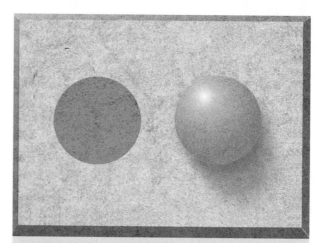

FIGURE 4.14 *The addition of a highlight and a shadow gives us the sense that the circle on the right is three-dimensional, or has depth.*

When you hold up two fingers at different distances, depth cues help you tell which finger is closer. One cue is retinal disparity. The images on the retinas of the closer finger are seen from wider angles and differ more than the images on the retina of the farther finger. What other cues help you perceive depth?

toward each other, the nearer the object they are looking at is. Like retinal disparity, convergence has stronger effects when objects are close.

Perceptual Constancies

Imagine that you are just leaving school and that you see your friends waiting for you under a tree some distance away. As you run over to them, they get closer and look larger because, as you have just learned, the image of your friends takes up more and more space on your retina. Why do you not think your friends are literally growing in inches? This would certainly appear to be the case judging from the sensory input. Or consider the problems of a pet owner who might recognize his or her dog from the side but not from above because the dog's shape would differ from above. The reason you know your friends are not actually getting taller by the second, and the pet owner recognizes the dog

from almost every angle, is experience. Each person's experience creates perceptual constancies—constancies of size, color, brightness, and shape.

Size Constancy   The image of a dog seen from a distance of 20 feet occupies about the same amount of space on the retina as an inch-long insect crawling in the palm of the hand. Yet we do not perceive the dog to be as small as the insect. Similarly, we may say that people on the ground look like ants when we are at the top of a tall building, but we know they remain people even if the details of their forms are lost in the distance.

Through experience, people acquire a sense of size constancy. Size constancy is the tendency to perceive an object as being of one size no matter how far away the object is, even though the size of its image on the retina varies with its distance. Through experience, humans learn about perspective—that the same object seen at a great distance

FIGURE 4.15 *Although the two gray squares are identical, the one on the left is perceived as brighter because it appears against a dark background.*

from the viewer will appear much smaller than when it is nearby.

How do we know that size constancy is something we learn? Some evidence comes from a study of the Mbuti people of Africa, who live in a dense forest. When anthropologist Colin Turnbull (1961) took one of the Mbuti guides out of the forest and onto a wide plain, they happened to see some

buffalo in the distance. The Mbuti guide mistook the buffalo for insects and would not believe Turnbull when he told him otherwise. The reason? Experience. The Mbuti man had seen buffalo before. However, having lived in a dense forest, he was not used to seeing them at great distances. He had therefore not developed size constancy in the way a plains dweller would have.

Color Constancy Imagine that Marc was wearing a tan sweatshirt and Linda had on a red blouse. Even in the darkened movie theater, Marc and Linda still knew that their shirts were tan and red. Because of their previous experience, they perceived their shirts as remaining tan and red even though both appeared gray in the darkness of the theater. Color constancy is the tendency to perceive objects as keeping their color even though different light might change the appearance of their color.

Brightness Constancy Brightness constancy is the tendency to perceive an object as being equally bright even when the intensity of the light around it changes. Look at Figure 4.15. Does the gray square in the black frame look brighter than the one in the white frame? If it does, it is because we judge the

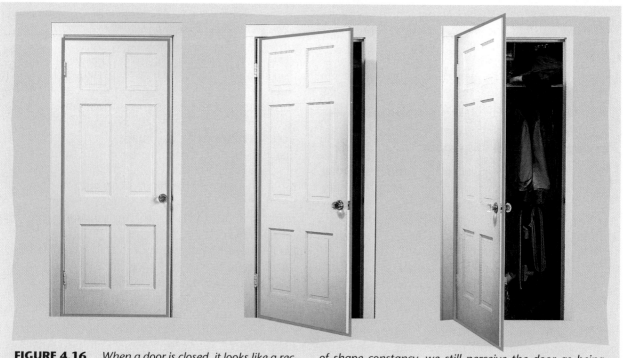

FIGURE 4.16 *When a door is closed, it looks like a rectangle. When it is open, it is trapezoidal. But because of shape constancy, we still perceive the door as being rectangular whether it is open or not.*

brightness of an object by the brightness of other objects around it. For example, a black object really looks almost gray in very bright sunlight, but we still perceive it as being black because everything else around it is also much brighter.

Shape Constancy Take a glass and look at it from directly above. You see a circle, right? Now move back slightly; it becomes an ellipse. When you look at the glass straight on, the image of the top of it is a line. So why would you still describe the rim of the glass as being a circle? Because of shape constancy—the knowledge that an item has only one shape no matter what angle you view that item from. Figure 4.16 shows another example. A door appears to be a rectangle only when you view it straight on. When you move to the side or open it, the left or right edge comes closer and appears to be larger, changing the retinal image of the door to a trapezoid. Yet because of shape constancy, you continue to think of doors as being rectangular.

Visual Illusions

Do your eyes sometimes "play tricks on you"? Actually, your eyes are not to blame, but your brain's use of perceptual constancies is responsible. Your brain can trick your eye through visual illusions.

Part A of Figure 4.17 shows the Müller-Lyer illusion. Look at the two lines at the top of the illustration. Do you think they are the same length? To most people, the line on the right, with its reversed arrows, looks longer. Why? Again, because of experience. In this culture, we are used to living in rooms in buildings. The line on the right may remind us of how a far corner of a room looks, while the line on the left reminds us of the outside near corner of a building. The rule of size constancy is that if two objects seem to be the same size and one is farther away, the farther object must be larger than it actually seems. How did psychologists come to the conclusion that we are reminded of buildings and rooms in this illusion? Because they found that the illusion does not work

FIGURE 4.17 *(A) Which line at the top is longer? If you measure them, you will find that they are exactly the same. Notice how the line on the left resembles the near corner of a building and the line on the right looks like the far corner of a room. (B) The two horizontal lines are equally long, but the top line seems longer. Why?*

in cultures that do not live in the same types of structures that we do (Segall, Campbell, & Herskovits, 1966).

Now look at Part B of Figure 4.17, which shows the Ponzo illusion. Which of the two horizontal lines do you think is longer? Do you perceive the top line as being longer? The rule of size constancy may also afford insight into this illusion. Perhaps the converging lines strike you as receding into the distance. If so, you assume from experience that the horizontal line at the top is farther down the track—farther away from you. The rule of size constancy is at work again.

SECTION 5 REVIEW

go. hrw .com Homework Practice Online

Keyword: SY7 HP4

1. List and explain three rules of perceptual organization.

2. Explain the cues people use to perceive motion and depth.

3. Describe four perceptual constancies.

4. **Critical Thinking** *Analyzing Information* Describe how a person's perceptions affect that person's points of view. What are some examples of bias related to various points of view?

Writing a Summary

Using standard grammar, spelling, sentence structure, and punctuation, summarize the information in this chapter. Consider:
• how sensation and perception differ
• how people see, hear, feel, taste, smell, touch, and otherwise perceive the world around them

Identifying People and Ideas

Identify the following terms or people and use them in appropriate sentences.

1. sensation
2. perception
3. difference threshold
4. retina
5. conductive deafness
6. gate theory
7. continuity
8. stroboscopic motion
9. monocular cue
10. binocular cues

Understanding Main Ideas

SECTION 1 (pp. 78–80)
1. What is the difference between sensation and perception?

SECTION 2 (pp. 80–85)
2. How do pupils adjust to the amount of light available?

SECTION 3 (pp. 85–88)
3. How does the ear transmit sound to the brain?

SECTION 4 (pp. 88–92)
4. How are smell and taste related?

SECTION 5 (pp. 93–99)
5. What is the difference between monocular cues and binocular cues? Give examples of each.

Thinking Critically

1. **Making Generalizations and Predictions** What do you think life would be like if human beings lacked sensory adaptation?

2. **Analyzing Information** What would happen if our eyes were unable to control the amount of light that entered them?

3. **Summarizing** The process of hearing is considered a chain reaction. Why?

4. **Drawing Inferences and Conclusions** How might people's perceptions and senses affect their choice of a career?

5. **Evaluating** Give an example of a situation in which monocular cues could be used to determine how far away an object is.

Writing About Psychology

1. **Summarizing** Recall an experience in which one of your senses produced such an impact that you still remember it. Write two or three paragraphs to re-create the experience in vivid detail.

2. **Analyzing Information** With three classmates, take a 10-minute walk outside. Stay together, but do not talk to one another or take any notes. After the walk, divide a sheet of paper into four columns. Write the following headings at the top of each column: *See, Hear, Smell, Feel.* Write down what you experienced during your walk. Compare your list with those of the others in your group. How do people exposed to the same stimuli perceive them differently? Use the graphic organizer below to help you with your chart.

See	Hear	Smell	Feel

Interpreting Graphs

Study the graph below. Then use the information in the graph to help you answer the questions that follow.

**Comparing Senses:
Perceptions of Hearing and Seeing**

Perceived Duration of Stimulus (seconds)

auditory

visual

Real Duration of Stimulus (seconds)

Source: Marks, *The Unity of the Senses*, 1978

1. Which of the senses has a perceived duration of stimulus that is equal to the real duration of stimulus?

a. sight

b. hearing

c. hearing and sight

d. smell

2. What does this graph reveal about the differences between the senses?

Analyzing Primary Sources

Read the following excerpt, in which Constance Classen discusses the ways different cultures understand the senses. Then answer the questions that follow.

66 Different cultures present strikingly different ways of 'making sense' of the world. The Ongee of the Andaman Islands in the South Pacific, for example, live in a world ordered by smell. According to the Ongee, odour is the vital force of the universe and the basis of personal and social identity. Therefore, when an Ongee wishes to refer to 'me,' he or she points to his or her nose, the organ of smell. Likewise, when greeting a friend, an Ongee will ask 'How is your nose?' The primary concern of Ongee culture is to maintain a proper state of olfactory [sense of smell] equilibrium within individuals and within the cosmos. 99

3. Which of the following statements reflects the argument that Classen makes in the excerpt?

a. The Ongee are a strange people.

b. The sense of smell is the sharpest and most accurate sense.

c. Cultural values shape the way in which people use and understand the senses.

d. Island peoples are more likely to rely on smell than sight.

4. Which sense do you regard as the most important in your culture? Provide an example to support your answer.

PSYCHOLOGY PROJECTS

Linking to Community

Using Your Observation Skills   Conduct an experiment to show the relationship of the senses of taste and smell. Ask several friends to participate. Select four foods that are similar in texture, such as an apple, an onion, a pear, and a potato. Peel and cut the food into pieces. Blindfold the participants and ask them to hold their noses. Guide each person's hand to each bit of food and ask him or her to taste it and guess what it is. Write a report describing how accurately the participants guessed the same foods.

🖬 **internet** connect

Internet Activity: go.hrw.com
KEYWORD: SY7 CH4

Create an activity on sensation and perception to:

• create a drawing or model of the parts of the eye.
• make an oral presentation on the brain and sound processing.
• conduct an Internet scavenger hunt on perception and the senses.

CONSCIOUSNESS

5 Chapter

Read to Discover

1 What is consciousness?

2 What are the stages of sleep, and what are several sleep problems?

3 What are meditation, biofeedback, and hypnosis?

4 In what ways do various kinds of drugs affect consciousness?

A DAY IN THE LIFE

"I had an extremely strange dream last night," Linda said as she, Marc, and Todd were standing around at school waiting for the bell to ring.

"What was it about? Was I in it?" Marc wanted to know.

"Sorry, Marc, you weren't," Linda replied. "Actually, you know who was in it? Nick. And it was weird because it was Nick the way he used to be before he had the drug problem, before he started spacing out all the time. Back when you could talk to him and know that he was actually listening."

The group was silent for a few seconds while they recalled the way Nick used to be. They were all glad his parents had convinced him to go to a treatment center for help.

"But Nick wasn't the only person in my dream," Linda continued. "The thing is, I can't remember who else was there. It was someone I know, but I can't think of who!" She was obviously annoyed.

"Hey, in a movie I saw last weekend, this guy used hypnosis to help a woman remember her dreams," said Todd.

"Did it work?" asked Linda.

"Well, in the movie it did," said Todd. "But I read in a magazine article that you can only be hypnotized if you want to be."

"How did he hypnotize her in the movie?" Linda wanted to know. "What kinds of things did he do?"

"Well, first he got out a chain with something hanging from it. He began to swing it slowly back and forth in front of the woman's eyes, and he told her to concentrate on it. Then he told her that she was getting sleepy, very sleepy, and that her eyelids were getting heavy. Once he'd put her in a trance, he asked her some questions about her dreams, and she was able to answer them. It was amazing."

"Huh," pondered Linda. "Sounds a little creepy to me." Just then the bell rang, and everyone went off to class. Linda never did figure out who else had been in her dream.

- - -

Key Terms

- consciousness
- selective attention
- preconscious
- unconscious
- nonconscious
- altered state of consciousness
- circadian rhythm
- rapid-eye-movement sleep
- insomnia
- night terror
- sleep apnea
- narcolepsy
- meditation
- biofeedback
- hypnosis
- posthypnotic suggestion
- addiction
- depressant
- intoxication
- narcotic
- stimulant
- amphetamine
- hallucination
- delusion
- hallucinogen
- detoxification

Linda's dream, Nick's behavior while on drugs, and Todd's description of hypnotism all have to do with **consciousness**, or awareness of things inside and outside ourselves. Many psychologists believe that we cannot capture the richness of the human experience without talking about consciousness.

You may be fairly certain that you are conscious right now. For example, you are conscious, or aware, that you are reading this page. But what about tonight, when you are asleep? Sleeping and dreaming are related to consciousness. There are also several altered states of consciousness, such as those that occur when a person is in a hypnotic trance or is under the influence of certain drugs. These topics and others that have to do with consciousness will be discussed in this chapter.

HOLT

Psychology Video Program

Watch the video to explore how some companies use meditation.

TRUTH OR fiction?

Read the following statements about psychology. Do you think they are true or false? You will learn whether each statement is true or false as you read the chapter.

- If it were not for cues such as the sunrise and sunset, people would act as if a day were 25 hours long.
- The only time people dream is just before they wake up.
- It is possible to hypnotize any person at any time.
- People who are drunk always know that they are drunk.
- Smoking leads to more deaths in the United States than automobile accidents do.

The Study of Consciousness

Psychologists have not always thought that consciousness should be part of the study of psychology. In 1904 William James wrote an article titled "Does Consciousness Exist?" In this article, James questioned the value of studying consciousness because he could not think of a scientific way to observe or measure another person's consciousness. His point was that even though we can see other people talking or moving around, we cannot actually measure their consciousness.

John Watson, the founder of behaviorism, agreed with James. In 1913 Watson wrote an article called "Psychology as the Behaviorist Views It." In this article, he stated, "The time seems to have come when psychology must discard all references to consciousness". Watson, like James, questioned whether consciousness could be studied scientifically. He chose instead to focus only on observable behaviors.

Consciousness as a Construct

Not all psychologists dismissed the possibility of studying consciousness. Today many psychologists believe that consciousness can be studied because it can be linked with measurable behaviors, such as talking, and with brain waves.

Consciousness is a psychological construct. Intelligence and emotion are also psychological constructs. None of them can be seen, touched, or measured directly. However, they are known by their effects on behavior and play roles in psychological theories. For example, we can theorize as to how sleep or alcohol affects consciousness and devise ways of testing our theories. When people behave in certain ways, we may conclude that the behaviors result from, say, intelligence even though there is no way to be certain. Although consciousness cannot be seen or touched, it is real enough to most people.

Meanings of Consciousness

Generally speaking, consciousness means awareness. But there is more than one type of awareness. Thus, the term *consciousness* is used in a variety of ways. Sometimes consciousness refers to sensory awareness. At other times, consciousness may mean direct inner awareness. A third use of the term *consciousness* refers to the sense of self that each person experiences.

Consciousness as Sensory Awareness When you see a raindrop glistening on a leaf, when you hear your teacher's voice, or when you smell pizza in the cafeteria, you are *conscious* of all of these sensations around you, including sights, sounds, and smells. Your senses make it possible for you to be aware of your environment. Therefore, one meaning of consciousness is sensory awareness of the environment. In other words, you are conscious, or aware, of things outside yourself.

Focusing on a particular stimulus is referred to as **selective attention.** To pay attention in class, you must screen out the rustling of paper and the scraping of chairs. To get your homework done, you must pay more attention to your assignments than to your hunger pangs or the radio playing in the background. Selective attention makes our senses keener (Basic Behavioral Science Task Force, 1996). We may even be able to pick out the speech of a single person across a room at a party.

We tend to be more conscious of some things than others. We tend to be particularly conscious of sudden changes, as when a cool breeze enters a sweltering room. We also tend to be especially conscious of unusual stimuli—for example, a dog entering the classroom. Intense stimuli—such as bright colors, loud noises, or sharp pains—also tend to get our attention.

Consciousness as Direct Inner Awareness

Imagine jumping into a lake or a swimming pool on a hot day. Can you feel the cool, refreshing water all around you? Although this image may be vivid, you did not really experience it. No sensory organs were involved. You are conscious of the image through what psychologists call direct inner awareness.

Anytime you are aware of feeling angry, anytime you remember a best friend you had when you were younger, anytime you think about abstract concepts such as fairness or love, you do so through direct inner awareness. In other words, you do not hear, see, smell, or touch thoughts, images, emotions, or memories. Yet you are still conscious of them. This meaning of consciousness, then, is being aware of things inside yourself.

Consciousness as Sense of Self

Have you ever noticed how young children sometimes refer to themselves by their names? For example, they do not say, "I want milk" but "Taylor wants milk." It is only as they grow older that they begin to understand that they are unique individuals, separate from other people and from their surroundings. From then on, they have a sense of self, no matter how much they or the world around them might change. In some uses of the word, *consciousness* is this sense of self in which we are aware of ourselves and our existence.

Levels of Consciousness

So far, we have discussed only one of the levels of consciousness—the level at which people are aware of something and are aware of their awareness. But many psychologists speak of other levels of consciousness as well. These include the preconscious level, the unconscious level, and the nonconscious level. At these levels of consciousness, awareness is more limited.

The Preconscious Level

What if someone asked you what you wore to school yesterday? Or what you did after school? Your class schedule? Your next vacation? Although you were not consciously thinking about any of this information before you were asked about it, you will probably be able to come up with the answers. **Preconscious** ideas are not in your awareness right now, but you could recall them if you had to. You can make these preconscious bits of information conscious simply by directing your inner awareness, or attention, to them.

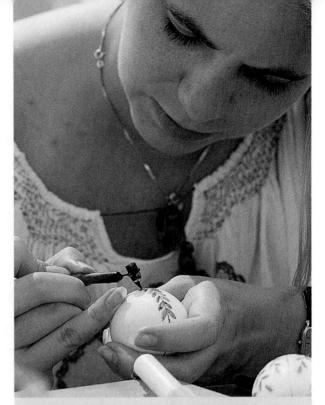

When people are engaged in activities that require close attention to detail, they screen out many sensations to stay focused on the task at hand.

The Unconscious Level

Sigmund Freud theorized that people have an unconscious mind. Information stored in the **unconscious** (sometimes called the subconscious) is unavailable to awareness under most circumstances. In other words, this information is hidden. For example, imagine that you are planning to go to a party. Without realizing why, you find yourself continually distracted from getting ready. First, perhaps, you cannot find a pair of shoes. Then maybe you become involved in a lengthy phone call. Can you guess what information was stored in your unconscious? It may be that you did not want to go to the party. But according to Freud's theory this desire to avoid the party was unconscious—you were not aware of it.

Freud believed that certain memories are painful and that some of our impulses, such as aggressiveness, are considered unacceptable. He stated that we use various mental strategies, called defense mechanisms, to push painful or unacceptable ideas out of our consciousness. In this way, we protect ourselves from feelings of anxiety, guilt, and shame. (See Chapter 14.)

The Nonconscious Level

Many of our basic biological functions exist on a **nonconscious** level.

Freud's Levels of Consciousness

CONSCIOUS LEVEL

Perceptions

Thoughts

PRECONSCIOUS LEVEL

Memories   Stored knowledge

UNCONSCIOUS LEVEL

Selfish needs   Violent motives

Immoral urges   Fears

Irrational   Shameful   Unacceptable
wishes   experiences   desires

FIGURE 5.1 *According to Sigmund Freud, many memories, impulses, and feelings exist below the level of* conscious awareness. **On what level did Freud place irrational wishes?**

For example, even if you tried, you could not sense your fingernails growing or the pupils in your eyes adjusting to light. You know that you are breathing in and out, but you cannot actually feel the exchange of carbon dioxide and oxygen. You blink when you step from the dark into the light, but you cannot feel your pupils growing smaller. It may be just as well that these events are nonconscious. After all, how much can a person hope to keep in mind at once?

Altered States of Consciousness

The word *consciousness* sometimes refers to the waking state—the state in which a person is awake. Yet there are also **altered states of consciousness**, in which a person's sense of self or sense of the world changes. When you doze off, you are no longer conscious of what is going on around you. Sleep is one altered state of consciousness. When Nick was under the influence of drugs, he also experienced

altered states of consciousness. Other altered states of consciousness occur through meditation, biofeedback, and hypnosis. The rest of this chapter explores these altered states of consciousness.

1. What are three psychological constructs?

2. List and describe three levels of consciousness at which awareness is limited.

3. **Critical Thinking** *Analyzing Information* Do you think that a person can study or understand the consciousness of another person? Why or why not?

SECTION 2

Sleep and Dreams

Are you aware that you spend about one third of your life asleep? Why do we sleep? Why do we dream? Why do some of us have trouble getting to sleep or experience nightmares?

Much of how people, animals, and even plants function is governed by **circadian rhythms**, or biological clocks. The word *circadian* comes from the Latin words *circa*, meaning "about," and *dies*, meaning "a day." The circadian rhythms in humans include a sequence of bodily changes, such as those in body

The Stages of Sleep

Awake

Stage 1

Stage 2

Stage 3
(deep sleep)

Stage 4
(deep sleep)

REM sleep

└──┘ = 1 second

FIGURE 5.2 *These are the typical EEG patterns for the stages of sleep. During rapid-eye-movement, or REM, sleep, EEG patterns resemble those of stage 1 sleep. Most people dream or have nightmares during REM sleep.*

temperature, blood pressure, and sleepiness and wakefulness, that occurs every 24 hours. The human circadian rhythms usually operate on a 24-hour day. For example, body temperature falls to its lowest point between 3:00 A.M. and 5:00 A.M. each day.

The most-studied circadian rhythm is that of the sleep-wake cycle. Because people normally associate periods of wakefulness and sleep with the rotation of Earth, a full sleep-wake cycle is 24 hours. However, when people are removed from cues that signal day or night (such as clocks, radio or television programs, sunrise, and sunset), their cycle tends to expand to about 25 hours (National Sleep Foundation, 2000). Researchers are unsure why this happens. This and many other issues concerning sleep have been, and continue to be, the subject of much research.

It is true that if it were not for cues such as the sunrise and sunset, people would act as if a day were 25 hours long. Because of Earth's rotation, a day is 24 hours. For reasons not fully understood, however, people may be more suited to a 25-hour day.

The Stages of Sleep

Sleep researchers have discovered that we sleep in stages. (See Figure 5.2.) Sleep stages are defined in terms of brain-wave patterns, which can be measured by an electroencephalograph (EEG). Brain waves, like other waves, are cyclical, and they vary on the basis of whether we are awake, relaxed, or sleeping. Four different brain-wave patterns are beta waves, alpha waves, theta waves, and delta waves.

When we are awake and alert, the brain emits beta waves, which are short and quick. As we begin to relax and become drowsy, the brain waves slowly move from beta waves to alpha waves, which are a little slower than beta waves. During this relaxed state, we may experience visual images such as flashes of color or sensations such as feeling as if we are falling. This state is followed by five distinct stages of sleep.

Stage 1 is the stage of lightest sleep. As we enter stage 1 sleep, our brain waves slow down from the alpha rhythm to the slower pattern of theta waves. This transition may be accompanied by brief dreamlike images that resemble vivid photographs. Because stage 1 sleep is light, if we are awakened during this stage, we will probably recall these images and feel as if we have not slept at all.

If we are not awakened, we remain in stage 1 sleep no more than 30 to 40 minutes. Then we move into sleep stages 2, 3, and 4. During stages 3 and 4, sleep is deep, and the brain produces delta waves—the slowest of the four patterns. Stage 4 is the stage of deepest sleep, meaning that it is the one during which someone would have the greatest difficulty waking us up.

After perhaps half an hour of stage 4 sleep, we begin a relatively quick journey back to stage 3 to stage 2 to stage 1. About 90 minutes will have passed since we fell asleep. Now something strange happens. Suddenly, we breathe more irregularly,

blood pressure rises, and the heart beats faster. Brain waves become similar to those of stage 1 sleep. Yet this is another stage of sleep—the stage called **rapid-eye-movement sleep**, or REM sleep, because beneath our closed lids, our eyes are moving rapidly. The preceding four stages are known as non-rapid-eye-movement, or NREM, sleep because our eyes do not move as much during them.

During a typical eight-hour night of sleep, most people go through these stages about five times, each of which constitutes one sleep cycle. (See Figure 5.3.) As the night goes on, periods of REM sleep become longer. The final period of REM sleep, toward morning, may last half an hour or longer.

Why Do We Sleep?

People need sleep to help revive the tired body and to build up resistance to infection. Sleep also seems to serve important psychological functions. It may, for example, help us recover from stress. We seem to need more sleep when we have problems in school, with our families and friends, or at work.

What would happen if people forced themselves to go without sleep? In 1964 Randy Gardner, age 17, tried to find out as part of a science project. Under the supervision of a physician, Randy stayed awake almost 11 days. He became irritable, could not focus his eyes, and had speech difficulties and memory lapses. (Because of these types of effects and others that are potentially dangerous, sleep deprivation experiments like Gardner's should be conducted only by trained professionals in laboratory settings.) William Dement, an early sleep

FIGURE 5.3 *This is a typical sleep pattern. Most people go through the cycle five times in eight hours.* *As the night progresses, stages 3 and 4 become shorter, and REM sleep becomes longer.*

The mystery of dreams has occupied artists, philosophers, and scientists for centuries. Les Valeurs Personnelles (Personal Values), a painting by French artist Rene Magritte, shows a variety of dreamlike images.

researcher, tracked Gardner's recovery. He found that Gardner slept an extra 6.5 hours for the first three days following the experiment. On the fourth night he slept 2.5 extra hours (Gulevich, Dement, & Johnson, 1966).

In some studies, animals or people have been deprived only of REM sleep. People and animals deprived of REM sleep tend to show what psychologists call REM-rebound. They catch up on their REM sleep by having much more of it when they sleep later on. REM sleep seems to serve particular psychological functions. Animals and people who are deprived of REM sleep learn more slowly than usual. They also forget more rapidly what they have learned (Gais & Born, 2004; Ribeiro & Nicolelis, 2004). Other research findings suggest that REM sleep may help brain development in infants and "exercise" brain cells in adults (McCarley, 1992).

Dreams

It is during REM sleep that we have the most vivid dreams. Linda's dream, for example, probably occurred while she was in REM sleep. Dreams are a mystery about which philosophers, poets, scientists, and many others have theorized for centuries.

Did you know that dreams can be in black-and-white or in full color? Some dreams seem very realistic. You may have had a dream of going to class and suddenly realizing that there was going to be a test in the class. You had not studied. You started to panic. Then you woke up. The dream felt very real, and you were relieved to find that it was only a dream after all. Other dreams are disorganized and seem less real.

We may dream every time we are in REM sleep. During REM sleep, dreams are most likely to have clear imagery and plots that make sense, even if some of the events are not realistic. During NREM sleep, plots are vaguer and images more fleeting.

TRUTH OR fiction
■ R E V I S I T E D ■

It is not true that the only time people dream is just before they wake up. The most vivid dreams occur during REM sleep, the final part of the sleep cycle. Most people go through the sleep cycle about five times a night.

Interestingly, if the events in a person's dream seemed to last 10 minutes, she or he was probably dreaming for 10 minutes. That is, people seem to dream in "real time." Although some dreams involve fantastic adventures, most of the dreams people have—particularly REM-sleep dreams experienced early in the night—are simple extensions of the

A DAY IN THE LIFE

activities of the day. The characters in dreams are more likely to be friends and neighbors than spies, monsters, or princes. Linda suspected that the other person in her dream was someone she knew, and she was probably right.

Like Linda, we sometimes have difficulty recalling all, or even a few, of the details of our dreams. This may be because we are often unable to hold on to information from one state of consciousness (in this case, sleeping/dreaming) when we move into another (in this case, wakefulness).

The Freudian View   Have you ever heard the song "A Dream Is a Wish Your Heart Makes" from the Disney film *Cinderella*? Is it true that your dreams reveal what you really want? Sigmund Freud thought so—he theorized that dreams reflect a person's unconscious wishes and urges—"wishes your heart makes."

However, some unconscious wishes may be unacceptable, perhaps even painful. Those, Freud thought, would be the ones that would most likely appear in dreams, although not always in direct or obvious forms. Freud believed that people dream in

symbols. He thought that these "symbolic" dreams give people a way to deal with painful material that they cannot deal with consciously.

The Biopsychological Approach   Some psychologists believe that dreams begin with biological, not psychological, activity. According to this view, during sleep, neurons fire in a part of the brain that controls movement and vision. These neuron bursts are random, and the brain tries to make sense of them. It does so by weaving a story—the dream. When neurons fire in the part of the brain that controls running, for example, we may dream we are running toward or away from something.

The biopsychological approach suggests an explanation for why people tend to dream about events that took place earlier in the day. The most current activity of the brain concerns the events or problems of the day. Thus, the brain uses everyday matters to give structure to the random bursts of neurons during REM sleep.

Today most psychologists caution that there are no hard-and-fast rules for interpreting dreams. And we can never be sure whether a certain interpretation is correct.

Sleep Problems

Even when we need sleep, we may have trouble getting to sleep or sleeping soundly. When these troubles last for long periods of time or become serious, they are considered to be sleep problems.

Insomnia   **Insomnia** is the inability to sleep. The word comes from the Latin *in-,* meaning "not," and *somnus,* meaning "sleep." The most common type of insomnia is difficulty falling asleep. People with insomnia are more likely than others to worry and to have "racing minds" at bedtime. For many people, insomnia comes and goes, increasing during periods of anxiety or tension and decreasing or disappearing during less stressful periods.

People can actually make insomnia worse by *trying* to get to sleep. The effort backfires because it increases tension. We cannot force ourselves to fall asleep. We can only set the stage by lying down and relaxing when we are tired. Yet millions of people go to bed each night dreading the possibility that they will not be able to fall asleep.

Some people use sleeping pills to cope with insomnia, but many psychologists believe that the safest, simplest, most effective ways of overcoming insomnia do not involve medication. Psychologists recommend that people with insomnia try the following techniques:

- Tense the muscles, one at a time, then let the tension go. This helps relax the body.
- Avoid worrying in bed. If worrying persists, get up for a while.
- Establish a regular routine, particularly for getting up and going to sleep each day.
- Use pleasant images or daydreams to relax. These may occur naturally, or people may have to focus on creating them.

Many psychologists also note that occasional insomnia is fairly common and is not necessarily a problem. It becomes a problem only if it continues for long periods of time.

Nightmares and Night Terrors You have probably experienced one or more nightmares in your lifetime. Common nightmares involve snakes or murderers. Some nightmares are specific to a particular activity or profession. For example, the "actor's nightmare" involves being on stage in front of an audience. The dreamer (an actor, naturally) has no idea what play is being presented, much less what any of the lines are.

In the Middle Ages, nightmares were thought to be the work of demons who were sent to make people pay for their sins. Today we know that nightmares, like most other dreams, are generally products of REM sleep. In one study, college students kept dream diaries and reported having an average of two nightmares a month (Wood & Bootzin, 1990). Upsetting events can produce nightmares, as reported in a study of people who experienced the San Francisco earthquake of 1989 (Wood et al., 1992). People who are anxious or depressed are also more likely to have nightmares.

Night terrors (also called sleep terrors) are similar to, but more severe than, nightmares. Dreamers with night terrors feel their hearts racing, and they gasp for air. They may suddenly sit up, talk incoherently, or thrash about. They do not fully wake up. In the morning, they may recall a feeling or an image from the night terror. Unlike the case with nightmares, however, memories of night terror episodes usually are vague.

Night terrors also differ from nightmares in when they occur. Night terrors tend to occur during deep sleep (stages 3 and 4), whereas nightmares occur during REM sleep. Night terrors happen during the first couple of sleep cycles, nightmares more toward morning. Night terrors are most common among

This person with sleep apnea is hooked up to equipment that applies continuous pressure through the nose to keep airways open during sleep.

young children and may reflect immaturity of the nervous system.

Sleepwalking Many children walk in their sleep. Sleepwalkers may roam about almost nightly during stages of deep sleep. They may respond to questions while they are up and about, but when they wake up they typically do not remember what they did or said. Contrary to myth, there is no evidence that sleepwalkers become violent or upset if they are awakened. However, because sleepwalkers are not fully conscious and thus may be prone to accidentally hurting themselves, they should be supervised if possible.

Most children outgrow sleepwalking as they mature. As is true of night terrors, sleepwalking may reflect immaturity of the nervous system.

Sleep Apnea We all have occasional apneas, or interruptions in breathing. **Sleep apnea** is a breathing interruption that occurs during sleep. People with sleep apnea do not automatically start breathing again until they suddenly sit up and gasp for air. Once they begin breathing again, they fall back asleep. They usually do not wake up completely, so they may not even be aware of what has happened during the night. However, they often feel tired during the day.

Sleep apneas occur when a person's air passages are blocked. Thus, they are sometimes accompanied by snoring. A nasal mask that provides a steady air flow can help prevent breathing interruptions.

About 10 million Americans have apnea, and it is associated with obesity as well as snoring. Apnea is more than a sleep problem. It can lead to high blood pressure, heart attacks, and strokes (Lavie et al., 2000; Peppard et al., 2000).

Narcolepsy Narcolepsy is a rare sleep problem in which people suddenly fall asleep no matter what time it is or where they are. One minute they are awake. The next, their muscles completely relax, and they are in REM sleep. Drug therapy and frequent naps have been used to treat narcolepsy.

Although people usually awaken from an episode of narcolepsy feeling refreshed, such episodes may be dangerous. For example, they can occur while people are driving or operating machinery. No one knows for sure what causes narcolepsy, but it is believed to be a genetic disorder of REM-sleep functioning.

SECTION 2 REVIEW

Homework Practice Online
Keyword: SY7 HP5

1. Describe the five stages of sleep.

2. Describe three kinds of sleep problems.

3. **Critical Thinking** *Comparing and Contrasting* How are nightmares and night terrors similar and different? Why might it be difficult to differentiate between the two in a young child?

SECTION 3
Meditation, Biofeedback, and Hypnosis

People who are asleep and dreaming are in an altered state of consciousness. Other altered states of consciousness occur when we are awake. These states of consciousness can be achieved through meditation, biofeedback, and hypnosis.

Meditation: Narrowing Consciousness

Meditation is a method some people use to try to narrow their consciousness so that the stresses of the outside world fade away. Numerous techniques have been used to accomplish this. The ancient Egyptians gazed upon an oil-burning lamp. The yogis of India stare at an intricate pattern on a vase or carpet. Other meditators repeat pleasing sounds called mantras, such as *om* or *sheereem,* and mentally focus on these sounds.

All of these methods of meditation share a common thread—they focus on a peaceful, repetitive stimulus. This focus helps people narrow their consciousness and become relaxed. By narrowing their consciousness, people can suspend planning, worrying, and other concerns. Meditation is an important part of some religions, such as Buddhism. Some meditators claim that meditation helps them achieve "oneness with the universe," pleasure, or some great insight. These claims have never been scientifically proven, but evidence does suggest that meditation can help people relax. Studies have found that meditation can also help people lower high blood pressure (Alexander et al., 1996; Schneider et al., 1995).

Biofeedback: Feeding Back Information

Biofeedback is a system that provides, or "feeds back," information about something happening in the body. Through biofeedback training, people have learned to control certain bodily functions, such as heart rate. Some people have used biofeedback to learn to create the brain waves produced when relaxing—alpha waves—as a way of coping with tension (Budzynski & Stoyra, 1984). Figure 5.4 shows a biofeedback system designed to record the tension in the forehead muscle of a person who suffers from headaches. As the forehead muscle relaxes, the line on the screen levels off. The patient's task is to keep the line on the screen as level as possible—in other words, the patient needs to keep his or her forehead muscle relaxed. Using biofeedback, people have learned not only to treat tension headaches, but also to lower their heart rates or blood pressure. However, as with

A monk meditates in Thailand. Meditation is important in both Buddhism and Hinduism.

Biofeedback Training

2. Receives signal

3. Processes signal

5. Feedback

4. Displays signal

1. Senses signal

FIGURE 5.4 *By using a biofeedback system to monitor the level of tension in the forehead muscle, a person can learn to control the level of tension and thereby cut down on tension headaches.*

all treatments, biofeedback should be attempted only under the direct supervision of a medical professional.

Hypnosis: Myths and Realities

Perhaps you have seen movies like the one Todd described to Linda, in which one character hypnotized another. Or perhaps you have seen audience members hypnotized in a magic show. If so, chances are you found that these people seemed unable to open their eyes, could not remember their own names, acted out scenes from childhood, or behaved in other unusual manners. But hypnosis is not always what it seems to be in movies and magic shows.

What Is Hypnosis? The word *hypnosis* is derived from the Greek *hypnos,* meaning "sleep." Some psychologists believe that **hypnosis** is an altered state of consciousness during which people respond to suggestions and behave as though they are in a trance. Other psychologists, however, wonder whether hypnosis truly is an altered state of consciousness. Studies have shown that some of the same effects achieved by hypnosis can also occur without hypnosis. Furthermore, brain-wave patterns (as measured by an EEG) of people in hypnotic states look the same as brain-wave patterns produced in the waking state.

Hypnosis began with the ideas of German physician Franz Mesmer in the late 1700s. Mesmer thought that the universe was connected by forms of magnetism. To cure his patients, he would pass magnets over their bodies. Some of them would fall into a trance, then awaken feeling better. Eventually, scientists decided that Mesmer's so-called cures had little scientific basis.

Hypnotism, however, may have more validity than Mesmer's magnet treatment. Today hypnotism may be used in a variety of ways. For example, some doctors use hypnosis as an anesthetic in certain types of surgery (Montgomery et al., 2000; Lang et al, 2000). Some psychologists use it to help clients reduce anxiety, manage pain, or overcome fears (Pinnell & Corino, 2000). Nevertheless, there is still a great deal about hypnosis that is not understood. Thus, hypnosis should be left in the hands of professionals. Do not attempt hypnotism on your own.

CASE STUDIES

AND OTHER TRUE STORIES

Taking Psychology to Heart Through Biofeedback

Suppose that someone told you to lift your arm. Could you do it? Of course—all you would have to do is decide to do it. Lifting your arm is an example of *voluntary* behavior. Walking and talking are other examples. You can walk and talk simply by deciding that you are going to.

But suppose someone told you to lower your blood pressure or your heart rate. Could you do *that*? Perhaps, but not directly. To lower your blood pressure, you might eat less salt, lose weight, or lie down and relax. To lower your heart rate, you might sit down and take it easy for a while. But you cannot lower your blood pressure or heart rate directly. Blood pressure and heart rate are *involuntary* forms of behavior.

Or are they?

A few decades ago, psychologists thought they knew the difference between voluntary and involuntary behavior of the body. They thought voluntary behaviors (such as lifting an arm or a leg) were conscious. People could make them happen simply by directing their attention to having them happen. Psychologists thought other behaviors, such as heartbeat and blood pressure, were involuntary. They were automatic. They could not be consciously controlled, at least not on an immediate basis.

Then, in 1969, psychologist Neal E. Miller made an exciting discovery. He was able to train laboratory rats to increase or decrease their heart rates voluntarily. But why would rats do such a thing in the first place? Miller already knew that there is a pleasure center in the hypothalamus of a rat's brain. Whenever a rat was given a small burst of electricity in this center, the rat felt pleasure, and it wanted more.

Because the rats would do whatever they could to continue feeling this pleasure, they quickly learned that whenever they pressed a lever in their cage, they received this bit of pleasure-producing electric shock. Miller's rats pressed this lever to the point of exhaustion.

Miller designed a study to find out what the rats would do for pleasure. He implanted electrodes in the rats' pleasure centers. Then some of the rats were given shocks whenever their heart rates happened to increase. Other rats received shocks when their heart rates happened to decrease. In other words, some rats were rewarded when their heart rates were faster, whereas others were rewarded when their heart rates were slower. After a training session that took only 90 minutes, the rats learned to change their heart rates—either up or down, depending on when they had been rewarded—by as much as 20 percent. In other words, they seemed to be *voluntarily* changing their heart rates.

Miller's research was an example of biofeedback training (BFT). If it could be done with rats, could people, too, control bodily behavior thought to be involuntary? Instead of implanting electrodes in people's brains, researchers used monitors to let people know when, for example, their heart rates were slower. A biofeedback system does not actually control any of the bodily behaviors. Instead, like a mirror, the biofeedback monitor reflects a person's own efforts and enables him or her to see how various voluntary behaviors affect the involuntary ones. For example, a person might be able to observe that breathing slower reduced his or her heart rate. Indeed, some people have learned to control their heart rates using biofeedback.

Studies have shown that biofeedback has numerous other applications. For example, biofeedback is moderately effective in reducing the intense pain of migraine headaches and other painful conditions.

THINKING CRITICALLY

1. **Finding the Main Idea** How can people learn to control involuntary behaviors?
2. **Identifying Cause and Effect** How does the use of biofeedback help people who are experiencing pain?

How Is Hypnosis Achieved?   Professional hypnotists may put people in a state of consciousness called a hypnotic trance by asking them to focus on something specific—a spot on the wall, an object held by the hypnotist, or merely the hypnotist's voice. Hypnotists usually suggest that people's arms and legs are becoming warm, heavy, and relaxed. They may also tell people that they are becoming sleepy or are falling asleep. Hypnosis is not sleep, however. People who are sleeping have very different brain waves from people in trances. But hearing the word *sleep* often does help a person enter a hypnotic trance.

People who are easily hypnotized are said to have hypnotic suggestibility. They can focus on the instructions of the hypnotist without getting distracted. Suggestible people also usually *like* the idea of being hypnotized and are not resistant to it. Todd was correct when he told Linda that people can only be hypnotized if they want to be.

This photograph shows French doctors putting a patient into a trance in the 1890s. Hypnosis gained widespread popularity in the late 1800s.

TRUTH
OR
fiction
■ R E V I S I T E D ■

It is not true that it is possible to hypnotize any person at any time. People must have a positive attitude toward hypnosis and a willingness to cooperate with the hypnotist for hypnosis to be successful.

How Can We Explain Hypnosis?   Psychologists offer various explanations for the behavior of people under hypnosis. According to Freud, hypnotized people permit themselves to return to childish ways of behaving. For instance, they allow themselves to put fantasy and impulse before fact and logic. Therefore, they believe what the hypnotist tells them. They also enjoy becoming passive and waiting for the hypnotist to tell them what to do.

According to another view, called role theory, people who are hypnotized are playing a part as if they are in a play. However, unlike actors in a play, hypnotized people may believe that what they are doing is real. Research suggests that many people in hypnotic trances may *not* be faking it (Kinnunen et al., 1994). Rather, they become engrossed in playing the part of a hypnotized person. They use their imaginations to try to experience what the hypnotist tells them to experience. If they are told that they are blind, for example, and then are handed a book, they may think of a white curtain coming down over the page. Then they believe they cannot see or read anything. People with vivid imaginations are especially suggestible.

Is Hypnosis Effective?

Psychologists continue to debate whether hypnosis has a scientific basis. They also continue to research what hypnosis can and cannot do. Some of the research on hypnosis has addressed the effects of hypnosis on memory, on feelings of pain, and on the quitting of habits such as smoking or overeating.

Hypnosis and Memory   Police have occasionally used hypnosis to jog the memories of witnesses to a crime. At times this approach has worked with dramatic success. Nevertheless, studies have shown that unhypnotized people are just as likely as hypnotized people to remember details of a crime. More important, hypnotized people are just as likely to make *mistakes* about those details as are others. Many psychologists thus argue that material recalled under hypnosis should not be used as testimony in trials.

One interesting finding about hypnosis and memory has to do with memory of events that occur during the hypnotic trance itself. If so directed by the hypnotist, many people will act as if they do not recall what happened while they were hypnotized (Barber, 2000; Bowers & Woody, 1996). They may not even remember that they were hypnotized at all.

Reprinted with special permission of King Features Syndicate

Hypnosis and Pain Prevention   Under certain circumstances and with careful application, hypnosis has been used to help people prevent feelings of pain (Patterson, 2004). For example, dentists have used hypnosis successfully to help people avoid feeling pain during certain procedures. Some people are so suggestible that they can even undergo surgery without anesthesia if they are hypnotized and told they feel no pain. On the other hand, some studies have shown that a similar effect can sometimes be achieved through relaxation techniques.

Hypnosis and Quitting Bad Habits   To help someone quit a habit such as overeating or smoking, a therapist may use **posthypnotic suggestion**. In this technique, the therapist gives instructions during hypnosis that are to be carried out after the hypnosis session has ended. Often, psychologists link the habit with something repulsive, something that would make the person feel ill or disgusted. Then whenever that person begins the habit, such as lighting up a cigarette, that sickening image appears in his or her mind. Sometimes hypnotists give more positive posthypnotic suggestions—for example, telling a person that he or she now has the willpower to resist sweets. But the effectiveness of hypnosis for helping people quit smoking is uncertain (Lancaster et al., 2000).

SECTION 3 REVIEW

1. Define *meditation*.
2. Explain how biofeedback works.
3. **Critical Thinking**   *Drawing Inferences and Conclusions*   Why do you think hypnosis is not used more often to relieve pain or help people change habits?

go.hrw.com
Homework Practice Online
Keyword: SY7 HP5

SECTION **4**

Drugs and Consciousness

A DAY IN THE LIFE

Linda recalled that Nick had started "spacing out" when he had a drug problem. Some drugs slow down the nervous system, while others spur it into rapid action. Some drugs, such as alcohol and nicotine (the drug found in tobacco), are believed to be connected with serious diseases. Many drugs are addictive. **Addiction** to a drug means that after a person takes that drug for a while, his or her body craves it just to feel normal. Alcohol, nicotine, and many other drugs are considered addictive.

Drugs also have a number of effects on consciousness. They may distort people's perceptions, change their moods, or cause them to see or hear things that are not real. Categories of drugs that affect consciousness include depressants, stimulants, and hallucinogens.

Depressants

Depressants are drugs that slow the activity of the nervous system. They generally give people a sense of relaxation but can have many negative effects. Depressant drugs include alcohol and narcotics.

Alcohol   Few drugs are as widely used in the United States as alcohol. Alcohol is a depressant. Small amounts of alcohol may have little effect, or they may be relaxing. High doses of alcohol can put a person to sleep. Too much alcohol can be lethal, either in the long term or the short term—people have died from drinking too much at one time.

Alcohol also intoxicates. **Intoxication** is another word for drunkenness. The root of the word *intoxication* is *toxic*, which means "poisonous." Intoxication slurs people's speech, blurs their vision, makes them clumsy, and makes it difficult for them to concentrate. They may bump into things or be unable to write. It also affects their judgment. In fact, they may not even realize that they are intoxicated. Therefore, they may try to do things that require a clear mind and good coordination, such as drive a car, when they are incapable of doing these things correctly. Alcohol is involved in more than half of all fatal automobile accidents in the United States.

These Civil War casualties may have been treated with morphine, a painkiller introduced during the war.

TRUTH OR fiction ■ REVISITED ■

It is not true that people who are drunk always know that they are drunk. Because intoxication impairs judgment, people who are drunk may believe that they can drive just as well as they can when they are sober.

Some drinkers do things they would not do if they were sober. Why? When intoxicated, people may be less able to focus on the consequences of their behavior. Alcohol can also bring feelings of elation that wash away inhibitions. Furthermore, it provides an excuse for behaviors that sober people know are unwise. Drinkers may place the blame for their behavior on the alcohol. But, of course, drinkers *choose* to drink. Thus, people remain responsible for actions taken while intoxicated.

Regardless of why people start drinking, regular consumption of alcohol can lead to addiction. Once people become addicted to alcohol, they may continue drinking to avoid withdrawal symptoms such as tension and trembling. Long-term heavy drinking has been linked to liver problems, heart problems, and cancer.

Narcotics   The word *narcotic* comes from the Greek *narke,* meaning "numbness" or "stupor." **Narcotics** are addictive depressants that have been used to relieve pain and induce sleep.

Many narcotics—such as morphine, heroin, and codeine—are derived from the opium poppy plant. Morphine is a narcotic that was introduced during the Civil War to deaden the pain from battle wounds. Therefore, addiction to morphine became known as "the soldier's disease."

Heroin, also introduced in the West in the 1800s, was hailed as the "hero" that would cure addiction to morphine. It was named heroin because it made people feel "heroic." This drug, which is now illegal, is a powerful narcotic that can give the user feelings of pleasure. However, coming off heroin can plunge the user into a deep depression. Furthermore, high doses impair judgment and memory and cause drowsiness and stupor. High doses of heroin can also depress the respiratory system so much that they lead to loss of consciousness, coma, and, in some cases, even death.

The use of heroin can also lead to death indirectly because it is often taken intravenously—that is, injected with a needle into a vein. Sometimes such needles are shared among users. If one user is infected with the virus that causes AIDS, needle sharing can infect other users as well.

People who are addicted to narcotics experience withdrawal symptoms when they try to stop using them. These withdrawal symptoms may include tremors, cramps, chills, rapid heartbeat, insomnia, vomiting, and diarrhea.

Stimulants

Stimulants, in contrast to depressants, increase the activity of the nervous system. They speed up the heart and breathing rate. Stimulants include nicotine, amphetamines, and cocaine.

Nicotine   Nicotine, the drug found in tobacco leaves, is one of the most common stimulants. The leaves are usually smoked in the form of cigarettes, cigars, and pipe tobacco. They can also be chewed, as in chewing tobacco.

Nicotine spurs the release of the hormone adrenaline, which causes the heart rate to increase. As a stimulant, nicotine may make people feel more alert and attentive, but research has shown that it does not improve the ability to perform complex tasks, such as solving difficult math problems.

Nicotine reduces the appetite and raises the rate at which the body changes food to energy. For these reasons, some smokers do not try to quit for fear that they will gain weight. But weight gain can be controlled by diet.

Through regular use, people can become addicted to nicotine. In fact, evidence suggests that cigarette smoking is as addictive as the use of heroin. People who stop smoking can experience symptoms such as nervousness, drowsiness, loss of energy, headaches, lightheadedness, insomnia, dizziness, cramps, heart palpitations, tremors, and sweating. Nonetheless, many people have successfully quit smoking.

Smoking has also been associated with serious health risks. All cigarette advertisements and packs sold in the United States carry a message such as:

"Warning: The Surgeon General Has Determined That Cigarette Smoking Is Dangerous to Your Health." Each year, more than 400,000 Americans die from smoking-related diseases. This is more than the number who die from motor-vehicle accidents, abuse of alcohol and all other drugs, suicide, homicide, and AIDS combined.

TRUTH OR **fiction** ▪ R E V I S I T E D ▪

It is true that smoking leads to more deaths in the United States than automobile accidents do. In fact, almost one out of every five deaths in the United States is caused by smoking. Lung cancer and heart disease are the most common smoking-related diseases.

Smokers are 12 to 20 times as likely as nonsmokers to die of lung cancer. Moreover, the substances in cigarette smoke have been shown to cause several other kinds of cancer in laboratory animals. Cigarette smoking is also linked to death from heart disease, chronic lung and respiratory diseases, and other illnesses. Pregnant women who smoke risk miscarriage, premature birth, and babies with birth defects. Perhaps due to the risks involved in smoking, the percentage of American adults who smoke has declined from more than 40 percent in the 1960s to less then 25 percent today.

Research indicates that secondhand smoke, the cigarette smoke exhaled by smokers, can even increase the health risk of nonsmokers who inhale it. Secondhand smoke is connected with lung cancer, breathing problems, and other illnesses. It accounts for thousands of deaths per year. Because of the effects of secondhand smoke, smoking has been banned from many public places, such as government buildings, airports, and restaurants.

Amphetamines   **Amphetamines** are another kind of stimulant. They are especially known for helping people stay awake and for reducing appetite. Amphetamines are made from the chemical alpha-methyl-beta-phenyl-ethyl-amine, which is a colorless liquid made up of carbon, hydrogen, and nitrogen.

Amphetamines were first used by soldiers during World War II to help them remain awake and alert during the night. Sometimes called "speed" or "uppers," amphetamines can produce feelings of pleasure, especially in high doses.

EXPLORING
DIVERSITY

Multicultural Perspectives on Consciousness

Visions, dreams, meditation, and hallucinations are important parts of many cultures, reflecting the human desire to reach beyond what the senses can directly perceive. The methods for reaching these altered states of consciousness, however, are as diverse as the people who inhabit this planet.

The Aborigines of Australia believe that there are two worlds: the ordinary, physical world and another world called Dreamtime. Ritual songs, dances, stories, and dreams create the Dreamtime world. Frans Hoogland, a Dutchman who lived for 15 years among the Aborigines, described the process: "We start with nothing—a total emptiness—a void. Then we have some singing and dancing. . . . [T]he singing creates the sound and the vibration forms a shape; and the dancing helps solidify it. . . . The process, the Dreaming itself, becomes a reality" (Maybury-Lewis, 1992, pp. 197–202). For the Aborigines, dream and actuality are just different states of the same consciousness.

The Mevlevi, a Muslim sect in Turkey, also use dancing to create an altered state of consciousness. The Mevlevi are known as whirling dervishes because they whirl around until they are in a trance. This trance, they believe, brings them closer to Allah, or God.

Some religions use meditation to achieve an altered state of consciousness. According to the yoga school, a part of Hinduism, every human being consists of two parts. The first is a person's body, mind, and conscious self. The second part is the soul—pure empty consciousness. The yoga school uses certain exercises, including bodily postures, control of breathing, and meditations, to help teach people understanding of their soul.

Accompanied by music, whirling dervishes spin around until they are in a trance.

The followers of Buddhism meditate to achieve a state of enlightenment called *nirvana.* Buddhists believe that nirvana can be achieved through control of the mind, or mental discipline. Certain yoga techniques help followers achieve this control.

People in some cultures use drugs to produce a religious trance. The Inca in the Andean highlands of South America use a drug called yage while a shaman, or holy man, watches them. Once past an initial drug-induced nausea, they begin to hallucinate. The hallucinations range from pleasurable to terrifying. The Inca will endure even the terrifying visions because they believe that terror is something that needs to be overcome in order to gain knowledge, look into the future, and communicate with the spirit world.

The Huichol Indians in central Mexico make a sacred pilgrimage to a place hundreds of miles from their homes. Once they arrive, they fast, pray, dance, and chant. The next day, they hunt for peyote, a strong stimulant that comes from a cactus plant. They then sit with their shaman-priest, talk, eat peyote, and begin to hallucinate. They believe that the hallucinations help them achieve a state of fusion with their ancestors and the universe. The shaman must always be present to help them return from the experience. Many fear that if they stay too long "in paradise," their souls will be lost forever.

Think About It

Analyzing Information In some cultures, people view altered states of consciousness as something to be avoided whenever possible, not something to be sought out. Why do you think some people feel this way?

Various advertising campaigns have helped make people more aware of the dangers of drugs. Posters such as this one encourage people to refuse drugs and enjoy life without them.

Amphetamines can be taken in the form of pills. They can also be injected directly into the veins in the form of liquid methedrine, the strongest form of the drug. People who take large doses of amphetamines may stay awake and "high" for days. Such highs must come to an end, however. People who have been on prolonged highs usually "crash." That is, they fall into a deep sleep or depression. Some people even commit suicide when crashing. Nick's spaced-out, inattentive behavior may have been the result of his coming down from an amphetamine high.

High doses of amphetamines can cause restlessness, insomnia, loss of appetite, and irritability. They also affect consciousness. For example, people who have taken amphetamines sometimes experience frightening hallucinations. A **hallucination** is a perception of an object or a sound that seems real but is not. One hallucination that people under the influence of amphetamines commonly experience is that bugs are crawling all over them.

Use of amphetamines can also cause the user to have delusions. A **delusion** is a false idea that seems real. If you thought you could fly (without the aid of an airplane), that would be a delusion. Overdoses of amphetamines are sometimes connected with delusions of being in danger or of being chased by someone or something.

Cocaine   Cocaine is a stimulant derived from the leaves of the coca plant, which grows in the tropics of South America. Cocaine produces feelings of pleasure, reduces hunger, deadens pain, and boosts

self-confidence. Because cocaine raises blood pressure and decreases the supply of oxygen to the heart while speeding up the heart rate, it can sometimes lead to death.

Cocaine has been used as a painkiller since the early 1800s. It came to the attention of Sigmund Freud in 1884. Freud, then a young neurologist, first used the drug to overcome depression. He even published an article on cocaine called "Song of Praise." But Freud's excitement about cocaine's healing powers was soon cooled by his awareness that the drug was dangerous and addictive.

Overdoses of cocaine can cause symptoms including restlessness, insomnia, trembling, headaches, nausea, convulsions, hallucinations, and delusions. A particularly harmful form of cocaine is known as crack. Crack is very powerful. However, crack is impure, and therefore it is even more dangerous than other forms of cocaine. Because of the strain crack and other forms of cocaine can put on the heart, overdoses of these drugs are sometimes fatal.

Hallucinogens

A **hallucinogen** is a drug that produces hallucinations. In addition, hallucinogens may cause relaxation or feelings of pleasure. However, hallucinogens can also cause feelings of panic. Marijuana and LSD are examples of hallucinogens.

Marijuana   Marijuana is a hallucinogenic drug produced from the leaves of the *cannabis sativa* plant, which grows wild in many parts of the world. Marijuana may produce feelings of relaxation and mild hallucinations. Hashish, or "hash," comes from the sticky part of the plant. Hashish has stronger effects than marijuana.

Marijuana impairs perception and coordination, making it difficult to operate machines, including cars. It also impairs memory and learning. In addition, marijuana can cause anxiety and confusion. It increases the heart rate up to 140 to 150 beats per minute and in some people raises blood pressure. These effects thus pose a particular threat to people with high blood pressure or heart problems.

One hundred years ago, marijuana was used by some people almost the way aspirin is used today—to treat headaches and other minor aches and pains. It could be bought without a prescription in any drugstore. Because it carries a number of health risks, marijuana use and possession are now illegal in most states.

Marijuana has distinct effects on consciousness. People who are very intoxicated with marijuana may think time is passing more slowly than usual. A song might seem to last an hour rather than a few minutes. Some people experience increased consciousness of bodily sensations such as heartbeat. Experiencing visual hallucinations is also fairly common while under the influence of marijuana.

Strong intoxication gives some marijuana smokers frightening experiences. Sometimes marijuana smokers become confused and lose their sense of self—their consciousness of who and where they are. Some fear they will lose themselves forever. Consciousness of a rapid heart rate leads others to fear that their hearts will "run away."

LSD Lysergic acid diethylamide (LSD) is a hallucinogen. LSD is sometimes simply called acid. It is much stronger than marijuana and can produce intense hallucinations. Some of these hallucinations can be quite bizarre. Users of LSD claim that it expands consciousness and "opens new worlds." Sometimes people are convinced that they have achieved great insights while using LSD. But when its effects wear off, they often are unable to recall or use these "discoveries."

LSD's effects are not predictable. Some LSD experiences are so frightening that the users, in a state of panic and confusion, injure themselves seriously or even commit suicide. In addition, some users of LSD experience lasting side effects. These side effects include memory loss, violent outbursts, nightmares, and feelings of panic.

Another long-term effect of LSD use is the experience of flashbacks. Flashbacks are hallucinations that happen weeks, months, or even years after the LSD was used. Some psychologists believe that flashbacks stem from LSD-induced chemical changes in the brain.

Treatments for Drug Abuse

Treatment for drug abuse varies, depending on the drug abused. Forms of treatment include detoxification, maintenance programs, and therapy. Some people also join support groups.

Detoxification One form of treatment for drug abuse is detoxification. **Detoxification**, the removal of the harmful substance from the body, is a way of weaning addicts from the drug while restoring their health. This treatment is most commonly used with people addicted to alcohol and narcotics.

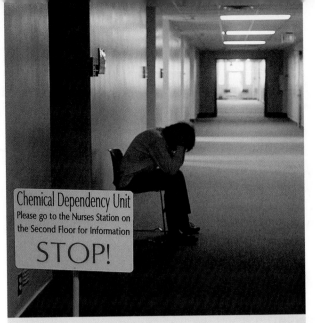

Many hospitals have chemical dependency units to help treat drug abusers.

Maintenance Programs Maintenance programs are sometimes used for people addicted to narcotics. Participants in these programs are given controlled and less dangerous amounts of the drug or some less addictive substitute. This treatment is very controversial because the users never actually become completely free of drugs.

Counseling Counseling can be conducted either individually or in a group. Both individual and group methods are used for treating stimulant and depressant abuse.

Support Groups Support groups usually consist of several people who share common experiences, concerns, or problems. These individuals meet in a group setting to provide one another with emotional and moral support. Alcoholics Anonymous is an example of a support group that encourages members to live without drugs—in this case, alcohol—for the rest of their lives.

SECTION 4 REVIEW

go.hrw.com
Homework Practice Online
Keyword: SY7 HP5

1. Describe the effects of depressants, stimulants, and hallucinogens on consciousness. Give examples of each type of drug.

2. **Critical Thinking** *Evaluating* Do you think people use drugs to heighten consciousness or to escape from it? Explain your answer.

Writing a Summary

Using standard grammar, spelling, sentence structure, and punctuation, summarize the information in this chapter. Consider:
- the nature of consciousness, the stages of sleep and possible sleep problems
- the effects of meditation, biofeedback, hypnosis, and drugs on consciousness

Identifying People and Ideas

Identify the following terms or people and use them in appropriate sentences.

1. consciousness
2. altered state of consciousness
3. rapid-eye-movement sleep
4. insomnia
5. sleep apnea
6. meditation
7. biofeedback
8. depressant
9. stimulant
10. detoxification

Understanding Main Ideas

SECTION 1 (pp. 104–106)
1. What does it mean to say that consciousness is a construct?

SECTION 2 (pp. 106–112)
2. What are circadian rhythms, and how do they influence human behavior?
3. What are the five stages of sleep? What brain-wave patterns occur in each stage?

SECTION 3 (pp. 112–116)
4. In what way is biofeedback training useful?

SECTION 4 (pp. 116–121)
5. Describe one of the three major groups of drugs, including their effects and problems.

Thinking Critically

1. **Comparing and Contrasting** How are REM and NREM sleep similar and different?

2. **Drawing Inferences and Conclusions** Why do you think many people use medication to try to overcome insomnia? Why might medication not be an effective cure?

3. **Evaluating** Identify the pros and cons of using biofeedback instead of medication to reduce high blood pressure.

4. **Analyzing Information** Why might some people drink or use other drugs even though they know that the drugs can be harmful?

Writing About Psychology

1. **Making Generalizations and Predictions** Design, but do not actually do, an experiment or survey to study the effects that altered states of consciousness have on sensation and perception. Begin by writing down a question. For example, you might ask, "How do people perceive pain when they are dreaming?" After you have prepared a question, form a hypothesis about the answer to the question. Write a paragraph explaining your hypothesis, then write another paragraph analyzing what results would indicate that your hypothesis was correct.

2. **Summarizing** Create an outline describing the four levels of consciousness. Then, using your outline, write a summary of what you have learned. Use the graphic organizer below to help you with your summary.

Consciousness

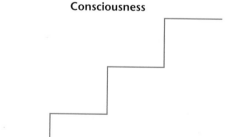

Interpreting Graphs

Study the graph below. Then use the information in the graph to help you answer the questions that follow.

Time Spent Sleeping

Source: Carskadon, *Encyclopedia of Sleep and Dreaming*, 1993

1. How many minutes do most people spend sleeping per night?

  a. less than 300

  b. 420–479

  c. 480–539

  d. more than 600

2. What statement can be made about people who get less than 300 minutes of sleep and people who get more than 600 minutes of sleep?

Analyzing Primary Sources

Read the following excerpt, in which E. Thomas Dowd provides some warnings about selecting a hypnotherapist. Then answer the questions that follow.

❝One should be wary of hypnotists with no formal training in medical, psychological, or other established professions who claim to be able to cure such entrenched [long-term] habits as overeating and smoking in one or two sessions. Such individuals prey on the universal human desire for quick and easy relief from their distress, relief that involves little or no effort on the part of the hypnotized. They take advantage of the common misconception [misunderstanding] that hypnosis is somehow magic in its effects. It takes little time and effort to teach someone how to enter, or help others to enter, a hypnotic trance, but considerably more training and experience to know how to use trance behavior effectively and appropriately.❞

3. Which of the following statements best reflects Dowd's attitudes toward many hypnotists.

  a. Patients seeking assistance should never be hypnotized.

  b. All hypnotists are fakes.

  c. Professionals with proper training can use hypnosis to help patients.

  d. Hypnosis can cure bad habits such as smoking with little effort.

4. According to the excerpt, how does popular misunderstanding of hypnosis lead to misuse of the technique?

PSYCHOLOGY PROJECTS

Cooperative Learning

Creating a Case Study Imagine that a friend tells you the following dream: He is sunbathing on a beach with a friend. Suddenly, other people on the beach begin screaming, and he sees a huge tidal wave. Before he can run, he feels himself being swept away. Working in groups, use the Freudian and biopsychological theories about dream interpretation to analyze the dream. Then write a summary, comparing the interpretations suggested by each approach. Finally, share the analysis with the class.

🗷 **internet** connect

Internet Activity: go.hrw.com
KEYWORD: SY7 CH5

Choose an activity on consciousness to:
- make a drawing that illustrates the levels and meanings of consciousness.
- create a multimedia display on sleep patterns and dreaming.
- write a research paper on altered states of consciousness.

PSYCHOLOGY IN ACTION

YOU SOLVE THE PROBLEM . . .

How can a psychologist help a client with a sleep disorder?

Complete the following activity in small groups. Imagine that a psychologist has asked your group for advice on helping a client with insomnia. She has asked for a report outlining the best way for her to treat the client.

1. Gather Information. Use your textbook and other resources to find information that might influence your plan of action for preparing the report. Remember that your report must include information that will convince the psychologist that your suggested method should be used. This information might include charts and graphs to show the psychologist which treatment method is most effective. You may want to divide up different parts of the research among group members.

2. List and Consider Options. After reviewing the information you gathered, list and consider the options you might use to help the psychologist choose how to treat her patient. Your final solution to the problem may be easier to reach if you consider as many options as possible. Be sure to record all your options for the preparation of your report.

3. Consider Advantages and Disadvantages. Now consider the advantages and disadvantages of choosing each option. Ask yourselves questions such as,

- What seems to be causing the client's insomnia?
- Is the client taking any medication that might affect his sleeping patterns?

Once you have considered the advantages and disadvantages, record them as notes for use in preparing your report.

4. Choose and Implement a Solution. After considering the advantages and disadvantages, you should choose a solution. Next, plan and create a report that describes how your solution will be implemented. Be sure to make the solution you have chosen very clear.

5. Evaluate the Effectiveness of the Solution. Once you have prepared your report, write a paragraph evaluating how effective your recommendation will be for the psychologist. Explain why you believe that your solution will be more effective than other possible solutions you considered. When you are ready, decide which group members will present which parts of the report. Then take your report to the psychologist (the rest of the class). Good luck!

UNIT 3
LEARNING AND COGNITION

6 Chapter

LEARNING

A DAY IN THE LIFE

Linda, Marc, Dan, and Janet were in the library studying after school. "I don't feel like studying," Marc complained. "Let's shoot some hoops instead."

"Come on," Linda protested. "It's interesting stuff—it's all about how people learn. And don't you want to get a good grade on Thursday's psychology test?"

"Yeah, I suppose," Marc said, playing with his pencil. "But why do we even care about grades anyway? I mean, they're just letters. They don't really *mean* anything."

"Try saying that to the college admissions officers or at a job interview," chimed in Janet. "Even though a grade doesn't mean anything by itself, it means a lot in terms of what it can get you."

"And don't forget the district's new rule—you *have* to get at least a C in order to be on a sports team. Marc, the soccer team can't afford to lose you this year—you *have* to do well in the class," Dan pleaded.

"But what happens if I study a lot and *still* don't do well on the test? That's what happened to me last week on that test in Ms. Kramer's class. I studied for *hours* the night before, and I *still* only got a C on the test. So what's the point in studying if it's not going to help anyway?" asked Marc gloomily.

"There's more to good studying than just memorizing," Linda pointed out. "Hey, why don't we all study together? We can review the chapter and quiz one another. And when we're finished, we can do something fun. Any suggestions?"

Dan made a face. "Anything that doesn't involve eating ice cream. I ate a whole half-gallon of ice cream Monday night, and now the thought of it makes me sick."

"I wasn't thinking about food anyway. How about Marc's idea of playing basketball? Or maybe we could go to a movie," suggested Linda. "But we can't go until we really know the chapter."

"If I knew I'd get to do something fun every time I studied, maybe I'd study more often," Dan reflected thoughtfully.

. . .

Marc, Linda, and the others were studying material about learning. When you hear the word *learning*, you probably think of school—of listening to teachers and studying and taking tests. But people are learning all the time.

Learning is achieved through experience. Anything we are born knowing how to do is not a result of learning. For example, babies do not learn to cry. But people do need experience to learn how to walk, how to speak the languages of their parents and communities, and how to read. The experiences through which we learn all of these things, however, can vary. Sometimes we learn to do things by trying them ourselves; at other times, we learn by watching others or by reading books. This chapter explores several types of learning and the processes involved in each type.

Key Terms

- stimulus
- response
- conditioning
- classical conditioning
- unconditioned stimulus
- unconditioned response
- conditioned response
- conditioned stimulus
- taste aversion
- extinction
- spontaneous recovery
- generalization
- discrimination
- flooding
- systematic desensitization
- counterconditioning
- operant conditioning
- reinforcement
- primary reinforcers
- secondary reinforcers
- positive reinforcers
- negative reinforcers
- schedule of reinforcement
- continuous reinforcement
- partial reinforcement
- shaping
- latent learning
- observational learning

HOLT

Psychology Video Program

Watch the video to explore how dogs learn.

SECTION 1

Classical Conditioning

A DAY IN THE LIFE Presumably, Linda and her friends were hoping to get a good grade on the psychology test they were studying for. But Marc wanted to know why grades mattered, and it was a good question. After all, people are not born with instinctive attitudes regarding the letters used for grades, such as A and F. So why do most students like As and try to avoid Fs?

As Janet and Dan pointed out by mentioning the relationship between grades and college, jobs, and participation in team sports, grades have meaning because they are associated with other things. Most of us are familiar with this concept of association. Have you ever been listening to the radio and heard a song that was popular a few years ago—maybe a song that you really liked back then? Did you feel a rush of the sensations that you used to feel back when the song was popular?

If so, this reaction was probably a result of associations between the song and the events of the time in your life when the song was popular. In other words, the song served as a stimulus. A **stimulus** is something that produces a reaction, or a **response**, from a person or an animal. In this case, the response consisted of the feelings brought about by hearing the song.

Here is a simple experiment that also demonstrates associations. Think of a food you really like, such as lasagna or enchiladas. Is your mouth watering? If it is, you are experiencing the results of **conditioning**, or learning. Conditioning works through the pairing of different stimuli. In particular, your reaction demonstrates a type of conditioning known as classical conditioning. **Classical conditioning** is a simple form of learning in which one stimulus (in this case, the thought of the food) calls forth the response (your mouth watering) that is usually called forth by another stimulus (the actual food). This occurs when the two stimuli have been associated with each other.

Ivan Pavlov Rings a Bell

Some of the earliest findings about classical conditioning resulted from research somewhat similar to your own experiences in thinking of food. However, that early research was with dogs, not people. Russian physiologist Ivan Pavlov (1849–1936) discovered that dogs, too, learn to associate one thing with another when food is involved.

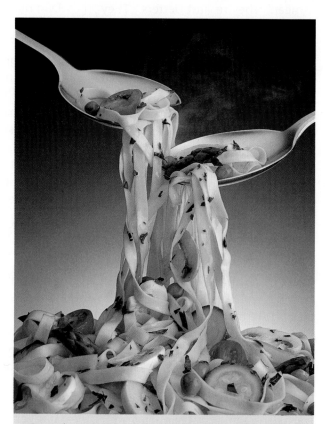

Does the sight of this pasta make your mouth water? If so, the reaction is a result of classical conditioning.

FIGURE 6.1 *Pavlov strapped dogs into harnesses and collected their saliva in a tube. After several pairings of a bell and meat powder, the dogs learned to salivate at the sound of the bell by itself.*

Pavlov did not set out to learn about learning. Rather, he was interested in the relationship between the nervous system and digestion. In particular, Pavlov was studying salivation, or mouth-watering, in dogs. He knew that dogs would salivate if meat was placed on their tongues because saliva aids in the eating and digestion of the meat. In other words, meat on the tongue is a stimulus for the production of saliva.

But Pavlov discovered that the dogs did not always wait until they had received meat to start salivating. For example, they salivated in response to the clinking of food trays. The dogs would also salivate when Pavlov's assistants entered the laboratory. Why? Because the dogs had learned from experience that these events—the clinking of the trays, the arrival of the assistants—meant that food was coming.

At first, Pavlov viewed the dogs' unwanted salivation as a nuisance because it was getting in the way of what he was trying to study. But soon he decided that the "problem" was worth looking into. If the dogs could learn to salivate in response to the clinking of food trays because this clinking was associated with the bringing of meat, could they learn to salivate in response to any stimulus that signaled meat? Pavlov predicted that they could. He set out to show that he could train his dogs to salivate in response to any stimulus he chose.

The stimulus Pavlov chose was the ringing of a bell. He strapped the dogs into harnesses and rang a bell. (See Figure 6.1.) Then about half a second after the bell rang, meat powder was placed on the dogs' tongues. As expected, the dogs salivated in response to the meat powder. Pavlov repeated this process several times.

After several pairings of the meat and the bell, however, Pavlov changed the procedure: he sounded the bell but did not follow the bell with the meat. Yet the dogs salivated anyway—they had learned to salivate in response to the bell alone.

US, UR, CR, and CS: Letters of Learning

The dogs' salivation in response to the bell demonstrates classical conditioning. Terms that are important in understanding classical conditioning include *unconditioned stimulus, unconditioned response, conditioned response,* and *conditioned stimulus.*

The meat in Pavlov's research was an example of an unconditioned stimulus. An **unconditioned stimulus** (US) is a stimulus that causes a response that is automatic, not learned. That automatic response, in turn, is called an **unconditioned response** (UR). Salivation in response to the meat was an unconditioned response. In other words, the dogs did not *learn* to salivate in response to the meat—they did so naturally, by instinct, because of their biology.

The dogs' salivation in response to the bell was a conditioned response. A **conditioned response** (CR) is a learned response to a stimulus that was previously neutral, or meaningless. In Pavlov's research, the bell was a neutral stimulus. That is, before Pavlov associated it with the meat, it might have made the dogs' ears perk up, but it would not have made the dogs salivate because it had nothing to do with food. Through repeated association with meat, however, the bell became a learned stimulus, or a **conditioned stimulus** (CS), for the response of salivation.

A conditioned response is often the same as or very similar to an unconditioned response. With Pavlov's dogs, for example, salivation in response to the meat was the UR. But salivation in response to the bell was the CR. In other words, salivation was both the UR and the CR. (See Figure 6.2.)

Adapting to the Environment

Classical conditioning helps organisms adapt to their surrounding environment. For example, just as Pavlov's dogs learned that the bell signaled meat, a person's pet dog may learn that the sound of a can opener (CS) means that dog food (US) will soon appear in the dog's bowl. Thus, the dog comes running to the bowl (CR).

Sometimes classical conditioning helps animals and people avoid or deal with danger. For example, a bear cub may learn to associate a particular scent (CS) with the appearance of a dangerous animal (US). The cub can then hide or run away (CR) when it catches the scent. Or a new car owner may hear his or her car alarm go off (CS). Thinking that someone is breaking into the car (US), the car owner calls the police (CR).

Taste Aversions   One form of classical conditioning that can be particularly useful to people is called a taste aversion. A **taste aversion** is a learned avoidance of a particular food. Have you ever eaten a food that made you ill, perhaps because it was spoiled? Did you then stay away from that food for a long time? If so, you had probably developed a taste aversion to it.

Often when foods make us ill, it is because they are unhealthy, even poisonous. A taste aversion helps us avoid these foods by keeping us away from

FIGURE 6.2   *Before conditioning, food (US) elicits salivation (UR). The bell (a neutral stimulus at first) elicits no response. Then, during conditioning, the bell precedes the food. After several repetitions, the bell (now a CS) elicits salivation (CR).* **What do US, UR, CS, and CR stand for?**

© 1995 Grimmy Inc. Distributed by Tribune Media Services. Reprinted with permission.

A DAY IN THE LIFE

them. Psychologists would call Dan's response to eating a half-gallon of ice cream all at one time a taste aversion. Dan had felt nauseated after eating so much ice cream. Ice cream was the unconditioned stimulus (US) that had caused the unconditioned response (UR) of nausea. As a result of his one experience, even the thought of ice cream served as a conditioned stimulus (CS) that made him feel nauseated (CR). The taste aversion was strong. Even though Dan knew that he could probably eat smaller amounts of ice cream safely, the thought of any ice cream at all made him feel ill.

It is useful for people and animals to develop taste aversions readily. With other examples of classical conditioning, an association must be made several times before the conditioned response occurs. Pavlov had to pair the bell with meat several times before the dogs would begin to salivate at the sound of the bell. In taste aversions, however, just one pairing of food and illness may be all that is necessary to create the aversion.

- - - - - - - -

TRUTH
OR
fiction
■ R E V I S I T E D ■

It is true that becoming sick from eating a certain food can be a genuine learning experience. Avoidance of a food that once caused illness is called a taste aversion. Taste aversions are a result of classical conditioning.

- - - - - - - -

Extinction Classical conditioning helps people and animals adapt to their environments. But things can change, and what once was dangerous may no longer be so. What threatens a bear cub may lose its menace once the bear matures. Or the signal for

danger may lose its meaning. A car alarm may be set off so often by accident (such as by a harmless gust of wind) that the car owner no longer rushes to call the police.

When a conditioned stimulus (such as the scent of an animal or a car alarm) is no longer followed by an unconditioned stimulus (a dangerous animal, the car being broken into), it will eventually lose its ability to bring about a conditioned response. In classical conditioning, this is called **extinction**. Extinction occurs when the conditioned stimulus

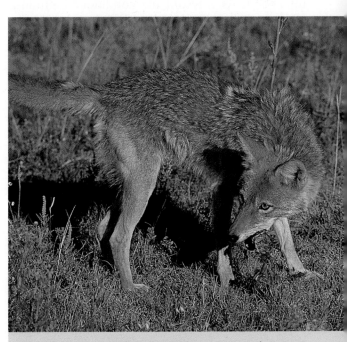

Researchers used classical conditioning to teach coyotes not to eat sheep by feeding them poisoned lamb meat. Because the poisoned meat made the coyotes sick, they developed a taste aversion to the lamb. Thus, they no longer attacked the livestock, solving an economic problem for many ranchers.

Key Concepts in Classical Conditioning

	Procedure	Result
Classical Conditioning	Before conditioning is begun, an unconditioned stimulus (US) such as meat brings forth an unconditioned response (UR) such as salivation. During conditioning, a neutral stimulus such as a bell is paired with the unconditioned stimulus (US).	The neutral stimulus becomes a conditioned stimulus (CS). The CS (bell) brings forth the CR (salivation).
Example	A child waits for her parents to come home. She hears a car drive up (neutral stimulus). Then her parents come inside (US). She becomes excited (UR) when she sees her parents come in.	After a few repetitions in which hearing the car is followed by her parents' coming in, she becomes excited (CR) when she hears the car drive up (CS).
Related Concepts	Taste aversion, extinction, spontaneous recovery, generalization, discrimination	

FIGURE 6.3 *The more times the unconditioned stimulus is paired with the neutral stimulus, the stronger the neutral stimulus (now the CS) becomes.* **What happens** **when the conditioned stimulus is presented repeatedly without the unconditioned stimulus?**

(CS) is disconnected from the unconditioned stimulus (US). As a result, the conditioned stimulus (CS) no longer causes the conditioned response (CR) to occur.

Pavlov found that with repeated ringing of the bell (CS) not followed by meat (US), the dogs eventually stopped salivating (CR) when they heard the bell (CS). The dogs had learned that the bell no longer meant that food was on the way. The conditioned response of salivating at the sound of the bell had been extinguished.

Spontaneous Recovery An extinguished response is not necessarily gone forever. In what psychologists have termed **spontaneous recovery**, organisms sometimes display responses that were extinguished earlier. This revival of the response follows a period in which the conditioned stimulus was not presented. For example, after the response of salivating at the sound of the bell had been extinguished in Pavlov's dogs, a day or two passed during which the dogs did not hear the bell at all. After this rest period, the bell was rung again. Even though the salivation response had earlier been extinguished, it was now back. It was, however, a little weaker than it had been when it was in full force—the dogs produced less saliva.

Think again of the song that brought back old feelings. If the song were again to become popular and you started hearing it every day, you probably would no longer experience the same rush of feelings after hearing it over and over. After all, your life has changed now, and when the song is continually played without actually transporting you into the past, it loses the ability to spark those old feelings—the response has undergone extinction. But if a month passes without your hearing the song at all, the next time you hear it, those old feelings may well return. In other words, they will have been spontaneously recovered.

Generalization and Discrimination Dan's half-gallon of ice cream was probably all one flavor, perhaps chocolate. But Dan did not say, "I can eat any flavor of ice cream except chocolate." Rather, he wanted to avoid ice cream of all flavors. This is called generalization. **Generalization** is the act of responding in the same ways to stimuli that seem to be similar, even if the stimuli are not identical.

In a demonstration of generalization, Pavlov first conditioned a dog to salivate when it was shown a circle. On several occasions, the dog was shown a circle (the CS), then given meat (the US). After several pairings, the dog salivated when presented with only the circle. Pavlov demonstrated that the dog would also salivate in response to the sight of many other geometric figures, including ellipses, pentagons, and squares. The more closely the figure resembled a circle, the greater the strength of the response (the more drops of saliva that flowed).

The dog's weaker response to figures that looked less like a circle was an example of discrimination. **Discrimination** is the act of responding differently to stimuli that are not similar to each other. Dan did not want to eat ice cream, but he probably would not have objected to eating other types of food—such as, chocolate pudding. This is because ice cream and pudding are sufficiently different that Dan was able to discriminate them from each other.

Both generalization and discrimination help people and animals adapt to their environments. For example, a bear cub who has a bad experience with a wolf may generalize from that experience that all big furry animals that growl (other than adult bears) should be avoided. On the other hand, the bear cub probably discriminates between the wolf and a mouse. The mouse might be furry, but it is not big and does not growl. Thus, the mouse is not a danger. A child who has been frightened by a dog may generalize and stay away from all dogs. But because of discrimination, the child continues to play with his or her stuffed animals, even the ones that look like dogs.

Applications of Classical Conditioning

Classical conditioning is the means by which stimuli come to serve as signals for other stimuli. It is a major avenue of learning in our daily lives. It also can be used to solve specific problems that people have. For example, classical conditioning can help people overcome their fears of various objects and situations. It can even help children stop wetting their beds.

Flooding and Systematic Desensitization
Many fears—such as fear of heights, of snakes, and of speaking in front of the class—are out of proportion to the harm that could happen. Some people fear looking out of windows in tall buildings, even though they cannot fall. Many people fear snakes, even snakes that are small and nonpoisonous.

Two methods for reducing such fears are based on the principle of extinction. In the method called **flooding**, a person is exposed to the harmless stimulus until fear responses to that stimulus are

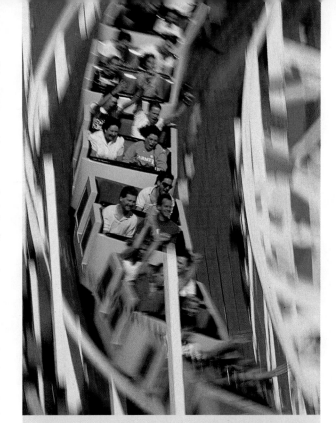

People on a roller coaster discriminate between the real danger of an automobile careening out of control and the ride in an amusement park.

extinguished. A person with a fear of heights might look out from a sixth-story window until she or he is no longer upset by it. A person with a fear of snakes might be put in a room with lots of harmless snakes crawling around in the room.

TRUTH
OR
fiction
■ REVISITED ■

It is true that if you are afraid of snakes, it may help to surround yourself with them. This is a method of therapy called flooding. In flooding, an application of classical conditioning, a person is exposed to a fear-provoking but harmless stimulus until the fear is extinguished.

Although flooding is usually effective, it tends to be quite unpleasant. When people fear something, forced exposure to it is the last thing they want. For this reason, psychologists usually prefer to use **systematic desensitization** to help people overcome their fears. In this method, people are taught relaxation techniques. Then they are exposed gradually to whatever stimulus they fear while they

CASE STUDIES
AND OTHER TRUE STORIES
The Story of Little Albert

In 1920, psychologists John B. Watson and Rosalie Rayner published an article describing an experiment they had done with an infant named Albert. The experiment had such an impact on the field of psychology that the boy became known as "Little Albert" and the story of the experiment became a classic. Even today, psychologists and psychology students are still familiar with it.

What was the experiment? It was a very small but very significant demonstration that emotional reactions such as fears can be acquired through principles of classical conditioning.

Albert was the 11-month-old son of one of Watson's and Rayner's acquaintances. Watson and Rayner observed that Albert did not become easily frightened. They also observed that he had a white laboratory rat for a playmate. To demonstrate that fears can be learned through associations, Watson and Rayner decided to see if they could condition Albert to fear the white rat rather than be amused by it. All they had to do, they reasoned, was pair the rat with something that Albert would find frightening.

What does an 11-month-old instinctively find frightening? Loud, harsh noises—such as the clanging of steel bars. Every time Albert played with the rat, Watson clanged steel bars behind the infant. Sure enough, after seven pairings, Albert showed fear of the rat even when there was no more clanging. The rat had at first brought pleasure to Little Albert. Now, through no fault of its own, it had become a source of fear and trembling. Through association, the animal had taken on the meaning of the jangling, jarring steel bars to Little Albert.

In the terms used in classical conditioning, the clanging of the steel bars was the unconditioned stimulus (US) that led to the unconditioned

Why do children fear some objects but not others?

response (UR) of fear. The rat was the conditioned stimulus (CS) that, through association with the clanging of the bars, also led Albert to feel fear—now the conditioned response (CR).

Little Albert's newfound fear, however, did not stop with the innocent rat. It spread, or generalized, to objects similar in appearance to the rat, such as a rabbit and a fur coat. Because of his experiences with the rat and the steel bars, Albert learned to fear other objects that were white and furry.

Unfortunately, Watson and Rayner never had the chance to help Little Albert overcome his conditioned fear of rats. Therefore, his fear may never have become extinguished. Somewhere out there may be an older man who cringes at the sight not only of rats but also of little girls wearing fluffy sweaters, of small dogs, or maybe even of Santa Claus's beard. Moreover, because the conditioning was carried out at such a tender age, Little Albert—now Big Albert?—may have no idea why he fears these things. He would not remember the original experience.

Was it ethical for Watson and Rayner to experiment on such a small child—especially when the experiment involved repeatedly frightening him and teaching him to fear something that had previously given him pleasure? Today most psychologists would say no, it was not ethical. For this reason, this experiment would never be duplicated today. Psychologists would have to find some other way of demonstrating their theories.

THINKING CRITICALLY

1. **Explaining** How did Watson and Rayner condition Little Albert to fear white rats?
2. **Drawing Inferences and Conclusions** Why do you think most psychologists today consider Watson and Raynor's experiment to be unethical?

remain relaxed. For example, people who fear snakes are shown pictures of snakes while they are relaxed. Once they can view pictures of snakes without losing the feeling of relaxation, they are shown some real snakes from a distance. Then, after some more time, the snakes are brought closer, and eventually the people no longer fear snakes. Systematic desensitization takes longer to work than flooding, but it is not as unpleasant.

Counterconditioning Can cookies help children overcome their fears? Perhaps. Early in this century, University of California professors Mary Cover Jones (1924) and Harold Jones reasoned that if fears could be conditioned by painful experiences, perhaps fears could be counterconditioned by pleasant experiences. In **counterconditioning**, a pleasant stimulus is paired repeatedly with a fearful one, counteracting the fear.

The Joneses tried out their idea with a two-year-old boy named Peter, who feared rabbits. The Joneses gradually brought a rabbit closer to Peter while they fed Peter candy and cookies. Peter seemed nervous about the rabbit, but he continued to eat his treat. Gradually, the animal was brought even closer. Eventually, Peter ate treats and petted the rabbit at the same time. Apparently, his pleasure at eating the sweets canceled out his fear of the rabbit. Dentists might caution against overusing this "cookie treatment," however. While it might help children overcome their fears, it might also give them cavities.

The Bell-and-Pad Method for Bed-Wetting
By the time children are five or six years old, most of them wake up when their bladders are full. They stop themselves from urinating, which is an automatic response to bladder tension, and go to the bathroom. But some children do not respond to sensations of a full bladder when they are asleep. They remain asleep and often wet their beds.

To help children stop wetting their beds, psychologists came up with the bell-and-pad method. This method teaches children to wake up in response to bladder tension. A child with a bed-wetting tendency sleeps on a special pad placed on his or her bed. When the child starts to urinate, the water content of the urine triggers a bell, and the ringing wakes the child up.

Unlike the case in Pavlov's experiments with the dogs, in which the bell was a conditioned stimulus, the bell in the bell-and-pad method is an unconditioned stimulus (US). That is, it wakes up the child because of the child's biological makeup; people instinctively wake up when they hear loud noises. Waking up to the bell is the unconditioned response (UR).

Because of repeated pairings, a stimulus that precedes the bell becomes associated with the bell. It also gains the capacity to wake up the child. What is this stimulus? It is the sensation of a full bladder. In this way, bladder tension is the conditioned stimulus (CS) that comes to wake up the child even though the child is asleep during the classical conditioning procedure. Waking up in response to bladder tension is the conditioned response (CR).

After a couple of weeks of using the bell-and-pad method, most children no longer wet their beds. Similar methods have been used to aid in the toilet training of children.

SECTION 1 REVIEW

go.hrw.com
Homework Practice Online
Keyword: SY7 HP6

1. Explain the principles of classical conditioning by describing Pavlov's classic experiment with dogs using the following terms: *unconditioned stimulus, unconditioned response, conditioned response, conditioned stimulus.*

2. Explain what is meant by extinction, spontaneous recovery, generalization, and discrimination in classical conditioning.

3. **Critical Thinking** *Drawing Inferences and Conclusions* Describe and explain learning as an adaptation to the environment.

SECTION 2
Operant Conditioning

In classical conditioning, we learn to associate one stimulus with another. Pavlov's dogs learned to associate a bell with meat. Because of classical conditioning, the response made to one stimulus (for example, meat) is then made in response to the other (for example, the bell).

Classical conditioning, however, is only one type of learning. Another type of learning is operant conditioning. In **operant conditioning**, people and animals learn to do certain things—and not to do others—because of the results of what they do. In other words, they learn from the consequences of their actions. Linda and Janet, for example, had learned that studying would result in good grades. Because they desired good grades, they studied. In operant conditioning, organisms learn to engage in behavior that results in desirable consequences, such as receiving food, an A on a test, or social approval. They also learn to avoid behaviors that result in negative consequences, such as pain or failure.

In classical conditioning, the conditioned responses are often involuntary biological behaviors, such as salivation or eye blinks. In operant conditioning, however, voluntary responses—behaviors that people and animals have more control over, such as studying—are conditioned.

B. F. Skinner's Idea for the Birds

The ideas behind a secret war weapon that was never built will help us learn more about operant conditioning. The weapon was devised by psychologist B. F. Skinner, and it was called Project Pigeon. During World War II, Skinner proposed training pigeons to guide missiles to targets. The pigeons would be given food pellets for pecking at targets on a screen. Once they had learned to peck at the targets, the pigeons would be placed in missiles. Pecking at similar targets on a screen in the missile would adjust the missile's flight path to hit a real target. However, the pigeon equipment was bulky, and plans for building the missile were abandoned.

 It is not true that pigeons were used to guide missiles during World War II. B. F. Skinner, however, proposed that with the proper conditioning, pigeons would be able to guide missiles by pecking at targets on a screen.

Although Project Pigeon was scrapped, the principles of learning Skinner applied to the project are a fine example of operant conditioning. In operant conditioning, an organism learns to do something because of its effects or consequences. Skinner reasoned that if pigeons were rewarded (with food) for pecking at targets, then the pigeons would continue to peck at the targets.

Reinforcement

To study operant behavior, Skinner devised an animal cage that has been dubbed the "Skinner box." A Skinner box is ideal for laboratory experimentation. Treatments can be introduced and removed, and the results can be carefully observed.

In a classic experiment, a rat in a Skinner box was deprived of food. The box was designed so that when a lever inside was pressed, some food pellets would drop into the box. At first, the rat sniffed its way around the box and engaged in random behavior. The rat's first pressing of the lever was accidental. But lo and behold, food appeared.

Soon the rat began to press the lever more frequently. It had learned that pressing the lever would make the food pellets appear. The pellets are thus said to have reinforced the lever-pressing behavior. **Reinforcement** is the process by which a stimulus (in this case, the food) increases the chances that the preceding behavior (in this case, the lever pressing) will occur again. After several reinforced responses, the rat pressed the lever quickly and frequently, until it was no longer hungry.

In operant conditioning, it matters little why the person or animal makes the first response that is reinforced. It can be by chance, as with the rat in the Skinner box, or the person or animal can be physically guided into the response. In training a dog to sit on command, the dog's owner may say, "Sit!" and then push the dog's rear end down. Once sitting, the dog's response might be reinforced with a pat on the dog's head or a food treat.

People, of course, can simply be told what they need to do when they are learning how to do things such as boot up a computer or start a car. In order for the behavior to be reinforced, however, people need to know whether they have made the correct response. If the computer does not turn on or the car lurches and stalls, the learner will probably think he or she has made a mistake and will not repeat the response. But if everything works as it is supposed to, the response will appear to be correct, and the learner will repeat it next time. Knowledge of results is often all the reinforcement that people need to learn new skills.

Types of Reinforcers

The stimulus that encourages a behavior to occur again is called a reinforcer. There are several different types of reinforcers. Reinforcers can be primary or secondary. They can also be positive or negative.

Key Concepts in Operant Conditioning

	Procedure	Result
Operant Conditioning	A behavior is followed by a consequence or reinforcement.	The behavior increases in frequency.
Example	When a child cleans his room, his parents read him a story.	The child cleans his room more often, so as to hear more stories.
Related Concepts	Primary and secondary reinforcers, positive and negative reinforcers, schedules of reinforcement, extinction	

FIGURE 6.4 *In classical conditioning, a neutral stimulus becomes a conditioned stimulus that brings forth the desired behavior. In operant conditioning, on the other hand, reinforcements are used to increase the frequency of the desired behavior from the organism.*

Primary and Secondary Reinforcers Reinforcers that function due to the biological makeup of the organism are called **primary reinforcers**. Food, water, and adequate warmth are all primary reinforcers. People and animals do not need to be taught to value food, water, and warmth.

The value of **secondary reinforcers**, however, must be learned. Secondary reinforcers initially acquire their value through being paired with established reinforcers. Money, attention, and social approval are all usually secondary reinforcers. Money, for example, is a secondary reinforcer because we have learned that it may be exchanged for primary reinforcers such as food and shelter.

Sometimes secondary reinforcers acquire their value only through a long chain of associations. Janet pointed out that good grades (secondary reinforcers) were important because they could help with college admission or jobs. College admission and jobs (also secondary reinforcers) might lead to money or social approval (other secondary reinforcers). As a result of such a chain of associations, secondary reinforcers—such as good grades—sometimes come to be desired in and of themselves.

Positive and Negative Reinforcers Reinforcers can also be positive or negative. **Positive reinforcers** increase the frequency of the behavior they follow when they are applied. Food, fun activities, and social approval are usually examples of positive reinforcers. In positive reinforcement, a behavior is reinforced because a person (or an animal) receives something he or she wants following the behavior.

Different reinforcers work with different people. For people who enjoy sports, for example, receiving the opportunity to participate in a sport is a positive reinforcer. For people who do not enjoy sports, however, receiving the opportunity to participate in a sport would not be an effective reinforcer. Similarly, what serves as a reinforcer at one time for a person may not be effective at another time for that same person. When a person is hungry, food will work well as a positive reinforcer. But once the person has eaten and is full, food will no longer have an effect.

Unlike with positive reinforcement, with negative reinforcement, a behavior is reinforced because something unwanted *stops* happening or is removed following the behavior. **Negative reinforcers** increase the frequency of the behavior that follows when they are removed. Negative reinforcers are unpleasant in some way. Discomfort, fear, and social disapproval are negative reinforcers.

Daily life is filled with examples of negative reinforcement. When we become too warm in the sun, we move into the shade. When we are tired at the end of the day, we go to sleep. When a food particle is stuck between our teeth, we floss to remove it. And when we have an itch, we often scratch it (even when advised not to do so). All of these situations involve some uncomfortable stimulus—a negative reinforcer—that we act on to make the discomfort disappear. When a specific behavior reduces or

Reinforcement and Punishment

	Behavior		Result		Change
Positive Reinforcement	Studying	→	Enjoyment of the material (Positive reinforcer)	→	Student studies more. (Increase)
Negative Reinforcement	Studying	→	Decreases fear of doing poorly on test (Negative reinforcer)	→	Student studies more. (Increase)
Punishment	Littering	→	Person has to pay fine. (Punishment)	→	Person stops littering. (Decrease)

FIGURE 6.5 *Both positive and negative reinforcers increase the frequency of a behavior. Punishment, however, is intended to decrease or eliminate a particular behavior.* **Which type of reinforcer increases the behavior when it is removed?**

removes the discomfort, that behavior is reinforced, or strengthened.

Linda wanted to study for her psychology test in part because she thought the material was interesting. In this case, her interest in the material was a positive reinforcer for her. But Linda was also probably studying because she did not want to do poorly on the test. In this case, fear of doing poorly was a negative reinforcer. She wanted to study because studying would remove her fear of getting a bad grade. In addition, Linda's efforts showed that she understood the importance of monitoring and evaluating her work for timeliness, accuracy, and goal attainment.

Rewards and Punishments

Many people believe that being positively reinforced is the same as being rewarded and that being negatively reinforced is the same as being punished. Yet there are some differences, particularly between negative reinforcement and punishment.

Rewards When Linda suggested that she and her friends do something enjoyable after they finished studying, she was proposing that they give themselves a reward. Rewards, like reinforcers, increase the frequency of a behavior, and some psychologists do use the term *reward* interchangeably with the term *positive reinforcement*. But Skinner preferred the concept of reinforcement to that of reward because the concept of reinforcement can be explained without trying to "get inside the head" of an organism to guess what it will find rewarding. A list of reinforcers is arrived at by observing what kinds of stimuli increase the frequency of a behavior.

Punishments While rewards and positive reinforcers are similar, punishments are quite different from negative reinforcers. Both negative reinforcers and punishments are usually unpleasant. But negative reinforcers increase the frequency of a behavior by being removed. Punishments, on the other hand, are unwanted events that, when they are applied, decrease the frequency of the behavior they follow. (See Figure 6.5.)

It is not true that negative reinforcement is the same thing as punishment. Both punishments and negative reinforcers are unpleasant, but negative reinforcers encourage a behavior by being removed. Punishments, on the other hand, discourage a behavior by being applied.

In school districts such as Marc's that tie participation in athletic programs to academic grades, both punishment and negative reinforcement are involved. To the athlete on the team who does not achieve the required grades, being removed from the team is a punishment. But once the student is off the team, the disappointment of being banned from participation is a negative reinforcer. The student may work harder to raise his or her class grades in order to gain permission to rejoin the team, thus ending the disappointment.

Strong punishment can rapidly end undesirable behavior. Yet many psychologists believe that in most cases punishment is not the ideal way to deal with a problem. They point to several reasons for minimizing the use of punishment:

- Punishment does not in itself teach alternate acceptable behavior. A child may learn what not to do in a particular situation but does not learn what to do instead.

- Punishment tends to work only when it is guaranteed. If a behavior is punished some of the time but goes unnoticed the rest of the time, the behavior probably will continue.

- Severely punished people or animals may try to leave the situation rather than change their behavior. For example, psychologists warn that children who are severely punished by their parents may run away from home.

- Punishment can create anger and hostility. A child who is punished may take out such anger on other children.

- Punishment may have broader effects than desired. This can occur when people do not know why they are being punished and what is wanted of them.

- Punishment may be imitated as a way of solving problems. As discussed in the next section, people learn by observing others. Psychologists warn that when children are hit by angry parents, the children may learn not only that they have done something wrong, but also that people hit other people when they are upset. Thus, children who are hit may be more likely to hit others themselves.

- Punishment is sometimes accompanied by unseen benefits that make the behavior more, not less, likely to be repeated. For instance, some children may learn that the most effective way of getting attention from their parents is to misbehave.

Most psychologists believe that it is preferable to reward children for desirable behavior than to punish them for unwanted behavior. For example, parents and other authority figures should pay attention to children, and praise them, when the children are behaving well. If good behavior is taken for granted, and only misbehavior receives attention, misbehavior may be getting reinforced.

Psychologists also point out that children need to be aware of, and capable of performing, the desired behavior. Consider a situation in which parents punish a child for not listening to directions only to find out much later that the child has a hearing problem and could not *hear* the directions.

Schedules of Reinforcement

A major factor in determining how effective a reinforcement will be in bringing about a behavior has to do with the **schedule of reinforcement**—when and how often the reinforcement occurs.

Continuous and Partial Reinforcement Up to now, we primarily have been discussing **continuous reinforcement**, or the reinforcement of a behavior every time the behavior occurs. For

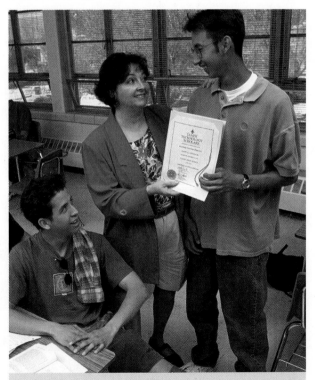

An effective way of encouraging someone to "keep up the good work" is to reward them, as with a prize.

example, the rats in the Skinner box received food every time they pressed the lever. If you walk to a friend's house and your friend is there every time, you will probably continue to go to that same location each time you want to visit your friend because you have always been reinforced for going there. New behaviors are usually learned most rapidly through continuous reinforcement.

It is not, however, always practical or even possible to reinforce a person or an animal for a behavior every single time the behavior occurs. Moreover, a person or animal who is continuously reinforced for a behavior tends to maintain that behavior only as long as the reinforcement is still there. If for some reason the reinforcement stops occurring, the behavior disappears very quickly. For example, if you walk to your friend's house only to find that your friend no longer lives there, you almost certainly will not return to that house again in search of your friend.

The alternative to continuous reinforcement is partial reinforcement. In **partial reinforcement**, a behavior is not reinforced every time it occurs. People who regularly go to the movies may not enjoy every movie they see, for example, but they continue to go to the movies because they enjoy at least *some* of the movies. Behaviors learned through partial reinforcement tend to last longer after they are no longer being reinforced at all than do behaviors learned through continuous reinforcement.

There are two basic categories of partial reinforcement schedules. The first category concerns the amount of time (or interval) that must occur between the reinforcements of a behavior. The second category concerns the number of correct responses that must be made before reinforcement occurs (the ratio of responses to reinforcers).

Interval Schedules   If the amount of time—the interval—that must elapse between reinforcements of a behavior is greater than zero seconds, the behavior is on an interval schedule of reinforcement. There are two different types of interval schedules: fixed-interval schedules and variable-interval schedules. These schedules affect how people allocate the persistence and effort they apply to certain tasks.

In a fixed-interval schedule, a fixed amount of time—say, five minutes—must elapse between reinforcements. Suppose a behavior is reinforced at 10:00 A.M. If the behavior is performed at 10:02, it will not be reinforced at that time. However, at 10:05, reinforcement again becomes available and will occur as soon as the behavior is performed. Then the next reinforcement is not available until five minutes later, and so on. Regardless of whether or how often the desired behavior is performed during the interval, it will not be reinforced again until five minutes have elapsed.

The response rate falls off after each reinforcement on a fixed-interval schedule. It then picks up

FIGURE 6.6   *Some teachers like to surprise students with pop quizzes. Students tend to study more regularly when they do not know when the next quiz will be. Unpredictable pop quizzes are on a variable-interval schedule.*

As harvest time draws nearer, the corn farmer begins to check the crop more often. Typically, by late summer, the corn crop will have been completely harvested, and the farmer will not have to check it again until after the next year's replanting. **What type of reinforcement schedule do the corn farmer's actions indicate?**

as the time when reinforcement will be dispensed draws near. For example, in a one-minute fixed-interval schedule, a rat may be reinforced with food the first time it presses the lever after a minute has elapsed since the previous reinforcement. After each reinforcement, the rat's rate of lever pressing slows down, but as a minute approaches, lever pressing increases in frequency. It is as if the rat has learned that it must wait a while before reinforcement is available. Similarly, if you know that your teacher gives a quiz every Friday, you might study only on Thursday nights. After a given week's quiz, you might not study again until the following Thursday. You are on a one-week fixed-interval schedule.

Farmers and gardeners are quite familiar with one-year fixed-interval schedules. If a particular type of fruit ripens only in the spring, for example, the farmer probably will not check to see if the fruit is ripe in the autumn or winter. However, as spring begins, the farmer will probably check more and more frequently to see if the fruit is ripe. Once all the fruit has ripened and been picked, the farmer will stop checking for it until the next spring.

In a variable-interval schedule, varying amounts of time go by between reinforcements. For example, a reinforcement may occur at 10:00, then not again until 10:07 (7-minute interval), then not again until 10:08 (1-minute interval), then not again until 10:20 (12-minute interval). In variable-interval

schedules, the timing of the next reinforcement is unpredictable. Therefore, the response rate is steadier than with fixed-interval schedules. If your teacher gives unpredictable pop quizzes, you are likely to do at least some studying fairly regularly because you do not know when the next quiz will be. And if it turns out to be tomorrow, you want to be prepared.

Ratio Schedules If a desired response is reinforced every time the response occurs, there is a one-to-one (1:1) ratio of response to reinforcement (one response: one reinforcement). If, however, the response must occur more than once in order to be reinforced, there is a higher response-to-reinforcement ratio. For example, if a response must occur five times before being reinforced, the ratio is 5:1. As with interval schedules, there are fixed-ratio schedules and variable-ratio schedules.

In a fixed-ratio schedule, reinforcement is provided after a fixed number of correct responses have been made. The rat in the box would have to press the lever, say, five times, and always exactly five times, in order to receive the food. Some stores use fixed-ratio schedules to encourage people to buy more. A video rental store, for instance, may promise customers a free video rental after payment for five rentals.

With a fixed-ratio schedule, the person or animal tends to try to get its fixed number of responses "out of the way" as quickly as it can to get to the reward. With the free video rental offer, for example, a customer may rent the five required videos as soon as possible so as to get to the free one sooner. If the ratio is very high, however, it is often less effective, particularly with people.

In a variable-ratio schedule, reinforcement is provided after a variable number of correct responses have been made. Sometimes the rat might have to press the lever 5 times to receive the food; at other times, 8 times; and at still other times, 14 times. The rat cannot predict how many times the lever must be pressed because the number changes each time.

With a variable-ratio schedule, reinforcement can come at any time. This unpredictability maintains a high response rate. Slot machines tend to work on variable-ratio schedules. Even though the players do not know when (or even if) they will win, they continue to drop coins into the machines. And when the players do win, they often continue to play because the next winnings might be just a few lever-pulls away.

Extinction in Operant Conditioning

In operant conditioning, as in classical conditioning, extinction sometimes occurs. In both types of conditioning, extinction occurs because the events that had previously followed a stimulus no longer occur.

In operant conditioning, the extinction of a learned response results from repeated performance of the response without reinforcement. In Skinner's experiment with the rats, lever pressing was followed by—and reinforced by—food. But if a rat presses a lever repeatedly and no food follows, it will eventually stop pressing the lever. The lever-pressing behavior will have been extinguished.

Marc's reluctance to study for the psychology test may have been an example of extinction. The previous week, he had studied very hard for a test in another class but had done poorly on the test anyway. In other words, his studying behavior had not been reinforced by doing well on the test. As a result, he began to question whether studying was helpful at all. If Linda and the others had not been there to persuade him that it was necessary to study, he might very well not have studied for the psychology test. Marc's studying behavior would have been

extinguished because of the previous week's lack of reinforcement. After a rest period, though, it might have been spontaneously recovered, as in classical conditioning.

Applications of Operant Conditioning

As we have seen, even people who have never had a course in psychology use operant conditioning every day to influence other people. For example, parents frequently use rewards, such as a trip to the park, to encourage children to perform certain tasks, such as cleaning their rooms.

Techniques of operant conditioning also have widespread application in the field of education. Some specific applications of operant conditioning in education include shaping, programmed learning, and classroom discipline.

Shaping If you have ever tried to teach someone how to do a complex or difficult task, you probably know that the best way to teach the task is to break it up into parts and teach each part separately. When all the parts have been mastered, they can be put together to form the whole. Psychologists call this shaping. **Shaping** is a way of teaching complex behaviors in which one first reinforces small steps in the right direction.

Learning to ride a bicycle, for example, involves the learning of a complex sequence of behaviors and can be accomplished through shaping. First, people must learn to move the bike forward by using the pedals. Then they must learn to balance the bicycle and then to steer it. You may remember when you learned to ride a two-wheeler, or you may have seen a parent help a young child by holding the seat as the child learned to pedal. At first, each of these steps seems difficult, and people must pay close attention to each one. After many repetitions, though, and much praise and reassurance from the instructor, each step—and eventually bicycle riding itself—becomes habitual. Close attention no longer needs to be paid.

Psychologists have used shaping to teach animals some complex behavior patterns. For example, they have trained rats to pedal toy cars by first reinforcing the rats' behavior of turning toward the cars. Next they wait until the rats approach the cars before providing further reinforcement. Then they wait until the rats touch the cars, and so on. In this way, rats have been trained to run up ramps, cross bridges, climb ladders, and the like.

PSYCHOLOGY
IN THE WORLD TODAY

Technology and Learning

Changes in technology have strongly affected the way we learn. One of the most significant changes is the availability of information on the Internet. Many of the world's libraries and archives can be searched from any computer with online access. The wealth of online information has changed people's behavior in a variety of ways. For example, persons wishing to earn college credit from home can do so by "attending" virtual classes online. Taking classes for credit online reflects one way technology has affected people's growth and development.

Thanks to the Internet, medical patients can more easily learn about issues of importance to them. The widespread availability of medical data on the Internet helps people to ask their physicians more informed questions. As a result, many patients are taking more active roles in their own health care.

Advances in technology have enriched the lives of people throughout society. Children now converse online with other children around the world. As children's understanding of other cultures increases, their beliefs about and attitudes toward those cultures changes. Scientific advances have also enriched the lives of disabled and elderly people. Developments in voice technology allow some people who previously could not speak to communicate orally. For example, British physicist Stephen Hawking, who has a motor neuron disease, can speak and write with the help of a voice synthesizer. This technology has helped him remain active in research and teaching. Improvements in medical care have also enhanced the quality of life for many elderly persons.

Students around the world use computers to learn online.

Scientific and engineering achievements have also expanded people's understanding of the world around them. Research of animal behavior carried out by psychologists and other scientists has increased many people's interest in, and understanding of, the natural world. Knowledge of outer space has similarly increased. The 1969 Moon landing demonstrated the feasibility of lengthy manned space flights. The flight was the culmination of a long-range American goal of landing a human on the Moon, and the mission's success expanded people's belief in the feasibility of space travel. The landing, and subsequent travels to the Moon, inspired many Americans to study science and math.

Space travel had advanced enough by the end of the 1900s that persons other than trained astronauts could travel in space. Interest in space exploration continued to grow as unmanned spacecraft made successful trips to Mars. Vast amounts of information about these voyages have been placed on NASA's Web sites and other sources, sparking further interest in the sciences. In addition, the 1998 flight of then 77-year old U.S. senator John Glenn changed many people's attitudes about what elderly persons could accomplishment with the help of technology.

Think About It

1. *Finding the Main Idea* How have people's attitudes, beliefs, and behaviors been affected by changes in technology?
2. *Analyzing Information* Evaluate the impact of changes in technology on personal growth and development.

*Building on a squirrel's natural tendency to use its paws, this animal was taught to ride a remote-controlled hang glider. **What steps do you think were reinforced to produce this final behavior?***

Programmed Learning B. F. Skinner developed an educational method called programmed learning that is based on shaping. Programmed learning assumes that any task, no matter how complex, can be broken down into small steps. Each step can be shaped individually and combined to form the more complicated whole.

In programmed learning, a device called a teaching machine presents the student with the subject matter in a series of steps, each of which is called a frame. Each frame requires the student to make some kind of response, such as answering a question. The student is immediately informed whether the response was correct. If it was correct, the student goes on to the next frame. If the response was incorrect, the student goes back over that step until he or she learns it correctly.

Teaching machines can be mechanical hand-held devices. They can also be books or papers, such as worksheets. These days, however, teaching machines are most likely to be computers that are programmed so that the material can branch off in several different directions, depending on where the student needs the most instruction and practice. The use of computers in learning is called computer-assisted instruction.

Programmed learning does not punish students for making errors. Instead, it reinforces correct responses. Eventually, all students who finish the program earn "100 percent," but they do so at their own pace. The machines are infinitely patient with the learner. They are also highly efficient. Most people, however, believe that teaching machines should not be used to replace human teachers—only to assist them.

Classroom Discipline Sometimes when we think we are reinforcing one behavior, we are actually unknowingly reinforcing the opposite behavior. For instance, teachers who pay attention to students who misbehave may unintentionally give these students greater status in the eyes of some of their classmates (Wentzel, 1994). Some teacher training programs show teachers how to use principles of learning to change students' negative patterns of behavior. In these programs, teachers are taught to pay attention to students when they are behaving appropriately and to ignore their misbehavior as long as the misbehavior is not harmful to themselves or to others. If misbehavior is ignored, or unreinforced, it should become extinct, according to the theory.

Teacher attention and approval may have more influence with elementary school students than with high school students, however. Among some adolescents, peer approval can be more powerful than teacher approval. Peer approval may reinforce misbehavior even when teachers choose to ignore it. Moreover, ignoring adolescents' misbehavior may only encourage other students to become disruptive as well.

Instead of ignoring misbehaving adolescents, therefore, teachers may decide to separate them from the rest of the class or group. Teachers and parents frequently use a technique called time-out to discourage misbehavior. Time-out involves placing students in dull, confining environments for a short period of time, such as 10 minutes, when they misbehave. Students who are isolated cannot obtain the attention of peers or teachers, and no reinforcing activities are available.

SECTION 2 REVIEW

go.hrw.com
Homework Practice Online
Keyword: SY7 HP6

1. Explain the differences between classical conditioning and operant conditioning.

2. Describe the roles of reinforcement and punishment in determining persistence-and-effort allocation.

3. In what ways are the principles of operant conditioning applied?

4. **Critical Thinking** *Analyzing Information* How do parents and teachers use rewards and punishments to influence children's behavior? Give an example of a reward or punishment that works with some people but not with others.

Cognitive Factors in Learning

A DAY IN THE LIFE

If B. F. Skinner had heard Dan speculate that he might study more often if he got to do something enjoyable every time he studied, Skinner probably would have paid little attention. For Skinner, what was important was what organisms actually do, not what they say or think they might do. Skinner was interested only in organisms' behaviors.

Cognitive psychologists, however, are willing to speak about what people and animals know because of learning—not just about what they do. Cognitive psychologists see learning as purposeful, not mechanical. They believe that a person can learn something simply by thinking about it or by watching others. They see people and even some animals as searching for information, weighing evidence, and making decisions. Two kinds of learning that involve cognitive factors are latent learning and observational learning.

Latent Learning

How do you know where objects are in your home, in your school, or in your neighborhood? You probably have a mental picture, or "cognitive map," of the area. Because you are very familiar with your school, for example, you know the locations of your locker, the main office, the cafeteria, the gymnasium, and your psychology classroom. Chances are, no one has reinforced your creation of a mental picture of the school's layout; you have simply created it on your own.

In the past, many psychologists argued that organisms only learn behaviors that are reinforced. Today, however, most psychologists believe that much learning can occur without reinforcement. Support for this view came from the work of E. C. Tolman. Tolman showed that rats will learn about their environments even in the absence of reinforcement. Tolman trained some rats to run through mazes to reach food. Other rats were simply permitted to explore the mazes. They received no food or other rewards. After the unrewarded rats had run around in the mazes for 10 days, food was placed in a box at the far ends of the mazes. The previously unrewarded explorers reached the food as quickly as the rewarded rats after only one or two reinforced efforts (Tolman & Honzik, 1930).

Tolman concluded that the rats had learned about the layouts of the mazes even when they were unrewarded for their learning. Tolman distinguished between what organisms learn and what they do. Rats would learn about the mazes even when they roamed about without a goal. However, they had no reason to run efficient routes to the far ends of the mazes until they were rewarded for doing so. Therefore, even though they had knowledge of the most rapid routes all along, this knowledge had been hidden, or latent, until the rats had reason to use it—when there was food at the ends. Learning that remains hidden until it is needed is called **latent learning**.

On your way to school each morning, you may pass a particular street corner at which you have never had any reason to stop. But if a friend wants to meet you at that corner on Saturday, you will still know how to get there, even though you may never have stopped there before. This is an example of latent learning.

Observational Learning

How many things have you learned from observing other people, from reading books, and from watching films and television? No doubt you have picked

A mouse will learn its way through a maze even if it is not reinforced with food for turning left or right.

up a few ideas about how to act in certain situations. Certainly, cooking programs on television are based on the premise that people learn by watching or being told how others do things. People also learn to predict likely outcomes of actions by watching others.

Albert Bandura In his research on social learning, Albert Bandura (1925–) has shown that we acquire knowledge and skills by observing and imitating others (Bandura et al., 1963). Such learning is called **observational learning**. For example, a new student in a class might model his or her behavior after other students. The new student might learn that it is acceptable behavior to speak up in class by watching other students. In learning that classroom discussion is encouraged, the new student has demonstrated the ability to learn by a process known as vicarious reinforcement.

Observational learning accounts for much human learning. Children learn to speak, eat, and play at least partly by observing their parents and others do these things. Modern advertising also uses elements of social learning—people often decide what products they would like to purchase based on advertisements they have seen. You learn to pronounce words in your foreign language class by hearing your teacher pronounce them. We may not always be able to do something perfectly the first time we try it, but if we have watched others do it first, we probably have a head start over people who are coming into it without any previous exposure.

Many people believe that because cartoons are aimed at young children, cartoon violence should be kept to a minimum or eliminated altogether.

The Effects of Media Violence We learn by observing parents and peers, attending school, reading books, and watching media such as television and films. Television is one of our major sources of informal observational learning. Children are routinely exposed to scenes of violence just by turning on the TV set. If a child watches two to four hours of TV a day, she or he will have seen 8,000 murders and another 100,000 acts of violence by the time she or he has finished elementary school (Eron, 1993). Are G-rated movies safe? Perhaps not. One study found that virtually all G-rated animated films have scenes of violence, with a mean duration of 9 to 10 minutes per film (Yokota & Thompson, 2000). Many video games are also full of violent activity (Anderson & Dill, 2000).

Most health professionals agree that media violence contributes to aggression. A joint statement issued by the American Psychological Association and several medical associations (Holland, 2000) made the following points:

- Media violence supplies *models* of aggressive "skills," which children may learn by watching. Media violence also provides viewers with aggressive *scripts*—that is, ideas about how to behave in situations like those they have observed.

- Children who see a lot of violence are more likely to view violence as an effective way of settling conflicts. Children exposed to violence are more likely to assume that acts of violence are acceptable behavior.

- Viewing violence can lead to emotional desensitization toward violence in real life. It can decrease the likelihood that one will take action on behalf of a victim when violence occurs.

- Viewing violence may lead to real life violence. Children exposed to violent programming at a young age have a higher tendency for violent and aggressive behavior later in life than children who are not so exposed.

TRUTH OR fiction ▪ REVISITED ▪ *It is true that people who watch a lot of violence on television are more likely to be violent themselves, as compared with people who watch less violence on television.* People sometimes imitate the behavior they observe in real life and in the media. This is called observational learning.

Just as observational learning may contribute to violent behavior, it may also be used to prevent it. Television networks, for example, have recently made some attempts to limit the amount of violence in programs intended for children. But it is probably not practical to hope to shield children from all violence—after all, even religious texts, the evening news, and classic works such as Shakespeare's *Macbeth* contain violence. Instead, young people can be informed that the violence they see in the media does not represent the behavior of most people in society. Most people resolve their conflicts without resorting to violence. Children also can be told that the violence they see on TV shows is not real; it involves camera tricks, special effects, and stunts.

A person who has observed a behavior in others does not necessarily begin to display that behavior himself or herself. There is a difference between what people learn and what they do. Of all the children who are exposed to media violence, only a few of them become violent. Furthermore, it may be that people who *choose* to watch violent television programs are more likely to be violent in the first place. It is difficult to prove a cause-and-effect relationship based only on correlation. (See Chapter 2.) If young people consider violence wrong for them, they will probably not be violent, even if they know how to be violent. The same applies to other behaviors as well.

SECTION 3 REVIEW

Homework Practice Online
go.hrw.com
Keyword: SY7 HP6

1. What cognitive factors are involved in learning?

2. Identify elements of social learning theory in modern advertising.

3. **Critical Thinking** *Summarizing* Describe the processes of modeling and vicarious reinforcement in typical classroom situations.

SECTION 4

The PQ4R Method: Learning to Learn

If you put a sponge in a bathtub, it will soak up the water. Many students assume that simply by attending a course (such as history, biology, or even psy-

chology) they will somehow soak up the subject matter of that course. Not so. Students are not sponges. Courses are not water.

Students learn more when they take an active approach to learning. One such active approach is called the PQ4R method. Based on the work of educational psychologist Francis P. Robinson, the PQ4R method has six steps: Previewing, Questioning, Reading, Reflecting, Reciting, and Reviewing. Following these six steps will help you get the most out of your textbooks.

Preview

Previewing the subject matter in a textbook means getting a general picture of what is covered before you begin reading a chapter. If you are in the library or the bookstore looking at books to decide which ones you would like to read for pleasure, you may flip rapidly through the pages to get some idea of what the books are about. Thumbing through the pages is one way of previewing the material. In fact, many textbooks are designed with devices that encourage students to preview chapters before reading them.

This book, for instance, has Read to Discover chapter questions, Truth-or-Fiction sections, lists of key terms, major and minor section headings in each chapter, section review questions, and chapter reviews. If drama and suspense are your goals, read each chapter page by page. But if learning the material is your aim, it may be more effective to first read the opening chapter questions, skim the pages, and read the questions in the section and chapter reviews.

Familiarity with the overall picture will give you a cognitive map of a chapter. Your map will have many blank areas, but it will have an overall structure. You can fill in the details of the map as you read through the chapter page by page.

Question

Learning is made easier when we have goals in mind, when there is something in particular we want to learn. When we want to learn something, we become active learners.

One way to create goals is to phrase questions about the subject matter in each chapter. You may wonder what is a good way to come up with the questions without reading the chapter first. Look at each heading. Write down all the headings in a notebook. If a book you are reading does not have helpful headings, you might try looking at the first sentence of each paragraph instead. Phrase questions as you proceed. With practice, you will develop questioning skills, and your questions will help you grasp the subject matter.

The following questions are based on the major and minor headings at the beginning of this chapter: What is classical conditioning? Who is Ivan Pavlov? (See Figure 6.6.) You may have come up with different questions after reading the headings. Your questions might have been as useful as these, or more useful; there is always more than one "right" question. As you study, you will learn what works for you.

Read

Once you have formulated your questions, read the chapter with the purpose of answering them. A sense of purpose will help you focus on the key points of the material. As you answer each question,

you can jot down a few key words in your notebook that will remind you of the answer when you recite and review later. You may find it helpful to keep two columns in your notebook: one column for the questions themselves and the other column for the key words that relate to the answer to each question.

Reflect

Reflecting on subject matter is an important way to understand and remember it. As you are reading, think of examples or create mental images of the subject matter.

One way to reflect is to relate new information to old information. You may remember some facts about B. F. Skinner from Chapter 1, for example. What you learned about him there can serve as a springboard for you to learn about him and about his work in greater detail in this chapter. Take advantage of what you already know.

Another way to reflect is to relate new information to events in your personal life. For instance, you can reflect on classical conditioning by thinking of times when you have experienced it. Then you will find it easier to remember that classical conditioning involves learning through the association of stimuli with each other.

Even if you cannot think of any way to relate the material to your own life, you probably know other people who provide examples of the kinds of behavior discussed throughout this book. To help yourself understand and remember the subject matter of psychology, think of ways in which the behavior of people described in the text and by your teacher is similar to—or different from—the behavior of people you know.

Recite

Do you remember when you learned the alphabet? If you were like many children, you probably learned it by saying it—or singing it to the tune of the "Alphabet Song"—over and over again. This is an example of how reciting something can help a person learn. The same thing can work with your textbook. (You will have to make up your own song, however.)

Once you have read a section and have answered your questions, reciting the answers will help you understand and remember them. You can recite aloud or repeat words silently to yourself. You can also do your reciting alone or with others. Many

Using PQ4R

I. What is classical conditioning?

  A. Who is Ivan Pavlov?

  B. What do US, UR, CR, and CS mean?

  C. How is adaptation to the environment related to conditioning?

    1. What is a taste aversion?

    2. What is extinction?

    3. What is spontaneous recovery?

    4. How do generalization and discrimination relate to classical conditioning?

  D. What are some applications of classical conditioning?

    1. What are flooding and systematic desensitization?

    2. What is counterconditioning?

    3. How does the bell-and-pad method for bed-wetting work?

FIGURE 6.6 *An actual PQ4R notebook might include a column for answers in addition to the questions.*

A DAY IN THE LIFE

students learn by quizzing each other with their questions, taking turns reciting the answers. This may have been what Linda had in mind when she suggested that she and her friends study together for the psychology test.

Review

When Marc said that he had been studying for the test in Ms. Kramer's class the night before the test, he may have given the explanation for why he did not do as well on the test as he would have liked. For one thing, learning takes time. That means that we usually have to repeat or reread things before we know them well.

Second, "distributed" learning is more effective than "massed" learning. That is a scientific way of saying what most students already know but that Marc apparently did not: it is more effective to study regularly (to distribute the learning over several days or weeks) than to try to cram just before a test (to mass all the learning at once). Actually, distributed learning usually takes no more work than cramming. But it means that we have to plan ahead and try to stick to some sort of schedule.

Review the material for each subject you are studying according to a reasonably regular schedule, such as once a week. Reviewing leads to relearning, and relearning on a regular schedule is easier than learning something the first time. By reviewing material regularly, we understand and remember it better.

It may seem like a large time commitment to study regularly when there is no apparent immediate need to do so, but it will reduce the amount of time you need to study right before a test. It may also help reduce the amount of anxiety you feel about the test the day before (negative reinforcement) because you know that you have already mastered at least some of the material. And it also helps keep you prepared for pop quizzes.

Once you have set aside enough time to review the material, you will need to figure out what techniques will help you most. One way to review the material is to go back to the questions and key words in your notebook. Cover up the answer column and read the questions in the left column as though they were a quiz. Recite your answers and check them against the key words in the right column. When you forget an answer or get an answer wrong, go back and reread the subject matter in the textbook. (In this technique, your notebook

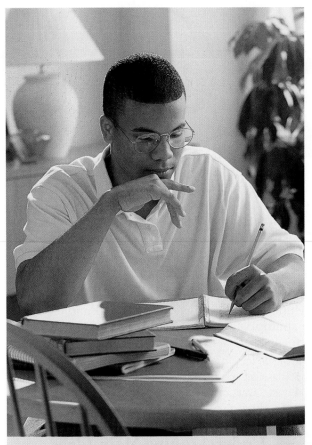
The PQ4R method helps students take an active approach to learning.

becomes a type of teaching machine used in programmed learning.)

Another way of reviewing the subject matter, as already mentioned, is for you and other classmates to quiz each other. By taking a more active approach to learning, you may find that you are earning higher grades and gaining more pleasure from the learning process.

SECTION 4 REVIEW

go. hrw .com **Homework Practice Online** Keyword: SY7 HP6

1. What are the steps in the PQ4R method?

2. What purposes does it serve for a person to reflect on information she or he has read? What purposes does reciting the information out loud serve?

3. **Critical Thinking** *Analyzing Information* Prepare a learning and studying schedule for yourself for one of your classes. Use PQ4R as a basis for the schedule.

Writing a Summary

Using standard grammar, spelling, sentence structure, and punctuation, summarize the information in this chapter. Consider:
• the principles of classical and operant conditioning
• cognitive factors in learning and the steps of the PQ4R method of learning

Identifying People and Ideas

Identify the following terms or people and use them in appropriate sentences.

1. stimulus
2. response
3. classical conditioning
4. taste aversion
5. flooding
6. operant conditioning
7. reinforcement
8. positive reinforcers
9. shaping
10. observational learning

Understanding Main Ideas

SECTION 1 (pp. 128–135)
1. How do people and animals learn responses through classical conditioning?

SECTION 2 (pp. 135–144)
2. How does a fixed-interval schedule of reinforcement differ from a fixed-ratio schedule?

SECTION 3 (pp. 145–147)
3. What are two types of learning that involve cognitive factors?

SECTION 4 (pp. 147–149)
4. List the six steps of the PQ4R method and explain the purpose of each step.

Thinking Critically

1. **Analyzing Information** How might a therapist help cigarette smokers quit smoking by using each of these types of learning: classical conditioning, operant conditioning, and cognitive learning?

2. **Drawing Inferences and Conclusions** How might the principles of classical conditioning lead to the formation of superstitions? How might the principles of operant conditioning help keep superstitions alive?

3. **Categorizing** Explain how flooding, desensitization, and counterconditioning can help a person overcome a problem. Give one example for each.

4. **Supporting a Point of View** Many psychologists believe that punishment is not the ideal way to change behavior. Do you agree or disagree? Give examples to support your opinion.

Writing About Psychology

1. **Analyzing Information** Use the PQ4R method to create a plan for improving your understanding of the material in this chapter. Create an outline setting forth how you intend to use your plan to achieve your goal of better understanding the chapter. After trying your new system, write a one-page report of your progress. Monitor and evaluate your system for how timely you are able to complete your work, whether your understanding of the material is more accurate, and whether you achieved your goal of better understanding the material.

2. **Making Generalizations and Predictions** People learn about the consequences of courses of action by observing others. Consider what a child might learn from observing an adult who refuses to pay taxes, register to vote, or obey the speed limit. Write a one-page paper predicting the likely outcome of these courses of action. Use the graphic organizer below to help you write your paper.

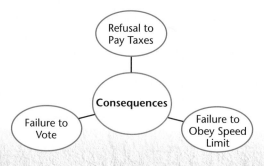

Interpreting Graphs

Study the graph below. Then use the information in the graph to help you answer the questions that follow.

Conditioning

Number of Times a Rat Presses a Lever to Receive Food

50

25

0

15   30   45

Time in Minutes

Source: Blackman, *Operant Conditioning*, 1993

1. What psychological principle does the above graph illustrate?
   a. classical conditioning
   b. operant conditioning
   c. shaping
   d. latent learning

2. What conclusions can you draw from the graph about the rat's behavior and what predictions can be made from the graph?

Analyzing Primary Sources

Read the following excerpt, in which Russian physiologist Ivan Pavlov explains one aspect of the principle of conditioning. Then answer the questions that follow.

"It is pretty evident that under natural conditions the normal animal must respond not only to stimuli which themselves bring immediate benefit or harm, but also to other physical or chemical agencies—waves of sound, light, and the like—which in themselves only *signal* the approach of these stimuli; though it is not the sight and sound of the beast of prey which is in itself harmful to the smaller animal, but its teeth and claws."

3. Which of the following statements best reflects the ideas that Pavlov was trying to convey in the excerpt?
   a. The sight and sound of a beast of prey are unconditioned stimuli.
   b. The sight and sound of a beast of prey are unconditioned responses
   c. The sight and sound of a beast of prey are conditioned stimuli.
   d. The sight and sound of a beast of prey are conditioned responses.

4. According to the excerpt, why must a normal animal respond to the sight and sound of a beast of prey?

PSYCHOLOGY PROJECTS

Cooperative Learning

Reading About Psychology Form a study group with two or three other students in your psychology class. Using material from Chapter 6, practice the recite step of the PQ4R method. Discuss with the other members of the group why this step is helpful. Then make a brief oral report to the rest of the class describing how the recite step helped you learn the material you were studying.

internet connect

Internet Activity: go.hrw.com
KEYWORD: SY7 CH6

Choose an activity on learning to:
- create an exhibit for "The Museum of Classical Conditioning."
- make an action plan using operant conditioning to teach a dog to fetch.
- research the processes of modeling, imitation, and vicarious reinforcement for a classroom.

Chapter 7

MEMORY

Read to Discover

1 What are the three kinds of memory?

2 What are the three processes of memory?

3 What are the three stages of memory related to?

4 In what ways can memory be improved?

A DAY IN THE LIFE

"Wow, this song really brings back memories of being in seventh grade," said Linda. She was talking to Marc and Todd at a party Hannah was holding. "Classical conditioning in action, I guess. Hearing it almost makes me feel 13 again. It was so relevant to the things I was feeling then—I used to think Ashley Austin must have written this song just for me."

"Except for one problem," said Todd. "This isn't an Ashley Austin song. It's by . . . I can't think of her name. It starts with an M, . . . Mary? Maria? Something like that. It's on the tip of my tongue."

Marc jumped in. "You're right. Marina Crossley."

At that moment, Dan bounded up and said, "Hey, guess what? I just met the most amazing girl! And she told me her phone number. Quick, before I forget it, someone give me something to write it down on."

While Linda was digging in her bag to find a pencil and a piece of paper, Todd decided to have a little fun with Dan. "What time is it?" he asked him innocently.

"What?" asked Dan in a distracted tone of voice.

"What time is it?" Todd repeated. "Look at your watch."

Dan glanced at his watch. "It's 9:37," he said. By this time, Linda had found a pencil and a scrap of paper and had given them to Dan. He started to write down the number, only to realize that he had forgotten it. He gave Todd a nasty look. "Thanks a lot," Dan said sarcastically. "If you hadn't asked me for the time, I would have remembered the phone number."

"Don't worry, you can look it up in the phone book," said Todd. "That is, assuming you can still remember her *name!*"

Everybody laughed—that is, everybody except Dan, who realized he had, in fact, forgotten her name.

- - -

As Linda, Todd, Marc, and Dan were demonstrating at the party, people use memory all the time. Some things we never seem to forget—visual images such as the faces of family members and friends and basic kinds of information such as the alphabet or simple math. Some of the physical skills we learn, such as walking and swimming, can also last a lifetime.

Much of what is stored in our memory was stored there with no conscious effort on our part. Sometimes it takes only a visual image, a sound, or an odor to bring back a memory. That was what happened when Linda heard the song. It brought back memories of when she was in the seventh grade. Other things in our memory take more effort to store.

This chapter discusses what psychologists have learned about memory. You will read about the "three threes" of memory—the three kinds, the three processes, and the three stages. You will also read about forgetting and learn some ways to improve your memory.

Key Terms

- memory
- episodic memory
- flashbulb memories
- semantic memory
- explicit memory
- implicit memory
- encoding
- storage
- maintenance rehearsal
- elaborative rehearsal
- retrieval
- context-dependent memories
- state-dependent memories
- tip-of-the-tongue phenomenon
- sensory memory
- iconic memory
- eidetic imagery
- echoic memory
- short-term memory
- primacy effect
- recency effect
- chunking
- interference
- long-term memory
- schemas
- recognition
- recall
- relearning
- decay
- infantile amnesia
- anterograde amnesia
- retrograde amnesia

HOLT

Psychology Video Program

Watch the video to explore how driving a taxi can improve memory.

Read the following statements about psychology. Do you think they are true or false? You will learn whether each statement is true or false as you read the chapter.

- Once people learn to ride a bicycle, they probably will never forget how.
- The best way to remember something is to repeat it many times.
- People with photographic memory are rare.
- There is no known limit to how much information you can remember.
- You can remember important events from the first two years of life.
- There are certain tricks you can use to improve your memory.

SECTION 1

Three Kinds of Memory

Look at Figure 7.1. Copy the names of the two objects you see ("eyeglasses" and "hourglass") on a sheet of paper. Do not copy the drawings themselves. Put the sheet of paper aside, but do not discard it. You will need it later in the chapter as a demonstration of one characteristic of memory.

What is memory? **Memory** is the process by which we recollect prior experiences and information and skills learned in the past. There are different kinds of memory. One way to classify memory is according to the different kinds of information it contains: events, general knowledge, and skills.

FIGURE 7.1 *Look at these two drawings for a moment. Write the labels of the two drawings on a sheet of paper, then continue reading. You will need the sheet of paper later in this chapter.*

Episodic Memory

Episodic memory is memory of a specific event. The event took place in the person's presence, or the person experienced the event. Your memories of what you ate for dinner last night and of your last quiz are examples of episodic memory.

Some events are so important that it seems as if a flashbulb goes off and we photograph it in every detail. Such memories are called **flashbulb memories**. Linda and Marc would never forget the first time they went out, or the time when they first thought they were in love. Linda would always recall how the sky and the streets and the trees looked different that day. Marc would remember how kind he was to everyone on that day. Both would laugh when they recalled how they were convinced that all of life's problems suddenly seemed solved. But Linda would never laugh when she recalled September 11, 2001.

On that morning, she received a cell phone call that a tower of the World Trade Center in New York City was in flames. She would remember turning on her TV set and watching in horror as the second tower was struck by an airplane and it became clear that terrorism was at work. She would vividly remember the slant of light in her window. She would continue to see the lower part of Manhattan covered with flames, black smoke, and ashen debris after the towers collapsed (Otani et al., 2005).

There are several reasons why certain memories become etched in our minds when the "flashbulb" goes off. One reason is the distinctness of the memories. We pay more attention to events that have a special meaning for us. Such events usually arouse powerful feelings. Also, we tend to think about flashbulb memories often, especially if they are positive ones—first love, the birth of a child, or a special accomplishment.

Sometimes places or events make an impression on us—and thus become flashbulb memories—because they are connected to other events that are important at the time, such as a major disaster or tragedy. Then, if we think of the important event later, it will trigger memories of things that were connected to it. Many older Americans have flashbulb memories of the assassination of President John F. Kennedy, which occurred in 1963.

Semantic Memory

General knowledge that people remember is called **semantic memory**. For example, we "remember" that George Washington was the first president of the United States. Unlike with episodic memory, we

After the attacks, firefighters raised the flag at the World Trade Center site.

instrument, and driving a car are other examples of implicit memory. Once such a skill has been learned, it usually stays with you for many years. Even if you do not use the skill for a long time, you are unlikely to forget it. Once skills have been learned, they tend to stay remembered for many years—perhaps even a lifetime.

TRUTH OR fiction ▪ REVISITED ▪

It is true that once people learn to ride a bicycle, they probably never will forget how. Once people learn a skill, there is little chance they will ever forget it. Skill memories tend to last, even when they are not used regularly.

usually do not remember *when* we acquired the information in our semantic memory. We probably cannot remember when we first learned about George Washington, for instance.

A DAY IN THE LIFE

The memory Marc had at Hannah's party was a semantic memory. He remembered that Marina Crossley wrote the song, not Ashley Austin, as Linda had thought. Most likely, Marc did not remember when he learned that Marina Crossley wrote the song. Still, he remembered correctly that she did.

Here are two more examples of semantic memory. You remember the alphabet, but you probably do not remember where, when, or how you learned it. So, too, you know that humans need oxygen, but you may not recall learning this piece of information. Most of what you have learned in your classes at school has become part of your semantic memory.

Episodic and semantic memories are both examples of **explicit memory**. Things that are *explicit* are clear, or clearly stated or explained. An explicit memory is memory of specific information. That information may be autobiographical (episodic) or refer to general knowledge (semantic).

Implicit Memory

The opposite of explicit is *implicit,* and another kind of memory is **implicit memory**. Things that are implicit are *implied,* or not clearly stated. Implicit memories consist of the skills or procedures you have learned. These skills might include throwing a ball, riding a bicycle, skipping rope, or swimming. Skills such as typing, using a computer, playing a musical

SECTION 1 REVIEW

go.hrw.com **Homework Practice Online**
Keyword: SY7 HP7

1. Describe the three kinds of memory.
2. Explain what flashbulb memories are.
3. **Critical Thinking** *Categorizing* Write down the three kinds of memory you have learned about so far. Next to each, give an example of how you have used that type of memory recently.

SECTION 2

Three Processes of Memory

Computers and people both process information. Computers use electronic circuits to process the information they receive, while people use their brains. But the processes used by computers and people are very similar. Both computers and people encode, store, and retrieve information.

Encoding

Imagine writing an essay or a story on a computer. You use the keyboard to type information in the form of letters and words. The information is usually stored on a hard drive or compact disk. But if you were to put the hard drive or compact disk under a

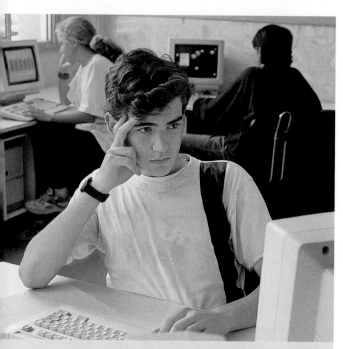

Computers use electronic circuits to process information; humans use their brains. Both use similar processes of encoding, storing, and retrieving information.

microscope, would you be able to see the letters or words you typed? No. This is because the computer changes, or encodes, the information into a form that it can store. **Encoding** is the translation of information into a form in which it can be stored. When people place information in their memory, they, like computers, encode it. For both the computer and the human brain, encoding is the first stage of processing information.

Initially, we receive information through our senses in a physical form—such as light waves or sound waves. When we encode it, we convert the physical stimulation we have received into psychological formats that can be mentally represented. To do so, we use different types of codes.

On a sheet of paper, write this list of letters:

OTTFFSSENT

Look at the letters for 30 seconds and memorize as much of the list as you can in that time. Then continue reading this section to find out which type of code—visual, acoustic, or semantic—you used to remember the letters.

Visual Codes   When you tried to memorize the letters, did you attempt to see them in your mind as a picture? If you did, you used a visual code. That is,

you tried to form a mental picture of the letters in your mind.

Acoustic Codes   Another way that you may have tried to remember the letters might have been to read the list to yourself and repeat it several times. That is, you may have said the letters (either out loud or silently) one after another: O, T, T, and so forth. This way of trying to remember the letters uses an acoustic (or auditory) code. An acoustic code records the letters in your memory as a sequence of sounds.

Semantic Codes   Still another way that you may have tried to remember the list might have been to attempt to make sense of the letters, that is, to figure out what they might mean. For example, you may have noticed that the last four letters spelled the word *sent.* You may then have tried to see if the letters made up a phrase or sentence with the word *sent* in it. The word *semantic* means "relating to meaning," so this type of code is called a semantic code. A semantic code represents information in terms of its meaning. If you tried to figure out a possible meaning for the letters, you were searching for a semantic code.

Another way that you could try to remember the letters by using a semantic code would be to find words that begin with each of the letters in the list and then make up a sentence using those words. Such an approach might result in a sentence that begins "Only Tiny Tots Feel Friendly . . ." By using all 10 letters in a sentence, you would then have to remember only the sentence, not the list of letters.

Yet another way you might use semantic coding to remember the letters would be to use the phrase "other flowers sent" and then make a few changes in the spelling—that is, "OTTher FFlowerS SENT." You would then have to remember the phrase with its "OTTities" (oddities) of spelling!

What you may *not* have realized when you first examined the list is that the letters **OTTFFSSENT** stand for the first letter of the series of numbers from one (O) through ten (T)—that is, One, Two, Three, Four, Five, Six, Seven, Eight, Nine, Ten. Obviously, if you had known that in the first place, remembering the letters would have been much easier. All you would have had to remember was that the letters were the first letters of the numbers 1 through 10. Remembering this rule would certainly be easier than remembering an apparently meaningless list of 10 letters. By using semantic (meaningful) codes, you can memorize lists of letters and other items more easily and will probably remember them for a longer amount of time than you would otherwise.

Storage

After information is encoded, it must be stored. **Storage**, the second process of memory, is the maintenance of encoded information over a period of time. As with encoding, human storage of information is not all that different from a computer's storage of information. With a computer, however, the user must instruct the machine to save information in its memory. Otherwise, it will lose the newly encoded information when the user shuts off the computer. People who want to store new information in their memory use a variety of strategies. These strategies are related closely to the strategies people use for encoding.

Maintenance Rehearsal

As Dan found out at the party when he tried to remember the phone number of the girl he had met, once we encode information we need to do something more to keep from forgetting it. If you were in a similar situation in which you wanted to remember a name or phone number, how would you do it? One way would be to keep repeating the name or number to yourself to keep it in your memory. If you were concerned that you might forget it before you could write it down, you might need to repeat it several times. Repeating information over and over again to keep from forgetting it is called **maintenance rehearsal**.

The more time spent in rehearsing, or repeating information, the longer the information will be remembered. Actors and actresses know this well. That is why they rehearse their lines again and again until they know them as well as they possibly can. Because maintenance rehearsal does not try to make information meaningful by connecting it to past learning, however, it is a relatively poor way to put information in permanent storage.

Elaborative Rehearsal

A more effective and lasting way to remember new information is to make it meaningful by relating it to information you already know well (Woloshyn et al., 1994). This method, called **elaborative rehearsal**, is widely used in education because it has proved to be a much more effective method than maintenance rehearsal. For example, language arts and foreign language teachers recommend elaborative rehearsal when they encourage their students to use new vocabulary words in sentences instead of just repeating individual words by themselves.

Organizational Systems Memories that you store become organized and arranged in your mind for future use. If you are a fairly organized person, you probably have a place for everything. When you bring items home, you probably do not just throw them on the floor or stick them haphazardly in a closet. You probably sort them and put them in their place. That way you have a better chance of finding them when you need them. You have probably learned from experience that not knowing where items are means that you end up spending a lot of time looking for them when you need them.

In some ways, your memory resembles a vast storehouse of files and file cabinets in which you store what you learn and need to remember. The more you learn, the more files you need and the more elaborate your filing system becomes. When you started attending school, the first facts you learned about American history, for example, may have been about Pocahontas, the Pilgrims, or George Washington. Your first "American history" file probably had only a couple of pieces of information in it.

However, as you progressed and learned more about American history, you had to expand your filing system. As you learned about the presidents, for example, you found new ways to file the information in your memory. You may have filed the presidents in chronological order, that is, in the order in which they held office. In that file you put Washington first, followed by others such as Jefferson, Lincoln, and Theodore Roosevelt. You may also have filed more recent presidents according to the events in American history with which they are associated, such as Franklin Roosevelt with the New Deal and World War II, Richard Nixon with Watergate, and George W. Bush with the war in Iraq.

As your memory develops, it organizes the information you learn into files and then files within files. Your memory organizes the new information it receives into certain groups, or classes, according to common features. For example,

The "American history" file in your brain might remind you that Mount Rushmore has the largest figures of any statue in the world and that the faces are those of Washington, Jefferson, Theodore Roosevelt, and Lincoln.

mammals share certain features. They are warm-blooded, and they nurse their young. If you knew that whales are warm-blooded and nurse their young, you probably filed them in your memory as mammals. If you did not know that about them, you might have filed them as fish because they swim and live in the water.

Classes can contain smaller classes and can also be part of a larger class. For example, the class mammals includes monkeys, rats, and other warm-blooded, nursing creatures. At the same time, mammals are part of a larger class—animals. Much of our semantic memory that is stored as we get older and acquire more knowledge is organized into groups or classes.

Filing Errors   Our ability to remember information—even when we are healthy and functioning well—is subject to error. Some memory errors occur because we "file" information incorrectly. Psychologists have discovered that when we classify pieces of information accurately—that is, when we place items in the correct file—we have a much better chance of recalling accurate information about them (Hasselhorn, 1992; Schneider & Bjorklund, 1992). Nevertheless, filing systems are not perfect. Have you ever misplaced a paper? For example, have you ever brought home a science paper and mistakenly filed it in your history folder? Our mental filing systems sometimes make similar errors.

Linda's memory had made a filing mistake. This became evident at the party when she said that Ashley Austin wrote the song that reminded her of being back in the seventh grade. Todd knew the song had not been written by Ashley Austin, but he was unable to remember who did write it. Marc was the one who finally came up with the right answer—Marina Crossley. Linda had apparently put the "wrong label"—Ashley Austin rather than Marina Crossley—on her file of information about the song.

Retrieval

The third memory process is retrieval. **Retrieval** consists of locating stored information and returning it to conscious thought. Retrieving information stored in our memory is like retrieving information stored in a computer. To retrieve information stored in a computer, we have to know the name of the file and the rules for retrieving information. Retrieval of information stored in our memory requires a similar knowledge of proper procedures.

Some information in our memory is so familiar that it is readily available and almost impossible to forget. Examples of this type of information include our own names and those of our friends and family members. But when it comes to trying to remember lines from a play or a mathematical formula, retrieval may be more difficult.

Remember the list of letters discussed earlier in the section? What were they? Write them down now. How did you retrieve them from your memory? The method of retrieval you used might have had to do with the way you encoded them to begin with. If you had encoded the series of letters—OTTFFSSENT—as a three-word phrase ("other flowers sent"), you would try to retrieve the letters by recalling the three words and the rule you needed to use to convert them into the 10 letters. But you might make a mistake. For example, you might recall "other flowers senD" rather than "other flowers senT." Or you might correctly recall "other flowers sent" but then not remember that you have to double the T, the F, and the S.

However, by remembering the semantic code that the letters stand for the numbers 1 through 10, your memory could accurately recall, or retrieve, the letters. Using this semantic code may be more complex than seeing the list in your mind's eye (using a visual code), and it might take you a little longer to reconstruct the list of letters. However, by using the 1–10 device, you have a much better chance of remembering the letters—and of remembering them for a longer time.

Before reading on, take this very brief spelling quiz: Which of the following words is spelled correctly—*retrieval* or *retreival*? Because you know how the word is pronounced, regardless of how it is spelled, saying the word to yourself (using an acoustic code) will not help you remember the correct spelling, which is retr*ie*val. How might you go about remembering the correct spelling? Repeating it over and over (maintenance rehearsal) is certainly one way, and that method might work. However, a much better way would be to remember a spelling rule, such as "*i* before *e* except after *c*," as a semantic code. That rule enables you to reconstruct the correct spelling without having to memorize the order of the letters.

Context-Dependent Memory   Have you ever been to a place that brought back old memories? Perhaps you went back to your elementary school or to a neighborhood where you once lived. The memories that came back to you in that place are called **context-dependent memories**. The context of a memory is the situation in which a person first had the experience being remembered. Such memories are dependent on the place where they were encoded and stored. If you had not returned to the place where your memories were encoded, you probably would not have retrieved them.

A fascinating experiment in context-dependent memory involved some students who belonged to a swimming club. They were asked to memorize lists of words while they were in the water of a pool (Godden & Baddeley, 1975). Other students in the club tried to memorize the lists while they were out of the water. Later, the students who had studied the lists in the water did a better job of remembering them when they were in the water again. Students who had worked on the lists out of the water, on the other hand, remembered more words when they were dry. These findings suggest that the ability to retrieve memories is greater when people are in the place or situation in which they stored the memories to begin with.

Another study of context-dependent memory indicated that students do better on tests when they study for a test in the room where the test will be given (Isarida & Isarida, 1999). If possible, try to do some studying for your tests in the classrooms where you will take the tests. Of course, you should study in a variety of other settings as well to

Context-dependent memories are dependent on the place where they were encoded and stored. This teenager may be remembering childhood friends and the games they played here years ago.

improve your recollection of the material after the tests are over.

When police and lawyers ask witnesses to describe a crime, they ask the witnesses to describe the scene as clearly as possible. By doing this, witnesses are better able to recall details that they might otherwise have forgotten. Police sometimes take witnesses to the scene of the crime in the hope that such visits will improve their memories of what they witnessed.

At Hannah's party, Linda heard the song that brought back memories of being in the seventh grade. Seventh grade was when she heard the song (probably many times), encoded it, and stored it in her memory. Hearing the song again brought back context-dependent memories connected to that earlier period in her life. As Linda put it, "Hearing it almost makes me feel 13 again." In fact, one reason some people like to hear familiar music is that it brings back old and happy memories.

State-Dependent Memory   Not only do people tend to retrieve memories better when they are in the same place they were in when they first stored the memories, but people also retrieve memories better when they are in the same emotional state they were in when they first stored the memories. Memories that are retrieved because the mood in which they were originally encoded is re-created are called **state-dependent memories**. For example, feelings of happiness tend to bring back memories from other times when we were happy, while feelings of sadness can trigger memories from other times when we were sad.

To demonstrate this phenomenon, Gordon Bower (1981) conducted experiments in which study participants were instructed, while in a hypnotic trance, to experience happy or sad moods. Then, while still in the trance, the participants tried to memorize a list of words. People who had studied the list while in a happy mood were better able to recall it when they were put into a happy state again. People who had studied the list while in a sad mood showed better recall when placed back in a sad mood. Bower's explanation of these results is that moods influence memories.

Not only is memory better when people are in the same moods as when the memories were acquired, it is also better when people are in the same states of consciousness. Drugs, for example, alter a person's state of consciousness and thus result in state-dependent memories. (See Chapter 5.) Things that happen to somebody while under the influence of a drug may be remembered most accurately when the person is again under the influence of that drug (Atkinson et al., 1996).

On the Tip of the Tongue At Hannah's party, when Linda said she used to think Ashley Austin wrote the song just for her, Todd knew it was not an Ashley Austin song. However, when he then went on to say who did write it, he could not think of the artist's name. "It's on the tip of my tongue," he said.

As in Todd's experience, memories can sometimes be difficult to retrieve. Either they are not very well organized, or they are incomplete. Trying to retrieve such memories can be highly frustrating. Sometimes we come so close to retrieving information that it seems as though the information is on the "tip of the tongue." Psychologists call this the **tip-of-the-tongue phenomenon**. It is sometimes also referred to as the "feeling-of-knowing experience." You feel you know something. In fact, you are sure you know it. However, you just cannot seem to verbalize it. It is on the tip of your tongue, but that is as far as it goes.

Because the files in our memory have labels, so to speak, that include both the sounds and the meanings of words, we often try to retrieve memories that are on the tip of the tongue by using either acoustic or semantic cues. Sometimes we try to summon up words that are similar in sound or meaning to a word that is on the tip of the tongue. We might make a remark like Todd's: "I can't think of her name. It starts with an M. Mary? Maria? Something like that."

SECTION 2 REVIEW **Homework Practice Online**
Keyword: SY7 HP7

1. List the three processes of memory.

2. What is the difference between maintenance rehearsal and elaborative rehearsal?

3. How are memories organized?

4. **Critical Thinking** *Analyzing Information* When was the last time you had a tip-of-the-tongue experience? Explain what you did to try to retrieve the memory.

SECTION 3
Three Stages of Memory

We do not store in our memory everything we experience. The world provides us with a rich display of colors, sounds, tastes, and other sources of stimulation, but we can only take in and remember so much. How much of what our senses experience will we encode and remember? That depends on what happens to the information as it flows through each of the three stages of our memory. The three stages of memory are sensory memory, short-term memory (STM), and long-term memory (LTM).

Sensory Memory

Sensory memory is the first stage of memory. It consists of the immediate, initial recording of information that enters through our senses. If we were to see a row of letters or numbers flash briefly on a screen, the memory trace—or impression made on our senses by the image—would last for only a fraction of a second. A memory trace of a visual stimulus held in our sensory memory decays within a second. So if we want to remember it, we have to do something with the information very quickly.

Psychologists believe that all of our senses have sensory registers. The mental pictures we form of visual stimuli are called *icons*. Icons are held in a sensory register called **iconic memory**. Iconic memories are like snapshots. They are accurate, photographic memories. However, these iconic memories are extremely brief—just a fraction of a second. The ability to remember visual stimuli over long periods of time (what most of us think of as photographic memory) is called **eidetic imagery**.

About 5 percent of children have eidetic imagery. They can look at a photograph and remember it in remarkable detail several minutes later. It is as if they were still looking at it (Haber, 1980). This keen ability usually declines with age, however. By adolescence it is nearly gone.

. . . .

TRUTH OR fiction ▪ R E V I S I T E D ▪ *It is true that people with photographic memory are rare.* All of us have split-second iconic memories that register in our visual sensory register when we see something. However, what most people usually think of as photographic memory is rare. Some children have the ability to remember what they see in remarkable detail, but that ability usually fades as they become older.

. . . .

Mental traces of sounds, called *echoes*, are held in a sensory register called **echoic memory**. While icons (memory traces of visual stimuli) are held only for a fraction of a second, echoes can last for several seconds. For this reason, acoustic codes are easier to remember than visual codes. That is, it is easier to remember a spoken list of letters than to try to remember a mental picture of the letters. Saying things to yourself or out loud makes them easier to remember.

Short-Term Memory

If you pay attention to iconic and echoic memories held ever so briefly in a sensory register, you can transfer that information into your **short-term memory**. The information will remain there after the sensory memory trace has faded away. Short-term memory is also called working memory.

A DAY IN THE LIFE At Hannah's party, Dan tried to use his short-term memory to help himself remember the phone number of the girl he had met. After she gave him her number, he converted that echoic memory, which lingered in his sensory register for a few seconds, into his short-term memory. He hoped to keep it there until he could find a piece of paper and write it down.

We use our short-term memory a great deal of the time. Whenever you are thinking about something, it is in your short-term memory. When you are trying to solve a math problem, the elements of the problem are in your short-term, or working, memory. When you meet someone new, you put the person's name in your short-term memory, perhaps by using the name or by repeating it to yourself several times. Similarly, when a teacher assigns homework or changes the date on which a paper is due, you place that information in your short-term memory until you can write it down or store it in long-term memory.

When you are told a new phone number, you can keep it in short-term memory by repeating it over and over. Repeating the number will give you time to look for a pencil and paper. The more times you rehearse a piece of information, the more likely you are to remember it. If you rehearse information often enough, as actors do when they learn lines, you will probably remember it for a long time.

When you look up a number in the phone book and then walk across the room to reach the phone, you try to keep the number in your short-term memory long enough to dial it. You may repeat or rehearse the number on your way across the room

After people look up a phone number, they keep it in short-term memory until it has been dialed.

to improve your chances of keeping it in your short-term memory. If the number you dial is busy, you can dial it again a few minutes later if you have been able to keep it in your short-term memory. Otherwise, you will have to look it up again.

Information in short-term memory begins to fade rapidly after several seconds. If you want to remember it longer, you need to keep rehearsing the information or take other steps to prevent it from fading. People can sometimes keep visual images in short-term memory. But it is usually better to encode information as sounds so that you can rehearse or repeat the sounds.

At the party, Dan probably would have remembered the phone number of the girl he had just met if he had been able to repeat it until he could write it down. Instead, unable to contain his excitement about meeting her, he stopped to share the good news with his friends. That was Dan's mistake. Talking to Linda and Todd prevented him from rehearsing the number enough times to keep it in his short-term memory.

The Primacy and Recency Effects   When we try to remember a series of letters or numbers, our memories of the first and last items tend to be sharper than our memories of the middle items of the list. The tendency to recall the initial items in a series of items is called the **primacy effect**. (The root *prim-* means "first.") Perhaps we remember the first few items of a series better because, due to their placement early in the list, we have more time to rehearse them than we do for later items. Also, we may remember first items better because our minds are fresher when we first see or hear them.

The tendency to recall the last items in a series is called the **recency effect**. Since the last items in a series are likely to have been perceived and rehearsed most recently, they tend to be fresher in our memory and therefore probably more easily remembered than items in the middle of a series.

Chunking   When we try to keep something in our short-term memory by rehearsing it, it is usually better to organize the information into manageable units that are easy to remember. **Chunking** is the organization of items into familiar or manageable units. Return for a moment to **OTTFFSSENT**. If you tried to remember it letter by letter, there were 10 distinct pieces, or chunks, of information to retain in your short-term memory. When you tried to repeat the list as consisting of 10 meaningless

chunks, you probably had a difficult time. It is not easy to repeat 10 meaningless letters, let alone remember them.

If you tried to encode **OTTFFSSENT** as "other flowers sent" you reduced the number of chunks you needed to remember from 10 to 3. (Of course, you also needed to remember the variations in spelling.) Psychologist George Miller (1956) found that the average person can hold a list of seven items in short-term memory. This, conveniently, is the number of digits in local telephone numbers. Nearly everyone can remember a ZIP code, which is five numbers long. Some people can remember a list of nine items, but very few people can remember more than nine.

Businesses try to obtain telephone numbers with as many zeros or repeated digits as possible because they are easier to remember. For example, 222-2000 is easier for customers to remember than 792-6873. Numbers with zeros and repeated digits contain fewer chunks of information. Alternatively, a business may try to get a telephone number that can be spelled out as a word or phrase (because most digits on the telephone are associated with a set of letters). Thus, people need only remember the word or phrase, not the seven numbers. For instance, a clinic that helped people quit smoking was able to get a telephone number that spelled out the phrase NO SMOKE. This phrase worked well as a semantic code.

How do people remember long-distance telephone numbers? With area codes included, such phone numbers are 10 digits long. Actually, most people do not try to remember the numbers as a series of 10 separate items. They try to remember the area code as a single, separate chunk of information. They become familiar with the area codes of surrounding areas and places where their long-distance friends and relatives live. When they know where someone lives, they sometimes already know and remember the area code.

If you had known that **OTTFFSSENT** stood for the first letters of the numbers 1 through 10, you could have reduced the number of chunks of information you needed to hold in short-term memory from 10 down to 1. That one chunk would have been a single rule: make a list of letters in which each letter is the first letter of the numbers 1 through 10. Of course, your ability to remember the 10 letters rested on the fact that you already knew the numbers 1 through 10 (and how to spell them). But most likely, you learned this information by heart when you were much younger.

Three Stages of Memory

Sensory input → Attention → **Rehearsal** → **Rehearsal** / **Storage** / **Retrieval**

Sensory registers

Sensory Memory   **Short-Term Memory**   **Long-Term Memory**

FIGURE 7.2 *Psychologists have identified three stages of memory. Outside stimuli first enter sensory memory. Here most stimuli are soon forgotten. Certain pieces of information—those to which attention is paid—enter* *short-term memory, where they remain if they are rehearsed. Information that is not rehearsed is forgotten. Information needed for future use is stored in long-term memory, where it can be retrieved when necessary.*

Interference   Short-term memory is like a shelf that holds only so much. Once a shelf is full, you cannot put something on it without shoving something else off. Only a limited amount of information at a time can be retained in short-term memory. **Interference** occurs when new information appears in short-term memory and takes the place of what is already there.

A classic experiment by Lloyd and Margaret Peterson (1959) showed how new information can cause problems with what is stored in short-term memory. The Petersons asked college students to remember three-letter combinations, such as ZBT. Because most students can remember seven chunks of information, this task was fairly easy. Nearly 100 percent of the students could recall the three-letter sequences when asked to repeat them immediately. But then the Petersons asked the students to count backward from a number such as 142 by threes (142, 139, 136, 133, and so forth). After a certain amount of time passed, the students were then asked to stop counting backward and to report the letters they had been asked to remember. After only three seconds of this interference, the percentage of students who could recall their letters dropped by about half. After 18 seconds had elapsed, practically nobody could recall the letters. The numbers that entered the students' short-term memory while they were counting backward had displaced the letters in nearly all cases.

Interference was what happened to Dan at Hannah's party. His conversation with Linda and Todd, especially when Todd asked him the time, interfered with his short-term memory of the phone number. When Dan looked at his watch and told Todd it was 9:37, it was as if the new numbers bumped the old numbers off the shelf of his short-term memory.

Short-term memory is very useful, but it is only a temporary solution to the problem of remembering information. It allows us just enough time to find a way to store the information more permanently. Short-term memory is the bridge between sensory memory and long-term memory.

Long-Term Memory

Long-term memory is the third, and final, stage of memory of information. (Figure 7.2 shows all three stages of memory.) If you want to remember something more than just briefly, you have to take certain steps to store it in your long-term memory. Mechanical repetition (maintenance rehearsal) is one way of transferring information from short-term memory to long-term memory. Relating new information to information that you already know (elaborative rehearsal) is another.

New information is constantly being transferred into your long-term memory. Your long-term memory already contains far more information than an encyclopedia or a computer's hard drive. It holds names, dates, places, the memory of how you kidded around with the student in front of you in second grade, and the expression on your mother's face when you gave her the picture you drew of her in fourth grade. Your long-term memory contains more words, pictures, sounds, smells, tastes, and touches than you could count.

When Linda heard the song at the party, it brought back images and feelings stored in her long-term memory. The song reminded her of being back in the seventh grade. Had she been asked to reminisce about what she remembered, she probably could have talked for a long time about many of the feelings and experiences she had when she was 13, with all their rich sights, sounds, smells, and even tastes.

Capacity of Memory Our long-term memory holds the equivalent of vast numbers of videos and films of our lifetime of experience. All of them are in color (as long as we can perceive color). They also come with stereo sound (as long as we can hear), with smells, tastes, and touches thrown in. This light and sound show will never fit on any stage. But all of it is contained comfortably within our long-term memory. And there is room for more, much more. How much more? Psychologists have yet to discover a limit to how much can be stored in a person's long-term memory.

It is true that there is no known limit to how much information a person can remember. **There seems to be no restriction on** the capacity of long-term memory.

Although there is apparently no limit to how much we can remember, we do not store all of our experiences permanently. Not everything that reaches our short-term memory is transferred to our long-term memory. Our memory is limited by the amount of attention we pay to things. We are more likely to remember the things that capture our attention. If we are distracted or uninvolved with what is occurring around us, we are not going to remember as much as we will if we are interested and paying attention. The memories we have stored in our long-term memory are the incidents and experiences that have had the greatest impact on us.

Memory as Reconstructive Some psychologists once thought that nearly all the perceptions and ideas people had were stored permanently in their memory. Supporters of this view often pointed to the work of Wilder Penfield (1969), a brain surgeon. Many of Penfield's patients reported that they had experienced images that felt like memories when parts of their brain were stimulated electrically during surgery. From this information, some observers inferred that experiences become a physical part of the brain and that proper stimulation can cause people to remember them.

Today psychologists recognize that electrical stimulation of the brain does not bring about the accurate replay of memories. Memory expert Elizabeth Loftus, for example, notes that the memories stimulated by Penfield's instruments had little in the way of detail and were often factually incorrect (Loftus, 1983; Loftus & Loftus, 1980).

We now know that memories are not recorded and played back like videos or movies. Rather, they are reconstructed from the bits and pieces of our experience. When we reconstruct our memories, we tend to shape them according to the personal and individual ways in which we view the world. Thus, we tend to remember things in accordance with our beliefs and needs. That is, we put our own personal stamp on our memories. This is one of the reasons brothers and sisters can have differing memories of the same family events. Each sibling has interpreted the information differently.

Schemas The mental representations that we form of the world by organizing bits of information into knowledge are called **schemas**. To understand better what is meant by a schema, take out the sheet of paper on which you wrote the names of the objects you saw in Figure 7.1. Without looking back at Figure 7.1, draw the items on your sheet of paper. Try to make your drawings as similar to the originals as you can. (But again, no peeking!)

Now turn to Figure 7.3 on page 166. Are your drawings more similar to those in Group 1 or those in Group 2? Because of the labels you had already written on the sheet of paper, your drawings probably look more like the ones in Group 1. The labels

PSYCHOLOGY
IN THE WORLD TODAY

Can We Trust Eyewitness Testimony?

Jean Piaget, the renowned child psychologist, described an attempt to kidnap him from his baby carriage along the Champs-Élysées in Paris. He portrayed the excited people, the scrapes on the face of the nurse who rescued him, the police officer's baton, and the escape of the kidnapper. Although Piaget's memories were clear, they were false. Years later, the nurse admitted that she had made up the tale.

Can eyewitness testimony be trusted? Is the testimony of eyewitnesses any more factual than that of Piaget? Legal professionals are concerned about the accuracy of our memories as reflected in eyewitness testimony (Wells et al., 2000). Misidentification of suspects "creates a double horror: The wrong person is devastated by this personal tragedy, and the real criminal is still out on the streets" (Loftus, 1993, p. 550).

One problem with eyewitness testimony is that the words chosen by a lawyer interviewing a witness can influence the reconstruction of memories (Wells et al., 2000). For example, as in the experiment described on page 166, a lawyer might ask the witness, "How fast was the car going when it *smashed* into the other car?" In such a case, the car might be reported as going faster than if the question had been: "How fast was the car going when the accident occurred?" (Loftus & Palmer, 1974). Could the use of the word *smashed* bias the witness? What about jurors who heard the word *smashed*? Would they assume that the driver had been reckless?

Children tend to be more suggestible witnesses than adults, and preschoolers are more suggestible than older children (Ceci & Bruck, 1993). But when questioned carefully, even young children may be able to provide accurate and useful testimony (Ceci & Bruck, 1993).

There are cases in which the memories of eyewitnesses have been "refreshed" by hypnosis. But hypnosis does more than enhance memories; it can

Even when witnesses believe they are telling the truth, their memories may be inaccurate.

also distort them (Loftus, 1994). Witnesses may accept suggestions made by the hypnotist as their own memories. Witnesses may report false memories obtained through hypnosis as forcefully as if they were real (Loftus, 1994).

There are also problems in the identification of criminals by eyewitnesses. Witnesses may pay more attention to the suspect's clothing than to more important characteristics such as facial features, height, and weight. In one experiment, viewers of a videotaped crime incorrectly identified a man as the criminal because he wore the eyeglasses and T-shirt that had been worn by the actual criminal on the tape (Sanders, 1984).

Other problems with eyewitness testimony include the following:

- Identification of suspects is less accurate when suspects belong to ethnic or racial groups that differ from that of the witness (Egeth, 1993).
- Identification of suspects is confused when interrogators make misleading suggestions (Loftus, 1997).
- Witnesses are seen as more believable when they claim to be certain in their testimony, but there is little evidence that such claims are accurate (Wells et al., 2000).

There are thus many problems with eyewitness testimony. Yet even Elizabeth Loftus (1993), who has extensively studied the accuracy of eyewitness testimony, agrees that it is a valuable tool in the courtroom. After all, identifications made by eyewitnesses are frequently correct, and what, Loftus asks, is the alternative? If we were to prevent eyewitnesses from testifying, how many criminals would go free?

Think About It

Drawing Inferences and Conclusions How do you think eyewitness testimony could be made more reliable?

served as schemas for the drawing—they helped you mentally represent the objects. When you drew the items, you did not draw them exactly from memory. Rather, you drew them to fit the schemas. Therefore, you did not recall them exactly. You reconstructed them from your ideas about what eyeglasses and hourglasses look like. People who have been told that the initial drawings are of a dumbbell and a table, on the other hand, reconstruct drawings more similar to those in Group 2 (Carmichael et al., 1932).

Elizabeth Loftus and J. C. Palmer (1974) conducted a classic experiment on the role of schemas in memory. They showed people a film of a car crash. Then they asked them to complete questionnaires about the film. One question asked for an estimate of how fast the cars were going when they collided. However, the phrasing of the question differed for different participants. Some participants were asked how fast the cars were going when they "hit" each other. Other participants were asked how fast the cars were going when they "smashed" into each other.

The participants who had been asked how fast the cars were going when they "hit" each other estimated an average speed of 34 miles per hour. Those who had seen the word "smashed," on the other hand, estimated an average speed of 41 miles per hour. In other words, which schema people used—"hit" or "smashed"—influenced how they mentally reconstructed the crash.

The participants were questioned again a week later. They were asked if they had seen any broken glass. There was no broken glass in the film; thus, a yes answer was incorrect. Of participants who had been told that the cars had hit each other, 14 percent incorrectly said yes, there was broken glass. However, 32 percent of those who had been told that the cars had smashed into each other—more than twice the percentage of the other group—incorrectly reported seeing broken glass. Schemas influence both the ways we perceive things and the ways our memories store what we perceive.

SECTION 3 REVIEW

**Homework
Practice
Online**

Keyword: SY7 HP7

1. What are the three stages of memory?

2. How does information move through each of the three stages of memory?

3. **Critical Thinking** *Analyzing Information* Give an example of a situation in which a schema might distort a person's memory.

Memory as Reconstructive

Figures Shown

Group 1

Eyeglasses

Hourglass

Group 2

Dumbbell

Table

FIGURE 7.3 *Are your drawings more like those in Group 1 or those in Group 2? Although you may not have recalled the drawings exactly, you reconstructed them from a schema, or mental representation. Your drawings were probably more like those in Group 1 because of the labels you copied from Figure 7.1.*

Forgetting and Memory Improvement

Forgetting is the flip side of memory. Forgetting may seem simple enough. If you do not think about something, you forget it, right? Not really. It is not that simple.

Forgetting can occur at any one of the three stages of memory—sensory, short-term, or long-term memory. Information encoded in sensory memory decays almost immediately unless you pay attention to it and transfer it into short-term memory. A memory trace in a visual sensory register decays in less than a second, and a sound recorded in echoic memory lasts no more than a few seconds.

Information in short-term memory does not last much longer. It will disappear after 10 or 12 seconds unless you find a way to transfer it into your long-term memory. As Dan found out at the party, information stored in short-term memory is lost when it is displaced, or crowded out, by new information.

Information in long-term memory also can be lost. Because long-term memory holds such vast amounts of material and the material is represented in an abstract form, forgetting and other memory errors (such as recalling information incorrectly) occur. Sometimes new information becomes mixed with material you already know. Old learning can interfere with new learning. For example, if you study a new foreign language, your knowledge of a language you already know or are studying at the same time can interfere with your new learning. This is more likely to happen if the languages are somewhat similar.

Consider the example of French, Spanish, and Italian. All three are closely related to each other because they are all based on Latin, the language of the ancient Romans. French, Spanish, Italian, and Latin have similar roots and spellings. Anyone who has ever tried to learn two or more of these languages, especially at the same time, knows how easy it is to confuse them.

Basic Memory Tasks

Do you know what DAL, RIK, and KAX are? They are nonsense syllables, or meaningless sets of two

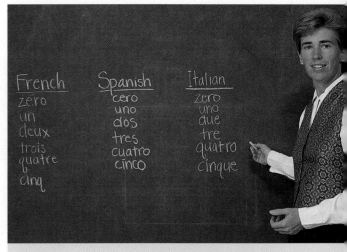

In long-term memory, old learning can interfere with new learning. If you try to learn more than one foreign language at a time, especially similar ones such as the Romance languages, you might become confused.

consonants with a vowel in the middle. Nonsense syllables provide psychologists with a way to measure three basic memory tasks: recognition, recall, and relearning.

The first researcher to use nonsense syllables to study memory and forgetting was German psychologist Hermann Ebbinghaus (1850–1909). Today his experiments are regarded as the first scientific study of forgetting, and psychologists continue to use nonsense syllables in their studies. Because nonsense syllables are meaningless, remembering them depends on acoustic coding (saying them out loud or in one's mind) and mechanical repetition (maintenance rehearsal). These tasks play a part in recognition, recall, and relearning.

Recognition　One of the three basic memory tasks is **recognition**, which involves identifying objects or events that have been encountered before. It is the easiest of the memory tasks. That is why multiple-choice tests are often considered easier than other tests. In a multiple-choice test, you need only recognize the right answer. You do not have to come up with the answer on your own.

In some experiments on recognition, psychologists ask people to read a list of nonsense syllables. The participants then read a second list of nonsense syllables and are asked whether they recognize any syllables in the second list as having appeared in the first list. In this instance, forgetting is defined as failure to recognize a nonsense syllable that had been read before.

Ebbinghaus's Curve of Forgetting

FIGURE 7.4 *Ebbinghaus found that people's ability to recall lists of words dropped sharply during the first hour after learning. After the first hour, however, losses then became more gradual.*

A classic study by Harry Bahrick and his colleagues (1975) examined recognition using a different technique. Bahrick took pictures from the yearbooks of high school graduates and mixed them in with four times as many photos of strangers. Recent graduates correctly picked out their former classmates 90 percent of the time. Graduates who had been out of school for 40 years recognized their former schoolmates less often, but not by too much—they recognized them 75 percent of the time. Keep in mind that only one photo in five was actually of a former schoolmate. Thus, if the graduates had been guessing, they would have picked out former schoolmates only 20 percent of the time. The participants recognized the photos of their former classmates far more easily than they recalled their classmates' names. The study showed that the ability of people to recognize familiar faces remains strong and lasting.

Recall The second memory task is recall. To **recall** something means to bring it back to mind. In recall, you do not simply recognize whether you have come across something before. Rather, you try to reconstruct it in your mind.

Hermann Ebbinghaus sometimes studied his own recall ability. For example, he would read a list of nonsense syllables aloud to himself while a metronome (an instrument that marks exact time) was ticking. He would then see how many nonsense syllables he could recall from memory. After reading through his list one time, Ebbinghaus could typically recall seven nonsense syllables. As noted earlier, this is the number of items most people can keep in short-term memory.

If a person memorizes a list of nonsense syllables or words and is asked to repeat the list immediately, there is generally no memory loss. But the ability to recall the list drops dramatically within an hour after learning it. In fact, about half of the nonsense syllables or words on the list are forgotten within the first hour. After that first hour, memory loss becomes more gradual. For instance, the amount of material a person remembers is cut in half again in about a month. The person continues to forget as time goes on, but the rate of forgetting slows down considerably. (See Figure 7.4.)

Psychologists also use paired associates to measure recall. Paired associates are lists of nonsense syllables, as shown in Figure 7.5. In this method, people read a list pair by pair. Later they are given the first member in each pair and are asked to recall the other one. That is, the people try to retrieve one syllable with the other serving as the cue.

Learning the vocabulary of a foreign language is something like learning paired associates. For example, a student studying Spanish might try to remember a Spanish word by pairing it with an English word that has a similar meaning. The student could most easily remember that the Spanish word *mano* means "hand" by creating a meaningful link between the words. She or he could do that by remembering that to do something *manually* is to do it by *hand*. Otherwise, the only way to remember the foreign word is by mechanical repetition (maintenance rehearsal).

Relearning The third basic memory task is **relearning**. Sometimes we do not remember things we once knew. For example, people who have been out of school for 25 years might not remember the algebraic formulas they learned when they were in high school. However, they could probably relearn them very quickly if someone showed them how to use them again. With some study and effort we can usually relearn fairly rapidly things we once knew but have forgotten.

Ebbinghaus (1885) used nonsense syllables to study relearning and other memory tasks. First, he would record how many repetitions a particular person needed to memorize a list of nonsense syllables. Then, after a few months had passed, Ebbinghaus would check on the person again. Typically, the person could not recall or even recognize the list of nonsense syllables that she or he had memorized. However, Ebbinghaus found that the person was able to relearn the list more quickly than she or he had learned it the first time.

Different Kinds of Forgetting

Much of the time, forgetting is due to interference or decay. As you have already learned, interference occurs when new information shoves aside or disrupts what has been placed in memory. **Decay**—the fading away of a memory—is similar to a burning candle. The candle burns down until it goes out. Both decay and interference are part of normal forgetting. They occur when memory traces fade from sensory or short-term memory. Memory loss also occurs in long-term memory when something that has been stored there cannot be retrieved. However, there are more extreme kinds of forgetting.

Repression

According to Sigmund Freud, the founder of psychoanalytic theory, we sometimes forget things on purpose without even knowing we are doing it. Some memories may be so painful and unpleasant that they make us feel anxiety, guilt, or shame. To protect ourselves from such disturbing memories, said Freud, we forget them by pushing them out of our consciousness. Freud called this kind of forgetting *repression*. For example, a person might forget to go to a dentist appointment because he or she expects the experience to be unpleasant. However, the extent to which repression occurs—and even *whether* repression occurs—is controversial in contemporary psychology.

Paired Associates

FIGURE 7.5 *Psychologists often use paired associates, such as those shown here, to measure recall. The task is to recall the second syllable in the pair when given the first syllable as a cue.*

Amnesia

Psychoanalysts believe that repression is responsible for a rare but severe kind of forgetting called dissociative amnesia. Amnesia is severe memory loss caused by brain injury, shock, fatigue, illness, or repression. Dissociative amnesia is thought to be caused by psychological trauma (an extremely upsetting experience or series of experiences). Other kinds of amnesia include infantile amnesia, anterograde amnesia, and retrograde amnesia.

Infantile Amnesia Some people think that they can remember special events that took place in their infancy, but they cannot. After many years of hearing his patients talk about their childhoods, Freud found that they could not remember things that had happened to them before the age of three. This forgetting of early events is called **infantile amnesia**.

People who think that they can remember their birth have probably constructed the memory from other memories. For example, they may remember being told about their birth by a parent or another family member. Or they may remember the birth of a younger sibling and then use that information to create a memory of their own birth.

The reason people have infantile amnesia is not that the events happened a long time ago. People in their 70s and 80s have many precise memories of their life between the ages of 6 and 10, even though the events they remember occurred 60 or 70 years earlier. College freshmen, meanwhile, have difficulty remembering events that occurred before the age of 6, even though these events occurred only 13 or 14 years earlier (Wetzler & Sweeney, 1986). Thus, failure to recall events from infancy or early childhood is not simply a matter of gradually forgetting information over many years.

Freud explained infantile amnesia in terms of repression. He believed that young children often have aggressive and sexual feelings toward their parents but that they forget these feelings as they get older. However, repression may not be the reason, or at least the only reason, people forget events from their earliest years. The fact that people tend to forget boring and bland events from their early childhoods casts doubt on Freud's theory.

Infantile amnesia probably reflects biological and cognitive factors. For example, a part of the brain (the hippocampus) that is involved in the storage of memories does not become mature until we are about two years old (Squire, 1993, 1996). Also, myelination of brain pathways is incomplete for the first few years, so memory formation remains somewhat inefficient.

There are also cognitive reasons for infantile amnesia:

- Infants are not particularly interested in remembering the past year (Neisser, 1993).
- Infants, unlike older children and adults, tend not to weave episodes together into meaningful stories of their lives. Information about specific episodes thus tends to be lost.
- Infants do not make reliable use of language to symbolize or classify events. Their ability to encode sensory input is therefore limited.

TRUTH OR fiction ▪ REVISITED ▪

It is not true that you can remember important events from the first two years of life. Apparent infant memories are reconstructed and probably inaccurate. Many factors contribute to and help explain this memory loss during the first two years of life.

Note that infantile amnesia refers to memory of specific events (episodic memory). We certainly learn and remember many other things during infancy and early childhood using semantic and implicit memory. For example, we learn who our parents are and learn to have strong feelings for them. We learn and remember the language spoken at home. We learn how to encourage other people to care for us. We learn how to get from one part of the home to another. We remember such information and skills quite well.

Anterograde Amnesia   Trauma to the brain caused by a blow to the head, electric shock, or brain surgery can cause memory loss of events that took place both before and after the trauma. Memory loss from trauma that prevents a person from forming new memories is called **anterograde amnesia**. Certain kinds of brain damage, such as damage to the hippocampus, have been linked to anterograde amnesia (Corkin et al., 1985; Squire et al., 1984).

Retrograde Amnesia   In **retrograde amnesia**, people forget the period leading up to a traumatic event. For example, many people who are injured in auto accidents do not remember that they were in the car before the accident. Similarly, athletes who are knocked unconscious during a game often have no memory of what happened before the play in which they were injured. Some cannot even remember starting the game.

In the most severe cases of retrograde amnesia, the person cannot remember a period of several *years* prior to the traumatic incident. One man with retrograde amnesia received a head injury in a motorcycle accident (Baddeley, 1982). When he woke up after the accident, he had no memory of anything that had happened since he was 11 years old. As a matter of fact, he thought that he was still 11. Over a period of months, he regained much of his memory, but he never did remember what happened just before the accident.

Improving Memory

Memory can be improved, and there are specific ways to go about improving it. As a result of studies of memory and forgetting, psychologists have been able to identify different strategies people can use to improve their memory. Some of the methods they recommend are discussed in the rest of this section. You may find them helpful.

Drill and Practice   One basic way to remember information is by going over it again and again, that

CASE STUDIES
AND OTHER TRUE STORIES

The Case of H.M.

Studies of people who have undergone brain surgery to reduce epileptic seizures have helped provide a clearer picture of the relationship between amnesia and damage to certain parts of the brain. In the operations, which are now performed only rarely, the patients had one or both of their temporal lobes surgically removed to stop the epileptic seizures. One of the most famous of these cases was that of a man known by his initials: H.M.

H.M. suffered from severe epileptic seizures beginning at the age of 16. His seizures became worse as he reached adulthood. By the time he was 27, he could no longer function at work or live a normal life. At that point, he agreed to undergo surgery to reduce the rate and severity of the seizures. Surgery was performed to remove part of his hippocampus.

Following the operation, H.M.'s personality and mental functioning seemed to be normal. However, as time went on, it became increasingly difficult for him to process new information. His memory of events during the year leading up to the operation was weak, and his ability to learn and store new information was almost nonexistent. For example, two years after the surgery, H.M. thought he was still 27 years old. His memory was so poor that he forgot something as soon as he was distracted from rehearsing it.

When he moved with his family to a new home, he could not remember his new address or how to reach his new home. When his uncle died, he expressed appropriate grief at the loss. However, he then began asking about his uncle and wanting to know why he did not visit. Each time he was told that his uncle was dead, H.M. grieved as if he were hearing the information for the first time.

The formal testing that was done on H.M. showed that he could remember verbal information for as long as 15 minutes if he was allowed to rehearse it. However, it soon became clear that H.M.'s operation had caused him to lose the ability to transfer information from his short-term memory to his long-term memory. As soon as his short-term memory capacity reached its limit, or he was distracted from the rehearsing he had to do to keep new information in his short-term memory, he would forget the information. His capacity to remember nonverbal material was even more impaired. With or without distractions, he forgot even simple figures, such as circles, squares, and triangles.

Despite this severe memory loss, H.M. retained a limited capacity to learn, although the learning process was very slow and difficult. For example, H.M. had to exert great effort to learn to navigate a very short visual maze. What took most people only a couple of trials to master took H.M. 155 trials. Surprisingly, a week after he did so, H.M. remembered what he had painstakingly learned. Two years later he still retained some of what he had learned. At that time, it took him only 39 trials to relearn his way through the maze (116 fewer trials than he had needed to learn it originally).

H.M. showed learning ability in other situations as well. When he was asked to trace the drawing of a star by looking at its reflection in a mirror, he completed the task successfully. Not only did he draw the star as well as other people do, but his ability to retain what he had learned was also normal. For example, on the second and third days, he performed as well on the first trial of the day as he had on the last trial of the day before. That was evidence that there was no memory loss from day to day. Apparently, the operation he had did not significantly impair his ability to retain motor skills even though his ability to transfer information from short-term memory into long-term memory was impaired.

THINKING CRITICALLY

1. **Summarizing** How did H.M.'s operation affect his memory and capacity to learn?
2. **Drawing Inferences and Conclusions** What conclusions can psychologists draw from the case of H.M?

JUMP START reprinted by permission of United Feature Syndicate, Inc.

is, by repetition, or drill and practice. Repetition is one fairly effective way to transfer information from sensory memory to short-term memory and from short-term memory to long-term memory.

Mechanical repetition may sound boring. Nevertheless, it was by repetition that we all learned the alphabet and how to count. We can memorize the spellings and meanings of new vocabulary words by repeating them over and over again. Math students can memorize formulas by writing and rewriting them. They can then use their time on tests to figure out how to use the formulas rather than spending time trying to remember what they are.

You can remember facts in social studies and other courses by pairing different pieces of information with each other and then drilling yourself on the connections between the items. This is what flash cards do. Use flash cards and write each word or phrase from the pair on a different side of a card. For example, write, "The U.S. president during the Persian Gulf War" on one side of the card and "George Bush" on the other. If you make a set of flash cards and then go over them again and again, drilling yourself on the information, eventually you will know it by heart.

You can use this method to learn new vocabulary words as well. Put the words on one side of the cards and the definitions on the other, and then test yourself both ways. You can read the definitions first and see if you know the words that go with them. Then you can read the words and see if you can remember their definitions. You might then want to go on to practice using the words in sentences. If you rehearse what you have learned by going through this procedure with the cards at regular intervals, including just before a test, you should do well on the test.

Douglas Herrmann (1991) has some advice about how to remember the names of people you meet. He recommends using the names right away. This will help you remember them later. If you are introduced to a new person, for example, say his or her name aloud when you are introduced. Instead of saying, "Glad to meet you," say, "Glad to meet you, Sam." You can also use his or her name in a question, such as, "Where do you live, Sam?" As you continue to talk, use the person's name some more. You might find it even more helpful, says Herrmann, to write the name down, if you can, at the end of the conversation. If you need to remember the names of several different people you meet, you may want to write down a brief description of each person next to the listing of the person's name.

At Hannah's party, Dan concentrated so hard on remembering the telephone number of the girl he had met that he ended up forgetting her name as well as her number. He forgot her number because he did not write it down soon enough while it was still in his short-term memory. He then forgot her name, too, because he was so confident he would remember it that he did not bother to rehearse it sufficiently to keep it in his short-term memory.

Relate to Things You Already Know Relating new information to what you already know (elaborative rehearsal) is not as mechanical and repetitious as drill and practice (maintenance rehearsal). Relating new information to what you already know requires you to think more deeply about the new information (Willoughby et al., 1994). As a result, you may remember the new information better.

There are many situations in which elaborative rehearsal can be helpful. For example, if you were trying to remember the spelling of the word *retrieve,* you would probably do it by recalling the rule "i before e except after c." But then how would you remember the spelling of the word *weird,* which does not follow the rule? One way would be to use elaborative rehearsal on the word by recalling that it does not follow the "*i before e*" rule because it's a "weird" word.

Learning to expand our knowledge by relating new information to things we already know begins early. For instance, children learn that a lion is like a house cat, only bigger and more dangerous.

Form Unusual Associations

It is sometimes easier to remember a piece of information if you can make an unusual or even humorous association between that piece of information and something else. That will make it stand out from ordinary things and thus help you recall it. For example, suppose that you wanted to memorize the symbol for the chemical element tin. You could remember that *Sn* is the symbol for tin by thinking of a *snake* in a *tin* can. The more unusual the association, the more effective it will probably be.

Sometimes people can enhance memory by forming a group of unusual associations. Suppose that you need to buy groceries but do not have time to write out a shopping list. How will you remember what items to buy? First, think of a group of related images, such as the parts of your body. Then picture each dish you plan to cook as hanging from a different body part. For example, you might envision lasagna hanging off your left shoulder. When you are at the supermarket, mentally go through the body parts you have designated and see what is connected to each one. When you get to the left shoulder and envision the lasagna, tick off the items you want to buy in order to make the lasagna: lasagna noodles, tomato paste, mozzarella cheese, and so forth.

Construct Links

Constructing links between items is another way elaborative rehearsal can help improve memory. You may find it easier to remember vocabulary words from a foreign language if you construct a meaningful link between each foreign word and its English equivalent (Atkinson, 1975). One way to create such a link is to find part of the foreign word and construct a sentence or phrase that includes that part of the word in English. For example, suppose that you are trying to remember that a *peso* (PAY-soh) is a unit of Mexican money. You might note that *peso* contains the letters *pe,* and then construct the following sentence: "*Pe*ople *pay* with money." Then, when you come across the word *peso,* you recognize the *pe* and retrieve the sentence that serves as the link. From that sentence, you can then reconstruct the meaning of the word *peso* as "a unit of money."

Use Mnemonic Devices

All these methods for improving memory are called *mnemonics* (ni-MAH-niks). Mnemonic devices are systems for remembering information. Such devices usually combine chunks of information into a format, such as an acronym, phrase, or jingle. For example, many psychology students have used the acronym *Roy G. Biv* to remember the colors of the spectrum (*r*ed, *o*range, *y*ellow, *g*reen, *b*lue, *i*ndigo, and *v*iolet).

In biology, you can remember that dromedary camels have one hump, whereas Bactrian camels have two humps. How? Just turn the uppercase letters D and B on their sides and count the "humps" in each one. In geography, the acronym HOMES stands for the Great Lakes: *H*uron, *O*ntario, *M*ichigan, *E*rie, and *S*uperior.

Douglas Herrmann (1991) recommends using a mnemonic device to remember the name of someone new. He suggests that you make up a little rhyme that uses the name. For example, suppose

the name of the girl Dan met at the party was Kate. When he stopped talking to her, he might have made up this rhyme: "I've met my next date; her name is Kate." However, he wanted to remember her telephone number as well as her name. Since poetry and telephone numbers do not mix very well, a poem would not have been much help in this case.

TRUTH *OR* **fiction** ■ REVISITED ■

It is true that there are certain tricks you can use to improve your memory. Such tricks are called mnemonic devices. These devices provide people with systems for remembering information.

SECTION 4 REVIEW

go.hrw.com **Homework Practice Online**
Keyword: SY7 HP7

1. Explain how psychologists use nonsense syllables to study both memorization and forgetting.

2. How can memory be improved?

3. What are the differences between infantile, anterograde, and retrograde amnesia?

4. **Critical Thinking** *Drawing Inferences and Conclusions* How can you test whether you really remember something that happened in early childhood?

7 REVIEW
Chapter

 Writing a Summary

Using standard grammar, spelling, sentence structure, and punctuation, summarize the information in this chapter. Consider:
- the kinds, processes, and stages of memory
- how memory can be improved

 Identifying People and Ideas

Identify the following terms or people and use them in appropriate sentences.

1. memory
2. semantic memory
3. retrieval
4. sensory memory
5. primacy effect
6. recency effect
7. recall
8. relearning
9. infantile amnesia
10. retrograde amnesia

Understanding Main Ideas

SECTION 1 (pp. 154–155)
1. How is a flashbulb memory like a photograph?

SECTION 2 (pp. 155–160)
2. What are maintenance rehearsal and elaborative rehearsal?

SECTION 3 (pp. 160–166)
3. What are icons, and where are they held?

SECTION 4 (pp. 167–173)
4. What are mnemonics? Give an example.

 Thinking Critically

1. **Categorizing** Name the type of memory involved in each of the following situations: (a) You can recite the capitals of every U.S. state. (b) You and your friends laugh every time you think about the fun you had last summer. (c) You know how to program a VCR to tape your favorite TV show.
2. **Contrasting** Why might you and another family member have different memories of the same vacation?

3. **Analyzing Information** Which type of forgetting is usually to blame when people cannot find their car keys?
4. **Drawing Inferences and Conclusions** If you were asked to identify all the students in a photo of your third-grade class, which memory task would be involved? Why might the task be easier if you were supplied with a list of their names?
5. **Analyzing Information** Give several reasons why you may be unable to recall your fifth birthday.

 Writing About Psychology

1. **Comparing** Interview a person who must memorize a great deal of information to perform a task or job well. For example, you might interview a classmate who acts in school plays or a person who works for the U.S. postal service. Ask the person what techniques he or she uses to memorize material. Compare these techniques with information you read in this chapter. Write up your findings in a "helpful tips" column for the school newspaper.
2. **Analyzing Information** Ask your parents or older adults to describe where they were and what they were doing when they heard the news of some shocking event, such as the assassination of President John F. Kennedy or the explosion of the space shuttle *Challenger*. Ask them to describe details surrounding the event, such as what they were doing or who else was with them. Write a one-page report describing what the person remembers. Be sure to note what kind of memory the person is demonstrating. Use the graphic organizer below to help you write your report.

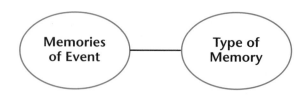

Interpreting Graphs

Study the bar graph below. Then use the information in the graph to help you answer the questions that follow.

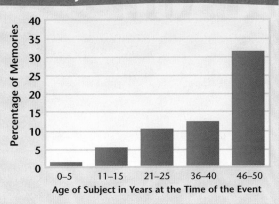

The Memory of Events from a Person's Life

Percentage of Memories (y-axis: 0, 5, 10, 15, 20, 25, 30, 35, 40)

Age of Subject in Years at the Time of the Event (x-axis: 0–5, 11–15, 21–25, 36–40, 46–50)

Source: Bjork and Bjork, *Memory*, 1996

1. Which of the following statements best reflects the information contained in the bar graph?

   a. The highest percentage of memories is of events from the recent past.

   b. The percentage of memories increases consistently as one moves from childhood to older age.

   c. People have no memories of early childhood.

   d. Adolescence is the time when most memories are formed.

2. From a psychological perspective, what unusual or interesting information does the graph reveal?

Analyzing Primary Sources

Read the following excerpt from a poem written by American poet Emily Dickinson. Then answer the questions that follow.

"The Brain—is wider than the sky—
For—put them side by side—
The one the other will contain
With ease—and You—beside—

The Brain is deeper than the sea—
For—hold them—Blue to Blue—
The one the other will absorb—
As Sponges—Buckets—do—"

3. Which of the following statements reflects one meaning of Dickinson's poem?

   a. The human brain is a surprisingly large organism.

   b. The world does not exist outside of human thought.

   c. The functioning of the human brain is a mystery that only poetry is capable of explaining.

   d. The human brain is able to "contain" the world around us through memory and thought.

4. Why, according to Dickinson, is the brain "wider than the sky" and "deeper than the sea"?

PSYCHOLOGY PROJECTS

Cooperative Learning

Using Your Observation Skills Working in groups, conduct an experiment on the primacy and recency effects. Make up a list of 15 items. Have everyone in the group show a copy of the list to friends, and then see how many items the friends can remember and write down. Pool your findings and, calculate what percentage of participants were able to recall the first item, the second item, and so on. Make a line graph of the results. Does the graph demonstrate the primacy and recency effects?

internet connect

Internet Activity: go.hrw.com
KEYWORD: SY7 CH7

Choose an activity on memory to:

- create a mnemonic device on the types and stages of memory.
- make a flowchart or diagram on memory processes.
- design and test a method of memory improvement.

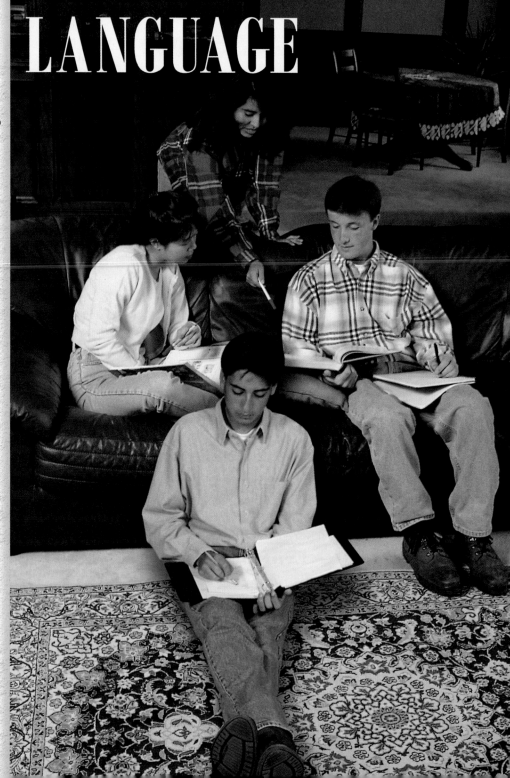

Chapter 8

THINKING AND LANGUAGE

Read to Discover

1 What are the three units of thought?

2 What steps can be used to solve problems?

3 How do deductive reasoning and inductive reasoning differ?

4 What strategies can be used in decision making?

5 What are the basic elements of language?

A DAY IN THE LIFE

"I can*not* figure out this trig problem!" Dan sighed. He, Marc, Linda, and Hannah were studying. "This is so frustrating!"

"I know what you mean," replied Hannah. "I'm stumped on this crossword puzzle assignment for world history. Here's one of the clues: 'The _____ Republic.' Five letters, C _ _ C H. What could that be?"

After a brief pause, Linda blurted out, "The *Czech* Republic!"

"Oh, of course. The CZ was throwing me off," stated Hannah.

Dan smiled and said, "Very good, Linda. Now does someone want to help with my trig problem?"

"I have problems of my own to solve," said Marc. "Like whether to take Japanese or creative writing next semester. Hannah, how hard will Japanese be?"

"How should I know?" she asked.

"Because you speak Korean, right? Korea and Japan are pretty near each other, so I figured the languages would be similar."

"As far as I know, Korean and Japanese are completely different."

"Oh. That's no help, then. Well, either way, I have to figure out how to tell Mr. Hochberg I'm not taking computer science, which is what *he* suggested I take." Mr. Hochberg is the school's guidance counselor.

"Mr. Hochberg will understand. When I talked to him last year about what courses to take, he was very open to my ideas," said Linda.

"Oh!" Dan exclaimed. "I just figured out the trig problem. Weird. I had stopped thinking about it."

"I think we should all stop thinking about studying for a moment," Linda stated. "Tonight is my night to cook dinner for my family. What am I going to make?"

"How about making macaroni and cheese?" Dan suggested.

"Had it last night," said Linda.

"Tacos?" put in Hannah.

"My sister doesn't eat red meat," Linda replied.

"Chicken stew?" Marc proposed.

"I don't have all the ingredients."

"So go to the store and get them!" the other three said together.

"I guess I could do that," Linda reflected. "That sounds like a pretty good idea, come to think of it."

• • •

This chapter is about thinking. When you are awake, you are probably thinking nearly all the time. But the type of thinking you are doing may vary from moment to moment. You may be solving a problem, such as Dan's math problem, Hannah's crossword puzzle, or Linda's dinner dilemma. Or you may be reasoning—using information to draw a conclusion. Or perhaps you are making a decision, such as Marc's decision about which course to take. Problem solving, reasoning, and decision making are three types of thinking explored in this chapter. And because thinking often relies on language, this chapter also deals with language.

thinking
symbol
concept
prototype
algorithm
heuristic
difference reduction
means-end analysis
incubation effect
mental set
functional fixedness
convergent thinking
divergent thinking
reasoning
deductive reasoning
premise
inductive reasoning
confirmation bias
representativeness
  heuristic
availability heuristic
anchoring heuristic
framing effect
language
phoneme
morpheme
syntax
semantics
overregularization
language acquisition
  device

HOLT

Psychology Video Program

Watch the video to learn about a parrot who has a way with language.

TRUTH OR fiction?

Read the following statements about psychology. Do you think they are true or false? You will learn whether each statement is true or false as you read the chapter.

- The most reliable way of solving a problem correctly is not always the best way of solving it.
- If you do not see the answer to a problem right away, you will probably not be able to solve it.
- Scientists can never prove for certain that their theories are true.
- Most people easily change their opinions when presented with convincing arguments.
- Once a child learns the correct form of a word, he or she will never use the incorrect form.

SECTION 1

What Is Thinking?

Thinking is the mental activity that is involved in the understanding, processing, and communicating of information. But how is all this accomplished? Thinking is made possible through the use of symbols, concepts, and prototypes. These are all units of thought.

Symbols

When we think, we use symbols to represent the things about which we are thinking. A **symbol** is an object or an act that stands for something else. As you are probably aware, symbols are a part of our daily lives. Your school mascot and the American flag are both examples of symbols. Different types of symbols are found in mathematics. Plus and minus

A DAY IN THE LIFE

signs, for example, are both symbols: the plus sign signifies "add," and the minus sign signifies "subtract." Dan probably was all too familiar with various mathematics symbols from his trigonometry class.

Letters and words are also symbols. After all, a word actually stands for something else—it is not the thing itself. For example, the word *plate* is not itself a plate—it only refers to an object that is called a plate in English.

Even your mental images are a type of symbol. If you picture a dog in your mind, that image stands

Shown here is the Greek letter psi—the symbol of the American Psychological Association.

for a dog, but of course it is not itself a dog. If it were not for symbols, we would be unable to think about things that were not present.

Concepts

What do dogs, horses, and elephants have in common? You may say that they are all animals, or perhaps you may say that they are all mammals. When we think, we tend to mentally group together objects, events, or ideas that have similar characteristics, as dogs, horses, and elephants do. Such a grouping is called a **concept**. "Animal" and "mammal" are both examples of concepts.

Much thinking involves categorizing new items and manipulating the relationships among them. Think of a new kind of animal, for instance—just make one up. What makes it an animal? You have used the concept "animal" to create a new item that fits into the "animal" category. Now imagine your new animal in a tree eating a piece of fruit. You are thinking about relationships among concepts (your animal, the tree, and the fruit).

People organize concepts in hierarchies, series of levels that go from broad to narrow. As we saw above, dogs, horses, and elephants can be grouped both as animals and as mammals. The "animal" concept is higher up in the hierarchy than is the "mammal" concept because it is broader, or contains more elements. Sparrows, goldfish, and spiders are all animals, but they are not mammals.

People learn concepts through experience. Simple concepts such as "ball" and "vegetable" are taught by means of examples. We point to a baseball or a basketball and say, "Ball" or "This is a ball" to a child. We point to broccoli or carrots and say, "Eat your vegetables." Communication of the meaning of abstract concepts such as fairness, beauty, and goodness may require detailed explanations, a variety of personal experiences, and many examples. Even then, people may still disagree about what is fair, beautiful, or good.

Prototypes

Often when we think about a concept, we have an image in our minds of a particular example of that concept, even though a concept is a category and contains many different examples. For instance, picture a shoe in your mind. What does the shoe you pictured look like? Does it have shoelaces, straps, or neither? Does it have a heel, or is it flat-soled?

The shoe you imagined was a **prototype**—an example of a concept that best exemplifies that concept. A prototype does not have to be an actual, experienced example, such as a particular shoe you have seen. Instead, a prototype can be more like an average of all experienced examples. You may never have seen a shoe that looks exactly like your shoe prototype, but your prototype probably contains elements of many different shoes you have seen.

Which do you think is a better example of a shoe: a loafer or a slipper? You probably said a loafer. Why? Because a loafer is probably closer to your "shoe" prototype than is a slipper. Most people think of shoes as items that are worn outside or in public, and slippers usually are worn only around the house. But a slipper is a type of shoe.

Even though there are many, many different types of shoes, you probably picture only one type when you hear the word shoe. *What you picture is your prototype of a shoe.*

SECTION 1 REVIEW

 Homework Practice Online
Keyword: SY7 HP8

1. Define *thinking*.
2. List and describe three units of thought.
3. **Critical Thinking** *Drawing Inferences and Conclusions* Is a concept a type of symbol? Why or why not?

SECTION **2**

Problem Solving

A DAY IN THE LIFE

People solve many different kinds of problems. Some, such as Dan's trigonometry problem, are in math and science. In such cases, people often use formulas and scientific facts to solve the problems. For example, they may need to know the formula for the area of a circle or how many protons oxygen contains.

Other problems concern fitting things into a busy schedule or paying for what we need. Such problems are best solved by budgeting. Still other problems are social problems, such as how Marc should approach Mr. Hochberg about his choice of an elective for next semester. How should Marc tell Mr. Hochberg that he really wants to take Japanese or creative writing rather than computer science?

Solving problems involves a series of processes including analyzing the problem, breaking it into component parts, and establishing goals. Intermediate goals address parts of the problem that must be solved to arrive at the terminal goal—that is, the final solution to the problem.

Figure 8.1 on the next page shows some more problems. Try to solve them now. If you have difficulty with any of them, do not worry—you will learn the answers as you read.

Algorithms and Heuristics

In many cases, people do not go straight from a problem to its solution in one giant leap. Rather, they move toward the solution in a series of steps. Ideally, each step taken moves the problem solver closer to the solution. But how do people know what steps to take? If they do not know the solution, how can they know where to start?

Through experience, people know that different types of problems must be approached in different ways. By simply identifying the type of problem it is, people have an idea of which method to use—which steps to take—in solving the problem.

Algorithms Some types of problems are best approached with the use of an algorithm. An **algorithm** is a specific procedure that, when used

Six Problems to Solve

A

Naomi, Marquita, and Kim are planning to go to a party, and they want to prepare for the party together. The party is across the street from Naomi's home, so the three meet there an hour before the party. When, at the end of the hour, they are ready to go to the party, they discover that it has started to rain heavily. None of them wants to get wet because they are all wearing nice clothing. Unfortunately, they only have one umbrella for the three of them, and the umbrella is big enough to protect only two people from the rain. How can all three of them get to the party without becoming drenched?

B

Imagine that you are a doctor. One of your patients has a stomach tumor that must be destroyed if the patient is to live. Certain rays will destroy the tumor if they are intense enough. To reach the tumor, however, the rays need to pass through the healthy tissue that surrounds it, and at the intensity needed to destroy the tumor, the rays will also destroy the healthy tissue. How can you use the rays to destroy the tumor without damaging the healthy tissue? (Adapted from Duncker, 1945)

C Copy this dot formation on a sheet of tracing paper. Then connect all four dots with two straight lines without lifting your pencil from the paper.

D Imagine that you are in a room with a candle, a box of matches, and some thumbtacks. Your task is to use these objects to attach the candle to the wall. How do you do it? (Adapted from Duncker, 1945)

E Imagine that you are in a room in which two strings are hanging from the ceiling. Your task is to tie the two strings together, but they are so far apart that you cannot reach both of them at the same time. The only other object in the room is a pair of safety scissors. How can you tie the strings together? (Adapted from Maier, 1931)

F An airplane crashes on the border of Mexico and the United States. Where do you bury the survivors?

FIGURE 8.1   *Try solving these problems. You will learn the answers as you read the section.*

properly and in the right circumstances, will always lead to the solution of a problem.

Formulas are examples of algorithms. If you know the radius (r) of a circle and you want to find the area (A) of that circle, you can apply the formula $A = \pi r^2$ to get the correct answer. As long as you know the formula and how to use it correctly, you need know nothing else to solve the problem.

Many algorithms are more complex and time-consuming than simple formulas, however. One such complex algorithm is called a systematic search. In a systematic search, each possible solution to a problem is tried and tested according to a certain set of rules.

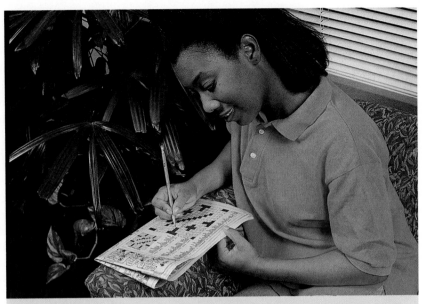

People who do crossword puzzles regularly know of several heuristics that often help lead to solutions quickly. For example, if a word ends in G, the previous two letters are often I and N.

For example, suppose that you, like Hannah, are working on a crossword puzzle. You are trying to fill in a word for which you have all but one letter—say, C L _ F F. Using a systematic search, you would try putting every letter of the alphabet, starting with A, in that blank middle space until you found the letter that formed a word that fit the clue. In other words, first you would try C L A F F, then you would try C L B F F, then C L C F F, and so on, until you came to the right letter, which would probably be an I (C L I F F). It might take some time, but as long as you had all the other letters in the word correct and as long as you were able to recognize the word once you found it, this method would be guaranteed to work.

Heuristics While algorithms are guaranteed to work, they are not always practical. Suppose, for example, that you were missing not one, but two letters of your crossword puzzle word—C _ _ F F. In order to have success with the systematic search, not only would you have to try every letter of the alphabet in each of the two spaces, but you would have to fill in one of them with a placeholder while you tried letter after letter in the other space.

In other words, first you would have to fill the first blank space with an A, then you would have to run through all 26 letters in the second blank space. And when that did not work, you would have to try a B in the first space, and then run through all the letters *again* in the second space. By the time you arrived at C L I F F, you would have already run through 294 other possible solutions.

Needless to say, although this algorithm would eventually lead to success, it would not be a very efficient way to do a crossword puzzle, nor would it be very interesting or rewarding. This is why, for many types of problems, people use heuristics rather than algorithms. **Heuristics** are rules of thumb that often, but not always, help us find the solution to a problem. They are shortcuts.

In the first crossword puzzle problem, where only one letter is missing, you probably would use the following heuristic: in a five-letter word in which four of the letters are consonants, the fifth letter will be a vowel. Thus, instead of trying *eight* possible combinations before you arrived at the letter I, you would try only *two*: A and E (the only vowels that precede I). In the second crossword puzzle problem, in which two letters are missing, a heuristic might involve deciding that certain letters of the alphabet (B, C, D, F, and so on) would be unlikely to follow the first letter C, and thus you would not even try them as possibilities. Rather, you might focus on the letters that you know are likely to follow C.

Heuristics are faster than algorithms, but they are not as reliable. For example, we might forget that if C is the first letter of a word, the letter L (a consonant rather than a vowel) might be the second. And in some circumstances, we might miss some more unusual words. This is probably what happened to Hannah with C _ _ C H. She did not try a Z in the first blank space because the letter Z usually does not directly follow the letter C. As Hannah put it, "The CZ was throwing me off." Thus, she was unable to come up with the word C Z E C H.

Problem-Solving Methods

Algorithms and heuristics are general approaches to problem solving. There are also specific methods of problem solving. Systematic searching, which we have already discussed, is one of these methods. Others include trial and error, difference reduction, means-end analysis, working backward, and use of analogy.

Trial and Error Sometimes we have little choice but to resort to trial and error in solving a problem. We know what our goal is, but we have absolutely no idea how to reach it, and all we can do is try different things and see what happens with each one until we arrive at our goal more or less by chance. Trial and error is somewhat similar to systematic searching, except that it is more haphazard and less reliable. In trial and error, we often do not keep track of which possibilities we have already tried.

If you have ever tried to work on a complicated maze puzzle, you probably found that the only thing you could do was just to pick one possible route and see where it took you. When you hit a dead end, you came back and tried something else. In other words, you used trial and error—trying one thing until it is proved to be an error.

Difference Reduction In a method called **difference reduction**, we identify our goal, where

we are in relation to it, and the direction we must go to move closer to it. In other words, we want to *reduce the difference* between our present situation (problem unsolved) and our desired situation (problem solved).

Suppose you are standing blindfolded on the side of a hill. Your goal is to get to the top of the hill, but because you cannot see, you do not know which way to go. So what do you do? You take a step. If you feel yourself moving downward, then you know that you are going the wrong way and that you must change direction. But if you feel a pull in your legs that means you are moving upward, you know you are getting closer to the top of the hill. You have identified which direction to go in to move closer to your goal.

The difference-reduction method is a heuristic, however, and thus is not always reliable. Sometimes we may think we have reached our goal when we have not. Suppose that the hillside levels off for a bit and then continues upward to the top, for instance. You may think you have reached the top when you arrive at this level place, and you may stop there. You do not know that there is more hill ahead.

Furthermore, sometimes we have to take what seems to be a step away from our goal in order to

This woman will probably use trial and error to figure out which key is the correct one.

achieve that goal. For example, to straighten up your desk, you might have to take everything out of the drawers first, to organize the contents—even though this would seem to be a step in the wrong direction (since at first, things will become messier rather than neater). Similarly, what seems to be moving us closer to a goal may actually be moving us farther away.

Problem A in Figure 8.1 highlights some of the pitfalls of the difference-reduction method. In order for Naomi, Marquita, and Kim to get to the party dry, two of them (say, Marquita and Kim) must cross the street to the party first, leaving the third one (Naomi) back at Naomi's home. But then either Marquita or Kim must *leave* the party and go back with the umbrella for Naomi. In other words, they must temporarily increase, rather than decrease, the difference between the goal (all three of them at the party) and their present situation (two of them at the party but one of them not). One of the two currently at the party must temporarily leave the party.

When people set out to cook or bake something, they use means-end analysis to break the task down into individual steps.

Means-End Analysis Another heuristic problem-solving technique is called means-end analysis.

A DAY IN THE LIFE

In **means-end analysis**, we know that certain things we can do (means) will have certain results (ends). If the stew Linda is making for dinner seems bland, adding pepper will probably help. Adding water probably will not.

As with the difference-reduction method, means-end analysis aims to reduce the difference between where we are and where we want to be. But means-end analysis goes beyond difference reduction in its awareness that a particular action will have a particular effect. Whereas the difference-reduction user asks, "What direction must I move in to get from here to there?" the means-end-analysis user asks, "What can I do to get there?"

Those who use means-end-analysis often break a problem down into parts and then try to solve each part individually, recognizing that solving each of the parts will contribute to solving the entire problem. We do this all the time without realizing it.

Once Linda had decided to make chicken stew for dinner, for example, she first had to identify the ingredients she needed. Then she had to figure out how to obtain these ingredients—a trip to the grocery store seemed necessary. Next, she had to figure out which store to go to, how to get there, how to find what she needed once she arrived at the store, and how to pay for what she bought. Finally, she had to figure out how to put the ingredients together in the way that would yield the taste and flavor she was trying to achieve—in other words, she had to do the actual cooking. Each of these steps was one means toward the end of serving chicken stew for dinner.

Working Backward Related to means-end analysis is the technique known as working backward. As in means-end analysis, working backward involves breaking a problem down into parts and then dealing with each part individually. In working backward, however, the problem solver starts by examining the final goal, then works back from the final goal to the present position to determine the best course of action.

This method is particularly useful when we know what we want to accomplish but are not sure how best to begin. Working backward helps ensure that we start off on the right path and avoid having to retrace our steps if we discover that the path we have chosen does not lead where we want to be.

vote too. That expectation is an anchor in your life. Beliefs about politics, religion, and way of life are common anchors. When something happens that makes people question the beliefs they have grown up with, they may change their beliefs a bit. But most people change only reluctantly.

When people form judgments or make estimates, they begin with an initial view, called a presumption. The initial view serves as the anchor. As they receive additional information, they make adjustments. But such adjustments are often difficult for people to make, and sometimes people are unwilling to make them.

The Framing Effect

Suppose that once Linda arrived at the store, she "chickened out" of making chicken stew from scratch and decided instead to buy canned stew. She noticed that there were two brands to choose from. One brand called the stew "zesty" and "hearty." The other brand simply contained the name of the stew. As far as Linda could tell, the two brands were identical in every other respect. Which one do you think Linda decided to buy? Probably the zesty, hearty one.

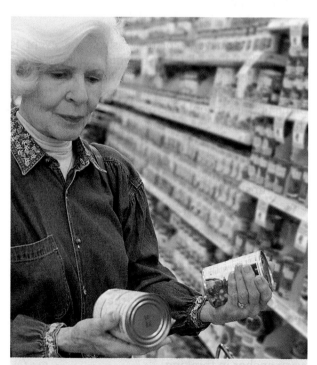

The way information is presented, or framed—such as on product labels—can affect our decisions.

If so, this decision was based on the framing effect. The **framing effect** refers to the way in which wording affects decision making. Advertisers try to use the framing effect to get people to decide to buy a particular product. They are very careful in choosing what words to put on a product. Foods with fewer calories, for example, are advertised as being "light," not "thin." A "thin" food does not sound as appetizing as a "light" food.

Advertisers are not the only people who use the framing effect to their advantage. Political groups also are very aware of the framing effect. Most political groups, for example, pick names that sound positive—they know that people are more likely to support a cause that they feel good about rather than a cause that merely opposes something. This is why groups are usually "pro" something rather than "anti" something.

Experienced parents, too, know all about the framing effect, particularly when dealing with very young children. They know that they have to choose their words carefully to encourage the children to give the desired responses. Thus, when parents want the child to take a bath, they might say, "Mr. Duck is waiting for you in the tub!" and not "You'll be cleaner after your bath."

Overconfidence

People tend to have a great deal of confidence in their decisions, whether the decisions are right or wrong (Gigerenzer et al., 1991; Lundeberg et al., 1994). For instance, many students refuse to change their opinions about how well they did on a test they have just taken even when other students point out that their answers were wrong. Likewise, have you ever known anyone who kept unrealistic confidence in a baseball team, even though the team was far behind in the standings?

There are a number of reasons why people tend to be overconfident, even when they are wrong:

- People are often unaware of how flimsy their supporting evidence is.

- People tend to pay attention to examples that confirm their opinions and to ignore examples that do not.

- People tend to bring about things they believe in. If students believe that they are capable of getting an A on next week's test, for example, they are more likely to study for the test and prepare for it in ways that might just help get them that A.

- Even when people are told that they tend to be overconfident in their decisions, they usually do not make use of this information (Gigerenzer et al., 1991).

SECTION 4 REVIEW

go.
hrw
.com

Homework Practice Online

Keyword: SY7 HP8

1. What is the main drawback of basing decisions on the availability heuristic?

2. Give two reasons why people tend to be overconfident about their decisions?

3. **Critical Thinking** *Summarizing* What are several strategies that can be used in decision making?

SECTION 5

Language

Language is the communication of ideas through symbols that are arranged according to rules of grammar. Language makes it possible for people to share knowledge. People can use language to describe what they ate for breakfast or what they thought of the movie they just saw. They can use language to set down the learning of past generations and store it for people who will live hundreds or even thousands of years in the future. Language also permits people to use the eyes and ears of other people to learn more than they ever could from their own individual experiences.

The Basic Elements of Language

Languages contain three basic elements: phonemes (sounds), morphemes (basic units of meaning), and syntax (grammar). Combinations of these units create the words, phrases, and sentences that people use to communicate ideas.

Phonemes The basic sounds of a language are called **phonemes**. (Languages that do not consist of sounds, such as American Sign Language, do not have phonemes.) There are 26 letters in the English alphabet, but there are many more than 26 phonemes. Phonemes include consonants, such as the *d* and *g* in *dog*. They also include vowels, such as the *o* in *dog* and the *o* in *no*. Even though *no* and *dog* each contain an *o*, the *o* sound is different in each word, and thus the two *o* sounds are two different phonemes. Other phonemes in the English language cannot be represented by a single letter—for example, the sound *sh*.

English contains some phonemes and phoneme distinctions that are not found in other languages. French has no equivalent for the English *th,* for example, which is why native French speakers often use a *z* sound to approximate the *th* in an English word: "Zee book is on zee table." Chinese does not distinguish between a *p* sound and a *b* sound; Japanese does not distinguish between *r* and *l*.

Morphemes The units of meaning in a language are called **morphemes**. Morphemes are made up of phonemes. Some morphemes, such as *car* and *bike,* are words in and of themselves. Other morphemes are prefixes (for example *pre,* which means "before"), while still others are suffixes (for example, *-ness* and *-ence*). Many words use combinations of morphemes. English uses morphemes such as *z* and *s* to make objects plural. Adding the *z* morpheme to *car* makes the word plural; adding the *s* morpheme to *bike* makes it plural.

In English, the past tense of regular verbs is formed by adding the *ed* morpheme to the end of the present-tense verb. The past tenses of *walk* and *talk,* for example, are *walked* and *talked*. Verbs such as *to be, to run,* and *to think* do not follow this rule, however. Thus they are considered irregular verbs.

Syntax The way in which words are arranged to make phrases and sentences is **syntax**. The rules for word order are the grammar of a language. English syntax usually follows the pattern of subject, verb, and object of the verb. For example:

Linda (subject)→cooked (verb)→dinner (object).

Many other languages have a different word order. Whereas in English the verb usually goes in the middle of the sentence, between the subject and the object, in German the verb often is placed at the end of a sentence. In the vast majority of languages, however, the subject precedes the object. And in no languages does the object appear first in a sentence (Slobin, 1983).

Semantics

Compare these two sentences:

It will be a long time before dinner is served.

The members of Linda's family long for a tasty dinner.

In the first sentence, *long* is an adjective. The sentence means that there is still much time before dinner. In the second sentence, on the other hand, *long* is a part of a verb—"to long for." The word *long* has more than one meaning.

The study of meaning is called **semantics**. Semantics involves the relationship between language and the things depicted in the language. Words that sound alike, such as *right* and *write,* can have different meanings, depending on how they

are used. So can words that are spelled alike, as we saw with *long.*

How a sentence is structured also affects meaning. Compare these two sentences:

Linda's chicken is ready to eat.

Linda's family is ready to eat.

The first sentence probably means that Linda has prepared the chicken and that it is ready to be eaten. The second sentence looks similar, but it most likely means that Linda's family is hungry—that the members of her family want to eat as soon as possible.

Sentences have a surface structure and a deep structure. The surface structure is what you see, the actual words of a sentence. Both "ready to eat" sentences have the same surface structure. The deep structure of a sentence is its deeper meaning, the message the speaker is trying to communicate. The "ready to eat" sentences differ in meaning.

Some sentences, such as "Make me a sandwich," have an unclear surface structure—you cannot be certain of the deep structure based on the surface structure. If you ask someone with a sense of humor to make you a sandwich, don't be surprised if the reply is, "Poof! You're a sandwich!"

The Stages of Language Development

Children develop language in a sequence of steps. The sequence is the same for nearly all children. It begins with crying, cooing, and babbling, then moves into the learning of words, and finally, the learning of grammar.

Crying, Cooing, and Babbling Crying, cooing, and babbling are not considered true language because they do not use symbols with specific meanings. Nevertheless, crying is a highly effective form of verbal expression for newborn infants—it usually gets the attention of caregivers.

During their second month, babies begin to coo. Coos are vowel-like and resemble "oohs" and "ahs." Cooing seems to express feelings of pleasure. Tired, hungry babies do not coo. Cries and coos can communicate discomfort, hunger, or enjoyment of being rocked, held, or fed.

At about six months of age, infants begin to babble. Unlike crying and cooing, babbling has the sounds of speech. Babies often babble consonant and vowel combinations, as in *ba, ga,* even the

This infant may coo to indicate satisfaction at being fed. Cooing is a form of verbal expression that precedes the development of actual language.

EXPLORING

DIVERSITY

Language and Culture

Nearly all humans are born with the capacity to learn language. But the languages used in different cultures vary widely.

List 10 basic colors. Would it surprise you to know that the Dani, a people who live in New Guinea, have only two words for colors: *mili,* used to describe dark, cool shades, and *mola* for bright, warm shades?

You might think that any word in one language can be translated into another language, but this is not true. Many languages contain words that have no direct equivalent in other languages. The Arabic language contains more than 250 words for camel. The Hanunoo people of the Philippines have some 90 words for rice. And the Inuit, who live near the Arctic, have many terms describing different types and conditions of snow.

According to the Whorfian hypothesis (named after its originator, Benjamin Whorf), differences such as these indicate that language determines how people perceive the world. In other words, someone who has many words for snow actually perceives snow differently than someone who only has one word for snow.

Most research evidence, however, does not support the Whorfian hypothesis. The Inuit may have many different words for snow, but that does not mean that they perceive snow differently from other people. Rather, because snow is a basic part of their daily existence, the Inuit may have more of a need and more of a use for several snow terms than do people who have less exposure to snow.

Vocabulary is only one of the ways in which languages differ. Languages also differ from each other in the phonemes, or sounds, they use. The Spanish rolled *r,* for example, does not appear in English and is difficult for some native English speakers to pronounce. Similarly, German contains some vowel sounds (such as *ä, ö,* and *ü*) that are not generally used in English. One Khoisan language of southern Africa contains four different clicking sounds. And in some languages, even the pitch or tone of the speaker's voice can change the meaning of a word.

Think About It

Drawing Inferences and Conclusions Think of an item that Americans use many different words to identify. What does the large number of words indicate about the importance of the item in American culture?

Calvin and Hobbes   by Bill Watterson

highly valued *mama* and *dada.* At first, however, combinations with actual meaning, such as *mama* and *dada,* are purely coincidental.

Crying, cooing, and babbling are basic human abilities. Children from cultures whose languages sound different all babble similar sounds, including sounds they have not heard. In fact, children babble phonemes found in languages spoken around the world. By 9 or 10 months of age, however, children pick out and repeat the phonemes used by the people around them. Other phonemes start to drop away.

Babies understand much of what other people are saying before they can talk. They demonstrate understanding with their actions and gestures.

Words, Words, Words After babbling comes the learning of words—the start of true language. Most children acquire new words slowly at first. After they speak their first word, it may take another three or four months before they have a 10-word vocabulary. By about 18 months of age, children are saying about two dozen words. Most early words are nouns—names for things. Research indicates that reading to children increases their vocabulary.

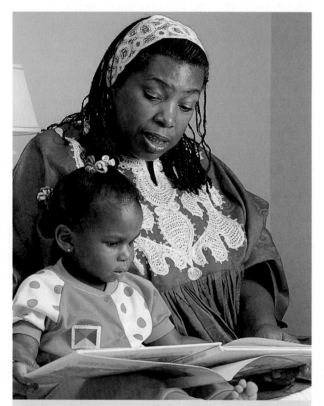

Studies have shown that reading to children can increase their vocabulary.

It is thus a good idea for parents to pull out the storybooks and read to their children (Arnold et al., 1994; Robbins & Ehri, 1994).

Children sometimes overreach—they try to talk about more things than they have words for. Often they extend the meanings of words to refer to things for which they do not have words. This behavior is called overextension. For example, if a child sees a cow but does not know the word *cow,* she or he might call the cow a doggie.

Development of Grammar The first things children say are usually brief, but they have the meanings of sentences. That is, these utterances have a grammar. Even one word can express a complete thought, such as "Sit!" Children just starting to use language use only the words essential to communicating their meaning.

Sometimes a word will have more than one meaning, depending on the circumstances. For example, *doggie* can mean "There is a dog," "That stuffed animal looks like my dog," or "I want you to give me the dog!" Most children readily teach their parents what they mean with their utterances. They are delighted when parents do as requested and may howl when they do not.

As they approach their second birthday, most children begin to use two-word sentences. "That doggie" might seem like just a phrase but is really a sentence in which *is* and *a* are implied: "That (is) (a) doggie." Two-word utterances such as this appear at about the same time in all languages (Slobin, 1983).

Even brief two-word utterances show understanding of grammar. A child who wants his or her mother to sit in a chair says, "Sit chair," not "chair sit." Similarly, the child says, "my doggy," not "doggy my," to show possession. "Mommy go" means Mommy is leaving. "Go Mommy" expresses the desire to have Mommy leave.

Between the ages of two and three, children's sentences expand to include missing words. They add articles (*a, an, the*), conjunctions (*and, but, or*), possessive and demonstrative adjectives (*your, her, that*), pronouns (*she, him, it*), and prepositions (*in, on, over, around, under, through*).

One interesting aspect of how children learn grammar has to do with irregular words. As you know, English has many irregular verbs and nouns. For example, the past tense of *am* is *was,* the past tense of *sit* is *sat,* and the plural of *child* is *children.* Children first learn irregular words by imitating their parents. Two-year-olds often use them correctly. But then a seemingly odd thing happens.

Even though the children have used these words correctly, they soon begin to use them incorrectly (Kuczaj, 1982). What has happened?

What has happened is that they have learned the rules for forming the past tense and plurals (in English, adding *d* or *ed* morphemes to make a word past tense and adding *s* or *z* morphemes to form plurals). Once they have learned these rules, they begin to make errors. For example, three- to five-year-olds may be more likely to say, "I runned away" than "I ran away." They are likely to talk about the "gooses" and "sheeps" they "seed" on the farm.

They make these errors because they have applied the normal rules to all words, even the words for which the rules do not work. This is called **overregularization**. Although it may seem like a bad thing when children begin to incorrectly use words that they previously used correctly, over-regularization represents an advance in the development of grammar. And in another year or two, children will learn the correct forms of the irregular words as well as the regular ones, and overregularization will stop.

TRUTH OR fiction ▪ REVISITED ▪ *It is not true that once a child learns the correct form of a word, he or she will never use the incorrect form.* Because of overregularization of the rules of grammar, children often begin to use words incorrectly that they once used correctly. However, the errors are only temporary.

How Do We Learn Language?

Billions of children have acquired the languages of their parents and have then proceeded to hand them down to their own children. In this manner, languages pass, with small changes, from generation to generation. How are languages learned? Both heredity and environment play a role.

Hereditary Influences   Many psychologists believe that people have a natural tendency to acquire language. Linguist Noam Chomsky and some other researchers refer to this tendency as a **language acquisition device** (LAD). These researchers assert that humans have a LAD. Animals do not.

The LAD enables the brain to understand and use grammar. It enables people to turn ideas into sentences (Pinker, 1990, 1994). People may not be

ready for chemistry and algebra until high school, but the LAD makes people most capable of acquiring language between about 18 to 24 months of age and puberty (Lenneberg, 1967). One- and two-year-olds seem to learn languages with ease. In many cases, they learn more than one language.

Environmental Influences   People may have an inborn ability to learn language, but environmental influences are important as well. Learning theorists claim that language learning is similar to other kinds of learned behavior (Gleason & Ratner, 1993). Children learn language, at least in part, by observing and imitating other people. For example, all children babble. But during the first year, children start to babble the sounds they hear around them more often and drop other sounds.

Bilingualism

A DAY IN THE LIFE   Hannah speaks both Korean and English. She most likely learned Korean at home and English in school, in other public places, and from English-speaking friends. Because she learned English very early, Hannah

It is becoming increasingly common in the United States to see signs in public places printed in several different languages.

CASE STUDIES
AND OTHER TRUE STORIES
Washoe and Kanzi: Chimps with Language?

Language is one of the things that sets people apart from other creatures. Sure, parrots can say a few words like "Polly wants a cracker." And your dog may respond to commands such as "Sit!" But animals cannot use language.

Or can they?

Over the past few decades, various researchers have made a number of attempts to teach language to chimpanzees (the animal that is biologically most similar to humans) and to other apes. One of the earliest efforts was aimed at getting a chimp to speak human words. But several years of work that yielded few positive results led to the conclusion that chimps cannot produce verbal speech (Hayes, 1951). Just because chimps cannot talk, however, does not necessarily mean that they are incapable of understanding language. Subsequent efforts therefore focused instead on teaching chimps to use symbols, such as those of American Sign Language (ASL).

Washoe, a female chimpanzee raised by Beatrice and Allen Gardner (1980), was one of the first chimps reported to use language. By the age of 5, Washoe could use more than 100 ASL signs. These included signs for actions (come, give, tickle), objects (apple, flower, toothbrush), and even for more abstract concepts such as more.

Moreover, Washoe could combine the signs to form simple sentences. The sentences were similar to those of two-year-old children: "More tickle," "More banana," "More milk." As time passed, Washoe signed longer sentences such as "Please sweet drink" and "Give me toothbrush hurry." However, Washoe had trouble with word order. One day she might sign, "Come give me toothbrush." The next she might sign, "Hurry toothbrush give me." Even one-year-old children use correct syntax more consistently.

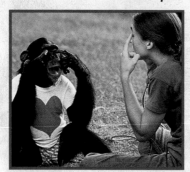

Can chimps use language?

Psychologist Sue Savage-Rumbaugh and her colleagues (1993) had somewhat better luck in terms of grammar with a bonobo, or pygmy chimpanzee, named Kanzi. Kanzi learned several hundred words and to correctly respond to commands in which these words were put together in ways that Kanzi had not previously heard. For example, he knew the words *dog, bite,* and *snake.* When Kanzi was given a stuffed dog and a stuffed snake and asked to "make the dog bite the snake," he put the snake to the dog's mouth, even though he had never before heard this sentence. Kanzi's grammatical ability, however, never surpassed that of the average two-and-a-half-year-old child.

So the question remains: Can chimps use language? The answer seems to hinge on the definition of language. It seems clear that chimps and even some other types of apes can learn to use signs and symbols and can follow some commands given to them. So if this is considered language, then yes, chimps can use language.

Most psychologists, however, use a more restrictive definition of language: the combination of symbols into original, grammatical sentences. If we use originality and mastery of grammar as the standards for defining language, there is little question that chimps fall short. For now, at least, the theory that language belongs to humans alone remains standing.

THINKING CRITICALLY

1. **Finding the Main Idea** What did Washoe and Kanzi learn to do?
2. **Supporting a Point of View** Do you agree with the broad definition or the restrictive definition of language? Why?

speaks it with no accent. Her parents, who learned English as adults, do have accents. If Marc decides to study Japanese, he will probably never be able to speak it without an American accent. He could become perfectly fluent, yet never speak it without an accent.

In general, the earlier in life a person learns a second language, the more likely the person is to become fluent in it and sound like a native speaker (Snow, 1993). This fact lends support to the theory that there is a period in life—a portion of childhood—during which language acquisition is easiest and most effective.

Although many people in the United States speak only one language, the number of people who (like Hannah) are bilingual, or speak two languages, is growing. In this respect the United States is becoming more similar to many other parts of the world. Many people throughout the world speak two or more languages. A number of countries have minority populations whose languages differ from the national tongue. A large percentage of Europeans are taught English and the languages of neighboring nations. Consider the Netherlands. Dutch is the native language, but children are also taught French, German, and English in the public schools.

For more than 40 million people in the United States, English is a second language. Spanish, French, Chinese, Russian, or Arabic is spoken in the home and, perhaps, in the neighborhood.

Many students in the United States are learning, or already know, more than one language.

A century ago it was widely believed that children reared in bilingual homes would be slowed in their cognitive and language development. It was thought that people who knew two languages were crowding their mental abilities because cognitive capacity is limited (Lambert, 1990). However, the U.S. Bureau of the Census reports that more than 75 percent of Americans who first spoke another language in the home also speak English "well" or "very well." Moreover, a careful analysis of older studies in bilingualism shows that the bilingual children often lived in poor families and had little education. Yet these bilingual children were compared to middle-class children who spoke English. In addition, achievement and intelligence tests were given in English, which was the second language of the bilingual children (Reynolds, 1991). Lack of education and poor testing methods, rather than bilingualism, accounted for the apparent differences in achievement and intelligence.

Today most psychologists believe that it is good for children's cognitive development to be bilingual. Knowledge of more than one language expands children's awareness of different cultures and broadens their outlooks on life (Cavaliere, 1996). For example, bilingual children are more likely to understand that the symbols used in language are arbitrary. Children who speak only English are more likely to think that the word *dog* is somehow connected with the nature of the animal. Bilingual children therefore have somewhat more cognitive flexibility. Learning a second language has been shown to increase children's expertise in their first (native) language. Research evidence reveals that learning French enhances knowledge of the structure of English among Canadian children whose native language is English (Lambert et al., 1991).

SECTION 5 REVIEW

go. hrw .com Homework Practice Online

Keyword: SY7 HP8

1. Identify and explain the three basic elements of language.

2. Define *overextension* and *overregularization*.

3. **Critical Thinking** *Finding the Main Idea* How do research findings about bilingualism indicate that language acquisition involves both environmental and hereditary influences?

Chapter **8** **REVIEW**

Writing a Summary

Using standard grammar, spelling, sentence structure, and punctuation, summarize the information in this chapter. Consider:
- how people solve problems and make decisions
- the basic elements of language, and deductive and inductive reasoning

Identifying People and Ideas

Identify the following terms or people and use them in appropriate sentences.

1. symbol
2. concept
3. prototype
4. mental set
5. functional fixedness
6. reasoning
7. confirmation bias
8. anchoring
9. phoneme
10. semantics

Understanding Main Ideas

SECTION 1 (pp. 178–179)
1. How do prototypes help people understand concepts?

SECTION 2 (pp. 179–188)
2. What is the purpose of an algorithm?

SECTION 3 (pp. 189–191)
3. What is confirmation bias, and which type of reasoning does it affect?

SECTION 4 (pp. 191–195)
4. How do people use each of the following shortcuts to make a decision: the representativeness heuristic, the availability heuristic, and the anchoring heuristic?

SECTION 5 (pp. 195–201)
5. What is a language acquisition device?

Thinking Critically

1. **Drawing Inferences and Conclusions** How could a child be taught the meaning of an abstract concept such as honesty?

2. **Evaluating** Explain how mental set might occasionally help problem solving rather than hinder it.

3. **Analyzing Information** Imagine that you are driving to a strange town to visit a friend. Using the ABCDEs of problem solving, explain how you would plan your trip.

4. **Categorizing** In addition to using words and sentences to communicate, human beings use sounds, symbols, gestures, and other means to communicate. Give five examples of how people communicate without using words, and the type of communication they use.

5. **Supporting a Point of View** Give reasons to support or reject a proposal to teach world languages in elementary schools.

Writing About Psychology

1. **Analyzing Information** Go to the library to find information about the development of language skills in young children. Write a one-page paper explaining why children are often able to learn more than one language with relative ease.

2. **Evaluating** Think of a problem facing your school or community for which there are two or more possible solutions or courses of action. On a sheet of paper, create a "balance sheet" listing each possible course of action and its pros and cons. Write a brief report explaining what your decision is, how you reached that decision, and how the balance sheet helped you arrive at your decision. Be sure to use standard grammar, spelling, sentence structure, and punctuation. Use the graphic organizer below to help you with your report.

Balance Sheet	
Pros	Cons

Interpreting Graphs

Study the bar graph below. Then use the information in the graph to help you answer the questions that follow.

Acquisition of Language Skills by Young Children

Age in Months

33
30
27
24
21
18
15
12
9
6

First words

Vocabulary increase

Sentences

Language Achievement

Source: Damon (Ed.), *Handbook of Child Psychology,* 1998

1. Which of the following statements best reflects the information given in the graph?
   a. A child who does not use words by its 12th month has a problem with language skills.
   b. A child who does not speak until its 17th month will not use sentences until it is 32 months old.
   c. All children experience a dramatic increase in vocabulary by their 8th month.
   d. Some children begin using sentences as early as their 18th month.

2. What conclusions can you draw from this graph about children and language development?

Analyzing Primary Sources

Read the following excerpt, in which psychologist Alan Lesgold discusses the role that problem solving plays in daily life. Then answer the questions that follow.

"Problem solving is a major human activity in our high-technology society. Many of the jobs currently available are characterized by the problem solving they require. Doctors have to solve the problem of what is causing their patients' symptoms. Auto mechanics have to determine why cars don't run properly. Counselors often perceive either their role, the client's role, or both as one of solving certain life problems. The political process, on both an international and a domestic level, is driven by the need to solve complex problems. College students have to schedule courses, jobs, and study time. Almost every aspect of daily life seems to involve problem solving."

3. Which of the following statements best reflects the meaning of the excerpt?
   a. Only professionals such as doctors and mechanics use problem-solving skills.
   b. Problems make daily life difficult for almost everyone.
   c. For most people, problem solving requires a college education.
   d. Problem solving is a regular activity used by many people every day in modern society.

4. According to the excerpt, why are problem-solving skills essential in today's society?

PSYCHOLOGY PROJECTS

Cooperative Learning

Applying Psychology With several of your classmates, play a popular board game. Team up with one other person in the group and play as partners. Decide together how you will make your moves. At the end of the game, have each set of partners give examples of the thought processes they used to make their moves during the game. You may want to discuss with the class how prior familiarity with the game helped or hindered your strategy.

⊠ internet connect

Internet Activity: go.hrw.com
KEYWORD: SY7 CH8

Choose an activity on thinking and language to:

- write a short analysis of your own methods of solving problems.
- role-play a conflict resolution process that uses persuasion, compromise, debate, and negotiation.
- research and evaluate theories of language acquisition and development.

INTELLIGENCE

Chapter 9

Read to Discover

1   How is intelligence defined, and what are the various theories of intelligence?

2   How do the various types of intelligence tests differ?

3   What are the characteristics of mental retardation and of giftedness?

4   How do heredity and the environment influence intelligence?

A DAY IN THE LIFE

Todd and Dan were at Todd's house after school. Todd had decided to go to college six months ago and had already begun applying. Dan, on the other hand, had not decided what he wanted to do. He noticed some of Todd's college catalogs sitting on the table and began looking through them.

"Todd, what made you decide to go to college?" Dan asked.

"I'm not really sure. I've always done well in school, and I love studying science. Why do you ask?"

"I don't know. I've just always wondered if I'm intelligent enough for college," Dan replied. "My older brother seems to get good grades without any effort at all, but I have to work hard for every A or B that I get. And we both have the same parents and have had the same upbringing."

"Yeah, but you and your brother aren't identical. You two only share some of the same genes, and you've had different experiences, especially in school," Todd said. "Plus, don't you think there might be different types of intelligence?"

"How so?" Dan asked.

"Well, have you ever heard Hannah play the violin?"

"Of course I have," Dan replied. "She's great at it."

"Right. Hannah has a special ability to read the music and play the right notes. You're the same way with sports, and you have great communication and people skills."

"But those are talents, not *intelligence*," Dan replied. "Talent is different from intelligence."

"Maybe," Todd pondered. "But I think any kind of learning ability is a type of intelligence."

"Okay then, what if I don't have enough learning ability to go to college? Don't they have some sort of test to tell you if you have enough intelligence for college?" Dan asked.

"I don't know," Todd replied honestly. "When I was younger I took some sort of intelligence test for placement. But I doubt that there are tests to tell you if you're intelligent enough for college. Why don't you talk to Mr. Hochberg, the guidance counselor?"

"I guess I could do that," Dan said. "Thanks, Todd."

"No problem. Hey, I have to work hard for every A that I get, too."

. . .

Intelligence is one characteristic that sets humans apart from other forms of life. Intelligence permits us to adapt to changing conditions and to challenge our physical limitations—to move faster and higher than any other animal. The human ability to think about abstract ideas, such as space and time, also sets us apart from all other species. Intelligence has even expanded our senses, enabling us to invent microscopes and telescopes to see things too small or distant for the naked eye to detect. This chapter examines how intelligence is defined and measured. It also discusses differences in intelligence and considers the factors that influence intelligence.

Key Terms

- achievement
- intelligence
- mental age
- intelligence quotient
- transformed score
- reliability
- test-retest reliability
- validity
- mental retardation
- gifted
- creativity
- heritability

HOLT

Psychology Video Program

Watch the video to learn about a man with exceptional intelligence.

INTELLIGENCE **205**

TRUTH OR fiction?

Read the following statements about psychology. Do you think they are true or false? You will learn whether each statement is true or false as you read the chapter.

- There may be more than one kind of intelligence.
- Two children can answer exactly the same items on an intelligence test correctly, yet one may have an above-average IQ and the other may have a below-average IQ.
- When we think we will not succeed at something, we may not try as hard as we can.
- Intellectually gifted people are by definition highly creative.
- Preschool programs have long-term benefits for the children who attend them.

What Is Intelligence?

A DAY IN THE LIFE

Todd and Dan raised many interesting points about the nature of intelligence. People can be very intelligent and not know a lot because they have not studied. People can also know a lot because they have worked hard, even if their intelligence is not particularly high. But what exactly is intelligence?

Some people, like Todd, have very strong science or math skills. Others, such as Hannah, are talented in music or art. Still others, including Dan, have the ability to get along well with other people. Are all of these abilities signs of intelligence? Are *any* of them? How many factors are involved in intelligence? Throughout human history, many philosophers and scientists have speculated about the answers to these questions.

Intelligence Versus Achievement

According to psychologists, one thing intelligence is *not* is achievement. **Achievement** refers to knowledge and skills gained from experience. In other words, achievement focuses on the things that you know and can do. Thus, achievement involves specific content, such as Spanish, calculus, history, psychology, biology, art, or music. The relationship between achievement and experience is obvious. If you have spent a lot of time reading about the Civil War, for example, then you will probably do well on a test about that period in U.S. history. You will have gained knowledge on the subject of the Civil War. But if you were tested on the Revolutionary War instead, you might not do as well.

Although intelligence is not the same as achievement, intelligence can provide the *basis* for achievement. Intelligence makes achievement possible by giving people the ability to learn. Todd pointed this out when he suggested that intelligence might be involved in Hannah's abilities to play the violin.

Now we know what intelligence is *not*. But what is it? **Intelligence** can be defined as the abilities to learn from experience, to think rationally, and to deal effectively with others. Within that general definition, psychologists have differing theories about what exactly makes up intelligence.

Spearman's Two-Factor Theory

About 100 years ago, psychologist Charles Spearman suggested that general intelligence, which he labeled

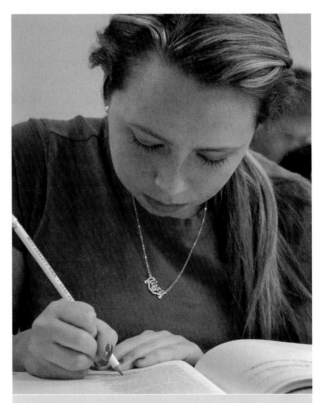

Research has shown that the SATs more or less reflect a person's general intelligence, which Spearman labeled g.

Gardner would probably suggest that architects excel in visual and spatial intelligence.

- naturalist intelligence (understanding of nature and the laws that govern natural behavior)
- existential intelligence (insight into the larger philosophical issues of life)

Gardner refers to these talents or abilities as intelligences because they can be quite different from one another. In addition, he proposes that the different intelligences are independent of each other. According to Gardner, a person might write novels yet be average in math or sports. Gardner would probably say that Todd, Dan, and Hannah are each intelligent in their own way. Todd has strong scientific ability. Dan, as an athlete, has highly developed bodily-kinesthetic skills. Whereas, Hannah undoubtedly has special musical-rhythmic ability.

Critics of Gardner's theory of multiple intelligences state that exceptional abilities in the musical or bodily-kinesthetic areas are not really what is meant by intelligence. His critics argue that those skills are special talents and that being talented is not the same thing as being intelligent. Dan, too, made this distinction when he asserted that talent and intelligence are two different things.

g, underlies all of our intellectual abilities. The g factor represents the abilities to reason and solve problems. The SATs, which break intellectual skills into verbal, quantitative, and writing subtests, have been shown to reflect a more or less unified factor, which some psychologists refer to as g (Frey & Detterman, 2004). At the same time, all people are better at some things than others—such as math, music, or writing. For this reason, Spearman suggested that specific, or s, factors account for people's specific abilities.

Gardner's Theory of Multiple Intelligences

Psychologist Howard Gardner (1983, 1993) proposes that there are actually multiple intelligences instead of just one.

- verbal, or linguistic, intelligence
- logical-mathematical intelligence
- visual-spatial intelligence
- bodily-kinesthetic intelligence (such as dancers and athletes have)
- musical-rhythmic intelligence
- interpersonal intelligence (sensitivity to other people's feelings)
- intrapersonal intelligence (insight into one's own inner feelings)

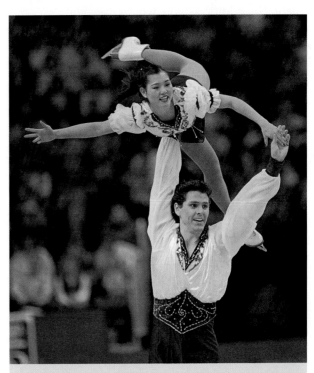

According to Gardner's theory, people can possess various kinds of intelligence. These skaters probably have highly developed bodily-kinesthetic intelligence.

Analytical Ability, Creativity, and Street Smarts

Psychologist Robert Sternberg (Sternberg, 1997, 2001; Sternberg et al., 2003) breaks intelligence into the following three factors (see Figure 9.1):

- analytical intelligence (the type of intelligence we use in academic courses)
- creative intelligence
- practical intelligence

Some people might excel in their school work, while other people might be more creative or have more practical intelligence, or "street smarts." Practical intelligence includes abilities such as knowing how to discuss a grade with a teacher or what to do if you're stuck somewhere and you've lost your wallet. Some students with moderate analytical skills do very well in school—and afterward—because they are creative or have street smarts.

We often use more than one of Sternberg's three factors at the same time. If you were doing an experiment for an upcoming science fair, you might use practical intelligence to plan your time and to obtain the materials you need. You would use your analytical intelligence to interpret the results of your experiment. In addition, you would use your creative intelligence to design the display for your project.

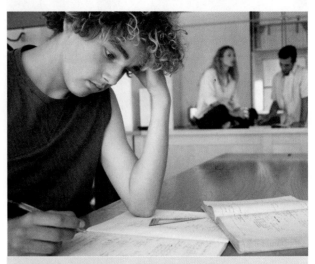

When you put off having fun until you finish studying, you are using impulse control, an emotional intelligence that aids in success.

Emotional Intelligence

Psychologist Daniel Goleman (1995) is interested in why smart people are not always as successful as might be expected. He proposes yet another kind of intelligence: emotional intelligence. Emotional intelligence, says Goleman, consists of five factors that are involved in success in school or on the job:

- **Self-awareness:** the ability to recognize our own feelings. If we know how we feel, we can better cope with our feelings.

- **Mood management:** the ability to distract oneself from an uncomfortable feeling. Although we may not be able to prevent feelings of anger or sadness, we do have some control over how long the feelings last. Rather than dwell on bad feelings, we can distract ourselves or make changes to improve our situation.

- **Self-motivation:** the ability to move ahead with confidence and enthusiasm. People who are self-motivators sometimes accomplish more than people who obtain higher scores on intelligence tests.

Sternberg's Triarchic Model

Problem-solving skills — analytic
Ability to deal with new situations — creative
practical
Ability to accomplish everyday tasks

FIGURE 9.1 *According to Sternberg, there are three types of intelligence: analytical (academic ability), creative, and practical ("street smarts"). Psychologists often talk about the relationship between intelligence and creativity, but according to Sternberg, creativity is a type of intelligence.*

PSYCHOLOGY
IN THE WORLD TODAY

Artificial Intelligence

In 1997 the reigning world champion chess player Gary Kasparov pitted his skills against an IBM computer known as Deep Blue. The event was captured live on an IBM Web site, where millions of chess fans logged on to watch the match. In two previous matches, Kasparov had beaten the best artificial intelligence IBM could muster. But this match would be different. In the sixth game a tired Kasparov accidentally reversed two steps in a well-known defensive maneuver. Deep Blue immediately took advantage of the situation by killing Kasparov's queen. After just 19 moves Kasparov admitted defeat.

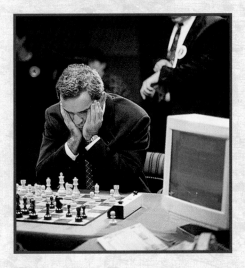

Kasparov versus the computer

Artificial intelligence (AI) is a broad field that involves the creation and development of "intelligent machines." These machines include industrial robots and computers such as the one that played chess with Gary Kasparov. Chess-playing computers are considered *expert systems*—computer programs that specialize in some particular field. Expert systems have been created not only to play chess but also to aid in medical diagnosis, the drilling of oil wells, and the mining of minerals.

But are these programs anything like human intelligence? Not really. For one thing, expert systems are very limited in their information. Prescriptive computer programs for psychologists are created by human experts who tell programmers all they know about their particular field. Then all the possible psychological symptoms—for depression, for example—and combinations of symptoms are included in the program. Under those limited conditions, the computer does well enough. But it is restricted by what it "knows," which is what it has been "told" by the programmer.

The human brain is a complicated machine. We may not be able to calculate numbers as quickly as a computer can, but we can deal with complex ideas and problems with remarkable ability. That is because our brains use what is known as "parallel processing." In other words, our thoughts analyze several different aspects of a problem at once. A computer, on the other hand, uses serial processing. The computer analyzes only one step at a time. Humans use serial processing, too, but parallel processing is what gives us the decided edge. Even highly sophisticated robots have difficulty moving with speed because it takes them so long to serially analyze all the stimuli necessary for coordinated motion.

Will we ever be able to create a computer or robot that thinks like the human brain? It does not seem likely anytime soon. Despite its electronic brainpower, AI is simply no match for human intelligence. Powerful computers can handle many problems and vast amounts of information. But they do not have the insights, intuitions, and creativity that humans have. They follow commands very well, but they have no originality. These limitations become quickly evident when, for instance, computers are asked to write poetry or compose music.

THINK ABOUT IT

Drawing Inferences and Conclusions If you were creating a new expert system of your own, in what area would it be? To whom would you go for expertise? What sort of problems can you anticipate?

Emotional intelligence includes mood management and people skills, qualities possessed by many airline flight attendants.

- Impulse control: the ability to delay pleasure until the task at hand has been accomplished. A student who resists the temptation to watch television until her or his homework is done may do better in school than a student who puts off homework until later.

- People skills: the ability to empathize, understand, communicate, and cooperate with others. People skills help us get along with others, and getting along with others helps us in school and on the job.

A DAY IN THE LIFE As Todd pointed out, Dan has exceptional people skills. According to Goleman's theory, Dan would be characterized as emotionally intelligent because of his ability to get along with others. Goleman's view has captured the interest of many psychologists and educators. However, research studies still need to be done to confirm Goleman's theory.

SECTION 1 REVIEW

go.hrw.com **Homework Practice Online**
Keyword: SY7 HP9

1. What is the difference between achievement and intelligence?

2. Describe the theories of intelligence that Spearman, Gardner, Sternberg, and Goleman have proposed.

3. **Critical Thinking** *Evaluating* Choose an occupation that interests you. List the types of intelligence, as outlined by any of the theories in this section, that a person should possess to succeed in that occupation.

SECTION 2

Measurement of Intelligence

You have probably taken many tests throughout your school career. Some of the tests you have taken or will take are achievement tests—they show what you have learned. Other tests are aptitude tests, which are intended to predict your ability to learn new skills. There are also tests that are designed to

 measure intelligence. The most widely used intelligence tests are the Stanford-Binet Intelligence Scale and the Wechsler scales. These are probably the types of tests Todd was given when he was younger.

The Stanford-Binet Scale

In the early 1900s, leaders of the French public school system were interested in finding a test that could identify children who were likely to need special educational attention. In response, French psychologist Alfred Binet devised the first modern intelligence test. The original version of the test was first used in 1905.

Binet assumed that intelligence increased with age. Thus, Binet's test contained questions for children of different age levels. (See Figure 9.2.) Older children were expected to answer more difficult questions. Children earned "months" of credit for correct answers.

Binet's test yielded a score called a mental age. A child's mental age is not the same thing as his or her chronological age. **Mental age** (MA) shows the intellectual level at which a child is functioning. For

Typical Items on the Stanford-Binet Intelligence Scale		
Age Level	**Item 1**	**Item 2**
2 years	Children know basic vocabulary words. When the examiner says, "Show me the eyes" (or ears), they can point to the proper parts of a doll.	Children can match a model by building a tower made up of four blocks.
4 years	Children show language and classifying ability by filling in a missing word: "Brother is a boy; sister is a _____."	Children show general understanding by answering questions such as: "Why do people have telephones?"
9 years	Children can point out absurdities. For example: "She dug up a coin dated 544 B.C. What is silly about that?"	Children show increased language ability, as shown by answering: "Can you tell me a number that rhymes with *gate*?"
Adult	Adults show knowledge of the meanings of words and conceptual thinking by correctly explaining the differences between word pairs such as "sickness and misery," "house and home," and "integrity and prestige."	Adults show spatial skills by correctly answering questions such as: "If a car turned to the right to head north, in what direction was it heading before it turned?"

FIGURE 9.2 *These items are similar to those that appear on the Stanford-Binet Intelligence Scale. The test includes tasks for age levels from two to adulthood. The test produces an intelligence quotient, or IQ, that reflects the relationship between a person's mental age and his or her chronological age.*

Note: Adapted from Stanford-Binet Intelligence Scale.

Writing a Summary

Using standard grammar, spelling, sentence structure, and punctuation, summarize the information in this chapter. Consider:
- the types of intelligences and intelligence tests
- mental retardation, giftedness, creativity, and the roles that heredity and environment play in intelligence

Identifying People and Ideas

Identify the following terms or people and use them in appropriate sentences.

1. achievement
2. intelligence
3. mental age
4. transformed score
5. reliability
6. test-retest reliability
7. validity
8. gifted
9. creativity
10. heritability

Understanding Main Ideas

SECTION 1 (pp. 206–210)

1. What is the relationship between achievement and intelligence?
2. Contrast Howard Gardner's theory of intelligence with Robert Sternberg's.

SECTION 2 (pp. 211–215)

3. Why are the Wechsler scales more widely used than the Stanford-Binet test?

SECTION 3 (pp. 215–218)

4. Give one characteristic of each of the following individuals: a person with moderate mental retardation, a person with profound mental retardation, a gifted person, a creative person.

SECTION 4 (pp. 218–221)

5. What have kinship and adoptee studies revealed about the genetic role in intelligence?

Thinking Critically

1. **Supporting a Point of View** Which theory of intelligence do you think is the most accurate? Use specific examples to explain your answer.

2. **Evaluating** Other than vocabulary and problem-solving methods, what else might cause intelligence tests to be culturally biased?

3. **Summarizing** List some examples of steps parents and educators can take to encourage highly creative children.

4. **Drawing Inferences and Conclusions** How might a person boost his or her score on an intelligence test?

5. **Analyzing Information** What are three activities that could help someone who is age 70 or older maintain a high level of intellectual functioning?

Writing About Psychology

1. **Drawing Inferences and Conclusions** Write a report describing the criteria you would use to select the most intelligent students for a student body hall of fame. You might want to compare your criteria with those prepared by other members of the class.

2. **Analyzing Information** Go to the library to find information about Gardner's "intelligences." Prepare brief biographies of three people who appear to exhibit one such intelligence. Be sure to use standard grammar, spelling, sentence structure, and punctuation. Use the graphic organizer below to help you write your biographies.

Person and Intelligence Type	Person and Intelligence Type	Person and Intelligence Type

Interpreting Graphs

Study the bar graph below. Then use the information in the graph to help you answer the questions that follow.

Similarity of IQ Scores Among Relatives

Source: Bouchard and McGue, *Genetic and Environmental Influences on Adult Personality*, 1981

1. Which statement best reflects the information presented in the graph?

  a. There is a significant correlation between IQ levels and how closely people are related.

  b. There is no relation between IQ levels and how closely people are related.

  c. A higher correlation between IQ levels exists between siblings than between identical twins.

  d. A higher correlation between IQ levels exists between fraternal twins than between identical twins.

2. What does the information in this graph suggest about the effect heredity has on intelligence?

Analyzing Primary Sources

Read the following excerpt, in which a group of psychologists discuss the use of intelligence tests. Then answer the questions that follow.

❝Critics . . . often stress the political history of IQ testing in the United States. . . . They highlight the use of IQ tests in the early to mid-twentieth century to . . . restrict immigration and defend segregation. . . . Based on this history, many dismiss testing. We do not take this approach, for two reasons. First, . . . testing in other countries shows that it is really a history of the *decisions* people made about how to use tests. In the United States, IQ tests were made for discriminatory purposes, but elsewhere, like Great Britain, liberal reformers used similar tests to find promising lower-class children and provide them with opportunities. Second, IQ and similar tests are widely used by educators and employers as gatekeeping mechanisms to determine who will or will not obtain scarce positions. It is highly unlikely that such tests will be discarded simply because people used them badly in the past.❞

3. Which of the following statements best reflects the meaning of the excerpt?

  a. The use of IQ tests must be abandoned entirely.

  b. Because people continue to use IQ tests, psychologists must continue to study and improve testing methods.

  c. British psychologists are superior to American psychologists.

  d. People today would never misuse an IQ test.

4. According to the excerpt, how have IQ tests been used in the past to benefit people?

PSYCHOLOGY PROJECTS

Cooperative Learning

Research in Psychology Fetal alcohol syndrome (FAS) is a cause of mental retardation. Work with a group to find out more about FAS. Then make a poster warning about the dangers of drinking alcohol during pregnancy. As you work on the project, keep in mind that members of your group should act in accordance with acceptable behavior to maintain group cohesion. Be sure to meet regularly and support the group. When your group has finished the poster, display it in the classroom.

⧉ internet connect

Internet Activity: go.hrw.com
KEYWORD: SY7 CH9

Choose an activity on intelligence to:

- make a news broadcast on theories of intelligence.
- write a report on the concept of "transformed score" as it applies to IQ scores and define and differentiate reliability and validity.
- design a program that has a positive impact on intelligence.

PSYCHOLOGY IN ACTION

YOU RESOLVE THE CONFLICT . . .

How can people settle a disagreement about how to complete a class assignment?

Complete the following activity in small groups. Imagine that two of your friends are having a disagreement about how to complete a class assignment. Prepare a presentation outlining ways to resolve the conflict.

1. Consider Persuasion. Encourage your friends to try to persuade one another to come around to the other's point of view. To help your friends come up with persuasive arguments for their side, list the reasons why they hold the positions that they do. Then rank each reason in order of persuasiveness. Finally, urge your friends to present the most persuasive reasons to one another in an effort to sway the other to his or her point of view.

2. Compromise. Explain to your friends that sometimes compromise is necessary to resolve a conflict. Tell them that each will have to give up something to reach an agreement. Consider what they would be willing to give up to resolve their disagreement. Then encourage your friends to meet and discuss what they would be willing to give up to reach an agreement.

3. Debate the Issue. Suggest to your friends that they hold a debate. Gather information about the advantages and disadvantages of each side of their disagreement. Ask questions such as,

- Has one friend worked on this type of assignment before?
- Has one of the friends already researched the assignment and thus gained a stronger understanding of how it should be carried out?

Then consider having your friends prepare flash cards outlining the best arguments they can come up with in support of their side. Finally, hold the debate. Your friends might want to include charts and graphs to better demonstrate their positions.

4. Consider Negotiation. Urge your friends to begin negotiations about the conflict. Suggest that they meet to discuss their positions and what they would be willing to agree upon. Tell them that perhaps by working together to resolve the conflict, they will arrive at a solution that neither had considered before. When you are ready, decide who in your group will make which part of the presentation. Then make your presentation to the class. Good luck!

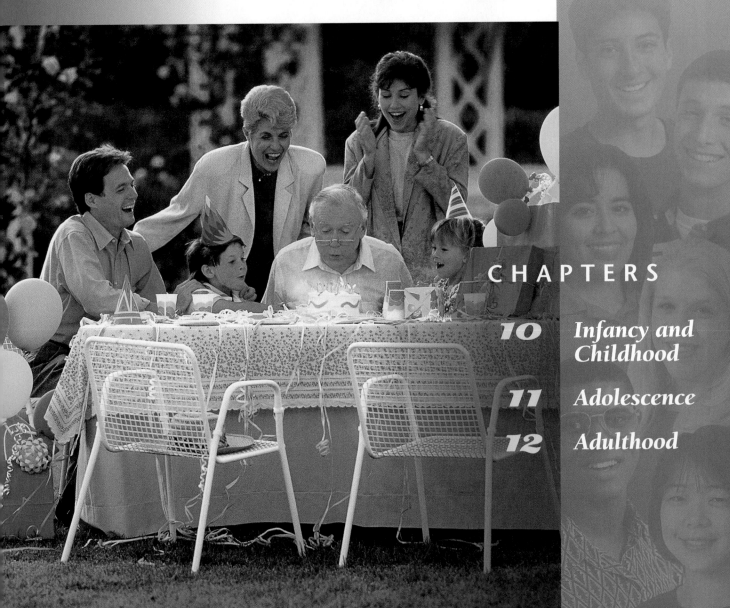

UNIT 4

DEVELOPMENT

10 Chapter

INFANCY AND CHILDHOOD

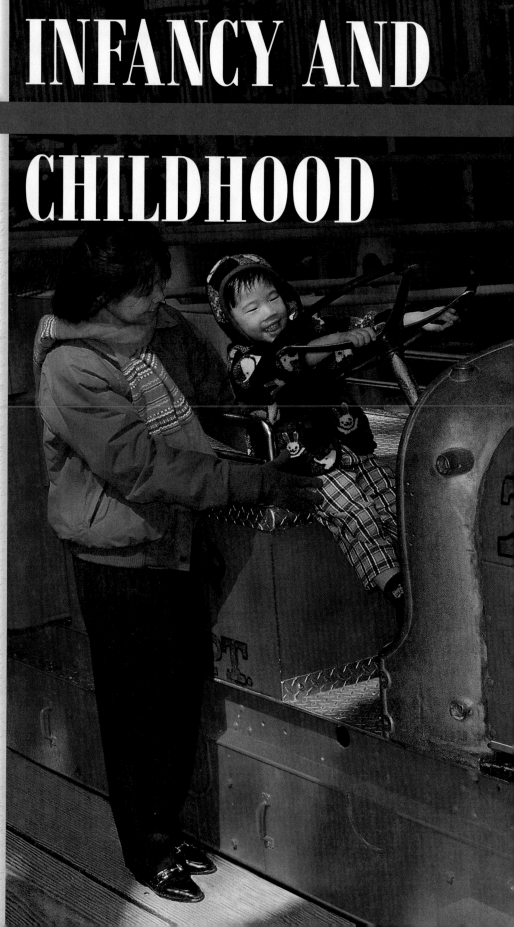

Read to Discover

1 What are the major theories of development?

2 How do infants develop physically?

3 What are some of the ways infants and children develop socially?

4 What are the stages in Piaget's theory of cognitive development and in Kohlberg's theory of moral development?

A DAY IN THE LIFE

Hannah and her friends were having a discussion with Hannah's three-year-old brother, Eddie. "Why does it get dark outside?" Hannah asked him.

"'Cause I go to sleep," Eddie answered emphatically.

"Why does the sun rise?" Todd asked Eddie.

"'Cause I get up!" Eddie said.

"And why does the sun move in the sky?" Linda asked, taking a turn.

Eddie thought for a moment, "To follow me!" he answered as he scampered off to play with Dan.

"He's really something else," Marc grinned. "It's like he thinks the world revolves just around him."

"You should see some of the other things he does," Hannah said. "The other day, I showed him two rows of pennies. There were five pennies in each row. But in the first row, the pennies were half an inch apart. In the second row, they were two inches apart. I asked Eddie which row had more pennies."

"Bet I know his answer," said Marc. "The longer row, right?"

"Right. But then I asked him to count both rows, which he did, and he counted five pennies in each row. Then I asked him again which row had more pennies. He pointed to the second row again!"

"Makes you wonder how his mind works, doesn't it?" asked Marc.

"He's grown so fast," Hannah replied after a bit. "Not so long ago, he couldn't even sit by himself, then he suddenly started crawling, then standing, then he was walking. Now just look at him go."

"I remember last year when all he wanted to do was stay next to his mother or you," Todd said. "Now all he wants to do is go and explore."

"Yeah," remembered Hannah, laughing. "He used to tug on my leg until I'd pick him up. Now he's so big, I can hardly lift him."

"Bet your parents are spoiling him rotten," said Marc.

"Actually, they're pretty strict. They say it's better for kids."

"Really?" asked Marc. "I don't believe that. I bet it's better just to love them a lot."

Hannah thought for a moment. "Parents can be strict and still love their kids."

"Well," Marc replied, "Eddie is turning out great. Guess your parents are doing something right."

• • •

Hannah and her friends had discovered that Eddie's view of the world was very different from theirs. Psychologists know that preschool children such as Eddie do not think like adults—or like teenagers. Children's thinking is truly in a class of its own. Psychologists know this because they have studied people of all ages—throughout the life span. This chapter is about two stages in the life span: infancy, the stage of life that lasts from birth until the second birthday, and childhood, the stage that follows infancy and spans the period from the second birthday to the beginning of adolescence.

Key Terms

- developmental psychology
- maturation
- critical period
- reflex
- infancy
- childhood
- attachment
- stranger anxiety
- separation anxiety
- contact comfort
- imprinting
- authoritative
- authoritarian
- self-esteem
- unconditional positive regard
- conditional positive regard
- assimilation
- accommodation
- sensorimotor stage
- object permanence
- preoperational stage
- conservation
- egocentrism
- concrete-operational stage
- formal-operational stage
- preconventional moral reasoning
- conventional moral reasoning
- postconventional moral reasoning

HOLT

Psychology Video Program

Watch the video to explore infant development.

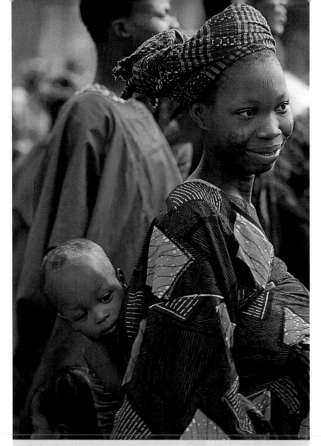

Cultural factors can influence when certain stages of motor development occur. Infants in some African countries, who spend much of their time being carried upright on their parents' backs, walk (on average) earlier than American infants.

months old, whereas in the United States, babies often do not start walking until around one year of age (Frankenberg et al., 1992). Why might this be? Perhaps because, while American babies spend much of their time lying in cribs, Ugandan babies spend much of their time being carried on their parents' backs. This contact with the parents, the sense of movement, and the upright position the babies maintain as they are being carried may help them learn to walk earlier (Bril, 1986).

Reflexes

Soon after a baby is born, the doctor or nurse places a finger against the palm of the baby's hand. Babies are not told how to respond and do not "know" what to do, of course. Even so, they usually grasp the finger firmly. Grasping is a reflex. Reflexes are inborn, not learned, and they occur automatically, without thinking.

Some reflexes are essential to our survival. Breathing is such a reflex. Although it is a reflex, we can also breathe consciously if we wish—slowly or quickly, deeply or shallowly. The breathing reflex works for a lifetime. Sneezing, coughing, yawning, blinking, and many other reflexes also continue for a lifetime.

Rooting is another reflex that babies are born with. Because of the rooting reflex, babies turn toward stimuli that touch their cheeks or the corners of their mouths. Once infants locate the source of a stimulus, they automatically begin sucking and swallowing. The sucking and swallowing reflexes are essential to an infant's survival; without them, newborns would not eat. Babies reflexively suck objects that touch their lips and reflexively swallow food in their mouths.

Babies also reflexively withdraw from painful stimuli. They pull up their legs and arch their backs in response to sudden sounds or bumps. This is known as the Moro, or startle, reflex. Babies also raise their big toes when the soles of their feet are touched, a behavior that is called the Babinski reflex. They also eliminate wastes by reflex.

As children develop, many reflexes, such as rooting and sucking, disappear. Other reflexes, such as swallowing, remain. And some reflexes, such as elimination of wastes, come under voluntary control. These changes are all part of the maturation process.

Perceptual Development

Imagine what the world must seem like to a newborn. Prior to birth, the baby has spent several months in a warm, wet, dark place. Now suddenly, it finds itself in a bright, noisy world full of sensory stimuli. Perceptual development is the process by which infants learn to make sense of the sights, sounds, tastes, and other sensations to which they are exposed.

Infants tend to prefer new and interesting stimuli. They seem to be "preprogrammed" to survey their environment and to learn about it. For example, a study by Robert Fantz (1961) found that two-month-old infants preferred pictures of the human face to any other pictures, such as newsprint, a bull's-eye, or colored disks without patterns.

Researchers have, however, discovered that infants' perceptual preferences are influenced by their age. For example, 5- to 10-week-old babies look longest at patterns that are fairly complex. It does not matter whether the pattern looks like a human face. What most interests them is the variety and complexity of the pattern. At this age, eyesight is not fully developed, so infants prefer to look at the most complex things they are capable of seeing reasonably well. By 15 to 20 weeks, patterns begin to matter. Babies then begin to stare longer at face-like patterns (Haaf et al., 1983).

These studies illustrate how nature and nurture work together. At first, infants seem to have an inborn preference for moderately complex visual stimuli. That is a result of nature. Their preference for human faces seems to appear only after they have had some experience with people. That results from the interaction of nature with nurture.

Other studies have focused on depth perception in infants. In some of these studies, researchers use what has become known as the "visual cliff." The visual cliff is a special structure, a portion of which has a surface that looks like a checkerboard. Another portion is a sheet of glass with a checkerboard pattern a few feet below it. It creates the illusion of a drop-off of a few feet—like a cliff.

One classic study with the visual cliff found that very young infants seem to be unafraid (as indicated by heart rate) when they are placed face down on the edge of the apparent drop-off. By nine months, however, infants respond with fear to the drop-off (Campos et al., 1970). Another classic study found that by the time infants learn to crawl, most of them will refuse to move onto the glass portion even when their mothers call them from the other side (Walk & Gibson, 1961). Perhaps crawling and exploring the world have taught the older infants that drop-offs are dangerous. Experience may have contributed to their ability to perceive depth. (See Chapter 4.)

Vision, of course, is only one type of perception. In general, infants' hearing is much better developed at birth than is their eyesight. When it comes to hearing, most newborns stop whatever they are doing to turn toward unusual sounds. They respond more to high-pitched sounds than to low-pitched ones, although they seem to be soothed by the sounds of someone singing softly or speaking in a low-pitched tone (Papousek et al., 1991). No wonder parents often sing lullabies to help their infants go to sleep.

Newborns immediately distinguish strong odors. They spit, stick out their tongues, and wrinkle their noses at pungent odors (as the rest of us do). But they smile and show licking motions in response to the sweet smells of chocolate, strawberry, and vanilla. They also like sweet-tasting liquid but refuse to suck salty or bitter liquids. A "sweet tooth" is of human nature.

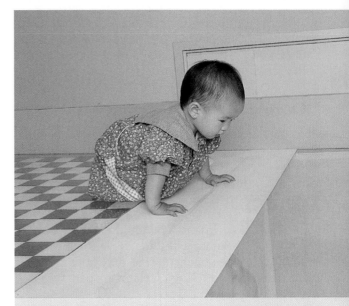

This visual cliff has a glass-covered drop-off. It is used in experiments to test the depth perception of infants. Most infants who can crawl refuse to cross the part that appears to be a cliff even if their mothers call them.

SECTION 2 REVIEW

Homework Practice Online
Keyword: SY7 HP10

1. How do babies develop physically during infancy?
2. Define *reflex* and give two examples.
3. Describe the purpose of research studies that use the visual cliff.
4. **Critical Thinking** *Drawing Inferences and Conclusions* Why are reflexes necessary for an infant's survival?

SECTION 3

Social Development

Social development involves the ways in which infants and children learn to relate to other people. For example, infants usually can be comforted by being held, and they soon respond to their mothers' voices. At first, they might cling to their mothers, but after a few months they venture out to explore the world and to make contact with strangers. Infants tend to play with toys by themselves, even when other children are around. As they grow older, however, they begin to play with others. All of these changes are part of social development.

Many important factors affect social development. Such factors include attachment, parenting styles, child care, child abuse and neglect (for some children), and self-esteem.

Attachment

Feelings of **attachment** are the emotional ties that form between people. Feelings of attachment keep people together. Because infants are basically helpless and are totally dependent on others to fulfill their needs, feelings of attachment are essential to their survival.

Infants and children try to stay in contact with the people to whom they are attached. That may be why Eddie used to tug on Hannah's pant leg.

Development of Attachment Psychologist Mary Ainsworth studied attachment in infants around the world (Ainsworth & Bowlby, 1991). What she observed in every place she studied was that, at first, infants prefer being held or even just being with someone—anyone—over being alone. By about four months of age, however, infants develop specific attachments to their main caregivers—usually their

Newborn infants can usually be comforted by being held. They prefer their mothers' voices to those of other women from the time they are a few days old.

mothers. This attachment grows stronger by six to seven months. Once they reach this point, infants and children try to maintain contact with their mothers and cry or complain when they are separated.

By the age of about eight months, some infants develop a fear of strangers. This fear is known as **stranger anxiety**. Infants who experience stranger anxiety cry and reach for their parents if they are near strangers. Their anxiety is somewhat less if the person to whom they are attached is holding them (Thompson & Limber, 1990). The closer they are to the strangers, however, the more upset they become (Boccia & Campos, 1989). They are most distressed when the strangers actually touch them.

At about the same age, infants may also develop separation anxiety. **Separation anxiety** causes infants to cry or behave in other ways that indicate distress if their mothers leave them. Why do infants become so attached to their primary caregivers? Research suggests that at least two factors are involved: contact comfort and imprinting.

Contact Comfort For a long time, psychologists thought that infants became attached to those who fed them. But then psychologist Harry F. Harlow observed that infant monkeys without mothers or companions became attached to pieces of cloth in their cages—even though, of course, the pieces of cloth did not provide food. The monkeys held on to their pieces of cloth and were upset when the cloth was taken away. Harlow conducted several experiments to find out why, and what types of objects to which the monkeys would and would not become attached (Harlow, 1959).

In one study, Harlow placed infant monkeys in cages, each of which had two "mother" objects. One object was made from wire and held a baby bottle. The other, which had no bottle, was made of soft terry cloth. The monkeys spent most of their time clinging to their cloth "mother," even though it did not feed them. Harlow thus concluded that the monkeys had a basic need for **contact comfort**, which is the instinctual need to touch and be

In Harlow's study of the importance of contact comfort, monkeys spent most of their time with their cloth "mother" even though it did not feed them.

touched by something soft, such as skin or fur. This need seems to be even stronger than the need for food. In other words, the monkeys and perhaps human babies may cling to their mothers because of the need for contact comfort rather than just because they are hungry. Based on such findings, researchers have concluded that attachment grows more from bodily contact than from feeding.

Bonds of attachment between mothers and infants also appear to provide a secure base from which the infants can explore their environments. Harlow and Zimmerman (1959) placed toys, such as stuffed bears and wooden insects, in cages with infant monkeys. Some of the cages had wire "mothers," and the others had terry cloth "mothers." The monkeys who were alone or with wire mothers cringed in fear as long as the bears or insects were in the cage. Infant monkeys in cages with terry cloth mothers, on the other hand, cringed for a while but eventually began to explore the bears or insects. The terry cloth mothers apparently gave the infant monkeys a sense of security that enabled them to explore the world around them.

Imprinting   For many animals, attachment is an instinct. Instinctive behavior develops during a critical period shortly after birth. Ducks, geese, and some other animals become attached to the first moving object they see. The moving object is said to become imprinted on the infant animal. **Imprinting** is the process by which some animals form immediate attachments during a critical period.

Researchers have shown that animals can become imprinted on some rather unusual objects. Using imprinting, researcher Konrad Lorenz (1937) acquired a family of goslings for himself. How did he do it? He was present when the goslings hatched, and he then allowed them to follow him. The critical period for imprinting in geese and some other animals begins when they can first move about on their own. Lorenz's "family" followed him wherever he went. They ran to him when they were frightened. They honked loudly when he left them alone—just as human infants cry when they are left by the people to whom they are attached.

TRUTH OR fiction
■ R E V I S I T E D ■

It is true that baby geese become attached to the first moving object that they see— even if the object is a human being. This is called imprinting. Imprinting is what caused baby geese to become attached to Konrad Lorenz, as if he were their mother.

Imprinting involves animals forming attachments during a critical period. Konrad Lorenz was present when these goslings hatched. Because he was the first moving object they perceived and could follow, they became attached to him.

Although the development of attachment may also be instinctive in people (Ainsworth & Bowlby, 1991), human attachments develop somewhat differently than attachments among ducks and geese. For example, children do not imprint on the first person they see or are held by. For humans, it takes several months before infants become attached to their main caregivers. There is also no known critical period for attachment in humans. Children can become strongly attached to their adoptive parents even when they are adopted after infancy.

Secure Versus Insecure Attachment When mothers or other primary caregivers are affectionate and reliable, infants usually become securely attached (Cox et al., 1992). Infants with secure attachment are very bonded to their caregivers. They cry or protest if the parent or caregiver leaves them. When the caregiver returns, the infants welcome that person back and are happy again.

When caregivers are unresponsive or unreliable, the infants are usually insecurely attached. They often do not seem to mind when the caregivers leave them. When the caregivers return, the infants make little or no effort to seek contact with them. Some insecure infants may cry when picked up, as if they are angry with the caregiver (Ainsworth, 1973, 1979; Ainsworth et al., 1978).

Secure infants may mature into secure children. Secure children are happier, friendlier, and more cooperative with parents and teachers than insecure children are. They get along better with other children than insecure children do (Belsky et al., 1991; Thompson, 1991a). Secure children are also less likely to misbehave and more likely to do well in school than insecure children (Lyons-Ruth et al., 1993; Youngblade & Belsky, 1992).

Styles of Parenting

Styles of parenting differ along two separate dimensions. One dimension is warmth-coldness; the other is strictness-permissiveness (Baumrind, 1991a, 1991b; MacDonald, 1992). Warm parents can be either strict or permissive, as can cold parents.

Warm or Cold? Warm parents show a great deal of affection to their children. For example, they hug and kiss them and often smile at them. They show their children that they are happy to have them and enjoy their company. Cold parents may not be as affectionate toward their children or appear to enjoy them as much.

Research suggests that children fare better when their parents are warm to them (Dix, 1991). The children of warm parents are more likely to be well adjusted. They are also more likely to develop a conscience—a sense of moral goodness or a sense of responsibility when they do wrong (MacDonald, 1992; Miller et al., 1993). Children of cold parents, on the other hand, are usually more interested in escaping punishment than in doing the right thing for its own sake.

Strict or Permissive? If you have younger brothers and sisters, you probably know that children do many things that anger or annoy other people. For example, they may make noise when other people are trying to sleep or concentrate on a difficult task. Sometimes they make messes. Children may also engage in behaviors that are unhealthy to themselves. They may have poor eating habits or watch too much television. They may neglect their schoolwork or play with dangerous objects.

Some parents are extremely strict when it comes to such behaviors. They impose many rules and supervise their children closely. Permissive parents, on the other hand, impose fewer rules and watch their children less closely. Permissive parents tend to be less concerned about neatness and cleanliness than are strict parents.

Parents may be strict or permissive for different reasons. Some extremely strict parents cannot tolerate disorder. Others fear that their children will run wild and get into trouble if they are not taught self-discipline. Some parents are permissive because they believe that children need freedom to express themselves if they are to become independent. Other parents are permissive because they are less concerned or have little time to monitor their children's activities. Without clear and consistent guidance, these children may become confused about which behaviors are acceptable and which are not.

Strictness can have positive and negative results, depending on how it is used. Strictness is not necessarily the same as meanness—as Hannah pointed out, parents can be strict but still love their children. Research suggests that consistent and firm enforcement of rules can foster achievement and self-control, especially when combined with warmth and support (Putallaz & Heflin, 1990). But physical punishment or constant interference may lead to disobedience and poor grades in school (Olson et al., 1992; Westerman, 1990).

Authoritative (meaning with authority) parents combine warmth with positive kinds of strictness. The children of authoritative parents are often more independent and achievement oriented than other children. They also feel better about themselves (Baumrind, 1991b; Dumas & LaFreniere, 1993). Parental demands for responsible behavior combined with affection and support usually pay off. Apparently, Hannah's parents knew this, and were raising Eddie with both strictness and warmth.

Be careful not to confuse the term *authoritative* with the word *authoritarian,* which means "favoring unquestioning obedience." **Authoritarian** parents believe in obedience for its own sake. They have strict guidelines that they expect their children to follow without question. Often they are rejecting and cold. Children of authoritarian parents may become either resistant to other people or dependent on them (Baumrind, 1989). They generally do not do as well in school as children of authoritative parents. They also tend to be less friendly and less spontaneous (DeKovic & Janssens, 1992; Maccoby & Martin, 1983).

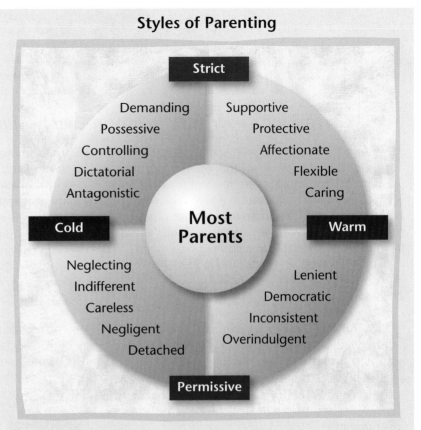

FIGURE 10.2 *Styles of parenting can be classified along the dimensions of warm-cold and strict-permissive. Both dimensions are continuums, and most parents do not lie at the extremes but cluster in the middle.*

Child Care

In the United States today, most parents—both fathers and mothers—work outside the home. More than half of mothers of children younger than one year of age are working mothers (Erel et al., 2000). For this reason, millions of preschoolers are cared for in day-care facilities. Parents and psychologists are concerned about the effects of day care on the development of children.

The effects of day care depend in part on the quality of the day-care center. One study found that children in day-care centers with many learning resources, many caregivers, and a good deal of individual attention did as well on cognitive and language tests as children who remained in the home with their mother (Azar, 1997). A Swedish study actually found that on tests of math and language skills, children in the best day-care centers outperformed children who remained in the home (Broberg et al., 1997).

Studies of the effects of day care on parent-child attachment have yielded mixed results. Children in full-time day care show less distress when their mothers leave them and are less likely to seek out their mother when they return. Some psychologists worry that this distancing from the mother could mean that the child is insecurely attached (Belsky, 1990). But other psychologists suggest that children may simply be adapting to repeated separations from and reunions with their mothers (Field, 1991; Lamb et al., 1992; Thompson, 1991b).

Day care seems to have mixed effects on other aspects of children's social development. First, the positive: children in day care are more likely to share their toys and be independent, self-confident, and outgoing (Clarke-Stewart, 1991; Field, 1991).

Helping Children with Protein-Energy Malnutrition (PEM)

Malnutrition can have harmful effects on a child's early physical and mental development. The most severe form of malnutrition is protein-energy malnutrition (PEM). This form of malnutrition can be damaging because protein is essential for growth. In addition, food energy from protein translates as calories.

The following are facts about PEM from the World Health Organization (2004).

- Protein-energy malnutrition (PEM) affects one child in four around the world. As a result of PEM, some 150 million children (27 percent) are underweight, and 182 million (33 percent) have stunted growth.
- More than 70 percent of children with PEM live in Asia. Some 26 percent live in Africa, and about 4 percent live in Latin America and the Caribbean.
- Children can develop PEM prior to birth if their mother is malnourished.
- Infants and young children are most vulnerable to PEM because of their high needs for protein and their susceptibility to infection.
- Children with PEM suffer up to 160 days of illness per year.
- Malnutrition contributes to about 60 percent of the 11 million deaths of children each year.

In 2003 the World Health Organization adopted methods for teaching health professionals how to treat children with PEM. These methods, listed below, include the use of psychological methods.

- Education as to the extent and severity of PEM
- Identifying children with severe malnutrition: Physical symptoms include hypoglycemia (shakiness due to low sugar levels), shock, dehydration, and anemia. Psychological symptoms include lack of energy and loss of interest.
- Ways to prepare feeding formulas and food supplements, and how to encourage malnourished infants to eat
- Using psychological tracking methods, including a weight chart, to monitor the child's intake of food and gain or loss of weight

- Monitoring the child's vital signs—pulse, respiration rate, and temperature—and being aware of signs of physical danger
- Bathing the child
- Using psychological methods to involve mothers in the care of malnourished infants so that mothers can continue care at home, including feeding and play activities (for purposes of stimulation); following up by visiting the mother and child in the home

The mortality rate of children with PEM can be as high as 30 to 50 percent. Yet, with adequate care, those rates can be reduced to less than 5 percent. If you are interested in learning more, contact the following organization.

Department of Nutrition for Health and Development
World Health Organization
1211 Geneva 27, Switzerland
Phone: +41 22 791 2624/4342
Fax: +41 22 791 4156

THINK ABOUT IT

Drawing Inferences and Conclusions Why do you think the World Health Organization adopted psychological methods for teaching health professionals how to treat children with PEM?

However, some studies have found that children in day care are less cooperative and more aggressive than are other children (Vandell & Corasaniti, 1990). Perhaps some children in day care do not receive the individual attention or resources they need. When they are placed in a competitive situation, they become more aggressive to try to meet their needs. Yet some psychologists interpret the greater aggressiveness of children in day care as a sign of independence rather than social maladjustment.

All in all, it would appear that nonparental care in itself may not affect child development very much (Erel et al., 2000). The quality of care seems to be more important than who provides it.

Child Abuse and Neglect

Most parents are kind and loving to their children. Yet child abuse—physical or psychological—is widespread. The incidence of child abuse is seriously underreported because children themselves often do not go to the authorities and abusive parents sometimes try to protect one another. It is estimated that nearly 3 million children in the United States are neglected or abused by their parents or other caregivers each year (Herman-Giddens et al., 1999). More than half a million of them suffer serious injuries, and thousands die.

Physical child abuse refers to a physical assault of a child. Neglect is failure to give a child adequate food, shelter, clothing, emotional support, or schooling. More health problems and deaths result from neglect than from abuse (Hamby & Finkelhor, 2000; Hashima & Finkelhor, 1999).

Why do some parents abuse or neglect their children? Psychologists have found the following factors to be associated with child abuse or neglect:

- stress, particularly the stresses of unemployment and poverty (Lewin, 1995; Trickett et al., 1991)
- a history of child abuse in at least one parent's family of origin
- acceptance of violence as a way of coping with stress
- lack of attachment to the child
- substance abuse
- rigid attitudes about child rearing (Belsky, 1993; Kaplan, 1991).

Studies show that children who are abused run a higher risk of developing psychological problems than children who did not grow up in an abusive environment. For example, they tend to be unsure of themselves. They are thus less likely than other children to venture out to explore the world around them (Aber & Allen, 1987). They are more likely to suffer from a variety of psychological problems such as anxiety, depression, and low self-esteem (Wagner, 1997). They are less likely to be close to their peers and more likely to engage in aggressive behavior (DeAngelis, 1997; Parker & Herrera, 1996; Rothbart & Ahadi, 1994). As adults, they are more likely to act in violent ways toward their dates or spouses (Malinosky-Rummell & Hansen, 1993).

Child abuse tends to run in families (Ertem et al., 2000). There are many possible reasons for this pattern. For one thing, children may imitate their parents' behavior. If children see their parents coping with feelings of anger through violence, they are likely to do the same. They are less likely to seek other ways of coping, such as humor, verbal expression of negative feelings, deep breathing, or silently "counting to 10" before reacting, thus giving the feelings of anger time to subside.

Children also often adopt their parents' strict ideas about discipline. Abused children may come to see severe punishment as normal. As a result, when they have children of their own, they may continue the pattern of abuse and neglect.

This pattern does not mean, however, that all people who were abused as children will in turn become abusers themselves. Most children who are victims of abuse do not later abuse their own children (Kaufman & Zigler, 1989). One study found that mothers who had been abused as children but who were able to break the cycle of abuse with their own children were likely to have received emotional support from a nonabusive adult during childhood. They were also likely to have participated in therapy and to have a nonabusive mate (Egeland et al., 1988).

It is not true that most abused children become child abusers themselves when they grow up. Although some children of abuse do become abusers, most do not.

Self-Esteem

The development of self-esteem begins in early childhood. **Self-esteem** is the value or worth that people attach to themselves. Self-esteem is important because it helps to protect people against the stresses and struggles of life. Although everyone experiences failure now and then, high self-esteem gives people the confidence to know that they can overcome their difficulties.

Influences on Self-Esteem   What factors influence self-esteem? Secure attachment plays a major role. Young children who are securely attached to their parents are more likely to have high self-esteem (Cassidy, 1988).

The ways in which parents react to their children can also make a difference. Research suggests that authoritative parenting contributes to high self-esteem in children (Baumrind, 1991). Children with high self-esteem tend to be close to their parents because their parents are loving and involved in their lives. Their parents also teach and expect appropriate behavior and thus encourage them to become competent individuals.

Psychologist Carl Rogers noted that there are two types of support parents can give to their children—unconditional positive regard or conditional positive regard. **Unconditional positive regard** means that parents love and accept their children for who they are—no matter how they behave. Children who receive unconditional positive regard usually develop high self-esteem. They know that even if they do something wrong or inappropriate, they are still worthwhile as people.

On the other hand, children who receive conditional positive regard may have lower self-esteem. **Conditional positive regard** means that parents show their love only when the children behave in certain acceptable ways. Children who receive conditional positive regard may feel worthwhile only when they are doing what their parents (or other authority figures) want them to do.

Once these children grow up, they often continue to seek the approval of other people. Excessive need for approval from other people is linked to low self-esteem (Ellis & Dryden, 1987). It is unrealistic for people to expect everyone to like and respect them. If they understand that it is natural for others to not always appreciate them, they may have higher self-esteem in the long run.

A sense of competence also increases self-esteem. By the age of about four, children begin to

When children are encouraged and given the means to develop skills, such as tending a garden, their self-esteem may rise.

judge themselves according to their cognitive, physical, and social competence (Harter, 1990). Children who know that they are good at something usually have higher self-esteem than others. Children may feel good about themselves if they are good at puzzles or counting (cognitive skills), if they are good at tying their shoelaces or swinging (physical skills), or if they have friends (social skills).

Both heredity and environment play a role in individual differences in skills. Some people are more physically coordinated than others and therefore naturally good at sports. Other people may take lessons and train to improve their athletic abilities. Part of becoming competent is setting realistic goals. Warmth and encouragement from parents and teachers can help children reach high levels of competence and self-esteem.

Gender and Self-Esteem   By the ages of five to seven, children begin to value themselves on the basis of their physical appearance and performance in school. Once in grade school, girls tend to display greater competence in the areas of reading and general academic skills. Boys tend to display competence in math and physical skills (Eccles et al., 1993; Marsh et al., 1991). (See Chapter 9.)

Does this mean that girls are genetically better in reading and boys better in math and sports? No. It may be that the reason girls and boys show greater competence, and thus higher self-esteem, in these areas is that people around them have suggested that this is what girls and boys are *supposed* to be good at. For example, girls predict that they will do better on tasks that are considered "feminine," and boys predict better performance for themselves when tasks are labeled "masculine" (Lips, 1993). When people feel they will do well at a particular task, they often do. People generally live up to the expectations that they have for themselves and that others have for them. Such expectations often become self-fulfilling prophecies.

Age and Self-Esteem   Children gain in competence as they grow older. Through experience they learn more skills and become better at them. Even so, their self-esteem tends to decline during the elementary school years. Self-esteem seems to reach a low point at about age 12 or 13 and increases again during adolescence (Harter, 1990; Pomerantz et al., 1993). How can we explain this pattern?

It appears that young children, such as Hannah's brother Eddie, assume that others see them as they see themselves. Thus, if they like themselves, they assume that other people like them too. As children develop, however, they begin to realize that some people might not see them the way they see themselves. They also begin to compare themselves to their peers. If they see themselves as less competent in some areas, their self-esteem may decrease.

TRUTH OR **fiction** ▪ R E V I S I T E D ▪

It is true that children's self-esteem tends to decrease as they go through elementary school. As children develop and mature, they begin to compare themselves to others of the same age. Sometimes they feel they do not measure up to their peers.

SECTION 3 REVIEW

go.hrw.com **Homework Practice Online**
Keyword: SY7 HP10

1. Define the terms *attachment, contact comfort,* and *imprinting.*

2. Describe several ways children develop socially.

3. **Critical Thinking** *Evaluating* What are three things you think parents and teachers can do to help children keep self-esteem high throughout the school years?

Cognitive Development

In addition to social development, psychologists are interested in studying cognitive development, or the development of people's thought processes. Two psychologists who are famous for their work on children's cognitive development are Jean Piaget and Lawrence Kohlberg.

Piaget's Theory of Cognitive Development

Jean Piaget

When Jean Piaget (1896–1980) was in his early 20s, he was employed at the Binet Institute in Paris. At the institute he worked on the Binet intelligence test, trying out potential test questions on children.

Before long, Piaget realized that the children he questioned gave certain types of wrong answers and that these wrong answers fit patterns from child to child. Piaget was so interested in these patterns that the study of children's thinking became his life's work.

Assimilation and Accommodation   Piaget believed that human beings organize new information in two ways: through assimilation and through accommodation. **Assimilation** is the process by which new information is placed into categories that already exist. For example, a child might know the word *doggie* because the family has a pet collie. If that child sees a Great Dane on the street and says "doggie," she or he has assimilated the new information about the Great Dane into the category "dog"—even though the Great Dane looks and may act differently from the collie familiar to the child.

If the same child sees a cat and says "doggie" again, some adults most likely will correct the child. Through such corrections, the child will learn that the category "dog" does not apply to cats and that a new category is needed. This adjustment is an example of **accommodation**—a change brought about because of new information.

Object permanence means understanding that objects exist even when they are out of sight. This toddler realizes that his brother still exists even when he is hidden behind the cushions.

Piaget theorized that children's thinking develops in a sequence of stages. Some children are more advanced than others at a given age. However, the developmental sequence is the same for everyone. Piaget identified four stages in the sequence: sensorimotor, preoperational, concrete operational, and formal operational.

The Sensorimotor Stage   The behavior of newborns is mainly reflexive. They are capable only of responding to their environment and cannot initiate behavior. Instead of acting, infants react. By about one month of age, however, infants begin to act with purpose. As they coordinate vision with touch, for example, they will look at objects they are holding.

The first stage of cognitive development is characterized mainly by learning to coordinate sensation and perception with motor activity. Infants begin to understand that there is a relationship between their physical movements and the results they sense and perceive. That is why Piaget called this stage the **sensorimotor stage**.

Infants who are three and four months old are fascinated by their own hands and legs. They are easily amused by watching themselves open and close their fists. If they hear an interesting sound, such as a rattle, they might do something to sustain the sound. By four to eight months, infants are exploring cause-and-effect relationships. They might, for example, hit mobiles that hang over their cribs so that the mobiles will move.

Perhaps you have heard the expression "Out of sight, out of mind." Before infants are six months old, objects out of their sight are truly out of their minds. The infants do not realize that objects out of sight still exist. They might stare at a stuffed animal, but if you were to put the stuffed animal behind a piece of paper, they would not look behind the paper or reach to find it. By eight months to a year, however, infants understand that things that have been taken away still exist. For example, a 10-month-old child probably would search for a stuffed animal that was hidden behind a screen. Piaget called this **object permanence**—the understanding that objects exist even when they cannot be seen or touched.

According to Piaget's theory, object permanence occurs because infants are able to hold an idea in mind. For instance, they learn that "stuffed animal" is a soft, fuzzy object. They can mentally picture a stuffed animal even when it is no longer in view. Therefore, they know to look for it when it is hidden behind a screen.

The Preoperational Stage   The sensorimotor stage ends at about the age of two years, when children begin to use words and symbols (language) to represent objects. At this point, children enter the **preoperational stage**.

A DAY IN THE LIFE

As we saw with Eddie, preoperational thinking is very different from more mature forms of thinking. Children's views of the world are different from those of adolescents and adults. For example, preoperational thinking is one-dimensional. In other words, preoperational children can see only one aspect of a situation at a time.

This one-dimensional thinking is most evident in the fact that in the preoperational stage children do not understand the law of **conservation**. The law says that key properties of substances, such as their weight, volume, and number, stay the same even if their shape or arrangement are changed. That is, the basic properties are *conserved*. Children in the preoperational stage cannot comprehend all the aspects at once, so they focus only on the most obvious one—the way a substance looks.

When preoperational children are shown two identical tall, thin glasses of water, each filled to the same level, they know that both glasses hold the

In the first photograph, the child looks at two tall glasses filled to the same level and understands that both glasses contain the same amount of liquid. In the second photograph, the child watches as the liquid from one of the tall glasses is emptied into a shorter glass. In the third photograph, the child indicates a belief that the tall glass that is still full contains more liquid than the short one simply because the taller glass looks larger.

same amount of water. However, if water from one of the tall glasses is poured into a short, squat glass, the children say that the other tall glass contains more liquid than the short one. They say this even if they have *watched* the water being poured. Because they can focus only on what they are seeing at a given moment—and on one dimension at a time—they incorrectly think that the tall glass now contains more water than the short glass. Their thinking is that it looks as if there is less water in the short glass (because the water level is lower) and therefore it must be so. Children in the preoperational stage do not realize that increases in one dimension (such as width) can make up for decreases in another (such as height).

A DAY IN THE LIFE Eddie—who at three years of age is in the preoperational stage—did not understand the law of conservation, as demonstrated by Hannah's experiment with the five pennies. Eddie insisted that the row of five pennies that were farther apart had more pennies in it than the row in which the pennies were close together. He said so even when Hannah had him count the pennies in both rows, which he did correctly.

Another characteristic of children in the preoperational stage is **egocentrism**—the inability to see another person's point of view. Remember how Eddie thought it became dark because he went to sleep and that the sun rose because he woke up? Preoperational children assume that other people see the world just as they do. They cannot imagine that things might happen to others that do not happen to them. They think that the world exists to meet their needs. Egocentrism is a consequence of the preoperational child's one-dimensional thinking. Egocentrism is not the same as selfishness. When a preschooler sits down in front of the television set blocking everyone else's view, he or she is not being rude. The child simply thinks you can see exactly what he or she can see.

Preoperational children are also artificialistic and animistic. They think that natural events such as rain and thunder are made by people (artificialism). They also think objects such as the sun and the moon are alive and conscious (animism).

The Concrete-Operational Stage Most children enter the **concrete-operational stage** at about the age of seven. In this stage, children begin to show signs of adult thinking. Yet they are logical only when they think about specific objects, not about abstract ideas. Their thinking is still grounded mostly in concrete experiences. This is one reason why many teachers assign them hands-on projects. Seeing, touching, and manipulating objects often help concrete-operational children understand abstract concepts.

Children at the concrete-operational stage can focus on two dimensions of a problem at the same time. For this reason, they understand the laws of conservation. They understand that a short, wide glass might contain the same amount of water as a tall, thin glass. They can focus on both the height

Examples of Preoperational Thought

Kind of Thinking	Sample Questions	Typical Answers
Egocentric *(thinking that the world exists to meet one's own needs)*	Why does it get dark out?	So I can go to sleep.
	Why does the sun shine?	To keep me warm.
	Why is there snow?	For me to play in.
	Why is grass green?	Because that's my favorite color.
	What are TV sets for?	To watch my favorite shows and cartoons.
Animistic *(thinking that inanimate objects are alive and conscious)*	Why do trees have leaves?	To keep them warm.
	Why do stars twinkle?	Because they're happy and cheerful.
	Why does the sun move in the sky?	To follow children and hear what they say.
	Where do boats go at night?	They sleep like we do.
Artificialistic *(thinking that natural things and events are made by people)*	Why is the sky blue?	Somebody painted it.
	What is the wind?	A man blowing.
	What causes thunder?	A man grumbling.
	What makes it rain?	Somebody emptying a watering can.

FIGURE 10.3   *The second stage of Piaget's theory of cognitive development is the preoperational stage. At about two years of age, the child begins to use words and symbols to represent things. Thinking tends to be one-dimensional, however. The child believes that the world exists to meet his or her needs.*

and the width of the glasses at the same time. They can therefore recognize that a gain in width compensates for a loss in height. Similarly, in a few years, Eddie will conserve numbers. He will understand that the two rows have the same numbers of pennies in them, even though one row is longer because the pennies are spaced farther apart.

Concrete-operational children are less egocentric than children in earlier stages. They can see the world from another person's point of view. They understand that people may see things differently because they have different experiences or are in different situations.

The Formal-Operational Stage   The final cognitive stage in Piaget's theory begins at about puberty and represents cognitive maturity. It is the **formal-operational stage**.

People in the formal-operational stage think abstractly. They realize that ideas can be compared and classified mentally just as objects can. For example, they understand what is meant by the unknown quantity x in algebra. They can work on geometry problems about lines, triangles, and squares without concerning themselves with how the problems relate to the real world. They can also deduce rules of behavior from moral principles. They focus on many aspects of a situation simultaneously when reasoning and solving problems.

During the formal-operational stage, people are capable of dealing with hypothetical situations. They realize that they may be able to control the outcome of a situation in several different ways. Therefore, if one approach to solving a problem does not work, they will try another. They think ahead, imagining the results of different courses of action before they decide on a particular one.

Criticism of Piaget's Theories   Over the years, a number of psychologists have questioned the accuracy of Piaget's views. Some believe his methods caused him to underestimate the abilities of children. Recent research using different methodology indicates that preschoolers are less egocentric

CASE STUDIES
AND OTHER TRUE STORIES

Bullying—An Epidemic of Misbehavior and Fear

Nine-year-old Stephanie did not want to go to school. It turns out that Stephanie had had a disagreement with Susan, another girl at school. Susan had then threatened to beat Stephanie mercilessly if Stephanie showed up at school again. To highlight her warning, Susan had shoved Stephanie across the school hall. Stephanie was a victim of bullying, and Susan was a bully.

Many students are bullied.

Was there something unusual about this situation? Not really. Although boys are more likely than girls to be bullies, many girls engage in bullying, too (Baldry, 2003; Griffin & Gross, 2004; Richter & Barbara, 2003). Overall, an estimated 70 to 75 percent of students are bullied at some point. Moreover, an estimated 10 percent of students are exposed to extreme bullying (Elias & Zins, 2003; Richter & Barbara, 2003; Swearer & Cary, 2003).

Bullying has devastating effects. Students come to think of school as a violent place rather than a safe place for learning (Laufer & Harel, 2003; Nansel et al., 2003). Even bullies come to see the school as a violent environment (Laufer & Harel, 2003). Bullying also impairs adjustment to middle school and high school, where older children sometimes bully younger children (Nansel et al., 2003). In particular, bullying impairs adjustment for children who speak another language in the home. Those children tend to experience bullying more often than other children.

Many but not all bullies have some things in common. First, their achievment tends to be lower than average. Perhaps peer approval—or the ability to control other students—becomes more important to bullies than learning and grades are (Laufer & Harel, 2003; Pereira et al., 2004). Second, bullies are more likely to come from homes that are characterized by violence between the parents (Baldry, 2003).

In addition, numerous studies have investigated the personalities of bullies. One study compared bullies to nonaggressive students from similar backgrounds (Coolidge et al., (2004). This study found that bullying was more often associated with delinquent behavior, attention deficit hyperactivity disorder, and depression. Bullies were also more likely to assume that others wanted to harm them, even when the assumption had no foundation.

Is there any cure for bullying? School systems and families have a stake in controlling bullying. Setting strict limits on bullies can sometimes help. Yet, much bullying—if not most—goes unreported. Some children do not report bullying because they are embarrassed. Other children do not report bullying because they fear retaliation. Many children simply learn to accommodate or avoid bullies until they are out of school (Hunter & Boyle, 2004).

THINKING CRITICALLY

1. **Finding Main Ideas** How does bullying affect students and the school atmosphere?
2. **Analyzing Information** How might schools decrease or prevent bullying?

than Piaget's research suggested. Some psychologists also assert that several cognitive skills appear to develop more continuously than Piaget thought. Nonetheless, his theories are still respected.

Kohlberg's Theory of Moral Development

Psychologist Lawrence Kohlberg (1927–87) devised a cognitive theory about the development of children's moral reasoning. Kohlberg used the following story in his research:

> A woman was near death from a special kind of cancer. There was one drug that the doctors thought might save her. It was a form of radium that a pharmacist in the same town had recently discovered. The drug was expensive to make, but the pharmacist was charging 10 times what the drug cost him to make. He paid $200 for the radium and charged $2,000 for a small dose of the drug. The sick woman's husband, Heinz, went to everyone he knew to borrow the money, but he could raise only about $1,000—half the amount he needed. He told the pharmacist that his wife was dying and asked him to sell it cheaper or let him pay later. But the pharmacist rejected the man's plea saying that he had discovered the drug and intended to make money from it. Heinz became desperate and broke into the man's store to steal the drug for his wife. (Adapted from Kohlberg, 1969, p. 379.)

Should Heinz have stolen the drug? Was he right or wrong? Kohlberg believed that there was no simple answer. Heinz was involved in what Kohlberg called a moral dilemma. In this case, laws against stealing contradicted Heinz's strong human desire to save his wife's life.

Kohlberg was not particularly interested in whether children thought Heinz was right or wrong to steal the drug. More important to Kohlberg were the reasons why children thought Heinz should or should not steal the drug. People arrive at answers for different reasons. Kohlberg classified these reasons according to levels of moral development.

Kohlberg, like Piaget, was a stage theorist. He believed that the stages of moral development always follow a specific sequence. People do not skip any stages or go backward. Children advance at different rates, however, and not everyone reaches the highest stage. Kohlberg theorized that there are three levels of moral development and two stages within each level.

The Preconventional Level   According to Kohlberg, through the age of nine, most children are at the preconventional level of moral development. Children who use **preconventional moral reasoning** base their judgments on the consequences of behavior.

In stage 1, children believe that what is "good" is what helps one avoid punishment. Therefore, children at stage 1 would argue that Heinz was wrong because he would be caught for stealing and sent to jail.

At stage 2, "good" is what satisfies a person's needs. Stage 2 reasoning holds that Heinz was right to steal the drug because his wife needed it.

The Conventional Level   People who are at the level of **conventional moral reasoning** make judgments in terms of whether an act conforms to conventional standards of right and wrong. These standards derive from the family, religion, and society at large.

At stage 3, "good" is what meets one's needs and the expectations of other people. Moral behavior is what most people would do in a given situation. According to stage 3 reasoning, Heinz should steal the drug because a good and loving husband would do whatever he could to save the life of his wife. But stage 3 reasoning might also maintain that Heinz should not steal the drug because good people do not steal. Both conclusions show conventional thinking. Kohlberg found stage 3 moral judgments most often among 13-year-olds.

Stage 4 moral judgments are based on maintaining the social order. People in this stage have high regard for authority. Stage 4 reasoning might insist that breaking the law for any reason sets a bad example and undermines the social order. Stage 4 judgments occurred most often among 16-year-olds (Kohlberg, 1963).

The Postconventional Level   Reasoning based on a person's own moral standards of goodness is called **postconventional moral reasoning**. Here, moral judgments reflect one's personal values, not conventional standards.

Stage 5 reasoning recognizes that laws represent agreed-upon procedures, that laws have value, and that they should not be violated without good reason. But laws cannot bind the individual in exceptional circumstances. Stage 5 reasoning might suggest that it is right for Heinz to steal the drug, even though it is against the law, because the needs of his wife have created an exceptional situation.

Kohlberg's Stages of Moral Development

Stage	Moral Reasoning Goal	What Is Right?
preconventional level		
1	Avoiding punishment	Doing what is necessary to avoid punishment
2	Satisfying needs	Doing what is necessary to satisfy one's needs
conventional level		
3	Winning approval	Seeking and maintaining the approval of others using conventional standards of right and wrong
4	Law and order	Moral judgments based on maintaining social order High regard for authority
postconventional level		
5	Social order	Obedience to accepted laws Judgments based on personal values
6	Universal ethics	Morality of individual conscience, not necessarily in agreement with others

FIGURE 10.4 *According to Lawrence Kohlberg, people's moral development follows a specific sequence. Not every person reaches the highest stage.*

Stage 6 reasoning regards acts that support the values of human life, justice, and dignity as moral and good. People at stage 6 rely on their own consciences. They do not necessarily obey laws or agree with other people's opinions. Using stage 6 reasoning, a person might argue that the pharmacist was acting out of greed and that survival is more important than profit. Therefore, Heinz had a moral right to steal the drug to save his wife's life. Post-conventional moral reasoning rarely occurs before adolescence and is found most often in adults.

Bias in Kohlberg's Theory Some studies have found that according to Kohlberg's stages, boys appear to reason at higher levels of moral development than do girls. Does this mean that boys are morally superior to girls? No. It may mean instead that Kohlberg's stages and scoring system were biased to favor males.

Psychologist Carol Gilligan argues that the differences between boys and girls are created because of what adults teach children about how they should behave as boys or girls (1982; Gilligan et al., 1989). For example, girls are often taught to consider the needs of others over simple right or wrong. Therefore, a girl might worry that both stealing the drug and letting Heinz's wife die are wrong. Such reasoning—involving empathy for others—would be classified as stage 3.

Boys, however, are often taught to argue logically rather than with empathy. Therefore, a boy might set up an equation to prove that life has greater value than property. This would be considered reasoning at stage 5 or even stage 6.

Gilligan suggests, however, that girls' reasoning is at as high a level as that of boys. Girls have, in fact, thought about the same kinds of issues boys considered. In the end, they have chosen to be empathetic, not because their thinking is simpler, but because it is very complex—and because of what they have been taught is appropriate for girls. Shortly before his death in 1987, Kohlberg had begun to correct the gender bias in his theory.

SECTION 4 REVIEW

go.hrw.com **Homework Practice Online**
Keyword: SY7 HP10

1. Identify and briefly describe Piaget's four stages of cognitive development.

2. List the three levels of moral development, as theorized by Kohlberg.

3. **Critical Thinking** *Comparing* In what way are Piaget's preoperational stage and Kohlberg's stage 2 similar?

10 REVIEW

Writing a Summary

Using standard grammar, spelling, sentence structure, and punctuation, summarize the information in this chapter. Consider:
• how people develop physically and socially
• cognitive and moral development

Identifying People and Ideas

Identify the following terms or people and use them in appropriate sentences.

1. developmental psychology
2. maturation
3. attachment
4. stranger anxiety
5. separation anxiety
6. imprinting
7. assimilation
8. object permanence
9. concrete-operational stage
10. postconventional moral reasoning

Understanding Main Ideas

SECTION 1 (pp. 228–230)
1. What is the main focus of developmental psychology?

SECTION 2 (pp. 230–233)
2. Describe motor development in infants.

SECTION 3 (pp. 233–241)
3. How does an authoritarian parenting style differ from an authoritative parenting style?

SECTION 4 (pp. 241–247)
4. According to Piaget, what allows object permanence to occur?
5. What is meant by the law of conservation in developmental psychology?

Thinking Critically

1. **Evaluating** Why might a child's learning to read be the result of both maturation and nurture?

2. **Summarizing** How do infants unknowingly encourage warmth and affection from their caregivers?

3. **Drawing Inferences and Conclusions** Provide an example of how cognitive development occurs gradually.

4. **Analyzing Information** How might a child's physical development influence his or her social development?

5. **Categorizing** Describe how each of the following types of parents might react to their child drawing a picture on the wall with crayons: a warm-permissive parent, a warm-strict parent, a cold-permissive parent, a cold-strict parent.

Writing About Psychology

1. **Analyzing Information** Use the library to find more information about Piaget's theories of child development. Then create an annotated time line that provides examples of growth and development of children based on cognitive theories.

2. **Evaluating** Write a one-page paper that evaluates theories of human development. Note the strengths and weaknesses of each theory. Be sure to use standard grammar, spelling, sentence structure, and punctuation. Use the graphic organizer below to help you write your paper.

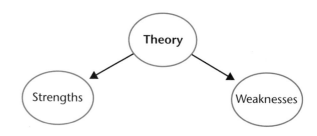

Interpreting Graphs

Study the graph below. Then use the information in the graph to help you answer the questions that follow.

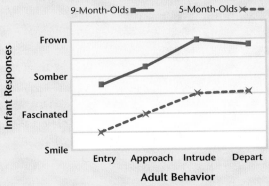

Responses of Infants to the Presence of a Strange Adult

9-Month-Olds ▬ 5-Month-Olds ✗▬ ▬

Infant Responses: Frown, Somber, Fascinated, Smile

Adult Behavior: Entry, Approach, Intrude, Depart

Source: Ruff and Rothbart, *Attention in Early Development*, 1996

1. Which of the following statements can be drawn from the information found in the graph?

    a. Five-month-old infants are afraid of strange adults.

    b. Infant responses to strangers do not change markedly between the ages of five months and nine months.

    c. Infants cannot tell the difference between family members and strangers.

    d. Nine-month-old infants respond differently to strangers than do five-month-old infants.

2. What conclusions can you draw about infant development based on the information in the graph?

Analyzing Primary Sources

Read the following excerpt, in which Swiss psychologist Jean Piaget considers the role of curiosity in child development. Then answer the questions that follow.

❝As sense organs . . . widen an organism's field of activity, then biological needs take on an aspect of implicit curiosity which keeps growing and flourishing. We see it already in primates, for example. Chimpanzees demonstrate intellectual curiosity.

For example, once when one of my children was in his playpen . . . I held out an object to him horizontally, so that if he tried to pull it towards himself, it was blocked by the rails of the playpen. He tried various positions, and finally got it in, but he got it in by chance, and he wasn't satisfied. He put it back outside the playpen and tried to do it again, and continued until he understood how he had to turn it to get it through the rails. He wasn't satisfied just to succeed. He wasn't satisfied until he understood how it worked.❞

3. According to Piaget's theory of cognitive development, at what stage was the child in the playpen?

    a. sensorimotor

    b. preoperational

    c. concrete-operational

    d. formal-operational

4. According to the excerpt, what role did curiosity play in the child's development?

PSYCHOLOGY PROJECTS

Cooperative Learning

Research in Psychology Working in small groups, construct a scenario in which a moral judgment must be made. Have one person write out the scenario and make a copy for each group member. Consider how people belonging to different age groups will respond to the scenario. Then have each member read the situation to a young child, an adolescent, and an adult, and record their responses. Evaluate the responses and compare them with Kohlberg's levels and stages of moral development.

📶 **internet** connect

Internet Activity: go.hrw.com
KEYWORD: SY7 CH10

Choose an activity on infancy and childhood to:

- write a report on the role of nature and nurture in development.
- create an annotated time line on human physical development.
- create a multimedia presentation on social and cognitive development in children and infants.

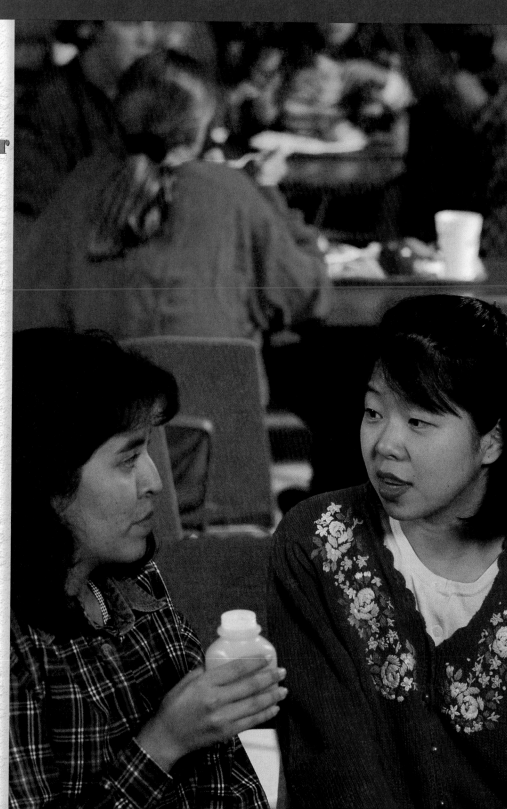

Read to Discover

1 How do males and females change physically during adolescence, and what are the psychological effects of these changes?

2 What role do parents and peers play in the lives of adolescents?

3 What is identity formation, and what are the four categories of adolescent identity status?

4 What are some of the challenges that adolescents face in today's society?

A DAY IN THE LIFE

Linda and Hannah feel very much a part of their circle of friends, which they often refer to as "the group." They are friendly with classmates outside the group, but when it comes to discussing the people and ideas they care about most, they talk to each other more than to anybody else except their parents. When they were concerned about Nick and his problems with drugs and alcohol, they could always talk to each other about it.

As it turned out, Nick wasn't the only one of their classmates they were concerned about. Linda and Hannah were eating lunch one day when Linda asked Hannah quietly, "Can I tell you something?"

"Sure," said Hannah. "Don't tell me Marc actually did something wrong. I thought he was supposed to be *perfect.*"

Linda laughed. "Hardly. No, Marc is wonderful." Her expression turned serious. "It's about Annie."

"Oh, Annie," said Hannah. "I bet I know what you're going to say."

They both liked Annie although she wasn't really a part of their group. She was a bright, quiet girl, well liked by her teachers—and everyone else for that matter.

"I'm worried about her," said Linda. "She keeps losing weight."

"I know," said Hannah.

"You've noticed too?" Linda asked with concern.

"How can you not notice it?" replied Hannah.

"She says she's on a diet. But she looks like a skeleton."

"I know," Hannah responded. "She's been skipping gym a lot too. I asked her when she was going to stop dieting. She said her weight was nearly where she wanted it to be and that she had never felt better."

"I don't know," said Linda. "Something's not right. Maybe I should talk to my parents about it. They might know how to help her."

"You're right," said Hannah. "We really should do something."

• • •

This chapter is about adolescence—the time between childhood and adulthood. For many teenagers, adolescence can be a rich and fulfilling time of life. Close friendships may develop. New opportunities to learn and grow present themselves. Most teenagers look to the future and see it as a time of hope and promise. However, adolescence can also be a confusing and difficult period. Rapid physical growth and sexual development bring dramatic changes. Teenagers must define who they are and what they stand for as they begin to establish identities as young adults. Even though they may be old enough to reproduce and be as big, or bigger, than their parents, adolescents sometimes feel they are treated like "big children." At other times, they must make adult decisions when they do not feel ready to make them. This chapter explores the physical changes that occur during adolescence, adolescent social development and identity formation, and the special challenges of adolescence.

Key Terms

- adolescent growth spurt
- puberty
- primary sex characteristics
- secondary sex characteristics
- menarche
- cliques
- crowds
- identity crisis
- identity status
- identity moratorium
- identity foreclosure
- identity diffusion
- identity achievement
- anorexia nervosa
- bulimia nervosa
- juvenile delinquency
- status offenses

HOLT

Psychology Video Program

Watch the video to explore how teenagers determine what is cool.

SECTION **1**

Physical Development

In earlier times in Western societies (and in some developing countries today), the period of transition from childhood to adulthood was very brief. Most people took over the responsibilities of adulthood—going to work, caring for children, and so on—shortly after they reached sexual maturity. The transition to adulthood was often marked by an elaborate ceremony that symbolized the passage from childhood to adulthood.

In the 1900s, however, all that has changed. In Western societies, required education has been extended, and the status and duties of adulthood have been delayed. As a result, adolescence has come to cover most of the teen years. Today the period known as adolescence is sometimes subdivided into smaller categories. These categories include early adolescence (ages 11 through 14), middle adolescence (15 through 18), and late adolescence (18 through 21).

The biological changes that occur during adolescence are greater than those of any other time of life, with the exception of infancy. In some ways, however, the changes in adolescence are more dramatic than those that occur in infancy—unlike infants, adolescents are aware of the changes that

are taking place and of what the changes mean. But no teenager can ever be quite sure how all these physical changes will turn out. There are many variables to consider. Different adolescents begin their growth spurts at different ages, and they grow at different rates. Even the different parts of an adolescent's body grow at different rates. Most adolescents can only wonder about the final shape and size of their body.

The Adolescent Growth Spurt

During adolescence the stable growth patterns in height and weight that mark early and middle childhood come to an end. Stability is replaced by an abrupt burst of growth. This **adolescent growth spurt** usually lasts two to three years. During this time of rapid growth, most adolescents grow 8 to 12 inches in height.

Girls begin the adolescent growth spurt earlier than boys. The growth spurt usually begins in girls at about the age of 10 or 11 and in boys about 2 years later. As a result, girls tend to be taller and heavier than boys during early adolescence. Then, during middle adolescence, most boys catch up and grow taller than their female classmates. However, the exact time when this growth will occur for any individual—boy or girl—is difficult to predict (Rathus, 2003).

It is not true that boys begin their adolescent growth spurt before girls do. Most boys begin their spurt at about 12 or 13 years of age, two years later than most girls.

By the time Linda entered her senior year of high school, she had been at her full height for about four years. At the same time, Marc had been at his full height for only about two years. In eighth grade, when Marc first noticed Linda, she was taller than he was. But then he caught up and passed Linda in height. His voice deepened, and by the time they were juniors, they seemed to be more or less equal in their level of physical maturity.

This period of sudden adolescent growth can be awkward for both boys and girls because different parts of their bodies grow and mature at different rates. For example, hands and feet may grow before arms and legs do. This growth spurt may cause adolescents to feel as if their hands or feet are too big or to worry that they "just don't look right."

Although some teenagers may feel that they look awkward, they tend to be well coordinated during adolescence. As adolescents become older and complete the growth spurt, their bodies usually reach their correct proportions. Once this has happened, the seeming awkwardness of the early teens becomes a thing of the past. Some psychologists believe that only a small percentage of adolescents—no more than about 15 percent—have difficulty adjusting to the adolescent growth spurt (Petersen, 1987).

Sexual Development

Adolescence begins with the onset of puberty. **Puberty** refers to the specific developmental changes that lead to the ability to reproduce. This biological stage of development ends when physical growth does.

During puberty the reproductive organs of both males and females develop and dramatically change the body of an adolescent. Characteristics that are directly involved in reproduction are called **primary sex characteristics**. Other characteristics that are not directly involved in reproduction—called **secondary sex characteristics**—also develop during puberty. These characteristics include the growth of hair on certain parts of the body, the deepening of the voice in males, and the rounding of the hips and breasts in females.

These changes are linked to changes in hormone levels. All hormones are present in children of both sexes from birth. During puberty, however, boys begin to produce higher levels of some hormones, while girls begin to produce higher levels of other hormones.

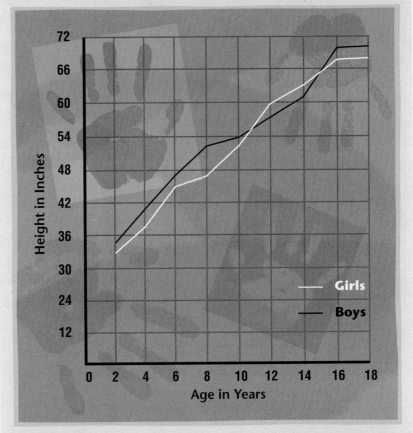

Average Growth Rates for Boys and Girls from Childhood Through Adolescence

FIGURE 11.1 *Throughout childhood, girls and boys are similar in height, with boys being slightly taller. At puberty, girls surge ahead for a short time. At about age 14, boys surge back ahead of girls.*

Source: Tanner, J.M. (1978). *Fetus into man: Physical growth from conception to maturity.* Cambridge, MA: Harvard University Press. (p. 118)

Changes in Males In boys, hormones from the pituitary gland cause the testes to increase output of the hormone testosterone. This causes boys' sexual organs to grow, their voices to deepen, and hair to grow on their faces and later on their chests. During the period of rapid growth, boys develop broader shoulders and thicker bodies. They also develop more muscle tissue and larger hearts and lungs.

Changes in Females In girls, hormones from the pituitary gland stimulate the ovaries to secrete more estrogen. Estrogen spurs the growth of breast tissue and supportive tissue in the hips and buttocks. As a result, the pelvic region widens and the hips become rounder. Girls also produce small amounts of androgens, which are similar to testosterone, in the adrenal glands. Androgens stimulate

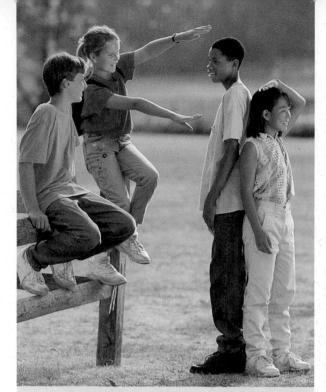

Adolescents develop physically at different rates. Both early- and late-maturing adolescents may experience difficulties associated with their rates of development, but these problems usually fade over time.

handle problems. Also, coaches, friends, and others may pressure them to perform beyond their abilities. They may not be prepared to live up to the expectations of others (Kutner, 1993). Boys who mature early may even be more likely than other boys to engage in types of problem behaviors (Andersson & Magnusson, 1990).

Furthermore, although early-maturing boys may have some advantages over their peers who develop later, these advantages fade over time. In fact, some longitudinal studies indicate that boys who mature later show better adjustment as adults than boys who mature early (Livson & Peskin, 1972). Of course, not all early maturing boys have problems, either as adolescents or as adults.

TRUTH OR fiction
▪ R E V I S I T E D ▪

It is true that boys who mature early have certain advantages over their peers. For example, they tend to be more popular and self-assured than their peers. However, early maturity may also carry certain disadvantages.

the growth of pubic and underarm hair. Estrogen and androgens work together to spur the growth of the female sex organs.

The production of estrogen, which becomes cyclical in puberty, regulates the menstrual cycle. The first menstruation, or **menarche**, is a major life event for most girls, and most societies consider it the beginning of womanhood. It usually occurs between the ages of 11 and 14.

Differences in Maturation Rates

Some adolescents reach physical maturity at a relatively early age, while others reach it later. Research suggests that boys who mature early have certain advantages over boys who mature later (Alsaker, 1992). They tend to be more popular and to be leaders within their circle of friends. Their greater size and strength may give them a competitive edge in sports. They also tend to be more self-assured and relaxed. Because they have matured early, they no longer need to worry about maturing later than their peers. This may boost their self-esteem.

However, boys who mature early physically are not necessarily more mature than their peers in some other ways, such as in how they approach and

Early maturation is somewhat different for girls. Girls who mature early may feel awkward because they are taller than their classmates, both male and female. They may be teased about their height. Early maturing girls may be tempted to associate with older teens, even when they are not emotionally ready for such associations. Moreover, older boys may assume that these girls are more mature than they really are and may expect them or pressure them to do things they do not want to do.

Needless to say, not all girls who mature early encounter problems. In any case, the differences between early and late-maturing girls usually do not last long. Once their peers catch up to them, the issue of differences in maturity generally disappears (Simmons & Blyth, 1987).

SECTION 1 REVIEW

go.
hrw
.com
Homework Practice Online
Keyword: SY7 HP11

1. List three characteristics of the adolescent growth spurt.
2. What physical changes occur in males during puberty? in females?
3. **Critical Thinking** *Finding the Main Idea* Identify some long-term effects of early maturation for girls and for boys.

EXPLORING
DIVERSITY

Rites of Passage

A rite of passage is a ceremony that marks a person's entrance into a new stage of life. Rites of passage include ceremonies such as baptism, graduation, and marriage. For many Americans, rites of passage such as school graduations and weddings signify the end of one period of life and the beginning of another.

Most rites of passage are characterized by three stages. In the first stage, the participant is separated from his or her previous status. The next stage is a transitional stage in which the participant learns the behavior and ideas appropriate to his or her new status. In some African societies, for example, boys who are on the verge of adulthood are separated from others for days or even months while they learn tribal traditions and skills. After the completion of the second stage, the participant is formally admitted into his or her new status. This is often marked by an elaborate ceremony.

People often pass through the stages of a rite of passage as a group. For example, in many graduation ceremonies in the United States, the graduating students sit together in a special area separated from their families and friends. The walk across the stage to receive their diploma symbolizes the transition from student to graduate. In some ceremonies, in which the graduates wear academic caps and gowns, they move the tassels on the caps from one side to the other to signify their entrance into the society of graduates.

Many cultures have special ceremonies to mark young people's passage from childhood to adulthood. In some societies, teenagers celebrate certain birthdays as rites of passage. For example,

In some Hispanic cultures, a girl's 15th birthday marks her passage into adulthood.

the 15th birthday is an important occasion for many Hispanic girls. It is celebrated by the girl, her family, and community members in an event called the *quinceañera.* A ceremony, usually in a church, is followed by a party.

Jewish adolescents mark their entrance into the adult religious community in a ceremony called (for boys) a bar mitzvah, which means "son of the commandment," or (for girls) a bat mitzvah, which means "daughter of the commandment." When a Jewish child reaches age 13, he or she is expected to observe the religious customs and obligations of Jewish adulthood. After much preparation, Jewish teens show what they have learned about Judaism.

Several Christian traditions—including Roman Catholicism, Eastern Orthodox, Lutheranism, and Episcopalianism—also have an initiation ceremony. It is called a confirmation, and it confers full adult membership in the church. At the confirmation service, young people renew, or confirm, promises made for them at baptism.

For many American teenagers, rites of passage are neither formal nor religious. Rather, they are a series of "first" events that signify assuming more responsibility and receiving adult treatment. Obtaining one's driver's license is one example. Getting one's first after-school job is another.

Think About It

Analyzing Information Besides the examples mentioned above, what are some other rites of passage for adolescents in the United States?

Social Development

About 100 years ago, G. Stanley Hall, the founder of the American Psychological Association, described adolescence as a time of *Sturm und Drang*. These are German words that mean "storm and stress." Hall attributed the conflicts and distress some adolescents experience to biological changes.

Research suggests that the hormonal changes of adolescence do have some effect on the activity levels, mood swings, and aggressive tendencies of many adolescents. However, contemporary studies suggest that cultural and social influences may have more of an effect on adolescent behavior than hormones do (Buchanan et al., 1992).

Adolescence is a psychological concept as well as a biological concept. Psychologically, the adolescent period ends when people become adults and take on adult responsibilities. How long adolescence lasts varies with each individual. For some people, adolescence may be quite extended; for others, it is quite short. For example, when a teenager finds himself or herself caring for family members, financially supporting the family, or assuming other significant responsibilities, adolescence for that individual has probably been quite short, at least in the psychological sense.

Certainly, adolescence can be a challenging time of life. Some teenagers may experience difficulties at home or at school that lead to psychological and social problems. Nonetheless, the vast majority of teenagers face the many challenges of adolescence and cope with them successfully. They form new friendships, increase their knowledge, build their self-esteem, and develop personal and social skills that enable them to become successful and competent adults.

Relationships with Parents

During adolescence, parent-child relationships undergo redefinition. However, the picture of adolescence as a state of constant rebellion against parents and society is exaggerated. The truth is that most of the changes that occur during adolescence are positive rather than negative (Collins, 1990; Steinberg, 1991).

As adolescents strive to become more independent from their parents, however, some conflicts may arise. This striving for greater freedom often results in bickering, especially in early adolescence (Smetana & Gaines, 1999). Conflicts typically center on such issues as homework, chores, money, appearance, curfews, and dating (Galambos & Turner, 1999). Arguments sometimes arise when adolescents maintain that personal choices, such as those that have to do with clothes and friends, should be made by them, not their parents (Smetana et al., 1991).

The adolescent quest for independence may lead to less time spent with family, greater emotional attachment to people who are not family members, and more activities outside the home. In one study, children ranging in age from 9 to 15 carried electronic pagers for a week so that when signaled they could report to researchers what they were doing and with whom (Larson & Richards, 1991). The study showed that the older the children were, the less time they spent with their families. The 15-year-olds spent only half as much time with their families as the 9-year-olds. For the older boys in the study, time spent with the family tended to be replaced by time spent alone. The older girls, on the other hand, tended to divide the time they spent away from their families between friends and solitude.

Greater independence from parents does not necessarily mean that adolescents withdraw emotionally from their parents or fall completely under the influence of their peers. Most adolescents continue to love, respect, and feel loyalty toward their parents (Montemayor & Flannery, 1991).

Linda and Hannah spent less time with their parents than they did when they were younger. They also talked to each other more than they did to either one of their parents. Still, they continued to love their parents and depend on them for emotional support. Adolescents who feel close to their parents tend to show greater self-reliance and independence than those who are distant from their parents. Adolescents who retain close ties with parents also tend to fare better in school and have fewer adjustment problems (Davey, 1993; Papini & Roggman, 1992; Steinberg, 1991).

Despite a certain amount of parent-adolescent conflict, parents and adolescents usually share similar social, political, religious, and economic views (Paikoff & Collins, 1991). For example, adolescents tend to share the religion of one or both of their parents. Rarely will a teenager break completely with his or her family and adopt a different

SNIFFF? BLEAH TOSS SLAM! SNORT! STOMP STOMP STOMP SMAK! I THOUGHT YOU WEREN'T COMING!!!

religion. Therefore, while there are frequent parent-adolescent differences of opinion about behavior and rules of conduct, conflict between the generations on broader issues is less common.

 TRUTH **OR** **fiction** ▪ REVISITED ▪ *It is not true that adolescents are in a constant state of rebellion against their parents. While there may be conflict with parents about family rules, most adolescents are in agreement with their parents about broader issues.*

Adolescents tend to interact with their mothers more than they do with their fathers. Most adolescents also see their mothers as more supportive than their fathers, as knowing them better, and as more likely to tolerate their opinions (Collins & Russell, 1991; Noller & Callan, 1990). Teenagers are also more likely to seek and follow advice from their mothers than from their fathers (Greene & Grimsley, 1991).

Relationships with Peers

The transition from childhood to adolescence involves an increase in the importance of peers. While most adolescents maintain good relations with parents, peers become more important in terms of influence and emotional support. For example, fourth-graders consider parents to be their most frequent providers of emotional and social support. If something upsetting happens at school, they are more likely to discuss it with their parents than with anybody else. However, by seventh grade, friends of the same gender are generally seen as providing more support than parents (Furman & Buhrmester, 1992).

Adolescent Friendships Friendship is a very important part of adolescence. Most adolescents tend to have one or two "best friends," but they have other good friends as well. Linda and Hannah probably considered themselves to be best friends, but they had other friends too, such as Annie. Adolescents may spend several

A DAY IN THE LIFE

Friends begin to take on greater importance during adolescence. Although most teenagers maintain loving relationships with their parents, they spend more time with friends, either in person or on the phone. Friendships provide adolescents with support and understanding and boost self-esteem.

together in larger, less intimate groups. These gender differences in patterns of friendship continue into adulthood (Dindia & Allen, 1992).

TRUTH OR fiction ■REVISITED■ *It is true that girls are more likely than boys to have close friendships.* Boys seem to be more comfortable spending time with friends in larger, less intimate groups.

hours a day with their friends (Hartup, 1993). When teenagers are not actually with their friends, they are often speaking with them on the telephone.

Friendships serve many purposes for adolescents. One teen girl described her best friend this way: "I can tell her things and she helps me talk. And she doesn't laugh at me if I do something weird—she accepts me for who I am" (Berndt & Perry, 1990, p. 269).

Adolescents also value loyalty as a key aspect of friendship. They say that true friends "stick up for you in a fight" and do not "talk about you behind your back" (Berndt & Perry, 1990, p. 269). In other words, having friends means more to adolescents than just having people to spend time with. Close friends provide support and understanding, strengthen one's ability to be a caring person, and contribute to self-esteem.

Adolescents usually choose friends who are similar to themselves in age, background, educational goals, and attitudes toward drinking, drug use, and sexual activity (Hartup, 1993; Youniss & Haynie, 1992). In addition, adolescents' closest friends are usually of their own sex (Hartup, 1993). The friendships of adolescent girls tend to be closer than those of boys (Berndt & Perry, 1990; Manke, 1993). Girls are more likely than boys to share their secrets, personal problems, and innermost feelings. While boys also have close friendships, they tend to spend time

Cliques and Crowds Adolescents not only have close friends; they also tend to belong to one or more larger peer groups. **Cliques** are peer groups of 5 to 10 people who spend a great deal of time with one another, sharing activities and confidences. Larger groups of people who do not spend as much time together but share attitudes and group identity are called **crowds**.

Marc, Linda, Hannah, Todd, Dan, Janet, and a few others were members of a clique, which they called "the group." Adolescent cliques often include members of both sexes, which may lead to romantic relationships such as the one between Marc and Linda. Most young people also belong to a larger crowd with whom they go to parties, play basketball or baseball, and participate in other activities.

Some adolescents join certain cliques in their search for the stability and sense of belonging that come from being part of such a group. They may imitate their peers' speech and adopt some of their values. Teens in the same clique may follow similar fads in the way they dress or style their hair. They and the other members of the group may even become intolerant of "outsiders"—people not in the group.

Peer Influences Parents often worry that their adolescent children's needs for peer approval will influence them to engage in risky or unacceptable behavior. However, the assumption that parents and peers often pull an adolescent in different directions does not seem to be borne out by reality. In fact, parental and peer influences often coincide to some degree (Brown et al., 1993; Youniss & Haynie, 1992). For example, research suggests that peers are more likely to urge adolescents to work for good grades and complete high school than they are to try to involve them in drug abuse, sexual activity, or delinquency (Brown et al., 1993).

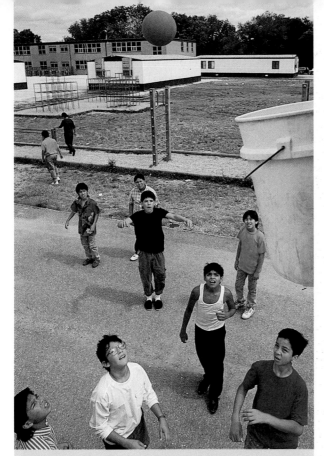

Studies show that while girls are more likely to develop close, personal relationships with a couple of other girls, boys are more likely to spend time in a larger group. Girls are also more likely to spend their time together talking and sharing thoughts and feelings, while boys are more likely to engage in an activity, such as a sport.

Nevertheless, adolescents are influenced by their parents and peers in different ways. Adolescents are more likely to follow their peers in terms of dress, hairstyles, speech patterns, and taste in music (Camarena, 1991). However, they are more likely to agree with their parents on issues such as moral values and educational and career goals (Savin-Williams & Berndt, 1990).

TRUTH OR fiction

■ REVISITED ■

It is true that many adolescents follow the example of their peers in matters of clothing, hairstyles, speech patterns, and musical tastes. However, they are likely to agree with their parents on important and broader issues, such as morality and educational goals.

In early adolescence, peer pressure is relatively weak, but it increases in middle adolescence, peaking at about the age of 15. Peer pressure seems to decrease after the age of 17 (Brown et al., 1993; Youniss & Haynie, 1992). Adolescents are strongly influenced by their peers for several reasons. They seek the approval of their peers and feel better about themselves when they receive it. Peers provide standards by which adolescents can measure their behavior as they grow more independent of their parents (Foster-Clark & Blyth, 1991). Also, because peers may share some of the same feelings, they can provide support in times of difficulty.

Dating and Romantic Relationships Many people begin dating during adolescence. Dating usually develops in stages (Padgham & Blyth, 1991). During the first stage, adolescents place themselves in situations where they will probably meet peers of the other sex—for example, at after-school events. In the next stage, adolescents participate in group dating, such as joining a mixed group at the movies. Finally, they may pair off as couples for traditional dating.

People date for several reasons. Obviously, people may date simply because they enjoy spending time with somebody they like. But dating may also help adolescents learn how to relate positively to other people. Furthermore, dating may help prepare adolescents for the more serious courtship activities that come later in life.

Among younger adolescents, dating relationships tend to be casual and short-lived. But in later adolescence, relationships tend to be more stable and committed (Feiring, 1993). As 18-year-olds, Marc and Linda were most likely thinking in terms of trust, commitment to each other, and honesty.

A DAY IN THE LIFE

SECTION 2 REVIEW

go.hrw.com **Homework Practice Online** Keyword: SY7 HP11

1. In what ways does a teen's relationship with his or her parents change during adolescence? How does it stay the same?

2. Suggest two reasons why adolescents are influenced by their peers.

3. What are the three stages of dating?

4. **Critical Thinking** *Evaluating* Why might adolescence be considered a time of "storm and stress"?

Identity Formation

Psychoanalyst Erik Erikson maintained that the journey of life consists of eight stages. (See Chapter 14.) At each stage, there is a task that must be mastered in order for healthy development to continue. Erikson said that young children must deal with issues of trust, autonomy (self-government), and initiative (taking the lead). Once children begin school, their main task becomes the development of competence, which is the sense that they can learn and achieve.

According to Erikson, the main task of the adolescent stage is the search for identity—a sense of who one is and what one stands for. Adolescents seek to identify their beliefs, their values, and their life goals. They also need to identify the areas in which they agree and disagree with parents, teachers, and friends.

Identity Development

According to Erikson, the task of establishing one's identity is accomplished mainly by choosing and developing a commitment to a particular role or

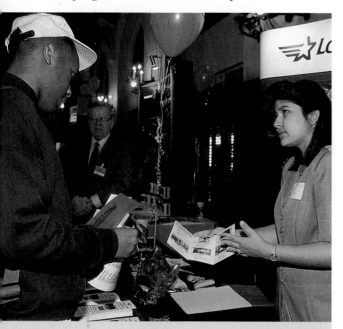

Investigating various career options at a career fair might be one step toward developing an identity, according to Erikson.

occupation in life. Accomplishing this task may also involve developing one's own political and religious beliefs.

To find an identity that is comfortable, adolescents may experiment with different values, beliefs, roles, and relationships. They may try out different "selves" in different situations. For example, the way they behave with their friends may be quite different from the way they behave with their parents. Adolescents who take on these different roles may sometimes wonder which one of their selves is the "real" one. Adolescent identity is achieved when different selves are brought together into a unified and consistent sense of self (Conger, 1978).

Erikson believed that teens who do not succeed in forging an identity may become confused about who they really are and what they want to do in life. They may have difficulty making commitments and may drift from situation to situation. Since they do not create a solid sense of self, they may remain overly dependent on the opinions of others.

One key aspect of adolescent identity development is what Erikson called an identity crisis. An **identity crisis** is a turning point in a person's development when the person examines his or her values and makes or changes decisions about life roles. Should I go to college? Which one? What type of job should I look for? What career is right for me? Adolescents can feel overwhelmed by the choices that lie before them and the decisions they must make (Crain, 2000).

Chapter 10 discussed Piaget's four stages of cognitive development. The final stage is the formal-operational stage. It generally begins at puberty and continues through adulthood. Formal-operational thinking involves abstract thinking, such as hypothetical situations. It enables people to find reasonable solutions to problems and to predict the possible consequences of the decisions they make. Formal-operational thinking helps adolescents make important life choices. Because their thinking is no longer tied to concrete experience, adolescents can evaluate the options available to them even though they may not have personally experienced them (Kahlbaugh & Haviland, 1991).

Identity Status

According to psychologist James Marcia (1966, 1993), the adolescent identity crisis arises as teenagers face decisions about their future work, moral standards, religious commitment, or political orientation. Marcia studied the different ways that

CASE STUDIES

AND OTHER TRUE STORIES

Adolescents on the Job

Kim, age 16, has a job at a fast-food restaurant in a suburban mall. She has already saved $1,000 toward a car and a stereo by working on weekends. Kim is worried, though, because her state legislature is considering reducing the number of hours that teenagers may work. What light can psychological research shed on the effects of working on adolescents?

Research shows that many adolescents work in addition to going to school. About half of all high school sophomores, two-thirds of juniors, and almost three-fourths of seniors have a job during the school year (Bachman et al., 2003). On average, girls and boys are equally likely to work, but boys tend to work longer hours (Mortimer & Johnson, 1998).

Millions of adolescents who work are legally employed. Yet, many other teens work illegally (Bachman et al., 2003; Holloway, 2004). Some of these teens receive cash payments so that their employers can avoid paying taxes or minimum wages. Other teens work too many hours, late hours on school nights, or at hazardous jobs.

Research also shows that which groups of teens are working has changed. In the past, teenagers from poorer households were more likely to work than wealthier teens. Poorer teens often worked to help support their families. Today employment is more common among middle-class adolescents. One of the reasons for this change might be the areas where middle-class families live. Middle-class families tend to live nearer to the locations where teens can easily find jobs, such as suburban shopping malls.

Many middle-class adolescents do not work for the same reasons that poorer teens do. Poorer teens tend to work to help support their families or to save money for college. In contrast, most middle-class teens use their income from working for personal purchases. These purchases might include clothing, music, sports equipment, TVs, and cars (Bachman et al., 2003).

Working can have benefits for teens. By holding a job, adolescents can:
- develop a sense of responsibility, self-reliance, and discipline;
- learn to appreciate the value of money and education;
- acquire positive work habits and values; and
- enhance their career aspirations.

On the other hand, some people question the benefits of the types of jobs that teenagers often get. For example, teenagers usually work in service and retail jobs. These jobs pay little, have high turnover, and offer little authority or chance for advancement. In addition, adolescent workers typically perform simple, repetitive tasks that do not require any special skills (Mortimer & Johnson, 1998).

Moreover, research has shown that working can negatively affect teenagers (Brandstätter & Farthofer, 2003; Holloway, 2004). For example, adolescents who work after school tend to have lower grades. Working long hours—more than 11 to 13 hours per week—has even more serious effects. Compared to students who do not work or who work only a few hours, teens who work long hours report
- lower grades,
- higher rates of drug and alcohol use,
- more delinquent behavior,
- lower self-esteem, and
- higher levels of psychological problems.

Many of you may have a job or may be considering getting one. Given the research, however, you might consider limiting the number of hours you work during the school year.

THINKING CRITICALLY

1. **Summarizing** How has adolescent employment changed in recent years?
2. **Evaluating** Do you think the benefits of teens working long hours during the school year outweigh the disadvantages? Why, or why not?

adolescents handle commitment and cope with the adolescent identity crisis. He concluded that there are four categories of adolescent **identity status**, or reaction patterns and processes. Adolescents do not remain in a single one of these categories throughout their entire adolescence, nor do they proceed through them in a particular order. Rather, they move in and out of the various categories, from one to another. The four categories are identity moratorium, identity foreclosure, identity diffusion, and identity achievement. (See Figure 11.2.)

Identity Moratorium   A moratorium is a "time out" period. Teens experiencing what Marcia termed **identity moratorium** delay making commitments about important questions. They are actively exploring various alternatives in an attempt to forge their identity. They may even experiment with different behaviors and personalities. Adolescents experimenting with different ways of life in their search for an identity may adopt distinctive ways of dressing or behaving. For example, they may cut or style their hair in a particular way. Or they might adopt a special article of clothing as their "trademark."

Adolescents who remain in moratorium longer than other teens may become somewhat anxious as they struggle to find anchors in an unstable world (Patterson et al., 1992). But for most high school students in moratorium who say, "I don't know what I want to do," it is enough to know that they are heading in a general direction even if they do not know where their journey will end. They may end up attending college, joining the armed services, or doing something completely different to reach their final goals. It is not unusual for young people to actively explore their life alternatives for a decade or more.

Identity Foreclosure   To avoid an identity crisis, adolescents in the **identity foreclosure** category make a commitment that forecloses (or shuts out) other possibilities. These adolescents make a definite commitment, but the commitment is based on the suggestions of others rather than on their own choices. They adopt a belief system or a plan of action without closely examining whether it is right for them. They may simply follow the model set by their parents, peers, teachers, or other authority figures in order to avoid uncertainty. For example, an adolescent who is "foreclosed" might decide to become a lawyer because one or both parents are lawyers. Adolescents in identity foreclosure tend to

be inflexible and intolerant of people who do not share their views and commitments (Berzonsky et al., 1993; Marcia, 1991).

Although following a path recommended by a respected adult eliminates the need to make some hard choices, some adolescents become foreclosed too early. After they find themselves dissatisfied with the direction of their lives, they may switch to the moratorium category. For instance, the adolescent who has chosen to be a lawyer simply because both parents are lawyers may discover in law school, or even after becoming a lawyer, that being a lawyer is not really what he or she wants to do. The individual may then enter moratorium to reassess life goals and to decide whether to make a career change.

Identity Diffusion   Adolescents in the category of **identity diffusion** seem to be constantly searching for meaning in life and for identity because they have not committed themselves to a set of personal beliefs or an occupational path. They tend to wander about without goals or interests and seem to live from crisis to crisis.

Identity diffusion is characteristic of children in middle school and early high school. However, if it continues into the 11th and 12th grades, identity diffusion can lead to an "I don't care" attitude. Some adolescents in this category become angry and rebellious. They may reject socially accepted beliefs, values, and goals (Archer & Waterman, 1990; Marcia, 1991).

Identity Achievement   Adolescents in the **identity achievement** category have coped with crises and have explored options. They have then committed themselves to occupational directions and have made decisions about important life questions. Although they have experienced an identity crisis, they have emerged from it with a solid set of beliefs or with a life plan. The plan might be to pursue a course of study that leads to a particular career. Identity-achieved teens tend to have feelings of well-being, high self-esteem, and self-acceptance. They are capable of setting goals and working toward attaining them (Berzonsky et al., 1993; Waterman, 1992). A teenager who decides to become a veterinarian or a businessperson, for example, may choose courses in high school or take an after-school job with that goal in mind.

Many young people do not reach identity achievement until well after high school. It is normal to change majors in college and to change

Marcia's Adolescent Identity Status Categories

Identity Status	Characteristics	Example
Identity Moratorium	Searching for identity Exploring various alternatives Delaying making commitments	"I don't know what I want to do when I graduate, so I'm going to apply to college and for jobs. Then I'll decide which would be best for me."
Identity Foreclosure	Conforming Accepting identity and values from childhood Choosing to identify with others rather than self Making commitments and adopting plans without self-examination Becoming inflexible	"Everyone in my family has gone into the military after high school, so that's what I'm planning to do."
Identity Diffusion	Making no commitment Doing no soul-searching Wandering without goals Becoming angry and rebellious	"I really have no idea what I'll do after graduation. I'll just have to see what happens."
Identity Achievement	Exploring options Committing self to direction in life and occupation Finding own identity	"I'm going to start college in the fall. My parents wanted me to go into the family business after I graduated, but I decided that what I really want to do is go to school and become a scientist."

FIGURE 11.2 *By studying how teenagers handle commitment and cope with the adolescent identity crisis, psychologist James Marcia identified four adolescent identity status categories.*

careers. Such changes, which may even be made several times, do not necessarily mean that these people are indecisive or that they have made wrong decisions. The changes may simply mean that these individuals are continuing to actively explore their options. College, vocational training, and jobs are broadening experiences that expose people to new ways of life, career possibilities, and belief systems. It is common to adjust one's personal goals and beliefs as one matures and views the world from a new or broader perspective.

Gender and Ethnicity in Identity Formation

All adolescents struggle at some point with issues concerning who they are and what they stand for.

However, the nature of the struggle is somewhat different for males and females and for adolescents from different ethnic backgrounds.

Gender and Identity Formation According to Erik Erikson's theory, identity development during adolescence means embracing a philosophy of life and a commitment to a career. However, his views of the development of identity were intended to apply primarily to boys (Archer, 1992; Patterson et al., 1992).

Erikson believed that people develop the capacity to form intimate relationships in the young adult stage of development. He also believed that the development of interpersonal relationships was more important than occupational issues and values to women's identity. Erikson, like Sigmund Freud,

The cultural heroes for adolescents from ethnic minority groups are often not as well known in other groups in society. Some, however—such as professional golfer Tiger Woods—are quite well known and respected.

believed that women's identities were intimately connected with their roles as wives and mothers. Men's identities, on the other hand, were not assumed to depend on their roles as husbands and fathers (Patterson et al., 1992).

Today many women work outside the home. Research shows that female adolescents are now more apt to approach identity formation like male adolescents (Archer, 1992). The concern of female adolescents about occupational plans is now about equal to that of males. However, there is a difference. Female adolescents also express concern about how they will balance the day-to-day demands of work and family life (Archer, 1992). Their concern is well founded. Despite their involvement in the workplace, women in the United States still bear most of the responsibility for rearing the children and maintaining the home (Archer, 1991).

Ethnicity and Identity Formation Identity formation is often more complicated for adolescents from ethnic minority groups (Collins, 2000; Phinney, 2000). These adolescents may be faced with two sets of cultural values: those of their ethnic group and those of the larger society (Phinney, 2000; Phinney & Devich Navarro, 1997). When these values are in conflict, minority adolescents need to reconcile the differences and, frequently, decide where they stand.

Prejudice and discrimination can also contribute to the problems faced by adolescents from ethnic minority groups as they strive to forge a sense of identity. For example, the cultural heroes for these adolescents may not be recognized by members of other groups in society.

Adolescents whose father and mother are from different cultural backgrounds must also wrestle with balancing two cultural heritages (Collins, 2000; Phinney, 2000). Parents from different ethnic groups may decide to spend their lives together, but their values sometimes do not dwell contentedly side by side in the minds of their children. As a result, the children may experience some emotional conflict.

SECTION 3 REVIEW

go.hrw.com Homework Practice Online

Keyword: SY7 HP11

1. What is an identity crisis?
2. Briefly describe the four adolescent identity status categories.
3. **Critical Thinking** *Supporting a Point of View* Do you agree that the main task of adolescence is the formation of identity? Why or why not?

SECTION 4
Challenges of Adolescence

A DAY IN THE LIFE

Adolescence is a rewarding time of life for many young people. Close friendships, such as the one between Hannah and Linda, develop. So do romantic relationships, such as that of Linda and Marc. While there are important choices to be made, the future seems exciting. Yet, for some, adolescence is a difficult time.

Some adolescents have problems that seem too large to handle. Nearly all teenagers know classmates who have school or family problems. Adolescents who are not accepted by their peers often experience loneliness and feelings of low self-esteem. Concerns about getting a good job, being able to support family members, and being accepted into college can be highly stressful.

Some young people, such as Annie, may develop an eating disorder. Others, such as Nick, may abuse alcohol or other drugs. Still others may turn to crime and acts of mischief. Tragically, a few take their own lives.

Eating Disorders

The adolescent growth spurt makes it especially important that teenagers receive adequate nutrition. The average girl needs about 2,200 calories a day, and the average boy needs about 3,000 (Ekvall, 1993). Adolescents also need sufficient protein, carbohydrates, fiber, vitamins, and minerals in their diet. Teens who primarily eat foods such as hamburgers, pizza, potato chips, and candy may not be getting the nutrients their growing bodies need.

Adolescents who develop eating disorders get neither the calories nor the nutrients their bodies need. Some, such as Annie, literally starve themselves. Eating disorders affect many teenagers and young adults, especially females. More attention has been focused on eating disorders in recent years. The two main types of eating disorders are anorexia nervosa and bulimia nervosa.

Anorexia Nervosa   In the United States the typical person with anorexia or bulimia is a young white woman of higher socioeconomic status. **Anorexia nervosa** is a life-threatening disorder characterized by self-starvation and a distorted body image. Adolescents with anorexia usually weigh less than 85 percent of what would be considered a healthy weight. By and large, eating disorders afflict women during adolescence and young adulthood (Heatherton et al., 1997; Winzelberg et al., 2000). Women with anorexia greatly outnumber men with the disorder.

In the typical pattern, an adolescent girl notices some weight gain and decides that it must come off. But even after she loses the "excess" weight, dieting—and, often, exercise—continue at a fever pitch. They persist even after she reaches an average weight, even after family members and others have told her that she is losing too much. Girls with anorexia usually deny that they are wasting away. Their body image is distorted (Williamson et al., 1993; Winzelberg et al., 2000). They focus on remaining pockets of fat—which may be nonexistent—while others see them as "skin and bones."

Many girls with anorexia become obsessed with food. They engross themselves in cookbooks, take on the family shopping chores, and prepare elaborate dinners—for others.

Women with anorexia may lose 25 percent or more of their body weight in a year. Their overall health declines. A British study found that for many women, anorexia is a prolonged problem. Of women

contacted 21 years after being hospitalized for the problem, only half had fully recovered (Zipfel et al., 2000). About 4 to 5 percent of women with anorexia die from causes related to the problem, such as weakness or imbalances in body chemistry.

It is true that excessive dieting may be a sign that a person has an eating disorder. Anorexia nervosa is an eating disorder characterized by self-starvation and a distorted body image. It can be life-threatening.

Bulimia Nervosa   **Bulimia nervosa** is characterized by recurrent cycles of binge eating followed by dramatic measures to eliminate food, such as vomiting. Binge eating frequently follows a pattern of severe dieting (Lowe et al., 1996). As with anorexia, the great majority of people with bulimia are female. In addition to vomiting, girls may seek to compensate for what they have eaten by fasting, strict dieting, and vigorous exercise. Girls with bulimia tend to be perfectionists about their body shape and weight (Joiner et al., 1997).

Origins of Anorexia Nervosa and Bulimia Nervosa   To understand anorexia and bulimia, let us return to the fact that so many more women than men develop these problems. Theorists account for the gender gap in different ways. Some psychodynamic theorists suggest that anorexia represents a woman's effort to return to a stage before puberty. Anorexia allows her to avoid growing up, separating from her family, and taking on adult responsibilities.

But the cultural aspects of eating disorders seem to be more important. Young people with eating disorders are often attempting to conform to an ideal body shape. Popular fashion models represent that ideal: they are 9 percent taller and 16 percent slimmer than the average woman (Williams, 1992). For most women, that 16 percent is at least 16 pounds. The feminine ideal has been becoming slimmer and slimmer. For example, winners of the Miss America contest have been getting thinner over the years. Since the beginning of the pageant in 1922, the annual winner of the contest has become taller but is 12 pounds lighter in weight. In the late 1920s, her height-to-weight ratio was what the World Health Organization (WHO) considers to be "normal" today (Rubinstein & Caballero, 2000). But in recent years, Miss America

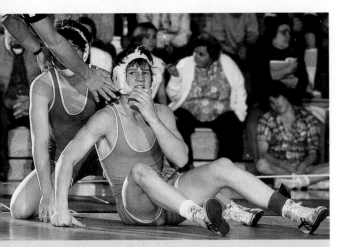

Anorexia nervosa and bulimia nervosa are much more common in adolescent girls than in boys, but boys can suffer from these disorders as well. Wrestlers are more likely to develop eating disorders than boys in general because their sport demands that they stay in a certain weight class during wrestling season.

has become "undernourished" according to the WHO's standards. As the feminine cultural ideal grows thinner, women with average or heavier-than-average figures feel more and more pressure to slim down (Winzelberg et al., 2000).

Many men with eating disorders are involved in sports or jobs that require them to retain a certain weight, such as wrestling, dancing, and modeling (Goode, 2000). Men are more likely than women to control their weight through intense exercise. Like women, men are under social pressure to conform to an ideal body image—one that builds their upper bodies and trims their abdomens (Goode, 2000).

Families also play a role in eating disorders. Parents of adolescent girls with eating disorders are relatively more likely to have problems with eating and dieting themselves, to think that their daughters should lose weight, and to consider their daughters to be unattractive (Baker et al., 2000; Pike & Rodin, 1991). Some researchers speculate that adolescents may develop eating disorders as a way of coping with feelings of loneliness and alienation they experience in the home.

Some cases of anorexia nervosa may even reflect exaggerated efforts to remain healthy by avoiding intake of fat and cholesterol, which are widely publicized as risk factors for heart problems. For example, a 15-year-old boy developed anorexia nervosa after his grandfather—a heavy man who enjoyed steak and deep-fried vegetables—died from a heart attack while he and the boy were playing checkers (Markel, 2000).

Anorexia nervosa and bulimia nervosa both tend to run in families (Strober et al., 2000). Researchers have found evidence pointing to genetic factors involving perfectionism as increasing the risk of these disorders (Kaye et al., 2000). Even so, they believe there is a role for cultural influences (Wade et al., 2000). Perhaps genetic factors contribute to a perfectionistic personality and then cultural and family influences direct the perfectionism toward concern about body shape (Baker et al., 2000).

Treatment Whatever the causes, eating disorders are a severe health problem, and people who have them require professional assistance to overcome them. Often a school psychologist or counselor can suggest possible courses of action.

Sometimes health professionals will give students with eating disorders a choice—either to enter a treatment program (where their caloric intake is closely monitored) or to remain in school as long as they stop losing weight and receive counseling. They may have to see a psychologist on a regular basis and have their weight checked weekly. Treatment for eating disorders is often a long and difficult process. Many issues are often involved, including some that have nothing to do with food.

Substance Abuse

Substance abuse usually begins with experimentation in adolescence (Chassin et al., 2000). Why do adolescents experiment with drugs? Reasons include curiosity, response to peer pressure, parental abuse, rebelliousness, escape from boredom or pressure, and looking for excitement or pleasure (Finn et al., 2000; Wills et al., 2000).

A government survey of more than 15,000 teenagers across the United States found that use of drugs and cigarettes increased over the 1990s, despite public education campaigns about the risks (Centers for Disease Control, 2000). Cigarette smoking was up slightly, with 35 percent of teenagers reporting lighting up in the previous month. The number of teens who reported smoking marijuana in the previous month nearly doubled from about 15 percent in 1991 to 27 percent in 1999. Self-reported cocaine use also doubled in the same period, from about 2 percent to 4 percent. Alcohol is used at least occasionally by the majority of high school and college students (Johnston et al., 2000). Drinking in early adolescence is a risk factor for alcohol abuse later in life (DeWit et al., 2000).

Adolescents often try alcohol and other substances because their peers recommend them or their parents use them. Adolescents also frequently turn to alcohol and other substances as a way of coping with stress (Armeli et al., 2000). In the short term, use of a substance may win the approval of peers or have a positive effect on one's mood. It may also reduce unpleasant sensations such as anxiety and tension (Bonin et al., 2000; Swendsen et al., 2000). But binge drinking—that is, having five or more drinks in a row—and long-term drinking are connected to aggressive behavior, poor grades, and accidents (Vik et al., 2000; Wilgoren, 2000). Alcohol is involved in about half of the fatal automobile accidents in the United States.

Some 430,000 Americans die from smoking-related diseases each year, including lung cancer, emphysema, and heart attacks (American Lung Association, 2000). Cocaine narrows blood vessels, thickens the blood, and quickens the heart rate. These events have caused the sudden deaths of a number of athletes who used cocaine to try to boost their performance and self-confidence (Moliterno et al., 1994). Marijuana contains more tars than cigarette smoke—a factor in lung cancer. Marijuana also elevates one's heart rate and blood pressure. Marijuana can also make it more difficult to retain information—that is, it can make it more difficult to learn both in and out of school (Sullivan, 2000). All in all, these substances cause many more problems than they solve.

Regular use of alcohol and some other substances—particularly nicotine, cocaine, barbiturates, and heroin—can cause teenagers, such as Linda's and Janet's friend Nick, to become addicted to them. Addicts experience intense cravings for the substances when their effects have worn off. They usually have to take more and more of the substance to achieve the same effects they once obtained with a small amount. The substance may eventually take control of the person's life.

Treatment Withdrawing from alcohol and other drugs can be a physically and psychologically painful experience for people of any age. After someone such as Nick is admitted to a hospital or a treatment center, the first step in his or her treatment is detoxification—the removal of the toxic, or poisonous, substance from the body. During this

Peer counseling is a valuable way of preventing substance abuse in teenagers. Scare tactics by adults can often backfire by making students more curious. Teenagers may be more willing to believe the warnings of other students who have actually used illegal substances.

process, the person is gradually and carefully taken off the drug. Both medical treatment and emotional support are very important to help the individual through the process.

Another important aspect of the treatment of adolescents with substance abuse problems is psychological in nature. Therapists can help young people understand the meaning of their drug use. For example, they can learn to recognize that they might be using drugs or alcohol to avoid facing the difficult issues in their lives: How are they doing in school? How are their relationships with their family? How do they feel about themselves? Therapy can help teenagers recognize that low self-esteem may be at the root of their problems.

Drug Prevention Most school drug-prevention programs are aimed at stopping the use of so-called gateway drugs. These drugs include alcohol, cigarettes, and marijuana. They are called gateway drugs because they are typically tried first—before teenagers "open the gate" to more powerful drugs, such as heroin and cocaine.

Research on the effectiveness of prevention programs shows mixed results. Attempts to scare students by warning them about the dangerous consequences of using drugs can backfire, possibly because scare tactics can arouse their curiosity and disbelief (Kazdin, 1993). Peer counseling is often effective because students are generally more willing to believe other students who have actually

In the United States, many babies are born to teenage mothers every year. Rearing a child is always challenging, even without the additional burdens teen parents usually face, such as a lack of money, education, and emotional maturity.

school (Brooks-Gunn & Furstenberg, 1989; Miller et al., 1986). About 10 percent of American girls between the ages of 15 and 19 become pregnant each year. This amounts to more than 900,000 pregnancies a year.

Teenage pregnancies can be devastating for adolescent mothers, their children, and society at large. Life for many teenage mothers is an uphill struggle. Teenage mothers are more likely to live in poverty and lack hope for their futures than teenagers of the same age who do not have children (Desmond, 1994; Grogger & Bronars, 1993). Half of all adolescent mothers quit school and go on welfare (Kantrowitz, 1990). Few receive financial or emotional help from the fathers of their children. The fathers—sometimes also adolescents—often cannot support themselves, much less a family. Most adolescents share the view that teenage parenthood is very undesirable (Moore & Stief, 1992).

Several factors contribute to the likelihood of teenage pregnancy (Rathus, 2003). These include the following:

- problematic relationships with parents or rebellion against parents
- emotional problems, such as feelings of emptiness or loneliness
- problems in school or lack of educational or vocational goals
- societal loosening of traditional prohibitions against adolescent sexuality and the portrayal of sexual themes in the media
- pressure from peers who are engaging in sexual activity
- misunderstanding or lack of knowledge about reproduction

Some adolescent girls intentionally become pregnant to try to strengthen relationships with their boyfriends or to fill an emotional void by having a child. However, the relationships with the fathers usually come to an end. Premature motherhood tends to make emotional problems worse, not better. It also has serious implications for the offspring. Teen mothers are more likely to give birth to premature babies and to babies who are below average in weight (Osofsky et al. 1988).

used the substances they are being warned against (Hawkins et al., 1992; Perry, 1991).

Sexuality

Many adolescents struggle with issues of how and when to express their sexual feelings. But they receive mixed messages. Their bodies may be giving them a powerful "go-ahead" signal at the same time that their parents and other adults are advising them of the dangers of early sexual relationships and encouraging them to practice abstinence. Yet other messages may come from media images—models in advertisements, television shows that revolve around sex, and popular songs with lyrics that contain powerful sexual messages. Many teenagers may assume that sexual activity is more widespread among their peers than it actually is. The truth is, however, that many adolescents are not sexually active.

People today often start dating and "going steady" at a younger age than people of earlier times. Adolescents who begin dating early are more likely to engage in sexual relations during high

Juvenile Delinquency

The term **juvenile delinquency** refers to many illegal activities committed by children or adolescents. The most extreme acts of delinquency include robbery, rape, and homicide, which are considered criminal acts regardless of the age of the offender. Less serious offenses, known as **status offenses**, are illegal only when they are committed by minors. Status offenses include truancy (unexcused absence from school), drinking, smoking, and running away from home.

Some people assume that teenagers from poor neighborhoods are more likely to break the law than other teens. However, this is not true. Research shows that low income is not a factor (Hinshaw, 1992; Zigler et al., 1992). Another common belief is that children whose mothers work outside the home are more likely to engage in delinquent behavior. Once again, research shows that this is not the case (Silverstein, 1991).

Many delinquent acts do not lead to arrest and prosecution but still have other serious consequences for the delinquent teenager. Status offenses tend to be handled by school officials, social workers, parents, and other such authorities. When adolescents *are* arrested and prosecuted, they are often referred to mental-health agencies and are not formally labeled as delinquents. Nonetheless, between 25 percent and 30 percent of the serious crimes in the United States are committed by teenagers under the age of 18.

Factors that contribute to juvenile delinquency are similar to those that contribute to substance abuse. They include the following:

- low self-esteem and feelings of alienation (Krueger et al., 1993)
- lack of affection, lax and ineffective discipline, and use of severe physical punishment in the home (Kopera-Frye et al., 1993)
- behavior problems that began at an early age (Brook et al., 1993)
- poor grades and lack of educational or vocational goals (Zigler et al., 1992)
- pressure from peers who engage in delinquent behavior (Etaugh & Rathus, 1995)
- having a parent or sibling who has been convicted of criminal behavior (Butterfield, 1992)

Avoiding Problems

Most adolescents who have clear educational and vocational goals manage to steer clear of problems. Adolescents who fear the onset of a particular problem are usually better off if they can talk things over with a trusted adult—a parent or another relative, a teacher, or a guidance counselor.

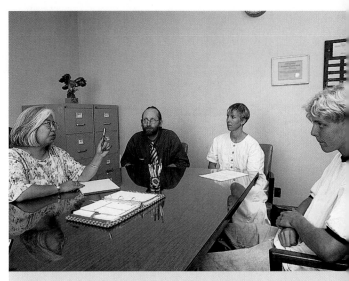

The most successful programs for dealing with juvenile delinquency try to address potential problems early. Many counselors focus their efforts on reducing school violence.

Unfortunately, many troubled adolescents do not get into programs developed to deal with juvenile delinquency until after the delinquent behavior pattern has become well established. At that late date, it is more difficult to help them. The most successful delinquency-prevention programs are those that address the potential problems early. These programs provide classes and support groups for parents, make home visits to families, and provide other effective services. And they encourage parents to become involved in the activities of their children both in and out of school.

Research shows that children who participate in prevention programs do better in school and are more likely to graduate from high school, go to college, and work at a steady job. They also seem less inclined to commit crimes (Zigler et al., 1992).

SECTION 4 REVIEW

go.hrw.com **Homework Practice Online**

Keyword: SY7 HP11

1. Describe the similarities and differences between anorexia and bulimia.

2. How do status offenses differ from other acts of delinquency?

3. List three factors that contribute to juvenile delinquency.

4. **Critical Thinking** *Categorizing* List several types of challenges faced by adolescents today.

Chapter 11 REVIEW

 Writing a Summary

Using standard grammar, spelling, sentence structure, and punctuation, summarize the information in this chapter. Consider:
- physical and psychological changes that occur during adolescence, and the role parents and peers play in a teen's life
- how teens form identity, and what challenges they face today

 Identifying People and Ideas

Identify the following terms or people and use them in appropriate sentences.

1. puberty
2. primary sex characteristics
3. menarche
4. cliques
5. identity crisis
6. identity foreclosure
7. identity achievement
8. anorexia nervosa
9. juvenile delinquency
10. status offenses

 Understanding Main Ideas

SECTION 1 (pp. 252–254)
1. Why do some adolescents feel awkward during the adolescent growth spurt?

SECTION 2 (pp. 256–259)
2. How is the behavior of adolescents influenced by fads and peers?

SECTION 3 (pp. 260–264)
3. What does it mean to find one's identity?
4. How is the concept of moratorium related to finding an identity?

SECTION 4 (pp. 264–269)
5. Describe the detoxification process in the treatment of substance abuse.

 Thinking Critically

1. **Drawing Inferences and Conclusions** Why do you think adolescence has become prolonged in Western societies?

2. **Categorizing** List several types of peer relationships that develop during adolescence. What are some of the advantages and disadvantages of these types of relationships?

3. **Summarizing** What factors might help a teenager in his or her search for identity?

4. **Contrasting** Other than physical changes, how does adolescence differ for boys and girls?

5. **Evaluating** Why might peer counseling be an effective way of helping teenagers deal with the challenges of adolescence?

 Writing About Psychology

1. **Evaluating** Read a short story or novel that features an adolescent as its main character. (Ask your school librarian or English teacher for suggestions on appropriate books.) As you read, try to connect the character to information you learned in this chapter about adolescent development and the challenges of adolescence. For example, is the character having an identity crisis? Is the character dealing with negative peer pressure? Write a profile of the character exploring these issues.

2. **Analyzing Information** Imagine that you are the writer of a newspaper column in which you answer letters from teens seeking advice. Think of a problem or concern that a teen might have. Compose a letter to "Dear (*your name*)" briefly describing the background of the problem. Then write a response that suggests a way to deal with the situation. Read your letter and response to the class. Use the graphic organizer below to help you write your letter and response.

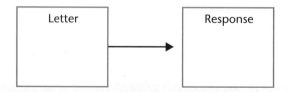

Interpreting Charts

Study the chart below. Then use the information in the chart to help you answer the questions that follow.

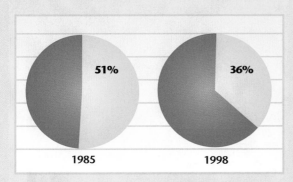

Percent of Adolescents Who Have Smoked Cigarettes

51% 1985

36% 1998

Source: U.S. Bureau of the Census, 2000

1. Which of the following statements can be made using information from the chart above?

   a. Cigarette smoking among teenagers increased consistently between 1985 and 1998.

   b. Cigarette smoking among teenagers declined from 1985 to 1998.

   c. Very few American adolescents smoke cigarettes.

   d. Adolescent use of cigarettes increased slightly between 1985 and 1990.

2. How might a psychologist use this information to assist in creating an effective antismoking program?

Analyzing Primary Sources

Read the following excerpt, in which several psychologists explain adolescence as a stage of life. Then answer the questions that follow.

❝How do we best characterize adolescence? Until recently, psychologists regarded it primarily in terms of age-related stress and crisis. Traditional psychoanalytic theory assumed that crisis is inevitable when adolescents, made particularly vulnerable to stressors by the biological changes of puberty, strive to develop self-identity and ego strength needed to deal with . . . adult roles. . . . Most researchers today argue that difficulties or problems presenting themselves during adolescence should not be considered solely in terms of their disruptive nature and their contribution to crisis and storm, but also with regard to the coping responses they evoke in the young people concerned. The focus is on coping rather than crisis.❞

3. Which of the following statements best reflects the authors' viewpoint?

   a. Adolescence is a time of crisis.

   b. Adolescents cannot cope with crises in their lives without professional help.

   c. The manner in which psychologists understood adolescence in the past was completely wrong.

   d. Psychologists are changing the way in which they view adolescence.

4. In view of the authors' argument, what skills would be most valuable to a person during adolescence?

PSYCHOLOGY PROJECTS

Cooperative Learning

Research in Psychology Working in small groups, survey the contents of several recent teen magazines. Identify the types of articles, features, and advertisements that appear most frequently. Discuss the overall message these magazines send to teenagers. Also consider whether the material appearing in the magazines is representative of the issues students at your high school face. Have one person in your group report your findings to the class.

🖅 internet connect

Internet Activity: go.hrw.com
KEYWORD: SY7 CH11

Choose an activity on adolescence to:

- write a report describing rites of passage.
- make a 3D model illustrating identity formation.
- create a pamphlet on challenges faced by adolescents.

12 ADULTHOOD

Read to Discover

1 What are the characteristics and issues of young adulthood?

2 What are the changes that occur and the issues that are faced in middle adulthood?

3 How do people's lives change in late adulthood?

4 What are the attitudes and issues related to death and dying?

A DAY IN THE LIFE

Marc and Linda had decided to volunteer at the local residential community for senior citizens. They had just finished for the day and were comparing experiences while they waited for the bus.

"So what did you do today?" asked Marc.

"I visited with the patients in the nursing home," said Linda. "At first it was upsetting because it reminded me of visiting my grandmother in the hospice before she died. I didn't think I'd ever get over missing her, but I guess I've adjusted."

"That must have been hard," Marc sympathized.

"I used to love spending time with my grandmother," Linda mused. "She would always think of fun things for us to do. Until she got sick, she was very energetic."

"She sounds like the people I met today," said Marc. "I was helping some of the people who live in their own apartments over by the recreation center. There was a man there in his late 70s who was doing yard work. He told me that he walks about five miles every day—he says that regular exercise keeps him

healthy. I hope I'm as fit as he is when I'm that age."

"My dad will be happy to hear about him," said Linda. "When Dad turned 40, he began worrying about aging. He started doing all these things he'd never done before, like exercising and taking classes. It's funny, but I really think he's actually happier now than he was when he was younger."

"That's fantastic," said Marc. "Turning 40 seems to make people really think about their lives."

"Yeah," answered Linda. "Janet said that when her parents hit their 40s, they finally realized how unhappy they were with each other."

"How's Janet been doing since her parents' divorce, by the way?" asked Marc.

"Well, it was really hard for her at first, but she's basically fine now. In fact, she told me she feels closer than ever to her mom."

Marc and Linda were both silent for a moment.

"Do you realize we'll be in our 20s soon?" asked Linda.

"I know. We'll be on our own then—we'll be independent," said Marc, obviously anticipating the arrival of that day.

• • •

Marc and Linda had just been confronted with what it means to be an adult, grow older, and eventually die. Development is a process that continues throughout one's lifetime. Many theorists believe that adult development, like childhood and adolescence, follows certain stages. Others believe that there is no "standard" life cycle with predictable life stages. Nowadays, people are living longer and, in some ways, are freer than ever to make their own life choices. The adult years are generally divided into three broad stages: young adulthood, middle adulthood, and late adulthood.

Key Terms

- patriarchy
- generativity
- midlife transition
- midlife crisis
- empty-nest syndrome
- menopause
- programmed theories
- cellular damage theories
- free radical
- cross-linking
- dementia
- senile dementia
- Alzheimer's disease
- ego integrity
- hospice
- euthanasia
- living wills
- bereaved

HOLT

Psychology Video Program

Watch the video to explore why some adults choose not to retire.

TRUTH OR fiction?

Read the following statements about psychology. Do you think they are true or false? You will learn whether each statement is true or false as you read the chapter.

- Many people in their 30s completely change the lives they created for themselves in their 20s.
- People in the United States have been marrying later than people did a few generations ago.
- Romantic love is a relatively new reason for marrying.
- Most parents feel a great sense of loss and loneliness when the youngest child leaves home.
- It is good for older people not to exercise.
- Everyone who lives long enough will eventually become senile.

SECTION 7

Young Adulthood

Young adulthood, also called early adulthood, covers a span of approximately 20 years—from about age 20 to about age 40. Most people reach their physical peak in their 20s. During their 20s and early 30s, they are faster, stronger, better coordinated, and have more endurance than they have ever had or will ever have again. Many people also are at the height of their cognitive powers during this period (Baltes, 1997).

Young adulthood is characterized by a desire to try new ways of doing things and by changing relationships with parents. In their late teens and early 20s, some people assume that they must live the way their parents do if they want to succeed in life. Some also assume that their parents will always be there to rescue them if their plans fail. As time passes, however, young adults learn to become independent and to take responsibility for themselves and the decisions they make.

Studies indicate that, in the United States, becoming independent from parental authority is a

 A DAY IN THE LIFE

key goal of development for most young adult men (Guisinger & Blatt, 1994). Although Marc is still in high school, his remark anticipating independence indicates that he, too, shares this goal. Women are generally less

concerned with seeing themselves as separate, independent individuals. They tend to be more interested in creating relationships with others (Gilligan et al., 1990, 1991; Jordan et al., 1991). Of course, these are generalizations only; many women in their 20s become independent and focus on their development as individuals (Helson, 1993). The creation and maintenance of relationships are also important concerns for many men.

Reassessment

Adults in their 20s often believe they have chosen the course in life that is exactly right for them. As they reach their 30s, however, they often reevaluate the decisions they have made in an effort to determine whether their chosen course is really the one that is right for them. Levinson (1978, 1996) has labeled the period of the late 20s and early 30s the "age 30 transition." For many young adults, this is a time to reassess earlier choices. People often ask themselves, "Why am I doing this?" or "Where is my life going?" Sometimes they find that the life paths they chose in their 20s are no longer the paths they truly want to follow.

This period of reassessment may bring about major life changes. Some people change jobs or start new careers. Many single people feel that this is the time to find a mate. People who have been working in the home, perhaps raising children, may feel the urge to find a job outside the home. Couples who are without children may now think about starting a family (Sheehy, 1995).

TRUTH OR fiction ▪ R E V I S I T E D ▪

It is true that many people in their 30s completely change the lives they created for themselves in their 20s. During their late 20s and early 30s, many young adults undertake a major reassessment of their lives. Sometimes this reassessment leads to major life changes.

Women in particular may find themselves reassessing their lives in their 30s. Some women in their 30s begin to think about the biological changes that lie ahead. Many women become concerned about how many childbearing years they have left, especially if they have not already had children. Furthermore, during their early 30s, many women begin to feel that they have been controlled by others and that they have never had the chance to shape their own lives (Helson & Moane, 1987). Today, as in years past, it is still mostly women who take care of family and household chores. As a result, women in the workforce may feel overwhelmed by the double duties of caring for their families and maintaining jobs.

In addition, research suggests that some working women have mixed feelings about success on the job. Even though the great majority of women are in the workplace, some still feel they must sacrifice their family lives to advance their careers. Although working men also have less time to spend with their families, many people still consider it more acceptable for men to work long hours than for women to do the same (Levinson, 1996).

Settling Down

After the upheaval of the early 30s, the mid- to late 30s are often characterized by settling down or "planting roots" (Levinson, 1978). People in their 30s may increase the financial and emotional investments they make in their lives. Many have been employed long enough to gain promotions and pay raises. They often become more focused on advancing their careers and gaining stability in their personal lives.

Figure 12.1 on page 276 lists some of the developmental tasks of young adulthood. Not every individual necessarily experiences all of these tasks. Nor does every young adult follow them in a particular order. For example, many people today choose to remain single or to postpone or forgo having and rearing children.

Marriage and Intimate Relationships

An important part of adolescence and young adulthood is the development of an identity—who you are and what you stand for (your values). Identity brings the personal stability that is needed to form lasting relationships. (See Chapter 11.) According to Erik Erikson (1963), one of the key tasks of young adulthood is the forming of relationships.

Relationships can be difficult to sustain when one or both of the people involved lack personal stability, which may be one reason why teenage marriages suffer a higher divorce rate than adult marriages. However, young adults who have developed a firm sense of identity during adolescence may be ready to join their lives with those of other

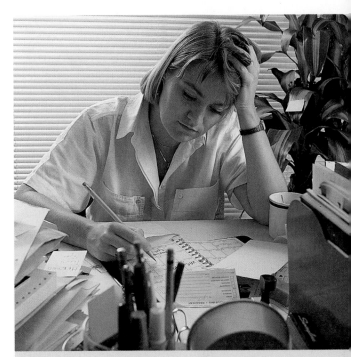

It is not unusual for women to feel torn between their obligations to their jobs and to their families. Many women still have the primary responsibility for taking care of the family and home in addition to working full-time.

people through friendships and marriage. Erikson believed that people who do not develop intimate relationships may risk falling into a pattern of isolation and loneliness. An intimate relationship is not necessarily a physical relationship. Rather, it is a trusting, close friendship with another person in which one can be honest without fear of rejection.

In the United States, 75 percent to 80 percent of people get married at least once (Marital Status, 1998). However, more people have been delaying marriage in recent decades to pursue educational and career goals. Therefore, the median age of marriage has risen in the past 30 years from about 23 to 27 for men and from about 21 to 25 for women (Marital Status, 1998).

TRUTH OR fiction
■ REVISITED ■

It is true that people in the United States have been marrying later than people did a few generations ago. Many people now wait until they have finished college or have their careers under way before they marry.

History of Marriage In most Western societies, men have traditionally played the dominant role in marriage as well as in the larger society. This system is known as a **patriarchy**. Over the past several decades, however, this situation has changed, and spouses are now more likely to be considered equal partners in marriage.

Marital roles in modern society are still changing. Some couples continue to adhere to roles in which the husband is the breadwinner and the wife is the homemaker. Other couples have begun to share, and even sometimes reverse, these roles. And many single or divorced individuals are alone responsible for fulfilling these roles.

In the United States today, most people marry primarily for love. The concept of romantic love as a reason for marriage, however, did not become widespread in Western societies until the 1800s. In the 1600s and 1700s, most marriages were arranged by the parents of the bride and groom, generally on the basis of how the marriage would benefit the two families. This practice permitted the orderly transferring of wealth from one family to another and from one generation to the next. Another purpose of marriage was to provide a stable home life in which to have and rear children.

Developmental Tasks of Young Adulthood

- Exploring adult roles
- Becoming independent
- Developing intimate relationships
- Adjusting to living with another person
- Starting a family and becoming a parent
- Assuming the responsibilities of managing a home
- Beginning a career or a job
- Assuming some responsibilities in the larger community—for example, participating in local government or religious organizations
- Creating a social network of friends and co-workers

FIGURE 12.1 *Erikson believed that each stage of life has its own developmental tasks. This chart lists some of the tasks associated with young adulthood. Not all young adults experience all of these tasks, nor do they experience them in a particular order.*

TRUTH OR fiction
■ REVISITED ■

It is true that romantic love is a relatively new reason for marrying. Historically, marriage was seen as an institution for rearing children and for providing for the transferring of wealth from one generation to another. Marriage was not viewed as an expression of romantic love.

Today, however, companionship and intimacy are central goals in most marriages. Marriage generally provides feelings of security and opportunities to share experiences and ideas with someone special. A *New York Times* poll found that the great majority of people in the United States still see marriage as permanent. The poll asked, "If you got married today, would you expect to stay married for the rest of your life, or not?" Some 86 percent of respondents said yes (Eggers, 2000).

Choosing Spouses Unlike in times past, in which marriages were arranged by the family, today young people in the United States typically select their own mates. Parents may, however, have at least some degree of influence over the choice.

People are also influenced in their marital decisions by factors such as ethnicity, level of education, social class, and religion. Generally, people marry others who are similar to themselves. For example, Americans tend to marry people who are from the same geographic area and social class—perhaps because they are more likely to meet such people in the first place.

People in the United States rarely marry people of different races or socioeconomic classes. According to the U.S. Census Bureau, only 2 percent of U.S. marriages are interracial. More than 90 percent of married couples are of the same religion. Similarity in attitudes and tastes is a key contributor to attraction and intimate relationships (Laumann et al., 1994; Singh & Ho, 2000; Watson et al., 2000).

PSYCHOLOGY

LOVE STORIES

Some couples seem perfectly happy. Then suddenly, to the surprise of all their friends, they divorce. Other couples seem to fight all the time and constantly complain about each other. Yet they stay married. Why does this happen? That is the question psychologist Robert Sternberg asked himself. After interviewing many people he formed the theory that "love is a story."

Sternberg maintains in his article "Love Stories" (1996) that through the interaction of our personalities and the environment, we create stories about love, which we then try to fulfill. Various potential spouses fit these stories to a greater or lesser degree. According to Sternberg, marriages tend to last when the partners fulfill the roles they have created for themselves in their love stories.

Sternberg explains how we develop these stories and why they are very different from culture to culture:

> The stories we invent draw on elements from our experience of living in the world—from the fairy stories we heard as young children, from the models of love relationships we observe around us in parents and relatives, from television and movies, from conversations with other people about their relationships, and so on. (p. 62)

According to Sternberg, love is not just a single story. He has come up with 24 model stories but cautions that there are probably many more. Two of Sternberg's stories are the "fantasy" story and the "gardening" story. The fantasy story is similar to a fairy tale. A woman who has a fantasy story expects her mate to be a "knight in shining armor" to protect her from danger. A man with a fantasy story expects his mate to be a "princess." The potential for the success of such a union depends on how much the people expect the fantasy to continue. If their expectations are too high, they may become disappointed.

In the "gardening" story, both partners tend and nurture the relationship as they would a beautiful rose. According to Sternberg, this relationship has potential for success as long as the partners continue to tend the "garden" (marriage).

Although people have created these stories, they are not aware that they have done so. Sternberg suggests what happens when we meet a person who might be a potential partner:

> . . . if our story is a fantasy story then the slot we want to fill is reserved for a knight or princess. . . . Thus . . . we are attracted to a person who (we think) can fill a slot in our story line and we will stay attracted as long as the person continues to fill the slot. (pp. 71–72)

If the potential mate does not meet our story ideals, we probably will not even consider him or her, but if the person comes close, we might fall in love. What matters more than the individual story itself is that both partners believe in the same story. That is what is needed for the success of the union, as stated in the following excerpt:

> Love stories have complementary roles. We look for someone who shares our story or who at least has a compatible story that can more or less fit it. (p. 69)

Sternberg's story theory might explain why some people stay with abusive partners:

> Abused individuals might stay with partners not only for reasons of finances or fear, but because they truly believe—perhaps from what they have seen as children or in movies—that abuse is part of love. (p. 73)

It is possible that both people in an abusive relationship share a terrible story—that love includes hurt and abuse. And stories, explains Sternberg, are hard to change or break.

Think About It

Categorizing What might be some other common love stories? Give three examples and explain what kinds of roles people would play in those stories.

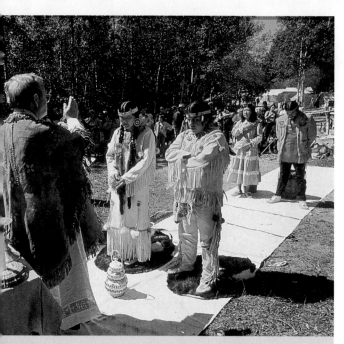
Many wedding ceremonies blend modern and traditional customs.

People also tend to choose marriage partners who are near their own age (Michael et al., 1994). This is especially true for couples who marry in early adulthood. People who meet in school and then marry each other tend to be similar in age. Most bridegrooms are about two to five years older than the women they are marrying (Buss, 1994). People who marry later in life or who remarry after being divorced or widowed are less likely to select partners who are as close in age.

Marriages between similar people may have a greater chance at survival because the partners probably share many of the same values and attitudes (Michael et al., 1994). Dissimilar couples, however, can work to overcome the differences that divide them by developing shared interests and mutual respect. Evidence that similarity between spouses is beneficial in the long run—the entire course of the marriage—remains somewhat limited (Karney & Bradbury, 1995).

Divorce

A DAY IN THE LIFE Although most couples get married because they are in love, about half of the marriages in the United States—such as the one between Janet's parents—end in divorce (Carrère et al., 2000). The divorce rate rose steadily throughout most of the last century before leveling off in the 1980s. More than one quarter of children live in single-parent households (USBC, 1998).

Reasons for Divorce Why is divorce such a common occurrence when most couples believe in marrying for life? One reason may be that obtaining a divorce has become easier than it used to be. Many states now have "no-fault" divorce laws. That means that a judge can grant a divorce without having one or both partners blaming the other. If both partners agree on issues of child custody, financial support, and the distribution of the couple's assets, the marriage is legally dissolved.

The increased economic independence of women also may have contributed to the rise in the divorce rate. Just 30 years ago, most women were homemakers with little or no work experience outside the home. Because there were relatively few opportunities for women to enter the paid workforce at that time, many women probably doubted whether they would be able to support themselves and their children on their own. Thus, they may have been inclined to remain in troubled marriages because they perceived that they had no realistic alternative. Today, however, more women have jobs outside the home and are therefore more likely to have the economic independence that makes it easier for them to break away.

Increasingly high expectations may also have made divorce more likely. Today many couples expect marriage to be constantly gratifying—and to be easy. Relationships, however, require work and commitment. Some couples no longer feel committed enough to the marriage to try to make it work. Of course, there are numerous other reasons why people get divorced, including spouse abuse, child abuse, infidelity, strains brought about by illness or financial hardship, and an inability to communicate effectively (Carrère et al., 2000; Gottman et al., 1998).

The Costs of Divorce Divorce has many financial and emotional costs. When a household splits, the financial resources, such as income and property, are usually divided. Often, neither partner can afford to maintain the standard of living he or she had while married. A woman who does not have an established career may find herself struggling to compete with younger, more experienced workers as she enters the workforce.

Women generally are granted custody of the couple's children. Thus, divorced mothers often face the primary responsibility for rearing the children and may need to increase income to make ends meet. These responsibilities can be extremely stressful. Divorced fathers, meanwhile, may find it difficult to pay child support and alimony—financial support paid to a former spouse.

Divorce can lead to feelings of failure, loneliness, fears about the future, and depression. Married people—especially happily married people—are usually better able to cope with the stresses of life, perhaps because they lend each other emotional support. Divorced and separated people have higher rates of physical and psychological disorders than do married people (Nevid et al., 2000).

Yet, for some people, divorce is a time of personal growth and renewal. When partners are convinced they cannot save their marriage, divorce may enable them to establish new and more rewarding lives. Despite the difficulties in adjusting to a divorce, most divorced people eventually recover. The majority remarry. Yet research suggests that remarriages are even more likely than first marriages to end in divorce (USBC, 1998). This may be because divorced people—having set a precedent by ending their first marriage—are inclined to leave a troubled second marriage fairly quickly. People in first-time marriages, on the other hand, may be more inclined to persist even if the marriage is difficult. In addition, many divorced people who remarry have alimony and child-support obligations that often place a financial strain on their new marriages.

The Children of Divorce Divorce can be difficult for the children, even when they are almost adults, as Janet was, when their parents get divorced. Research shows that the children of divorced people are more likely to have behavioral problems, engage in substance abuse, and earn lower grades in school (O'Connor et al., 2000). Sometimes a stepfamily introduces new family relationships. Parents may have to work more to support the family financially and have less time for the children. Nevertheless, like Janet, most children overcome an initial period of stress and eventually stop doubting their ability to adjust to their new situation. Boys have greater problems than girls in adjusting to parental conflict or divorce, such as conduct problems at school and increased anxiety and dependence (Grych & Fincham, 1993; Holden & Ritchie, 1991).

It also seems that it is not so much parental separation that affects the children as the breakdown in the quality of parenting that often follows separation (Erel & Burman, 1995). Clarke-Stewart and her colleagues (2000) analyzed data from the National Institute of Child Health and Human Development Study of Early Child Care to examine the effects of marital separation on children during the first three years of life. The families studied included nearly 100 separated or divorced mothers and a comparison group of 170 two-parent families. In general, the children in the two-parent families obtained higher scores on achievement and ability tests, showed more social skills, and experienced fewer problems and greater security. However, when the researchers considered the mothers' levels of education and income, the differences between the children in one-parent versus two-parent families became less significant. Thus, the psychological development of the children in this study was not affected by parental separation or divorce. Instead, the children's psychological development was related to the mother's income, level of education, and well-being. The results of this study suggest that children may fare better in homes with well-adjusted mothers than in homes with constantly bickering parents. In order to protect the children, psychologists usually advise parents who are getting divorced to

- try to agree on how they will interact with the children (for example, how to handle a situation where a child asks a parent for something after the other parent has said no),
- help each other maintain a good parent-child relationship, and
- avoid criticizing each other to or in front of the children.

Some people believe that parents in unhappy marriages should stay together for the sake of the children. While divorce can take its toll on children, so can living in a household with parents who are in constant conflict with each other.

Should parents in conflict stay together for the sake of the children? There is no easy answer to this question. Although divorce can have negative effects on children, so do marital conflicts. Marital conflict or fighting is also connected with serious psychological distress in children and adolescents. Marital conflicts make relationships between parents and children more difficult and are also connected with later conflict in the children's marriages.

SECTION 1 REVIEW

Homework Practice Online
go.hrw.com
Keyword: SY7 HP12

1. List some of the issues and characteristics of young adulthood.

2. According to Erikson, what are the risks for people who do not develop intimate relationships during young adulthood?

3. **Critical Thinking** *Supporting a Point of View* Do you agree or disagree with the following statement: "Parents in conflict should remain together for the sake of the children"? Provide evidence to support your answer.

SECTION 2
Middle Adulthood

Middle adulthood spans the years from 40 to 65. By age 40, most people have begun to lose some of the strength, coordination, and stamina they had in their 20s and 30s. This decline in physical ability is generally so gradual that it is hardly noticeable. It is often only of concern to people who rely on physical fitness for their livelihoods or interests. However, middle adulthood can also be the time when many people first *begin* to work on developing their physical potential, as Linda's father did when he was 40. Even someone who has been inactive for years might decide at 45 to train for a marathon. People who work at their conditioning can maintain excellent health and strength throughout middle adulthood.

Generativity

A DAY IN THE LIFE

Figure 12.2 on page 281 summarizes some of the developmental tasks of middle adulthood, according to Erik Erikson. Erikson believed that the greatest challenge for middle-aged adults is **generativity**—the ability to create, originate, and produce. According to Erikson, generativity adds meaning to the lives of adults, and it helps them to maintain and enhance their self-esteem.

Adults can be creative, or generative, in various areas of their lives, such as their career, their family, and their community. People in middle adulthood are often also in positions in which they can exercise a particularly important influence on the world around them. As experienced workers, they may improve methods and relationships in the workplace. As parents, they guide the next generation. As voters and residents, they can help make their communities safer, friendlier places. Erikson also believed that adults who are not generative become stagnant. Stagnation—lack of advancement or development—can result in feelings of emptiness and meaninglessness.

Transition

Some psychologists have noted that many people experience a midlife transition around the ages of 40 to 45. The **midlife transition** is a period in middle adulthood when people's perspectives change in a major way. Some adults in their 40s are struck with the dramatic realization that they have lived about half their lives. They see themselves as being at a turning point. Previously, they had probably thought of their ages mostly in terms of how many years had elapsed since their birth. Once the midlife transition occurs, however, they begin to think of their ages in terms of how many years they may have left.

People in their 30s may still think of themselves as the older sibling of brothers or sisters in their 20s. Then, in their early 40s, a critical event often occurs. It may be a serious illness, a change at work, the death of a friend or a parent, or even just losing at basketball to one's child. Whatever the event, it triggers a 40-year-old's realization that he or she has made a generational shift. For example, the death of a parent may mean that the 40-year-old is now the head of the family. Similarly, losing at basketball to one's child may trigger the realization that "I'm not a kid anymore."

Women tend to undergo their midlife transitions about five years earlier than men do, at about age 35 instead of 40 (Reinke et al., 1985; Sheehy, 1995). What makes the mid-30s so special for women? For some women, 35 is about the age when they have sent their youngest child off to grade school, an event that can illustrate that their children are quickly growing up. Many women, of course, are not finished (or have not begun) having children by the age of 35, and for women who become pregnant at age 35 or older, doctors advise routine fetal testing for Down syndrome and other chromosomal disorders. (See Chapter 3.) Thirty-five is often also the age at which women are given a baseline mammogram—a specialized X ray for early detection of breast cancer—and are considered at greater risk for various types of cancer. These are all events that can cause women to reflect on their age and mortality.

With the thought that their lives may be close to half over, many people—men and women—come face-to-face with their limitations. They may acknowledge that dreams they had when they were younger may never be realized. For instance, they probably will never be a professional baseball player, a movie star, or president of the United States. People begin to adjust to the idea that they are growing older. For some adults, entering midlife may trigger a sense of urgency—a "last chance" to do certain things.

Midlife Crisis or Age of Mastery?   In some people, the midlife transition triggers a second period of reassessment, often referred to as a **midlife crisis**. The middle-aged professional who sees younger people advancing at a faster rate may become seriously depressed. The parent with two or three teenagers may feel less needed by her or his children. Both may feel trapped and think they have lost their purpose in life.

The concept of the midlife crisis has often been treated as something generally negative. It suggests that people are overwhelmed by the crushing realities and the limits of their lives. Yet journalist Gail Sheehy (1995) is quite positive about the years from 45 to 65. She calls these years the "age of mastery."

Sheehy maintains that during these years, people are frequently at the height of their creative and productive powers. In many cases, they need only

Developmental Tasks of Middle Adulthood

- Helping one's children make the transition from home life to the outside world

- Strengthening one's relationship with one's spouse

- Helping make the world a better place by assuming leadership roles in social and civic activities

- Achieving mastery in one's career

- Adjusting to the physical changes that occur in middle age

- Making decisions about how to spend one's "second adulthood"

- Pursuing one's passions

- Coping with one's aging parents

FIGURE 12.2   *Earlier in the chapter you read a list of what Erikson believed are the developmental tasks of young adulthood. Erikson also believed that middle adulthood has its own developmental tasks. The focus of these tasks is on improving one's quality of life and strengthening relationships, both personal and in the community.*

find new outlets for their talents and experience. Therefore, Sheehy believes, the key task for middle-aged adults is to decide what they will do with the remainder of their lives. Because people are living longer than people did in previous generations, most American adults have 30 to 40 healthy years left after they reach middle adulthood. Men and women can continue to have fulfilling lives if they find careers, hobbies, or other activities that bring satisfaction and if they pursue these newfound interests wholeheartedly.

"Middlescence"   But how do people go about recognizing and finding these interests? The term *middlescence* is sometimes used to describe a period of searching that in some ways resembles adolescence. Both middlescence and adolescence are periods of transition. Just as a key task of adolescence is the formation of identity in becoming an adult, middlescence involves a search for a *new* identity, or a *second* adulthood.

By the time they reach their early 40s, women have already dealt with some of the fears and

TONIGHT'S TOPIC:

LIFE STAGES ←

HE SAYS YOUR LIFE GOES IN CYCLES.

OF COURSE! AS SOON AS YOU KNOW WHAT YOU'RE DOING, EVERYTHING CHANGES.

THAVES 3-19

© 1996 by NEA, Inc.

E-mail: FandEBobT@AOL.COM

FRANK & ERNEST reprinted by permission of Newspaper Enterprise Association, Inc.

uncertainties that are only just starting to confront men (Helson 1993). As women emerge from middlescence in their 40s and 50s, they frequently experience a renewed sense of self. Many women in this age group feel confident and secure. They extend their interests. For example, they may become more involved in their communities. They are committed to what they are doing and feel productive, effective, and empowered.

The Empty-Nest Syndrome

In the past, psychologists placed great emphasis on the so-called empty-nest syndrome. **Empty-nest syndrome** is the term applied to the feelings of emptiness and loss mothers and fathers sometimes feel after the children have left home to establish their own lives. For mothers who have never worked outside the home, it can be particularly difficult to adjust to the departure of the children whose upbringings have been a full-time job. After years of being totally committed to being a wife and mother, some women seem to lose their sense of purpose and become depressed after their children go out on their own.

Contemporary research findings, however, reveal a much more optimistic picture. Once the "nest" is empty, many women report that they are happier with their marriages and other aspects of their lives. Many women mention positive changes, such as greater peace of mind, self-confidence, and personal stability (Helson et al., 1995). Many middle-aged women become more self-assertive and achievement oriented. Furthermore, most women whose children have left home are already employed. With more energy and time to spend outside the home, many women become more influential in politics and careers. Many others return to school. And although there may be some problems of adjustment once children leave, those problems affect both parents, not just mothers.

While parents do encounter some adjustment problems when their youngest child leaves home, many actually experience a new sense of freedom.

TRUTH OR fiction ▪ REVISITED ▪

It is not true that most parents feel a great sense of loss and loneliness when the youngest child leaves home. Instead, many parents experience a new sense of opportunity.

There is much variation, of course. Some people in middle age feel hopeless and drained. But often middle age is a time of increased freedom. Many people have been successful enough to be free of financial worries. Many begin to travel extensively. They may have the leisure time to take up new hobbies or explore old interests. Therefore, middle age does not need to be a painful period. Rather, it can be a time to enjoy new freedoms and opportunities for self-development.

Menopause

Menopause, the end of menstruation, usually occurs in a woman's late 40s or early 50s, although it can occur earlier or later. It is caused by a decrease in the secretion of the hormones estrogen and progesterone. After menopause, a woman no longer produces egg cells that can be fertilized. Other body changes also occur. Breast tissue decreases, and the skin becomes less elastic. There may also be a loss in bone density that can lead to brittle bones—a condition called osteoporosis.

In some women, the hormonal changes of menopause may cause discomfort, such as hot flashes—sudden sensations of warmth, often accompanied by reddening and sweating, fatigue, and mood swings. However, in most cases, these symptoms are relatively mild. Some women cope with the more severe changes of menopause with hormone-replacement therapy—taking doses of hormones to replace those the body no longer produces.

The psychological meaning of menopause to a woman is often more important than the physical changes she experiences. Some women feel that they have become less attractive or even that they are losing their identity as women. These women are likely to be more distressed by menopause than those who do not have such feelings (Rathus et al., 2000). Women who feel that their primary purpose in life was birthing and rearing children are also likely to find menopause stressful.

Figure 12.3 highlights some myths and realities about menopause. Notice that all the myths are negative. The reality, however, is often positive. For

Myths and Realities About Menopause

Myth	Reality
Menopause is abnormal.	Menopause is a normal development in women's lives.
Doctors consider menopause to be a disease.	Not so. Again, menopause is a normal development in women's lives.
After menopause, women need estrogen-replacement therapy.	Not necessarily. Some estrogen is still produced by the body. Estrogen-replacement therapy is undertaken with caution because of possible health risks.
Menopause is accompanied by depression and anxiety.	Not necessarily. However, hormonal changes in the body can affect a woman's mood.
At menopause, women suffer crippling hot flashes.	Not necessarily. Women who do have uncomfortable hot flashes can often be treated successfully with estrogen replacement.
Menopause ends a woman's sex drive.	Not at all. In fact, many women feel a renewal of sexual interest.
A woman's general level of activity is lower after menopause.	Not so. Many women report having more energy after menopause.

FIGURE 12.3 *The left-hand side of this table shows several of the myths about menopause. The realities of menopause are shown on the right-hand side. Why do you suppose people have so many misconceptions about menopause? How might these misconceptions influence the way menopausal women are treated?*

example, many women report having more energy —not less—after menopause.

When someone is referred to as "menopausal," it is usually the mood swings and increased irritability that are being talked about. Unfortunately, this oversimplifies what menopause is all about for women, and it also reinforces the stereotype of menopause as a time when women are not in control of their emotions. Such stereotypes and myths often do not have anything to do with the biology or psychology of aging.

Do men undergo menopause? The quick answer is "of course not," since men have never menstruated. Yet occasionally one hears of a so-called male menopause. Men do experience a hormone decline. At about age 40 or 50, testosterone levels in men begin to decline. They may fall to one third or one half of their peak levels by age 80 (Brody, 1995c). However, this is a gradual drop-off. It does not resemble the sharp plunge in estrogen levels that women experience.

The decline in a man's testosterone level may be connected with such other age-related changes as loss of strength, weight gain, reduced energy, and decreased fertility. Some of these changes, however, could just as well be due to a gradual loss of the human growth hormone rather than a diminishing testosterone level.

SECTION 2 REVIEW

Homework Practice Online
Keyword: SY7 HP12

1. How does generativity contribute to a healthy middle adulthood?
2. List some of the changes that occur and issues that are faced in middle adulthood.
3. **Critical Thinking** *Evaluating* Do you think middle age is a time of crisis or a period of new opportunities? Explain your answer.

SECTION 3

Late Adulthood

Age 65 marks the beginning of late adulthood. People are living longer than ever before. In 1900 only one American in thirty was over 65. By the year 2020 nearly one American in five will be age 65 or older (Longer, 1997).

Some people view the later years as the beginning of the end of life, but they can be much more. In fact, the later years provide many opportunities for self-fulfillment. John Glenn served as a member of the space shuttle crew when he was 77; comedian George Burns performed his comedy routines into his late 90s.

Physical Changes

Many physical changes take place in late adulthood. Wrinkles and skin folds occur as the skin becomes less elastic. Some of the senses become less sharp. In general, older people do not see and hear as well as younger people. A decline in the sense of smell leads many older people to add more spices to their food for flavor. The reflexes and the reaction time of older people also tend to be a little slower than those of younger people.

A few of the physical changes cause health problems. For example, as bones become more brittle, they fracture more easily, and the risk is greater that they will break if the person falls. As people grow older, their immune systems also become less effective as a barrier against disease.

However, older adults can do many things to maintain their health, strength, and energy levels.

Many people continue to learn new skills and lead active lives well into late adulthood.

A DAY IN THE LIFE

Regular exercise and a healthful diet can contribute to making older adults feel well and also help them fight disease. The man whom Marc met doing yard work is a good example of the benefits of exercise.

Exercise helps people maintain flexibility and fitness at any age—including the years of late adulthood. Because brittle bones and stiff joints are part of the aging process, many older people may prefer walking and swimming to more weight-bearing exercises such as running and bicycling. The latter activities tend to cause more stress on bones and joints (Pena & Bricklin, 1990).

TRUTH OR fiction ■ REVISITED ■

It is not true that it is good for older people not to exercise. Exercise helps people maintain flexibility and fitness at any age. Many older adults enjoy walking and swimming.

Exercise is beneficial at every stage of life, especially late adulthood. Regular exercise can help older people stay healthy, flexible, and energetic.

Why Do People Age?

Why do some people seem to age faster than others? Many scientists hope that by understanding the process of aging, we may eventually be able to slow it down or even reverse some of its negative effects. Theories of aging fall into two categories: programmed theories and cellular damage theories.

Programmed Theories The developmental theories that maintain that aging is the result of genetics are called **programmed theories**. These theories of aging view people as having biological clocks that move forward at a predetermined pace. Studies show that people whose parents lived long lives are more likely to have long lives themselves. This suggests that genetics plays a significant role in the length of one's life.

Heredity influences our cells, our hormones, and our immune systems. The cells in our bodies divide and repair themselves only a specific number of times. After that, they become inactive and eventually die. Some researchers believe that the limitation on the number of times a cell can divide is less important than the fact that the cells are aging. As they age, cells become less able to repair themselves. This makes people vulnerable to diseases that involve cellular breakdown, such as cancer (Lehrman, 1995).

Heredity also affects our hormones. Hormonal changes in later life may leave the body more vulnerable to certain health problems, such as diabetes, osteoporosis, and heart disease. Researchers are investigating the possible role of certain hormones—such as melatonin and the human growth hormone—in the aging process.

In addition, heredity influences the immune system. According to programmed theories, genetics may predetermine the decline in our immune systems. Such a decline makes the body less able to fight off disease.

Cellular Damage Theories In contrast to programmed theories, **cellular damage theories** of aging suggest that cells malfunction as a result of damage, not heredity. The damage may come from internal body changes or from external causes, such as trauma or toxins.

The cells in our bodies are affected by the environment. If they are exposed to poisons or cancer-causing agents for long periods of time, they become less able to repair themselves and more vulnerable to disease. As time passes, cells and vital organs are worn down, like machines whose parts eventually wear out from constant use.

Some scientists blame free radicals for damage to our bodies. **Free radicals** are unstable molecules in our bodies. They are normally produced as a by-product of digestion. They may also be produced by exposure to environmental agents, including

Late adulthood can be a time of creativity and self-fulfillment.

(Teachout, 2000). Pablo Picasso was still painting quite exciting canvases in his 90s, and Grandma Moses did not begin painting until she was 78. Architect Frank Lloyd Wright designed New York City's innovative Guggenheim Museum when he was 89 years old.

Although people can lead creative lives throughout old age, memory ability does decline with age. It is common for older people to have trouble recalling the names of things or people. Memory lapses can be embarrassing, and older people sometimes lose confidence in their memory (Cavanaugh & Green, 1990). But declines in memory are not usually as great as people assume, and they can sometimes be reversed (Villa & Abeles, 2000). Memory tests usually measure ability to recall meaningless information. Older people show better memory in areas in which they can apply their special experiences to new challenges (Graf, 1990). For example, who would do a better job of learning and remembering how to solve problems in chemistry—a young expert in history or a retired chemistry teacher?

All in all, most older people do quite well intellectually. Late adulthood is a time to discover new skills and ways of thinking. Unfortunately, some older people do have cognitive problems, such as senile dementia and Alzheimer's disease.

Senile Dementia   The serious loss of cognitive functioning is called **dementia**. People with dementia show major losses in memory. They may also have speech problems or be unable to perform simple tasks, such as tying their shoes or buttoning a shirt, even if they are physically able to perform such tasks. They may also have difficulty concentrating or making plans.

Dementia that occurs after the age of 65 is called **senile dementia**. Only a minority of older people have senile dementia, sometimes called senility. Most cases occur in people over the age of 80 (Nevid et al., 2000).

ultraviolet light, air pollution, pesticides, and even extreme heat. According to this view, aging occurs because free radicals accumulate in the body. These molecules eventually damage cells, causing people to age faster and to become vulnerable to various diseases (Hayflick, 1994; Lehrman, 1995).

Another cause of aging may be **cross-linking**. According to this view, proteins within a cell bind together, toughening body tissues. This toughening eventually leads to the breakdown of various bodily processes and causes aging (Lamb, 1993).

Aging is a complex biological process. It may not be due to a single cause. It may not be explainable by a single theory. Aging may result from a combination of the processes described here, or it may involve factors we are not even aware of yet. For these reasons, researchers continue to study the aging process.

Cognitive Changes

Cognitive development is also affected by aging. Cognitive development in adulthood has many aspects—creativity, memory functioning, and intelligence. People can be creative for a lifetime. At the age of 80, Merce Cunningham choreographed a dance that made use of computer-generated images

It is not true that everyone who lives long enough will eventually become senile. Senile dementia (sometimes called senility) is not an automatic result of aging.

Alzheimer's Disease **Alzheimer's disease** is a progressive form of mental deterioration that affects about 10 percent of people over the age of 65 and nearly half of those over the age of 85 (Katzman, 2000). Although Alzheimer's is connected with aging, it is a disease and not a normal part of aging (Haan, 2000).

Alzheimer's disease is characterized by general, gradual deterioration in mental processes such as memory, language, and problem solving. As the disease progresses, people may fail to recognize familiar faces or forget their names. Eventually, people with Alzheimer's disease become helpless. They become unable to communicate or walk and require help eating.

Alzheimer's disease is characterized by reduced levels of the neurotransmitter acetylcholine (ACh) and by the buildup of a sticky plaque in the brain. The plaque is formed from fragments of a body protein (Cotman, 2000; Frangione, 2000). Normally, the immune system prevents the buildup of this plaque, but the immune system does not do its job effectively in the case of people with Alzheimer's disease. One form of drug therapy is aimed at boosting ACh levels by slowing its breakdown. This approach achieves modest benefits with many people. Another approach to the treatment of Alzheimer's is the development of a vaccine made of a harmful protein that will help the immune system to better attack the plaque (Schenk, 2000).

Vascular Dementia Another common kind of dementia is vascular dementia. Vascular dementia can be caused by the bursting of a blood vessel in the brain (as during a stroke) or by a decrease in the blood supply to the brain. Such a decrease happens when fatty deposits collect in the blood vessels that go to the brain. The deposits cause the blood vessels to narrow, impeding the blood flow. Various infections can also cause dementia.

Social Changes

In addition to physical and cognitive changes, aging also involves many social changes. People have to make decisions about their retirement, how much time to spend with their children and grandchildren, and where they should live.

Retirement Many people dream of retirement, the period when they no longer need to wake up early in the morning and go to work. Other people dread the idea of retirement, wondering what they will do with all their free time. In many cases, retirement is voluntary. But people in some jobs, including teachers in most school systems, must retire when they reach a certain age, usually 65 or 70. In other cases, older people find themselves forced out of jobs because of discrimination or for other reasons related to age.

Some people turn their attention to leisure activities when they retire. Others continue in part-time work, either paid or voluntary. Research indicates that there may be some common experiences involving retirement (Atchley, 1991). When people first retire, they often undergo a "honeymoon" phase. They feel very positive about their newfound freedom, and they do many of the things they had dreamed about doing once they had the time. During this honeymoon period, people are often quite busy.

After a while, however, many people become disillusioned with retirement. Their schedules slow down, and they discover that the things they had fantasized about are less stimulating than they had thought they would be. Retirement can also place stress on a marriage because spouses may suddenly be spending a great deal more time together than they ever have before. As people encounter such experiences, they tend to develop a more realistic view of retirement. They may join volunteer groups and participate more in community activities. Sometimes elderly persons begin entirely new careers—painting or writing, for example. In general, people establish a new routine, and stability sets in.

Grandparenthood Grandparents often have more relaxed relationships with their grandchildren than they had with their children. Their perspectives may have become broader as they have grown older. Many have become more tolerant and understanding over the years. And because they do not usually have to shoulder the major responsibility for the grandchildren, grandparents usually can enjoy them. Because of a variety of circumstances, increasing numbers of grandparents are in fact taking on the major responsibility for raising their grandchildren.

A DAY IN THE LIFE

Grandparents are frequently valued by their children for the roles they play with the grandchildren. For example, retired grandparents who live nearby can help baby-sit. Grandparents also often serve as special sources of wisdom and love for grandchildren, as Linda remembered about her own grandmother.

For many older adults, balancing a need for independence with a need to stay involved with their

To grandchildren, grandparents often serve as a source of love and understanding—and enjoyment.

Successful Aging

Some people age more successfully than others. Psychologists have found that "successful agers" have several characteristics that can inspire all people to lead more enjoyable and productive lives.

Ego Integrity   Erik Erikson (1963) believed that people in late adulthood, like those in other stages of life, face certain developmental tasks. (See Figure 12.4 on page 290.) He believed that one challenge facing people in late adulthood is the maintenance of **ego integrity**—the belief that life is meaningful and worthwhile even when physical abilities are not what they used to be. A person with ego integrity is able to accept his or her approaching death with composure.

People spend most of their lives developing relationships and gathering possessions. Erikson believed that ego integrity enables people to let go of relationships and objects as the end of life approaches. Older people who do not maintain ego integrity risk falling into despair because they feel as if they are losing everything that matters to them. Ego integrity is connected with the wisdom to accept that one's life span is limited and to realize that nothing will last forever. Successful agers have this wisdom.

Aging and Adjustment   Most people in their 70s report being largely satisfied with their lives (Margoshes, 1995). Despite the physical changes that occur with aging, more than 75 percent rate their health as good or excellent.

Older people tend to be more satisfied with their lives when they are in good health and when they are financially secure. In fact, there is a correlation between socioeconomic status and health (Leary, 1995). Economically disadvantaged people at any age are more likely to report ill health than people of higher socioeconomic status. People who are financially secure are usually able to afford better health care and preventive services. They tend to worry less, and thus their stress is reduced. It may also be true that throughout life, people who are healthy are able to work harder and earn higher incomes. Most older people have some degree of financial security, but about 10 percent of people age 65 or older do live below the poverty line.

Among older people, as among younger people, a strong connection exists between social support and personal well-being. Social support is provided by various relationships. Spouses, children, and

children and grandchildren is an important job. How often older adults see the children and grandchildren and whether they have the right to make "suggestions" become key issues. Although many older people worry that their families might no longer want them around, they are not usually rejected by their children. Most older people see or talk to their children regularly (Berger, 1994).

Living Arrangements   Some Americans hold certain stereotypes about older people's living arrangements. One stereotype portrays older people living with their children. Another has them in nursing homes and other institutions (Stock, 1995). Still another stereotype is that older people buy condominiums or move to retirement communities in areas with warmer climates.

Most older people are independent. Many of them are financially secure and own their own homes. It is true that nearly 30 percent of older people will spend some time in a nursing home (Kemper & Murtaugh, 1991). However, the populations of nursing homes usually consist of people who are 80 or older.

Most older people also remain in their hometowns rather than moving to other areas of the United States. They prefer to live in familiar surroundings where they have social and cultural ties (U.S. Bureau of the Census, 1995).

CASE STUDIES

AND OTHER TRUE STORIES

Making the Most of Late Adulthood

Late adulthood does not mean the end of achievement. In fact, many people reach the height of their productivity and accomplishments in late adulthood. Three people who have proved just how valuable the contributions of older people can be are Pablo Picasso, Mother Teresa, and Thurgood Marshall.

Pablo Picasso (1881–1973)

Many people consider Pablo Picasso to be the most influential artist of the 1900s. This Spanish-born artist experimented with various styles of painting, sculpture, and ceramics. His innovative art styles were sometimes viewed with surprise, even horror, as so often happens when something different is introduced. Throughout Picasso's life and career, he never stopped trying new things. The last major exhibition of his work during his own lifetime was mounted in 1973, when he was in his 90s. As with earlier shows, the public was once again surprised by the newness of his artistic vision. Many of the works in this exhibit were early expressions of a style that came to dominate the art of the early 1980s. Picasso never stopped working. He died in his sleep. Next to his bed was a bundle of crayons—placed there in case he woke with an inspiration. As he once said: "The painter never finishes . . . you can never write 'The End.'"

Mother Teresa (1910–1997)

Mother Teresa became a nun when she was only 18 years old. Known as Sister Teresa early on, she found herself in India teaching the daughters of middle-class Indians. Then one day she received what she referred to as "a call within a call." She believed that God wanted her to serve only the poorest people, the dying, and the homeless for the rest of her life. She left the convent with only the clothes she was wearing. In 1948 Sister Teresa opened her first school. Two years later, she founded the Order of the Missionaries of Charity, a congregation of women dedicated to helping poor people. She established schools and opened health centers for the care of the blind, the elderly, the sick, and the dying. In 1989, when she was 79, Mother Teresa suffered a heart attack and, soon after, resigned as head of the order. But by the end of 1990, she had returned to her post in India. Although Mother Teresa was a small, frail-looking woman, old age did little to weaken her. At the time she returned to the order, the Missionaries of Charity had more than 3,000 nuns.

Thurgood Marshall (1908–1993)

Thurgood Marshall was another extremely influential figure whose contributions continued throughout his life. He first made his mark as a young lawyer when he became the lead attorney for the National Association for the Advancement of Colored People (NAACP). Although it was often dangerous to do so, Marshall traveled across the country urging the courts to protect the constitutional rights of African Americans. He became famous for his leading work on the *Brown* v. *Board of Education of Topeka* case, which resulted in the historic 1954 Supreme Court ruling that segregation in the nation's public schools is unconstitutional.

In 1967 Marshall was appointed to the Supreme Court, the first African American to receive such an appointment. He worked to end political, economic, and social injustices in this country. Despite several serious illnesses, he continued to serve, noting that he had "a lifetime appointment." However, during his 80s, Marshall's health declined, and he retired from the bench in 1991. He will always be remembered for his strong convictions, especially regarding civil rights.

THINKING CRITICALLY

1. **Making Generalizations and Predictions** In general, how did Picasso, Mother Teresa, and Marshall make the most of late adulthood?
2. **Analyzing Information** How might you make the most of your late adulthood?

Developmental Tasks of Late Adulthood

- Adjusting to physical changes and keeping (or becoming) physically active

- Maintaining concern about other people so that one does not become preoccupied with one's own physical changes

- Shifting interests from work to retirement or leisure activity

- Adjusting to changes in financial status

- Establishing fulfilling living arrangements

- Learning to live with one's husband or wife in retirement (in that both spouses may now be together much of the time)

- Adjusting to the illness or the death of one's husband or wife

FIGURE 12.4 *Erikson also believed that late adulthood has its own particular developmental tasks. Acceptance and adjustment are primary tasks at this time in life.*

Paul and Margret Baltes (1995) noted that successful agers no longer try to compete with younger people in certain activities, such as athletics or business. Rather, they focus on matters that allow them to maintain a sense of personal control. They also try to find ways to make up for losses in some of their abilities. If their memories are not quite what they used to be, they may make notes or use other types of reminders. If their senses are no longer as sharp as they once were, they use devices such as hearing aids or eyeglasses. Some older people even develop creative solutions to their problems. The great pianist Arthur Rubinstein performed well into his 80s, even after he had lost much of his speed. To make up for this lack, he would slow down as he approached a passage in the music that required him to play faster. In this way, he gave the impression of speed during the more rapid passages (Margoshes, 1995).

friends may all provide social support, helping out in both practical and emotional ways when necessary. This may help explain the research finding that older couples generally are happier than older single or widowed people (Berger, 1994). Once couples are retired, they tend to spend more time together. Their relationships thus take on greater importance in their lives. When one spouse dies, however, children often are able to give needed support to the surviving spouse.

Reshaping One's Life Another component of successful aging is reshaping one's life to focus on what is important. Laura Carstensen's (1995) research on people aged 70 and above revealed that successful agers formulate specific goals that bring them satisfaction. For example, rather than becoming involved with many different causes or hobbies, they may focus on one particular interest. Successful agers may have less time left than people in earlier stages of adulthood, but they tend to spend it more wisely (Garfinkel, 1995).

A Positive Outlook A positive outlook is another component of successful aging. For example, some older people blame their occasional aches and pains on specific causes, such as a cold. Others simply blame old age itself. Not surprisingly, those who attribute their problems to specific causes are more optimistic that they will get better. Thus, they have a more positive outlook or attitude.

Researcher William Rakowski (1995) followed 1,400 people aged 70 and above who had common health problems, such as aches and pains. He found that those who blamed the problems on aging were more likely to die sooner than those who blamed the problems on specific factors.

Self-Challenge Yet another component of successful aging is challenging oneself. Many people look forward to late adulthood as a time when they can rest from life's challenges. However, sitting back and allowing the world to pass by is a prescription for becoming passive and for not living life to its fullest extent.

This view was confirmed in a study conducted by Curt Sandman and Francis Crinella (1995). They randomly assigned 175 participants, whose average age was 72, either to a foster-grandparent program or to a control group. They then followed the participants for 10 years. As compared to people in the control group, the foster grandparents faced greater physical challenges, such as walking a few miles each day. They also had new social experiences by getting to know the children and their families. The results of the study showed that people in the foster-grandparent program improved their overall cognitive functioning, including their memories. They even slept more soundly.

Withdrawing from life and avoiding challenges is clearly not the route to well-being and good health for older people. Focusing on what is important, maintaining a positive attitude, and accepting new challenges are as important for older people as for younger people.

SECTION 3 REVIEW

go.hrw.com **Homework Practice Online**
Keyword: SY7 HP12

1. What are some changes people face in late adulthood?

2. Why is ego integrity an important part of healthy aging?

3. **Critical Thinking** *Analyzing Information* Many older people experience memory losses. What are some ways older people can keep track of their medication and remember important telephone numbers or directions to the doctor's office?

SECTION 4

Death and Dying

We all must face death at some point in our lives. Yet most of us seem to want to turn away from such a thought. According to psychiatrist Elisabeth Kübler-Ross (1969), the subject of death is often avoided. We seem to do all kinds of things to avoid confronting the reality of death. For example, prior to burial, cosmetics are used to make the deceased person look as if he or she is asleep.

Because death often brings sadness, some people send their children away to friends or relatives so that they need not face the sadness and anxiety around the home. Children may be prevented from visiting dying grandparents. But part of healing after a death is having the chance to say good-bye. Therefore, some psychologists suggest that trying to protect children by keeping them away from a dying loved one may actually make it harder for them to cope with their grief.

Stages of Dying

Kübler-Ross (1969) worked with people who had terminal illnesses. An illness is terminal when it seems certain to lead to death. Some types of cancers are terminal illnesses. Kübler-Ross theorized that there are five stages through which many dying people pass. She believed that many older people have similar feelings when they suspect that death is near, even if they have not been diagnosed with a terminal illness. The stages are as follows:

1. *Denial.* For example, the dying person might think, "It can't be me. The doctor's diagnosis must be wrong."

2. *Anger.* People in this stage might think, "It's unfair. Why me?"

3. *Bargaining.* For instance, "I'll be kinder if I can just live to see my grandson graduate."

4. *Depression.* The person may despair and wonder, "What's the use of living another day?"

5. *Acceptance.* The person reasons, "I've had a good life. I'm ready to die."

Kübler-Ross's theory has met with considerable criticism. Some psychologists, such as Edwin Shneidman (1984), agree that many terminally ill people have the kinds of feelings described by Kübler-Ross. But Shneidman has not found that the feelings follow a particular sequence. Shneidman finds that people faced with approaching death show a variety of reactions. Some people have quickly shifting emotions that range from rage to surrender, from envying the young and healthy to yearning for the end. Some people accept death more easily; others feel despair. Still others feel terror. People's reactions to dying reflect their unique personalities and their philosophies of life.

Another problem with Kübler-Ross's theory is that it may tempt family members and health professionals to ignore the uniqueness of each individual's experiences at the end of life. If a dying person is angry or in despair, people may think that it is just a stage and not pay close attention to the dying

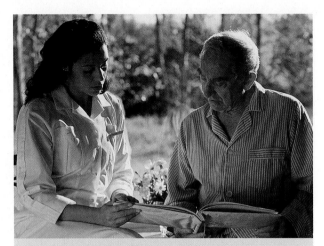

An alternative to hospitals, hospices are homelike places where dying people and their families are given the physical and emotional support to help them cope with terminal illness.

person's feelings. In addition, people might try to encourage the dying person to work through the sequence of stages in the belief that by doing so the dying person will reach the acceptance stage sooner. However, what a dying person may really need is to be treated as a living individual with hopes and feelings, not as someone undergoing predictable stages of behavior.

Dying with Dignity

Dying people, like other people, need security, self-confidence, and dignity. Dying people may also need relief from pain. One controversial issue is whether terminally ill individuals should be given painkilling drugs, such as narcotics, that are highly addictive. Physicians usually try to balance the patient's need for relief from severe and constant pain against the dangers of such drugs. However, some people feel that to worry about addiction does not make sense when a person is going to die soon.

Dying people, perhaps even more than other people, need to feel cared for and supported. Therefore, it is helpful for family members to encourage a dying person to talk about his or her feelings. Sometimes it is enough just to spend quiet time with the person—to let the person know that he or she is not alone. Family members and others also can help by assisting with the financial and legal arrangements to pay for medical care and distribution of property. The knowledge that one's final wishes will be carried out can help the dying person gain a sense of peace and completion.

Some dying people want to know all the details regarding their situation; others do not. Therefore, it is important for family members and health professionals to understand the extent of the person's need for details. It is also important to give the person accurate information about what she or he can expect to experience in terms of pain and loss of body functions and control. Old and dying people should not be treated like infants, but as adults who have dignity and a right to know what is going to happen to them.

The Hospice Alternative Linda mentioned that her grandmother had been in a hospice. A **hospice** is a homelike place where dying people and their families are given the physical and emotional support to help them cope with terminal illness. Unlike hospitals, hospices do not restrict visiting hours. Family members and friends work with trained staff to provide physical comfort and emotional support. Hospice care may be given in the patient's own home by visiting hospice workers.

In a hospital, rules determine a patient's treatment—usually the patient has little say in the matter. In a hospice, however, dying people are allowed more control over their lives. They are encouraged to make decisions about their diets, activities, and medication. Relatives and friends often remain in contact with the hospice staff to cope with their own feelings of grief after the person has died.

Euthanasia The term **euthanasia** comes from the Greek language and means "easy death" (*eu* means "well"; *thanatos* means "death"). Euthanasia—also called mercy killing—is another controversial issue regarding death and dying.

Some physicians may consider euthanasia when they are absolutely convinced that there is no hope for a person's recovery, such as when a person has been in a coma for a long time or when the pain of a terminal illness is so severe and constant as to be unbearable. Euthanasia is illegal in most states.

Opponents of euthanasia argue that no one has the right to take—or to help another person take—a life, even one's own life. Opponents also maintain that new medications and therapies are continually being developed and that a person who feels today that death is the most desirable option may feel more optimistic tomorrow or next week. In other words, the pain and suffering may be temporary, but death is permanent.

The Living Will Many people today write **living wills** to avoid being kept alive by artificial support systems (such as respirators) when there is no hope for recovery. The living will is a legal document.

A living will is intended to spare people the perceived indignity and cost of being kept alive when there is no hope of survival and to spare their families from having to make the decision to remove a loved one from an artificial life-support system. The idea is that once the person has died, the family members can grieve and move on with their lives. Of course, whether to have a living will is a choice that each individual must make.

The Funeral

The funeral is a traditional way for a community to acknowledge that one of its members has died. The rituals of the funeral also provide a framework for what to do and how to act when a family member or friend has died.

The specific kind of funeral chosen usually reflects religious beliefs and cultural customs. Some funeral services tie a person's death to the ongoing progression of time and the universe. Various professionals, such as undertakers and religious leaders, can be especially helpful when a family's grief adds to the difficulty of making decisions concerning the final arrangements for the deceased.

Funerals are a way of saying good-bye. But they accomplish much more. As the deceased is physically removed and prepared for burial or cremation, his or her body is both physically and symbolically separated from the living. In some religions and cultures, the transition is slow. Some customs provide periods of time during which mourners may view the body and meet with family members.

Funerals also provide a way to remember and celebrate the life of the deceased. Many funerals include a eulogy—a speech praising the person who has just died. Finally, there is the burial or the cremation of the body. This is when family and friends physically let go of the person who has died.

Bereavement

A DAY IN THE LIFE

Linda was sad when her grandmother died, but she may also have felt a sense of relief that her suffering was finally over. Such feelings of relief often seem disturbing, but they are rather common. The people who are left behind are said to be **bereaved**, which means mourning

Different cultures deal with death in different ways. Most cultures have rituals to commemorate the life and passing of the deceased. Here, a New Orleans jazz band is featured in a funeral procession known as a wake.

over something or someone precious who has been taken away. People who are bereaved may have feelings of sadness and loneliness, numbness, anger, and even relief. When the dying person suffers greatly, family members may feel they have reached the limits of their ability to be helpful. Therefore, it is normal for them to feel a certain amount of relief when death finally comes.

Some bereaved people may join support groups or seek professional help in dealing with their grief. With or without such help, most bereaved people eventually recover from their losses. They may never forget the person they have lost, but they usually become less preoccupied by the loss itself. They resume their lives at home and at work. They may always miss the person who died, but most of the time they are able to resume normal functioning. Sometimes the survivors grow in compassion because of their loss and gain a deeper appreciation of the value of life.

SECTION 4 REVIEW

go.hrw.com Homework Practice Online
Keyword: SY7 HP12

1. List two or three ways that people tend to try to push aside death rather than face it.

2. Identify three ways in which hospice care differs from hospital care.

3. **Critical Thinking** *Sequencing* List in order the five stages of death and dying in Kübler-Ross's theory.

12 REVIEW

Writing a Summary

Using standard grammar, spelling, sentence structure, and punctuation, summarize the information in this chapter. Consider:
- the issues faced by persons in young and middle adulthood
- issues of importance to elderly persons, and how people cope with issues related to death and dying

Identifying People and Ideas

Identify the following terms or people and use them in appropriate sentences.

1. patriarchy
2. generativity
3. midlife crisis
4. empty-nest syndrome
5. menopause
6. cellular damage theories
7. senile dementia
8. Alzheimer's disease
9. hospice
10. living wills

Understanding Main Ideas

SECTION 1 (pp. 274–280)
1. What factors typically influence a young adult's choice of a spouse?

SECTION 2 (pp. 280–284)
2. In what ways are middlescence and adolescence similar?

SECTION 3 (pp. 284–291)
3. Why is maintaining ego integrity important for older adults?

SECTION 4 (pp. 291–293)
4. List two ways in which family members and friends can help a dying person.

Thinking Critically

1. **Evaluating** Why do you think large numbers of middle-aged adults enroll in classes and programs offered by community organizations, schools, and colleges?

2. **Making Generalizations and Predictions** How could the concept of free radicals be used in a campaign to discourage teenagers from using drugs and alcohol?

3. **Analyzing Information** What strengths might workers in the different stages of adulthood bring to a business?

4. **Drawing Inferences and Conclusions** What steps might a young person take to prepare for a successful late adulthood?

5. **Categorizing** What are the advantages and disadvantages of classifying adult development into stages?

Writing About Psychology

1. **Summarizing** Read about the marriage or funeral customs in a different culture or during an earlier time in history. As you read, look for answers to the following questions: What people play important roles in the customs? What is the basis of the customs? How have the customs changed over time, if at all, and what has led to the changes? Write a brief report summarizing your findings.

2. **Categorizing** Create a two-page dialogue between the following fictional characters: a 25-year-old, his or her 50-year-old parent, and his or her 75-year-old grandparent. In the dialogue, have the characters discuss some of the challenges each of them is facing and the methods each character is using to face the challenges. Use the graphic organizer below to help you with your dialogue.

25-year-old	50-year-old	75-year-old

Interpreting Graphs

Study the graph below. Then use the information in the graph to help you answer the questions that follow.

Loss of Memory with Age

Source: Light and Burke, (eds.), *Language, Memory, and Aging,* 1988

1. Which of the following statements accurately uses the information found in the graph?

   a. The younger a person is, the better that person will perform on a vocabulary test.

   b. A person's age is never a factor in performance on vocabulary exams.

   c. People in their 20s and 30s are most able to write well.

   d. Performance on vocabulary tests declines after age 40.

2. How might a psychologist explain the improvement in scores that takes place during the period from 20 years of age to 30 years of age?

Analyzing Primary Sources

Read the following excerpt from *On Death and Dying,* in which Dr. Elisabeth Kübler-Ross discusses the behavior of a dying patient. Then answer the questions that follow.

❝Another patient was in utmost pain and discomfort, unable to go home because of her dependence on injections for pain relief. She had a son who proceeded with his plans to get married, as the patient had wished. She was very sad to think that she would be unable to attend this big day, for he was her oldest and favorite child. . . . She had made all sorts of promises if she could only live long enough to attend this marriage. The day preceding the wedding she left the hospital as an elegant lady. Nobody would have believed her real condition. She was the 'happiest woman in the whole world' and looked radiant. . . . I will never forget the moment when she returned to the hospital. She looked tired and somewhat exhausted and—before I could say hello—said, "Now don't forget I have another son!❞

3. According to Kübler-Ross's stages of dying, which stage had the patient in the excerpt reached?

   a. denial

   b. anger

   c. bargaining

   d. depression

4. Why do you think that the patient in the excerpt thought it important to tell Kübler-Ross that she had another son?

PSYCHOLOGY PROJECTS

Linking to Community

Using Interviewing Skills Working with a partner, create a chart or other visual that summarizes the physical, mental, and social characteristics and issues of young adulthood, middle adulthood, and late adulthood. Start off by filling in the visual with information from the chapter. Then interview people in each of the three stages to build on what you have already filled in. When your visual is completed, present your chart to the class.

🔲 **internet** connect

Internet Activity: go.hrw.com
KEYWORD: SY7 CH12

Choose an activity on adulthood to:

- create a product or advertisement applying various perspectives of motivation to target young adults.
- write a newspaper article on the challenges of middle adulthood.
- conduct a poll or interview regarding the joys and challenges of late adulthood.

PSYCHOLOGY IN ACTION

YOU MAKE THE DECISION . . .

Which college should you attend?

Complete the following activity in small cooperative groups. Your group is looking for information about a number of colleges to help the members of the group decide which one they would like to attend. Work together to prepare a flyer that describes one of the colleges that a member of your group would like to attend.

1. Gather Information. Use your textbook and other resources to find information that might help you decide what college the members of your group would like to attend. What characteristics are the group members looking for in a college? What type of information about colleges is available to the group? You may want to divide up different parts of the research among the various members of the group.

2. Identify Options. After reviewing the information that you have gathered, consider which college has characteristics that the members of your group find appealing. Your final decision may be easier to reach if you consider as many options as possible. Be sure to record the options your group has identified for your flyer.

3. Predict Consequences. Now take each option you and the members of your group came up with and consider how each college might meet the needs of each group member. Ask yourself questions such as,

- Does this college offer a major in the group member's area of interest?
- Is this college affordable?

Once you have predicted the consequences of each option your group has identified, record them as notes for your flyer.

4. Take Action to Implement Your Decision. After you have considered your options, you should create your flyer. Be sure that your flyer makes your decision about what college to attend very clear. You will need to support your decision by including information you gathered and by explaining why you rejected other options. You may want to create charts or graphs to support your decision. When you are ready, decide who in your group will present the flyer. Then make your presentation to the class. Good luck!

UNIT 5

PERSONALITY

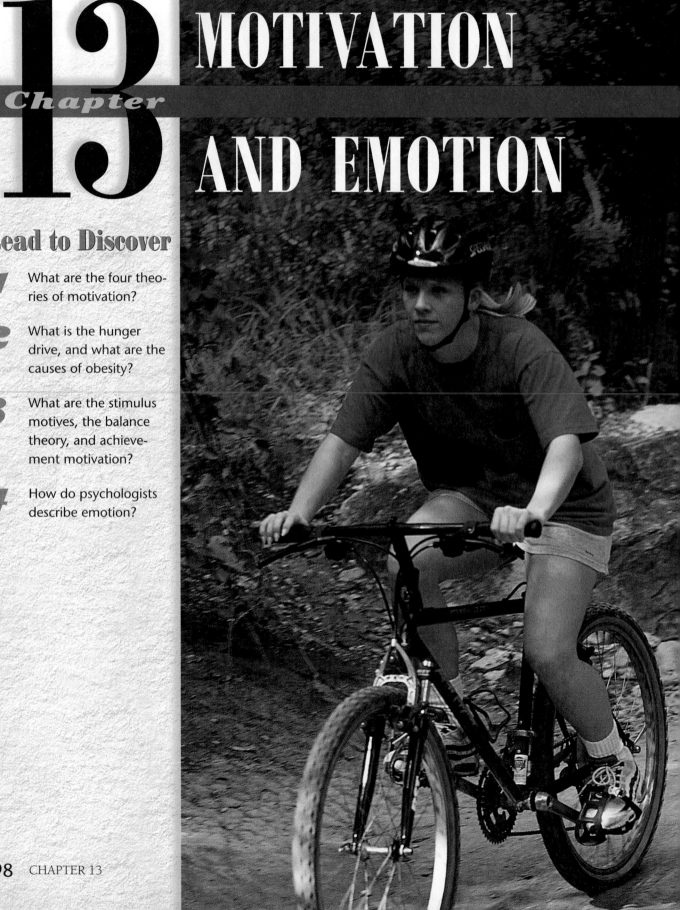

13 MOTIVATION AND EMOTION

Chapter 13

Read to Discover

1 What are the four theories of motivation?

2 What is the hunger drive, and what are the causes of obesity?

3 What are the stimulus motives, the balance theory, and achievement motivation?

4 How do psychologists describe emotion?

A DAY IN THE LIFE

Hannah, Todd, and Dan gathered at Hannah's house after school to study. Hannah was trying to work on her psychology assignment, but she could not seem to concentrate.

"Hannah, what are you thinking about?" Todd finally asked. "Every time I look at you, you're staring off into space and smiling."

"I'm sorry. I just can't stop thinking about my violin recital last night. I played better than I ever had in a recital before."

"I'm glad I was there to see it. You were great," Dan said.

"Thanks!" Hannah replied with enthusiasm. "At first, I was really nervous, but once I started playing, I was fine. Of course, it really helped that you, Marc, and Linda were all there with my parents. For some reason, I was so much more confident because I knew that all of you were in the audience."

"I really wish I could have been there," Todd commented, "but I had to study for that advanced biology test I had today."

Hannah knew how much Todd enjoyed studying science. "Don't worry about it," Hannah said. "You love science. And you need to do well in biology if you're going to get that scholarship."

"You'll have to try to go to the next recital, though, Todd. Hannah is really good," Dan added. "Hey, wasn't Janet going to study with us this afternoon?"

"She'll be here later," Hannah answered. "She wanted to stop by the recreation center after school. The youth group is planning a hiking trip and, knowing Janet, she'll probably be the first person to sign up. That is, of course, if she can fit it into her schedule."

Everyone laughed because they knew Hannah was right. Whenever Janet was not working at her part-time job or studying for her classes, she was outdoors playing basketball or riding her mountain bike.

Just then, Eddie, Hannah's three-year-old brother, came wandering into the room. "Hannah, I'm hungry," he announced as he walked over to sit with Dan.

Dan loved spending time with Eddie, so he welcomed the opportunity to take a study break. "You know what, Eddie?" Dan said. "I'm hungry too. Let's have a snack."

Why does Todd push himself to study advanced biology when he could be relaxing in front of the television set or outside playing ball? Why does Hannah spend hours, days, and weeks of her free time practicing the violin for a 40-minute recital? Is the elation Hannah feels after her recital worth the anxiety she felt on stage? The answers to these questions involve motivation (the elusive feelings that make us do the things we do) and emotions (the responses generated by certain situations). In this chapter, we will examine the ways in which our emotions lead us to behave in certain ways.

- motive
- need
- drives
- instincts
- homeostasis
- self-actualization
- obese
- stimulus motives
- sensory deprivation
- achievement motivation
- performance goals
- learning goals
- extrinsic rewards
- intrinsic rewards
- cognitive consistency
- balance theory
- imbalance
- nonbalance
- cognitive-dissonance theory
- affiliation
- emotions
- opponent-process theory

HOLT
Psychology Video Program
Watch the video to explore why some people have a need for speed.

SECTION 1

The Psychology of Motivation

Why do many people like to travel to faraway places or to try new foods? The answer to this question—and other questions about why people do the things they do—relates to motivation. A **motive** is a stimulus that moves a person to behave in ways designed to accomplish a specific goal. Motives are considered theoretical states because they cannot be seen or measured directly. Psychologists assume that people and other organisms are motivated when they observe the people trying to reach their goals. The psychology of motivation deals with the *whys* of behavior.

Needs

When psychologists speak of motives, they also often speak of needs. A **need** is a condition in which we require something we lack. People have both biological and psychological needs. People fulfill biological needs to survive. Examples of biological needs include the need for oxygen and food. Some biological needs such as for food or sleep occur in part because of physical deprivation. That is, people feel hungry or sleepy when they have not eaten or slept for a while.

Achievement, self-esteem, a sense of belonging, and social approval are examples of psychological needs. Like biological needs, psychological needs motivate people to accomplish certain goals. However, psychological needs differ from biological needs in two important ways. First, psychological needs are not necessarily based on deprivation. A person with a need to achieve an A on a test may already be an honor-roll student. Second, unlike biological needs, which are inborn, psychological needs may be learned. People possess common biological characteristics, thus they have similar physical needs. For example, all people must eat to survive, therefore all people need food. However, people have different psychological needs because they learn from a variety of experiences. Psychological needs are shaped by culture and learning, so people's psychological needs differ markedly. For example, some people prefer vegetarian diets because they believe it is morally wrong to kill animals for food.

Drives

Biological needs and psychological needs give rise to **drives**—the forces that motivate an organism to take action. The biological need for food gives rise to the hunger drive. The biological need for water gives rise to the thirst drive.

Although hunger and thirst are aroused by biological needs, the *experience* of them is psychological. The longer we are deprived of something such as food or water, the stronger our drive becomes. For example, our hunger drive is stronger 6 hours after eating than it is 20 minutes after eating.

Theories of Motivation

Psychologists agree that motives prompt behavior, but they are not in agreement about the nature of motivation. The leading theories of motivation are instinct theory, drive-reduction theory, humanistic theory, and sociocultural theory.

Instinct Theory Behavior patterns that are genetically transmitted from generation to generation are known as **instincts**. Sometimes they are called fixed-action patterns. Researchers have discovered that many animals are born to act in certain ways in certain situations. Studies have shown that birds acquire the songs characteristic of their species largely by instinct (Marler, 1991).

Siamese fighting fish reared in isolation also display instinctive behavior. Males fan their fins and gills in the typical threatening posture when other males are introduced into their tanks. Similarly, bees perform an instinctive "dance" to relay the location of food to other bees (Moffett, 1990).

Certain behavior patterns are largely instinctive and do not have to be learned. Birds raised in isolation will build nests characteristic of their species, despite the fact that they were never taught how to do this by other members of the species.

TRUTH OR **fiction** ∎ REVISITED ∎

It is not true that robins and other birds have to learn the songs that are characteristic of their species. These songs are largely inborn, or instinctive, not learned.

At one time, psychologists believed that human behavior, like that of animals, is instinctive. In the late 1800s and early 1900s, psychologists William James (1890) and William McDougall (1908) argued that people have instincts that foster survival and social behavior. Today, however, most psychologists do not believe that human behavior is primarily motivated by instinct. If a behavior pattern is instinctive, they argue, it must be found throughout a species. However, there is so much variation in the way people behave that much of human behavior is unlikely to be instinctive.

Drive-Reduction Theory Psychologist Clark Hull formulated the drive-reduction theory in the 1930s. Drive-reduction theory is based on learning as well as motivation. According to this theory, people and animals experience a drive arising from a need as an unpleasant tension. They learn to do whatever will reduce that tension by reducing the drive, such as eating to reduce their hunger drive.

Some drives, such as hunger, are caused by biological needs, which are inborn. Other drives, such as a drive for money, are learned from experience. According to drive-reduction theory, people will try to reduce these learned drives, just as they try to reduce biological drives.

Basic drives, such as hunger, motivate us to restore an internal state of equilibrium, or balance. The tendency to maintain this state of equilibrium in the body is called **homeostasis**. Homeostasis works like a thermostat. When room temperature drops below a certain point—called the set point—the heat comes on. The heat stays on until the set point is reached. Similarly, according to the theory, when people are hungry, they will eat until they reach a level at which they are no longer hungry.

Drive-reduction theory seems to apply to many biological drives, including hunger and thirst. Yet people sometimes eat when they are not hungry. They also often act to increase rather than decrease the tension they experience. For example, some people enjoy riding roller coasters and driving fast cars. Yet these activities *increase* rather than decrease the tension they experience. Clearly, drive-reduction theory does not explain all motivation.

Humanistic Theory Humanistic psychologists argue that instinct theory and drive-reduction theory suggest that human behavior is mechanical and directed only toward surviving and reducing tension. According to humanistic psychologists, however, people are also motivated by the conscious desire for personal growth and artistic fulfillment. In fact, they argue, sometimes our drive to fulfill such needs outweighs our drive to meet more basic needs. For example, some people seek artistic or political goals, even though they may have difficulty affording food or may have to give up a certain level of comfort or security to achieve their goals. Some artists, musicians, and writers commit themselves to their artistic goals even when they are unable to make a living by doing so.

Abraham Maslow, one of the pioneers of humanistic psychology, pointed out that some people are willing to tolerate pain, hunger, and other kinds of tension to achieve their artistic or political goals. Hannah undoubtedly spent countless hours prac- ticing the violin and learning new songs. Humanistic theory would suggest that her desire to achieve artistic fulfillment was worth sacrificing other desirable activities, such as spending time with her friends.

Maslow claimed that people strive to fulfill their capacity for self-actualization. The term **self-actualization** refers to the need to become what one believes he or she is capable of being. The desire to fulfill oneself takes one past the point of just satisfying one's physical needs. Maslow believed that striving to become something or to do something meaningful in one's life is as essential to human well-being as food.

Maslow (1970) organized human needs into a hierarchy—a ranking of items in order of importance. (See Figure 13.1.) At the bottom of the hierarchy are biological needs. The need for self-actualization is at the top. Maslow believed that once a person's needs are satisfied at one level, the person will try to satisfy needs at the next higher level. For example, once food and drink have satisfied a person's biological needs, that person will then seek means to satisfy safety needs, such as the needs for shelter and security. Maslow believed that people rise naturally through the levels of this hierarchy as long as they do not encounter overwhelming obstacles along the way. Many people seek self-actualization through work, hobbies, and aesthetic experiences such as music, art, and poetry.

Critics of Maslow's hierarchy of needs argue that it does not apply to everyone (Neher, 1991). For example, some people show little interest in satisfying higher-level needs such as achievement and social recognition, even after their biological and safety needs have been met. But, one might ask, does their apparent lack of interest stem from not being motivated to seek achievement or from having met with overwhelming obstacles?

Sociocultural Theory Sociocultural theorists argue that even if basic drives such as hunger are inborn, cultural experiences and factors influence the behavior that people use to satisfy those drives. The foods people eat and the way they eat those foods are shaped by culture. Cultural experience affects whether people prefer hot dogs or tacos, coffee or tea, apples or pineapples. Cultural experiences also affect whether people prefer kissing lips or rubbing noses to express feelings of affection.

Maslow's Theory of the Hierarchy of Needs

Self-Actualization
fulfillment of potential

Esteem
achievement, competence, recognition, respect from others

Love and Belongingness
love, acceptance belongingness

Safety
protection from danger, security, stability

Physiological
food, water, warmth, rest

FIGURE 13.1 *Maslow believed that people begin to fulfill higher psychological needs (such as achievement) only after their basic survival needs (such as hunger and thirst) have been at least partially met.* **Do you agree or disagree?**

SECTION 1 REVIEW

go.hrw.com **Homework Practice Online**
Keyword: SY7 HP13

1. Define the following terms: *motive, need,* and *drive.*

2. Briefly summarize the four leading theories of motivation.

3. **Critical Thinking** *Supporting a Point of View* Maslow believed that people seek to satisfy basic survival needs before they seek to satisfy higher psychological needs. Use specific examples to argue for or against Maslow's theory of the hierarchy of needs.

SECTION 2

Biological Needs: Focus on Hunger

Biological needs are based mainly on body tissue needs, such as the needs for food, water, air, temperature regulation, and pain avoidance. However, even basic biological needs can be complex because they involve psychological as well as physiological factors. People need food to survive, but food can mean much more than mere survival. Food can be a symbol of the closeness of the family or group of friends, or it can be something to make a stranger feel welcome. Food can also be part of a pleasurable

A DAY IN THE LIFE social experience with others. For example, when Dan took time out from studying for his class to share a snack with Hannah's little brother Eddie, it was an enjoyable break for both of them.

The Hunger Drive

Hunger is regulated by both biological and psychological factors. In this section, we will look at the mechanisms in the body that are involved in the hunger drive. We will also examine the psychological influences that are involved in hunger.

The Role of the Mouth The acts of chewing and swallowing provide certain sensations that help satisfy the hunger drive, as shown by "sham feeding" research with dogs. In a classic research experiment, tubes were implanted in dogs' throats so that the food they swallowed was dropped out of their bodies instead of moving into their stomachs (Janowitz & Grossman, 1949). Nevertheless, the dogs stopped feeding after a brief period. Based on the finding of this and other studies, researchers have concluded that chewing and swallowing apparently help reduce feelings of hunger in animals as well as in people.

The hunger drive is usually satisfied when the body digests food and the nutrients in the food enter the bloodstream. However, this takes time. Chewing and swallowing help let the body know that its hunger drive is being satisfied, thus saving us from eating more than is needed. Still, it is wise to stop eating *before* feeling completely full because it takes time for the digestive tract to metabolize

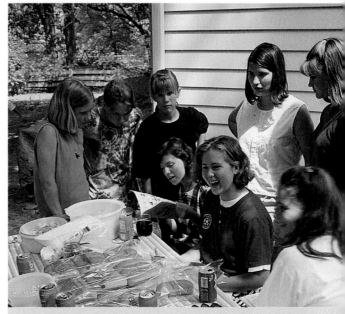

Although food is a basic biological need, it can also be part of a pleasurable social experience with others.

food and provide signals to the brain that the need for food has been satisfied.

The Role of the Stomach It was once believed that the growls and contractions (called hunger pangs) of an empty stomach were the cause of hunger. Researchers did, in fact, find that when a person is hungry, his or her stomach does contract. However, they also found that the stomach contracts at other times as well (Cannon, 1939). Furthermore, people who have surgery to remove their stomachs still experience hunger. Thus, the researchers concluded that hunger pangs felt in the stomach play a role in hunger but are not the main factor involved in signaling hunger.

The Hypothalamus The level of sugar in the blood and the part of the brain known as the hypothalamus are key influences on feelings of hunger. When people have not eaten for a while, their blood sugar level drops. Information about the sugar level is then communicated to the hypothalamus, which is known to be involved in the regulation of body temperature and various aspects of psychological motivation and emotion.

Researchers have learned more about how the hypothalamus functions through research conducted with laboratory animals. In these studies, researchers implanted electrodes on the hypothalami and observed the effects on the animals' behavior. They

MOTIVATION AND EMOTION **303**

Researchers have discovered that a part of the hypothalamus, called the ventromedial hypothalamus (VMH), serves as a "stop-eating" center. When this portion of the hypothalamus is destroyed, the rat will continue to eat until it is several times its normal weight. Eventually, the rat's food intake will level off enough to simply maintain the rat's higher weight; that is, the rat will no longer continue to gain weight.

found that the side of the hypothalamus, called the lateral hypothalamus (LH), appears to function as a "start-eating" center. If the LH is electrically stimulated, the rat will begin to eat, even if it has just finished eating a large meal (Miller, 1995). Conversely, if a lesion is made in the LH, the rat may stop eating altogether and eventually die of starvation if it is not force-fed.

The underside of the hypothalamus, called the ventromedial hypothalamus (VMH), apparently functions as a "stop-eating" center. When this center is electrically stimulated, the rat will stop eating. When this part of the hypothalamus is destroyed, the rat will continue to eat until it is several times its normal weight. The damage to the VMH interferes with the rat's ability to recognize that its hunger has been fulfilled and the rat simply continues to nibble. Eventually, the rat's eating will level off and the rat will maintain the higher weight (Miller, 1995).

Psychological Influences   Many biological factors affect the hunger drive. However, this is only part of the story. In human beings, psychological as well as biological factors affect feelings of hunger. For example, we usually eat more when we are in the presence of other people than when we are alone (Zajonc, 1965). Dan did not realize he was hungry until Eddie mentioned that he was hungry. Eddie, therefore, acted as a psychological influence on Dan's hunger drive.

A DAY IN THE LIFE

Learning that certain amounts of food or drink will produce a feeling of well-being and relaxation can cause people to eat and drink when they feel upset. For example, they may develop the habit of eating and drinking at the first sign of pressure or anxiety as a way to fend off feeling any negative emotions. People with a tendency to eat compulsively or drink alcohol excessively need to be alert to this tendency. Likewise, parents should consider whether it is wise to give children food as a reward for doing something good. Rewarding with food can cause a child to grow up associating food with parental approval, perhaps leading to dietary problems in later life.

Obesity

More than 6 out of 10 adult Americans are overweight. Moreover, 3 in 10 are obese—that is, weigh more than 30 percent greater than their recommended weight (Flegal et al., 2002). Problems with unhealthy weight gain are on the rise in the United States. For example, 60 percent of Americans were overweight in 1988–1994, but 64 to 65 percent were overweight in 1999–2000 (Flegal et al., 2002).

Obese people encounter more than their fair share of illnesses, including heart disease, stroke, diabetes, gall bladder disease, gout, respiratory problems, and certain kinds of cancer. It has been estimated that 300,000 people in the United States

Source: HAGAR THE HORRIBLE reprinted with special permission of King Features Syndicate.

die each year because of health problems related to excess weight and inactivity. Weight control is elusive for most obese people. They regain most of the weight they have lost, even when they have dieted successfully (Jeffery et al., 2000).

Losing Weight Psychologists have worked with other professionals to devise strategies to help overweight people lose weight. However, not everyone who is a few pounds overweight should be trying to slim down. For example, women in the United States today are often under social pressure to conform to an unnaturally slender feminine ideal. As a result, they tend to set unrealistic weight-loss goals (Sarwer & Madden, 1999).

Any teenager who considers going on a diet should proceed with caution because adolescents need a good deal of nourishment—perhaps more than any other age group. Adolescents should discuss the benefits and hazards of dieting with their parents and with a health professional, such as a doctor or school nurse.

A sound diet is one that is sensible, realistic, and well planned. Healthful weight-control programs do not involve fad diets such as fasting, eliminating carbohydrates, or eating excessive amounts of one particular food. Instead, they involve changes in lifestyle that include improving nutritional knowledge, decreasing caloric intake, exercising, and substituting healthful foods for harmful foods.

Most people in the United States eat too much fat and not enough fruits and vegetables. Fast foods like french fries, hamburgers, muffins, and candy tend to be particularly high in fat. Eating foods that are low in fat sets a good precedent for a lifetime of healthful eating. It is good for the heart and can also help in losing weight. Losing weight means "burning" or using more calories than you eat. Foods that are high in fat also tend to be high in calories. Nutritional knowledge helps people manage their consumption of food to take in fewer calories. Taking in fewer calories does not just mean eating smaller portions. It means switching to some lower-calorie foods—relying more on fresh, unsweetened fruits and vegetables (eating apples rather than apple pie), fish and poultry, and skim milk and cheese. It means cutting down on butter, margarine, oils, and sugar.

The same foods that help control weight—whole grains, fruits, and vegetables—also tend to be high in vitamins and fiber and low in fats. Such foods therefore may also reduce the risk of heart disease, cancer, and other illnesses.

Dieting plus exercise is more effective than dieting alone for shedding pounds and keeping them off. Exercise burns calories and builds muscle tissue, which metabolizes more calories than fatty tissue does.

Causes of Obesity Why are so many people obese? As with the hunger drive in general, both biological and psychological factors appear to contribute to obesity. Obesity seems to run in families. But does this mean that it is inherited? Not necessarily. For example, obese parents may simply encourage their children to overeat by having fattening foods around the house and by setting an example. However, research suggests that heredity plays a major role in obesity (Friedman & Brownell, 1995). One study showed that adopted children tend to more closely resemble their biological parents than their adoptive parents in terms of body weight (Stunkard et al., 1990).

MOTIVATION AND EMOTION **305**

Obese people are more likely to suffer from such health problems as heart disease, diabetes, gout, poor respiratory systems, and some types of cancer than are their slimmer counterparts.

One of the ways in which heredity may contribute to obesity is that certain people with a particular gene may not receive the biological signal that they have eaten enough to sustain them (Lindpaintner, 1995). Thus, they end up eating more than they need to.

Genes also help determine the number of fat cells a person has. People with a greater number of fat cells feel hungry sooner than people with fewer fat cells, even if they are of the same weight. When overweight people take off extra pounds, they do not reduce the number of fat cells in their body. Instead, the fat cells shrink. As they shrink, they signal the brain, triggering the hunger drive. For this reason, many people who lose weight complain that they feel hungry all the time.

People metabolize food—or burn calories—at different rates and in accordance with the amount of muscle and fat in their bodies. Since fatty tissue converts food to energy more slowly than muscle does, people with more body fat metabolize food more slowly than people who weigh the same but have a lower percentage of body fat. Men tend to have more muscle and less fat in their bodies than

women. The average man is approximately 40 percent muscle and 15 percent fat. The average woman is 23 percent muscle and 25 percent fat. Therefore, men tend to burn calories more quickly than women of the same weight. For this reason, men generally are able to lose weight more easily than women, and they can usually eat more than women can without putting on extra pounds.

Psychological factors also play a role in obesity. For example, people tend to eat more when they are under stress or experiencing certain negative emotions, such as anxiety (Cools et al., 1992; Greeno & Wing, 1994). Ironically, the stress of trying to diet can make some people want to eat even more.

Personal circumstances also affect people's ability to control their weight. For example, many people tend to overeat and ignore their diets when they are attending family gatherings, watching television, or experiencing tension at school, home, or at work (Drapkin et al., 1995).

SECTION 2 REVIEW

go.hrw.com **Homework Practice Online** Keyword: SY7 HP13

1. What is the hunger drive?
2. What is the relationship between heredity and obesity?
3. **Critical Thinking** *Analyzing Information* How might dieting actually cause the body to resist efforts to lose weight?

SECTION 3
Psychological Needs

Human beings and other organisms are motivated to reduce the tension or stimulation caused by biological drives such as hunger or thirst. The hungry person who "has a bite to eat" wants to reduce the feeling of being hungry. However, we experience psychological needs as well as biological needs. Some psychological needs motivate us to reduce tension or stimulation. Other psychological needs actually lead us to increase the amount of stimulation we experience.

Stimulus Motives

Desires for stimulation are called **stimulus motives**. Stimulus motives include sensory stimulation, activity, exploration, and manipulation of the environment. Some stimulus motives have clear survival value. Human beings and other organisms who are motivated to explore and manipulate their environments are more likely to survive (Keller & Boigs, 1991). Learning about one's surroundings increases usable information concerning resources and potential dangers. Manipulation allows people to change the environment in useful ways, thereby increasing and enhancing their chances of survival.

Sensory Deprivation During the 1950s, several student volunteers at McGill University in Montreal were paid $20 a day for participating in an experiment in which they did nothing—literally nothing. They were blindfolded and placed in small rooms (Bexton et al., 1954). Their arms were bandaged so that they could feel no tactile sensations (sensations of touch), and they could hear nothing except the dull hum of the air-conditioner. The intention of the experiment was to see how people would react to an absence of stimulation, a state referred to as **sensory deprivation**.

With nothing to do, some of the students slept. Those who remained awake began to feel bored and irritable. As the hours passed, the students felt more and more uncomfortable. Some reported having hallucinations. The study was scheduled to last for several days, but many students quit during the first day despite the monetary incentive and the desire to help in the research. Most of those who completed the study felt they had been through a terrible ordeal and, for several days after the experiment, found it difficult to concentrate on even simple matters. They reported feeling extreme boredom and disorientation for some time. The experiment demonstrated the importance of sensory stimulation to human beings.

TRUTH OR fiction
■ REVISITED ■

It is not true that "getting away from it all" by being in a place away from all sensory input is relaxing. The sensory deprivation experiments conducted at McGill University were shown to be very stressful to the participants.

Desire for Sensory Stimulation All people seek sensory stimulation, but it is clear that some need it more than others. Some people like being couch potatoes. They enjoy sitting and relaxing in front of a television set whenever possible. Other people prefer more active lifestyles. They are not happy unless they are out running or tossing a ball around.

A DAY IN THE LIFE

As Dan noted, Janet was always on the run. She seemed to be happiest when she was hiking or riding her mountain bike. Many psychologists would call Janet a sensation seeker. A sensation seeker is somebody who regularly seeks out thrilling activities such as riding mountain bikes, roller coasters, or even skydiving. They feel at their best when they are doing something active or adventurous.

It is not clear why some people seek high levels of sensation and others prefer lower levels. Inborn factors may play a role. So may learning experiences. For example, a child or adolescent whose parents ride motorcycles or skydive will be exposed to these activities at an early age. He or she may be inclined to want to try these activities.

Exploration and Manipulation

Anybody who has ever had the experience of bringing home a new cat knows that the animal's first reaction to totally new surroundings is to show anxiety. The frightened cat may hide under a bed or in a closet. However, eventually, the cat will feel adventurous enough to take a few tentative steps out. Then it will begin exploring its new surroundings. Within a few days, the cat will probably have explored every corner of the house. In this respect,

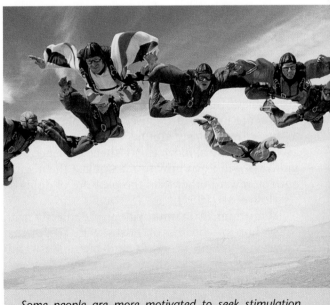
Some people are more motivated to seek stimulation than others. These people are called sensation seekers.

Both animals and humans seem to have a need to explore objects in their environments.

cats and people appear to behave in similar ways. Most people are also motivated to explore their immediate surroundings.

Once people and animals become sufficiently comfortable with their environment, they seek novel stimulation. That is, they seek new and varied experiences. For example, researchers have shown that laboratory rats who are not terribly hungry usually choose to explore unfamiliar parts of mazes rather than to head down familiar alleys directly to a food reward (Wilkie et al., 1992). Studies have also shown that monkeys learn to manipulate gadgets for the reward of being able to observe novel stimulation (Harlow et al., 1950).

Do people and animals explore and manipulate their environment because these activities help them meet their needs for food and safety? Or do they explore and manipulate these objects simply for the sake of novel stimulation? Many psychologists believe that exploration and manipulation are reinforcing in and of themselves. Monkeys appear to enjoy "monkeying around" with gadgets. If you leave mechanical devices in their presence, the monkeys will learn how to manipulate them without any reward other than the pleasure of doing so (Harlow et al., 1950).

Many human infants will play endlessly with "busy boxes"—boards or boxes with pieces that move, honk, squeak, rattle, and buzz. Most children seem to find pleasure in playing with new gadgets and discovering interesting new activities. This seems to support the view of psychologists who see the desire for novel stimulation as natural to both people and animals.

Achievement Motivation

People who are driven to get ahead, to tackle challenging situations, and to meet high personal standards of success are said to have high **achievement motivation**. For example, students who demonstrate high achievement motivation will work on difficult test items until they find the answer or run out of time. These students tend to earn higher grades than students with equal abilities but lower achievement motivation (Allen et al., 1992).

Adults with high achievement motivation may strive to move ahead in their careers. They may set challenging goals for themselves, broaden their skills, or simply recognize and take advantage of opportunities presented to them. Adults with high achievement motivation are more likely to be promoted and earn high salaries than less motivated people with similar opportunities. Research shows that people with high achievement motivation enjoy personal challenges and are willing to take moderate risks to achieve their goals (McClelland, 1965).

Types of Goals Achievement motivation can be fueled by different sources (Dweck, 1990). For some students, performance goals may be the reason for their achievement motivation. **Performance goals** are specific goals such as gaining admission to

college, earning the approval of parents or teachers, or even simply avoiding criticism. It was a performance goal—winning the science scholarship—that motivated Todd to study advanced biology.

Other students are driven mainly by learning goals. For some students, learning for learning's sake is the most powerful motivator. We call such motivators **learning goals**. People who demonstrate high achievement motivation may be influenced by more than one type of goal. For example, in addition to striving to win the scholarship, Todd enjoyed studying science.

Performance goals are usually satisfied by external or extrinsic rewards. **Extrinsic rewards** include good grades, a good income, and respect from others. On the other hand, learning goals are usually satisfied by internal or **intrinsic rewards**, such as self-satisfaction.

Development of Achievement Motivation

Where does achievement motivation come from? Parents and caregivers certainly play a crucial role. Their attitude toward achievement is instrumental in developing a child's motivation.

Research suggests that children with learning goals often have parents who encourage them to be persistent, to enjoy schoolwork, and to find their own ways to solve problems whenever possible (Ginsburg & Bronstein, 1993; Gottfried et al., 1994). Such parents create opportunities to expose their children to new and stimulating experiences. Parents of children with performance goals, on the other hand, are often more likely to reward their children with toys or money for good grades and to punish them for poor grades.

Achievement motivation can come from a variety of sources. This graduate's motivation probably includes earning the approval of parents.

Research also shows that parents of children with high achievement motivation tend to be generous with their praise when their children do well. Such parents are also less critical of their children when they do poorly (Ginsburg & Bronstein, 1993; Gottfried et al., 1994). The children themselves set high personal standards and relate their feelings of self-worth to their achievements (Dweck, 1990; Ginsburg & Bronstein, 1993).

Making Things Fit

The stimulus motives we have been discussing are examples of psychological needs aimed at increasing our level of stimulation. However, many psychological needs are aimed at reducing stimulation or tension, especially in interactions with other people. These types of psychological needs are based on people's need to maintain a balance between their personal beliefs, actions, and thoughts.

Cognitive Consistency   Cognitive theorists, such as Leon Festinger (1957) and Sandra Bem (1993), maintain that people are motivated to achieve **cognitive consistency**. That is, they seek to think and behave in a way that fits what they believe and how others expect them to think and behave. According to Festinger, people are primarily motivated to behave according to their beliefs. Therefore, a person who is politically liberal would find it difficult to support a conservative candidate. According to Bem, most girls and boys try to behave in ways that are consistent with what people expect of females and males in their society.

Most people prefer that the "pieces" of their lives fit together. They seek out as friends those who have values and interests similar to their own. As they grow older, most people try to find a set of beliefs that will help them understand the world in which they live. Most people feel better when the important relationships in their lives are stable and orderly. Two theories that address this need to create cognitive consistency are balance theory and cognitive-dissonance theory.

Balance Theory   According to **balance theory**, people need to organize their perceptions, opinions, and beliefs in a harmonious manner (Heider, 1958). They want to maintain a cognitive balance by holding consistent views and by being with people who share their beliefs and values. When the people we like share our attitudes, there is a state of balance that gives us a feeling that all is well.

A DAY IN THE LIFE

Hannah, Todd, Dan, Janet, Marc, and Linda are all very good friends. But why is this group of friends so close? According to balance theory, they have probably discovered that they share many of the same values, interests, and beliefs. Balance theory also suggests that, when we care about a person, we tend to share her or his interests. For example, prior to meeting Hannah, Dan may not have been very interested in attending a classical violin recital. However, because of his friendship with Hannah, he was introduced to, and developed positive feelings about, the things she liked.

Psychologists note that people who have strong feelings for each other, as Marc and Linda do, might be very upset to discover a major area of disagreement (Orive, 1988). Such a disharmony would place them in a state of **imbalance**. When someone we care about disagrees with us, an uncomfortable state of imbalance arises. We may attempt to end the uncomfortable state by trying to persuade the other person to change his or her attitude or by changing our feelings about the other person.

Relationships can usually survive disagreements about such things as different tastes in food or a difference of opinion about a movie. However, more basic conflicts such as over religion, politics, or personal values can create a state of imbalance.

When we dislike certain people or have no feelings toward them one way or another, their attitudes are not of much interest to us. Because we do not care about them, we are not greatly affected by the disharmony between their views and ours. We can be said to be in a state of **nonbalance**. Unlike imbalance, which tends to upset people, nonbalance usually leaves people feeling indifferent (Newcomb, 1981).

Cognitive-Dissonance Theory   Why do people find a state of imbalance uncomfortable? The answer is that most people want their thoughts and attitudes (cognitions) to be consistent with their actions. Awareness that our cognitions are inconsistent (dissonant) with our behavior is unpleasant. It causes an inner tension, which can be uncomfortable. According to **cognitive-dissonance theory**, people are motivated to reduce this inconsistency (Festinger, 1957; Festinger & Carlsmith, 1959).

Classic research on cognitive dissonance was conducted by Leon Festinger and James Carlsmith (1959). Participants in their experiment were divided into two groups. The people in one group were paid $20 to tell another person that a boring task—such as turning pegs—was interesting. The people in the second group were paid $1 to say that it was interesting. Afterward, the participants were asked to express their own feelings about the task. The people who received $1 rated the task *more* interesting than the people who were paid $20.

According to cognitive-dissonance theory, this occurred because the people who received $1 felt an inconsistency—a dissonance—between their cognition ("That was a boring task") and their action ("I just told someone that task was interesting"). The people who received $20 could easily justify lying about how they really felt about the task because doing so was worthwhile, financially. The people who received just $1 could not use that excuse. Instead, they changed their attitude about the task. By convincing themselves that the task was more interesting than it really was, they were able to reduce the inconsistency between their cognition and their action.

What happens when two people in a relationship disagree about a key issue, such as religion? A strong disagreement about an important issue can injure or even end a relationship. Cognitive-dissonance theory suggests that people having such a basic disagreement may seek to reduce the dissonance by trying to pretend that the differences between them are unimportant or even by denying that the differences exist. They may avoid thinking about those differences and put off dealing with them as long as possible.

Affiliation

Of course, if we never dealt with other people we would not need to worry about balance or cognitive dissonance. However, humans are social beings who have a need to be with other people. The desire to join with others and be part of something larger than oneself is called **affiliation**. The desire to affiliate is what prompts people to make friends, join groups, and participate in activities with others rather than by oneself. During adolescence, the motive for affiliation with one's peers is particularly strong. It is a time of life when one discovers the extent to which peers provide emotional support, useful advice, and pleasurable company.

Affiliation motivation helps keep families, groups, and nations together. However, some people are so strongly motivated to affiliate that they find it painful to be by themselves. Sometimes a strong need to affiliate may be a sign of anxiety.

Psychologist Stanley Schachter (1959) showed how anxiety increases the desire to affiliate. In a classic study, he manipulated people's anxiety levels. He told one group of people that they would be given painful electric shocks. He told another group of people that they would be given mild electric shocks. All participants were then asked to wait for the shock apparatus to be set up. They were given the choice of waiting alone or waiting in a room with other participants.

The majority (63 percent) of those who expected the painful shock chose to wait with other participants. In contrast, only one third of those who expected the mild shock chose to wait with other participants. Schachter concluded that anxiety tends to cause people to want to affiliate with other people.

TRUTH OR fiction ■ REVISITED ■

It is not true that when people feel anxious, they want to be alone. A classic experiment by Stanley Schachter found that the more anxious the participants were, the more they wanted to be with other participants.

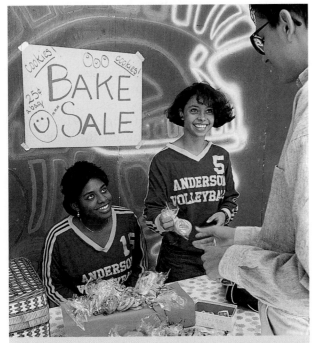

In general, individuals are motivated to make friends and participate in activities with others. This desire to join with others is known as affiliation motivation.

SECTION 3 REVIEW

Homework Practice Online
go.hrw.com
Keyword: SY7 HP13

1. What are stimulus motives?
2. Define *balance, imbalance,* and *nonbalance* in terms of balance theory.
3. **Critical Thinking** *Summarizing* What is achievement motivation, and where does it come from?

SECTION 4

Emotions

Anxiety and elation are two commonly experienced emotions. **Emotions** are states of feeling. For most people, positive emotions such as happiness and love make life worth living. Persistent negative emotions such as fear and sadness can make life difficult.

Some emotions arise in response to a situation.

At her violin recital, Hannah was anxious because she was uncertain about her ability to perform. Emotions can also motivate behavior. When Hannah remembered that her friends and family were in the audience, she felt their support and played with great confidence.

The Nature of Emotions

Emotions have biological, cognitive, and behavioral components. Strong emotions spark activity in the autonomic nervous system (LeDoux, 1997). For example, anxiety triggers activity of the sympathetic division of the autonomic nervous system. (See Chapter 3.) When people are anxious, their hearts race. They breathe rapidly, sweat heavily, and tense their muscles. The cognitive component of anxiety—the idea that something terrible might happen—may lead a person to try to escape from the situation. But where do emotions come from, and how many does the average person experience?

The ancient Chinese believed that there are four inborn (instinctive) human emotions: happiness, anger, sorrow, and fear (Carlson & Hatfield, 1992). Behaviorist John B. Watson (1924) believed that there are three instinctive emotions: fear, rage, and love. In 1932 psychologist Katherine Bridges proposed that people are born with one basic emotion: general excitement. This excitement then divides into other emotions as children develop.

Psychologist Carroll Izard (1984, 1990, 1994) suggests that all the emotions that people experience are present and distinct at birth. However, they do not all show up at once. Instead, they emerge as the child develops.

Many psychologists support Izard's view. In fact, they have found that infants show many emotions at ages earlier than those suggested by Bridges. In one study, the mothers of three-month-old babies were interviewed (Johnson et al., 1982). Results of the study revealed that 99 percent of the mothers reported that their babies showed curiosity; 95 percent of the mothers reported that the babies displayed joy; 84 percent, anger; 74 percent, surprise; and 58 percent, fear.

Questions concerning how many emotions there are, how they develop, and how they affect our lives remain unanswered (Fischer et al., 1990). Two emotions of great importance to most people, however, are happiness and anger.

Happiness William James (1902) said that the motive behind everything that people do is "how to gain, how to keep, how to recover happiness." Certainly our state of happiness or unhappiness affects nearly everything we do as well as our perception of our surroundings. People who are happy think the world is a happier, safer place (Johnson & Tversky, 1983), make decisions more readily (Isen & Means, 1983), and report greater satisfaction with their lives (Schwarz & Clore, 1983) than do people who are unhappy. When a person is unhappy, gloom seems to settle over everything he or she does. When his or her mood brightens, everything seems better—school, work, relationships, and self-image (Isen et al., 1987; Izard, 1989). It seems that happiness and unhappiness create their own momentum. When we feel good, the world looks good. But when we are feeling low, nothing seems to go right.

Moreover, many studies have found that the happier we are, the more likely we are to help others. When good things happen that lift our mood, we are more likely to volunteer our time to help other people (Khanna & Rathee, 1992).

Anger Anger is a common response to an insult or an attack. Anger can often make a person seem out of control. Angry people may even seek revenge. The ancient Roman poet Horace called anger "a short madness."

What makes people angry? In one study, participants were asked to keep a record of their experiences with anger (Averill, 1983). Most of the participants reported becoming at least moderately angry several times a week, while others became angry several times a day. Usually the anger was directed against someone close—a friend or family member—and over some alleged offense, especially if the act seemed deliberate or thoughtless. However, small annoyances such as a loud noise, an unpleasant odor, or an accidental injury can also make a person angry.

What is an effective way to handle anger? Hold it in? Lash out at the offender? The participants in Averill's study reported that when they became angry they tended to react by being assertive rather than hostile. Their anger frequently prompted them to discuss the situation with the offending person, thus easing the unpleasant feelings. Such controlled reactions are almost always more effective at reducing anger than hostile outbursts or suppression of the feelings of anger.

Facial Expressions

We often rely on the practice of "reading" people's faces. We can tell when people are happy from their smiles. We can see when they are fearful from their open mouths and the look in their eyes. We can read people's expressions and know when they are sad or surprised. Are these facial expressions of emotion instinctive, or do people learn to show these expressions to signify certain emotions on the basis of their cultural settings?

Cross-cultural evidence suggests that facial expressions are probably inborn. The ways in which many specific emotions are expressed appear to be the same around the world (Rinn, 1991). Certain facial expressions seem to suggest the same emotions in all people (Brown, 1991; Buss, 1992; Ekman, 1992, Izard, 1994). Smiling appears to be a universal sign of friendliness and approval. Baring the teeth may be a universal sign of anger. Charles Darwin, the evolution theorist, believed that the universal recognition of facial expressions had survival value by communicating motivation. For example, facial expressions could signal whether a group of approaching strangers were friendly or hostile.

In a classic study by Paul Ekman, people from around the world were asked to identify the emotions that were being expressed in a series of photographs. (The photos were of people showing anger, disgust, fear, happiness, sadness, and surprise.) Researchers interviewed people ranging

PSYCHOLOGY
IN THE WORLD TODAY

Is It Possible to Detect Lies?

For better or worse, lying is a part of life. A *New York Times* poll found that 60 percent of adults in the United States believe that it is sometimes necessary to lie, especially to protect people's feelings (Smiley, 2000). Some students lie about why they have not completed assignments. Research shows that the great majority of people lie to their boyfriends or girlfriends—most often about other relationships (Rowatt et al., 1999; Saxe, 1991). People also lie about their qualifications to obtain jobs, and some people lie when they deny guilt for crimes.

People's facial expressions often offer clues to whether or not they are telling the truth, but some people can lie with a straight face—or a smile. As Shakespeare wrote in his play *Hamlet*: "One may smile, and smile, and be a villain." The use of devices to try to detect lies has a long history. The Bedouin people of the Arabian Peninsula used to make parties involved in conflict lick a hot iron. They concluded that the one whose tongue was burned was lying. The ancient Chinese had a somewhat similar lie detection method. A person suspected of lying was made to chew rice powder and then spit it out. If the powder was dry, the suspect was judged to be guilty. The Chinese technique is, in fact, consistent with modern psychological knowledge. Anxiety about being caught in a lie is linked to activity of the sympathetic division of the autonomic nervous system. One sign of sympathetic activity is lack of saliva, or dryness in the mouth. The emotions of fear and guilt are linked to sympathetic activity, and so both of them are connected with dryness in the mouth.

In modern times, the close connection between emotions and the nervous system has led to the creation of devices called polygraphs, or lie detectors. The assumption behind the lie detector is that when somebody tells a lie, his or her body reacts in a way that can be detected with particularly sensitive equipment. Lie detectors detect something, but do they detect specific emotional responses that mean that the person is lying?

Modern lie detectors measure several signs of sympathetic activity while a witness or suspect is being questioned. These indicators include heart rate, blood pressure, rate of breathing, and perspiration. However, questions have been raised about the accuracy of assessing truth or fiction in this way (Saxe & Ben-Shakhar, 1999).

The American Polygraph Association claims that the use of the polygraph is 85 percent to 95 percent accurate. However, critics find polygraph testing to be less accurate and claim that it is sensitive to more than lies (Saxe & Ben-Shakhar, 1999). Factors such as tense muscles, drugs, and previous experience with polygraph tests can reduce their accuracy. In one experiment, people were able to reduce the accuracy of polygraph-based judgments to about 50 percent by biting their tongue to produce pain or by pressing their toes against the floor to tense muscles while being interviewed (Honts et al., 1985).

Psychologists William Iacono and David Lykken (1997) conducted a mail survey of members of the Society for Psychophysical Research and the American Psychological Association to see how much faith the members of these organizations put in polygraph testing. Response rates were high—91 percent and 74 percent, respectively. Most of the people who responded to the survey agreed on the following:

- Polygraph lie detection is not theoretically sound.
- Claims of the accuracy of polygraph testing are exaggerated.
- People can easily learn to beat the test.
- Polygraph results should not be admitted as evidence in courts of law.

It appears that no specific pattern of bodily responses pinpoints lying (Iacono & Lykken, 1997; Saxe & Ben-Shakhar, 1999). Because of problems in accuracy, results of polygraph examinations are not admitted as evidence in many courts.

Think About It

Supporting a Point of View Do you think lie detector tests are an accurate way to determine whether someone is lying? Why or why not?

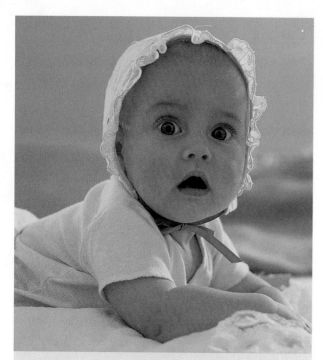

Many psychologists believe that all the emotions people experience are present at birth and that they emerge as the child develops.

from college students at a European university to tribal members in the remote highlands of New Guinea. All groups, including the New Guineans, who had had almost no contact with Americans or Europeans, agreed on the emotion that was being portrayed in each photograph (Ekman, 1982; Ekman & Friesen, 1984).

Theories of Emotion

Emotions are states of feeling that influence thought and behavior. People respond emotionally to events and situations in a variety of ways. Psychologists have different theories about what emotions are, where they come from, and how they operate.

The Opponent-Process Theory   According to the **opponent-process theory**, originated by psychologist Richard Solomon, emotions often come in pairs, with one emotion being followed by its opposite. That is, one emotion—for example, extreme happiness—tends to be followed by feelings that are opposite—for example, extreme sadness—rather than by a neutral feeling (Kimble, 1994; Solomon, 1980). Solomon and his colleague J. D. Corbitt (1974) suggested that people are inclined to

maintain balance in their emotional lives. When this balance is upset by a strong emotional response to a particular situation, an opponent process, or an opposite emotional response, occurs and eventually restores the balance.

A DAY IN THE LIFE

Although Hannah had practiced in preparation for her recital, she was anxious when she went on stage. Once she began to play, however, and focused on the music, her anxiety disappeared and was replaced by tremendous relief, even elation. The first emotion (anxiety) was followed by its opposite (relief). At the end of the performance, when she drew her bow across the strings for the final time, she knew she had played the piece very well.

The Commonsense Approach   You and most of your classmates would probably agree with a "commonsense approach" to emotions. According to this view, when something happens to a person in a certain situation, the person quickly interprets the situation. The interpretation triggers body sensations that signal a feeling, or emotion. The emotion, in turn, triggers a behavior. For example, a person who is walking down the street and encounters a large stray dog may sense that he or she is in danger. That person then feels anxious (body sensation) and quickly turns down the nearest side street to avoid the dog (behavior).

Many psychologists agree that thoughts (appraisal of the situation) come before our feelings and behavior (Lazarus, 1991). They maintain that people's appraisals of their situations are the keys to emotional response. That is, people's thoughts, feelings, and behavior are strongly intertwined, and their thoughts to some degree determine their emotional and behavioral responses.

Other psychologists, however, believe that it is important to understand the biology of emotion. According to these psychologists, the activities of the nervous system and hormones play a more important role in determining emotion than what people are thinking about their situations (Izard, 1984; Zajonc, 1984). Some psychologists even believe that people's behavior determines their thoughts and feelings. Three important theories of emotion are the James-Lange theory, the Cannon-Bard theory, and the theory of cognitive appraisal.

The James-Lange Theory   About 100 years ago, William James suggested that people's emotions follow, rather than cause, their behavioral reactions to their situations. That is, people act first and then react emotionally according to the way they acted. For example, a person crossing the street who looks up and sees a truck bearing down acts first to get out of the way, then feels fright. James would say that the emotions of fear and panic are the *result* of jumping out of the way of the truck, not the cause of the action. This theory was also proposed by the Danish biologist Karl G. Lange at about the same time. Hence, it is called the James-Lange theory of emotion.

According to James and Lange, certain situations trigger reactions, called instinctive bodily response patterns. These patterns include specific feelings and behaviors. For example, a physical threat can trigger one of two instinctive response patterns: fighting or fleeing from the situation. According to this view, people who would meet the threat by fighting would experience the emotion of anger *because* (and only *after*) they acted aggressively. People who would meet the threat by fleeing would experience the emotion of fear *because* (and *after*) they ran away from the situation. In other words, their behavior would come first, followed by the emotion that fit the behavior.

The James-Lange theory suggests that people can change their feelings by changing their behavior. Changing one's behavior to change one's feelings is an approach used in behavior therapy, a method that has been employed to treat certain psychological disorders. (See Chapter 19.)

The James-Lange theory has been criticized, however, because it downplays the role of human cognition. This theory views the cognitive appraisal of a situation as having little or no role in determining human behavior. The James-Lange theory also minimizes the role of personal values and choice as factors in human behavior.

The Cannon-Bard Theory Walter Cannon (1927) and Philip Bard (1934) suggested that emotions *accompany* the bodily responses that are aroused by an external stimulus. According to the Cannon-Bard theory, a situation triggers an external stimulus that is processed by the brain. The brain then stimulates bodily changes and cognitive activity (the experience of the emotion) simultaneously. Emotions are not produced by the bodily responses.

The central question raised by the Cannon-Bard theory is whether bodily responses and emotions do in fact occur at the same time. In some cases, it seems they do not. For example, pain or a threat may trigger bodily responses (such as rapid heartbeat) in someone before that person begins to experience distress or fear. Also, people who manage a "narrow escape" from a dangerous situation often become quite upset and shaken afterward, when they have had a chance to consider what might have happened to them. In such situations it seems that a two-stage reaction is involved—the bodily response is followed by the emotional reaction.

The Theory of Cognitive Appraisal Other theoretical approaches to emotion have focused on cognitive factors. One such theory argues that all emotions have basically similar bodily response patterns (Schachter & Singer, 1962). That is, the body reacts in physically similar ways even though different emotions are being experienced. This theory, called the theory of cognitive appraisal, maintains that the way people label an emotion depends largely on their cognitive appraisal of the situation.

Studies indicate that the facial expressions of basic emotions, such as anger, disgust, happiness, fear, sadness, and surprise, are universally recognized. What emotions do you think are being expressed in these four photographs?

Major Theories of Emotion

JAMES-LANGE

| External stimulus | Arousal and action | Evaluation of arousal and action | Experience of the emotion |

CANNON-BARD

| External stimulus | Mental processing | Experience of the emotion |

COGNITIVE APPRAISAL

| External stimulus and physiological arousal | Interpretation of arousal according to situation | Experience of the emotion |

FIGURE 13.2 *According to the James-Lange theory, emotions follow the evaluation of a bodily response. The Cannon-Bard theory maintains that bodily response and emotion occur simultaneously. The cognitive appraisal theory states that emotion is the result of the individual's evaluation of a situation.*

The cognitive appraisal that occurs is based on many factors. These factors include the person's analysis of the situation and the ways other people are reacting in the same situation. When other people are involved in the same situation, an individual will look at the way they are reacting and then compare his or her reaction to theirs to arrive at what seems to be the right response.

Critics of the theory of cognitive appraisal point out that studies designed to support the theory often yield different results when repeated (Ekman, 1993). In science, research studies must be replicated with the same methods used and similar results obtained. Since several studies designed to prove cognitive appraisal theory produced different results, some psychologists have questioned the theory's validity.

Evaluation of the Theories The theory of cognitive appraisal is quite different from the James-Lange theory. The James-Lange theory asserts that each emotion has distinct and easily recognized bodily sensations. The theory of cognitive appraisal asserts that all emotions are rooted in common bodily sensations but argues that we label these sensations differently according to the situation. The truth may lie somewhere in between.

In summary, it is possible that the bodily response patterns of different emotions are more distinct than Schachter and Singer suggested, but

are not as distinct as James and Lange suggested. In addition, research with PET scans suggests that different emotions involve different parts of the brain (Goleman, 1995). Furthermore, lack of control over our emotions and ignorance of what is happening to us appear to be distressing experiences (Zimbardo et al., 1993). Thus, it seems that our cognitive appraisals of our situations do affect our emotional responses but not to the extent envisioned by some cognitive-appraisal theorists.

People are complex, thinking beings who evaluate information both from their personal situations and from their bodily responses to their situations. Most likely, they process information from both sources to label their emotions and to decide what action to take. No one theory of emotion we have discussed applies to all people in all situations. That may not be a bad thing. People's emotions are not as easily understood or manipulated as some theorists have believed.

SECTION 4 REVIEW

go.hrw.com **Homework Practice Online**
Keyword: SY7 HP13

1. Identify three theories of emotion, and describe how each of the theories explains where emotions come from.

2. **Critical Thinking** *Analyzing Information* How have photographs of faces been used to prove the universality of emotions?

CASE STUDIES
AND OTHER TRUE STORIES

The Schachter-Singer Experiment

A classic experiment by Stanley Schachter and Jerome Singer (1962) showed that similar bodily responses can be labeled differently, depending on a person's situation. Participants were told that the purpose of the study was to examine the effects of a particular vitamin on eyesight.

Half of the participants were given an injection of adrenaline, a hormone that activates the autonomic nervous system. The other half—the control group—was given an injection of an inactive solution that had no effect on behavior. None of the participants were aware of the type of injection they received.

The participants in the group who received adrenaline were organized into three smaller groups. Group 1 was told nothing about the side effects of the adrenaline. Group 2 was told that the substance would cause itching and numbness. Group 3 was told that the injection would increase the activity of their nervous systems.

After the participants were given their injections, they were taken to a reception room and asked to wait, in pairs, for their "vision test." The participants did not know that the person with whom they were paired was a confederate—someone who was "in" on the experiment. The participants believed that the confederates had received the same injection they had. The confederates exhibited behavior that the participants would believe was caused by the injection.

Some of the participants were paired with confederates who acted in a happy-go-lucky manner. They joked, danced around, and made paper airplanes out of their questionnaires. Another set complained bitterly as they filled out their questionnaires. Some of them tore up the questionnaires and stormed out of the room. The researchers observed the reactions of the participants through a one-way mirror.

People in groups 1 and 2, who did not have accurate information about the effects of the injection, tended to imitate the confederates. Those exposed to the happy-go-lucky confederates acted happy and relaxed. Those paired with the angry confederates also tended to be angry and upset. The participants in group 3 (who had been told the truth) and the members of the control group were relatively uninfluenced by the behavior of the confederates.

Schachter and Singer concluded that those in groups 1 and 2, who felt aroused by the adrenaline injection but had no accurate information with which to interpret their bodily reactions, looked to the confederates for behavioral cues to better understand their reactions.

The participants in group 3, who were accurately informed about their adrenaline injection, expected arousal from the injection without any particular accompanying emotions. They watched as their confederates acted either happy or angry. They did not imitate the confederates because they had no reason to expect happiness or anger to be one of the consequences of receiving their adrenaline injection. Likewise, the participants in the control group were not inclined to imitate the behavior of the confederates. Since they had not been given adrenaline, they had no reactions that needed to be explained.

The experiment suggested those participants who had no way to interpret their reaction to the injection began feeling and acting the way they had been prompted. The experiment supports Schachter and Singer's theory that the body reacts in physically similar ways even though different emotions are being experienced. It also suggests that we interpret our emotions according to the behavior of those around us.

THINKING CRITICALLY

1. **Finding the Main Idea** What conclusions did Schachter and Singer draw from their experiment?
2. **Evaluating** Do you think you interpret your emotions according to the behavior of the people around you?

13 REVIEW

Writing a Summary

Using standard grammar, spelling, sentence structure, and punctuation, summarize the information in this chapter. Consider:
- theories of motivation and the causes of obesity
- stimulus and achievement motives, and theories of emotion

Identifying People and Ideas

Identify the following terms or people and use them in appropriate sentences.

1. motive
2. instincts
3. obese
4. stimulus motives
5. sensory deprivation
6. extrinsic rewards
7. cognitive consistency
8. balance theory
9. affiliation
10. emotions

Understanding Main Ideas

SECTION 1 (pp. 300–302)
1. How do biological and psychological needs differ?

SECTION 2 (pp. 303–306)
2. Why is knowledge of nutrition important as a strategy for weight loss?

SECTION 3 (pp. 306–311)
3. What are two examples of stimulus motives, and why are they important?

SECTION 4 (pp. 311–316)
4. What term explains why a person might feel "on top of the world" one day and "down in the dumps" another day?

Thinking Critically

1. **Drawing Inferences and Conclusions** Why is the instinct theory not used to explain human motivation?

2. **Comparing and Contrasting** How do the different theories of motivation explain why some people engage in high-risk behavior while other people prefer to avoid potentially dangerous situations?

3. **Evaluating** Why is sensory deprivation an important concept in the study of human motivation and emotion?

4. **Analyzing Information** List an example of the James-Lange and Cannon-Bard theories of emotion.

Writing About Psychology

1. **Supporting a Point of View** Imagine that a local school board is contemplating cutting all high school sports and extracurricular activities. Money, school officials say, should be spent on essentials such as books and equipment, teachers' salaries, and building maintenance. Write a letter to the school board in which you argue in favor of retaining extracurricular activities. Use your knowledge of humanistic theory of motivation to support your point of view.

2. **Analyzing Information** Identify a person in your school or community who has worked hard to achieve a specific goal. Interview that person and try to determine the motivation behind his or her success. Also find out if the person gave up anything or had to overcome obstacles to achieve his or her goal. Write a brief report summarizing your findings. Be sure to use standard grammar, spelling, sentence structure, and punctuation. Use the graphic organizer below to help you write your report.

Motivation → Obstacles → Goal

Interpreting Charts

Study the chart below. Then use the information in the chart to help you answer the questions that follow.

Percentage of Overweight Individuals Among U.S. Adolescents

5%   14%

1963–70   1999

Source: U.S. Surgeon General, 2001 Report on Overweight and Obesity

1. Which of the following statements can be drawn from the information presented in the chart above?
   a. Children are more obese than any other age group in American society.
   b. Diseases caused by obesity are leading killers of young people.
   c. Obesity is on the rise among young people in the United States.
   d. The United States leads the world in the number of obese children.

2. What cultural factors might psychologists point to in an effort to explain the information in the chart?

Analyzing Primary Sources

Read the following excerpt, in which Abraham Maslow describes people who are psychologically healthy. Then answer the questions that follow.

❝It would convey the wrong impression to say that they are self-satisfied. What we must say rather is that they can take the frailties and sins, weaknesses, and evils of human nature in the same unquestioning spirit with which one accepts the characteristics of nature. One does not complain about water because it is wet, or about rocks because they are hard, or about trees because they are green. As the child looks out upon the world with wide, uncritical, undemanding, innocent eyes, simply noting and observing what is the case, without either arguing the matter or demanding that it be otherwise, so does the self-actualizing person tend to look upon human nature in himself and in others.❞

1. With which of the following statements would Maslow most likely agree?
   a. Self-actualized people see human nature as it is, not as they want it to be.
   b. Self-actualized people behave like children.
   c. Self-actualized people like to go on nature hikes.
   d. Self-actualization requires people to try to change themselves and the world around them.

2. Drawing upon information in the excerpt, what is Maslow's concept of human nature?

PSYCHOLOGY PROJECTS

Cooperative Learning

Applying Psychology Working in small groups, prepare a chart about the four theories of motivation (Instinct Theory, Drive-Reduction Theory, Humanistic Theory, and Sociocultural Theory). Apply the various perspectives of motivation to a given economic situation. For example, you might want to consider the choice of car to purchase, personal budget priorities, and the choice of job. Present your chart to the class.

internet connect

Internet Activity: go.hrw.com
KEYWORD: SY7 CH13
Choose an activity on motivation and emotion to:
- create a comic strip to show cognitive consistency, balance, or cognitive-dissonance theory.
- apply various perspectives of motivation to a given economic situation.
- create a brochure that illustrates psychological and biological aspects of obesity.

14

THEORIES OF PERSONALITY

Read to Discover

1 What are the main features and limitations of the trait theory of personality?

2 What impact has the psychoanalytic theory of personality had, and how has the theory been modified since Freud's time?

3 What do learning theorists believe are the influences on and motivations for behavior?

4 How does the humanistic approach view the role of the self and free choice in shaping behavior?

5 How does the sociocultural approach view the importance of ethnicity, gender, culture, and socioeconomic status in the development of personality?

A DAY IN THE LIFE

Janet and Todd were having lunch together, and Todd, as usual, kept joking around. "Hey, Janet, look! Over there," Todd said as he stole one of her pretzels.

"I can't believe you're still pulling that same joke," Janet laughed.

"Well, I can't believe you're still falling for it," joked Todd. "You are so gullible."

"I'm not gullible; I'm just trusting," Janet said laughing. Just then Hannah came running up.

"Janet, Todd—I'm so glad I found you both. I have the best news!" Hannah was talking so fast they could barely understand her.

"Hannah, calm down a second. What's going on?" Janet asked.

"Mr. Hochberg just called me into his office because he said he had some news for me. Remember my violin recital last week?" Hannah asked, still trying to talk slowly. "Well, there was an arts foundation representative there, and she offered me a performing arts scholarship to almost any college I choose!"

"Hannah, that's great!" Janet exclaimed. "I always knew you could do it. Where do you think you'll go?"

"Well, I'm thinking about going to the same school where my brother goes. He loves it there. He said that there's a large Korean population. My parents have always raised us both to understand our heritage, but it will be really cool to meet lots of other people with the same background."

"Have you told your parents yet?" Todd asked.

"No, not yet. I want to tell them at the same time, and they're both at work right now," Hannah answered. "It would make them so happy if my brother and I were at the same school. It means a lot to them that we keep the family together as much as possible."

"Well, Hannah, congratulations," said Todd. "But you have to promise that you won't forget about us when you become a famous violinist!"

"Don't be silly," Hannah smiled. "Would I do a thing like that?"

- - -

Would Hannah do a thing like that? What influences the things people do and do not do? Some people might say that the answer is found in personality. But what exactly is personality? When people think of a person's personality, they usually think of the person's most striking characteristics, as in an "assertive personality" or an "artistic personality." Psychologists define **personality** as the patterns of feelings, motives, and behavior that set people apart from one another.

Psychologists seek to describe personality characteristics and to explain how personality develops. They try to predict how different people will respond to life's demands. In this chapter, we explore five approaches to the study of personality: trait theory, psychoanalytic theory, learning theory, humanistic theory, and sociocultural theory.

personality

trait

introverts

extroverts

id

ego

superego

defense mechanisms

repression

rationalization

displacement

regression

projection

reaction formation

denial

sublimation

collective unconscious

archetypes

inferiority complex

socialization

self-concept

congruence

acculturation

HOLT

Psychology Video Program

Watch the video to explore the personalities of great American presidents.

SECTION 1

The Trait Approach

A **trait** is an aspect of personality that is considered to be reasonably stable. We assume that a person has certain traits based on how the person behaves. If you describe a friend as shy, it may be because you have seen your friend looking anxious and trying to escape social encounters. Traits are assumed to account for consistent behavior in different situations. You would probably expect your shy friend to act withdrawn in most social situations. Todd, on the other hand, was constantly making jokes with

A DAY IN THE LIFE

his friends. Therefore, we might conclude that being outgoing and being humorous are two of Todd's personality traits. But if Todd made jokes only around his friends, we would not consider him to have these traits.

Trait theorists have generally assumed that traits are somehow fixed or unchanging. However, the question of where traits come from has been pondered through the ages.

Hippocrates

An early answer to where traits come from was offered by the ancient Greek physician Hippocrates. The ancient Greeks believed that the body contains fluids called humors. Hippocrates suggested that traits are a result of different combinations of these bodily fluids.

Hippocrates believed that there are four basic fluids, or humors, in the body:

- yellow bile, which was associated with a choleric, or quick-tempered, disposition
- blood, which was connected with a sanguine, or warm and cheerful, temperament
- phlegm, which was linked with a phlegmatic, or sluggish and cool, disposition
- black bile, which was associated with a melancholic, thoughtful temperament

Certain diseases and disorders were believed to reflect a lack of balance in these humors. Methods such as bloodletting (the removal of blood from the body) and vomiting were recommended to restore the balance of fluids and one's health. Although there is no scientific evidence for Hippocrates' biological theory, the terms based on his ideas remain in use today. A cheerful person, for example, may still be called sanguine.

Gordon Allport

In the 1930s, psychologist Gordon Allport (1897–1967) searched through a dictionary to find every term that could describe a person (Allport & Odbert, 1936). He cataloged some 18,000 human traits from a search through lists of descriptive words. Some of the words, such as *short* and *brunette*, describe physical traits. Others, such as *shy* and *emotional*, describe behavioral traits. Still others, such as *honest*, concern morality.

Allport assumed that traits can be inherited and that they are fixed in the nervous system. He conducted thorough and detailed studies of individuals, noting their outstanding traits as well as their behaviors. Allport's research led him to conclude that traits are the building blocks of personality. He believed that a person's behavior is a product of his or her particular combination of traits (Allport, 1937, 1961, 1965, 1966).

Hans Eysenck

British psychologist Hans J. Eysenck (1916–1997) focused on the relationships between two personality dimensions: introversion-extroversion and emotional stability-instability. **Introverts** tend to be imaginative and to look inward rather than to other people for their ideas and energy. **Extroverts**, on the other hand, tend to be active and self-expressive and gain energy from interaction with other people. The contrast between introversion and extroversion was first pro-

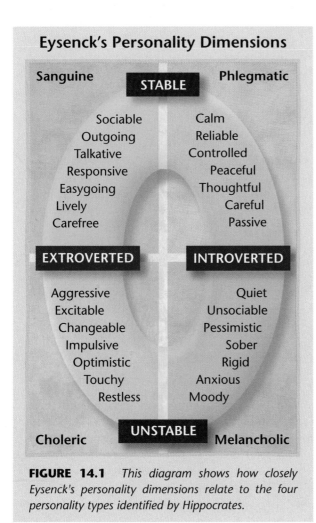

Eysenck's Personality Dimensions

STABLE

Sanguine

Sociable
Outgoing
Talkative
Responsive
Easygoing
Lively
Carefree

Phlegmatic

Calm
Reliable
Controlled
Peaceful
Thoughtful
Careful
Passive

EXTROVERTED

Aggressive
Excitable
Changeable
Impulsive
Optimistic
Touchy
Restless

INTROVERTED

Quiet
Unsociable
Pessimistic
Sober
Rigid
Anxious
Moody

Choleric

UNSTABLE

Melancholic

FIGURE 14.1 *This diagram shows how closely Eysenck's personality dimensions relate to the four personality types identified by Hippocrates.*

posed by Carl Jung, whom you will read about later in this chapter. Stable people are usually reliable, composed, and rational. Unstable people can be agitated and unpredictable.

Eysenck cataloged various personality traits according to where those traits appear within the dimensions of introversion-extroversion and emotional stability-instability. (See Figure 14.1 above.) For instance, an anxious person might be highly introverted and emotionally unstable. A reckless or impulsive person might be highly extroverted and unstable (Eysenck, 1953).

Eysenck's scheme is similar to the one suggested by Hippocrates. According to Eysenck's dimensions, the choleric type would be extroverted and unstable; the sanguine type, extroverted and stable; the phlegmatic type, introverted and stable; and the melancholic type, introverted and unstable.

The Five-Factor Model

The "big five" may sound like a description of a basketball team. In psychology, however, the term refers to recent research suggesting that there may be five basic personality factors. These include the two found by Eysenck—extroversion and emotional stability—along with conscientiousness, agreeableness, and openness to experience. (See Figure 14.2 on p. 324.) Many personality theorists, particularly Robert McCrae and Paul T. Costa, Jr., have helped in the development of the Five-Factor Model. Cross-cultural research has found that these five factors appear to define the personality structure of American, German, Portuguese, Jewish, Chinese, Korean, and Japanese people (McCrae & Costa, 1997). A study of more than 5,000 German, British, Spanish, Czech, and Turkish people suggests that the factors are related to people's basic temperaments, which are considered to be largely inborn (McCrae et al., 2000). The researchers interpreted the results to suggest that our personalities tend to mature rather than be shaped by environmental conditions, although personality traits are affected by culture. For example, a person who is open to new experience is likely to behave less openly in a restrictive society than in an open society.

A great deal of research is currently underway on the Five-Factor Model. There are hundreds of studies relating scores on the five factors, according to a psychological test constructed by Costa and McCrae (the NEO Five-Factor Inventory™), with various behavior patterns, psychological problems, and kinds of personalities. For example, consider driving. Research shows that people who are given more traffic tickets and who get into more accidents tend to score lower on the factor of agreeableness than do others (Cellar et al., 2000). In other words, it is safer to share the freeway with agreeable people. People who get along with nearly everybody tend to score low on conscientiousness—that is, they do not examine other people too closely, and high on agreeableness—they tend to go along with what other people want (Bernardin et al., 2000).

The Five-Factor Model also has been used to study politics. For example, studies in the United States (Butler, 2000), Belgium, and Poland (van Hiel et al., 2000) show that people who are authoritarians or dictators tend to score low on openness to experience—that is, they do not want people reading too much or watching the news too much.

Researchers are also studying how the five factors relate to the ways in which people interact with their friends and families (e.g., Wan et al., 2000;

The Five-Factor Model

Factor	Name	Traits
I	Extroversion	Contrasts talkativeness, assertiveness, and activity with silence, passivity, reserve
II	Agreeableness	Contrasts kindness, trust, and warmth with hostility, selfishness, and distrust
III	Conscientiousness	Contrasts organization, thoroughness, and reliability with carelessness, negligence, and unreliability
IV	Emotional Stability-Instability	Contrasts reliability and coping ability with nervousness, moodiness, and sensitivity to negative events
V	Openness to Experience	Contrasts imagination, curiosity, and creativity with shallowness and lack of perceptiveness

FIGURE 14.2 *The Five-Factor Model may be useful for helping people who suffer from a variety of psychological disorders.*

Wintre & Sugar, 2000). In the field of psychological problems, researchers are studying links between the five factors and a variety of disorders. These include anxiety disorders (Clarke et al., 1994), thinking that one is ill when there is no medical basis for the belief (Cox et al., 2000), depression and suicide attempts (Duberstein et al., 2000), schizophrenia (Gurrera et al., 2000), and personality disorders (Widiger & Costa, 1994). The Five-Factor Model helps in describing these disorders. It remains to be seen how well the model will enable psychologists to explain the disorders and control them—that is, prevent them or help people who develop them.

Psychologists continue to disagree about which personality factors are the most basic. However, nearly all psychologists would agree that the "big five" personality dimensions are important in defining a person's psychological makeup. Moreover, a person's position along these dimensions tends to be established at an early age and then remains stable through life.

Evaluation of the Trait Approach

One shortcoming of the trait approach is that it describes personality but does not explain where traits come from. The efforts of Allport and other trait theorists to link personality traits to biological factors have not been successful. Today trait theory focuses on describing traits rather than tracing their origins or investigating how people with certain traits can change for the better.

The work of trait theorists has, however, had a number of practical applications. In suggesting that there are links between personalities, abilities, and interests, trait theorists have alerted us to the value of matching people to educational programs and jobs on the basis of their personality traits.

SECTION 1 REVIEW

go.hrw.com **Homework Practice Online** Keyword: SY7 HP14

1. List the main features of the trait theory of personality.
2. List the "big five" personality factors.
3. **Critical Thinking** *Evaluating* What are the limitations of the trait theory?

SECTION 2

The Psychoanalytic Approach

The psychoanalytic approach to personality teaches that all people—even the most well-adjusted—undergo inner struggles. According to this approach, people are born with certain biological drives such as aggression, sex, and the need for superiority. These drives, however, may come into conflict with laws, social norms, and moral codes that have previously been internalized. At any moment, a person's behavior, thoughts, and emotions represent the outcome of inner contests between the opposing forces of drives and rules.

Sigmund Freud

The "inner conflict" approach to personality theory owes its origin to Sigmund Freud (1856–1939). Freud was trained as a physician. Early in his practice in Vienna, Austria, he was astounded to find that some people had lost feeling in a hand or had become paralyzed in the legs even though nothing was medically wrong with them. When Freud interviewed these individuals, he found that many things in their lives were making them very angry or anxious. Yet they refused to recognize their emotional or social problems. They were at the mercy of very powerful inner emotions, yet on the surface they seemed calm.

In psychoanalysis, the client is made comfortable, usually on a couch similar to Freud's original couch, which is shown here.

TRUTH OR fiction ▪ R E V I S I T E D ▪

It is true that people can lose feeling in their hands or legs even though nothing is medically wrong with them. Sigmund Freud directly observed such ailments.

Freud believed that conscious ideas and feelings occupy only a small part of the mind. Many of people's deepest thoughts, fears, and urges remain out of their awareness. These urges are pushed into an unconscious part of the mind.

One way in which Freud explored the unconscious is through psychoanalysis. In psychoanalysis, people are encouraged to talk about anything that pops into their minds. They do so in a comfortable and relaxed setting. The people Freud observed—those who had lost feeling in their hands or legs—regained much of their functioning when they talked about the things that were on their minds. For this reason, psychoanalysis has been called a "talking cure."

Freud also explored the unconscious through dream analysis. He believed that people experience unconscious wishes in their dreams—often in disguised form. Freud would ask people to record their dreams upon waking. He would then help them explore the dreams' possible hidden meanings.

Another technique that Freud used was hypnosis. He felt that people in a hypnotic state had better access to their unconscious thoughts. Freud eventually abandoned hypnosis, however, because many people later denied the things they said when they were in a hypnotic state.

Id, Ego, and Superego

Freud believed that the mind has three basic psychological structures: the id, the ego, and the superego. The id is like the stereotypical two-year-old: "I want what I want, and I want it now." The **id** represents basic drives such as hunger. It demands pleasure through instant gratification and pays no attention to laws, social customs, or the needs of others. It follows what Freud called the *pleasure principle*—the urge for an immediate release of energy or emotion that will bring personal gratification, relief, or pleasure.

According to Freud, the id is present at birth. The **ego**, however, develops because a child's demands for instant gratification cannot be met or because meeting these demands may be harmful. Freud wrote that the ego "stands for reason and good sense" (1964). It is guided by the *reality principle*—the understanding that in the real world we cannot always get what we want.

Calvin and Hobbes   by Bill Watterson

The ego seeks to satisfy the appetites of the id in ways that are consistent with reality. For example, the id lets you know that you are hungry, but the ego lets you know that certain ways of satisfying your hunger—such as cooking a hamburger—are more appropriate than others—such as eating raw hamburger. The ego also provides the conscious sense of self. Activities such as planning dinner and studying for a test are functions of the ego.

Although most of the ego is conscious, some of its business is carried out unconsciously. For instance, the ego acts as a censor that screens out the wild impulses of the id. When the ego senses that indecent or improper impulses are rising into awareness, it tries to repress them.

The third psychological structure Freud formulated is the **superego**. The superego develops throughout early childhood. It functions according to the *moral principle*. By incorporating the standards and values of parents and members of the community, the superego provides us with our moral sense. The superego acts as the conscience and floods the ego with feelings of guilt and shame when we think or do something that society defines as wrong.

The ego does not have an easy job. It is caught between the conflicting messages of the id and the superego. For example, the id may urge, "You want to go out with your friends. Don't study now!" while the superego warns, "You have to study or you will not pass the test." According to Freud, people with healthy egos—and thus healthy personalities—find ways to balance the id's demands and the superego's warnings. In this case, the healthy ego would probably conclude, "Study now, and after you do well on the test, you can spend time with your friends."

Defense Mechanisms

According to Freud, **defense mechanisms** are methods the ego uses to avoid recognizing ideas or emotions that may cause personal anxiety. These defenses operate unconsciously.

Repression   One of the main Freudian defense mechanisms is repression. **Repression** removes anxiety-causing ideas from conscious awareness by pushing them into the unconscious. To explain repression, Freud compared people's personalities to teakettles. Primitive urges such as aggression seek expression just like steam tries to escape from a boiling kettle. But acknowledging these urges would cause a person serious feelings of guilt, anxiety, and shame. Thus, the urges are repressed to keep the lid on the boiling kettle.

Repression, however, is not always successful. When enough steam builds up inside, the teakettle pops its lid. When people "pop their lids," the results are outbursts of anger and the development of other psychological and emotional problems.

Rationalization   Other defense mechanisms protect us from unacceptable ideas in a different manner. They do not completely repress such ideas, but they distort them in one way or another. One such defense mechanism is **rationalization**—the use of self-deception to justify unacceptable behaviors or ideas. For instance, a student who cheats during a test may explain, "I only cheated on a couple of questions—I knew most of the material."

Displacement   According to Freudian theorists, **displacement** is defined as the transfer of an idea or impulse from a threatening or unsuitable object to a less threatening object. For example, a football player who is yelled at by his coach may go home and yell at his little brother.

Regression   Freud believed that when an individual is under a great deal of stress he or she will return to behavior that is characteristic of an earlier stage of development. He termed this behavior **regression**. For example, an adolescent may pout and refuse to speak to her parents when forbidden to go out with friends. Similarly, an adult may become highly dependent on his parents following the breakup of his own marriage.

Projection   A motion picture projector thrusts an image outward onto a screen. Freud believed that people sometimes deal with unacceptable impulses by projecting these impulses outward onto other people. In other words, people see *their own* faults in other people. For example, hostile people, unable to think of *themselves* as hostile, may accuse other people of hostility. As a result of this **projection**, they may think of the world as a dangerous place.

Reaction Formation   People who use the defense of **reaction formation** act contrary to their genuine feelings in order to keep their true feelings hidden. A person who is angry with a coworker may behave in a "sickly sweet" manner toward that coworker. Someone who is unconsciously attracted to another person may keep the impulses out of mind by being mean to that person.

Denial   In the mechanism of **denial**, a person refuses to accept the reality of anything that is bad or upsetting. For example, people who smoke cigarettes may ignore the risks of lung cancer and heart disease from smoking because they think, "It can't happen to me."

Sublimation   Freud also believed that individuals can channel their basic impulses into socially acceptable behavior through a process called **sublimation**. For example, a hostile student may channel aggressive impulses into contact sports.

Effects of Defense Mechanisms   According to Freud, when used in moderation, defense mechanisms may be normal and even useful to protect people from painful feelings such as anxiety, guilt, and shame. Such defense mechanisms become unhealthy, he said, when they lead a person to ignore the underlying issues causing those feelings. However, Freud also noted that a person with a strong and healthy ego is able to balance the id and the superego without the use of such mechanisms. Therefore, the use of defense mechanisms may indicate the presence of inner conflict or personal anxiety.

Stages of Development

Freud believed that an individual's personality develops through a series of five stages. These stages of development begin at birth and continue to shape human personality through adolescence. He believed that people instinctively seek to preserve and extend life. He also thought that these instinctive efforts to survive are aided by a psychological energy he labeled libido. (*Libido* is the Latin word for "desire.")

Freud organized psychological development into five periods: oral, anal, phallic, latent, and genital. Children were said to encounter conflicts during each stage. If the conflicts were not resolved, Freud believed that the child might become fixated, or stuck, at an early stage of development. The child would then carry that stage's traits into adulthood. Thus, Freud believed that an adult's psychological problems might actually stem from unresolved childhood conflicts.

The Oral Stage   In Freud's theory, psychological development begins in the first year of life. He noted that infants are continually exploring their

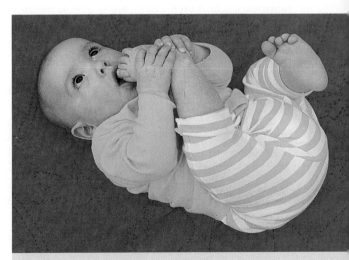

During the oral stage of development, an infant's first reaction to many objects is often to suck on them.

CASE STUDIES

AND OTHER TRUE STORIES

Identifying with the Team: "We're Number One!"

Think about when fall arrives each year. Cool air sweeps across the Great Plains. Across parts of the country, leaves turn rich hues of red and gold. And on hundreds of high school and college campuses, football teams, cheerleading squads, and marching bands can be heard practicing for the big game. Why is that football game so important? Does it really matter who wins or loses the game?

Psychologically speaking, it matters quite a lot. Many people form deep and lasting bonds of attachment with sports teams. Once fans identify with a team, their self-esteem rises and falls with the team's wins and losses (Cialdini, 2000; Wann et al., 2000; Wann & Waddill, 2003). When the team's fortunes are up, its fans feel up. When the team's fortunes are down, its fans feel down. At least, that is the message according to the research of personality, social, and sports psychologists.

For example, Arizona State psychologist Robert Cialdini found that college students were more likely to wear university-identifying clothes—such as sweatshirts bearing the school's name—on Mondays after the football team won. In addition, when asked, students described the team's wins and losses differently. When the team won, students typically said, "We won!" When the team lost, students would say, "They lost." In other words, the college students identified with the winners more than with the losers.

Freud's psychoanalytic theory suggests that children identify with parents and other "big" people in their lives. The reason for this identification is that "big" people seem to hold the keys to the resources needed for survival and excitement. Perhaps for similar reasons, entertainers have their fan clubs. Such fan clubs are filled with people who wish to connect their own smaller lights with the brilliant suns of their stars.

According to evolutionary psychologists, teams and sports heroes provide not only entertainment but the kind of gutsy competition that still whispers to us from our genes. These genetic whisperings push us toward aggression and the desire to rise to the top of the heap. If we cannot rise to the top on our own, we can do so *through* someone else.

Evolutionary psychologists also connect adoration of sports heroes to a time when people lived in small tribes and their warrior-protectors shared much of their genetic heritage. Today college and professional athletes may differ quite a bit from the rest of us, genetically speaking. Fans, however, can still identify with and worship their heroes, even if fans also recognize that doing so is silly. "Our sports heroes are our warriors," notes Cialdini (2000). "Whoever you root for represents you," he concludes.

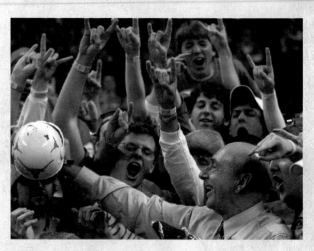

Fans celebrate a victory.

THINKING CRITICALLY

1. **Contrasting** According to Cialdini, how do college students' attitudes when the team is winning differ from their attitudes when the team is losing?

2. **Evaluating** Of the theories provided for why people identify so closely with sports teams, which one do you most agree with? Why?

world by picking up objects and putting those objects into their mouths. Infants also receive their main source of pleasure—food—with their mouths. For these reasons, Freud termed the first stage of development the oral stage. He theorized that the infant's survival is dependent on the attention of adults. A child whose caretakers do not meet his or her needs during this stage may become fixated at the oral stage. Some examples of this fixation might include smoking, overeating, excessive talking, and nail biting. In addition, as an adult, such a person might be inclined to have clinging, dependent interpersonal relationships.

TRUTH OR fiction • REVISITED • *It is true that according to Freud's theory, biting one's fingernails and smoking cigarettes are signs of early childhood conflicts. Such behavior might reflect fixation at the* oral stage of development.

The Anal Stage According to Freud, the anal stage occurs between the ages of one and a half and two and a half. During this stage, children learn that they can control their own bodily functions, and the general issue of self-control becomes a vital issue to children. Conflict during the anal stage can lead to two sets of adult personality traits. So-called anal-retentive traits involve an excessive use of self-control. They include perfectionism and excessive needs for order and cleanliness. People with anal-expulsive traits, on the other hand, are less restrained and may be careless and messy.

The Phallic Stage The third year of life marks the beginning of the phallic stage. Young girls and boys begin to discover the physical differences between the two sexes and become more focused on their own bodies. Children may also develop strong attachments to the parent of the opposite sex. At the same time, they may view the same-sex parent as a rival for the other parent's affections. Freud argued that the complex emotions of the phallic stage can lead to several psychological disorders later in life, including depression, excessive guilt, and anxiety.

The Latency Stage By the age of five or six, Freud believed, children would have been in conflict with their parents for several years. At this

Pictured here is a mandala, the symbol Carl Jung used to represent the collective nature, or oneness, of human experience.

point, they would retreat from the conflict and repress all aggressive urges. In so doing, they would enter the latency stage. *Latent* means "hidden," and during the latency period, impulses and emotions remain hidden, or unconscious.

The Genital Stage Freud wrote that people enter the final stage of psychological development, or the genital stage, at puberty. The adolescent does not generally encounter any new psychological conflicts during this period but does become more aware of his or her own gender identity. Instead, the conflicts of the early development stages resurface.

Carl Jung

Sigmund Freud had several intellectual heirs. The best known of these theorists was Carl Jung (1875–1961). Jung was a Swiss psychiatrist who had been a colleague of Freud's. He fell into disfavor with Freud, however, when he developed his own psychoanalytic theory—known as *analytic psychology*—which places a greater emphasis on the influences of mysticism and religion on human behavior.

Jung, like Freud, was intrigued by unconscious processes. But he dramatically altered Freud's theory of these processes. Jung believed that people

The deity is an example of an archetype. Although most cultures believe in deities, specific forms vary. Shown here are sculptures of the Aztec god Quetzalcoatl (left) and the Hindu god Rama (right).

TRUTH
OR
fiction
■ REVISITED ■

It is true that according to Jung, people can remember things that never happened to them personally. Jung believed that in addition to individual memory, all human beings share a collective unconscious in which we carry a store of some primitive concepts. He called these concepts archetypes.

Jung believed that every person's conscious sense of self can be characterized by four functions of the mind—thinking, feeling, intuition, and sensation. He argued that all four of these elements exist in every individual's unconscious. However, an individual can be identified by the function that becomes his or her primary form of expression. He thought that people could form healthy personalities by bringing together, or integrating, these conscious elements with the collective unconscious archetypes. His name for this integrating process is *individuation.*

Many psychologists consider Jung's theory of the collective unconscious to be mystical and unscientific. But Jungian theory has developed a tremendous following among the general public. Many people enter Jungian analysis to examine their dreams and to work toward individuation. Scholars explore the use of archetypical symbols as they appear in literature and the arts. In addition, Jung's focus on myth has made his theory very popular with those interested in the study of religion.

Alfred Adler

Alfred Adler (1870–1937) was another follower of Freudian psychoanalysis. Adler believed that people are basically motivated by a need to overcome feelings of inferiority. To describe these feelings of inadequacy and insecurity, Adler coined the term **inferiority complex**.

In some people, Adler theorized, feelings of inferiority may be based on physical problems and the need to compensate for them (Adler, 1927). This theory may have developed in part from Adler's own attempts to overcome repeated bouts of illness. As a child, Adler was crippled by a disease called rickets and suffered from pneumonia.

Physical problems are not the only source of feelings of inferiority, according to Adler. He believed that all of us have some feelings of inferiority

have not only a personal unconscious that stores material that has been forgotten or repressed but also an inherited collective unconscious. According to Jung, the **collective unconscious** is a store of human concepts shared by all people across all cultures (Jung, 1917, 1936).

The structural components of the collective unconscious are basic, primitive concepts, called archetypes. **Archetypes** are ideas and images of the accumulated experience of all human beings. Examples of archetypes include the supreme being, the young hero, the fertile and nurturing mother, the wise old man, the hostile brother, and even fairy godmothers, wicked witches, and themes of rebirth or resurrection. Jung found that each of these concepts appears in some form across most cultures and religions (Jung, 1936).

Jung argued that although these images remain unconscious, they often appear to us as figures in our dreams. He declared that these images influence our thoughts and feelings and that they help form a foundation on which personality develops. Despite his interest in the collective unconscious, Jung granted more importance to conscious thoughts than Freud did. Jung believed that one archetype is the sense of self. According to Jung, the self is a unifying force of personality that gives people direction and provides a sense of completeness.

because of our small size as children. He thought that these feelings give rise to a drive for superiority. Adler also introduced the term *sibling rivalry* to describe the jealousies that are often found among brothers and sisters.

Adler, like Jung, believed that self-awareness plays a major role in the formation of personality. Adler spoke of a creative self. The creative self is self-aware and strives to overcome obstacles and develop the individual's unique potential. President Theodore Roosevelt exemplified this personality. Roosevelt was a frail child who became not only president but also a strong and robust man. Similarly, football quarterback Boomer Esiason, who suffered from juvenile arthritis, overcame his disease to become a professional athlete.

Karen Horney

Karen Horney (HAWR-ny), who lived from 1885 to 1952, agreed with Freud that childhood experiences play a major role in the development of adult personality. She believed that the greatest influences on personality are social relationships.

Horney, like Freud, saw parent-child relationships to be of paramount importance (Horney, 1937). Small children are completely dependent. When their parents treat them with indifference or harshness, children develop feelings of insecurity that Horney termed *basic anxiety*. Because children also resent neglectful parents, Horney theorized that feelings of hostility would accompany the anxiety. Horney agreed with Freud that children would repress rather than express feelings of hostility because they would fear driving their parents away. In contrast to Freud, however, she also believed that genuine and consistent love could temper the effects of even the most painful childhoods.

Erik Erikson

Like Horney, Erik Erikson (1902–1994) believed that social relationships are the most important factors in personality development (Erikson, 1950). He placed great emphasis on the general emotional climate of the mother-infant relationship. Erikson also granted more powers to the ego than Freud had allowed. According to Freud's theory, people may think that they are making choices, but they may only be rationalizing the compromises forced upon them by inner conflict. According to Erikson's theory, however, people are entirely capable of making real and meaningful choices.

Erikson, like Freud, devised a developmental theory of personality. Erikson, however, expanded on Freud's five stages of development and formulated a psychosocial theory of development consisting of eight stages. Whereas Freud's developmental theory ends with adolescence, Erikson's includes the changing concerns of adulthood.

Erikson named his stages after the traits people might develop during each of them. (See Figure 14.3 on page 332.) For example, the first stage of psychosocial development is named the stage of trust versus mistrust. A warm, loving relationship with the mother (and others) during infancy may lead to a sense of basic trust in people and in the world. Janet, for example, had always maintained a very close relationship with her mother. Erikson's theories would indicate that Janet's trusting personality may have been a result of that warm relationship.

A cold, unfulfilling relationship may generate a broad sense of mistrust, which could damage the formation of relationships for a lifetime unless it is resolved successfully. Erikson believed that most people maintain a blend of trust and mistrust.

Evaluation of the Psychoanalytic Approach

Although psychoanalytic concepts such as libido and id strike many psychologists as unscientific today, Freud was an important champion of the idea that human personality and behavior are subject to scientific analysis. In Freud's day, serious psychological problems were still commonly seen as signs of weakness or so-called craziness. Freud's thinking contributed greatly to the development of compassion for people with psychological disorders.

Psychoanalytic theory also focused the attention of scientists and therapists on the far-reaching effects of childhood events. Freud and Erikson suggested that early childhood traumas can affect us for a lifetime. Psychoanalytic theorists have heightened society's awareness of the emotional needs of children.

Freud also helped us recognize that sexual and aggressive urges are common. He pointed out that there is a difference between recognizing these urges and acting on them. He realized that our thinking may be distorted by our efforts to avoid anxiety and guilt. And he devised an influential method of psychotherapy, which is described in Chapter 19.

Erik Erikson's Stages of Psychosocial Development

Infancy (0–1)	Early childhood (2–3)	Preschool years (4–5)	Grammar school years (6–12)
Trust versus mistrust	Autonomy versus shame and doubt	Initiative versus guilt	Industry versus inferiority
Coming to trust the mother and the environment—to associate surroundings with feelings of inner goodness	Developing the wish to make choices and the self-control to exercise choice	Adding planning and "attacking" to choice; becoming active and on the move	Becoming eagerly absorbed in skills, tasks, and productivity; mastering the fundamentals of technology

FIGURE 14.3 *Erik Erikson believed that social relationships are the most important factors in personality development. Shown here are the eight stages of Erikson's theory of psychosocial development.*

Psychoanalytic theories—particularly the views of Freud—have, however, been criticized on many counts. Even followers of Freud argued that he placed too much emphasis on unconscious motives and neglected the importance of social relationships. Opponents of Freud's theories also assert that people consciously seek self-enhancement and intellectual pleasures and do not merely try to gratify the dark demands of the id.

Critics have also questioned Freud's method of gathering evidence from clinical sessions (Hergenhahn, 2000). Using this method, therapists may subtly influence clients to say what the therapists expect to hear. Also, Freud and many other psychoanalytic theorists gathered their evidence only from case studies of white, middle-class individuals who had sought help for their psychological problems. These individuals may not have provided the most representative sample of the general population. (See Chapter 2.)

SECTION 2 REVIEW

Homework Practice Online
go.hrw.com
Keyword: SY7 HP14

1. Define the terms *id*, *ego*, and *superego*.
2. Trace the impact of Freud's theory.
3. How do the psychoanalytic theories of Jung and Horney disagree with the theories presented by Freud?
4. **Critical Thinking** *Summarizing* In what ways has the psychoanalytic theory of personality been modified since Freud?

The Learning Approach

A DAY IN THE LIFE
Some personality theorists might assume that Todd's sense of humor was largely a learned behavior. They might explain that Todd made jokes because he had learned that he would somehow be rewarded or positively reinforced for such behavior. Janet's laughter and obvious amusement would be examples of such positive reinforcement. Other theorists might suggest that Todd had learned to be comical by observing the behavior of other humorous people.

The two psychological approaches that might offer such explanations are, respectively, behaviorism and social-learning theory. Both are branches of a broader school of psychological thought called the learning approach.

Behaviorism

John B. Watson claimed that external forces or influences—not internal influences such as traits or inner conflict—largely shape people's preferences and behavior (Watson, 1924). In the 1930s, Watson's approach was taken up by B. F. Skinner. Skinner agreed that we should pay attention to how organisms behave and avoid trying to see within people's minds. Skinner also emphasized the effects of reinforcement on behavior (Skinner, 1938). (See Chapter 6.)

Adolescence (13–18)	Young adulthood (19–30)	Middle adulthood	Late adulthood
Identity versus role diffusion	Intimacy versus isolation	Generativity versus stagnation	Integrity versus despair
Connecting skills and social roles to formation of career objectives	Committing the self to another; engaging in sexual love	Needing to be needed; guiding and encouraging the younger generation; being creative	Accepting the timing and placing of one's own life cycle; achieving wisdom and dignity

Most of us assume that our wants originate within us. But Watson and Skinner largely discarded ideas of personal freedom, choice, and self-direction. Skinner suggested that environmental influences, such as parental approval and social custom, condition or shape us into wanting some things and not wanting others. **Socialization** is the process by which people learn the socially desirable behaviors of their particular culture and adopt them as part of their personalities.

In his 1948 novel, *Walden Two,* Skinner described a utopian (or ideal) society in which people are happy and content because every member of the society contributes to, and receives the benefits of, the society. They have been socialized from early childhood to help other people and society at large. Because of childhood socialization, people in the fictional community want to be decent, kind, and unselfish. They see their actions as a result of their own free will. According to Skinner, however, no one is really free. We may think of ourselves as being free because we can go after what we want and get it. But in Skinner's view, we are shaped into wanting what is good for society at an early age.

. . . .

TRUTH
OR
fiction
■ REVISITED ■

It is not true that all psychologists believe that humans possess the free will to make their own choices in life. Behaviorists believe that a person's actions and choices are shaped by environmental influences and cultural factors, such as socialization.

. . . .

Social-Learning Theory

Social-learning theory is a contemporary view of learning that is advocated by Albert Bandura and other psychologists. Social-learning theorists focus on the importance of learning by observation and on the role of the cognitive processes that produce individual differences (Bandura, 1986).

Unlike behaviorists, who believe that people are at the mercy of their environment, social-learning theorists argue that people can act intentionally to influence the environment. To behaviorists, learning is the mechanical result of reinforcement. To social-learning theorists, on the other hand, people engage in purposeful learning. Individuals seek to learn about their environment and have a certain degree of control over reinforcement. Observational learning extends to reading about others or watching them in media such as television and film.

According to social-learning theorists, behavior is not based solely on what is learned from observation. Internal variables also influence how we act in certain situations. These internal factors include the following:

- *Skills:* Skills include a person's physical and social abilities.
- *Values:* The value we put on the outcome of a certain behavior affects how we act. For example, if you value good grades, you will study.
- *Goals:* We regulate ourselves by setting goals. Once the goal is set, we plan the most effective way to achieve it.
- *Expectations:* Expectations are predictions of what will happen in certain situations.

Self efficacy expectation

Many behavior theorists believe that environmental factors, such as parental approval, condition us to exhibit certain behaviors and not others.

- *Self-efficacy expectations:* This term, coined by Bandura (1989), refers to beliefs people have about themselves. For example, if you believe that you are a good public speaker, you will be motivated to speak before the class assembly. People with high self-efficacy expectations are also more likely to persist at difficult tasks.

Evaluation of the Learning Approach

What are the strengths and weaknesses of learning theories? Learning theorists have made key contributions to the understanding of behavior, but their theories have left some psychologists dissatisfied. Psychoanalytic theorists and trait theorists focus on internal variables such as unconscious conflict and traits to explain behavior. Learning theorists emphasize the influence of environmental conditions on behavior. They have shown that people learn to do things because of reinforcements.

Behaviorism is limited in its ability to explain personality. Behaviorism does not describe, explain, or even suggest the richness of inner human experience. Behaviorism does not deal with thoughts, feelings, and people's complex inner maps of the world.

Social-learning theory does deal with these issues. But critics of social-learning theory argue that it has not come up with satisfying explanations for the development of traits or accounted for self-awareness. Also, social-learning theory—like behaviorism—may not pay enough attention to the

role genetic variation plays in determining individual differences in behavior.

SECTION 3 REVIEW

Homework Practice Online
Keyword: SY7 HP14

1. According to behaviorism, what is the main influence on how people act?
2. Many students strive to get good grades. How would social-learning theorists explain this behavior? How would behaviorists explain it?
3. **Critical Thinking** *Supporting a Point of View* Do you agree with the behaviorist view that true personal freedom does not exist? Why or why not?

SECTION 4

The Humanistic Approach

Behaviorists argue that psychologists should not attempt to study self-awareness. Humanists, on the other hand, begin with the assumption that self-awareness is the very core of humanity. They focus on people's pursuits of self-fulfillment and ethical conduct. To humanistic psychologists, people are truly free to do as they choose with their lives. Moreover, because people are free to choose, they are responsible for the choices that they make.

Abraham Maslow

Humanistic psychologist Abraham Maslow (1908–1970) believed that humans are separated from lower animals because they recognize their desire to achieve self-actualization—to reach their full potential. (See Chapter 13.) He also believed that because people are unique, they must follow their own paths to self-actualization. However, accomplishing this requires taking risks. Maslow argued that people who stick to what is tried and true may find their lives boring and predictable. Although Hannah was very close to her

A DAY IN THE LIFE

friends, she realized that she possessed a unique musical ability. According to Maslow's theory, Hannah's willingness to pursue her talent and her courage to go away to college were factors in her search for self-actualization.

Carl Rogers

Carl Rogers (1902–1987), another advocate of the humanistic approach, believed that people are to some degree the conscious architects of their own personalities. In Rogers's view, people shape their personalities through free choice and action (Rogers, 1961, 1977). Because Rogers's theory revolves around people's sense of self, it is termed *self theory.*

Rogers placed great emphasis on the human ability to derive a **self-concept**, a view of oneself as an individual. He also believed that the self is concerned with recognizing personal values and establishing a sense of one's relationships to other people. The self is the center of each person's experience, an ongoing sense of who and what one is. It provides the experience of being human in the world and it is the guiding principle behind both personality and behavior.

The Self-Concept and Congruence

Our self-concepts are made up of our impressions of ourselves and our evaluations of our adequacy. Rogers believed that the key to happiness and healthy adjustment is **congruence**, or consistency between one's self-concept and one's experience. For example, if you consider yourself to be outgoing and friendly, this self-concept will be reinforced if you have good relationships with other people. This will probably lead to feelings of happiness and a sense that your self-concept is accurate. If, however, you have difficulty getting along with others, the inconsistency between your self-concept and your experience will probably cause you to feel anxious or troubled.

Self-Esteem and Positive Regard

Rogers assumed that we all develop a need for self-esteem. Self-esteem is belief in oneself, or self-respect. At first, self-esteem reflects the esteem in which others hold us. As discussed in Chapter 10, parents help children develop self-esteem when they show them unconditional positive regard. Parents show unconditional positive regard when they accept children as they are, regardless of the children's behavior at the moment.

Parents show children conditional positive regard if they accept children only when they behave in a desired manner. Conditional positive regard may lead children to think that they are worthwhile only if they behave in certain ways.

Humanistic psychologists believe that each of us has a unique potential. Therefore, children who think that they are worthwhile only if they behave in certain ways will end up being disappointed in themselves. Humanistic psychologists believe that we cannot fully live up to the wishes of others and also remain true to ourselves.

The expression of the self does not always have to lead to conflict. Rogers was optimistic about human nature. He believed that we hurt others or act in antisocial ways only when we are frustrated in our efforts to develop our potential. When parents and others are loving and tolerant of the ways in which we are different, we, too, are loving.

However, Rogers believed that children in some families learn that it is bad to have ideas of their own, especially about political, religious, or sexual matters. When they perceive their parents' disapproval, they may come to see themselves as rebels and label their feelings as selfish, wrong, or evil. If they wish to retain a consistent self-concept and self-esteem, they may have to deny many of their genuine feelings. They may, in a sense, have to disown parts of themselves.

According to Rogers's theory, the path to self-actualization requires getting in touch with our

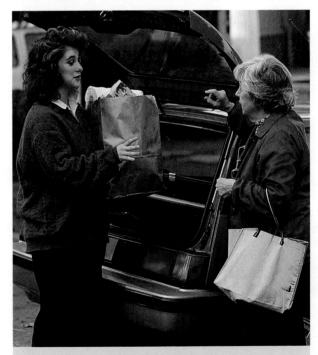

Carl Rogers argued that people shape their personalities through free choice and action. He believed that it is important for individuals to recognize their personal values and to establish a sense of their relationships with other people.

PSYCHOLOGY

WATSON AND ROGERS:
At Opposite Ends of the Theory Spectrum

The theories of behaviorist John B. Watson and humanist Carl Rogers are at opposite ends of the theoretical spectrum. Consider Watson's challenge to the field of psychology in his influential 1924 book, *Behaviorism*:

> Give me a dozen healthy infants, well-formed, and my own specified world to bring them up in and I'll guarantee to take any one at random and train him to become any type of specialist I might suggest—doctor, lawyer, merchant-chief and, yes, even beggar-man and thief, regardless of his talents, penchants, tendencies, abilities, vocations, and the race of his ancestors. (1924, p. 82)

With these words, Watson stated the classic behaviorist belief: Regardless of who we think we really are inside, we can be totally molded, or conditioned, by external stimuli. Our belief in individual choice is just an illusion.

Carl Rogers had a very different view of the freedom and dignity of the individual human being. He summarized this view in a 1974 article:

> My experience in therapy and in groups makes it impossible for me to deny the reality and significance of human choice. To me it is not an illusion that man is to some degree the architect of himself. (1974, p. 119)

About 10 years before writing this article, Rogers described an experience that helped confirm his conviction that life is more than a reaction to environmental forces:

> During a vacation weekend some months ago I was standing on a headland [piece of ground jutting out over water] overlooking one of the rugged coves which dot the coastline of northern California. Several large rock outcroppings were at the mouth of the cove, and these received the full force of the great Pacific combers [waves] which, beating upon them, broke into mountains of spray before surging into the cliff-lined shore. As I watched the waves breaking over these large rocks in the distance, I noticed with surprise what appeared to be a tiny palm tree on the rocks, no more than two or three feet high, taking the pounding of the breakers. Through my binoculars I saw that these were some type of seaweed, with a slender "trunk" topped off with a head of leaves. . . . In the interval between the waves it seemed clear that this fragile, erect, top-heavy plant would be utterly crushed and broken by the next breaker. When the wave crunched down upon it, the trunk bent almost flat, the leaves were whipped into a straight line by the torrent of the water, yet the moment the wave had passed, here was the plant again, erect, tough, resilient. It seemed incredible that it was able to take this incessant [never-ending] pounding hour after hour, day after night, week after week, for all I know, year after year, and all the time nourishing itself, extending itself, reproducing itself; in short, maintaining and enhancing itself in this process which, in our shorthand, we call growth. Here in this palmlike seaweed was the tenacity of life, the forward thrust of life, the ability to push into an incredibly hostile environment and not only hold its own, but to adapt, develop, become itself. (1963, pp. 1–2)

Rogers used this vivid metaphor to express the humanistic belief that living things, including people, struggle on, attempting in the toughest of conditions to actualize themselves.

Think About It

1. **Supporting a Point of View** Do you believe that anyone, regardless of ability, can be trained to become, say, a doctor, lawyer, or musician? Why or why not?
2. **Evaluating** Do you believe, like Rogers, that each individual takes charge of his or her environment? Explain your answer.

genuine feelings and acting on them. This is the goal of person-centered therapy, Rogers's method of psychotherapy. (See Chapter 19.)

Evaluation of the Humanistic Approach

For most animals, to be alive is to move, to eat, to breathe, and to reproduce. However, humanistic psychologists feel that humans are not merely animals. They believe that for human beings, an essential aspect of life is conscious experience—the sense of one's self as progressing through space and time. Humanists grant consciousness a key role in our daily lives. This focus on conscious experience is one reason that humanistic theories have tremendous popular appeal.

Another reason for their popularity is that they stress human freedom. Psychoanalytic theories see us largely as products of our childhoods. Learning theories, to some degree, see us as products of circumstances. Both theories argue that our sense of freedom is merely an illusion. Humanistic theorists, however, say that our freedom is real.

The primary strength of the humanistic theories—their focus on conscious experience—is also their main weakness. Conscious experience is private and subjective. Therefore, some psychologists question the soundness of framing theories in terms of consciousness (Liebert & Spiegler, 1982). Others, however, believe that the science of psychology can afford to relax its methods somewhat if loosening them will help it address the richness of human experience (Bevan & Kessel, 1994).

Critics also note that humanistic theories, like learning theories, have little to say about the development of traits and personality types. Humanistic theorists assume that we are all unique, but they do not predict the sorts of traits, abilities, and interests we will develop.

SECTION 4 REVIEW

Homework Practice Online
Keyword: SY7 HP14

1. Summarize Rogers's concept of congruence.

2. Trace the impact of humanism on current thinking in psychology.

3. **Critical Thinking** *Finding the Main Idea* According to the humanistic approach, what is the role of self and free choice in shaping human behavior?

The Sociocultural Approach

A DAY IN THE LIFE

The sociocultural perspective focuses on the roles of ethnicity, gender, and culture in the formation of personality. Hannah was raised by parents who had grown up in South Korea. She was also comfortable in an American school with her American friends. Sociocultural theorists would argue that her family and her environmental influences were key factors in the development of Hannah's personality.

Individualism Versus Collectivism

One aspect of culture that sociocultural theorists focus on is the level of individualism or collectivism in a society. Individualism is a trait valued by many people in the United States and in many European nations. Individualists tend to define themselves in terms of their personal identities. They usually give priority to their personal goals. When asked to complete the statement "I am . . . ," they are likely to respond in terms of their own personality traits or occupations. For example, they are likely to say, "I am outgoing" or "I am a nurse" (Triandis, 1990).

Collectivists, such as those pictured here, tend to define themselves in terms of the groups to which they belong. They often give priority to the goals of the group over their own individual needs.

The Self in Relation to Others from the Individualist and Collectivist Perspectives

Individualist

Collectivist

FIGURE 14.4   *An individualist sees the self as separate from other people. A collectivist, on the other hand, sees the self as complete only in terms of his or her relationships to other people.*

Based on Markus & Kitayama, 1991.

In contrast, many people from Africa, Asia, and Central and South America tend to be more collectivistic. (See Figure 14.4.) Collectivists tend to define themselves in terms of the groups to which they belong and often give priority to the goals of their group. They feel complete only in terms of their social relationships with others (Markus & Kitayama, 1991). When asked to complete the statement "I am . . . ," they are likely to respond in terms of their families, religion, or nation. For example, they are likely to say, "I am a father," "I am a Buddhist," or "I am Japanese" (Draguns, 1988; Triandis, 1994).

The Western capitalist system fosters individualism. It assumes that individuals are entitled to amass personal fortunes if they have the drive and ability to do so. The individualist perspective is found in the self-reliant heroes in Western entertainment—from Clint Eastwood's gritty cowboys to the character Belle in the Disney film *Beauty and the Beast*. The traditional writings of many non-Western cultures, on the other hand, have praised people who put the well-being of the group ahead of their personal ambitions.

There are, of course, conflicting ideals—as well as individual differences—within cultures. In the United States, for example, children are taught to share with other children as well as to be "Number One." But on the whole, the contrast between the individualist Western world and the more collectivist nations of other parts of the world is a generally reliable measure of some personality differences between individuals from these regions.

Sociocultural Factors and the Self

According to sociocultural theorists, social and cultural factors also affect the self-concept and self-esteem of the individual. Carl Rogers noted that our self-concepts tend to reflect how we believe other people see us. Members of ethnic groups who have been subjected to discrimination and poverty may have poorer self-concepts and lower self-esteem than people who have not experienced discrimination and poverty (Greene, 1993; Lewis-Fernández & Kleinman, 1994). Similarly, members of ethnic groups that have traditionally held power in society are likely to have a positive sense of self because they share in the expectations of personal achievement and respect that are typically given to members of such groups.

In some cases, however, things are not so simple. Many women in the United States, particularly white women, are unhappy with their appearance. This is in part because the current media ideal is found in female models who are on average 9 percent taller and 16 percent slimmer than the average woman in the United States (Williams, 1992). But a survey by the American Association of University Women (1992) found that African American girls are likely to be happier with their appearances than white girls are. Sixty-five percent of African American elementary-school girls said they were happy with the way they were, as compared with 55 percent of white girls. Among high school students, 58 percent of African American girls remained happy with the way they were, as compared with only 22 percent of white girls.

How do sociocultural theorists explain this difference? It appears that African American girls are taught that there is nothing wrong with them if they do not match the ideals of the majority culture. They come to believe that if the world treats them negatively, it is because of prejudice, not because of who they really are or what they do (Williams, 1992). White girls, on the other hand, may be more likely to look inward and blame themselves for not attaining the unreachable ideal.

Acculturation and Self-Esteem

Personalities are influenced by more than personal traits and learning experiences. They are also influenced by cultural settings. Hannah belonged to a traditional Korean family. At school, however, she was exposed daily to values that are in some ways unique to the United States.

Acculturation is the process of adapting to a new or different culture. People who immigrate to the United States undergo acculturation. If they come from Africa, Asia, or Latin America, they are likely to find that differences in language are only the tip of the iceberg of cultural differences.

Acculturation takes various patterns. Some immigrants become completely assimilated, or absorbed, into the culture of the area to which they move. They may stop using both the language and customs of their country of origin. Others choose to maintain separation. They retain the language and customs of their country of origin and never become completely comfortable with those of their adopted country. Still others become bicultural. That is, they successfully integrate both sets of customs and values.

Research suggests that people who are bicultural have the highest self-esteem (Phinney et al., 1992). For example, Mexican Americans who are fluent in English are more likely to be emotionally stable than Mexican Americans who do not speak English as well (Salgado de Snyder et al., 1990). Adopting the ways of the new society without giving up a supportive cultural tradition and a sense of ethnic identity apparently helps people function most effectively. According to the sociocultural approach, Hannah's musical and educational success and her high self-esteem may have been results of her ability to balance her Korean heritage with her cultural surroundings in the United States.

It is true that psychologists feel that culture, gender, and ethnicity are important in personality development. Sociocultural theorists believe that all of these factors contribute in some way to the development of personality.

Evaluation of the Sociocultural Approach

The sociocultural perspective provides valuable insights into the roles of ethnicity, gender, culture, and socioeconomic status in personality formation. Sociocultural factors are external forces that are internalized and affect all of us. They run through us deeply, touching many aspects of our personalities. Without reference to sociocultural factors, we may be able to understand generalities about behavior and mental processes. We cannot, however, understand how individuals think, behave, and feel about themselves within a given cultural setting. The sociocultural perspective also enhances our sensitivity to cultural differences and allows us to appreciate much of the richness of human behavior.

SECTION 5 REVIEW

Homework Practice Online
Keyword: SY7 HP14

1. Explain the difference between individualism and collectivist perspectives on personality.

2. What is acculturation and how can it affect self-esteem?

3. **Critical Thinking** *Analyzing Information* According to the sociocultural approach, what role do ethnicity, gender, culture, and socioeconomic status play in the development of personality?

14 REVIEW

Writing a Summary

Using standard grammar, spelling, sentence structure, and punctuation, summarize the information in this chapter. Consider:
• the main features of the trait and psychoanalytic theories of personality
• how behaviorists, learning theorists, humanists, and socioculturalists view the development of personality

Identifying People and Ideas

Identify the following terms or people and use them in appropriate sentences.

1. personality
2. trait
3. introverts
4. id
5. defense mechanisms
6. repression
7. regression
8. Erik Erikson
9. congruence
10. acculturation

Understanding Main Ideas

SECTION 1 (pp. 322–324)
1. What are five examples of personality traits?

SECTION 2 (pp. 324–332)
2. Describe Erikson's stages of psychosocial development.

SECTION 3 (pp. 332–334)
3. What is the impact of behaviorism on current thinking in psychology?

SECTION 4 (pp. 334–337)
4. How is congruence related to a person's self concept?

SECTION 5 (pp. 337–339)
5. What are examples of behaviors that would indicate whether a person is more individualistic or collectivistic?

Thinking Critically

1. **Analyzing Information** Describe a situation where an awareness of one's own traits and abilities might help in making important decisions.

2. **Making Generalizations and Predictions** What do you think would happen to society if people's minds had an id but not an ego or superego?

3. **Supporting a Point of View** Which do you think has a greater effect on people's behavior: the socialization received as children (nurture) or the natural instincts and feelings people are simply born with (nature)? Explain your answer.

4. **Categorizing** What are two positive and two negative aspects of individualism and of collectivism?

Writing About Psychology

1. **Evaluating** Prepare a fact sheet in which you evaluate the various perspectives of human learning. Be sure to specify the strengths and weaknesses of each.

2. **Categorizing** Write a report that gives examples of growth and development based on social-learning theories and behavioral theories. Be sure to use standard grammar, spelling, sentence structure, and punctuation. Use the graphic organizer below to help you write your report.

Social-Learning Theories	Behavioral Theories

Interpreting Graphs

Study the graph below. Then use the information in the graph to help you answer the questions that follow.

Early Infant Behavior

Visual Behavior (percentage of time) vs. Infant Age (days)

Source: Mischel, *Introduction to Personality*, 1986

1. Which of the following statements is supported by the information presented in the graph?

   a. Hearing is the primary means infants use to learn about the world.

   b. Infant use of visual behavior decreases with age.

   c. Infants do not rely upon other senses as much as they do visual behavior.

   d. Infant use of visual behavior increases with age.

2. How might a psychologist use this graph to criticize Freud's stages of development?

Analyzing Primary Sources

Read the following excerpt, in which psychologist Alfred Adler discusses why he believes people strive for superiority. Then answer the questions that follow.

"Now I began to see clearly in every psychical phenomenon the striving for *superiority*. It runs parallel to physical growth. It is an intrinsic necessity of life itself. It lies at the root of all solutions of life's problems, and is manifested in the way in which we meet these problems. All our functions follow its direction. . . . Willing, thinking, talking, seeking after rest, after pleasure, learning, understanding, work and love, betoken [show] the essence of this eternal melody. Whether one thinks or acts more wisely or less, one always moves along the lines of that upward tendency. In our right and wrong conceptions of life and its problems, in the successful or the unsuccessful solution of any question, this striving for perfection is uninterruptedly at work."

3. How does Adler define "striving for superiority" in this excerpt?

   a. attempting to achieve dominance over other people

   b. the effort to reach perfection

   c. trying to exercise complete control over one's environment

   d. receiving attention and praise from one's peers

4. How might a behaviorist such as John B. Watson have responded to Adler's arguments in this excerpt?

PSYCHOLOGY PROJECTS

Cooperative Learning

Writing About Psychology With a classmate, write a skit that shows someone using one of the defense mechanisms mentioned in the chapter. Act out your skit for the class, and have students guess which defense mechanism you are portraying. As a class, discuss situations in which defense mechanisms might be helpful and times when they might be harmful.

internet connect

Internet Activity: go.hrw.com
KEYWORD: SY7 CH14

Choose an activity on theories of personality to:

- create a theoretical profile of a noted personality theorist.
- identify elements of social-learning theory in modern advertising.
- write a dinner party conversation that could occur among theorists of different approaches to personality.

Chapter 15

PSYCHOLOGICAL TESTS

Read to Discover

1 What are the purposes and characteristics of psychological tests?

2 How are achievement tests, aptitude tests, and interest inventories used?

3 What are the two kinds of personality tests, and what are their uses?

4 What are some strategies for taking tests and for avoiding test anxiety?

A DAY IN THE LIFE

Marc and Todd were meeting Dan in the library to study for a history test. When they found him, he was reading something intently.

"Hi, Dan. What are you reading?" Todd asked curiously.

"Oh hi, guys," Dan answered. "I met with the guidance counselor, Mr. Hochberg, yesterday because I'm still having trouble figuring out what I want to do after high school. He asked me to take some tests, and now I'm trying to make sense of the results."

"Don't we take enough tests in school already?" Marc asked.

"These weren't *regular* school tests. Some tested my interests, and others looked at my aptitudes."

"I took some of those tests last year," Todd said. "I'd always known that I liked studying living things, but Mr. Hochberg showed me types of jobs I could pursue if I really took my biology courses seriously."

"So, Dan, what did your tests show?" Marc asked.

"Well, according to one of these tests, I have good communication skills and relate well to people. Both of those qualities are listed under guidance counselor and teacher."

"Guys, we really should start studying for this history test," Todd reminded them.

Suddenly Marc looked panicked. "I wish you hadn't reminded me."

"What's wrong?" Todd asked.

"I just don't like taking tests," Marc answered. "I get so nervous, and no matter how much I study, I always seem to draw a blank when I actually sit down to take the test."

"No one likes tests," Dan said.

"But I think I get more upset than most people. I know it's weird, but sometimes I get so nervous that I can't even think straight, even if I've studied enough."

Todd looked rather concerned about his friend. "Why don't you try talking to your teachers or maybe even to Mr. Hochberg? They might at least be able to give you some advice about how to study or how to concentrate during the actual test."

"I guess it's worth a try."

· · ·

As Dan discovered, there are many different kinds of psychological tests. In Chapter 9, you learned about one kind of psychological test: intelligence tests. The psychological tests that will be discussed in this chapter are achievement tests, aptitude and interest tests, and personality tests.

Tests to determine how much students have learned are called achievement tests. Mr. Hochberg gave Dan a test for special aptitudes and interests to help find out whether he is suited for certain occupations.

There are also tests that identify the psychological traits that make up a person's personality. Therefore, tests that measure psychological traits are also known as personality tests. Personality tests measure almost every known personality trait. Some tests measure a dozen or more traits at one time.

Key Terms

- behavior-rating scales
- self-reports
- standardized test
- validity scales
- norms
- norm group
- achievement tests
- aptitude tests
- vocational interest inventories
- forced-choice format
- objective tests
- projective tests
- open-ended format
- cognitive restructuring

HOLT

Psychology Video Program

Watch the video to explore the use of the Scholastic Assessment Test (SAT).

TRUTH OR fiction?

Read the following statements about psychology. Do you think they are true or false? You will learn whether each statement is true or false as you read the chapter.

- Psychologists can always tell whether a person has told the truth on a personality test.
- Some tests measure only aptitude.
- Psychologists agree that the Rorschach inkblot test is a reliable method for determining psychological health.
- You should always go with your first guess on a multiple-choice test.
- The longer your answer to an essay question, the better your score on that question is likely to be.

SECTION 1

What Are Psychological Tests?

Psychological tests assess abilities, feelings, attitudes, and behaviors. The responses a person gives on test items help psychologists predict a person's future behavior.

Psychological tests are hardly a new invention. It appears that over 2,500 years ago, during the golden age of Greece, people were selected for government service on the basis of psychological tests (Matarazzo, 1990). Those early tests measured physical as well as mental abilities. Evidence also suggests that psychological tests were used to select civil-service employees some 2,000 years ago in China (Bowman, 1989). The Chinese tests measured verbal and mathematical abilities as well as knowledge of law and geography.

Modern researchers have been using various types of psychological tests for about 100 years. Francis Galton, James Cattell, Alfred Binet, and other psychologists began constructing modern psychological tests in the late 1800s.

Uses of Psychological Tests

Psychological tests can be used to help people make important decisions. Tests can help indicate whether a person is suited for a certain line of work, for a particular class in school, or for medication to reduce agitation (Saccuzzo, 1994). Intelligence tests are often used

to indicate whether children are likely to profit from special kinds of educational experiences. Transformed score tests such as the Scholastic Assessment Test (SAT) are used to help determine whether students are likely to succeed in college. As part of their admissions process, college admissions personnel also often ask high school teachers and guidance counselors to rate applicants on scales that measure such traits as willingness to work hard and cooperativeness.

More specialized tests are used to measure students' prospects for success in graduate schools such as business, law, and medical schools. Many graduate schools use the Graduate Record Examination (GRE). Similarly, medical schools use the Medical College Admission Test (MCAT).

Some psychological tests measure behavior directly. For example, **behavior-rating scales** are used to measure behavior in such places as classrooms and hospitals. With behavior-rating scales, trained observers may check off each occurrence of a specific behavior within a certain amount of time, say, 15 minutes. For example, an observer might count how many times a person gestures while talking to someone else. This might be a measure of how outgoing the person is.

Behavior-rating scales are growing in popularity today, particularly for use with children (Kamphaus et al., 2000). However, most psychological tests rely on people's **self-reports** about their attitudes, feelings, and behavior.

Features of Psychological Tests

Psychological tests are sometimes frightening for the test takers and sometimes misleading for the evaluators. Tests such as the SAT can be particularly scary because the results on a test taken on one day can seem nearly as important as the grades earned over several years. The results can be misleading because a person may be ill or distracted on the day of the test and not perform as well as he or she might on another day.

For a psychological test to be useful and reasonably accurate, it has to have certain features, or characteristics. It has to be standardized, it has to show reliability and validity, and it has to have norms for scoring.

Standardization A **standardized test** is one that is administered and scored the same way every time. Psychologists and educators are trained in how to administer and score standardized tests accurately. For example, the two most widely used

Some psychological tests measure behavior directly by means of behavior-rating scales. With these scales, trained observers count the number of times a specific behavior occurs in a certain amount of time. For example, an observer might count how many times a person gestures during a conversation.

their problems on personality tests as a way to get attention. In addition, people may answer in the way they think is "correct," even if there are no objectively right or wrong answers. To avoid such distortion, some psychological tests have validity scales built into them.

Validity scales involve questions that, if answered in a certain way, let the psychologist know that the test taker is not answering the test questions honestly. Validity scales always depend on the answers to many interlinking questions. For example, there may be several test items on which a psychologist would expect to see a pattern of similar answers. If no such pattern is found, those answers, taken together, may indicate that the test taker is not answering the questions honestly. Validity scales are often quite helpful. However, they are not foolproof.

intelligence tests, the Stanford-Binet and Wechsler, are given individually. All test administrators are trained to ask the same questions in the same way. They also receive training in how to score the tests and interpret those scores.

Other tests such as the SAT are given to thousands of students at a time. All students receive the same instructions, and computers grade most of the answers. Essay questions on a standardized test are not graded by a computer. However, instructions for administrators on how to score essay questions are very clear and precise. This helps ensure that the same criteria will be used to score essay questions regardless of who is doing the scoring.

Reliability and Validity In Chapter 9, you learned that the *reliability* of a measure is its consistency. That is, an individual's score on a test should be the same or very nearly the same every time the individual takes that test. Test-retest reliability is demonstrated when a person receives similar scores on the same test taken on different occasions. *Validity* refers to the extent to which a test measures what it is intended to measure and predicts what it is intended to predict.

Test results can be distorted when people answer in ways they think will please the interviewer. People have also been known to exaggerate

TRUTH OR fiction
■ REVISITED ■

It is not true that psychologists can always tell whether a person has told the truth on a personality test. Validity scales help, but they cannot indicate with certainty whether a test taker has answered questions honestly.

In general, the tests you take in your classes are not psychological tests, and most are not constructed scientifically. Still, these tests should also be reliable and valid. Generally speaking, the longer a test is, the more valid it is. (Would you rather have your grade on a math test depend on solving just one problem, or would you prefer it to be based on your solutions to 10 or 20 problems?) Marc

A DAY IN THE LIFE

believes that the scores he receives on tests he takes in class are often not a valid measure of what he knows. He argues that the tests do not really measure what he has learned because his nervousness interferes with his ability to perform well.

PSYCHOLOGY
IN THE WORLD TODAY

Would You Tell Your Problems to a Computer?

Imagine you have been feeling tense lately and are wondering what is causing the tension. You decide to consult a psychologist. When you arrive at the psychologist's office, you are instructed to sit in a room with a computer that asks you several personal questions.

The fact is that computers have been "interviewing" people for more than 20 years. One computer program currently in use for this purpose is CASPER. CASPER stands for Computerized Assessment System for Psychotherapy Evaluation and Research. A CASPER interview lasts about 30 minutes. CASPER explores a wide variety of topics, including family relationships, social activities, overall life satisfaction, and specific behavior patterns that may be suggestive of physical and psychological disorders.

Questions and possible responses are displayed on the monitor. To answer a question, the test taker presses a number on the computer keyboard. CASPER then follows up with additional questions. For example, if you report difficulty sleeping, CASPER will inquire whether sleep has become a key problem. CASPER asks whether the sleep problem is "something causing you great personal distress or interfering with your daily functioning" (Farrell et al., 1987). If the answer is yes, the computer will explore further by asking more questions.

How well do people respond to being interviewed by a computer? Research shows that people find the computer program user-friendly. They also find that they are able to complete CASPER interviews with little difficulty. In fact, most people like the computerized interview (Bloom, 1992; Farrell et al., 1987). This is especially true for younger, better-educated people who are experienced with computers (Spinhoven et al., 1993).

A CASPER interview

People also seem to report more problems to CASPER than they do to a real, live psychologist. Why? Some people seem to prefer "speaking" with an impersonal computer to speaking with a person, who might disagree with or judge them.

Computer diagnostic programs apparently offer some advantages over human interviewers (Farrell et al., 1987):

- Standardization seems to be easier and more consistent. Computers can be programmed to ask specific questions in a prescribed sequence.
- People may be less embarrassed about reporting personal matters to a computer. Computers make no emotional or judgmental responses.
- Use of the computer for purposes of diagnosis frees clinicians to spend more of their time doing psychotherapy.

As computer programs become more sophisticated, they are also likely to become more accurate at diagnosis and better able to identify unusual problems. Because of its memory, a computer can also easily connect a person's complaints to similar cases and thus make the choice of treatment easier for the therapist.

A review of the research in computer diagnosis suggests that some computer programs are as capable of obtaining pertinent information from a client and arriving at an accurate diagnosis as trained clinicians (Bloom, 1992). Computer programs seem to be the wave of the future. Sophisticated diagnostic and treatment programs continue to be developed.

Think About It

Making Generalizations and Predictions What possible problems do you think might occur with computer diagnosis and treatment?

Norms Psychological tests are usually scored by comparing an individual's score to the norm. **Norms** are established standards of performance. They are designed to tell test administrators which scores are average, high, or low.

Norms for a test are usually established by administering the test to a large group of people who are similar to those for whom the test is intended. This group of test takers is called the **norm group**.

Imagine you are asked to create a psychological test for elementary school students. The tests would need to ask questions appropriate to the age of the children. You would establish the norm by administering the test to thousands of elementary school students of the same age or grade level. This would be your norm group. The average score of the norm group would become the norm for that particular test, and the scores of all other children taking the test in the future would be compared to that norm.

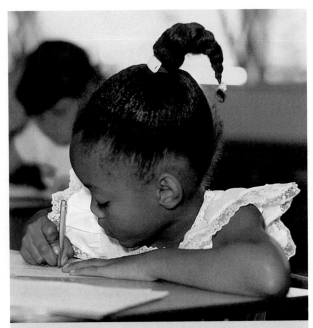

Achievement tests are given to most elementary and middle school students every year to assess basic skills such as reading and math.

SECTION 1 REVIEW

go.hrw.com **Homework Practice Online** Keyword: SY7 HP15

1. What is a standardized test?

2. Describe the purposes of psychological tests.

3. **Critical Thinking** *Analyzing Information* Explain the importance of reliability and validity in standardized tests.

Measuring Achievement, Abilities, and Interests

Achievement tests, aptitude tests, and tests of interests are all closely related. Most of the tests that you have taken in your classes at school have probably been achievement tests. There are also tests that measure people's abilities, or aptitudes. Still other tests help people identify their interests. Dan and his friends had been taking achievement tests for many years. Then when Dan was having difficulty deciding on a college major, Mr. Hochberg focused on testing Dan's abilities and interests.

Achievement Tests

Achievement tests measure people's skills and the knowledge they have in specific academic areas.

A DAY IN THE LIFE The history test Dan, Marc, and Todd were studying for was an achievement test. Throughout elementary and middle school, most students' basic skills are tested every year. They are tested in science, reading, math, and many other subject areas.

In high school, most students are tested repeatedly on their achievements in each of their courses. Factors such as intelligence and motivation play a role in achievement, but so does learning. For example, it should come as no surprise that students taking Spanish will have higher scores on a Spanish achievement test than students who are not taking Spanish, even though they may be equal in intelligence and motivation.

College students who wish to go to graduate school may be required to take standardized achievement tests in their major field of study—Spanish, political science, math, or psychology, for example. The tests are designed to determine whether the students have enough knowledge in the specific area to succeed in graduate school.

Aptitude Tests

Achievement tests measure a narrow range of skills. Intelligence tests, on the other hand, measure overall learning ability. Aptitude tests fall somewhere in

The Medical College Admission Test (MCAT) is an aptitude test that can help predict how well students will do in medical school. Aptitude tests are broader than intelligence tests but narrower than achievement tests.

on achievements in English (or the language in which the individual takes the test).

Moreover, the SAT consists of verbal and quantitative parts. The verbal sections rely heavily on vocabulary—that is, knowledge of the meaning of words. The quantitative part relies heavily on mathematical knowledge. Skill in these areas—knowledge of vocabulary and mathematics—depends on the amount one has learned or achieved. However, because performance on the SAT does not depend on one specific course, the SAT used to be called the Scholastic *Aptitude* Test. Recently, however, in recognition of the role that achievement plays in the SAT, the test was renamed the Scholastic *Assessment* Test.

It may be that there is no such thing as a "pure" aptitude test. All aptitude tests rely on some kind of prior achievement.

between. Aptitude tests measure more specific abilities or skills than intelligence tests but broader ones than achievement tests. **Aptitude tests** are generally used to determine whether a person is likely to do well in a given field of work or study.

The Scholastic Assessment Test is a general aptitude test. It is used to predict how well students are likely to do in college. The Law School Admission Test and the Medical College Admission Test are more specialized. They use percentile grade equivalent scores—the percent of scores at or below any given score—to predict how well students will do in law school and medical school, respectively. For example, success in medical school depends heavily on the ability to understand chemistry and biology. Therefore, the MCAT has many questions relating to these subjects.

Distinguishing Between Achievement and Aptitude

Sometimes it is difficult to distinguish between an achievement test and an aptitude test. Aptitude tests are intended to measure potential for learning in a specific area. An aptitude test is usually given to a person before that person has had any training in a specific area. It is used to predict how well the person will do in that area after receiving training. However, current abilities and future success are often based on past achievements. For example, the SAT is intended to measure the ability to do well in college, but it is given in specific languages. Therefore, the ability to do well on the SAT depends

TRUTH OR fiction ■ REVISITED ■

It is not true that some tests measure only aptitude. All aptitude tests rely on some kind of achievement. In recognition of this fact, the Scholastic Aptitude Test was renamed the Scholastic Assessment Test.

Vocational Interest Inventories

A DAY IN THE LIFE

When Dan was having difficulty deciding what to do after high school, Mr. Hochberg gave him some tests to help him figure out what his interests were. People usually perform better in jobs that interest them. Moreover, people who share interests with those who are successful in a given job are more likely to succeed in that job. Thus, many psychologists and educators use **vocational interest inventories** to help people determine whether their interests are similar to those of people in various lines of work. Two widely used interest inventories are the Kuder® Career Search and the Campbell™ Interest and Skills Survey (CISS®).

Kuder® Career Search Mr. Hochberg may have given Dan a test called a Kuder Career Search. This test has a **forced-choice format**, which means that the test taker is forced to choose one of the answers, even if none of them seems to fit his or her interests precisely. For example, test takers are asked to indicate which of a group of activities they like most and which they like least. They are not allowed to answer "none of the above."

The Kuder asks test takers to choose between activities such as the following:

a. hiking in the forest
b. giving someone advice
c. playing a musical instrument

The results are scored to show how much the person appears to be interested in areas such as science, music, art, literature, and outdoor work.

Campbell™ Interest and Skills Survey (CISS®) People taking a Kuder test can see where their interests lie and which areas they might want to look into for employment opportunities. Obviously, a person who repeatedly indicates a preference for music-related activities is showing a definite interest in music. The CISS is not as obvious or direct as the Kuder Career Serarch. The CISS includes many different kinds of items.

The CISS compares the test taker's interests with the interests of people who enjoy and are successful in various kinds of work. For example, if most successful accountants enjoy reading and solving puzzles, then a test taker who indicates these same preferences might also be a successful accountant. Therefore, the content of the test questions themselves may not be as important as the combinations of interests the test taker shares with people in certain occupations.

Evaluation of Interest Inventories Interest inventories are of great value to students such as Dan who do not have specific career goals. There are over 20,000 different occupations in the United States, and the task of trying to select one can be overwhelming to people who are unclear about their interests. Interest inventories can help point people in a direction they might find fulfilling.

On the other hand, interest in an area does not necessarily mean that one has the ability, or aptitude, to succeed in that area. Therefore, it is usually desirable to make vocational choices on the basis of one's abilities as well as one's interests.

No important life decisions should be made on the basis of a single psychological test. Tests provide only one source of information about an individual, and no test is perfectly reliable. Teachers' and counselors' personal knowledge of an individual should also be taken into account. People may also believe that the results of a single test may not be an accurate reflection of who they are.

Dan was pleased with the outcome of his interest test because it seemed to fit his own image of himself. If his test results had seemed wrong to him, it would be unwise for him to follow the directions suggested by the test results. For example, suppose the test showed that Dan likes outdoor activities, which suggests a career that includes working outdoors. Dan enjoys hiking and boating *occasionally*, but he also knows that he would dislike

The vast number of occupations available in the United States can make it difficult to know which career to pursue. Vocational interest inventories are often used to help people narrow down their career possibilities.

having to work outside all day and every day. He would have to carefully consider the test results in light of what he knows about himself. Taking additional interest tests might provide a clearer picture of the kind of career he would enjoy.

SECTION 2 REVIEW

Homework Practice Online
Keyword: SY7 HP15

1. What is the difference between an achievement test and an aptitude test?

2. What is the purpose of vocational interest inventories?

3. **Critical Thinking** *Summarizing* In what ways are achievement tests, aptitude tests, and interest inventories used?

SECTION 3
Personality Tests

An individual's personality consists of his or her characteristics, habits, preferences, and moods. Psychologists use personality tests to describe and measure various aspects of people's personalities. Sometimes, they also use personality tests to help diagnose psychological problems and disorders. There are two kinds of personality tests: objective tests and projective tests.

Objective Tests

Objective tests present test takers with a standardized group of test items in the form of a questionnaire. The Minnesota Multiphasic Personality Inventory® (MMPI®) and the California Psychological Inventory™ (CPI™), discussed below, are examples of objective personality tests. Sometimes test takers are limited to a specific choice of answers—true or false, for example. Sometimes test takers are asked to select the preferred answer from groups of three. In either case, though, the test takers must choose from a list of answers provided for them.

Minnesota Multiphasic Personality Inventory
The MMPI is the psychological test most widely used in clinical work (Helmes & Reddon, 1993; Watkins et al., 1995) and in research that requires measurement of personality traits. First developed

The results of the MMPI-2 can alert a psychologist to the possibility that the test taker may be suffering from a psychological disorder, such as depression. Most psychologists believe that the MMPI-2 scores should be supplemented and confirmed by interviews and observation.

in the late 1930s, the MMPI was intended for use by clinical and counseling psychologists to help diagnose psychological problems in people. A revised version of the test (the MMPI-2™) was released in 1989.

The MMPI-2 contains 567 items presented in a true-false format. Psychologists can score the MMPI-2 by hand, but they usually score it by computer. Computers generate reports by comparing the individual's score to group norms stored in the computer's memory. While the computer is certainly an objective (unbiased) scorer, most psychologists believe that the scores should be supplemented and confirmed by interviews and observation.

The MMPI-2 is organized into 10 clinical scales, up to 8 validity scales, and numerous subscales. The clinical scales reveal psychological problems. (See Figure 15.1) They also indicate whether people have stereotypical masculine or feminine interests and whether they are outgoing or shy.

To create the clinical scales of the MMPI-2, the designers interviewed people who had already been diagnosed with various psychological disorders. A test-item bank of several hundred items was derived from questions often asked in clinical interviews.

Commonly Used Validity and Clinical Scales of the Revised Minnesota Multiphasic Personality Inventory (MMPI-2™)

	Scale	Abbreviation	Possible Interpretations
Validity Scales	Cannot say	?	Corresponds to number of items left unanswered
	Lie	L	Lies or is highly conventional
	Infrequency	F	Exaggerates complaints or answers items haphazardly
	Correction	K	Denies problems
Clinical Scales	Hypochondriasis	Hs	Has bodily concerns and complaints
	Depression	D	Is depressed, guilty; has feelings of guilt and helplessness
	Conversion hysteria	Hy	Reacts to stress by developing physical symptoms; lacks insight
	Psychopathic deviate	Pd	Is immoral, in conflict with the law; has stormy relationships
	Masculinity-Femininity	Mf	High scores suggest interests and behavior patterns considered stereotypical of the other gender
	Paranoia	Pa	Is suspicious and resentful, highly cynical about human nature
	Psychasthenia	Pt	Is anxious, worried, high-strung
	Schizophrenia	Sc	Is confused, disorganized, disoriented; has bizarre ideas
	Hypomania	Ma	Is energetic, restless, active, easily bored
	Social introversion	Si	Is introverted, timid, shy; lacks self-confidence

FIGURE 15.1 *The MMPI-2 is the most widely used psychological test in clinical work. Although originally intended for use by psychologists to diagnose psychological disorders, it has now become the most widely used instrument of personality measurement in psychological research. This list describes the specific disorders that the MMPI-2 typically assesses.*

Here are some of the true-false items:

My father was a good man. **T F**
I am seldom troubled by headaches. **T F**
My hands and feet are usually warm enough. **T F**
I have never done anything dangerous for the thrill of it. **T F**
I work under a great deal of tension. **T F**

People with various psychological disorders, such as depression or schizophrenia, will answer certain questions in predictable ways. For example, a person suffering from depression might answer "true" to such questions as "I often feel sad for no reason" or "Sometimes I think life simply isn't worth living." These test items are then placed on scales to measure the presence of psychological disorders in other people. If a person taking the test answers the questions in ways that are similar to people who are known to have a particular psychological disorder, the psychologist administering the test is alerted to the possible presence of that disorder.

The validity scales are designed to detect distorted answers, misunderstood items, or an uncooperative test taker. For example, people with high "T" scores may answer questions in a way that makes them seem excessively moral or well behaved. Such people might answer the item "I never get angry" with "true." People with high "F" scores have a tendency to exaggerate complaints, or they may be trying to get attention by giving seemingly bizarre answers. (See Figure 15.1.)

However, there are questions concerning the usefulness of the validity scales (Helmes & Reddon, 1993). For example, people with serious psychological disorders may indeed see the world in an unusual way. Therefore, if they obtain high F-scale scores, it may be because of their problems and not because they are exaggerating their situation.

California Psychological Inventory   Because the MMPI-2 was designed to diagnose and classify psychological disorders, some psychologists prefer not to use it to measure the personality traits of "normal" clients. Many of these psychologists instead use the California Psychological Inventory, or CPI. The format of the CPI is similar to that of the MMPI-2, but it is designed to measure 15 "normal" personality traits, such as dominance, sociability, responsibility, and tolerance.

In many ways, the CPI is a much more valid instrument than the MMPI-2, even though it is not as widely used as the latter test. The norm group for the CPI is much larger than that for the MMPI-2,

and greater care was taken in controlling for factors such as age, socioeconomic status, and geographic location. Furthermore, the CPI has a much higher test-retest reliability than the MMPI-2 and seems to be a better predictor of such things as school and job success, leadership, and reactions to stress (Ross, 1987).

Projective Tests

Projective tests, unlike objective tests, have no clearly specified answers. Such tests use an **open-ended format**. People are presented with ambiguous stimuli such as inkblots, drawings of vague shapes, or pictures of people engaged in various activities. The test takers are then asked to report what the stimuli represent to them. They might also be asked to tell stories about the stimuli. Since the inkblots or drawings are open to interpretation, it is thought that people's interpretations of the pictures reveal something about their personalities. The Rorschach (RAWR-shahk) inkblot test and the Thematic Apperception Test (TAT) are two examples of widely used projective tests.

Rorschach Inkblot Test   Have you heard of a personality test that asks people to tell what a drawing or an inkblot looks like? There are actually a number of such personality tests. The Rorschach inkblot test is the best known of them. The Rorschach is named after its originator, Swiss psychiatrist Hermann Rorschach (1884–1922).

A Rorschach Inkblot

FIGURE 15.2   *While there is no "correct" response to a Rorschach inkblot test, certain answers are more in keeping than others with the features of the blot. What do you see?*

CASE STUDIES
AND OTHER TRUE STORIES
What Personality Type Are You?

Have you ever wondered how you or someone else would classify your personality? Whether you are an extrovert or an introvert? Whether you are logical or emotional?

Many people like to find out about themselves—to identify their characteristics and personalities. One of the most popular tests for that purpose is the Myers-Briggs Type Indicator® (MBTI®). Isabel Briggs Myers and her mother, Katharine Cook Briggs, began designing a personality test in the 1940s. Their goal was to create an objective test that would help employers hire the people who were best suited for particular kinds of jobs. Even today, the MBTI is popular in career and business counseling.

The MBTI is based on the personality theory of psychologist Carl Jung, who was one of Sigmund Freud's students. Jung believed that there are different personality types and that how a person acts in certain situations is based on the person's personality type. He also suggested that a person's personality preferences are present early in life and become more apparent as the person matures.

Each year, approximately 2 million people take the MBTI. The MBTI items are in forced-choice format. Typical questions include the following:

1. Which rules you more?
   (a) your head
   (b) your heart
2. At a party, do you
   (a) interact with many, including strangers?
   (b) interact with a few, known to you?

After choosing between (a) and (b) answers for 126 questions, the test taker's preferences are evaluated along four dimensions. The dimensions are extroversion versus introversion (E vs. I); sensing versus intuition (S vs. N) ; thinking versus feeling (T vs. F); and judging versus perceiving (J vs. P). Preferences may be classified as strong, moderate, or weak. The stronger one's preference along a dimension, the more one will exhibit the characteristics of that dimension.

Each preference is characterized by a particular way of seeing, or responding to, situations and other people. For example, extroverted people enjoy interacting with others, while introverted people prefer solitary activities. Intuitive people value creativity, while sensation-oriented people prefer practicality. Thinking people prefer to be logical and analytical when making decisions, while the decision-making process for feeling people relies more on interpersonal involvement and subjective values. Judgers typically prefer an environment that is ordered and structured, while perceivers tend to be more flexible and spontaneous.

The total possible combinations add up to 16 types, such as INTJ, ISFP, ESTJ, ENFP, and so on. In theory, each person is one of those 16 types. According to people who support the MBTI's results, how an individual sees the world and how he or she behaves can be predicted on the basis of the person's personality type.

The MBTI has received its share of criticism. One criticism has been that a person's type changes over time. Although Myers, Briggs, and Jung believed that an adult is one type and one type only, that appears to be untrue. The MBTI does not pass the test-retest standards for reliability.

Since the same test taker often obtains different results each time he or she takes the test, the MBTI cannot be considered an accurate predictor of behavior. In addition, the MBTI seems to label people in a prejudicial way. For these and other reasons, a National Academy of Sciences Study has concluded that the Myers-Briggs Type Indicator is not useful in career counseling programs.

THINKING CRITICALLY

1. **Summarizing** What are some criticisms of the Myers-Briggs Type Indicator?
2. **Predicting** How might being labeled as having a certain type of personality affect someone?

Interestingly, Rorschach's nickname as an adolescent was Klex, which means "inkblot" in German (Allison et al., 1988).

Figure 15.2 on page 352 shows a Rorschach inkblot. If you were taking the test, a psychologist would hand you a card with the inkblot and ask you what it looks like or what it could be. Because the Rorschach is a projective test, there is no list of clearly defined answers from which to choose. Instead, test takers provide their own responses to each inkblot. However, some answers are more in keeping than others with the features of the blot.

Look again at Figure 15.2. It could be a bat or a flying insect. It also could be an animal with a pointed face. It could be a jack-o'-lantern or many other things. But answers such as "diseased lungs" or "the devil in flames" are not readily suggested by the features of the blot. Therefore, a pattern of responses such as these is more likely than other patterns to suggest the presence of a personality disorder in the test taker.

Many attempts have been made to standardize the Rorschach. People's responses to the cards are usually interpreted according to factors such as location, determinants, content, and form level.

- *Location* is the part of the blot to which the person responds. Does he or she respond to the whole card or to a detail of the card?

- *Determinants* include features of the blot such as shading, texture, or color. People who are highly influenced by the texture and color are thought to be more emotional than those who do not focus on these aspects of the blot. Answers that incorporate many features of the blot are thought to reflect high intelligence.

- *Content* refers to the precise object the test taker reports seeing. Is he or she seeing a bat, a jack-o'-lantern, or a human figure?

- *Form level* indicates whether the answer is in keeping with the actual shape of the blot. Generally speaking, answers that fit the shape of the blot suggest that the individual sees the world the way most people do. (Some psychological disorders, such as schizophrenia, are characterized by bizarre perceptions.)

Supporters of the Rorschach test claim that it provides useful information that might not be obtained elsewhere. However, some researchers raise serious questions about the reliability and validity of the test. Because no two professionals interpret Rorschach responses in quite the same way, they argue that the test results can be arbitrary or biased to support the professional's point of view.

Thematic Apperception Test   The Thematic Apperception Test, or TAT, was developed in the 1930s by psychologists Henry Murray and Christiana Morgan at Harvard University. It is widely used in clinical practice and in motivation research (Watkins et al., 1995).

The TAT consists of drawings such as the one shown in Figure 15.3. These drawings, like the Rorschach inkblots, invite a variety of interpreta-

Thematic Apperception Test (TAT)

FIGURE 15.3   *Like the Rorschach inkblots, the TAT can invite a variety of interpretations. Test takers are asked to create a story for a variety of cards similar to the one pictured. From the responses, trained psychologists can derive achievement motivation scores.*

tions. As with the Rorschach, test takers are given the cards one at a time. They are then asked to create a story for each card. For example, people are asked what might have led to the scene depicted on the card, what the person (or people) in the picture is (are) doing, and how the story will end.

The idea behind the TAT is that people's needs and values emerge from the stories they tell. This can be especially true of attitudes toward other people, such as parents and romantic partners. The TAT is also used to measure achievement motivation. As you learned in Chapter 13, achievement motivation refers to the desire to do one's best and to realize one's goals.

For example, a TAT card may show an image of two women. However, it may be unclear exactly what their connection is. Are they mother and daughter? Do they have a close relationship? Are they friends? Here are two stories that could be told about this card:

Story 1 The mother and daughter are both annoyed. They dislike family gatherings. They have little in common and have nothing to say to one another, so they avoid even making eye contact. They are anxious for the awkward moment to be over.

Story 2 The mother and daughter are enjoying a quiet moment together. As they've gotten older, they don't have as much time to spend with one another. But they've remained close and have shared many special times. They feel lucky to have each other's support and love.

Psychologists are trained to derive attitudes and achievement motivation scores from stories such as these. As you might have guessed, the second story suggests a more positive attitude and achievement motivation than the first story.

Studying in a group can often be helpful. Members of the study group can pool their knowledge and take turns quizzing each other.

SECTION 3 REVIEW

go.hrw.com
Homework Practice Online
Keyword: SY7 HP15

1. What is the function of the validity scales in the MMPI-2?

2. How are the two types of personality tests used?

3. **Critical Thinking** *Supporting a Point of View* Because there are no standardized criteria for scoring answers on projective tests such as the Rorschach and the TAT, how accurate do you think they are? Support your answer.

S E C T I O N 4
Taking Tests

Many students think, "I know the material from my classes, but I just don't do well on tests." Sometimes they are right. But often they are wrong. When students are sure that they know something but cannot quite retrieve it—when it seems to be on the tip of their tongues—it may be that they did not learn it as well as they think they did. That is, some students have trouble on tests because they do not know the subject matter well enough, or they do not know it as well as they think they know it. For them, much of the cure lies in developing better study habits. (See Chapter 6.)

Some students, however, do know the material and yet they still perform poorly on tests. This section offers some general tips on taking tests, as well as specific ways of coping with certain types of test questions. Finally, the section analyzes the subject of test anxiety.

Tips for Taking Tests

Teachers generally determine the types of tests they give and when they give them. Midterm and final exams are usually a matter of school or department policy. And standardized tests, such as the SAT, are scheduled for certain dates throughout the year. You might think you have little control over the tests you take, but in reality there are many things students can do to help take charge of tests.

Gather Information   Learn where and when the next test will be given. Find out about the types of questions that will be asked and the topics you should study. Most teachers and other test administrators do not mind being asked questions. Some teachers may say that "everything" will be on the test, but others may offer specific information about what they consider important.

In addition, ask students who have already taken the course where test questions tend to come from. Do they tend to come from the textbook or from class notes?

Practice   Plan regular study periods. Use your reading assignments and class notes to create test questions that might be similar to those on the exam. Practice answering these test items with the members of your study group. Define key terms on your practice test. Outline the answers to possible essay questions. Try to answer all the questions and exercises in your textbook—even the ones that were not assigned as homework. Some of them may appear on the test. Even if they do not appear on it, they will provide useful practice.

Make the most of your study group. Pool your knowledge. Quiz one another and read the answers to your essay questions aloud. This is a good way to prepare yourself for writing the essays on the actual test. In the process, you will probably discover the areas that need further study.

Be Test-Wise   Small oversights can cause you problems on a test. For example, be sure you read the directions carefully and follow them precisely.

Bring the right equipment to tests. Avoid asking your teacher for a pen or a pencil during a test. Doing so communicates a message that you are not prepared for the test and that you do not take the course seriously.

Be sure your pencils are sharpened or that your pens have blue or black ink. Have some loose-leaf paper available, if only to use as scrap paper. Ask your teacher if you may use a pocket dictionary to check your spelling on essays. Teachers may also let you bring calculators and formulas to science tests.

Multiple-Choice Questions

Multiple-choice items are commonly used on many types of tests. They are used in standardized tests, such as the SAT, and they are also used in classroom quizzes and exams. Educators and psychologists often use multiple-choice questions because they encourage the student to focus on the right answer (and reject the wrong ones). They can also be graded quickly and objectively.

Below are two sample multiple-choice questions that might appear on a test for this chapter:

1. The Kuder Career Search is a(n)
   (a) achievement test.
   (b) aptitude test.
   (c) vocational interest inventory.
   (d) personality test.
2. Which of the following tests is an objective personality test?
   (a) the Thematic Apperception Test
   (b) the Minnesota Multiphasic Personality Inventory
   (c) the Standard Assessment Test
   (d) the Rorschach inkblot test

Here are some hints for doing well on multiple-choice tests:

- *Try to answer the question before you look at the choices.* When you see "Kuder Career Search," turn it into a question: "What is the Kuder Career Search?" If you can describe the test to yourself, it will be easy to select the correct choice.

- *Consider every possible choice.* The last choice may read "All of the above." If you have time, find a coherent reason for eliminating each choice you reject.

- *Look for answers that are opposites.* When you see two answers that are opposite in meaning, one of them is likely to be the correct choice.

- *Look for the best choice listed.* It may be that no choice is perfect, but one choice is probably better than the others.

- *Mark difficult questions so that you can come back to them later.* Do not let a tough question eat up your time.

- *Guess only when the odds of gaining points outweigh the odds of losing points.* For example, always guess when there is no penalty for wrong answers. But if full credit is subtracted for wrong answers and you have no idea which is the correct choice, do not guess.

- *Change your answer if you think you have made a mistake.* It is only a myth that you should go with your first hunch. Your hunch could be wrong, and by looking at the question again, you may come up with the right answer.

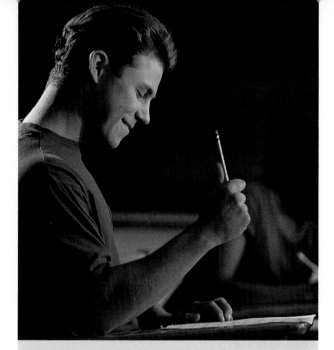

By staying relaxed and keeping certain rules of thumb in mind, students can improve their scores on a variety of types of tests. The most important rule of thumb is to study thoroughly.

TRUTH OR fiction ∎ R E V I S I T E D ∎

It is not true that you should always go with your first guess on a multiple-choice test. If you believe that you have made an error, you should change your answer. Often people arrive at the correct answer after thinking about the answer again.

True-False Questions

True-false questions can be tricky. After all, if half the questions are true and half are false, you could earn a grade of 50 percent simply by guessing. Below are two sample true-false questions that might appear on a test for this chapter:

1. The Minnesota Multiphasic Personality Inventory (MMPI-2) is a subjective personality test used in clinical work.
2. All psychologists consider the Rorschach inkblot test to be a valid measure for determining psychological health.

The following pointers can help you maximize your performance on true-false items:

- *For the item to be true, every part of it must be true.* If one part is false, then the entire item must be false. The question about the MMPI-2 correctly identifies it as a personality test used in clinical work, but it is an objective test, not a subjective test. Therefore, the answer to this question would be "false."

- *Be wary of items that use absolutes such as* all, always, *or* never. These items are usually false. Since only some, not all, psychologists consider the Rorschach to be a valid measure of psychological health, the answer to the second question would be "false."

- *Items that provide more information and are longer than others tend to be true.*

Keep in mind that these are only rules of thumb, however. They are not foolproof instructions. Your best strategy is still to study thoroughly and know the answers on your own.

Short-Answer Questions

Short-answer items ask the test taker to give a brief response to a question. Here are some sample short-answer questions:

1. What is an achievement test?
2. What is the difference between an objective test and a projective test?

Here are some pointers for responding to short-answer questions:

- *Answer in brief but complete sentences.* For example, the answer to the first question might be phrased as follows: "An achievement test measures a person's skill or knowledge in a specific subject or field of study."

- *Include significant terms in your answer.* In the answer to question 1, the significant terms would include *skill, knowledge, subject,* and *field of study.*

- *Use detail if time and space allow.* A detail added to the answer might be the following: "An achievement test is used to determine how much knowledge a person has acquired in a particular subject."

Essay Questions

The first step in answering an essay question is making certain you have understood the question. When students do not understand the question, the answer may draw comments such as the following: "Strays from the question" or "Nicely written, but misses the point."

Guiding Words Found in Essay Questions

Analyze	Identify
Compare	Illustrate
Contrast	Interpret
Criticize	Justify
Define	List
Describe	Prove
Discuss	State
Enumerate	Support
Evaluate	Trace
Explain	

FIGURE 15.4 *The first step in answering an essay question is to make sure that you understand the question. Look for key words such as those in the list above to guide your answer.*

Read the directions carefully and look for key words to guide your answer. Figure 15.4 lists some of these key words. Ignoring them increases the chances that you will omit important points from your answer.

Before beginning to write your essay, make a quick outline on a piece of scrap paper to help you organize your thoughts. The outline should help you keep track of the main points you wish to make in your answer. Mark where you will start and where you will end. Jot down key terms that represent ideas you wish to expand on in your essay. If you run out of time before you complete the essay, attach the outline to show where you were headed. It may help your grade (and it certainly will not hurt it).

Express your strongest ideas first. When you lead with the concepts you know best, you build a foundation for presenting a strong argument.

How long should your essay be? A good rule of thumb is "Don't count words; just answer the question." Teachers will reward you for being right on the mark as long as you have provided sufficient support for your argument.

TRUTH OR fiction ■ REVISITED ■ *It is not true that the longer your answer to an essay question is, the better your score on that question is likely to be.* Essay questions are graded on how completely and accurately you have covered the main points of the topic, regardless of how long the answer is.

Test Anxiety

A DAY IN THE LIFE Like Marc, some students become anxious before and during exams. The anxiety they experience consists of feelings of dread and foreboding. They may sense that something terrible—though they may not know what—is going to happen. Test anxiety ranges from increased tension to actual physical symptoms, such as rapid breathing, pounding heartbeat, light-headedness or dizziness, nausea, and diarrhea.

Anxiety may be very uncomfortable, but it is not always a bad thing. It is normal to feel somewhat anxious as a test approaches. Anxiety shows that we understand the importance of the occasion and that failure may have serious consequences. Test anxiety

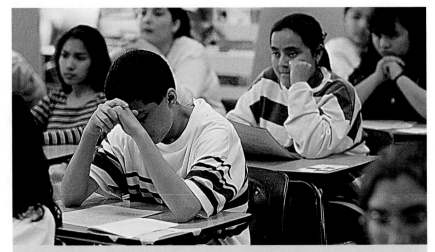

The test anxiety that many students feel before and during a test can often be overcome by being prepared and thinking positively.

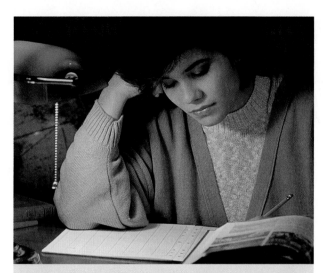

For those who suffer from test anxiety, practicing cognitive restructuring can eventually result in better grades.

reflects the thoughts of students before and during the test. Such thoughts might include the following:

- "I study as hard as I can, but my mind just blanks when the tests are distributed."

- "What's wrong with me? I know the material, but I just can't take tests."

- "I just know I'm going to flunk."

- "I wish I could get out of here. I wish the test was over."

- "I'm not going to have enough time to finish."

Test-anxious students allow these thoughts and self-doubts to distract them, preventing them from focusing on the test itself.

The good news, however, is that test anxiety can be overcome. The ways of handling test anxiety include being prepared, overlearning, and changing the way one thinks about tests. Changing the way one thinks about tests can also change the way in which one's body responds to test situations.

Be Prepared　One way to overcome test anxiety is to be prepared. Actors who have thoroughly memorized their lines may still be anxious when they hear their cue, but they are less likely to forget the line they have to speak. If you study carefully and review the material regularly, you can be confident that you will recall what you have learned.

Review the material regularly before a test and avoid cramming. Learning takes time. Studying a reasonable amount every day is far more effective than cramming suddenly the night before. You can

begin to cope with possible test anxiety right from the beginning of the semester—by planning a regular study schedule and sticking to it.

Overlearn　Overlearning means reviewing the material over and over, even after you think you have mastered it. Overlearning accomplishes two objectives: remembering the subject matter longer and building confidence. Overlearning makes you realize, "I *really* know this stuff!"

Think Helpful Thoughts　What if you are well prepared for tests and still make yourself anxious with self-defeating thoughts? There are strategies for ending upsetting thoughts and focusing on the task at hand—the test.

What are the negative thoughts that occur to you at test-taking times? Write them down. Once you are aware of these negative thoughts, you can replace them with positive ones. For example, replace "I'm probably going to fail this test" with "I'm prepared for this test, and I know I'll do well."

This method of coping is called cognitive restructuring. **Cognitive restructuring** means consciously changing the thoughts one has in a particular situation. Cognitive restructuring consists of the following four steps:

1. Identify self-defeating thoughts, paying special attention to the ones that seem exaggerated.
2. Replace self-defeating thoughts with positive and encouraging messages to yourself.
3. Imagine yourself in the testing situation and practice positive thinking.
4. Reward yourself for thinking positively.

If you consistently practice cognitive restructuring, chances are you will begin to see a change for the better. Eventually, you will become less anxious and more confident about taking tests. Your grades may reflect the changes.

SECTION 4 REVIEW

go.hrw.com　**Homework Practice Online**　Keyword: SY7 HP15

1. How does making an outline help one answer an essay question more effectively?

2. List the four steps of cognitive restructuring to cope with test anxiety.

3. **Critical Thinking** *Identifying Cause and Effect* What type of stress do some students feel before or during tests, and how might this stress affect their scores?

15 REVIEW

 Writing a Summary

Using standard grammar, spelling, sentence structure, and punctuation, summarize the information in this chapter. Consider:
- the purposes, characteristics, and types of psychological tests
- strategies for taking tests and avoiding test anxiety

 Identifying People and Ideas

Identify the following terms or people and use them in appropriate sentences.

1. behavior-rating scales
2. self-reports
3. standardized test
4. norms
5. achievement tests
6. aptitude tests
7. forced-choice format
8. projective tests
9. open-ended format
10. cognitive restructuring

 Understanding Main Ideas

SECTION 1 (pp. 344–347)
1. What are two examples of transformed score tests used by schools?

SECTION 2 (pp. 347–350)
2. How are aptitude tests generally used?

SECTION 3 (pp. 350–355)
3. How were the clinical scales of the Minnesota Multiphasic Personality Inventory (MMPI) originally created?

SECTION 4 (pp. 355–359)
4. What steps might a student take to overcome test anxiety?

 Thinking Critically

1. **Evaluating** Why is a longer test generally more valid and reliable?
2. **Analyzing Information** Why is it important not to depend too much on the results of interest inventories?

3. **Supporting a Point of View** Do you think it is possible for psychologists to accurately measure a person's personality using only multiple-choice and true-false questions? Explain your answer.
4. **Categorizing** What are the advantages and disadvantages of using self-reports, rather than observing behavior, to measure personality?
5. **Drawing Inferences and Conclusions** Why do you think people in the same occupation often share the same interests, even outside interests not directly related to their jobs?

 Writing About Psychology

1. **Analyzing Information** Popular magazines often include tests or self-inventories that claim to measure such diverse qualities as one's ability to handle money or how happy one's marriage is. Look through magazines at home or in the library and then create an outline that describes the test. Consider the following questions as you prepare your outline: What does the test claim to measure? Do you think it has any scientific validity? Why or why not? Why do you think these tests are so prevalent? Briefly present your outline to the class. As a class, discuss the kinds of issues these tests seem to focus on.

2. **Supporting a Point of View** The importance and the validity of the Scholastic Assessment Test (SAT) have been a subject of debate for the past several years. Research some of the issues surrounding the SAT. Write an essay stating your position on the use of the SAT as a part of the college admission process. Be sure to include references to your research to support your position. Use the graphic organizer below to help you write your essay.

For ← Use of the SAT → Against

Interpreting Graphs

Study the graph below. Then use the information in the graph to help you answer the questions that follow.

Age and Test Performance

Source: Sundberg, *Assessment of Persons*, 1977

1. Which of the following statements accurately reflects the information in the graph?

  a. Most 20 year-old test takers do not perform as well as most 10 year-old test takers.

  b. Growing older causes a decline in test performance.

  c. Performance on tests gradually declines after age 10.

  d. Test scores improve dramatically during adolescence.

2. What areas of research might this graph lead psychologists to investigate?

Analyzing Primary Sources

Read the following excerpt, in which Theodora Abel considers the issue of culture and testing. Then answer the questions that follow.

❝On the island of Montserrat in the Caribbean until recently there was no electricity, nor windowpanes in homes, and no motion picture houses, so that the idea of switching on lights, breaking windowpanes and replacing them, or knowing what to do in case of fire in a theater (items on various tests) would not have made much sense to children. At least these phenomena would not have had the same impact as they would if the children had had direct experience of them. Non-familiarity with the kind of stimuli presented or the kind of performance expected (looking at ink-blots, copying block designs, tracing through mazes, making up plots and stories) can cause test results to be incorrectly interpreted unless the psychologist takes these factors into account.❞

3. Which statement best reflects Abel's argument?

  a. Psychologists must be aware of cultural differences between groups when administering tests.

  b. People from poor backgrounds rarely do well on assessment tests.

  c. Cultural differences have no effect on psychological tests.

  d. Testing is an inherently flawed process and should be abandoned.

4. According to the excerpt, how can the test design itself lead to problems for test takers?

PSYCHOLOGY PROJECTS

Cooperative Learning

Applying Psychology With a partner, review the tips on taking tests that are discussed in this chapter. Decide on a visual—such as a booklet, flyer, or poster—that gives advice to other students about how to take tests. Be sure that the visual clearly illustrates the test–taking advice that you want to convey to your classmates.

🖅 internet connect ▤▤▤

Internet Activity: go.hrw.com
KEYWORD: SY7 CH15

Choose an activity on psychological tests to:

  • define the concept of "transformed score" and explain percentile grade equivalent scores.

  • write a report that describes psychological testing.

  • design questions for a personality test.

16 Chapter

GENDER ROLES

Read to Discover

1 What are gender roles and gender stereotypes, and how do they differ?

2 How have some studies indicated gender differences in cognitive abilities, personality, and behavior?

3 What is gender typing, and what are several theories that explain how it may occur?

4 How have gender roles changed over time, and in what ways can they vary from culture to culture?

A DAY IN THE LIFE

Marc, Janet, Dan, and Linda were at the recreation center following their school's annual career day. Suddenly, they were all thinking about their futures.

"What's wrong, Dan?" Janet asked. She had noticed that Dan seemed exceptionally quiet.

"This career fair just made me realize that I still don't know for sure what I want to do after graduation. I'm afraid that if I don't make some decisions I may end up just like my Uncle John," Dan said.

"Uncle John was laid off from his job, and my Aunt Debbie had to go to work to support the family. Now she's making more money than Uncle John ever did."

"That's great, isn't it?" Linda said.

"It should be, but ever since Aunt Debbie went to work, my uncle is always upset. I think he can't accept that my aunt is making more money than he did. All I know is, when I'm older I want to have a good career so I can support my family."

"Are you saying you wouldn't want your wife to work outside the home?" Janet asked defensively.

"It's not that I wouldn't *want* her to work. I just feel that she shouldn't *have* to work. I should be able to support her and our family."

"I don't understand that attitude," Linda said. "My parents both work, and usually they both help around the house. But when my grandparents visit from Mexico, my dad won't be caught doing any housework. I guess he doesn't want his parents to see him doing work they still consider 'women's work.'"

"Some people don't realize that times change," Janet responded. "Ever since my parents' divorce, my mom has had to work nights and take care of the house during the day. She still manages to have time for me, though. She's been great."

"I plan to have a career," Linda said. "I've always wanted to do something with math—maybe engineering or architecture."

Grinning, Linda turned to Marc and asked, "So, Marc, what would you think about staying at home while your wife went to work?"

• • •

Dan's uncle was having a hard time accepting his wife's new role, but she also was having a difficult time. She worked all day at her job and then had to take care of the home. She also had to deal with her husband's feelings of frustration and depression. Her husband was normally a good and generous person, but he was feeling trapped by his beliefs about the kinds of behavior that are appropriate for men and for women.

Some people, such as Dan's uncle, believe that a woman's place is in the home with the children and that a man's place is on the job, working to support them. Other people believe that a wide range of behaviors is appropriate for men and women. This chapter explores these and other beliefs about what it means to be male and what it means to be female.

Key Terms

- gender
- gender roles
- gender stereotypes
- nurturance
- gender typing
- lateralization
- modeling
- gender schema

HOLT

Psychology Video Program

Watch the video to explore how women bullfighters are changing gender stereotypes in Mexico.

Read the following statements about psychology. Do you think they are true or false? You will learn whether each statement is true or false as you read the chapter.

- Men generally demonstrate more aggressive behavior than women.
- Women tend to be more talkative than men.
- The qualities men look for in a potential mate are different from the qualities women look for.
- Boys and girls are treated in much the same way until about age three.
- Much of the behavior we think of as typical male or female behavior we are not born with but learn from other members of our culture.

SECTION 1

What Are Gender Roles?

We all have physical characteristics that make us different from other people. Height, hair color, eye color, and many other physical traits help to differentiate who we are. Possibly the most fundamental physical characteristic of any human being is his or her gender. **Gender** refers to the sex of an individual, either male or female. Like hair color and eye color, gender is a biological trait that is fixed by the genes before birth.

Gender Roles

Closely related to the concept of gender is the idea of **gender roles**—widely accepted societal expectations about how males and females should behave. Gender roles define what is considered to be appropriate masculine and feminine behavior in a particular culture.

A DAY IN THE LIFE

When Dan explained that he thought he should be able to support his wife and family, he was expressing his belief in the type of behavior that he considered appropriate for men in American society. That is, he was adhering to a gender role.

Unlike gender itself, gender roles are not genetically determined. Rather, gender roles appear to be a product of both biological and social factors.

Gender Trait Stereotypes Around the World

Stereotypes of Males	Stereotypes of Females
Active	Affectionate
Adventurous	Appreciative
Aggressive	Cautious
Arrogant	Changeable
Autocratic	Charming
Capable	Complicated
Coarse	Dependent
Conceited	Dreamy
Confident	Emotional
Courageous	Excitable
Cruel	Faultfinding
Determined	Fearful
Disorderly	Fickle
Enterprising	Foolish
Hardheaded	Forgiving
Individualistic	Fussy
Inventive	Gentle
Loud	Imaginative
Obnoxious	Modest
Opinionated	Nervous
Pleasure-seeking	Patient
Precise	Pleasant
Quick	Self-pitying
Rational	Sensitive
Realistic	Sentimental
Reckless	Sexy
Resourceful	Softhearted
Rigid	Sophisticated
Robust	Submissive
Sharp-witted	Suggestible
Show-off	Superstitious
Steady	Talkative
Stern	Timid
Stingy	Touchy
Tough	Unambitious
Unscrupulous	Understanding
	Unstable
	Weak
	Worrying

FIGURE 16.1 *Psychologists John Williams and Deborah Best (1994, p. 193, Table 1) found that people in 30 nations around the world tended to agree on the nature of masculine and feminine gender trait stereotypes.*

Many kinds of work that people do today can be done equally well by men and women. As an increased number of women have entered the workforce, gender roles have become less rigid. **How might this affect future generations?**

Although one speaks of "playing a role," people do not *play* gender roles in the same way that they play roles on the stage. That is to say, they do not usually see themselves as pretending to be someone they are not. Instead, for most people, gender roles are simply a part of who they are and how they see themselves.

Gender Stereotypes

Gender roles can become so rigid that they develop into **gender stereotypes**, which are fixed and oversimplified beliefs about the ways in which men and women ought to behave. Many gender stereotypes in the United States are linked to the traditional view of men as breadwinners and women as homemakers. In our society, people tend to see the feminine gender stereotypes as warm, emotional, dependent, gentle, helpful, mild, patient, submissive, and interested in the arts. The typical masculine gender stereotype is perceived as independent, competitive, tough, protective, logical, and competent at business, math, and science. Women are traditionally expected to care for the children and cook the meals. Cross-cultural studies confirm that these gender role stereotypes are widespread. (See Figure 16.1.) For example, in their survey of 30 countries, John Williams and Deborah Best

(1994) found that men are more likely to be judged to be active, adventurous, aggressive, arrogant, and autocratic. Women are more likely to be seen as fault finding, fearful, fickle, foolish, and fussy.

Even emotions are stereotyped. Subjects in one study believed that women more often than men experienced the emotions of sadness, fear, and sympathy (Plant et al., 2000). But they thought that men were more likely to feel anger and pride.

Gender stereotypes have tended to keep women in the home. Educational opportunities for women have traditionally been more limited. Today many jobs are still stereotyped as primarily for women—for example, nursing and teaching in elementary school. However, large numbers of women have entered some professions previously limited to men, such as medicine and law.

SECTION 1 REVIEW

go.hrw.com Homework Practice Online
Keyword: SY7 HP16

1. Define *gender, gender role,* and *gender stereotype.*

2. **Critical Thinking** *Contrasting* In what ways do *gender roles* and *gender stereotypes* differ?

Gender Differences

What kinds of differences actually exist between men and women? There are obvious physical differences between the sexes, but other, less obvious differences between men and women also seem to exist. These include differences in cognitive, or intellectual, abilities and differences in personality and behavior. As we shall see, psychologists disagree about whether these differences are biologically based or learned through experience.

It is important to note that *group* differences between men and women in certain traits and abilities says nothing about the differences among *individual* men and women. In fact, there is greater variation within each gender group than there is between the average man and the average woman.

Physical Differences

Several physical differences between the sexes are usually apparent because males and females differ in both primary and secondary sex characteristics. Primary sex characteristics refer to the organs of the reproductive system. For example, women have ovaries and men have testes. Secondary sex characteristics include such traits as deeper voices and greater amounts of facial hair in men and smaller body size and wider hips in women. These traits are controlled by sex hormones, which, in turn, are determined by genes.

Differences in Cognitive Abilities

It was once believed that men were more intelligent than women because they had greater knowledge of world affairs and skill in science and industry. Although men could demonstrate greater knowledge and skill in these areas, this did not reflect differences in intelligence. Rather, it merely reflected the exclusion of women from world affairs, science, and industry. Assessments of intelligence do not show overall gender differences in cognitive abilities (Halpern & LaMay, 2000). However, reviews of the research suggest that girls are somewhat superior to boys in verbal abilities, such as the ability to make up sentences and paragraphs, the ability to find words that are similar in meaning to other words, spelling, knowledge of foreign languages, and pronunciations (Halpern, 1997).

Girls seem to acquire language somewhat faster than boys do. Also, in the United States far more boys than girls have reading problems, such as reading below grade level (Halpern, 1997; Neisser et al., 1996). Men headed for college seem to catch up in verbal skills.

On the other hand, men seem to be somewhat superior in the ability to manipulate visual images held in memory. Psychological tests of spatial ability assess skills such as finding figures embedded within larger designs and mentally rotating figures in space. Men apparently excel in visual-spatial abilities of the sort used in mathematics, science, and even map reading (Grön et al., 2000; Halpern & LaMay, 2000). One study compared the navigation strategies of 90 male and 104 female college students (Dabbs et al., 1998). In giving directions, college men more often referred to miles and directional coordinates in terms of north, south, east, and west. College women were more likely to refer to landmarks and turns to the right or left.

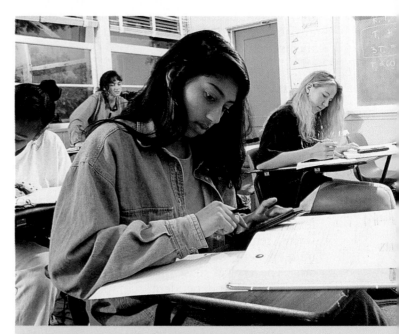

The gender gap in mathematical abilities seems to be closing, as more females are enrolling in advanced mathematics courses and obtaining bachelor's degrees in mathematics. These girls are solving problems in a high school math class.

Percentage of Bachelor's Degrees Awarded to Women in the Sciences

Bachelor's degrees	1970–1971	2001–2002
Biology	29	61
Chemistry	18	48
Computer Science	14	28
Engineering	1	19
Geology	11	45
Mathematics	38	47
Physics	7	23

FIGURE 16.2 *The number of women obtaining bachelor's degrees in math and the sciences has increased over the last 30 years.*
Source: Cox, W. Michael and Richard Alm, "Scientists are made, not born," *New York Times*, February 28, 2005.

Studies in the United States and elsewhere find that men generally obtain higher scores on mathematics tests than women (Beller & Gafni, 2000; Gallagher et al., 2000; Halpern & LaMay, 2000). Females excel in computational ability in elementary school, however. Males excel in mathematical problem solving in high school and college. Boys generally outperform girls on the mathematics section of the Scholastic Assessment Test (SAT).

These gender differences do appear to exist, at least for the time being. However, psychologists note the following:

- In most cases, the differences are small. Differences in math and visual-spatial abilities also appear to be narrowing as more women pursue course work in fields that had been typically preserved for men. More girls such as Linda are continuing to excel in mathematics. As Linda noted, her interest in mathematics could lead to a career in engineering or architecture—two fields previously dominated by men.
- These gender differences are *group* differences. There is greater variation in these skills between individuals *within* the groups than between men and women (Maccoby, 1990). That is, there may be a greater difference in, say, verbal skills between two women than between a woman and a man. Some men's verbal skills are better than those of the "average" woman, and millions of women outdistance the "average" man in math and spatial abilities.
- Some differences may largely reflect cultural influences. In our culture spatial and mathematics abilities are stereotyped as masculine. Women who are given just a few hours of training in spatial skills—for example, rotating geometric figures or studying floor plans—perform at least as well as men on tests of these skills (Baenninger & Elenteny, 1997; Lawton & Morrin, 1999).
- Last, as Figure 16.2 shows, a growing number of women are obtaining college degrees in mathematics and the sciences. Women now obtain most of the bachelor's degrees in biology and nearly half of the degrees in chemistry and math. Gains in computer science and engineering have also been dramatic. These trends disprove the stereotype that mathematics and the sciences are a male domain.

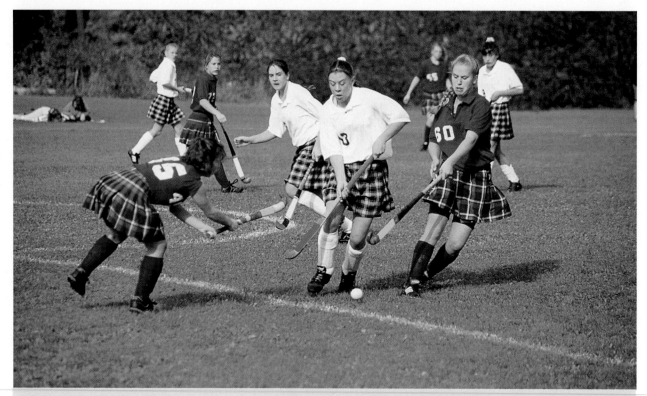

Although more men compete in sports in the United States, women's sports have become increasingly popular.
How might participation in sports help girls improve their visual-spatial skills?

Differences in Personality and Behavior

Many notable gender differences are found in personality and behavior. Women, for example, tend to exceed men in trust and **nurturance**, or affectionate care. Men tend to exceed women in such traits as assertiveness and tough-mindedness. Other gender differences in personality and behavior include differences in levels of aggression, communication styles, and traits desired in a mate (Feingold, 1994).

Aggression In most cultures, it is primarily the men who fight in war and compete in sports and games. This is, in part, because men tend to be physically larger and stronger than women, as previously mentioned. Yet men may be more suited to these activities for another reason as well—their generally higher level of aggression.

Most psychological studies of aggression have found that men tend to be more aggressive than women (Eagly & Wood, 1991; Knight et al., 1996). Not only are men more likely than women to act aggressively, particularly if provoked, but they are also more likely to use physical forms of aggression,

such as hitting and shoving. Women act aggressively less often, and when they do, they tend to use indirect forms of aggression. (Bjorkqvist et al., 1992; Lagerspetz et al., 1988).

 It is true that men generally demonstrate more aggressive behavior than women do. According to several studies, men are also more likely than women to be physical in the expression of their aggression.

Although it is clear that men tend to be more aggressive than women, the origins of this gender difference are not as clear. Some experts believe that gender differences in aggression are primarily due to biological differences between men and women (Baron & Richardson, 1994). For example, aggressive behavior has been linked with high levels of testosterone (Berman et al., 1993; Olweus, 1986).

Although biology may help explain gender differences in aggression, it is likely that the

PSYCHOLOGY

GENDER DIFFERENCES IN INTIMACY AND INDEPENDENCE

In her book *You Just Don't Understand* (1990), psychologist Deborah Tannen discusses the human needs for intimacy and independence. Although males and females both need intimacy and independence, Tannen believes that women tend to focus on the former and men on the latter. The difference, Tannen argues, rests on how men and women interact with the world around them and how they view relationships. The difference can lead to problems in communication between men and women.

According to Tannen, most women tend to live in a world of connection with others. They negotiate complex networks of friendship, try to reach consensus, minimize differences, and avoid the appearance of superiority because this tends to highlight differences. Intimacy with others is key for individuals with this view of relationships.

In contrast, Tannen sees the majority of men as living in a world of status, where they must establish their own place in a hierarchy of others. Here independence is key. This is because telling others what to do is a primary means of increasing status. Taking orders from others, on the other hand, is a mark of low status.

These differing perspectives of the two sexes can lead women and men to interpret and react to the same situation in very different ways. Tannen provides the example of a couple, Nancy and Josh, to illustrate how these differing views of relationships create problems in communication.

Nancy and Josh When Josh's old high school buddy called him at work and said he would be in town on business the following month, Josh invited him to stay for the weekend. That evening he informed Nancy that they were going to have a houseguest and that he and his buddy would be going out together like they did in high school.

When Josh told Nancy about the plans he had made, she was upset. Nancy reminded Josh that she was going to be away on business the week before his buddy's visit. The Friday night that Josh would be out with his buddy would be her first night home. What upset Nancy the most, however, was that Josh had made the plans on his own and only later informed her of them rather than discussing them with her first.

Nancy would never have made plans, even for an evening, let alone a whole weekend, without first checking with Josh. She could not understand why Josh did not show her the same courtesy and consideration that she would show him. When she protested, Josh responded, "I can't say to my friend, 'I have to ask my wife for permission'!"

To Josh, checking with his wife means seeking permission, and that, in turn, implies that he is not independent and free to act on his own. It would make him feel like a child. To Nancy, checking with her husband has nothing to do with permission. She thinks husbands and wives should discuss their plans with each other because their lives are connected and the actions of one have consequences for the other. Not only does Nancy not mind telling someone, "I have to check with Josh," but on the contrary, she likes it. It makes her feel good to know and to show that her life is connected with another's.

Conclusion Nancy and Josh were more upset about the incidents described above, as well as by others like them, than seemed warranted. This is because the incident reflected basic gender differences in how they view the world of relationships. Nancy was upset because she sensed a failure of connectedness and intimacy in her relationship with Josh. Josh was upset because he felt as though Nancy was trying to control him and limit his independence.

Think About It

Identifying Cause and Effect How do the perspectives of men and women differ, and how do these differences affect communication between men and women?

All of these predominantly male sports are based on aggressive behavior: hockey in Canada, judo in Japan, rugby in England, and boxing in the United States. **Why do men tend to dominate aggressive sports?**

differences are also at least partly due to predominant male and female gender roles (Eagly & Steffen, 1986). In many societies, men are expected and socialized, or taught through the influence of social pressures, to be tougher, more assertive, and more aggressive than women (Eagly, 1987).

Communication Styles A common gender stereotype is that of the "strong, silent" man. Many people believe that women talk more than men do, but some research suggests that the opposite is actually true. Although girls tend to be more talkative than boys during early childhood, by the time they enter school, boys usually dominate classroom discussions (Sadker & Sadker, 1994). Indeed, as girls mature, they do less of the talking in most mixed-sex groups. By adulthood, men generally spend more time talking than women do in many situations. Men are also more likely to introduce new topics and to interrupt others (Rathus, 2003).

TRUTH OR fiction
■ REVISITED ■

It is not true that women tend to be more talkative than men. Girls may be more talkative when they are young, but as they mature, they generally talk less than men do.

Men tend to talk less than women do about their feelings and personal experiences (Dindia & Allen, 1992). Women often talk with other women—mothers, sisters, roommates, and friends—about intimate matters. Men talk about intimate matters much less often. When they do discuss personal matters, they generally do so with women rather than with other men, perhaps because women tend to be better at using and understanding nonverbal communication (Hall, 1978, 1984). Women are also more likely to offer understanding and support (Hall, 1984; Reisman, 1990). Dan, for example, was experiencing several issues that he was having difficulty working through. Rather than discuss these issues with Marc, he chose to confide in Janet.

A DAY IN THE LIFE

Whether these gender differences in communication styles are biologically based or socially learned is still unclear. Male and female children tend to be treated differently from birth in both the number and nature of verbal and nonverbal communications directed toward them.

Mate Selection Many physical features, such as cleanliness, good complexion, clear eyes, strong teeth and healthy hair, firm muscle tone, and a steady gait, are found to be universally appealing to both genders (Buss, 1999). However, studies on mate selection find that men tend to be more swayed than women by a partner's physical appearance. Women tend to place greater emphasis than men on traits such as professional status, consideration, dependability, kindness, and fondness for children (Buss, 1994; Feingold, 1992). In a survey of more than 13,000 people in the United States, psychologist Susan Sprecher and her colleagues asked a series of questions relating to characteristics that people find appealing in a mate. Questions included how willing a person would be to marry someone who was older, younger, of a different religion, unlikely to hold a steady job, and not good-looking. Each item was answered by choosing a number on a 7-point scale on which 1 meant "not at all" and 7 meant "very willing." Women were more willing than men to marry someone who was not good-looking, but they were less willing to marry someone who was unlikely to hold a steady job.

Some psychologists believe that men and women originally valued different characteristics in potential mates because they are the traits that help ensure successful reproduction (Buss, 1994; Feingold, 1992; Fisher, 1992). However, this explanation cannot be proved conclusively. Gender differences in socialization may also influence which traits men and women look for in a mate. Regardless of the cause, however, the differences between the sexes in the traits they consider important in a mate are real, and they can be found in many different cultures (Buss, 1989).

TRUTH OR fiction
■ R E V I S I T E D ■

It is true that the qualities men look for in a potential mate are different from the qualities women look for. Men tend to focus more on the physical attractiveness of potential mates, whereas women tend to place greater emphasis on personal qualities, such as kindness.

As discussed earlier, actual differences in cognitive abilities, personality, and behavior are quite small and may be diminishing. Furthermore, many differences between men and women appear to be due largely to environmental influences and cultural expectations and not to inborn biological differences between men and women.

SECTION 2 REVIEW

go.hrw.com **Homework Practice Online** Keyword: SY7 HP16

1. What evidence suggests that gender differences in cognitive abilities are at least partly due to differences in boys' and girls' life experiences?

2. What hormone is linked to aggressive behavior?

3. **Critical Thinking** *Analyzing Information* Give three examples of ways that children might be socialized to be more or less aggressive.

Gender Typing

As you have learned, differences do exist between the genders. If these differences are not based solely on biological factors, however, how do they develop into gender roles? As in many areas of psychology, several different theories have been proposed to explain gender role development, which is also known as **gender typing**.

Research has shown that children as young as two and a half years of age have begun to develop ideas about traits and behaviors they consider characteristic of males and females (Rathus, 2003). These findings suggest that gender typing takes place at an early age. Exactly how and why gender roles develop, however, is a subject of considerable debate among psychologists. A number of theories have been proposed to explain gender typing. These theories fall into two general categories: those that explain gender typing as a biological process and those that explain it as a psychological process.

Biological Views

Biological views of gender typing focus on the impact of such factors as genes and hormones in the development of gender-related behavior.

Genetics Most biologists believe that genes for traits that help individuals survive and reproduce tend to be passed on to future generations. Some psychologists have argued that the traits that ensured the survival and reproductive success of early humans made early men successful hunters and warriors and early women successful child rearers (Buss, 2000). For men, these would have included such traits as good visual-spatial skills and aggression. For women, such traits would have included good nonverbal communication skills and nurturance. According to the theory, genes for these traits would have been passed on to future generations, and the traits would eventually come to characterize humans as a species.

The genetic view of gender role origins is highly controversial. Critics argue that a person's biological makeup does not predetermine how that person will behave. Instead, they point to cross-cultural research that suggests that gender roles are largely learned and not inherited (Mead, 1935). In their view, genes are important determinants of physical traits such as strength, but complex social behaviors such as aggression involve learning and cultural influences as well as heredity.

Hormones Some psychologists believe that gender typing occurs because men and women differ in the organization and functioning of their brains. According to this view, sex hormones sculpt the brains of men and women differently before birth. To understand this theory, some background on brain structure and function is necessary.

The two hemispheres, or right and left sides, of the brain are somewhat specialized to carry out different functions. In most people, the right hemisphere tends to be better specialized to perform visual-spatial tasks, whereas the left hemisphere tends to be better specialized to perform verbal tasks. This does not imply a strict division of roles, because neither hemisphere is solely responsible for any cognitive abilities. However, some cognitive tasks appear to be performed more quickly and efficiently by one hemisphere than by the other (Bradshaw et al., 1981). (See Chapter 3.)

This specialization of the two sides of the brain is called **lateralization**. Lateralization occurs during fetal development and is apparently influenced by sex hormones. Thus, lateralization may occur somewhat differently in boys and girls, resulting in some gender differences in brain organization and function (Collaer & Hines, 1995; Tan, 1994).

There is some evidence to suggest that testosterone leads to relatively greater growth of the right hemisphere as compared with the left hemisphere (Grimshaw et al., 1995). This evidence is consistent with research that indicates that females tend to show less lateralization than males (Grön et al., 2000). Taken together, these studies could help explain why males seem to be better at visual-spatial tasks, which tend to be processed by the right hemisphere, and why females seem to be better at verbal tasks, which tend to be processed by the left hemisphere of the brain.

Some psychologists also believe that gender typing may be a result of subtle prenatal changes to the brain caused by sex hormones. These psychologists suggest that boys' inclinations toward aggression and rough-and-tumble play, for example, might also be due to the influence of testosterone on the brains of developing male fetuses (Collaer & Hines, 1995). However, other psychologists argue that social influences are more important than hormones in shaping gender typing (e.g., Wood & Eagly, 2000).

Psychological Views

Although many psychologists believe that genes and sex hormones play some role in gender typing (Money, 1987), others believe that psychological processes play a more important role. Among the psychological theories that have been suggested to explain how gender typing comes about are psychoanalytic theory, social-learning theory, and gender-schema theory.

Psychoanalytic Theory   Sigmund Freud's psychoanalytic theory argues that gender typing can be explained in terms of gender identification. According to Freud, boys come to identify with their fathers and girls with their mothers. This occurs between the ages of three and five.

At the beginning of this period, Freud argued, children seek the attention of the parent of the opposite sex and perceive the parent of the same sex as a rival for that attention. By the end of the period, however, children no longer feel this way and instead identify with the parent of the same sex. (See Chapter 14.)

According to Freud, it is through this process of identification with the same-sex parent that a child comes to develop the behaviors that are associated with his or her own sex. The child internalizes the standards of the same-sex parent and eventually adopts that parent as a role model for behavior.

There are several problems with Freud's psychoanalytic theory, one of the most apparent being the age at which gender typing occurs. According to Freud, the complex feelings that children have for the parent of the opposite sex are not resolved until children reach age five. However, as noted previously, children tend to display gender typing much earlier. Even in infancy, boys have been found in some studies to be more independent than girls. Also, between the ages of one

and three, many girls appear to show preferences for dolls and soft toys, whereas many boys, on the other hand, prefer hard transportation toys (Rathus, 2003).

Social-Learning Theory   According to social-learning theory, gender role behavior, like other behavior, is acquired through two different learning processes—reinforcement and modeling.

Reinforcement occurs when a behavior has favorable consequences. Because it is rewarded, the behavior is more likely to be repeated. In contrast, behaviors that are not rewarded and behaviors that are punished are less likely to be repeated, because they are not reinforced. (See Chapter 6.)

Social-learning theorists argue that reinforcement of appropriate gender role behavior starts very early. Almost from the moment of birth, the way

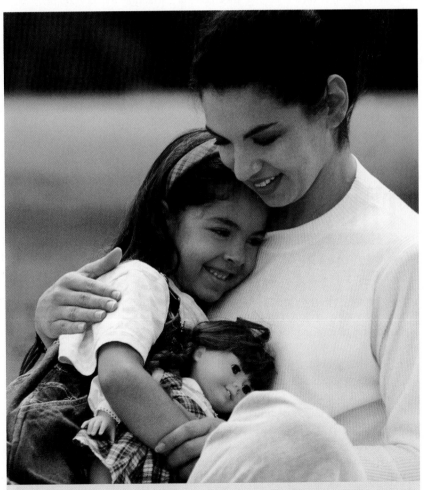

Girls are often given "girls' toys," such as dolls. Whereas boys are often given "boys' toys," such as toy trucks, weapons, and the like. Do you think that such toys teach children what our society expects them to do?

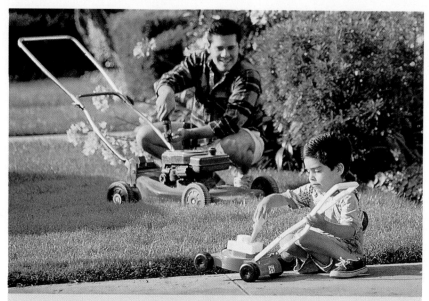

Social-learning theorists suggest that parents encourage the development of stereotypical gender roles by rewarding behavior they consider gender appropriate.

appropriate for girls, such as dolls. They may frown, make sarcastic comments, and even physically separate the child from the toy (Langlois & Downs, 1980). Girls, however, are less likely to receive negative reactions from their fathers for playing with toys considered more appropriate for boys, such as trucks (Siegal, 1987).

From an early age, boys are also more likely to be given toy cars, toy guns, and athletic equipment. Girls, on the other hand, are more likely to receive dolls and other soft toys (Smith & Daglish, 1977). When playing with their children at home, parents also tend to reach first for toys considered appropriate for the child's sex, even when the child owns toys that are generally considered appropriate for both sexes (Eisenberg et al., 1985; Schau et al., 1980).

Aggression provides a good example of how behavior is learned through reinforcement. In one study (Fagot et al., 1985), one-year-old boys and girls were found to be equally likely to use aggressive actions, such as pushing or grabbing, in order to obtain what they wanted. They were also equally likely to use communication, such as whining or gesturing. However, adults' reactions to their efforts varied greatly, depending on the children's sex. The adults tended to respond positively when the girls tried to communicate and solve the dispute in a nonaggressive manner but showed little response when the boys did. On the other hand, the adults tended to ignore aggression in the girls and respond positively to it in the boys.

Not surprisingly, by age two the girls in the study no longer acted aggressively. They had apparently learned through reinforcement to communicate their wants verbally. The boys had learned the opposite lesson, and their level of aggression remained high. As a result of such differences in reinforcement, girls tend to develop more anxiety about aggression and greater inhibitions against displaying it (Maccoby & Jacklin, 1974).

Even in the absence of reinforcement, social learning can occur through observation and imitation of others. This process is known as **modeling**. Children learn about both male and female gender

babies are treated may depend on their sex. When children are old enough to understand language, parents and others begin to instruct them about how they are expected to behave. Parents tend to talk and read more to baby girls, for example, and fathers often engage in more rough-and-tumble play with boys (Jacklin et al., 1984).

TRUTH OR fiction ■ REVISITED ■

It is not true that boys and girls are treated in much the same way until about age three. Studies have shown that gender-typed treatment of children begins at a very early age. Thus, gender differences in the behavior of very young children are not necessarily due to biological differences between boys and girls.

Parents are also likely to reward children for behavior they consider appropriate for their gender and punish, or at least fail to reward, them for behavior they consider inappropriate. For example, studies have found that parents tend to react positively when their children play with toys considered appropriate for their gender. On the other hand, parents often react negatively when children play with toys considered inappropriate for their gender. Fathers especially are likely to react negatively when their sons play with toys considered more

CASE STUDIES
AND OTHER TRUE STORIES

Women Enter the Sciences and the Professions

Traditionally, not many women in the United States pursued careers in the sciences. Several reasons lay behind the low number of women in the sciences. Up through the 1960s, many colleges did not admit women into science programs. Some colleges did not admit women at all. Moreover, the commonly held belief was that a woman's place was in the home.

No longer is this situation the case in the United States. For example, the number of women in the United States receiving bachelor's degrees in the sciences has mushroomed over the last 30 years (Cox & Alm, 2005). In 1970–71, women did not receive even 1 percent of the U.S. degrees in engineering. Women now receive about 19 percent of those degrees—an increase of a factor of 20. In addition, women now make up more than half of the U.S. graduates in biology and nearly half of the graduates in chemistry, math, and geology.

As you can see in the chart, American women have also made dramatic gains in entering prestigious professions over the past 30 years (Cox & Alm, 2005). Women now make up the vast majority of veterinarians and pharmacists. In addition, women now receive about half of the professional degrees in law and medicine, and more than 40 percent of the degrees in business and dentistry.

Are women suited to the sciences and to prestigious professions? The answer, as affirmed by the number of women earning these degrees, is a resounding yes.

THINKING CRITICALLY

1. **Explaining** Why did so few women in the United States pursue the sciences in the past?
2. **Predicting** How do you think women's gains in the sciences and in other prestigious professions have affected women?

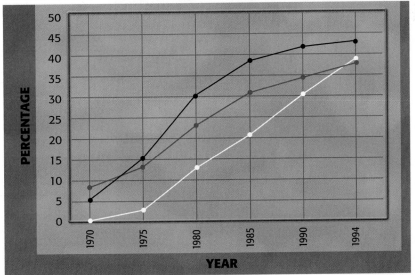

Percent of First Professional Degrees Conferred to Women, 1970–1994

○ **Dentistry** ● **Medicine** ● **Law**

role behavior by observing the behavior of the males and females with whom they commonly interact. However, the children are more likely to model, or imitate, individuals, particularly parents, who are of the same sex as themselves. Children are also more likely to be positively reinforced for imitating the behavior of the parent of the same sex (Golombok & Fivush, 1994).

Observational learning and imitation were illustrated in a classic experiment by David Perry and Kay Bussey (1979). In their study, eight- and nine-year-old boys and girls watched adult models indicate their preferences for one of the items in each of 16 different pairs of items. The adults chose among such pairs as toy cows versus toy horses and oranges versus apples. The children in the study did not realize that the adults' preferences were purely arbitrary. When the children were asked to indicate their own preferences for the items in the pairs, the boys' choices matched the adult men's choices 14 out of 16 times, and the girls' choices matched the adult women's choices 13 out of 16 times. Thus, both boys and girls tended to model their behavior after role models of their own sex, even though the behavior was arbitrary and unrelated to gender.

If gender roles are learned, as social-learning theory suggests, then they should be flexible, or capable of changing. Indeed, there are indications that this is the case. Today, as more women are working outside the home,

gender roles seem to be changing. Janet's mother is a good example. After Janet's parents divorced, her mother took on the role of wage earner in addition to her roles as parent and homemaker. Another indication of gender role change is that parents are more likely now than in the past to encourage their daughters to play sports and follow careers. They are also more likely to encourage their sons to be nurturing and cooperative.

Gender-Schema Theory   Social-learning theory has made important contributions to our understanding of how reinforcement and modeling promote gender-typed behavior. A related but somewhat different view of gender typing is provided by gender-schema theory. According to this theory, children themselves play an active role in developing gender-appropriate behavior. Children form their own concepts about gender and then shape their behavior so that it conforms to their gender concepts.

Specifically, children develop a gender schema in order to organize their perceptions of the world (Bowes & Goodnow, 1996). A **gender schema** is a cluster of physical qualities, behaviors, and personality traits associated with one sex or the other. It is argued that because society places so much emphasis on gender, children organize their perceptions along gender lines.

Gender-schema theorists suggest that as soon as children learn whether they are boys or girls, they begin to seek information concerning gender-typed traits. Even very young children start to mentally group people of the same sex according to the traits they believe are representative of that gender.

Once their gender schema is formed, children strive to live up to it. They begin to judge themselves according to the traits they believe are relevant to their sex, using their gender schema as a standard for comparison. In so doing, children blend their developing self-concepts with the prominent gender schema of their culture. For example, boys may react aggressively when provoked because they perceive that is what society expects males to

Children may be less likely to adopt traditional gender behaviors if they are allowed to play freely with both masculine and feminine toys.

do. Girls, on the other hand, may try to cooperate because they perceive that society expects such behavior from females.

Across both genders, children's self-esteem depends in part on how similar their own personalities, behaviors, and physical appearances are to those of the prominent gender schema of their culture. In other words, boys who see themselves as fitting their culture's idea of masculinity are more likely to develop higher self-esteem than boys who do not. Similarly, girls who see themselves as fitting their culture's idea of femininity are more likely to develop higher self-esteem than girls who do not (Bem, 1993).

Children's gender schema also determines how important particular traits are to them. Consider the dimensions of strength-weakness and kindness-cruelty. Children are likely to learn that the strength-weakness dimension is more important to males, whereas the kindness-cruelty dimension is more important to females. Thus, a boy is more likely to be concerned about how strong he is, whereas a girl is more likely to be concerned about being kind.

In summary, both biological and psychological views of gender typing can help us understand why males and females behave as they do. This is because differences in gender roles are likely to be influenced by differences in biology, life experiences, and cultural expectations. All of these factors appear to play some role in determining how individual males and females behave.

Regardless of how gender typing occurs, it should not be viewed as an inevitable process. In early human societies, it may have seemed appropriate for males and females to have very different roles. Today, however, many people believe that these strict gender roles no longer suit our contemporary way of life.

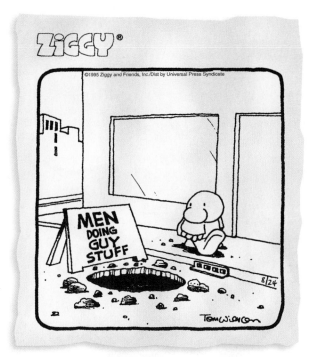

SECTION 3 REVIEW

go.hrw.com
Homework Practice Online
Keyword: SY7 HP16

1. Why do some theorists believe that brain lateralization leads to gender-typed behaviors and abilities?

2. Give an example to show how reinforcement could influence the types of toys children choose to play with.

3. **Critical Thinking**   *Supporting a Point of View*   What role do you think television might play in the development of a child's gender schema? Give examples to support your answer.

SECTION 4

Variation in Gender Roles

Both social-learning theory and gender-schema theory proposes that learning plays the key part in gender role development. They suggest that gender roles are not inborn or fixed at birth but may vary from person to person. Indeed, as the increasing participation of women in activities long considered appropriate only for men—business, sports, and politics, to name a few—demonstrates, gender roles have changed dramatically over time. Research has also shown that gender roles can vary from culture to culture. In other words, what is considered gender-appropriate behavior in one society may be viewed differently in another cultural setting.

Variation Through Time

In the past, gender roles were more distinct and rigid than they are today. There were distinct female and male worlds that were clearly set apart from each other. Throughout most of history, women in many parts of the world were expected to be the

In the 1950s most American families lived on one income. It was typical then for the husband to work outside the home and the wife to stay home and care for the house and family.

and raising a family was not very widespread. According to the dominant ideas of the time concerning gender roles, the ideal woman was the devoted wife who kept a clean house and had dinner waiting when her husband returned from work.

Over the past several decades, women in the United States have entered the workforce in increasing numbers. Today many women work outside the home because they enjoy the financial rewards and the social and intellectual stimulation their jobs provide. In other instances, economic conditions have led women into the workplace. Many working women are single mothers; others work because their families cannot afford to live on the husband's income alone. In some families, the wife works to support the family while the husband remains at home, either by choice or because he is unable to find a job.

Not surprisingly, male and female gender roles in the United States are much more flexible today than they were just a few decades ago. In many marriages, for example, husbands and wives share household chores, child rearing, and wage earning equally (Goodnow & Bowes, 1994). This is the case

A DAY IN THE LIFE

with Linda's parents. As Linda noted, her father, like an increasing number of men in American society, is willing to take on at least some of the tasks that were once performed almost solely by women.

homemakers and child rearers, and men were expected to be the providers for and protectors of women and children.

These differences in gender roles were based in part on the different biological characteristics of the two sexes. Women were more restricted in their activity and mobility by childbearing and the need to nurse their young children. In the earliest human societies, women typically stayed home and assumed responsibility for the homemaking and child-rearing chores. Men, being larger, stronger, and biologically less tied to childbearing and rearing, were considered better suited for hunting and similar activities. These roles remained largely unchanged until quite recently.

Just a generation or two ago, the accepted pattern was for a woman to marry, stay at home, and care for the house and children. She was expected to put the needs of her husband and children ahead of her own. The idea that a woman should put her own career or personal ambitions ahead of marriage

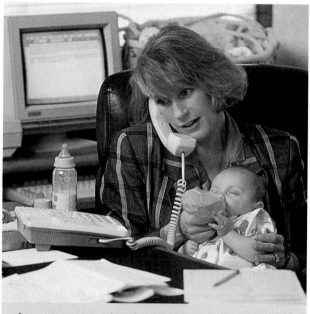

In contemporary American society, women often balance two full-time jobs—their careers and motherhood.

Both men and women of Arapesh society were taught from birth that aggressive behavior is unacceptable.

The Tchambuli differed from both the Mundugumor and Arapesh in their gender roles. Mead reported that their behavior was the opposite of traditional gender roles in the United States. Tchambuli men spent most of their time caring for children, gossiping, bickering, primping, and haggling over prices. Tchambuli women, on the other hand, spent most of their time catching the fish that made up the bulk of the Tchambuli diet. Tchambuli women also kept their heads shaved, disliked wearing ornaments, and were more aggressive than the men.

Margaret Mead's interpretation of her New Guinea study has been criticized as being too subjective, or biased by her personal views concerning gender roles (Errington & Gewertz, 1987). However, the data Mead collected suggests that what is considered to be appropriate behavior for men and women can differ from one culture to another. Thus, the data may support the claim that many gender differences are learned, not inborn.

 It is true that much of the behavior we think of as typical male or female behavior we are not born with but learn from other members of our culture. Because gender roles differ from culture to culture, it is likely that they are learned and not the result of inborn traits.

However, most women who work outside the home are still expected to retain traditional feminine gender roles in the household (Crosby & Jaskar, 1993; Deaux & Lewis, 1983). Dan's Aunt Debbie is a good example. In addition to her outside work, she is expected to maintain the household and care for the children.

Cultural Variation

Gender roles not only vary through time, but they also vary from culture to culture. A famous study by anthropologist Margaret Mead (1935) explored this issue. In the 1930s, Mead studied three different groups of people—the Mundugumor, the Arapesh, and the Tchambuli—on the South Pacific island of New Guinea.

According to Mead, the Mundugumor were a warlike people, and both men and women were very aggressive. Mundugumor women looked down on bearing and rearing children because this interfered with their ability to go to battle. In contrast, the neighboring Arapesh were a gentle and peaceful culture. In this group, both men and women played an equal role in caring for the children and maintaining the land.

 A DAY IN THE LIFE Linda's father grew up in a culture in which the roles of men and women were strictly defined. His parents supported these roles. In his own marriage, however, he adopted a less stereotypical role. Clearly, gender roles are not only learned but can be unlearned as well.

SECTION 4 REVIEW go.hrw.com **HOMEWORK Practice Online** Keyword: SY7 HP16

1. What biological factors have been suggested to explain the historic division between male and female gender roles?

2. How have gender roles in the United States changed in the past few decades?

3. **Critical Thinking** *Comparing and Contrasting* Describe how gender roles can vary from culture to culture.

Chapter 16 REVIEW

Writing a Summary

Using standard grammar, spelling, sentence structure, and punctuation, summarize the information in this chapter. Consider:
- gender roles and stereotypes, and how men and women differ in cognitive abilities, personality, and behavior
- gender typing, and how gender roles have changed over time

Identifying People and Ideas

Identify the following terms or people and use them in appropriate sentences.

1. gender
2. gender roles
3. gender stereotypes
4. nurturance
5. Deborah Tannen
6. gender typing
7. lateralization
8. modeling
9. gender schema
10. Margaret Mead

Understanding Main Ideas

SECTION 1 (pp. 364–365)
1. How have gender roles in the United States changed over the past few decades?

SECTION 2 (pp. 366–371)
2. What are two differences in the typical communication styles of men and women?

SECTION 3 (pp. 372–377)
3. What roles do reinforcement and modeling play in gender typing?

SECTION 4 (pp. 377–379)
4. How has the entrance of large numbers of women into the workforce affected current expectations concerning women's roles?

Thinking Critically

1. **Drawing Inferences and Conclusions** What evidence suggests that gender roles are in a state of transition?

2. **Making Generalizations and Predictions** How might the results of gender role studies change as more women work outside the home?

3. **Evaluating** Why do you think the increase in the number of women in the workplace has helped change gender stereotypes in the United States?

4. **Categorizing** List the advantages and disadvantages that you might think would exist for girls educated in female-only classes.

Writing About Psychology

1. **Comparing and Contrasting** Go to the library to learn more about psychological views of gender typing. Write a one-page report comparing and contrasting the various theories. Be sure to use standard grammar, spelling, sentence structure, and punctuation.

2. **Categorizing** Create a detailed chart listing actual gender differences between men and women as well as the stereotyped differences between them. Cite evidence that supports or refutes each difference shown in the chart. Use the graphic organizer below to help you complete your chart.

Gender Differences	
Actual Differences	Stereotyped Differences

Interpreting Graphs

Study the bar graph below. Then use the information in the graph to help you answer the questions that follow.

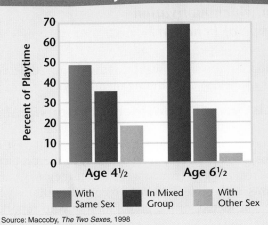

Gender and Play Behavior in Children

Percent of Playtime

Age 4½   Age 6½

- With Same Sex
- In Mixed Group
- With Other Sex

Source: Maccoby, *The Two Sexes*, 1998

1. Which of the following statements best reflects the information presented in the graph?

   a. Children rarely play with members of the opposite sex.

   b. Mixed-group play declines dramatically during the early years of childhood.

   c. As children grow older, they play less with members of the opposite sex.

   d. Boys are less willing to play with girls than girls are willing to play with boys.

2. What questions might this graph raise in the mind of a psychologist?

Analyzing Primary Sources

Read the following excerpt from *The Two Sexes: Growing Up Apart, Coming Together,* in which Eleanor Maccoby explains the ways in which parents influence gender roles. Then answer the questions that follow.

❝In a study done in the 1970s, parents got their first view of their newborn infant through a hospital window, and were asked to describe the child. Although the infant boys and girls in this study did not differ on objective measures of size or activity, parents saw their infant sons as robust, strong, alert, and large-featured, while they saw daughters as fine-featured, small, delicate, and 'soft.' (Rubin, Provenzano, and Luria, 1974). These parental reactions seemed to indicate that, from the very beginning, the way parents perceived their infants was strongly biased by their expectations about femaleness and maleness.❞

3. Which of the following statements best reflects Maccoby's point of view?

   a. Parental biases influence a child's perception of self from the day of birth.

   b. Fathers are more biased in their expectations for their children than mothers are.

   c. Parental bias plays a minimal role in a child's development.

   d. Many parents are biased in their perceptions of their children from birth.

4. How else might this study have been conducted to learn more about parental expectations?

PSYCHOLOGY PROJECTS

Linking to Community

Using Surveys With several of your classmates, carry out a survey to assess gender stereotypes in your community. Work together as a group to brainstorm a list of questions and develop a questionnaire that will reveal how people think about men and women and what behaviors they think are appropriate for each. Then work individually to interview at least three or four people. Include people from a wide range of ages. Summarize the results in an oral report to the class.

🖉 **internet** connect

Internet Activity: go.hrw.com
KEYWORD: SY7 CH16

Choose an activity on gender roles to:

- create a poster illustrating gender roles and how roles are reinforced by the media.
- research gender roles of the past and create a pamphlet showing how contemporary roles differ from those in the past.
- make a chart outlining theories of gender typing.

PSYCHOLOGY IN ACTION

YOU SOLVE THE PROBLEM . . .

How can a psychologist learn which motivation theory explains a certain type of behavior?

Complete the following activity in small cooperative groups. Imagine that a psychologist has requested your help in studying why people act in certain ways. Choose a behavior to be studied, and help the psychologist determine which motivation theory best explains the behavior. He has asked you to prepare a report outlining the solution to this problem.

1. Gather Information. Use your textbook and other resources to find information that will help your group prepare the report. Remember that your report must include information that will convince the psychologist which motivation theory best explains the behavior. This information might include charts and graphs to show the psy-

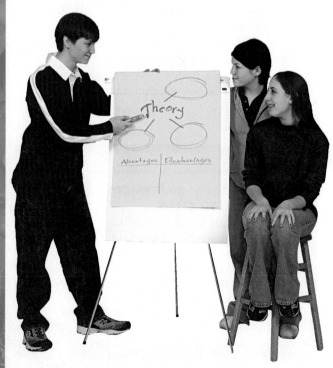

chologist. You may want to divide up different parts of the research among members of the group.

2. List and Consider Options. After reviewing the information you have gathered, list and consider the theories that you might suggest to the psychologist. Your final solution to the problem may be easier to reach if you consider as many options as possible. Be sure to record the options you have considered for the preparation of your report.

3. Consider Advantages and Disadvantages. Now consider the advantages and disadvantages of each option. Ask questions such as,

- Does the patient's behavior seem to be driven only by biological needs?
- Is the patient's behavior motivated by a desire for personal growth?

Once you have considered the advantages and disadvantages, record them as notes for use in preparing your report.

4. Choose and Implement a Solution. After considering the advantages and disadvantages, you should choose a theory. Next, plan and create a report that describes how your solution will be implemented. Be sure that your report makes your solution very clear.

5. Evaluate the Effectiveness of the Solution. Once you have prepared your report, write a paragraph evaluating how effective your recommendation will be for the psychologist. Explain why you believe that your solution will be more effective than other possible solutions you considered. When you are ready, decide which group members will present which parts of the report. Then take your report to the psychologist (the rest of the class). Good luck!

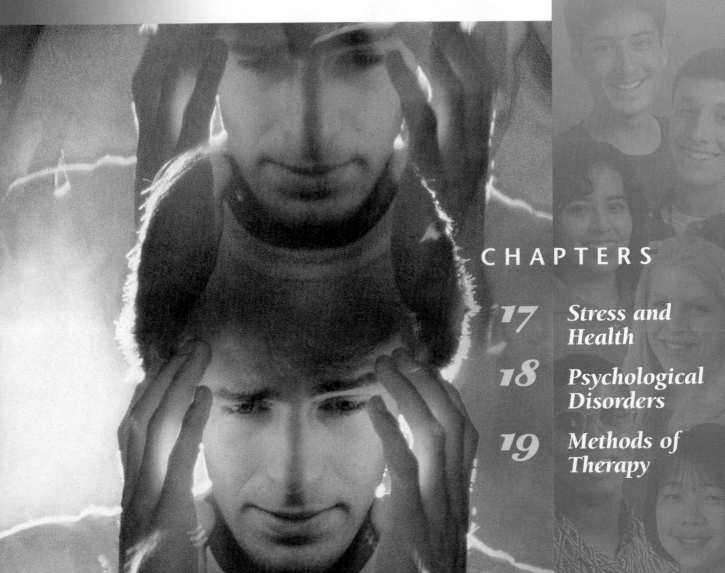

UNIT 6

HEALTH AND ADJUSTMENT

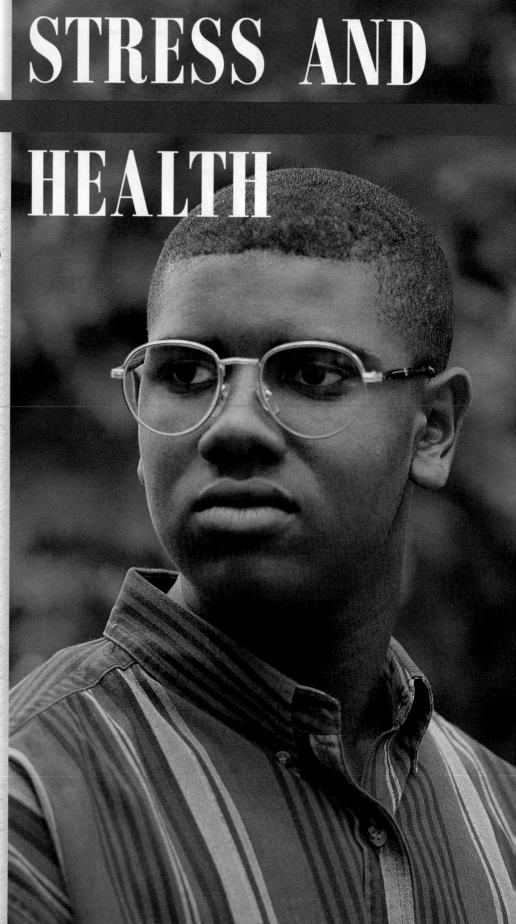

17 STRESS AND HEALTH

Read to Discover

1 What are some of the main causes of stress?

2 What are the factors that determine one's responses to stress?

3 What is the general adaptation syndrome, and how does stress affect the immune system?

4 How can psychological factors contribute to headaches, heart disease, and cancer?

5 In what ways can people cope with stress?

A DAY IN THE LIFE

Linda, Marc, and Janet were relaxing after a frantic day at school when they saw Todd rush by. Until recently, Todd was the one person they knew who never seemed to be stressed out.

"Hey, Todd," Marc called out. "Slow down a second. Why are you in such a hurry?"

"Sorry, guys. I really can't talk," Todd answered. "I have to get this scholarship application to Mr. Hochberg, then I have to finish my biology project. Then my dad and I are going to sit down and decide what college I should go to."

"Stay and talk with us for a second," Janet suggested. "You have time to get the application to Mr. Hochberg. And, Todd, you really shouldn't be so stressed. You've already been accepted by almost every college you applied to."

"I know I was accepted, but now I have to decide which one I want to go to. And what if I don't get this scholarship . . . ? Oh, my headache's coming back again."

"Todd, you're going to make yourself sick if you don't calm down a little," Linda warned.

"Thanks for worrying, but I'll be fine," Todd insisted.

"Don't you remember when my dad got sick last year?" Marc reminded Todd. "My dad always seemed like the healthiest guy in the world. Then he got so stressed over work that he started having serious heart problems."

"He's right, Todd," Janet added. "I don't want you to get sick."

"I know, but I have to decide what school to attend, I have to finish my homework, and I'm still working at my part-time job. These aren't things I can just ignore."

"We just want you to find a way to take it easy. We're worried about you," Linda told him.

"Well, I'm open to suggestions if you have any ideas," Todd said as he tried to smile.

"Okay, then," Janet said suddenly. "Why don't you and I play a little basketball tonight? It'll take your mind off things, and the exercise will make you feel better."

"Okay, you're on," said Todd smiling. "Now may I go to Mr. Hochberg's office?"

"Sure," laughed Janet, "but I hope it won't add to your stress when I beat you at basketball."

• • •

With some help from his friends, Todd recognized that he was stressed out and needed to ease up on himself. Many young people and adults alike experience a great deal of stress. This chapter is about the relationship between stress and health. We will explore the many sources of stress and some specific behavior patterns that contribute to stress. We then will look at the psychological factors associated with stress, the body's response to stress, and the effect of stress on one's health. Finally, we will examine the various ways in which people cope with stress.

Key Terms

- stress
- eustress
- distress
- stressor
- approach-approach conflict
- avoidance-avoidance conflict
- approach-avoidance conflict
- multiple approach-avoidance conflict
- self-efficacy expectation
- general adaptation syndrome
- migraine headache
- defensive coping
- active coping

HOLT

Psychology Video Program

Watch the video to explore the science of stress and its effects.

- Changes are stressful, even when those changes are for the better.
- Laughter can help people cope with stress.
- Few people are exposed to microorganisms that cause disease.
- Many people develop cancerous cells but do not become ill from them.

Students' Reasons for Seeking Counseling

REASON REPORTED	PERCENT REPORTING REASON
Stress, anxiety, nervousness	51
Romantic relationships	47
Low self-esteem, self-confidence	42
Depression	41
Family relationships	37
Academic problems, grades	29
Transition to the career world	25
Loneliness	25
Financial problems	24

FIGURE 17.1 *This table lists some of the reasons college students give for seeking counseling.*

Source: Data are from "College Youth Haunted by Increased Pressures" by B. Murray, 1996, *APA Monitor, 26* (4), 47.

SECTION 1

What Is Stress?

In physics, stress is defined as pressure, or a force. Examples of physical stress include tons of rock crushing the earth or water pressing against a dam. Psychological forces, or stresses, can "crush" and "press" people. People may feel crushed by the burden of making an important decision, or they may feel pressed by a lack of time in which to complete a major task.

In psychology, **stress** is the arousal of one's mind and body in response to demands made upon them. Stress forces an organism to adapt, to cope, to adjust. There are different sources of stress, including frustration, daily hassles, life changes, and conflict. Furthermore, the word *stress* is used differently by different psychologists. Some psychologists describe stress as an event that causes tension. Others describe stress as a person's response to a disturbing event. Still others define stress as a person's perception of an event.

Not all stress is bad. Stress can increase sharpness and motivation and can keep people alert and involved. This kind of positive stress is called **eustress**. Positive stress can be a sign that a person is taking on a challenge or trying to reach a goal. For example, you might experience eustress as you participate in a classroom activity, whether you are leading or following the activity.

Negative stress—called **distress**—is linked to intense pressure or anxiety that can have severe psychological and physical effects. When stress becomes too severe or prolonged, it can strain people's ability to adjust to various situations. Negative stress can dampen people's moods and impair their ability to experience pleasure. Negative stress can even harm the body.

High school and college students often experience stress that is related to family problems, relationships, pressures at school, loneliness, and general nervousness. In fact, stress is one of the main reasons that college students seek help at college counseling centers (Murray, 1996). Figure 17.1 lists a number of the reasons students give for seeking counseling.

Sources of Stress

The event or situation that produces stress is called a **stressor**. However, what is a stressor for one person may not be a stressor for another. For example, two people might react to a long bus trip quite differently. For one it might be a relaxing vacation, while for another person it could be stressful and unpleasant. However, some stressors are common to most people. For example, a loud, continuous drilling noise outside one's window would be irritating to just about everyone.

When stressors and stresses pile up on each other, we can reach a point where we have difficulty coping. To avoid reaching that point, it is important to recognize some of the causes of stress.

Frustration   One of the most common sources of stress is frustration—being blocked from obtaining a goal. Examples include being delayed from keeping an appointment, lacking enough money to buy an item we need or want, or forgetting something important. Sometimes life seems full of frustrations. Although many frustrations are minor, the more serious ones can be extremely stressful—for example, working for weeks on an important project, only to lose it and have to create it all over again.

Daily Hassles   The everyday frustrations we all experience are called daily hassles. They come in different forms, but they have one thing in common—they all create stress. When daily hassles become severe or frequent enough, they can threaten a person's well-being. Psychologist Richard Lazarus and his colleagues (1985) found that there are eight main types of hassles:

- household hassles, including preparing meals, cleaning, shopping, and mowing the lawn
- health hassles, including illness, anxiety about medical or dental treatment, and the side effects of medications
- time-pressure hassles, including the feeling that there are too many things to do, too many responsibilities, and not enough time to do what needs to be done
- inner-concern hassles, including feelings of low self-esteem and loneliness
- environmental hassles, including noise, crowding, pollution, traffic, and crime
- financial hassles, including concerns about paying current bills, repaying loans, and saving for the future
- work hassles, including unhappiness with one's job and problems with coworkers
- future-security hassles, including concerns about job security, taxes, investments, and retirement income

These hassles can result in feelings of tension, nervousness, worry, and sadness.

Life Changes   British writer Samuel Johnson wrote, "Change is not made without inconvenience, even from worse to better." Next year, when Todd goes to college, he will be living away from home for the first time. Right now, he may not know where he is going or even where he wants to go. He is, however, undergoing a major life change.

Life changes—such as moving, serious illness, or a death in the family—are another source of stress. Life changes differ from daily hassles in two important ways: (1) All hassles are annoying or irritating, but many life changes go "from worse to better." That is, they are positive and desirable changes. (2) Hassles occur regularly, often on a daily basis; life changes tend to happen less frequently, often after a long, stable period of little or no change.

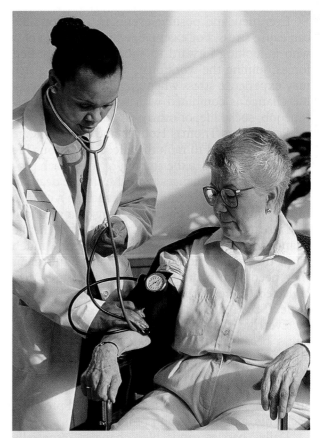

Daily hassles, such as anxiety about medical tests, can create stress. When daily hassles become severe enough, they may threaten a person's well-being.

The Four Types of Conflict

Type of Conflict	Definition	Example
Approach-approach	A choice between two equally attractive alternatives	Choosing between cake and ice cream for dessert
Avoidance-avoidance	A choice between two equally unattractive alternatives	Going to the dentist or letting a toothache get worse
Approach-avoidance	A choice of whether or not to do something when part of the situation is attractive but the other is not	Deciding whether or not to buy a new CD player because it will cost a lot of money
Multiple approach-avoidance	A choice between alternatives that have both good and bad aspects	Deciding to stay at home to study for a test or to go out to the movies with friends

FIGURE 17.3 *Conflict, the feeling that you are being pulled in two or more directions by opposing forces or motives, can be a source of stress. Psychologists have identified four types of conflict.*

persistent self-doubts about whether he or she has made the right decision. The decision maker may not feel settled until he or she is in the new situation and knows that things are working out. For example, even after Todd talks with his father and decides which college he will attend, he may still feel uncertain until he settles into his dorm, meets his roommates, and begins classes.

An **avoidance-avoidance conflict** is more stressful. People in this type of conflict are forced to choose "the lesser of two evils"—that is, to choose between two unsatisfactory alternatives. People are motivated to avoid each of two negative goals, but the problem is that avoiding one requires approaching the other. For example, a student may be faced with the choice of dropping a course in which he or she is doing poorly and may receive a failing grade. However, by dropping the course, the student will not have enough credits to graduate. Both alternatives have a negative side.

A single goal can produce both approach and avoidance motives. This is called an **approach-avoidance conflict**. People face an approach-avoidance conflict when a choice is both good and bad at the same time. For Todd, it might be a college that has an excellent reputation and exactly the program he is looking for, but the college is very far away and visiting home will be difficult and costly.

The most complex form of conflict is a **multiple approach-avoidance conflict**. In this kind of conflict, each of several alternative courses of action has its advantages and disadvantages. Todd may face this type of conflict when he has to decide which college courses to take. The factors he will consider may include his level of interest in the subject, the reputation of the teacher, the usefulness of the course to his overall plan, and the difficulty of the course (does he have the educational background necessary to succeed).

When making a decision about what to eat in a restaurant, you might have to decide between food that is healthful but not very tasty, tasty food that is not very healthful, and food that is both tasty and healthful but is too expensive. In such a situation, you would be faced with a multiple approach-avoidance conflict.

When conflicting motives are strong, people may encounter high levels of stress and confusion about what course of action to choose. They need to make a decision to reduce the stress, yet decision making itself can be quite stressful, especially when there is no clear right choice. Some people cope with such difficult decisions by making a two-column list, jotting down all the reasons for and against a particular choice. The thought that goes into making the list sometimes helps people decide what to do.

CASE STUDIES

AND OTHER TRUE STORIES

Ten Doorways to Distress

According to psychologist Albert Ellis, people's beliefs about events, as well as the events themselves, can be stressful. For example, a student who suddenly finds out she must move with her family to another state may feel a great deal of stress as she wonders how her life will change. Although the move itself may be stressful, anticipating the change and worrying about possible consequences may prove even more stressful.

Ellis uses an A-B-C approach when looking at each situation. For example, moving to another state is an activating event (A). The consequence (C) is stress. Between the activating event (A) and the consequence (C) lie beliefs (B). These beliefs may include such thoughts as "I may not be able to make friends in my new school." Anxieties about the future are normal and to be expected. However, according to Ellis, people tend to have some irrational beliefs that can lead to both depression and stress. He calls these beliefs "personal doorways to distress" because they create problems themselves and, at the same time, aggravate problems from other sources.

Ellis has identified some of these unrealistic expectations and beliefs, which are described below.

Irrational Belief 1: I must have sincere love and approval just about all the time from the people who are important to me.

Irrational Belief 2: I must prove myself to be thoroughly adept at something important. (This belief is called perfectionism.)

Irrational Belief 3: Things have to go the way I want them to go. Life is awful when I can't have my first choice in everything.

Irrational Belief 4: Other people must treat me fairly and justly. When people act unfairly or unethically, they are bad.

Irrational Belief 5: When I see something that is dangerous or makes me afraid, I must concentrate on it and become upset.

Irrational Belief 6: People and things should turn out better than they do. It is terrible when I do not find quick solutions to life's hassles.

Irrational Belief 7: My emotional misery stems from outside pressures that I have little or no ability to control. Unless these pressures change, I am going to have to stay stressed out.

Irrational Belief 8: It is easier to evade life's responsibilities and problems than to face them and try to work them out.

Irrational Belief 9: My past influenced me immensely and must therefore continue to determine the way I feel and act today.

Irrational Belief 10: I can achieve happiness by staying on my present path or by just enjoying myself from day to day.

In the case of the first irrational belief, for example, Ellis finds it understandable that people want the approval of others. However, he thinks it is irrational for them to believe that they cannot survive without it. The belief invites disappointment since it is unrealistic to expect approval all the time. Ellis allows that childhood experiences often explain where such beliefs come from. He also notes, however, that to retain those beliefs can cause much unhappiness.

THINKING CRITICALLY

1. **Finding the Main Idea** According to Ellis, what are "personal doorways to distress"?
2. **Identifying Cause and Effect** How do these "personal doorways to distress" affect people?

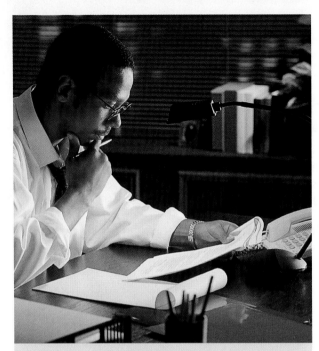

Here is a classic example of a type A personality—highly driven, intense, and impatient.

Personality Types

Some people actually create their own stress. Psychologists have classified people into two basic personality types: type A (intense) and type B (laid-back). Type A people are always on the go; they put pressure on themselves and thus are constantly under stress. They are highly driven, competitive, and impatient. Type A people always feel rushed and pressured because they operate at full speed and become annoyed when there is even the slightest delay. They are irritable when they have to wait in line. Type A people never seem to have enough time, especially since they often try to do several things at once. They walk, eat, and talk faster than other people, and they are generally quick to become angry.

Type B people, in contrast, are more relaxed. They are more patient, do not become angry as easily, and are typically less driven than type A people. While type A people often earn more money than type B people do, type A people pay a high price for their success. They must live with the heightened stress they create for themselves. Research shows that type A personalities run a much greater health risk than type B people. If they do not loosen up and relax, but instead continue their type A behavior, they are in greater danger of suffering coronary heart disease.

SECTION 1 REVIEW

Homework Practice Online
Keyword: SY7 HP17

1. What are the differences between daily hassles and life changes?
2. List the main causes of stress.
3. **Critical Thinking** *Supporting a Point of View* Do you agree that some people create their own stress through type A behavior? Explain your answer.

SECTION 2
Responses to Stress

Psychological factors play an important role in people's responses to stress. People with different types of personalities respond to stress in different ways (Vaillant, 1994). People who are more relaxed and free of conflict are less likely than others to become sick when they do experience prolonged stress (Holahan & Moos, 1990).

A DAY IN THE LIFE

The stress of an event depends largely on what the event means to the person involved (Whitehead, 1994). Going to college is important to Todd, but leaving home and being away from his family and friends also means a great deal to him. Moving can be a positive or a negative event, depending on whether one moves to where one wants to be and on the difficulties of packing, unpacking, and paying for the move. Even

In contrast to type A individuals, those with type B personalities tend to be more relaxed, less ambitious, and more patient.

a positive move, such as moving to a larger house, creates some stress. However, a negative move, such as an eviction, is much more stressful because of the fear, anxiety, anger, and depression it can trigger.

Biological factors also account for some of the differences in people's responses to stress. Research suggests that some people inherit the tendency to develop certain health problems under stress. Yet most people can do things to influence or reduce the effects of their stress. Factors that influence the effects of stress include self-efficacy expectations, psychological hardiness, a sense of humor, predictability, and social support.

Self-Efficacy Expectations

Do you remember the story "The Little Engine That Could"? In an effort to pull a heavy load up a great hill, the engine repeated to itself, "I think I can, I think I can . . ." The engine succeeded because of its self-efficacy expectations. **Self-efficacy expectations** are the beliefs people have that they can accomplish goals that they set for themselves. The goal might be to write a persuasive essay, dunk a basketball, or learn to solve math problems. Believing one can do it helps one reach the goal.

Self-efficacy expectations are closely related to self-confidence. Self-confidence affects people's abilities to withstand stress (Basic Behavioral Science Task Force, 1996; Maciejewski et al., 2000). For example, when people are in frightening situations, self-confidence reduces the level of adrenaline in the bloodstream (Bandura et al., 1985). As a result, people are less likely to experience panic and nervousness. People with more self-confidence—a strong belief that they can handle difficult situations—are also less likely than those with less self-confidence to be upset by stress. In other words, a self-confident person is more likely to keep cool under pressure.

Psychological Hardiness

Psychological hardiness is a personality characteristic that helps people withstand stress. The research on psychological hardiness is based on the pioneering work of Suzanne Kobasa and her colleagues (1994). They studied business executives who were able to resist illness despite heavy workloads and stress. The researchers found that these psychologically hardy executives differed from other executives in three important ways:

- *Commitment.* The hardy executives were highly committed to their jobs; they believed

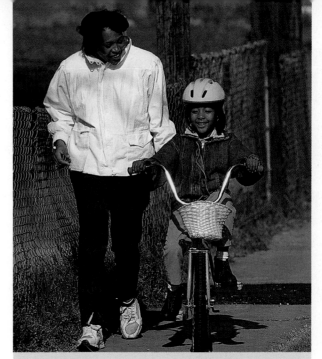

A child who develops strong self-efficacy expectations will probably have a greater sense of self-confidence as an adult.

that their work was meaningful, though it was also demanding and stressful; they regarded their stress as a source of motivation rather than as something that was victimizing them.

- *Challenge.* The hardy executives sought out challenges; they preferred change to stability even though change required adjustment; they regarded change as interesting rather than threatening.

- *Control.* The hardy executives viewed themselves as being in control of their lives and able to influence and control the rewards and punishments they received; they did not feel helpless in the face of the forces that were involved in shaping their lives.

Other researchers have also found that believing that one is in control of one's situation tends to enhance one's ability to withstand stress (Folkman & Moskowitz, 2000; Tennen & Affleck, 2000).

Sense of Humor

When Janet jokingly hinted that she would beat Todd at basketball, she instinctively knew that humor was what the situation needed. Do you remember the old saying "Laughter is the best medicine"? The idea that

Both scientific studies and anecdotal evidence suggest that humor has positive effects on one's health.

Predictability

The ability to predict a stressor seems to reduce the amount of stress it causes. Predictability allows people to brace themselves for an event and, in many cases, to plan various ways to cope with it. Since having control of the situation helps reduce stress, having prior information about the expected stressor gives people a feeling that they will be able to deal with it. For example, ill people who ask about the medical procedures they will undergo and the pain they will experience tend to cope with the stress better than ill people who do not know what to expect (Ludwick-Rosenthal & Neufeld, 1993).

Social Support

The presence and interest of other people provide the social support that helps people cope with stress. Todd's friends realized he was under stress and tried to find ways to help him cope with it. Like psychological hardiness, social support helps insulate people from the effects of stress (Folkman & Moskowitz, 2000a; Uchino et al., 1996). People who lack social skills and spend most of their time alone seem more likely to develop infectious diseases when they are under stress (Cohen & Williamson, 1991).

There are several ways to provide social support to people who are under stress.

- Express your concern by listening to people's problems and offering sympathy, understanding, and reassurance.

- Provide physical relief by offering the material support and services that help people adjust to stress—for example, financial assistance, food, and temporary shelter.

- Offer information, including advice, that helps people cope with stress.

- Provide feedback to help people understand or make sense of what they have experienced.

- Socialize, which includes talking, playing, or just being with the people who are under stress. While this may not directly solve people's problems, it helps them feel less isolated.

Research clearly suggests the value of social support. For example, older people who have social support recover more rapidly from physical problems than older people who have no support (Wilcox et al., 1994). People who have buddies who help them begin an exercise program are more

humor lightens the burdens of life is one that dates back to ancient times. One study found that students who had a sense of humor and saw humor in difficult situations experienced less stress than students who were not able to find humor in the same situations (Martin & Lefcourt, 1983).

Research suggests that emotional responses, such as happiness and even anger, may have beneficial effects on the immune system as well (Kemeny, 1993). Since humor and laughter are connected with feelings of happiness, they probably really are good "medicine" for the body. In *Anatomy of an Illness as Perceived by the Patient,* Norman Cousins (1979) reported his experience with a painful illness that is similar to arthritis. He found that laughing at Marx Brothers movies eased his pain. Laughter also helped him sleep better. He believed that it even reduced the painful inflammation of his joints.

TRUTH
OR
fiction
■ R E V I S I T E D ■

It is true that laughter can help people cope with stress. Research studies and the personal experiences of many people suggest that laughter is healthy and can actually reduce certain physical symptoms.

likely than others to stay with the activity (Gruder et al., 1993; Nides et al., 1995). Social support also appears to shield people and help them recover from feelings of depression (Holahan et al., 1995; Lewinsohn et al., 1994; McLeod et al., 1992).

Social support helps many immigrants to cope with the stresses of adapting to life in the United States. For example, social support helped children cope with the stresses of Hurricane Andrew and helped Chinese villagers cope with a major earthquake (Wang et al., 2000). Social support also helps people remain healthy and in good spirits when caring for other people who have serious health problems.

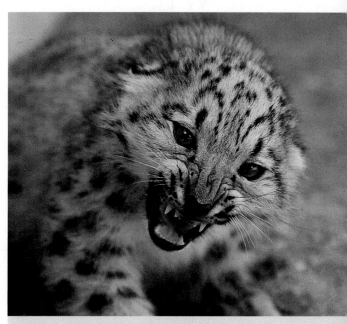

When an animal is confronted by a stressor, it prepares itself for defensive action. *During which stage of the GAS does this occur?*

SECTION 2 REVIEW

Homework Practice Online
Keyword: SY7 HP17

1. What is psychological hardiness?

2. Describe five kinds of social support.

3. **Critical Thinking** *Summarizing* What types of factors determine one's response to stress?

SECTION 3
Physical Effects of Stress

How is it that daily hassles, life changes, conflict, and other sources of stress often make people ill? Stress researcher Hans Selye (1976) suggested that the body under stress is like a clock with an alarm that does not shut off.

The General Adaptation Syndrome

Selye observed that different stressful situations each produced similar responses by the body. Whether the source of stress was a financial problem, a physical threat, or a bacterial invasion, the body's response was the same. Selye labeled this response the **general adaptation syndrome** (GAS). The GAS has three stages: an alarm reaction, a resistance stage, and an exhaustion stage.

The Alarm Reaction The alarm reaction is initiated when a stressor is perceived. This reaction mobilizes the body for defensive action. In the early 1900s, physiologist Walter Cannon described this alarm system as the fight-or-flight reaction.

Animals and human beings experience this fight-or-flight reaction in similar ways. Consider an animal's reaction when a stranger approaches or when the animal notices some other change in its environment that signals possible danger. A person might react the same way. Imagine that as you are about to go to sleep, you hear a loud noise in another room. Like the animal, you also become alert to your environment and sensitive to any sight, sound, or other stimulus around you that might indicate danger. Your body is in a state of high alert. Your heart is beating faster, your breathing is quicker, and your muscles are tense. Your body is in the fight-or-flight mode that occurs when danger is perceived to be present.

During the alarm reaction, the sympathetic nervous system is activated (Gallucci et al., 1993). (See Chapter 3.) This produces a flood of stress hormones, including adrenaline, noradrenaline, adrenocorticotropic hormone (ACTH), and corticosteroids. These hormones act in different ways to prepare the body to deal with the stressor.

Adrenaline and noradrenaline arouse the body to help it cope with threats and stress. They do this by speeding up the heart rate and causing the liver to release glucose (sugar), which provides energy for the body under stress. Corticosteroids and ACTH protect the body from allergic reactions (such as difficulty breathing). They also produce an inflammation that increases circulation to the part of the body that may be injured. Finally, they send

The Fight-or-Flight Response

- **Air passages widen to allow more air intake**
- **Hair stands on end**
- **Level of blood sugar increases**
- **Heart rate increases**
- **Muscles tighten up**
- **Blood pressure rises**
- **Senses sharpen and become more alert**
- **Steroids and adrenaline are secreted**

FIGURE 17.4 *When a person first perceives a stressor, the body initiates an alarm reaction, which mobilizes the body for defensive action. This reaction is known as the fight-or-flight response.*

white blood cells to the injury to fight off invading germs. Some of the changes that occur as a result of the alarm reaction are shown in Figure 17.4. Once the stressor or threat is removed, the body returns to its previous state.

The Resistance Stage If the alarm reaction mobilizes the body and the stressor is not removed, people enter the resistance stage of the GAS. During this stage, people attempt to find a way to cope with the stressor to avoid being overwhelmed by their negative reactions to the stressor. Hormones are still being released but at lower levels than in the alarm reaction stage. The body tries to regain its lost energy, repair damage, and restore balance. However, at this stage, people may still feel enough of a strain to continue to experience some physical symptoms.

The Exhaustion Stage If the stressor is still not removed, people may enter the exhaustion stage of the GAS. The capacity to resist stress varies from person to person, but everyone eventually becomes exhausted when severe stressors persist. At this stage, the adrenal and other glands activated by the fight-or-flight reaction can no longer continue to secrete hormones. People's muscles become worn out. Their heart and breathing rates slow down.

As the resources available to combat stress become depleted, people reach a breaking point. Continued stress during the exhaustion stage may cause people to develop health problems ranging from allergies and hives to ulcers and heart disease—and even death.

Effects of Stress on the Immune System

Stress also affects the body's ability to cope with disease. Research shows that chronic stress suppresses the activity of the body's immune system (Coe, 1993; Delhanty et al., 1996; O'Leary, 1990).

The Immune System You might think that some people, luckily, are not exposed to the kinds of organisms that cause serious health problems.

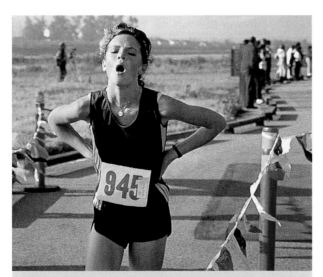

This marathon runner has probably entered the exhaustion stage, during which the adrenal gland and other glands that were activated by the alarm reaction can no longer continue to secrete hormones and the runner's muscles become worn out.

Actually, that is not true. Most people are exposed to a great variety of disease-causing organisms. However, an intact immune system manages to fight off most of them.

How does the immune system fight against disease? The immune system prevents disease by producing white blood cells that destroy disease-causing microorganisms (bacteria, fungi, and viruses), worn-out body cells, and cells that have become malignant (cancerous). White blood cells engage in "search-and-destroy missions." They first recognize and then destroy foreign bodies and unhealthy cells.

Some white blood cells produce antibodies—chemicals that attach to harmful cells and microorganisms, marking them for destruction. Other white blood cells destroy the foreign bodies by surrounding and digesting them. The immune system "remembers" these invaders and maintains antibodies in the bloodstream to fight them, often for years.

TRUTH
OR
fiction
■ REVISITED ■

It is not true that few people are exposed to the microorganisms that cause disease. Most people are continuously exposed to a great variety of disease-causing microorganisms. However, a healthy immune system produces white blood cells that fight off most of them.

Stress and the Immune System   One of the reasons that stress eventually exhausts people is that it stimulates their bodies to produce steroids, which suppress the functioning of the immune system. Persistent secretion of steroids interferes with the formation of antibodies, which are crucial in fighting germs. In the case of some serious diseases, such as cancer, the added stress that results from having a life-threatening disease contributes to the suppression of the immune system, thus leading to further health problems (Andersen et al., 1994).

A study of dental students showed the effects of stress on the immune system (Jemmott et al., 1983). To test the functioning of each student's immune system, researchers measured the level of antibodies in the students' saliva at different times during the school year. The lower the level of antibodies, the lower a person's immune-system functioning.

Students showed lower immune-system functioning during more stressful school periods than during the periods immediately after vacations. The study also showed that students with many friends had healthier immune systems than students with fewer friends. The study suggests that social support may have been a factor in insulating some students from the detrimental effects of stress.

Other studies have found that the stress of examinations weakens the capacity of the immune system to combat certain viruses, such as the Epstein-Barr virus, which causes fatigue and other health problems (Glaser et al., 1991, 1993). In another study researchers found that training aimed at improving coping skills and relaxation techniques improved the functioning of the immune systems of the participants (Glaser et al., 1991).

These studies prove that stress causes the immune system to function less effectively. They also indicate that social support, which reduces stress, makes the immune system function better.

SECTION 3 REVIEW

go.
hrw
.com
Homework Practice Online

Keyword: SY7 HP17

1. List and describe the three stages of the general adaptation syndrome.

2. How does the immune system protect people against disease?

3. **Critical Thinking**   *Analyzing Information* What advice for maintaining his or her immune system would you give to a student who was in a high-stress situation?

Psychological Factors and Health

Why do some people develop cancer or have heart attacks? Why do others seem immune to these health problems? Why do some people seem to fall prey to just about everything that is going around, while others ride out the longest winters with hardly a sniffle?

Biological factors play an important role in physical illness. For example, family history of a particular disease can certainly increase a person's susceptibility to that disease. Other biological factors that are involved in the development of illness include exposure to disease-causing microorganisms, inoculations against certain diseases, accidents and injuries, and age.

A family history of health problems, such as heart disease and cancer, may tempt some people to assume there is little they can do to influence their health. But one's family history (or genetic inheritance) merely suggests a potential for developing an illness. Health writer Jane Brody (1995) noted that a bad family medical history should not be considered a sign of doom. She noted that, instead, it should be welcomed as an opportunity to keep the harmful genes from expressing themselves.

Prolonged stress may have caused Marc's father to develop heart problems. This does not necessarily mean, however, that Marc will develop similar health problems. Instead, it has helped Marc to recognize how harmful stress can be and prompted him to take steps to manage the stress in his own life—and advise his friend Todd to do the same.

While biological factors are important, many health problems are affected by psychological factors, such as one's attitudes and patterns of behavior (Ader, 1993; Salovey et al., 2000). Psychological states of anxiety and depression can impair the functioning of the immune system and make people all the more vulnerable to physical health problems (Penninx et al., 1998; Salovey et al., 2000).

Health psychology is concerned with the relationship between psychological factors and the prevention and treatment of physical illness (Taylor, 1990). In recent years, health psychologists have been exploring the various ways in which states of mind influence physical well-being. Because of the growing recognition of the link between psychological factors and health, an estimated 3,500 psychologists are now on the faculties of medical schools (Matarazzo, 1993; Wiggins, 1994).

This section examines the interrelationship of biological and psychological factors in the development and treatment of three fairly common health problems: headaches, heart disease, and cancer. Health psychologists have made important contributions to the understanding and treatment of all three of these medical problems.

Headaches

Among the most common stress-related health problems are headaches. People under stress will sometimes get a headache as a direct result of feel-

ing tense. Todd felt a headache developing as he was trying to deal with the stress of getting his scholarship application in on time. It is estimated that 20 percent of Americans experience intense stress-induced headaches such as the one Todd suffered.

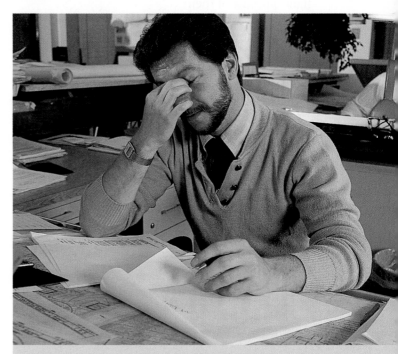

Headaches are among the most common stress-related health problems. They can be treated with medicine and various behavioral methods, such as progressive relaxation and biofeedback.

Types of Headaches   There are several types of headaches. The most frequent kind is the muscle-tension headache. When people are under stress, the muscles in their shoulders, neck, forehead, and scalp tend to tighten up. Prolonged stress can lead to prolonged muscle contraction, which causes muscle-tension headaches. Such headaches usually come on gradually. They are characterized by dull, steady pain on both sides of the head and by feelings of tightness or pressure.

The next most common kind of headache is the **migraine headache.** Migraine headaches usually have a sudden onset and are identified by severe throbbing pain on one side of the head. Migraines affect 1 American in 10. They may last for hours or days. Some people have warning "auras" before attacks. These warnings include visual distortions or the perception of unusual odors. The migraines themselves may be accompanied by sensitivity to light, loss of appetite, nausea, vomiting, loss of balance, and changes in mood. Brain imaging suggests that when something triggers a migraine, neurons at the back of the brain fire in waves that ripple across the top of the head then down to the brainstem, which has many pain centers.

Triggers for migraines include barometric pressure, pollen, some drugs, monosodium glutamate—better known as MSG, a chemical often used to enhance the flavor of food. Other triggers are aged cheese and the hormonal changes connected with menstruation (Mulvihill, 2000).

Psychological factors also trigger or worsen migraines. For example, the type A behavior pattern apparently contributes to migraines. In one study, 53 percent of people who had migraine headaches showed the type A behavior pattern, compared with 23 percent of people who had muscle-tension headaches (Rappaport et al., 1988). Another study compared 26 women who had regular migraines with women who did not get migraines. The migraine sufferers were more sensitive to pain, more self-critical, more likely to believe that stress and pain were awful things, and less likely to seek social support when they were under stress (Hassinger et al., 1999).

Regardless of the source of the headache, people can unwittingly propel themselves into a vicious cycle. Headache pain is a stressor that can lead to an increase in, rather than a relaxing of, muscle tension in the neck, shoulders, scalp, and face.

Treatment   Aspirin, acetaminophen, and many prescription drugs are used to fight headache pain.

Some inhibit the production of the prostaglandins that help initiate transmission of pain messages to the brain. Newer prescription drugs can help prevent many migraines. Behavioral methods can also help. Progressive relaxation focuses on decreasing muscle tension and has been shown to be highly effective in relieving muscle-tension headaches. Biofeedback training has also helped many people with migraine headaches. However, these methods should only be attempted under the supervision of a trained health-care professional.

Heart Disease

Nearly half the deaths in the United States each year are caused by heart disease (American Heart Association, 2000), making it a major national health problem. Marc's father is just one of the people who have developed heart disease. There are many risk factors associated with heart disease.

- *Family history (genetics).* People with a family history of heart disease are more likely than others to develop heart disease themselves (American Heart Association, 2000).
- *Physical conditions.* Obesity, high serum cholesterol levels, and hypertension all contribute to heart disease. About one American in five has hypertension—abnormally high blood pressure. Although there appears to be a genetic component to hypertension (Levy et al., 2000; Williams et al., 2000), many other factors are also involved. These factors include smoking, obesity, and excessive salt in one's diet. Blood pressure also rises when people become angry or are on guard against threats (Suls et al., 1995).
- *Patterns of consumption.* Heavy drinking, smoking, overeating, and eating food high in cholesterol can also contribute to heart disease (Stampfer et al., 2000). Smoking, for example, raises the level of cholesterol in the blood and weakens the walls of blood vessels (Bartecchi et al., 1994).
- *Type A behavior.* People who exhibit type A behavior are more likely than people who exhibit type B behavior to develop heart disease (Thoresen & Powell, 1992).
- *Anger and hostility.* A constant need to control angry and hostile impulses increases the risk of developing heart disease (Birks & Roger, 2000; Richards et al., 2000).

EXPLORING

DIVERSITY

Cultural Differences in Diet and Health

How important is an individual's diet to his or her health? In their search for evidence about the relationship between diet and health, researchers often look at Asian countries, where rates for cancer, heart disease, and other degenerative diseases are considerably lower than in Western nations.

Research indicates that death rates from cancer and heart disease are relatively high in Western nations such as the Netherlands, Denmark, the United Kingdom, Canada, and the United States, where people eat foods with a high fat content (Cohen, 1987). Death rates from cancer, heart disease, and other serious conditions are lower in Asian nations such as Thailand, the Philippines, Japan, and China, where the consumption of fat is lower.

Studies have shown that the difference has more to do with diet than with race. For example, the diets of Japanese Americans are similar in fat content to those of other Americans—and so are their death rates from cancer. Because of dietary differences, Japanese American men living in California and Hawaii are also much more likely to become overweight than Japanese men who live in Japan (Curb & Marcus, 1991).

One of the most extensive nutrition research projects ever undertaken was conducted by T. Colin Campbell, professor of nutritional biochemistry at Cornell University, and colleagues from China and Oxford Universities. Begun in 1983, the China Diet and Health Study used the vast population of China to study the relationship between

The low-fat diet in many Asian countries has been linked to lower rates of cancer, heart disease, and other degenerative diseases than the rates in Western countries.

dietary intake and health. Beginning in 1983, the study collected information about the eating habits and health records of thousands of people in 65 Chinese provinces. The researchers studied the kinds of foods eaten, examined medical records, took blood samples, and made other tests on thousands of rural Chinese.

In 1991, Campbell's team published an 896-page report containing their initial findings, which they are continuing to analyze and add to as the study progresses. So far, the researchers have found that the Chinese consume far greater amounts of rice and other grains, vegetables, and legumes (beans and peas) than Americans do. They also found that Asian diets are much lower in protein than the average American diet. On average, Asians eat far less meat and dairy products than Americans do. The Chinese plant-based diets were found to be much more healthful because they consist of significantly less fat and animal protein.

The preliminary conclusion of this ongoing study is that the Chinese diet of good-quality plant foods is preventing a wide range of degenerative diseases. "Our study suggests," says Campbell, "that the closer one approaches a total plant food diet, the greater the health benefits."

Think About It

Analyzing Information What are some positive dietary changes that Americans could make to ensure longer and healthier lives?

- *Job strain.* Overtime work, assembly-line labor, and exposure to conflicting demands on the job can all contribute to heart disease (Jenkins, 1988).
- *Lack of exercise.* People who do not get regular exercise are more likely to suffer from coronary heart disease than those who do exercise regularly (Stampfer et al., 2000).

Once heart disease has been diagnosed, various medical treatments, such as surgery and medication, are available. However, people can also benefit from behavioral changes that reduce the risks of heart disease. Among these behavioral changes are the following:

- Quitting smoking. The links between smoking and heart disease (and lung cancer) make quitting smoking the single best way to reduce the risks of serious health problems.
- Controlling weight. Maintaining a healthy weight appropriate to one's body proportions, not being either overweight or underweight, can help reduce the risk of heart disease.
- Reducing hypertension. Relaxation training, meditation, exercise, weight control, and a reduction in the intake of salt all help control blood pressure.
- Lowering serum cholesterol levels. Behavioral methods for lowering cholesterol include cutting down on foods high in cholesterol and saturated fats and exercising regularly (Stampfer et al., 2000).
- Changing type A behavior patterns. Learning to slow down and relax can decrease the risk of heart attacks. This is especially true for people who exhibit type A behavior and who have had previous heart attacks (Friedman & Ulmer, 1984; Roskies et al., 1986).
- Exercising regularly. A sustained program of exercise protects people from heart disease (Stampfer et al., 2000). People should consult their physicians before beginning an exercise program.

Cancer

Cancer is a disease that involves the rapid and abnormal growth of malignant cells. Cancerous cells can take root anywhere—for example, in the blood, skin, digestive tract, lungs, or reproductive organs. If not controlled early, cancer cells can spread and establish masses, or tumors, elsewhere in the body. People actually develop cancer cells frequently, but the immune system normally succeeds in destroying them. Individuals whose immune systems are weakened by physical or psychological factors appear to be more likely candidates than others for getting cancer (Azar, 1996).

TRUTH OR fiction ▪ REVISITED ▪ *It is true that many people develop cancerous cells but do not become ill from them.* A strong immune system regularly rids the body of such cells. A weakened immune system has a more difficult time destroying them.

Risk Factors People may inherit a tendency to develop certain kinds of cancer. The genes involved may remove the normal controls on cell division, allowing cancer cells to multiply wildly (Lichtenstein et al., 2000). Certain kinds of behavior also increase the risk of cancer. These behaviors include smoking, sunbathing (ultraviolet light can cause skin cancer), and eating animal fats (Bartecchi et al., 1994; Willett et al., 1990). Substances in cigarette smoke may damage the genes that would otherwise block the development of many types of cancers. Psychological problems such as prolonged anxiety and depression may also heighten the risk of cancer (Penninx et al., 1998; Salovey et al., 2000).

Research suggests that stress may be an additional risk factor for the development of cancer. In one study, researchers separated mice into one of two groups. One group was regularly subjected to stressful conditions, while the other group was not. The immune systems of the mice in the group that was exposed to stressful conditions showed a reduced ability to kill cancer cells compared to the mice that were not exposed to stressful conditions (Kandil & Borysenko, 1987). Other experiments with animals have suggested that once cancer has taken root, stress can affect the course of its development (Visintainer et al., 1982).

In one study, researcher V. Riley (1981) examined the effects of a cancer-causing virus that can be passed from female mice to their nursing offspring. The virus usually produces breast cancer in 80 percent of the female offspring by the time they have reached the age of 400 days.

Riley placed one group of female offspring that had been infected with the virus into a stressful environment with loud noises and unpleasant odors. She placed another group in a less stressful environment. By the age of 400 days, 92 percent of the female mice in the stressful environment had developed breast cancer, as compared with 7 percent of those in the other group. The mice that underwent stress also had increased levels of steroids that suppress the functioning of the immune system.

However, by the time another 200 days had elapsed, the mice that had been placed in the nonstressful environment showed about the same incidence of cancer as those that had experienced the stressful environment. Exposure to stress seemed to hasten the development of cancer in the mice infected with the cancer-causing virus. Nevertheless, the absence of stress did not prevent mice placed in a less stressful atmosphere from ultimately developing cancer as well.

Psychological Aspects People with cancer must cope with the many biological aspects of their illness, ranging from possible weakness and pain to the side effects of their medications. They also face many psychological effects of cancer. Anxiety about the medical treatment itself and about the possible approach of death are common psychological effects of cancer. Additionally, severe depression and feelings of vulnerability often accompany the diagnosis of cancer (Jacox et al., 1994).

Many people who are diagnosed with cancer are also burdened by the necessity of dealing with the insensitivity of others. Other people may actually criticize the person with the illness for feeling sorry for himself or herself or for "giving up" the fight against the disease (Andersen et al., 1994; Rosenthal, 1993).

Painful side effects sometimes accompany the treatment for certain types of cancer. For example, nausea frequently accompanies chemotherapy. People receiving chemotherapy are sometimes taught relaxation and guided imagery techniques, which have been shown to significantly reduce the nausea and vomiting associated with chemotherapy (Burish et al., 1987).

Studies with children and adolescents who have cancer have found that playing video games also reduces the discomfort of chemotherapy (Kolko &

Rickard-Figueroa, 1985; Redd et al., 1987). By allowing the children to focus their attention on battling computer-generated enemies, such games help keep the children distracted from the discomfort caused by the treatment.

Cancer requires medical treatment, and in some cases there are too few available treatment options. However, the attitudes people have about their cancer do seem to make a difference. A 10-year follow-up of women with breast cancer found a significantly higher survival rate among women who met their diagnosis with a "fighting spirit" rather than with resignation (Pettingale et al., 1985). A desire to fight the illness is apparently a key component of successful treatment. Social support also increases the survival rate of people who have cancer (Sleek, 1995).

Psychologists have found that the feelings of hopelessness that sometimes accompany the diagnosis of cancer may hinder recovery because they can suppress the person's immune system (Brody, 1994; Levy et al., 1985). Hospitalization itself is stressful because it removes people from the familiar surroundings of home and the sources of social support. Furthermore, being in the hospital and subject to hospital routines—for any reason—reduces one's sense of control.

In some cases, there may not be a great deal that a person with cancer can do to affect the eventual outcome of the disease. However, there are numerous ways to reduce the risk of developing cancer. The most effective way is to avoid behavioral risk factors for cancer by reducing the intake of fats and increasing the intake of fruits and vegetables (Mevkens, 1990; Willett et al., 1990). Limiting the amount of stress one is exposed to and having regular medical checkups are also vital factors in the reduction of the risk of developing cancer.

SECTION 4 REVIEW

go.hrw.com **Homework Practice Online**
Keyword: SY7 HP17

1. What psychological factors contribute to headaches, heart disease, and cancer?

2. Explain how stress might affect the progression of cancer.

3. **Critical Thinking** *Summarizing* How can psychological methods be used to help people prevent or deal effectively with health problems?

Ways of Coping with Stress

Because stress harms people's physical and psychological well-being, it is important to know how to cope with or reduce the stress in one's life. In this section we consider various ways of handling stress, including defensive coping and active coping.

Defensive Coping

Defensive coping is one way to reduce the immediate effects of a stressor, but it is probably not the most desirable way. Defensive coping may involve socially unacceptable behavior (substance abuse or aggression), running away from one's problems (withdrawal), or self-deception (use of defense mechanisms).

Defensive coping may give people time to gather their resources, but it does not eliminate the source of stress or improve the effectiveness of one's response to stress. In fact, in the long run, defensive methods are self-defeating and usually harmful.

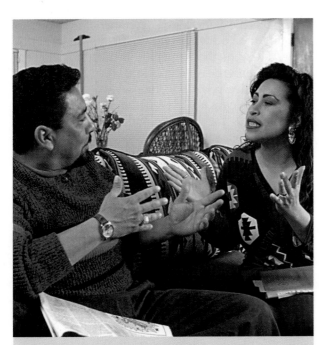

Some people use aggression to cope with stressful situations. However, aggressive behavior can often increase conflict rather than resolve it.

Substance Abuse   Some adolescents and adults use alcohol, tranquilizers, and other drugs to try to reduce feelings of stress (Wills et al., 1996). People may become psychologically dependent on these substances as they try to decrease their awareness of stress or to disguise what has become, for them, an unpleasant reality. That dependence only makes a problem worse because it makes people less able and less willing to deal with it.

Aggression   Some people use aggression and violence to cope with stressful situations, such as those that involve feelings of frustration or a difference of opinion with another person. However, violence rarely, if ever, provides solutions to people's problems. In fact, aggressive behavior often heightens interpersonal conflict because it may motivate an injured party to seek revenge.

Withdrawal   Some people withdraw from a stressful situation because they are frightened, feel helpless, or believe that any decision they make will be a mistake. Withdrawal can be emotional (loss of interest in life, turning away from friends and family), or it can be physical (moving to a new location to avoid dealing with an old problem).

Suicide   Suicide is the ultimate form of withdrawal. Some people experience so much stress and feel so hopeless about solving their problems that they believe the only way out is to commit suicide. Of course, suicide does not solve or reduce problems. It usually only increases the pain of those who are left to deal with its aftermath.

Defense Mechanisms   Sigmund Freud believed that defense mechanisms protect the ego from anxiety that may be produced by an awareness of unacceptable ideas or impulses. (See Chapter 14.) Defense mechanisms become problematic when they are the only means used to cope with stress.

Active Coping

Active coping involves changing the environment or situation (in socially acceptable ways) to remove stressors or changing one's response to stress so that stressors are no longer harmful. Todd was actively coping with the stressors in his life by submitting his scholarship application, talking with his father about his college selection, and completing his biology project.

Changing Stressful Thoughts

Stressful Thoughts	Calming Thoughts
"I feel like I'm losing control."	"This is painful and upsetting, but I don't have to go to pieces."
"This will never end."	"This will come to an end even if it's hard to see it right now."
"How can I go out there? I'll look like a fool."	"So you're not perfect. That doesn't mean that you're going to look stupid. And so what if someone thinks you look stupid? You can live with that too. Just stop worrying and have some fun."
"My heart is beating so fast. I feel like it's about to leap out of my chest."	"Calm down—hearts don't leap out of chests. Stop and think! Distract yourself. Breathe slowly, in and out."
"There's nothing I can do!"	"Stop and think—just because you can't come up with a solution right now doesn't mean there's nothing you can do. Take it one minute at a time. Breathe easy."

FIGURE 17.5 *Some people think stressful thoughts, which increases the stress they experience. People can actively cope with stress by becoming aware of these thought patterns and changing them.*

Sometimes stressors cannot be reduced, eliminated, or changed. In such cases, active coping involves adjusting to the stressors by reducing their impact. When Janet suggested playing basketball with Todd, she was trying to help him soften the effect of the stressors he was experiencing. Some methods of active coping include changing stressful thoughts, relaxing, and strengthening one's ability to withstand stress through exercise.

Changing Stressful Thoughts Have you ever had any of these thoughts?

"I feel like I'm losing control."

"This will never end."

"How can I go out there? I'll look like a fool."

"My heart is beating so fast. I feel like it's about to leap out of my chest."

"There's nothing I can do!"

Each of these thoughts increases the amount of stress people experience. However, people who have stressful thoughts can learn to recognize and change them before becoming overwhelmed by them. Through careful study, people can learn to identify self-defeating thoughts. Whenever a person feels tense or anxious, he or she should pay close attention to such thoughts and transform them into calming ones. (See Figure 17.5.) A sign that this is working is evident when the person begins to automatically have calming thoughts rather than stressful ones.

Relaxation Stress can cause strong bodily reactions, such as muscle tension, rapid breathing, high blood pressure, sweating, and a rapid heart rate. These reactions are signs that something is wrong. They prompt people to survey the situation and try to make things right. Psychologists and other researchers have developed a number of methods for reducing the bodily changes that are brought on by stress. These methods include meditation, biofeedback, and progressive relaxation. (See Chapter 5.)

Progressive relaxation helps lower stress in the body by reducing muscle tension. Reducing tension also affects the heart and breathing rates. Progressive relaxation teaches people how to relax by having them purposely tense a specific muscle group and then relax it. This process of tensing and then relaxing helps people develop awareness of muscle tension and distinguish between feelings of tension and feelings of relaxation. For example, a person can experience muscle relaxation in the arms while leaning back in a reclining chair by first tightening one fist, then the other, and gradually increasing the pressure (Wolpe & Lazarus, 1966).

Changing stressful thoughts and lowering the level of bodily reactions to stress reduce the effects of stressors and give the person more time to develop a plan for effective action. When there is no way to reduce or eliminate the stressors, thinking calming thoughts and relaxing the body will increase the ability to endure stress.

Exercise Exercise fosters physical health, enhances people's psychological well-being, and helps people cope with stress (Jonsdottir et al., 2000; Tkachuk & Martin, 1999). Janet knew that. That is why she suggested to Todd that they play basketball. Other kinds of stress-reducing exercise include activities such as running and jogging, running in place, brisk walking, swimming, bicycle riding, jumping rope, and playing team sports.

Sustained physical activity reduces the incidence of heart attacks (Stampfer et al., 2000). In one long-term research project, Paffenbarger and his colleagues (1993) studied 17,000 people. They

Exercise is one of the most effective ways to control stress and maintain physical and psychological well-being.

Incidence of Heart Attacks and Level of Physical Activity

Number with Heart Attack *

70
60
50
40
30 — **Total Heart Attacks**
20 — **Nonfatal Heart Attacks**
10
Fatal Heart Attacks
0

500 1,000 2,000 3,000 4,000
Physical Activity Index in Calories per Week

* per 10,000 people

FIGURE 17.6 *Research suggests that sustained physical activity reduces the incidence of heart attacks. In one study, researchers (1993) correlated the incidence of heart attacks with the level of physical activity. Their results showed a decline in the incidence of heart attacks as the activity level rose. The decline seemed to level off at the activity level of burning approximately 2,000 calories a week.*

Source: Paffenbarger et al. (1993). *New England Journal of Medicine, 328,* 538–545.

examined the relationship between the incidence of heart attacks and the levels of physical activity in the people they studied. As shown in Figure 17.6, the incidence of heart attacks began declining when the physical activity level rose to that of burning as few as 500 calories a week.

Inactive people run the highest risk of heart attacks. People who burn at least 2,000 calories a week through physical activity live two years longer, on average, than less active people. Sustained exercise also appears to strengthen the functioning of the immune system (Jonsdottir et al., 2000; Tkachuk & Martin, 1999).

SECTION 5 REVIEW

Homework Practice Online
Keyword: SY7 HP17

1. What is the difference between defensive coping and active coping?

2. How do people's thoughts affect the amount of stress they experience?

3. **Critical Thinking** *Drawing Inferences and Conclusions* How can methods of defensive coping become harmful rather than helpful?

Chapter 17 REVIEW

Writing a Summary

Using standard grammar, spelling, sentence structure, and punctuation, summarize the information in this chapter. Consider:
- the causes of stress and the general adaptation syndrome
- the effects of stress on health, and the ways people try to cope with stress

Identifying People and Ideas

Identify the following terms or people and use them in appropriate sentences.

1. stress
2. eustress
3. distress
4. stressor
5. avoidance-avoidance conflict
6. multiple approach-avoidance conflict
7. self-efficacy expectation
8. general adaptation syndrome
9. defensive coping
10. active coping

Understanding Main Ideas

SECTION 1 (pp. 386–392)
1. What are the benefits of eustress?

SECTION 2 (pp. 392–395)
2. How do self-efficacy expectations affect the way a person responds to stress?

SECTION 3 (pp. 395–397)
3. What is the general adaptation syndrome?

SECTION 4 (pp. 398–402)
4. What are some behavioral methods for reducing the pain of headaches?

SECTION 5 (pp. 403–405)
5. List two defensive coping methods and two active coping methods.

Thinking Critically

1. **Categorizing** Which of the following reactions to stress are defensive coping and which are active coping: overeating, leaving for work early to avoid rush-hour traffic, lying down while listening to music?

2. **Supporting a Point of View** Should companies that provide health and life insurance be allowed to charge higher rates to people under high levels of stress? Support your answer.

3. **Analyzing Information** Under what circumstances might eustress help a person perform better?

4. **Summarizing** What are three behavioral changes that help reduce the risk of heart disease?

Writing About Psychology

1. **Analyzing Information** Research how stress in the workplace, along with other stress, can affect a person's health and well-being. What kinds of situations contribute to job stress? How do employers try to deal with job stress? Write a report summarizing your findings.

2. **Comparing and Contrasting** Reread the chapter's section on type A and type B personalities. Think of famous people (present or past) or fictional characters that exemplify either type of personality. Write a paragraph to explain each choice. Be sure to use standard grammar, spelling, sentence structure, and punctuation. Use the graphic organizer below to help you write your paragraph.

Interpreting Graphs

Study the graph below. Then use the information in the graph to help you answer the questions that follow.

Test Anxiety

Percentage of Errors

Number of Steps to Answer Math Problem

■ Student Reporting High Anxiety   ■ Student Reporting Low Anxiety

Source: Goldbrger and Breznitz, *Handbook of Stress*, 1982

1. Which statement is the best conclusion that can be made from the information in the graph?

   a. Students with low anxiety levels are more intelligent than those with high anxiety levels.

   b. Anxiety levels play an unimportant role in the testing process.

   c. Psychologists should take test anxiety into account when assessing test performance.

   d. Students with high anxiety levels will never do well in math.

2. Which factors played a role in causing the greatest number of errors?

Analyzing Primary Sources

Read the following excerpt, in which Anne Petersen and Ralph Spiga look at school as one of the sources of adolescent stress. Then answer the questions that follow.

❝Indeed, the school may provide major stress during the adolescent years. In early adolescence, young people in our society move from a single classroom, with one teacher and the same group of classmates, into a middle school or junior high school, where they pass from class to class, most often with different teachers and different students. For many young people, this transition may be smooth, but for others it appears to be untimely and stressful. . . . Little research has focused on the transition from eighth or ninth grade into senior high school. Research with early adolescents, however, would suggest that this change also involves stress.❞

3. According to this excerpt, what is a key source of school-related stress for adolescents?

   a. greater demands placed on students at higher-grade levels

   b. fear of being unpopular

   c. meeting new teachers

   d. the change in the students' routine and environment

4. Using material from this excerpt, offer ideas as to how educators can make school less stressful for adolescents.

PSYCHOLOGY PROJECTS

Cooperative Learning

Using Your Observation Skills The Social Readjustment Rating Scale (shown on page 389) focuses primarily on life changes experienced by adults. In small groups, create a social readjustment scale for teens. Make a list of 20 events and assign a rating to each item on the basis of a consensus of group members. Post the completed scales in the classroom. Join in a class discussion of the similarities and differences between the scales. Participate in the discussion as a leader and as a follower.

☑ **internet** connect

Internet Activity: go.hrw.com
KEYWORD: SY7 CH17

Choose an activity on stress and health to:

- create a newspaper that discusses how to cope with stress.
- research the impact of stress on everyday life.
- create case studies regarding psychological factors and health.

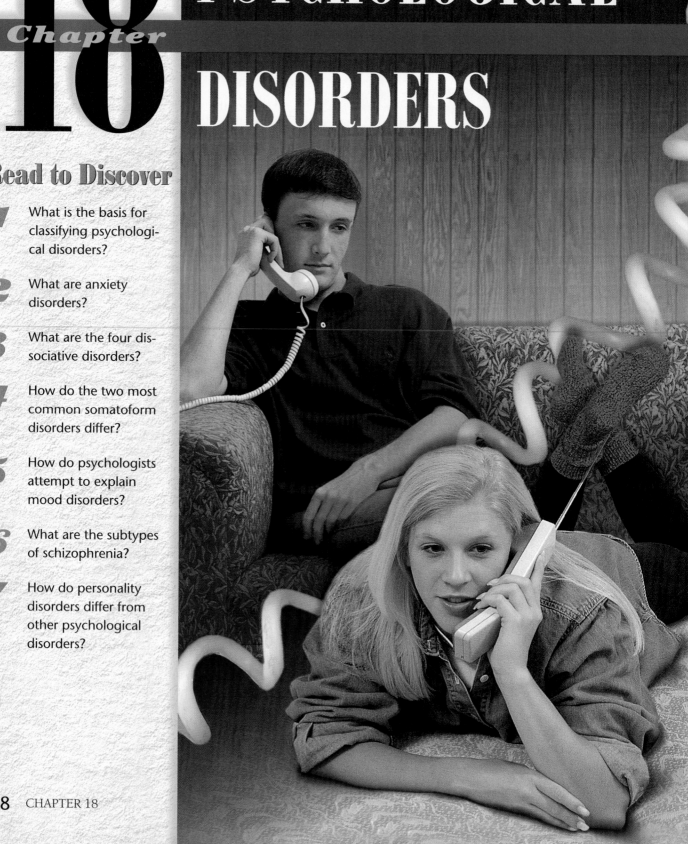

18 Chapter

PSYCHOLOGICAL DISORDERS

Read to Discover

1 What is the basis for classifying psychological disorders?

2 What are anxiety disorders?

3 What are the four dissociative disorders?

4 How do the two most common somatoform disorders differ?

5 How do psychologists attempt to explain mood disorders?

6 What are the subtypes of schizophrenia?

7 How do personality disorders differ from other psychological disorders?

A DAY IN THE LIFE

Janet was at home studying in her bedroom when the phone rang. "Hello?" she answered.

"Hey, Janet, it's me—Dan. Can you talk for a minute?"

Janet and Dan had been friends for years, and she could always tell when he sounded sad. "Of course I can. What's up?" Janet answered, trying to sound positive.

"It's Michelle again," Dan said.

About a year ago, Dan's older sister, Michelle, had been diagnosed with a serious psychological disorder called schizophrenia. Michelle was 23 years old and lived with her husband, Jeff, in a small house in the country. Accepting the fact that Michelle had a psychological disorder had been difficult for Dan. At first, he didn't talk about it with anyone outside his family. Then, after a while, he began confiding in Janet.

"It's so hard sometimes," Dan said sadly. "I really thought she was going to be okay after the doctors finally diagnosed and started treating her last year."

"Did something happen?" Janet asked, genuinely concerned.

"Well, I hadn't seen her in weeks because Jeff was the only person she would talk to. I finally saw her tonight, and I could tell that something was happening again. She always seems so distracted. It's like she's listening to something only she can hear."

"Has she been taking the medicine that the doctor prescribed?" Janet asked.

"I don't know for sure," Dan answered. "I asked her about it tonight, but she got really defensive. She kept saying that I was trying to confuse her, and then she insisted that Jeff take her home."

"I'm sorry, Dan. I wish there were something I could do," Janet responded sympathetically.

"Thanks," Dan said. "It really helps to be able to talk to someone. At least I'm handling it a lot better than my parents are. My mom thinks that somehow it's her fault—like it is hereditary or Michelle caught it as a baby."

"Do the doctors have any idea how she *did* get it?" Janet asked.

"Not really," Dan said. "They have a bunch of different theories, but I don't think they know for sure. I'm just hoping that somehow they'll figure out exactly what's wrong so they'll be able to really help her."

"Me, too," Janet replied softly.

- psychological disorders
- culture-bound syndromes
- anxiety
- phobia
- simple phobia
- social phobia
- panic attack
- agoraphobia
- obsessions
- compulsions
- post-traumatic stress disorder
- dissociation
- depersonalization
- somatization
- depression
- bipolar disorder
- mania
- schizophrenia
- catatonic stupor

Dan's sister, Michelle, has schizophrenia, a serious psychological disorder that causes her to hear things that others cannot hear and, in general, often to lose touch with reality. Most psychological disorders are less serious than schizophrenia, but they still may cause great distress for affected individuals and their families and friends. This chapter describes several types of psychological disorders, including schizophrenia. The treatment of psychological disorders is the focus of Chapter 19.

HOLT

Psychology Video Program

Watch the video to explore the stigma of mental illness in America.

TRUTH?
OR
fiction?

Read the following statements about psychology. Do you think they are true or false? You will learn whether each statement is true or false as you read the chapter.

- Very few people are actually affected by psychological disorders.
- People sometimes forget a very traumatic event as a way of coping with the psychological stress of the trauma.
- People whose illnesses are "all in their heads" do not really have symptoms of disease.
- Depression is the most common type of psychological disorder.
- Some people do not feel guilty, even when they commit serious crimes.

Estimates suggest that about one out of every three people in the United States will experience a psychological disorder at some point in life.

What Are Psychological Disorders?

Psychology is the scientific study of behavior and mental processes. **Psychological disorders** are behavior patterns or mental processes that cause serious personal suffering or interfere with a person's ability to cope with everyday life.

Many people believe that psychological disorders are uncommon, affecting relatively few individuals. It is true that the great majority of people are never admitted to mental hospitals, and most people never seek the help of psychologists or psychiatrists. And although many people have relatives they consider eccentric, few people have family members they consider to be truly abnormal.

Estimates suggest, however, that almost one third of the adults in the United States have experienced some type of psychological disorder (Goldstein et al., 1986). In addition to the many people with substance abuse problems, 23 percent of people in the United States experience some type of psychological disorder in their lifetime. In any given month, the figure is appoximately 13 percent (Regier, 1993). As Dan's family discovered, psychological disorders can affect almost anyone.

A DAY IN THE LIFE

TRUTH
OR
fiction
■ REVISITED ■

It is not true that very few people are actually affected by psychological disorders. Millions of people are affected by psychological disorders during their lifetimes.

Identifying Psychological Disorders

Deciding whether particular behaviors, thoughts, or feelings are "normal" or "abnormal" can be difficult. What is normal is often equated with what is average for the majority of people. Using this definition of normality, deviation from the majority becomes the primary criterion for abnormality.

People with psychological disorders usually do not differ much from "normal" people. In fact, the primary difference is the simple exaggeration of certain behaviors or mental processes. For example, laughing is a normal and healthy response to humorous situations. However, someone who laughs all the time, even in very inappropriate situations, might be considered abnormal.

Symptoms of Psychological Disorders

Several behavior patterns and mental processes may suggest that an individual has a psychological disorder. The word *suggest* is important here because diagnosing an individual with a psychological disorder is often difficult, and diagnoses are not always simple or straightforward.

However, psychologists generally use several criteria to determine whether a person's behavior indicates the presence of a psychological disorder. These criteria include how typical the behavior is of people in general, whether the behavior is maladaptive, whether the behavior causes the individual emotional discomfort, and whether the behavior is socially unacceptable.

Typicality   As previously noted, the normality of a behavior or mental process is often determined by the degree to which it is average, or typical, of the behavior or mental processes of the majority of people. There are, however, problems with defining normality in terms of what is typical of most people. The fact that a behavior is not typical of most people does not mean it is abnormal. Scientific and artistic geniuses, such as Marie Curie and Pablo Picasso, certainly are not typical of people in general. That does not mean, however, that such people are abnormal.

Maladaptivity   Many psychologists believe that what makes a behavior abnormal is the fact that it is maladaptive (Coleman et al., 1984). That is, the behavior impairs an individual's ability to function adequately in everyday life. Behavior that causes misery and distress rather than happiness and fulfillment may be considered maladaptive. Alcohol abuse is one such behavior. Alcohol abuse often has strong negative effects on the drinker's health, work, and family life. Abuse of alcohol may discourage the drinker from seeking healthier solutions to the problem of anxiety as well as create additional problems of its own.

Behavior that is hazardous to oneself or to others may also be considered maladaptive. This type of maladaptive behavior may include threatening or attempting suicide as well as threatening or attacking other people.

It is important to note that most people who commit violent crimes do not have psychological disorders. This is because most criminals are fully aware of what they are doing. That is, they know that their behavior is illegal and that they can be held responsible for it. Equally important, the majority of people with psychological disorders, even severe psychological disorders, are not violent or dangerous.

Emotional Discomfort   Psychological disorders such as anxiety and depression cause most people great emotional discomfort. For example, people who are depressed often suffer feelings of helplessness, hopelessness, worthlessness, guilt, and extreme sadness. They may lose interest in virtually everything they once enjoyed and believe that life is no longer worth living. Such feelings are so stressful that they may lead the affected individual to consider suicide. Thus, severe emotional discomfort may be a sign of a psychological disorder.

Socially Unacceptable Behavior   Behavior that violates a society's accepted norms may also be an indication of a psychological disorder. However, whether a behavior is socially unacceptable may depend on the particular society or culture in which it occurs. What is considered normal behavior in one culture may be considered abnormal in another. Therefore, the cultural context of a behavior must be taken into account before deciding that the behavior indicates a psychological disorder.

The importance of culture is demonstrated by **culture-bound syndromes**, clusters of symptoms that define or describe an illness. Many behaviors associated with culture-bound syndromes would be considered abnormal by people who are unaware of the syndrome's cultural context. For example, many people in Middle Eastern cultures believe that certain inappropriate behaviors, such as banging one's head, are due to possession of the body by a spirit. In the United States, such a belief would likely be considered a sign of a serious psychological disorder. However, in the cultural context of some areas in the Middle East, spirit possession is considered to be a rational explanation for certain types of behavior, and the affected individual is not thought to have a psychological disorder. There are many examples of culture-bound syndromes, some of which are listed in Figure 18.1 on page 413.

Classifying Psychological Disorders

Most psychologists believe that it is important to have a widely agreed upon classification of psychological disorders. Unless there is agreement about how to classify psychological disorders, it is difficult to know how many people have a given disorder or what other factors, such as socioeconomic status, heredity, or gender differences, may be associated with it. It is also important to classify psychological disorders so that individuals can be correctly diagnosed and treated.

CASE STUDIES
AND OTHER TRUE STORIES

Not Guilty by Reason of Insanity

The vast majority of people with mental illnesses are not dangerous to others. Some, however, do commit crimes. Many people have been found not guilty of serious crimes—even murder—"by reason of insanity." Typically, they are sent to psychiatric institutions instead of prison. They may be released when they are judged no longer to be a threat to others.

John Hinckley's lawyers used the insanity defense at his trial.

A well-known use of the insanity plea occurred in the case of John Hinckley, the man who attempted to assassinate President Ronald Reagan in 1981. Not only did Hinckley attempt to murder the president, but he did so in front of millions of television witnesses. Nevertheless, Hinckley was found not guilty by reason of insanity after expert witnesses testified that he had schizophrenia. Rather than being sent to prison, Hinckley was committed to a psychiatric institution.

In using an insanity defense, lawyers apply a modified version of the M'Naghten Rule, which states that if it can be proved that at the time of committing a criminal act a person either did not understand the nature of the act or did not know that it was wrong, then the person is insane and not responsible for the act.

The M'Naghten Rule goes back to 1843, when a Scotsman named Daniel M'Naghten was found not guilty of murder by reason of insanity. M'Naghten had tried to kill the British prime minister, Sir Robert Peel, because he had delusions that Peel was persecuting him. In the assassination attempt, Peel's secretary was killed. However, the court found M'Naghten not guilty of murder, stating that he was insane and thus not responsible for his criminal act.

Typically, when an accused person pleads insanity, prosecuting attorneys try to demonstrate that the accused was sane at the time of the crime, while the defense tries to prove that the accused was not sane. Both rely on the testimony of expert witnesses, usually psychologists or psychiatrists, who have interviewed the accused after the crime or who have previous knowledge of the accused.

Many people worry that criminals are literally "getting away with murder" because of the insanity defense. However, the defense is actually used in just 1 percent of felony cases and is unsuccessful in three fourths of those. Recent reforms have made it more difficult to use the insanity plea successfully. These reforms include the following:

- In many states, to be considered insane the accused now must be diagnosed with a severe psychological disorder.

- The burden of proof has been shifted from the prosecution to the defense. It is now up to the defense to prove the accused was insane.

- Some states have gone even further and abolished the insanity plea altogether.

Insanity is a legal concept, not a psychological one, and to be legally useful, it must be all or nothing—one is either sane or insane. In reality, most psychological disorders are a matter of degree. The distinction is important. One can be just a little depressed, for example, but according to the law, one cannot be just a little insane. Because of its all-or-nothing nature, deciding on someone's sanity can be a very difficult decision for the courts to make.

THINKING CRITICALLY

1. **Summarizing** In general, what criteria must someone meet to be ruled legally insane?

2. **Supporting a Point of View** Do you support the use of the insanity plea? Why, or why not?

The most widely used classification system for psychological disorders is the DSM, or *Diagnostic and Statistical Manual of Mental Disorders*, published by the American Psychiatric Association. The most recent version of the manual, the DSM-IV-TR™, was published in 2000.

The classification of psychological disorders has changed significantly from earlier classifications. Until 1980, when the third edition of the DSM was published, psychological disorders were classified on the basis of their presumed causes. For many decades, the most widely accepted causes were those suggested by Freud's psychoanalytic theory.

Many psychologists criticized early versions of the DSM because very diverse psychological disorders were grouped together under the labels "neuroses" and "psychoses." As a result, beginning with the DSM-III in 1980, psychological disorders have been categorized on the basis of observable signs and symptoms rather than presumed causes.

The DSM is subject to ongoing revision. New categories are added and old ones deleted as knowledge of psychological disorders increases. For example, post-traumatic stress disorder was added to the DSM only after the Vietnam War, when many soldiers were found to suffer from the disorder.

The remainder of this chapter focuses on six major types of psychological disorders: anxiety disorders, dissociative disorders, somatoform disorders, mood disorders, schizophrenia, and personality disorders. Many of the symptoms of these disorders are simply exaggerations of normal thoughts, feelings, or behaviors. As a result, as you read about the different symptoms, you may feel that you have one or more of the disorders being described. Such a feeling is common among most people who read about psychological disorders for the first time. Keep in mind that only trained professionals can diagnose psychological disorders, and they can do so only after careful evaluation.

Some Culture-Bound Syndromes

Latah

Malaysia and elsewhere:
hypersensitivity to sudden fright, often with nonsense mimicking of others; trance-like behavior

Hwa-byung

Korea:
panic, depression, or other symptoms believed to be due to the suppression of anger

Zar

Middle East:
shouting, laughing, head banging, or other inappropriate behavior that is believed to be caused by possession of the body by a spirit

Susto

Latino groups in the United States and the Caribbean:
unhappiness and illness following a frightening event that is believed to cause the soul to leave the body

Ghost sickness

Native Americans in the United States:
bad dreams, hallucinations, fainting, and other symptoms believed to be due to preoccupation with death and the dead

Mal de ojo

Mediterranean and elsewhere:
sufferers, mostly children, are believed to be under the influence of an "evil eye," causing fitful sleep, crying, and sickness

FIGURE 18.1 *Several patterns of abnormal behavior are recognized in specific cultures and may or may not be linked to an official category of psychological disorder. Listed here are a few of these culture-bound syndromes.* **Why is it important to consider the cultural context of a behavior before classifying it as a psychological disorder?**

Source: Adapted from the DSM-IV-TR, 2000.

Types of Anxiety Disorders

Phobic Disorder	A persistent, excessive or irrational fear of an object or a situation. Acrophobia is a fear of heights; claustrophobia is a fear of enclosed places. Fear of public speaking is an example of a social phobia.
Panic Disorder and Agoraphobia	Recurring, unexpected panic attacks characterized by rapid heart rate. Agoraphobia is a panic disorder in which people fear being caught in crowded, public places when they have an attack.
Generalized Anxiety Disorder	Excessive or unrealistic worry that appears to be present nearly all the time.
Obsessive-Compulsive Disorder	Unwanted thoughts or ideas (obsessions); impulses that are difficult or impossible to resist, such as repeated hand washing (compulsions) connected with the idea that one's hands remain unclean (an obsession).
Stress Disorders	Intense, persistent feelings of anxiety that follow traumatic events. PTSD may be accompanied by flashbacks, nightmares, and avoidance of stimuli connected with the traumatic event.

Explaining Anxiety Disorders

Psychoanalytic theory	Anxiety represents the "leakage" of primitive aggressive or sexual ideas or urges that were repressed during childhood.
Learning theory	Phobias are conditioned, or learned in childhood, either through direct experience or observing others. People avoid threatening situations to reduce anxiety.
Cognitive theory	People exaggerate threats and believe they are helpless to deal with them.
Biological factors	Anxiety disorders tend to run in families, suggesting a role for genetic factors. Anxiety disorders may be exaggerated descendants of adaptive fears.

FIGURE 18.2 *Anxiety is a state of dread or uneasiness that occurs in response to danger. When a person has an anxiety disorder, the amount of anxiety they experience is out of proportion to the actual or perceived threat.*

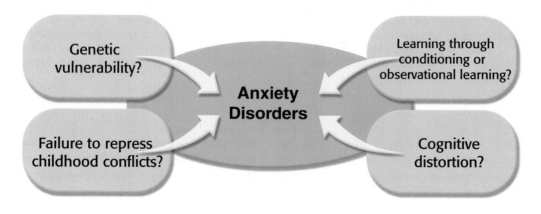

SECTION 1 REVIEW

go.
hrw
.com

Homework Practice Online

Keyword: SY7 HP18

1. Identify three problems with defining normal behavior as the behavior displayed by the majority of people.

2. How have the criteria for the classification of psychological disorders been arranged since 1980?

3. **Critical Thinking** *Categorizing* Give an example of a feeling or a behavior that would be considered normal in one circumstance but might be considered a sign of a psychological disorder in another circumstance.

SECTION 2
Anxiety Disorders

Anxiety refers to a general state of dread or uneasiness that occurs in response to a vague or imagined danger. It differs from fear, which is a response to a real danger or threat. Anxiety is typically characterized by nervousness, inability to relax, and concern about losing control. Physical signs and symptoms of anxiety may include trembling, sweating, rapid heart rate, shortness of breath, increased blood pressure, flushed face, and feelings of faintness or light-headedness. All are the result of overactivity of the sympathetic branch of the autonomic nervous system. (See Chapter 3.)

Everyone feels anxious at times—for example, before a big game or an important test. In such situations, feeling anxious or worried is an appropriate response that does not indicate a psychological disorder. However, some people feel anxious all or most of the time, or their anxiety is out of proportion to the situation provoking it. Such anxiety may interfere with effective living, the achievement of desired goals, life satisfaction, and emotional comfort. When these problems occur, anxiety is considered a sign of a psychological disorder. Anxiety-based disorders are among the most common of all psychological disorders in the United States (Gorman et al., 1989).

Types of Anxiety Disorders

Anxiety disorders classified in the DSM-IV include phobic disorder, panic disorder, generalized anxiety disorder, obsessive-compulsive disorder, and stress disorders. A description of each follows.

Phobic Disorder The word **phobia** derives from the Greek root *phobos,* which means "fear." **Simple phobia**, which is the most common of all the anxiety disorders, refers to a persistent excessive or irrational fear of a particular object or situation. To be diagnosed as a phobic disorder, the fear must lead to avoidance behavior that interferes with the affected person's normal life.

Almost any object or situation may lead to a phobic reaction. Several phobias, however, are especially common. The most common include:

- zoophobia: a fear of animals
- claustrophobia: a fear of enclosed spaces
- acrophobia: a fear of heights
- arachnophobia: a fear of spiders

Other relatively common phobias include fear of storms, blood, snakes, dental procedures, driving, and air travel.

When people with simple phobias are confronted with the object or situation they fear, they are likely to feel extremely anxious. As a result, they tend to avoid what they fear. For example, someone with hematophobia (a fear of blood) might avoid needed medical treatment. Someone with aviaphobia (a fear of air travel) might turn down a job

This person is waiting anxiously to be interviewed for a job. **What situations make you feel anxious?**

Someone with agoraphobia or panic disorder would be likely to avoid this crowded shopping mall. Why might these disorders lead to similar avoidance behaviors?

promotion because the new position involves air travel. Thus, although most people with simple phobias never seek treatment for their disorders, a simple phobia can seriously disrupt a person's life.

Social phobia is characterized by persistent fear of social situations in which one might be exposed to the close scrutiny of others and thus be observed doing something embarrassing or humiliating. Some people with social phobias fear all social situations; others fear specific situations, such as public speaking, eating in public, or dating.

People with social phobias generally try to avoid the situations they fear. They may invent excuses to avoid going to parties or other social gatherings, for example. If avoidance is impossible, the situations are likely to cause great anxiety. In addition, the avoidance behavior itself may greatly interfere with work and social life.

Panic Disorder and Agoraphobia People with panic disorder have recurring and unexpected panic attacks. A **panic attack** is a relatively short period of intense fear or discomfort, characterized by shortness of breath, dizziness, rapid heart rate, trembling or shaking, sweating, choking, nausea, or other distressing physical symptoms. It may last from a few minutes to a few hours. People having a panic attack may believe they are dying or "going

crazy." Not surprisingly, they usually have persistent fears of another attack.

For most people who suffer panic disorder, attacks have no apparent cause. However, many people with panic disorder also have agoraphobia. **Agoraphobia** is a fear of being in places or situations in which escape may be difficult or impossible. People with agoraphobia may be especially afraid of crowded public places such as movie theaters, shopping malls, buses, or trains.

Agoraphobia is a common phobia among adults. In fact, according to the DSM-IV, people with one or both disorders make up about 50 to 80 percent of the phobic individuals seen in clinical practice.

Most people with agoraphobia have panic attacks when they cannot avoid the situations they fear. They are afraid they will have a panic attack in a public place, where they will be humiliated or unable to obtain help. Panic disorder and agoraphobia both lead to avoidance behaviors. These behaviors can range from avoiding crowded places to never leaving home at all. Thus, these phobias can be very serious.

Generalized Anxiety Disorder According to the DSM-IV, generalized anxiety disorder (GAD) is an excessive or unrealistic worry about life circumstances that lasts for at least six months. The worries must be present during most of that time in order to warrant a diagnosis of GAD. Typically, the worries focus on finances, work, interpersonal problems, accidents, or illness.

GAD is one of the most common anxiety disorders, yet few people seek psychological treatment for it because it does not differ, except in intensity and duration, from the normal worries of everyday life. It is difficult to distinguish GAD from other anxiety disorders, and many people with GAD have other anxiety disorders as well, most often phobic disorders (Barlow et al., 1986).

Obsessive-Compulsive Disorder Among the most acute of the anxiety disorders is obsessive-compulsive disorder (OCD). **Obsessions** are unwanted thoughts, ideas, or mental images that occur over and over again. They are often senseless or repulsive, and most people with obsessions try to ignore or suppress them. The majority of people with obsessions also practice compulsions, which may reduce the anxiety their obsessions produce. **Compulsions** are repetitive ritual behaviors, often involving checking or cleaning something.

The following examples are typical of people with OCD. One person is obsessed every night with doubts that he has locked the doors and windows before going to bed. He feels driven to compulsively check and recheck every door and window in the house, perhaps dozens of times. Only then can he relax and go to sleep. In another example, a team of researchers reported the case of a woman who was obsessed with the idea that she would pick up germs from nearly everything she touched. She compulsively washed her hands over and over again, sometimes as many as 500 times a day (Davison & Neale, 1990).

People who experience obsessions are usually aware that the obsessions are unjustified (March et al., 1989; Rapoport, 1989; Swedo et al., 1989). This distinguishes obsessions from delusions. Although obsessions are a sign of a less serious psychological disorder than delusions, they still can make people feel extremely anxious, and they can seriously interfere with daily life. Compulsions may alleviate some of the anxiety associated with obsessions, but the compulsions themselves are time-consuming and usually create additional interference with daily life.

Constant organizing and cleaning are common compulsions in people who experience obsessive-compulsive disorder.

Stress Disorders Stress disorders include post-traumatic stress disorder (PTSD) and acute stress disorder. The two disorders have similar symptoms, but they differ in how quickly they occur after the traumatic event that triggers the disorder. They also differ in how long they last.

Post-traumatic stress disorder refers to intense, persistent feelings of anxiety that are caused by an experience so traumatic that it would produce stress in almost anyone. Experiences that may produce PTSD include rape, severe child abuse, assault, severe accident, airplane crash, natural disasters, and war atrocities. It appears to be a common syndrome in people who have experienced extensive trauma. For example, more than one third of the victims of Hurricane Andrew in 1992 developed PTSD (Ironson, 1993).

People who suffer from PTSD may exhibit any or all of the following symptoms (American Psychiatric Association, 2000):

- flashbacks, which are mental reexperiences of the actual trauma

- nightmares or other unwelcome thoughts about the trauma

- numbness of feelings

- avoidance of stimuli associated with the trauma

- increased tension, which may lead to sleep disturbances, irritability, poor concentration, and similar problems

The symptoms may occur six months or more after the traumatic event, and they may last for years or even decades. The more severe the trauma, the worse the symptoms tend to be.

Acute stress disorder is a short-term disorder with symptoms similar to those of PTSD. Also like PTSD, acute stress disorder follows a traumatic event. However, unlike with PTSD, the symptoms occur immediately or at most within a month of the event. The anxiety also lasts a shorter time—from a few days to a few weeks. Not everyone who experiences a trauma, however, will develop PTSD or acute stress disorder.

Explaining Anxiety Disorders

Several different explanations for anxiety disorders have been suggested. As is true for most of the psychological disorders discussed in this chapter, the explanations fall into two general categories: psychological views and biological views.

PSYCHOLOGY
IN THE WORLD TODAY

Terrorism and Anxiety

The September 11, 2001, terrorist attacks shocked people in the United States and around the world. The scale, surprise, and violence of the attacks provoked a wide variety of psychological responses both in those who survived the attacks and those who followed the events through the media.

Shortly after the attacks, many people were stunned. The reality of the attacks began to sink in as television stations repeatedly played images of the World Trade Center towers ablaze and collapsing, the Pentagon burning, and of the airplane crash site in Pennsylvania. Fears that more attacks were imminent quickly spread across the United States. Meanwhile, people desperately sought information about friends and relatives who worked in or near the World Trade Center towers and the Pentagon. The confusion and lack of information shortly after the attacks resulted in anxiety and frustration for many people.

After the initial shock of the attacks passed, people across the nation began to feel new anxieties as they struggled to cope with what had happened. New York City residents—particularly those who worked in or near the World Trade Center on September 11—grieved and experienced a range of unsettling and disturbing feelings. Some workers relived the fear they felt the day of the attacks every time they passed by "ground zero" on their way to work. Others were gripped with passing moments of fear whenever an airplane would pass overhead.

People in New York City and throughout the United States experienced other reactions as well. Many people reported unusually vivid and terrifying dreams related to the terrorist attacks. For example, one woman in Oregon dreamed she was trapped in a World Trade Center tower when it was hit by an airplane. A person in California

President George W. Bush met with rescue personnel after the attacks.

dreamed of a beautiful bald eagle that was suddenly transformed into a snarling bird with glowing red eyes.

Some people who experienced terrifying dreams were suffering from the crippling anxiety of post-traumatic stress disorder. People with this disorder may have sleep problems, irritable outbursts, and difficulty concentrating on their work. Many people continued to experience intrusive memories for weeks and months after the attacks. Others experienced flashbacks—the sudden feeling that the events were happening again. These sudden feelings were prompted by a variety of sights and sounds. Sirens, television images, tall buildings, and construction crews sparked anxiety in many people. These flashbacks and memories reflected the difficult struggle people were having to regain their emotional balance.

People tried to cope with the stress of the terrorist attacks in a number of ways. Many took the advice of psychologists who recommended that they limit their exposure to the horrific images of the attacks and that they seek social support among families and friends. Church membership grew after the attacks. Others flew flags at half staff or held quiet vigils to remember the victims and their families. Many people participated in the national day of mourning called for by President George W. Bush. In these ways, people across the nation tried to restore their sense of security.

Think About It

Analyzing Information What were some ways that people tried to deal with unsettling events such as the terrorist attacks of September 11, 2001?

Psychological Views For anxiety disorders, as well as the other disorders discussed later in this chapter, psychoanalytic views are presented even though they are no longer widely accepted. These views are included because they influenced later theories and had a major impact on the classification of psychological disorders until recently, as discussed earlier.

According to psychoanalytic theory, anxiety is the result of "forbidden" childhood urges that have been repressed, or hidden from consciousness (Freud, 1936). If repressed urges do surface, psychoanalysts argue, they may do so as obsessions and eventually lead to compulsive behaviors. For example, if one is trying to repress "dirty" sexual thoughts, then repetitive hand washing may help relieve some of the anxiety.

Learning theorists believe that phobias are conditioned, or learned, in childhood. This may occur when a child experiences a traumatic event—such as being lost in a crowd or frightened by a bad storm—or when a child observes phobic behavior in other people (Bandura, 1986). If a parent screams or faints when a child picks up a spider, for example, the child may learn that spiders are things to be feared and develop a fear of them. Learning theorists argue that such conditioned phobias may remain long after the experiences that produced them have been forgotten.

Learning theorists also believe that people will learn to reduce their anxiety by avoiding the situations that make them anxious (Gorman et al., 1989). For example, a student who feels anxious speaking in front of others in class may learn to keep quiet because it reduces his or her feelings of anxiety. However, by intentionally avoiding the anxiety-producing behavior, the student has no chance to learn other ways of coping with or unlearning the anxiety. As a result, the anxiety may worsen or be generalized to other situations that involve speaking in front of others.

Cognitive theorists, on the other hand, believe that people make themselves feel anxious by responding negatively to most situations and coming to believe they are helpless to control what happens to them. This creates great anxiety.

Biological Views Research indicates that heredity may play a role in most psychological disorders, including anxiety disorders. For example, one study showed that if one of a pair of identical twins exhibited an anxiety disorder, there was a 45 percent chance that the other twin would also exhibit the disorder. This was true even of twins raised in different families. By contrast, the chances of fraternal twins both developing anxiety disorders was only about 15 percent (Torgersen, 1983). Similarly, adopted children are more likely to have an anxiety disorder if a biological parent has one than if an adoptive parent does. Both types of studies suggest that genes play at least some role in the development of anxiety disorders.

How did genes get involved? Some psychologists believe that people are genetically inclined to fear things that were threats to their ancestors (Mineka, 1991). These psychologists argue that people who rapidly acquired strong fears of real dangers—such as large animals, snakes, heights, and sharp objects—would be more likely to survive and reproduce. To the extent that the tendency to develop such fears is controlled by genes, they conclude, the tendency would be passed on to future generations, causing the disorders to be relatively common today.

Interaction of Factors Some cases of anxiety disorder may reflect the interaction of biological and psychological factors. People with panic disorder, for example, may have a biologically based tendency to overreact psychologically to physical sensations (Ciesielski et al., 1981; Turner et al., 1985). The initial physical symptoms of panic—such as rapid heart rate and shortness of breath—cause these people to react with fear, leading to even worse panic symptoms. They may think they are having a heart attack and experience severe psychological stress. Anxiety about having another panic attack becomes a psychological disorder itself— one that originated in a biological reaction.

Regardless of their cause, anxiety disorders are both common and disabling. In serious cases, they lead to tremendous restrictions and limitations in lifestyle, relationships, and work. They can also lead to great personal distress. Fortunately, most people who suffer from anxiety disorder respond well to treatment, which is covered in Chapter 19.

SECTION 2 REVIEW

go.hrw.com Homework Practice Online Keyword: SY7 HP18

1. How does anxiety differ from fear?

2. Describe the relationship between panic disorder and agoraphobia.

3. **Critical Thinking** *Analyzing Information* Explain why studies of twins are important for determining whether a disorder has a biological basis.

Dissociative Disorders

Dissociation refers to the separation of certain personality components or mental processes from conscious thought. In some situations, dissociation is normal. Someone may be so engrossed in reading a book or watching a television program, for example, that he is unaware that his name is being called. Someone else may become so involved in watching the road that she misses the sign for her exit on the highway. Perhaps the most common form of normal dissociation is daydreaming, in which the person's thoughts may be "a million miles away." In each of these cases, dissociation usually does not indicate a psychological disorder.

However, when dissociation occurs as a way to avoid stressful events or feelings, it is considered to be a sign of a psychological disorder. People with dissociative disorders may lose their memory of a particular event or even forget their identity. It is believed that dissociation occurs when individuals are faced with urges or experiences that are very stressful. By dissociating, they are able to remove themselves from the source of stress and lessen their feelings of anxiety.

There are no current statistics on the prevalence of dissociative disorders. In part, this is because the DSM-IV classifies them somewhat differently than they were classified in the past. However, dissociation is a common psychological symptom.

Types of Dissociative Disorders

In the DSM-IV, the dissociative disorders are classified as dissociative amnesia, dissociative fugue, dissociative identity disorder, and depersonalization disorder. These disorders are described next.

Dissociative Amnesia Formerly called psychogenic amnesia, dissociative amnesia is characterized by a sudden loss of memory, usually following a particularly stressful or traumatic event. A person experiencing dissociative amnesia typically cannot remember any events that occurred for a certain period of time surrounding the traumatic event. Less commonly, a person may forget all prior experiences and may be unable to remember his or her name, recognize friends and family, or recall important personal information. Dissociative amnesia may last for just a few hours, or it may persist for

years. Memory is likely to return just as suddenly as it was lost, and the amnesia rarely recurs.

The term *psychogenic* means "psychological in origin." Dissociative amnesia cannot be explained biologically—as the result of a head injury, for example. Most often, a traumatic event, such as witnessing a serious accident, precedes the amnesia. Not surprisingly, the incidence of dissociative amnesia rises markedly during wartime and crises such as natural disasters.

TRUTH OR fiction ■ R E V I S I T E D ■

It is true that people sometimes forget a very traumatic event as a way of coping with the psychological stress of the trauma. This occurrence is called dissociative amnesia.

Dissociative Fugue Dissociative fugue—previously called psychogenic fugue—is characterized not only by forgetting personal information and past events but also by suddenly relocating from home or work and taking on a new identity. Like dissociative amnesia, dissociative fugue usually follows a traumatic event that is psychologically very stressful. It is reported most frequently during wartime and natural disasters.

When individuals with dissociative fugue travel away from their home or workplace, they may take on a new name, residence, and occupation. They may become socially active in their new identity and not appear to be ill in any way. When the fugue comes to an end, they no longer remember what happened during the fugue state.

Dissociative Identity Disorder Formerly called multiple personality disorder, dissociative identity disorder involves the existence of two or more personalities within a single individual. The various personalities may or may not be aware of the others, and at least two of the personalities take turns controlling the individual's behavior.

Each personality is likely to be different from the others in several ways, including in such observable traits as voice, facial expressions, and handedness, as well as self-perceived age, gender, and physical characteristics. The personalities may even have different allergies and eyeglass prescriptions. They may also behave very differently from one another.

People who are diagnosed with dissociative identity disorder usually were severely abused in childhood. They typically suffered severe physical, sexual, and/or psychological abuse (Spanos, 1994). Less often, dissociative identity disorder is preceded by other types of trauma.

Depersonalization Disorder   Depersonalization refers to feelings of detachment from one's mental processes or body. People with this disorder describe feeling as though they are outside their bodies, observing themselves at a distance.

Depersonalization is a common symptom of other psychological disorders in addition to being a disorder in its own right. After depression and anxiety, it is the most common complaint among psychiatric patients. Like the other dissociative disorders, depersonalization disorder is likely to be preceded by a stressful event.

Explaining Dissociative Disorders

Dissociative disorders have been explained primarily by psychological views. According to psychoanalytic theory, people dissociate in order to repress unacceptable urges. In dissociative amnesia or fugue, for example, the person forgets the disturbing urges. In dissociative identity disorder, the person expresses undesirable urges by developing other personalities that can take responsibility for them. In depersonalization, the person goes outside the self, away from the turmoil within.

According to learning theorists, individuals with dissociative disorders have learned not to think about disturbing events in order to avoid feelings of guilt, shame, or pain. They dissociate themselves from the stressful events by selectively forgetting them. This is reinforced by the reduced anxiety they feel when the trauma is forgotten.

Neither cognitive nor biological theorists have offered a complete explanation for dissociative disorders. At present, there is no convincing evidence that either biological or genetic factors play a role in the development of dissociative disorders.

SECTION 3 REVIEW

go.hrw.com
Homework Practice Online
Keyword: SY7 HP18

1. Describe the four dissociative disorders.

2. **Critical Thinking** *Evaluating* In some cultures, people are encouraged to go into trancelike states. Should this type of dissociation be considered a sign of a psychological disorder? Why or why not?

Somatoform Disorders

Somatization, which comes from the Greek word for "body," refers to the expression of psychological distress through physical symptoms. People with somatoform disorders have psychological problems (such as depression) but experience inexplicable physical symptoms (such as paralysis).

It is important to distinguish between somatoform disorders and malingering, or the conscious attempt to "fake" an illness in order to avoid work, school, or other responsibilities. People with somatoform disorders do not intentionally fake their illnesses. They honestly feel pain or believe they cannot move their limbs.

TRUTH OR fiction
■ R E V I S I T E D ■

It is not true that people whose illnesses are "all in their heads" do not really have symptoms of a disease. Although psychological in origin, the physical symptoms of somatoform disorders are very real to the people who experience them.

Reliable statistics on the incidence of somatoform disorders are not available. Many diagnoses of somatoform illness later prove to be incorrect when patients are found to have medical illnesses that account for their symptoms. On the other hand, cases of somatoform disorders may go undiagnosed because of the focus on physical, as opposed to psychological, symptoms.

Types of Somatoform Disorders

The DSM-IV identifies six types of somatoform disorders. The two most common are conversion disorder and hypochondriasis. The symptoms of these two disorders are described below and summarized in Figure 18.3 on page 422.

Conversion Disorder   People with conversion disorder experience a change in or loss of physical functioning in a major part of the body for which there is no known medical explanation. For example, they may suddenly develop the inability to see at night or to move their legs, even though no medical explanation can be found for their sudden physical disability. These behaviors are not, however, intentionally produced. That is, the person is not faking it.

Conversion disorder is further complicated because many people who experience conversion disorder show little concern about their symptoms, no matter how serious or unusual those symptoms may be. This lack of concern about the symptoms may help in the diagnosis of conversion disorder.

Hypochondriasis   Also called hypochondria, hypochondriasis is defined as a person's unrealistic preoccupation with thoughts that he or she has a serious disease. People with hypochondriasis become absorbed by minor physical symptoms and sensations, convinced that the symptoms indicate a serious medical illness. These people maintain their erroneous beliefs despite reassurances from doctors that there is nothing physically wrong with them. Some people with hypochondriasis visit doctor after doctor, seeking the one physician who will find the cause of their symptoms.

Explaining Somatoform Disorders

Explanations for somatoform disorders in general, and specifically conversion disorder or hypochondriasis, are primarily psychological. According to psychoanalytic theory, somatoform disorders occur when individuals repress emotions associated with forbidden urges and instead express them symbolically in physical symptoms. The physical symptoms thus represent a compromise between the unconscious need to express feelings and the fear of actually expressing them.

More recently, other psychologists have argued that people with conversion disorder "convert" psychological stress into actual medical problems. For example, a fighter pilot may lose the ability to see at night as a response to the great anxiety he feels

Two Examples of Somatoform Disorders

Type	Characteristics
Conversion Disorder	Sudden and severe loss of physical functioning, as in blindness or paralysis, despite the fact that no medical explanation can be found for the physical symptoms; usually characterized by the person's apparent lack of concern about his or her physical symptoms
Hypochondriasis	An unhealthy fear of having, or the unsubstantiated belief that one has, a serious disease; characterized by the person's misinterpretation of his or her normal bodily symptoms or functions

FIGURE 18.3   *People with somatoform disorders have psychological problems that express themselves in physical symptoms. There is, however, no known medical basis for the physical symptoms. The two most prevalent of the somatoform disorders are conversion disorder and hypochondriasis, the symptoms of which are described here.*

Source: Adapted from the DSM-IV, 1994.

about flying nighttime bombing missions. Another individual may suffer paralysis of the legs after nearly being in a car accident.

Some behavioral theorists have suggested that somatoform symptoms can serve as a reinforcer if they successfully allow a person to escape from anxiety. There are also some indications that biological or genetic factors may play a role in the development of somatoform disorders (Kellner, 1990).

SECTION 4 REVIEW   go.hrw.com   **Homework Practice Online**   Keyword: SY7 HP18

1. Define malingering. How does somatization differ from malingering?

2. How do conversion disorder and hypochondriasis differ?

3. **Critical Thinking**   *Analyzing Information* How do you think learning theorists might explain somatoform disorders? Do you agree with this type of explanation? Why or why not?

NEUROSIS CLINIC

PHOBIA CLINIC

HYPO- CHONDRIA CLINIC

CLOSED DUE TO POSSIBLE ILLNESS

THAVES 7-18

©E-mail: FandEBobT @aol.com

© 1996 by NEA, Inc.

Source: FRANK & ERNEST reprinted by permission of Newspaper Enterprise Association, Inc.

SECTION 5
Mood Disorders

Most people have mood changes that reflect the normal ups and downs of daily life. They feel down when things go wrong, such as failing an important test, and they feel up when good things happen, such as when their team wins a championship. Dan felt down when his sister's condition worsened. Janet noted that Dan was depressed, but she also realized that Dan's mood was a normal reaction to his situation.

Some people, however, experience mood changes that seem inappropriate for or inconsistent with the situations to which they are responding. These people feel sad when things are going well, or they feel elated for no apparent reason. People who have abnormal moods such as these may have a mood disorder.

Mood disorders fall into two general categories. **Depression** typically involves feelings of helplessness, hopelessness, worthlessness, guilt, and great sadness. **Bipolar disorder** involves a cycle of mood changes from depression to wild elation and back again.

Mood disorders—particularly depression—are very common psychological disorders. In any six-month period, about 8 percent of women and 4 percent of men are likely to be diagnosed with some form of depression (Myers et al., 1984).

Types of Mood Disorders

The DSM-IV classifies mood disorders into several different types of depressive and bipolar disorders. These are summarized in Figure 18.4 on page 424.

Major Depression Depression is by far the most common of all the psychological disorders. It has been estimated that depression affects more than 100 million people worldwide and that between 8 and 18 percent of the general population will experience depression in their lifetime (Boyd & Weissman, 1982).

TRUTH
OR
fiction
■ REVISITED ■

It is true that depression is the most common type of psychological disorder. At least 8 percent of the general population will experience depression.

According to the DSM-IV, major depression is diagnosed when an individual experiences at least five of the following nine symptoms of depression:

- persistent depressed mood for most of the day
- loss of interest or pleasure in all, or almost all, activities
- significant weight loss or gain due to changes in appetite
- sleeping more or less than usual
- speeding up or slowing down of physical and emotional reactions
- fatigue or loss of energy
- feelings of worthlessness or unfounded guilt
- reduced ability to concentrate or make meaningful decisions
- recurrent thoughts of death or suicide

For a diagnosis of major depression to be made, at least one of the individual's five symptoms must be one of the first two symptoms in the list.

PSYCHOLOGICAL DISORDERS **423**

Additionally, the symptoms must be present for at least two weeks, and occur nearly every day during that period (American Psychiatric Association, 2000).

Severely depressed individuals may become consumed by feelings of worthlessness or guilt. Severe depression calls for immediate treatment—as many as 15 percent of severely depressed individuals eventually commit suicide (Hirschfield & Goodwin, 1988).

Bipolar Disorder Formerly called manic depression, bipolar disorder is characterized by dramatic ups and downs in mood. Periods of **mania**, or extreme excitement characterized by hyperactivity and chaotic behavior, can change into depression very quickly and for no apparent reason.

The manic phase is characterized by a mood that is persistently and abnormally elevated. In some people, however, this phase may be characterized by irritability instead of elation. Manic moods are also characterized by at least some of the following traits:

- inflated self-esteem
- inability to sit still or sleep restfully
- pressure to keep talking and switching from topic to topic
- racing thoughts (referred to as "flight of ideas")
- difficulty concentrating

Individuals in the manic phase may appear highly excited and act silly or argumentative. In severe cases, they may have delusions (beliefs that have no basis in reality) about their own superior abilities or about others being jealous of them. They may also experience hallucinations (sensory perceptions that occur in the absence of sensory stimuli) such as hearing imaginary voices or seeing things that are not really there. These individuals may also engage in impulsive behaviors, such as going on wild spending sprees, quitting their jobs to pursue wild dreams, or making foolish business

Irrational, Depressing Thoughts and Rational Alternatives

Irrational Depressing Thought	Rational Alternative
"There's nothing I can do."	"I can't think of anything to do right now, but if I work at it, I may."
"I'm no good."	"I did something I regret, but that doesn't make me evil or worthless as a person."
"This is absolutely awful."	"This is pretty bad, but it's not the end of the world."
"I just don't have the brains for this course."	"I guess I really need to go back over the basics in the course. Who can I turn to for help?"
"I just can't believe I did something so terrible!"	"That was a bad experience. Well, I won't be likely to try that again soon."
"I can't imagine ever feeling right."	"This is painful, but if I try to work it through step by step, I'll probably see my way out of it eventually."

FIGURE 18.4 *Psychologists point out that many of us create or worsen feelings of depression through irrational thoughts. We can make mountains out of molehills and make it seem as if we cannot change things for the better. This figure shows the kinds of thoughts that can be depressing, and the kinds of more realistic thoughts that make it possible for people to take charge of their lives.*

investments. Thus, the manic phase of bipolar disorder can be very disruptive to an individual's life.

Explaining Mood Disorders

Psychological and biological theories have been proposed to explain why such a large number of people experience mood disorders, particularly depression. These theories are explained here.

Psychological Views The psychoanalytic view of depression is that some people are prone to depression because they suffered a real or imagined loss of a loved object or person in childhood. According to this view, the child feels anger toward the lost object or person but, instead of expressing the anger, internalizes it and directs it toward himself or herself. This leads to feelings of guilt and loss of self-esteem, which in turn lead to depression.

Learning theorists have suggested other explanations for depression. Some believe that *learned helplessness* makes people prone to depression. Psychologist Martin Seligman (1975) demonstrated the concept of learned helplessness in a classic experiment in which he taught dogs that they were helpless to escape from electric shock. First, he placed a barrier in the dogs' cage to prevent them from leaving when shocks were administered. Later the barrier was removed. However, when shocks were again administered, the dogs made no effort to escape. They had apparently learned there was nothing they could do to prevent the pain.

This helpless behavior has been compared to the helplessness often seen in people who are depressed. Learning theorists argue that people prone to depression have learned through experience to believe that previous events in their lives were out of their control. This leads them to expect that future events will be out of their control as well. As a result, whenever a negative event occurs, these people feel helpless, and this leads to depression.

In contrast, cognitive theorists have suggested that some people are prone to depression because of their habitual style of explaining life events. According to this view, people assign different types of explanations to most events—internal or external, stable or unstable, and global or specific. These attributional styles affect people's self-esteem and self-efficacy. These styles also relate to expectancy—what people expect based on prior experiences. Suppose, for example, that someone goes on a date that does not work out. Different ways to explain this might include the following:

- "I really messed up" (internal explanation, places blame on self).

- "Some people just don't get along" (external explanation, places the blame elsewhere).

- "It's my personality" (stable explanation, suggests problem cannot be changed).

- "It was my head cold" (unstable explanation, suggests problem is temporary).

- "I have no idea what to do when I'm with other people" (global explanation, suggests problem is too large to deal with).

- "I have difficulty making small talk" (specific explanation, suggests problem is small enough to be manageable).

Research shows that people who are depressed are more likely than other people to explain their failures on internal, stable, and global causes—causes they feel helpless to change. Cognitive theorists argue that such explanations give rise to feelings of helplessness, which in turn lead to depression. Dan's hope that the doctors would find a treatable (unstable,

A DAY IN THE LIFE

specific) cause for Michelle's disorder would be considered a healthy outlook.

Another cognitive theory was proposed by Aaron Beck (1976), who suggested that people who are depressed have a negative view of themselves, their experiences, and their future. According to Beck, this is because people who are depressed have negative self-schemas, developed from negative experiences in early childhood. This leads them to filter out positive information and perceive negative information as more negative than it really is. Such negativity, Beck argued, makes people prone to depression.

Biological Views Other researchers have investigated biological factors in mood disorders. Mood disorders, like anxiety disorders, tend to occur more often in the close relatives of affected individuals than they do in the general population (Rose, 1995; Wachtel, 1994). Between 20 and 25 percent of people with mood disorders have a family member who is affected by a similar disorder (Hirschfeld & Goodwin, 1988). Moreover, identical twins of affected individuals are more likely to be affected than fraternal twins (Goodwin & Jamison, 1990). These studies seem to indicate that mood disorders have a genetic basis.

Scientists believe that two neurotransmitters, or chemical messengers, in the brain—serotonin and noradrenaline—may at least partly explain the connection between genes and mood. Serotonin and noradrenaline both play a role in mood regulation (Cooper et al., 1991; Michels & Marzuk, 1993). Low levels, or deficiencies, of serotonin may create a tendency toward mood disorders in general. Deficiencies of serotonin *combined* with deficiencies of noradrenaline, however, may be linked to depression specifically. These findings have been important in the development of drug therapy for the treatment of mood disorders. (See Chapter 19.)

Biological and Psychological Factors Many cases of depression may reflect the interaction of biological factors such as neurotransmitter levels and psychological factors such as learned helplessness. This has been demonstrated with laboratory animals. Seligman (1975) and Weiss (1982) found that dogs that learned they were helpless to escape electric shocks also had less noradrenaline activity in their brains. Helplessness is thus linked to specific neurotransmitter deficiencies. The relationship may result in a vicious cycle. A depressing situation may slow down the activity of noradrenaline in the brain; in turn, the chemical changes may then worsen the depression.

SECTION 5 REVIEW

Homework Practice Online
Keyword: SY7 HP18

1. What is the difference between depression and bipolar disorder?
2. List five symptoms of major depression.
3. **Critical Thinking** *Summarizing* Describe and explain self-esteem, self-efficacy, and expectancy from the perspective of attribution theory.

SECTION 6

Schizophrenia

Schizophrenia, usually considered the most serious of the psychological disorders, is characterized by loss of contact with reality. Schizophrenia can be very disabling, and even lead to the affected person's inability to function independently. Typically, schizophrenia first appears in young adulthood, but it may occur at other ages. Although it usually develops gradually, it can also appear suddenly. Schizophrenia can now be treated more effectively, although if untreated it can worsen over time.

The most obvious symptoms of schizophrenia include hallucinations, delusions, and thought disorders. In most cases, the hallucinations are audi-tory—voices may tell the individual what to do or comment on the individual's behavior. This is what Dan's sister Michelle experienced. Sometimes the voices may tell the individual to harm herself or himself or others.

Individuals with schizophrenia may experience delusions of grandeur—beliefs that they are superior to other people. For example, such individuals may believe that they are famous or on a special mission to save the world. Sometimes the delusions are of persecution. For example, a person with schizophrenia might believe that he or she is being pursued by the CIA, FBI, or some other government agency. Other delusions may include beliefs that one has committed unpardonable sins or even that one does not really exist.

Thought disorders involve problems in the organization or the content of mental processes. The thoughts of a person with schizophrenia may skip from topic to topic in an apparently illogical way. This is reflected in the person's speech, which sounds disorganized and confused. A person with schizophrenia may also repeat the same word or phrase over and over, repeat words or phrases that another person has spoken, or invent new words.

People with schizophrenia experience other symptoms that result in a decreased ability to function. These symptoms include social withdrawal, loss of social skills, and loss of normal emotional responsiveness. Some people with schizophrenia may even go into a **catatonic stupor**—an immobile, expressionless, comalike state.

Understandably, these symptoms cause tremendous stress to individuals with schizophrenia and their families. It has been estimated that as many as 20 percent of people with schizophrenia attempt suicide and that 10 percent actually do kill themselves (Caldwell & Gottesman, 1990).

Schizophrenia is found in all cultures and has been recognized for several thousand years. A large number of people have schizophrenia—an estimated 2 million in the United States alone (Regier, 1993).

Types of Schizophrenia

Individuals with schizophrenia vary greatly in the symptoms they exhibit, although virtually all have thought disorders. Most people with schizophrenia exhibit a combination of symptoms.

The disturbed thoughts of people with schizophrenia sometimes appears in their artwork and in their speech.

The DSM-IV classification of schizophrenia and other psychotic disorders is based primarily on the duration and recurrence of symptoms. The types of schizophrenia include paranoid, disorganized, and catatonic schizophrenia.

Paranoid Schizophrenia People with paranoid schizophrenia have delusions or frequent auditory hallucinations, all relating to a single theme. These people may have delusions of grandeur, persecution, or jealousy. For example, an individual with paranoid schizophrenia may be convinced that people have been plotting against him or her even when there is no evidence of such.

Dan's sister, Michelle, was distrustful of everyone except her husband. She even accused Dan of trying to confuse her when he asked how she was feeling. Although people with this type of schizophrenia tend to have less disordered thoughts and bizarre behavior than do people with other types of schizophrenia, they may be agitated, confused, and afraid.

Disorganized Schizophrenia People with disorganized schizophrenia are incoherent in their thought and speech and disorganized in their behavior. They usually have delusions or hallucinations as well, but these tend to be fragmentary and unconnected, unlike the more ordered and systematic delusions of those with paranoid schizophrenia.

People with disorganized schizophrenia are also either emotionless or show inappropriate emotions. Typically, they act silly and giddy, and they tend to giggle and speak nonsense. They may neglect their appearance and hygiene and even lose control of their bladders and bowels.

The following case description (adapted from Spitzer et al., 1988, pp.137–138) illustrates several symptoms of disorganized schizophrenia. A 40-year-old man was brought to the hospital by his mother, who reported that she was afraid of him. It was his twelfth hospitalization. The man was dressed in a tattered overcoat, a baseball cap, and house slippers. He spoke with a childlike quality and walked with exaggerated movements. His emotions ranged from anger (hurling obscenities) to silliness (giggling for no apparent reason).

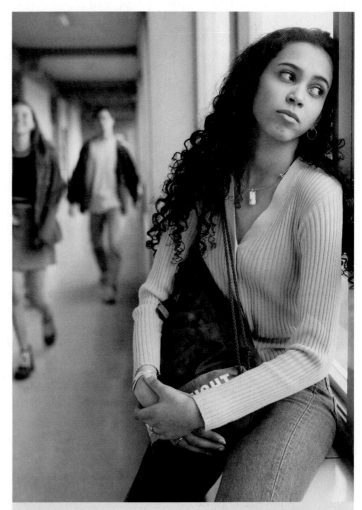

Schizophrenia and other serious psychological disorders affect many people in the United States and around the world.

Since stopping his medication about a month prior to his hospitalization, the man had been hearing voices and looking and acting more bizarre. He told the interviewer that he had been "eating wires and lighting fires." His speech was generally incoherent and consisted frequently of rhymes.

Catatonic Schizophrenia The most obvious symptom of catatonic schizophrenia is disturbance of movement. Activity may slow to a stupor and then suddenly switch to agitation. Individuals with this disorder may hold unusual, uncomfortable body positions for long periods of time, even after their arms and legs swell and stiffen. They may also exhibit waxy flexibility, a condition in which other people can mold them into strange poses that they continue to hold for hours.

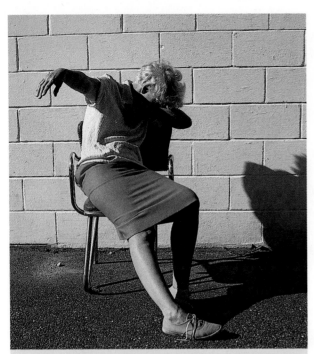

Individuals with catatonic schizophrenia may hold unusual positions for hours. Many of these people alternate between periods of immobility and periods of frenzied physical activity.

Explaining Schizophrenia

Many different theories have been proposed to explain schizophrenia. These theories include both psychological and biological views.

Psychological Views   According to the psychoanalytic perspective, schizophrenia is the result of the overwhelming of the ego by urges from the id. The urges threaten the ego and cause intense conflict. In response, the individual regresses to an early phase of the oral stage of development in which the infant has not yet learned that it is separate from the mother. (See Chapter 14.) In this condition, fantasies become confused with reality, leading to hallucinations and delusions. Like many psychoanalytic theories, this one has fallen into disfavor over the years.

Other psychological views focus on the family environment as the root of schizophrenia. One such theory suggests that a family environment in which a parent frequently expresses intense emotions and has a pushy, critical attitude puts children at risk of developing schizophrenia (Leff & Vaughn, 1985). It is possible, however, that such a family environment may only increase the chances of relapse in individuals who have schizophrenia. That is to say the family environment does not actually *produce* schizophrenia.

Biological Views   Schizophrenia appears to be a brain disorder, and many studies have been done to determine how the brains of schizophrenic people differ from those of other people. One avenue of brain research connects the major problems found in schizophrenia—problems in attention, memory, abstract thinking, and language—with differences in the frontal part of the brain. Schizophrenic people have smaller brains than other people and, in particular, a smaller frontal region (Selemon, 2000). Research suggests that the difficulties may reflect a loss of synapses, the structures that connect neurons and make it possible for neurons to communicate with one another (Glantz & Lewis, 2000; Selemon, 2000).

What might cause the loss of synapses? Research evidence suggests that there are three biological risk factors for schizophrenia: heredity, complications during pregnancy and birth, and birth during winter (Carpenter & Buchanan, 1994). Schizophrenia, like many other psychological disorders, runs in families, a view to which Dan's mother had alluded (Cannon et al., 1998; Kendler et al., 1997). People with schizophrenia constitute about 1 percent of the population. However, children with one parent who has been diagnosed as schizophrenic have about a 10 percent chance of being diagnosed as schizophrenic themselves. Children with two such parents have about a 35 to 40 percent chance of being so (Gottesman, 1991; Straube & Oades, 1992). When one identical twin has schizophrenia, the other has about a 40 to 50 percent chance of being diagnosed with it. Many studies have been carried out to try to isolate the gene or genes involved in schizophrenia. Some studies have found locations for multiple genes on several chromosomes. Recent research suggests that particular genes may provide the vulnerability to schizophrenia (Brzustowicz et al., 2000).

Many people with schizophrenia have experienced complications during pregnancy and birth (Rosso et al., 2000). For example, the mothers of many people with schizophrenia had influenza during the sixth or seventh month of pregnancy (C. E. Barr, et al., 1990). People with the disease are also somewhat more likely to have been born during the winter than would be predicted by chance (Carpenter & Buchanan, 1994). Maternal starvation has also been related to schizophrenia (Susser & Lin, 1992). These biological risk factors suggest that schizophrenia involves abnormal prenatal brain development.

Problems in the central nervous system may involve neurotransmitters as well as brain structures, and research has focused on one particular neurotransmitter: dopamine (Carpenter & Buchanan, 1994). According to the dopamine theory of schizophrenia, people with schizophrenia *use* more dopamine than other people do, although they may not *produce* more of it. Why? They may have more dopamine receptors in the brain than other people, or their dopamine receptors may be hyperactive (Davis et al., 1991).

A Multifactorial Model of Schizophrenia The multifactorial model of schizophrenia illustrates how several biological and psychological factors may interact in the development of the disorder. In this model, genetic factors create a vulnerability, or susceptibility, to schizophrenia. Among people who are genetically vulnerable, other factors, such as trauma during birth, may lead to brain injury and the subsequent development of schizophrenia. Once the disorder develops, its course may be negatively affected by the family environment.

The model also suggests that environmental factors alone are not enough to lead to the development of schizophrenia. Thus, people who are not genetically vulnerable are unlikely to develop the disorder, regardless of the environmental risk factors to which they are exposed.

SECTION 6 REVIEW

Homework Practice Online
Keyword: SY7 HP18

1. List four symptoms of schizophrenia.
2. How does paranoid schizophrenia differ from disorganized schizophrenia?
3. **Critical Thinking** *Drawing Inferences and Conclusions* Explain why a multifactorial model of schizophrenia may help in explaining the disorder.

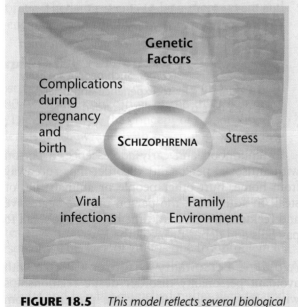

Multifactorial Model of Schizophrenia

Genetic Factors

Complications during pregnancy and birth

SCHIZOPHRENIA

Stress

Viral infections

Family Environment

FIGURE 18.5 *This model reflects several biological and psychological factors that may interact in the development of schizophrenia.*

Source: Adapted from the DSM-IV-TR, 2000.

SECTION 7
Personality Disorders

Personality disorders are patterns of inflexible traits that disrupt social life or work and/or distress the affected individual. They usually show up by late adolescence and affect all aspects of the individual's personality, including thought processes, emotions, and behavior.

It is important to note the distinction between personality disorders and other psychological disorders that they may resemble. Psychological disorders, such as schizophrenia or phobic disorder, for example, are episodes of illness that an individual experiences. They can be distinguished from the individual's personality. In contrast, personality disorders are enduring traits that are major components of the individual's personality.

Antisocial personality disorder, described in detail below, is the only personality disorder for which there are data on prevalence. The estimates as to the number of affected individuals vary widely—from less than 1 percent to almost 10 percent of the population (Robins, 1987).

Types of Personality Disorders

Figure 18.6 on page 430 shows the DSM-IV classification of personality disorders. Four of these personality disorders—paranoid, schizoid, antisocial, and avoidant—are described next.

19 METHODS OF THERAPY

Chapter

Read to Discover

1 What is psychotherapy, and what are the advantages of each method of psychotherapy?

2 What are the major techniques of psycho-analysis?

3 What are the primary goals and methods of humanistic therapy?

4 How do cognitive and behavior therapists try to help people?

5 What are the three major biological treat-ments for psychological disorders?

appropriate degrees help ensure that the professional is properly trained.

- Is the professional licensed by the state? All states require licensing of psychologists and psychiatrists. Some states also require the licensing of social workers and nurses. To be issued a state license, professionals must pass exams or demonstrate expertise and knowledge in other ways.

- What are the therapist's plans for treatment, and how long will treatment likely take? There is considerable variation in the nature and duration of treatment for different methods of psychotherapy. For example, traditional psychoanalysis tends to take longer than other psychotherapy methods. The individual should know in advance what to expect from the treatment method.

- What is the estimated cost of treatment? Psychotherapy can be expensive, and it is not always covered by health insurance plans. Although cost should not have to be the deciding factor in choosing a therapist, for some people, it must be.

People in group therapy usually sit in a circle as they share their thoughts and feelings. A therapist is usually present to guide and facilitate the discussion.

Individual Versus Group Therapy

Methods of psychotherapy are practiced either with individuals or in groups. Frequently, people who seek help for psychological problems have a choice between individual and group therapy. To make the best choice, it is important to be aware of the advantages of each type.

Advantages of Individual Therapy Some people do better with individual therapy because they need more personal attention than they would receive as part of a group. Moreover, some people feel uncomfortable talking about their problems in front of other people. These individuals are likely to talk more openly and freely if they are alone with their therapist.

Advantages of Group Therapy Group therapy can, however, have certain advantages over individual therapy. In fact, many people who begin seeing a therapist individually eventually switch to group therapy.

One advantage of group therapy is that it helps individuals realize that they are not alone. People can see other group members struggling with problems similar to their own. Members of the group can often benefit from the insights gained by other group members who have gone through similar struggles. Group members can support each other because they all have had similar experiences—they have "been there" themselves. Group therapy also gives individuals a chance to practice coping and other social skills in a supportive environment.

One of the most significant advantages of group therapy is that it shows individuals that therapy can work. People see other members of the group recovering, and this gives them hope of recovery for themselves.

From a practical standpoint, group therapy enables the therapist to work with several people at once. In addition, it often allows a therapist to immediately see people who might otherwise have to be placed on a waiting list to receive individual help. It is also more affordable for clients because they share the cost of the therapist's time.

TRUTH OR **fiction** ■ REVISITED ■

It is not true that it is always preferable to see a therapist alone rather than in a group. In group therapy, members of the group can provide support and understanding and serve as role models for each other.

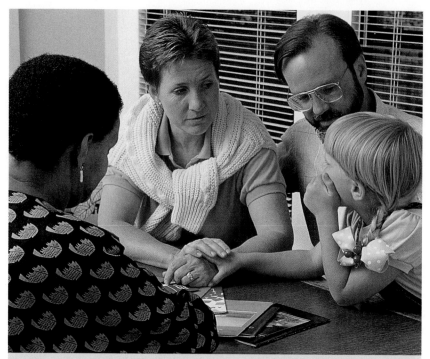

In family therapy, the therapist often can help family members see problems in their relationships more clearly.

Types of Group Therapy There are several types of group therapy. These include couples therapy, family therapy, and therapy for people who are dealing with similar problems, such as an eating disorder or the loss of a loved one.

Couples therapy tries to help two people improve or find more satisfaction in their relationship with each other. In particular, it helps them communicate more effectively by helping them learn new ways to listen to each other and to express their feelings (Rathus & Sanderson, 1999). Such therapy also helps couples discover healthy ways to resolve conflicts and handle intense emotions.

Family therapy aims to help troubled families by improving communication and relations among family members. It also seeks to promote the family's emotional growth (Prochaska & Norcross, 1999). Family therapy is based on the assumption that the lives of family members are so intertwined that the family as a whole is likely to suffer when one member has a problem. A parent may

be addicted to alcohol, for example, and become abusive when intoxicated. The abuse may lead to low self-esteem, anxiety, and depression in other family members. Dan's family provides another example. They sought family

therapy to help them cope with Michelle's schizophrenia. Janet and her mother also sought family therapy to help them adjust to the divorce.

Self-help groups are composed of people who share the same problem, such as overeating, drug addiction, or compulsive gambling. Members of a self-help group meet regularly—often without a therapist—to discuss their problem, share solutions, and give and receive support. One of the best-known self-help groups is Alcoholics Anonymous (AA). AA has served as a developmental model for many other self-help programs.

Encounter groups differ from these other kinds of groups. They are composed of strangers who do not necessarily share a common problem. In fact, encounter group members do not necessarily have psychological problems at all. Encounter groups are sometimes made up of people who simply desire emotional growth.

Encounter groups promote emotional growth by helping group members become more aware of their own feelings and the feelings of others. Under the guidance of a leader, group members share their feelings through role-playing and other group techniques. The fact that group members are strangers makes it easier for some people to reveal their private feelings in an encounter group. However, other people are often unprepared for the intense emotions they experience in encounter therapy. For this and other reasons, encounter groups are somewhat controversial and less popular today than they were in the 1960s and 1970s.

SECTION 1 REVIEW

1. What is psychotherapy?
2. What questions should one ask when selecting a psychotherapist?
3. **Critical Thinking** *Evaluating* What are the advantages of each type of psychotherapy?

SECTION 2

The Psychoanalytic Approach

Psychoanalysis, the model of therapy developed by Sigmund Freud, literally means "analysis of the psyche (mind)." Psychoanalysis was the first formal method of psychotherapy used in Western countries. For many years, it was the only method used. In recent decades, however, it has become less popular (Arlow, 1989).

As you may recall from Chapter 14, Freud believed that most of people's psychological problems originate in early childhood experiences and inner conflicts. These conflicts can cause people to develop unconscious sexual and aggressive urges that, in turn, cause anxiety. According to Freud, guilt occurs when the urges enter conscious thought or when the individual acts upon them. Guilt also leads to more anxiety. For example, someone may experience feelings of anxiety and guilt caused by repressed rage toward a parent.

Psychoanalysts try to reduce anxiety and guilt by helping clients become aware of the unconscious thoughts and feelings that are believed to be at the root of their problems. Psychoanalysts call this self-awareness *insight*. Once insight has been gained, clients can use the knowledge to resolve the problems that arise in their daily lives. Some of the techniques psychoanalysts use to help clients gain insight include free association, dream analysis, and transference.

Free Association   The primary technique of psychoanalysis is **free association**. In free association, the analyst asks the client to relax and then to say whatever comes to mind. Free association developed from Freud's early use of hypnosis to tap into his clients' unconscious thoughts and feelings. The use of free association instead of hypnosis enables the client to participate more actively in the analysis.

The topic of the free association might be a memory, dream, fantasy, or recent event. The analyst may say nothing, occasionally ask a question, or attempt to lead the client in a particular direction. The assumption is that, as long as the client associates freely, unconscious thoughts and feelings will "break through" and show up in what the client says. The client is encouraged to say whatever comes to mind, no matter how trivial, embarrassing, or painful the ideas may seem. In fact, psychoanalysts believe that the more hesitant the patient is to say something, the more likely it is that the hesitancy reflects an unconscious thought or feeling.

Resistance is the term psychoanalysts use to refer to a client's hesitancy or unwillingness to discuss issues raised during free association. An experienced psychoanalyst can recognize a client's resistance. It may occur when the client makes a joking remark about a serious subject, for example, or when the client changes the subject entirely. Resistance is believed to reflect a defense mechanism, such as the repression or denial of painful feelings. (See Chapter 14.)

The role of the analyst in free association is to point out the types of things the client is saying—or resisting saying—and to help the client interpret the meaning of the utterances or lack thereof. Psychoanalysts believe that free association allows the client to express troubling, unconscious thoughts and feelings in a safe environment where those thoughts and feelings may be explored. Through such means, clients are thought to gain insight into their problems.

Dream Analysis   Freud believed that dreams express unconscious thoughts and feelings. He called them the "royal road into the unconscious." In a technique called **dream analysis**, the analyst interprets the content of clients' dreams to unlock these unconscious thoughts and feelings.

Freud also distinguished between the manifest and latent content of dreams (Freud, 1952). **Manifest content** refers to the actual content of the dream as it is remembered by the client. **Latent content** refers to the hidden meaning in the dream, which the therapist interprets from the manifest content. For example, a client may dream about falling from a mountain and being unable to grab anything to break his fall (manifest content). The therapist might interpret the dream to mean that the client has repressed feelings that his life is out of control (latent content).

TRUTH OR fiction ▪REVISITED▪   *It is true that some therapists analyze people's dreams.* Most psychoanalysts believe that dreams are an expression of unconscious thoughts and feelings.

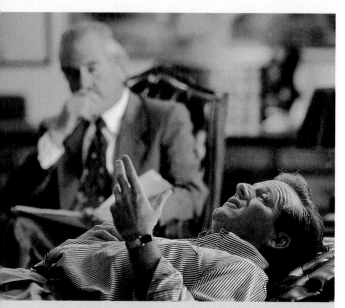

Traditionally, psychoanalysis was conducted with the patient lying on a couch and the analyst sitting out of the patient's line of vision in order to be less of a distraction. Today psychoanalysis is often conducted with patient and analyst sitting face-to-face.

Transference As analysis proceeds, many clients begin to view their relationship with their analyst as being similar to one they have or had with another important person in their lives, often a parent. They experience similar feelings toward the analyst and expect the analyst to feel and behave as the other person did. In other words, the client is transferring feelings and expectations from one person to another. This process is called **transference**.

Psychoanalysts make use of transference to help the client express and analyze unconscious feelings he or she has toward that other important person. In fact, establishing a transference relationship is a major goal of psychoanalysis. Psychoanalysts believe that transference exposes unresolved problems in earlier relationships. The client can then work through these problems, with the help of the analyst, in order to solve similar problems in current relationships.

It is not true that people should avoid relating to their therapist as a parent or other authority figure. People in psychoanalysis are often encouraged to relate to their therapist in this way.

The following example makes the concept of transference easier to understand. Consider a client who has repressed feelings of anger toward her mother because of her mother's cold, critical attitude toward her throughout her childhood. During the course of psychoanalysis, the client transfers the unconscious anger at her mother to the therapist. She falls into patterns of interaction with the therapist that are characteristic of her relationship with her mother.

The therapist, however, does not react as the client's mother would. Instead, he or she remains neutral and helps the patient examine her feelings. Through this process, the client gains insight into her relationship with her mother and how it affects her current relationships. The client begins to understand, for example, that problems with her boss at work may stem from unconscious and unresolved feelings of anger toward her mother.

Evaluation of Psychoanalysis Many psychologists believe that Freud placed too much emphasis on sexual and aggressive urges. Some argue that he underestimated the importance of conscious ideas and changes in behavior. Despite these criticisms, however, a classic review of dozens of studies concluded that people who had received psychoanalysis showed greater well-being than 70 to 75 percent of those who had not received treatment (Smith & Glass, 1977). Psychoanalysis has proved especially useful in the treatment of anxiety, mild depression, and difficulty in handling social relationships. However, it is generally not useful for the treatment of major depression, bipolar disorder, or schizophrenia (Melle & Friis, 1991).

The techniques of traditional psychoanalysis often require clients to meet with their analyst four or five times a week, for a period of months or years. For some clients, this provides a supportive, long-term relationship that fosters emotional growth and insight. For others, however, the cost of therapy in time, money, and emotional distress is too great to make psychoanalysis a real option.

Psychoanalysis does not work for everyone. For example, it is not the most effective type of psychotherapy for individuals who are less verbal or who have limited educational background. Psychoanalysis also is not useful for people who are too seriously disturbed to gain insight into their problems. For example, a person with schizophrenia may lose touch with reality. Such an individual is unlikely to be able to gain the insight needed for effective psychoanalytic treatment.

CASE STUDIES

AND OTHER TRUE STORIES

Overcoming Fears with Virtual Reality

The curtain opens and you step out onto the stage. Before you even start speaking, you are certain the audience is bored. People stretch and cough. Is that a snore you hear? The palms of your hands turn sweaty. Your stomach flutters. Suddenly, you feel dizzy, like you might pass out at any moment.

The anxiety you feel is real, but the scene is not. What you are seeing is a virtual scene created by a company. The virtual scene is designed to help people overcome stage fright. Researcher Albert Rizzo notes, "To help people deal with their problems, you must get them exposed to what they fear most" (Lubell, 2004). Companies create virtual scenes and experiences by combining video clips of real people with special effects. In this way, people can face their fears in a controlled environment.

To experience a virtual scene, a person wears a helmet with screens over the eyes to create a 3-D effect. A motion sensor in the helmet changes the scene with the wearer's head position. For example, if you were wearing one of these helmets, each time you turned your head, you would see a different part of the virtual scene.

With virtual scenes, an operator can control the level of intensity a person experiences. As the person begins to overcome his or her fear, the intensity can be increased. For example, people who fear flying can experience a virtual airplane flight that is smooth and short or bumpy and prolonged. People receiving virtual treatment work with psychologists before and after the sessions to learn ways to cope with their anxiety. The key element of treatment, however, is enabling people to face and experience their fears.

Is it real or virtual therapy?

Virtual therapy can be used to tackle many problems: stage fright, fear of elevators, fear of heights, fear of flying, and fear of bad weather are just a few. Engineers have even created a virtual re-enactment of the terrorist attacks on September 11, 2001. With this re-enactment, people can step back in time to learn to cope with their memories of the attacks.

Virtual therapy is not without its critics, and controversy exists as to whether such therapy is truly useful. Jill of Manhattan is happy with the results of her virtual therapy, however. Before therapy, Jill was so afraid of flying that she turned down a free trip to Europe rather than board an airplane. Yet, after three months of sessions on a virtual airplane, Jill can now ride airplanes with ease. "I wouldn't believe it if it weren't me," Jill remarks (Lubell, 2004).

THINKING CRITICALLY

1. **Analyzing Information** Why might a person be more willing to face their fears in a virtual setting than in a real one?
2. **Drawing Inferences and Conclusions** Why might virtual therapy have some limits in its usefulness?

Brief Psychoanalysis Over the past several decades, shorter terms of psychoanalysis have become more common. In traditional psychoanalysis, a client and therapist may meet almost daily over the course of several years. By contrast, in brief psychoanalysis, client and analyst typically meet just 10 to 20 times over the course of a few months to a year. The shorter duration of treatment makes brief psychoanalysis available to a wider range of people (Prochaska & Norcross, 1999).

The techniques used in brief psychoanalysis are generally the same techniques that are used in traditional psychoanalysis. The primary difference between the two approaches is that brief psychoanalysis has a more limited focus. Whereas traditional psychoanalysis examines the client's entire personality, brief psychoanalysis concentrates on fixing a specific problem. For brief psychoanalysis to be effective, clients usually must be highly motivated and actively involved in applying the insights gained in therapy to the events in their lives.

SECTION 2 REVIEW

Homework Practice Online
go.hrw.com
Keyword: SY7 HP19

1. Identify and describe the three techniques used in psychoanalysis.
2. **Critical Thinking** *Drawing Inferences and Conclusions* According to psychoanalytic theory, what effect do unconscious thoughts and feelings have on a person's ability to form meaningful personal relationships?

SECTION 3

The Humanistic Approach

The primary goal of **humanistic therapy** is to help individuals reach their full potential. It does this by helping individuals develop self-awareness and self-acceptance. The method assumes that most people are basically good and have a natural tendency to strive for self-actualization—that is, to become all that they are capable of being. The method also assumes that people with psychological problems merely need help tapping their inner resources so that they can grow and reach their full potential. Among the several types of humanistic therapy, person-centered therapy is the most widely used.

Person-Centered Therapy **Person-centered therapy** was developed in the early 1950s by psychologist Carl Rogers. According to Rogers, psychological problems arise when people stop being true to themselves and instead act as others want or expect them to act (Rogers, 1986). The role of therapy is to help clients find their true selves and realize their unique potential.

Person-centered therapy is sometimes called client-centered therapy. The use of the term *client* instead of *patient* reflects the status given to individuals seeking help. Clients are seen as equals in a working relationship with the therapist rather than as inferiors who are ill. Clients are encouraged to take the lead in therapy, talking openly about whatever may be troubling them. This method is called **nondirective therapy** because it is not directed by the therapist. The therapist's role is to act as a mirror, reflecting clients' thoughts and feelings back so that the clients can see themselves more clearly.

Techniques of Person-Centered Therapy **Active listening** is a widely used communication technique in which the listener repeats, rephrases, and asks for clarification of the statements made by the speaker. Facial expressions and body language are also important. The goal is to convey to the speaker that his or her words are being heard and that his or her thoughts and feelings are being understood.

The therapist also must remain nonjudgmental, accepting, and supportive, regardless of what the client says, providing what Rogers calls *unconditional positive regard.* The acceptance and support of the therapist help the client accept himself or herself and his or her true feelings. Self-esteem also rises, giving the client the confidence to make his or her own choices, take responsibility for those decisions, and form healthy relationships.

Other Applications Person-centered therapy is practiced widely by school and college counselors. It not only helps students deal with anxiety, depression, and other psychological problems but also helps students make decisions. Counselors try to provide a supportive atmosphere in which students feel free to explore alternatives and make their own choices. Dan's school counselor, Mr. Hochberg, is not a psychologist, but he took a person-centered approach in helping Dan decide on a career. He helped Dan identify options, but he did not make a decision for him.

EXPLORING
DIVERSITY

Therapy and Culture

Increasingly in the United States, people who seek help for psychological disorders come from a wide range of cultures. This has led to a growing awareness on the part of therapists that culture is a significant factor in the diagnosis and treatment of psychological disorders. People differ in how they describe or even experience problems such as anxiety and depression. Their ideas about psychological disorders—and in some cases even the disorders themselves—are influenced by their culture.

The relevance of culture to the diagnosis and treatment of psychological disorders is illustrated by the case of a woman, originally from Ecuador, who was taken to a psychiatric hospital in the United States by her relatives. The woman seemed to be seriously disturbed. She was listless and withdrawn, complaining only that she had "lost her soul" (Goleman, 1995c).

Many therapists probably would have diagnosed the woman with schizophrenia and labeled as a delusion her belief that she had lost her soul. However, the psychiatrist who interviewed the woman at the hospital was familiar with her cultural background. He recognized the woman's "soul loss" as a symptom of *susto*.

Susto is a term used only in Latin American cultures. The condition is believed to occur when a person's soul is captured by spirits and taken from the body. The condition often develops after a frightening or stressful event, such as a serious injury or the death of a loved one. The symptoms of *susto* include loss of appetite, loss of weight, listlessness, apathy, and withdrawal from normal activities. Do these symptoms sound familiar?

The symptoms of susto *include loss of appetite, listlessness, and apathy.*

They should—they are also the symptoms of what Western psychiatrists call depression.

In the case of the Ecuadoran woman, the psychiatrist determined that her problem had started when a close relative in Ecuador had died unexpectedly. In her grief, the woman had developed all the typical symptoms of *susto*. In Western psychiatric terms, the woman was depressed. However, the psychiatrist did not prescribe antidepressants, as he might have for some other depressed patients. Instead, he decided on a form of therapy that was culturally more relevant.

In Ecuador, a mourning ceremony would have been held to help family members adjust to the loss of the loved one. Therefore, with the help of the woman's family, the therapist arranged a mourning ceremony to help the woman confront and accept the death of her relative. Openly mourning the death in a supportive circle of family and friends was apparently what the woman needed to begin healing from her loss and recovering from her depression. Soon her symptoms had improved and she was functioning normally again.

This example illustrates the relevance of culture to therapy. Clearly, both the diagnosis and the treatment of psychological disorders should take into account a person's cultural background.

Think About It

Making Generalizations and Predictions What do you think might have happened to the woman from Ecuador if she had been diagnosed incorrectly with schizophrenia?

Evaluation of Humanistic Therapy In a review of several studies, nearly three fourths of people obtaining person-centered therapy showed greater well-being, on average, than people who did not receive therapy (Smith & Glass, 1977). Like psychoanalysis, person-centered therapy seems to be most helpful for well-educated, motivated people. Humanistic therapy in general works best for people who experience anxiety, mild depression, or problems in their social relationships. However, it is ineffective for people who have major depression, bipolar disorder, or schizophrenia.

SECTION 3 REVIEW

go.hrw.com **Homework Practice Online**
Keyword: SY7 HP19

1. Describe the methods of humanistic therapy.

2. What is the goal of active listening?

3. **Critical Thinking** *Analyzing Information* What role does the therapist play in person-centered therapy?

SECTION 4
Cognitive Therapy and Behavior Therapy

Cognitive therapy and behavior therapy are considered together because both methods share the same goal—to help clients develop new ways of thinking and behaving. Both cognitive and behavior therapists encourage the clients to focus on their thoughts and actions. Advocates of these two theories contend that only by modifying self-defeating thoughts and behavior patterns will the client truly be able to solve his or her own problems. Thus, the aim of these therapies is to eliminate troubling emotions or behaviors rather than to help patients gain insight into the underlying cause of their problems, which is a key goal of psychoanalysis and humanistic therapy.

Cognitive Model of Depression

FIGURE 19.3 *Cognitive psychologists believe that some people develop ways of thinking that can lead to emotional and behavioral problems. In this example, we will call the person on the left Person A and the person on the right Person B. A's positive thinking gives him the motivation to keep practicing and to try to make the team. B's negative thinking leads to depression, feelings of worthlessness, and a reluctance to try again.*

Cognitive Therapy

The aim of cognitive therapy is to help people learn to think about their problems in more productive ways. Cognitive psychologists focus on the beliefs, attitudes, and thought processes that create and compound their clients' problems (Beck, 1993; Ellis, 1995). They believe that some people develop ways of thinking that are illogical or based on faulty assumptions. Such ways of thinking can lead to emotional and behavioral problems for these people. This idea is illustrated in Figure 19.3 on page 446.

Figure 19.3 shows how two different individuals, whom we will call Person A and Person B, react to the same event—being rejected for the swim team. Person A has a positive, logical way of thinking. His ability to look forward gives him the motivation to continue practicing and to try again next year. Person B's negative way of thinking, on the other hand, leads to feelings of worthlessness and depression. It is highly unlikely that Person B will continue practicing, let alone try out for the team again next year.

TRUTH OR fiction ▪ R E V I S I T E D ▪ *It is true that people's reactions to life events are based not on the events themselves but on their ways of thinking about the events.* This is why cognitive therapists try to help people who are having emotional problems change the ways that they think.

Cognitive therapists help people change their ways of thinking. These therapists also try to help people develop more realistic and logical ways of thinking. Cognitive psychologists argue that once people have changed their ways of thinking, they become more capable of solving their emotional and behavioral problems.

The two most widely used cognitive therapy methods are rational-emotive therapy and psychiatrist Aaron Beck's model of therapy, sometimes called cognitive restructuring therapy. Both of these methods aim at modifying people's ways of thinking as a means of improving their emotional health. However, the two methods differ somewhat in the aspects of thinking they maintain must be changed and in the approach they take to bring about those changes.

Rational-Emotive Behavior Therapy   First developed by psychologist Albert Ellis in the 1950s, **rational-emotive behavior therapy** (REBT) is based on Ellis's belief that people are basically logical in their thinking and actions. However, the assumptions upon which they base their thinking or actions are sometimes incorrect. According to Ellis, people may develop emotional problems when they base their behavior on these faulty assumptions (Ellis & Dryden, 1996).

An example of a commonly held false assumption that leads to emotional problems is "I must do everything perfectly." People who believe they must do everything perfectly in order to be happy must also believe that if they are unhappy, it is because they did something imperfectly. Thus, their unhappiness is their own fault. In addition, no matter how hard these people try, they are unlikely to be able to live up to their own unrealistically high standard of perfection. It is easy to see why belief in this false assumption could lead a person to experience anxiety or severe depression.

People are often unaware of their false assumptions even though the assumptions influence their conscious thoughts and actions. The role of the therapist in REBT is first to identify and then to challenge the false assumptions. To teach individuals to think more realistically, REBT therapists use techniques such as role-playing and modeling. Role-playing helps individuals see how their assumptions affect their relationships. Modeling is used to show individuals other, more realistic assumptions they might adopt.

Individuals in rational-emotive behavior therapy may also receive homework assignments. For example, they may be asked to read relevant literature, listen to tapes of psychotherapy sessions, or carry out experiments designed to test their assumptions. The more faithfully patients complete their homework, the more likely it is that their therapy will succeed (Ellis & Dryden, 1996).

Beck's Cognitive Therapy   Another form of cognitive therapy was introduced in the 1960s by psychiatrist Aaron Beck. In contrast to REBT's focus on faulty assumptions, the focus of Beck's cognitive therapy is on restructuring illogical thought processes. Beck (1993) has noted several types of illogical thought processes that may lead to emotional problems, particularly depression. Some of these include the following:

- *Arbitrary inference,* or drawing conclusions for which there is no evidence. For example, when a teacher passes a student in the hall and does not smile, the student may arbitrarily conclude that the teacher is planning to fail her.

■ *Selective abstraction,* or drawing conclusions about a situation or event on the basis of a single detail and misinterpreting or ignoring other details that would lead to a different conclusion. For example, a person may look at his reflection in a mirror, but instead of feeling happy about his good features—say, a handsome smile and a muscular build—all he notices is the small blemish on his chin.

■ *Overgeneralization,* or drawing a general conclusion from a single experience. For example, a person may conclude that she is worthless because she failed one test.

Instead of confronting and challenging clients about the errors in their ways of thinking, as the REBT therapist does, the therapist using Beck's approach gently guides clients in testing the logic of their own thought processes and developing more logical ways of thinking. One technique for doing this is to train clients to observe and record their thoughts in response to the events of daily life. Therapists can later review events with clients and help them see the illogical thought processes that are causing them emotional problems.

Evaluation of Cognitive Therapy Cognitive therapy tends to be a short-term method, making it a realistic option for more people than traditional psychoanalysis. Clients generally meet with their therapist once a week for 15 to 25 weeks.

Studies of cognitive therapy show that modifying irrational beliefs of the type described by Albert Ellis helps people with problems such as anxiety and depression. Modifying self-defeating beliefs of the sort outlined by Aaron Beck also frequently alleviates anxiety and depression (Robins & Hayes, 1993; Whisman et al., 1991). Cognitive therapy has also helped people with personality disorders (Beck & Freeman, 1990).

Cognitive therapy is helpful with people with major depression who had been considered responsive only to medicine and other kinds of biological therapies. Many studies show that cognitive therapy is as effective or even more effective than antidepressant medication (Antonuccio, 1995; Muñoz et al., 1994). For one thing, cognitive therapy provides coping skills that reduce the risk of recurrence of depression once treatment ends. A combination of cognitive therapy and antidepressant medication may be superior to either treatment

A person who has a phobia of snakes may seek behavior therapy as a means of confronting and overcoming the phobia. According to behavior theorists, a client who fears snakes can be counterconditioned to react to snakes in a relaxed manner.

alone in the case of people with persistent depression (Keller et al., 2000).

Behavior Therapy

The goal of behavior therapy, which is also called *behavior modification,* is to help people develop more adaptive behavior. Some people seek behavior therapy to eliminate undesirable behaviors, such as overeating or smoking. Others seek behavior therapy to acquire desirable behaviors, such as the skills needed to develop healthy social relationships or confront phobias.

Behaviorists believe that both desirable and undesirable behaviors are largely learned and that people with psychological problems have learned unhealthy ways of behaving. The aim of behavior therapy is to teach people more desirable (or healthier) ways of behaving. To behaviorists, the reasons for the undesirable behavior are unimportant. Changing the behavior is what matters. For example, in Marc's case, changing his study habits led to a decrease in his test anxiety, but it did not help him understand why he had test anxiety in the first place.

Many behavioral techniques fall into two categories: counterconditioning, which helps people to unlearn undesirable behaviors, and operant conditioning, which helps in the learning of desirable behaviors. The choice of behavioral techniques for an individual client depends largely on the nature of the individual's psychological disorder.

Counterconditioning   If undesirable behaviors are conditioned, or learned through reinforcement, then presumably they can be unlearned, or counterconditioned. Counterconditioning pairs the stimulus that triggers an unwanted behavior (such as fear of spiders) with a new, more desirable behavior. (See Chapter 6.) For example, a client who reacts with fear to spiders can be counterconditioned to respond to spiders in a relaxed manner instead. Counterconditioning techniques include systematic desensitization, modeling, and aversive conditioning.

Systematic desensitization was developed by psychiatrist Joseph Wolpe in the 1950s as a treatment for phobias and other anxiety disorders. The assumption underlying systematic desensitization is that a person cannot feel anxious and relaxed at the same time. The therapist therefore trains the client to relax in the presence of an anxiety-producing situation (Wolpe, 1990).

This is done in a systematic way. First, the therapist teaches the client how to relax completely. Once this has been accomplished, the therapist gradually exposes the client to the object or situation that causes the phobic response. For a person who fears spiders, the therapist might first ask the person to simply imagine a spider. If the thought of a spider makes the client feel anxious, the client is told to stop thinking about the spider and relax again. This is done repeatedly until the thought of a spider no longer causes anxiety.

Gradually, the stimulus is increased—the person might be shown pictures of spiders, asked to hold a toy spider, and eventually asked to handle a real spider. In each case, the person is trained to respond with relaxation until the stimulus no longer provokes anxiety.

Systematic desensitization may be combined with other counterconditioning measures, such as modeling and aversive conditioning. Modeling involves observational learning. The client observes and then imitates the therapist or another person coping with the feared object or situation. For the person with a fear of spiders, the therapist might ask the person to observe someone calmly watching a spider make a web. The client would then be encouraged to behave in the same way.

Aversive conditioning is, essentially, the opposite of systematic desensitization. In aversive conditioning, the therapist replaces a positive

Someone who has a fear of water may gradually lose that fear through the behavior therapy technique of systematic desensitization. Once a person has overcome the fear of water, she may actually enjoy the experience of swimming. **What other fears might be overcome through systematic desensitization?**

response to a stimulus with a negative response. For example, for a person who wants to stop smoking, the therapist might replace the pleasant feelings associated with smoking with unpleasant ones. The person might be asked to smoke several cigarettes at once through a device that holds two or more cigarettes. This overexposure to cigarette smoke makes smoking an unpleasant experience. With repetition, the person may come to avoid smoking.

People who learn more desirable behaviors through counterconditioning often experience a boost in their self-esteem as well. Furthermore, by confronting, challenging, and overcoming their fears or bad habits, such people will increase their opportunity to lead less restrictive lives.

Operant Conditioning The behavioral technique of operant conditioning is based on the assumption that behavior that is reinforced tends to be repeated, whereas behavior that is not reinforced tends to be extinguished. Behavioral therapists reinforce desirable behaviors with rewards and at the same time withhold reinforcement for undesirable behaviors. In other words, therapists teach clients in a given situation, or antecedent, to behave in a certain way to achieve a desired consequence. The rewards for desirable behavior might be praise or treats, for example, depending on the client and the setting. For Marc, reducing his test anxiety may be all the reward he needs to motivate him to continue his new study habits.

Operant conditioning has sometimes proved effective in more severe cases, such as schizophrenia and childhood autism, that were previously resistant to other types of treatment. Operant conditioning is often used in institutional settings, such as mental hospitals. In such settings, the therapist may set up a system of rewards, called a **token economy**. When people in these settings begin to demonstrate appropriate behavior, they are rewarded with a plastic coin or token. The tokens can be accumulated and exchanged for real rewards, such as snacks, extra television time, a trip to town, or a private room.

The staff at one mental hospital used operant conditioning to convince withdrawn schizophrenic patients to eat their meals (Ayllon & Haughton, 1962). The more the staff coaxed the patients to eat—sometimes even hand-feeding them—the worse the problem became. The extra attention from the staff was apparently reinforcing the patients' lack of cooperation: the greater the refusal to eat, the more attention the patients received.

The solution was to stop reinforcing the uncooperative behavior and instead reinforce cooperative behavior. Patients who arrived late at the dining hall were locked out, and hospital staff were prevented from helping patients at mealtime. Thus, uncooperative behavior was no longer rewarded with extra attention. Only those who cooperated received food. As a result, the uncooperative patients quickly changed their eating habits.

Sometimes people find it difficult to adopt a new behavior all at once, finding it easier to change their behavior gradually. Another method of operant conditioning, called successive approximations, is useful in such situations. The term **successive approximations** refers to a series of behaviors that gradually become more similar to a target behavior. Through reinforcement of behaviors at each stage, the target behavior is finally achieved.

The technique of successive approximations is best understood by considering an example. Suppose a student wants to increase his studying

Aversive Versus Operant Conditioning

	Aversive	Operant
Goal	End maladaptive (harmful) behavior	Encourage adaptive behavior, or end maladaptive behavior
Technique	Associate the maladaptive behavior with aversive (painful) stimulation	Reinforce adaptive behavior, or avoid reinforcement of maladaptive behavior
Rationale	Associating a goal with aversive stimulation makes the goal aversive	Reinforcement increases the frequency of behavior, and lack of reinforcement extinguishes behavior

FIGURE 19.4 *Operant conditioning applies reinforcement to increase the frequency of desirable behavior and withholds reinforcement to extinguish undesirable behavior. Aversive conditioning makes use of punishment to make a once-desired goal unpleasant.*

time to two hours a day. However, he is not used to studying that long and cannot maintain his concentration for more than half an hour at a time. Instead of trying to study for two hours the first day, he studies for half an hour and then gives himself a small reward, such as shooting baskets or watching television for 15 minutes. Each night he adds five minutes to his study time, and each time he meets his new goal he reinforces his behavior with a small reward. Within a few weeks, through successive approximations, he reaches his goal of studying for two hours a day.

The relationship between antecedents, behavior, and consequences can be seen when operant conditioning is used for social skills training. People with severe psychological problems may lack social skills because of isolation and social withdrawal. In fact, lacking the social skills needed for independent living is one of the major symptoms of schizophrenia. A therapist might assist a client by teaching him or her to say "hello" in a friendly way when meeting someone. This technique would help the client function more comfortably in society—that is, it would help the client achieve a desired consequence.

Behavior therapists help people build their social skills by advising clients on their behavior, modeling effective behaviors, and encouraging clients to practice effective behaviors. Such techniques have proved successful in helping students build social relationships. They have also been used to help people with severe psychological disorders. With social skills training, a person who otherwise would be dependent on others might be able to hold a job and live on her or his own.

Evaluation of Behavior Therapy Behavior therapy tends to be somewhat more effective overall than psychoanalysis or person-centered therapy. It is also a short-term therapy, sometimes bringing about lasting results in just a few months.

Behavior therapy is especially effective for well-defined problems such as phobias, post-traumatic stress disorder, and compulsions (Borkovec & Costello, 1993; Thom et al., 2000). It has also helped many people overcome depression, social problems, and problems with self-control (as in quitting smoking or drinking). In addition, behavior therapy has proved very useful for managing the care of people living in institutions, including people with schizophrenia and people with mental retardation (Spreat & Behar, 1994).

Behavior therapy is less useful for some other disorders. For example, it is not usually effective for

treating the thought disorder of schizophrenia (Wolpe, 1990).

SECTION 4 REVIEW

go.hrw.com
Homework Practice Online
Keyword: SY7 HP19

1. Identify related antecedents, behavior, and consequences in a provided behavioral situation.
2. What is aversive conditioning?
3. **Critical Thinking** *Summarizing* What techniques do cognitive and behavior therapists use to help people?

SECTION 5
Biological Therapy

The methods of psychotherapy described so far rely on verbal interactions between the psychotherapist and the individual seeking help. As you have seen, psychotherapists may give their clients emotional support, advice, and help in understanding and changing their thoughts and behaviors.

Biological therapy, on the other hand, relies on methods such as medication, electric shock, and even surgery to help people with psychological disorders. All of these biological methods affect the brain in some way.

Because these treatments are medical in nature, they must be administered or prescribed by psychiatrists or other physicians. Psychologists do not prescribe drugs or administer biological treatments, but they may help decide whether a certain kind of biological therapy is appropriate for the treatment of a particular individual.

Drug Therapy

Drug therapy is the most widely used biological treatment for psychological disorders. It works well for several different problems. Four major types of medication are commonly used: antianxiety drugs, antidepressant drugs, lithium, and antipsychotic drugs. All of these medications can be obtained only with a prescription.

Antianxiety Drugs Also called minor tranquilizers, **antianxiety drugs** are used as an outpatient treatment to help people with anxiety disorders or panic attacks. (See Chapter 18.) They are also prescribed for people who are experiencing serious distress or tension in their lives.

Antianxiety drugs work by depressing the activity of the nervous system. They lower the heart rate and respiration rate. They also decrease feelings of nervousness and tension. Although antianxiety medications help control the symptoms of anxiety, they are not a permanent cure for anxiety disorders. Thus, most people use them for a short period of time (Shader & Greenblatt, 1993). The longer a person takes an antianxiety medication, the less effective the drug may become. Higher doses may be needed in order to achieve the same effect.

The major side effects of antianxiety medications are feelings of fatigue (Shader & Greenblatt, 1993). It is also possible to become dependent on antianxiety drugs. People who are dependent on these drugs may lose the ability to face the stresses and strains of everyday life without them.

Antidepressant Drugs

People who suffer from major depression are often treated with **antidepressant drugs**. Antidepressant drugs are also sometimes used in the treatment of eating disorders and panic disorder (Craighead & Agras, 1991).

Antidepressants work by increasing the amount of one or both of the neurotransmitters norepinephrine (noradrenaline) and serotonin. They tend to be most helpful in reducing the physical symptoms of depression. They increase activity levels and reduce the severity of eating and sleeping problems.

In order to work effectively, antidepressant medications must build up in the body to a certain level. This may take anywhere from several days to a few weeks. Severely depressed people who are at risk of suicide are sometimes hospitalized until the medication reaches the level required to improve their depressed mood. This is to prevent them from taking an overdose, which could be lethal. In addition, antidepressants sometimes have negative side effects, such as escalated heart rate and excessive weight gain (Sleek, 1996). For these and other reasons, some psychologists believe that antidepressant medications should be reserved for people who fail to respond to psychotherapy.

Lithium

The ancient Greeks and Romans may have been the first people to use the metal **lithium** to treat psychological disorders. They discovered that mineral water helped many people with what is now called bipolar disorder. (See Chapter 18.) It has been speculated that the mineral water may have contained lithium.

Today lithium carbonate, a salt of the metal lithium, is given in tablet form to help people with bipolar disorder. Lithium seems to flatten out their cycles of mania and depression. How lithium does this is not completely understood, although it is known to affect the functioning of several neurotransmitters (Price & Heninger, 1994).

Lithium may have side effects such as shakiness, memory impairment, and excessive thirst (Price & Heninger, 1994). Memory problems are reported to be the major reason that people stop using the drug.

Antipsychotic Drugs

People with schizophrenia, such as Dan's sister, are likely to be prescribed **antipsychotic drugs**, also called major tranquilizers.

Antipsychotic medications are effective for reducing agitation, delusions, and hallucinations (Kane, 1996). Their use has enabled many thousands of people with schizophrenia to live outside of mental hospitals and even to hold jobs.

Schizophrenia is associated with high levels of dopamine activity. (See Chapter 18.) Antipsychotic medications are thought to work by blocking the activity of dopamine in the brain. Unfortunately, prolonged use of these medications can lead to problems in balance and coordination and produce tremors and twitches (Kane, 1996).

Electroconvulsive Therapy

Electroconvulsive therapy (ECT), commonly called electric-shock therapy, was introduced as a treatment for psychological disorders in the 1930s by Italian psychiatrists Ugo Cerletti and Lucio Bini. Before ECT is given, anesthesia is administered to render the person unconscious throughout the procedure. Then an electric current is passed through the person's brain. The electric current produces convulsions (violent involuntary contractions of muscles) throughout the body. In some cases, muscle relaxant drugs are given to prevent injury during the convulsions.

When ECT was first introduced, it was used for many psychological disorders, including schizophrenia. However, once antipsychotic drugs became available, ECT was used much less often. In fact, in 1990 the American Psychiatric Association recommended that ECT be used primarily for people with major depression who do not respond to antidepressant drugs.

ECT is controversial for many reasons. For one thing, many professionals are distressed by the thought of passing an electric shock through a patient's head and producing convulsions. There are also side effects, including memory problems (Lisanby et al., 2000; Weiner, 2000). However, research suggests that for most people, cognitive impairment tends to be temporary. One study followed up on 10 adolescents who had received ECT an average of three and a half years earlier. Six of the ten had complained of memory impairment immediately after treatment, but only one complained of continued problems at the follow-up. Nevertheless, psychological tests did not reveal any differences in cognitive functioning between severely depressed adolescents who had received ECT and others who had not (Cohen et al., 2000). Despite the controversies surrounding ECT, it appears to help many people who do not respond to antidepressant drugs (Thase & Kupfer, 1996).

TRUTH
OR
fiction
■ R E V I S I T E D ■

It is true that severe depression is sometimes treated by passing an electric current through the brain. This is called electroconvulsive therapy. It is a biological treatment used primarily for patients with severe depression who do not respond to antidepressants.

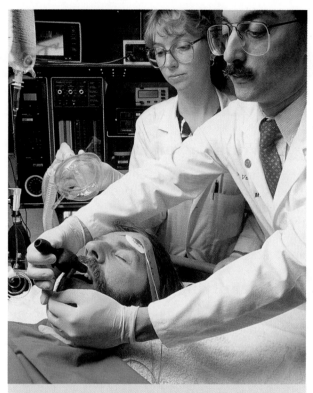

When a person with severe depression fails to respond to medications, electroconvulsive therapy may be considered. It is a drastic treatment that is used only in extreme cases.

Psychosurgery

Psychosurgery is brain surgery that is performed to treat psychological disorders. The best-known technique, **prefrontal lobotomy**, has been used to reduce the agitation and violence of people with severe psychological disorders.

The method was developed by Portuguese neurologist António Egas Moniz in the 1930s. The procedure involves cutting nerve pathways in the brain between the prefrontal lobes and the thalamus. (See Chapter 3.) However, the treatment produces several serious side effects, including distractibility, reduced learning ability, overeating, apathy, social withdrawal, seizures, reduced creativity, and occasionally even death.

Not surprisingly, prefrontal lobotomy is an even more controversial procedure than ECT. The original rationale behind the surgery has been challenged, and early success rates are now known to have been exaggerated (Valenstein, 1986). Because of the side effects of the surgery and the availability of antipsychotic drugs, prefrontal lobotomies are now performed only rarely.

Drug therapies, and to a limited extent ECT, seem to be effective for some psychological disorders that do not respond to psychotherapy. It is important to realize, however, that medications and electric shocks cannot help a person develop more rational ways of thinking or solve relationship problems. Changes such as these are likely to require psychotherapy.

SECTION 5 REVIEW

go.
hrw
.com

**Homework
Practice
Online**

Keyword: SY7 HP19

1. Describe the three major biological treatments for psychological disorders.

2. Explain why electroconvulsive therapy is a controversial treatment for psychological disorders.

3. **Critical Thinking** *Categorizing* Describe the type of biological therapy that might be prescribed for each of the following: panic disorder, bipolar disorder, schizophrenia, and severe depression.

Writing a Summary

Using standard grammar, spelling, sentence structure, and punctuation, summarize the information in this chapter. Consider:

• the methods and goals of psychotherapy
• humanistic, cognitive, and behavioral therapies, and biological therapies for psychological disorders

Identifying People and Ideas

Identify the following terms or people and use them in appropriate sentences.

1. psychotherapy
2. encounter group
3. free association
4. latent content
5. humanistic therapy
6. active listening
7. aversive conditioning
8. token economy
9. antianxiety drug
10. psychosurgery

Understanding Main Ideas

SECTION 1 (pp. 436–440)

1. In what ways do all methods of psychotherapy help troubled individuals?

SECTION 2 (pp. 441–444)

2. What is the difference between the manifest content and the latent content of dreams?
3. Give an example of a transference relationship. Why might a therapist encourage the formation of such a relationship?

SECTION 3 (pp. 444–446)

4. What is the primary goal of humanistic therapy?

SECTION 4 (pp. 446–451)

5. List and describe two counterconditioning techniques.

SECTION 5 (pp. 451–453)

6. When do therapists use electroconvulsive therapy, and why is it a controversial form of treatment?

Thinking Critically

1. **Summarizing** Why did Freud think that free association can reveal unconscious thoughts and feelings?
2. **Drawing Inferences and Conclusions** How could belief in the assumption "I must be loved by everyone to be happy" lead to unreasonable expectations and feelings of depression?
3. **Analyzing Information** Other than examples given in the text, what is an example of the use of systematic desensitization?
4. **Contrasting** What are the advantages of treating depression with cognitive therapy instead of with antidepressant drugs?

Writing About Psychology

1. **Summarizing** Research how the social and cultural conditions of Sigmund Freud's time influenced his ideas about the causes of psychological problems. Think about how Freud's era differed from the present. How did conditions then influence Freud's ideas? Write a brief summary of what you have learned.
2. **Comparing and Contrasting** In addition to person-centered therapy, there are other types of humanistic therapy. Three of these are existential therapy, Gestalt therapy, and transactional analysis. Read more about these other types of humanistic therapy, then write a report of their similarities and differences. Use the graphic organizer below to help you write your report.

Existential	Gestalt	Transactional

Interpreting Graphs

Study the graph below. Then use the information in the graph to help you answer the questions that follow.

The Effect of Desensitization and Therapy on Persons with a Phobia of Snakes

Snake Avoidance Scale (Greater ↔ Lesser)

Before Relaxation Therapy / After Relaxation Therapy

■ Group Not Desensitized   ■ Group Desensitized to Snakes

Source: Rachman, *Phobias*, 1968

1. Which of the following statements best reflects the information presented in the graph?
   a. Relaxation therapy worked best when used with desensitization.
   b. Relaxation therapy was useless in helping people with phobias.
   c. Some people feared snakes no matter what therapy or help they received.
   d. Desensitization rarely helps people with phobias.

2. Using information from this graph, what general statements can be made about relaxation therapy and the treatment of phobias?

Analyzing Primary Sources

Read the following excerpt from *The Story of Psychology,* in which Morton Hunt describes aspects of psychologist Aaron Beck's personal life. Then answer the questions that follow.

❝As a child, he had had a series of operations, and from then on the sight of blood would make him feel faint. By the time he reached his teens he decided to defeat the phobia. 'One of the reasons I went into medicine was to confront my fear,' he has said, and in his first year in medical school he made himself watch operations from the amphitheater and in his second year elected to be a surgical assistant. By making himself experience blood as a normal phenomenon, he dispelled his fear. Later in life he similarly tackled a fear of tunnels, manifested as involuntary shallow breathing and faintness (he attributes the phobia to a childhood fear of suffocation caused by a bad bout of whooping cough). He got rid of the fear by pointing out to himself repeatedly that the symptoms would show up even before he entered a tunnel.❞

3. Which method of therapy did Beck use to end his phobia of blood?
   a. psychoanalysis
   b. cognitive therapy
   c. behavior therapy
   d. biological therapy

4. Use Beck's experiences and his method of cognitive therapy to explain how personal background can shape a psychologist's views.

PSYCHOLOGY PROJECTS

Cooperative Learning

Writing About Psychology With a partner, write a skit showing how a client and a person-centered therapist might interact. First, select a suitable problem based on the text. Then write dialogue and descriptions for body language and facial expressions that illustrate active listening and unconditional positive regard. Rehearse the skit, and then present it to the rest of the class. After performing the skit, ask the class to identify examples of active listening and unconditional positive regard from the skit.

🖊 **internet** connect

Internet Activity: go.hrw.com
KEYWORD: SY7 CH19

Choose an activity on methods of therapy to:
- make a series of drawings illustrating the principles of humanistic therapy.
- create a graphic organizer for cognitive and behavior therapy.
- create a chart tracing changes in biological therapy over the years.

PSYCHOLOGY IN ACTION

YOU RESOLVE THE CONFLICT . . .

*How could two people settle a disagreement
in order to reduce stress in their lives?*

Complete the following activity in small groups. Imagine that two of your friends are having a disagreement about the best way to prepare for an upcoming test. Both friends are very distressed by their disagreement, but they are unsure how they can go about resolving the situation. Prepare a presentation outlining ways to help your friends.

1. Consider Persuasion. Encourage your friends to try to persuade one another to come around to the other's point of view. To help your friends come up with persuasive arguments for their side, list reasons why they have the points of view that they do. Then rank each reason in order of persuasiveness. Finally, urge your friends to present the most persuasive reasons to one another in an effort to sway the other to his or her point of view.

2. Compromise. Explain to your friends that sometimes compromise is necessary to resolve a conflict. Tell them that each of them will have to give up something in order to reach an agreement. Have them consider what they would be willing to give up to resolve their disagreement. Then encourage your friends to get together to discuss a compromise that they could both agree to.

3. Debate the Issue. Suggest to your friends that they hold a debate. Tell them to gather information about the advantages and disadvantages of each side of their disagreement. Ask questions such as,

- Should your friends have one cram session the night before the test?

- Should your friends study a little each night during the week leading up to the test?

Then consider having your friends prepare flash cards outlining the best arguments that they can come up with in support of their side. Finally, hold the debate. Your friends might want to include charts, graphs, or other visuals to better demonstrate their positions.

4. Consider Negotiation. Urge your friends to negotiate their conflict. Have them meet to discuss their positions and what they would be willing to agree to. Tell them that perhaps by working together to resolve the conflict, they will arrive at a solution that neither had considered before. Have your group decide who will prepare which part of the presentation. Then make your presentation to the class. Good luck!

UNIT 7
SOCIAL PSYCHOLOGY

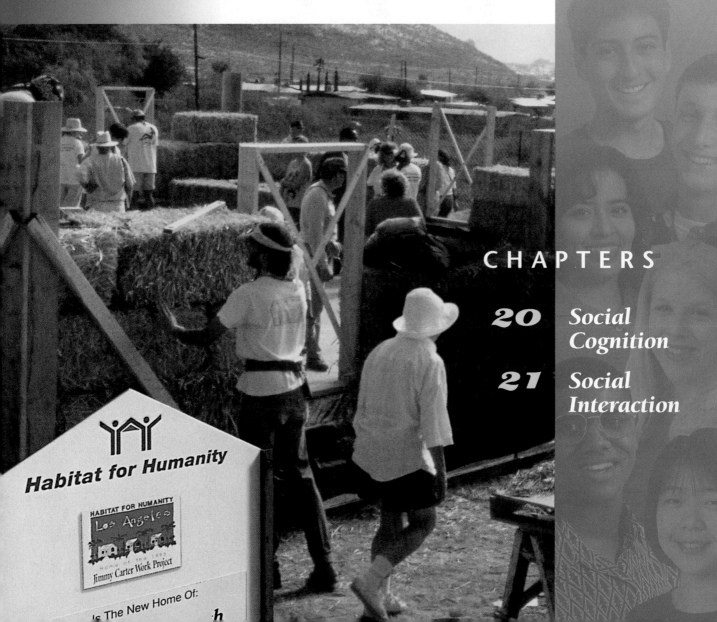

CHAPTERS

Habitat for Humanity

HABITAT FOR HUMANITY
Los Angeles
Jimmy Carter Work Project

Is The New Home Of:

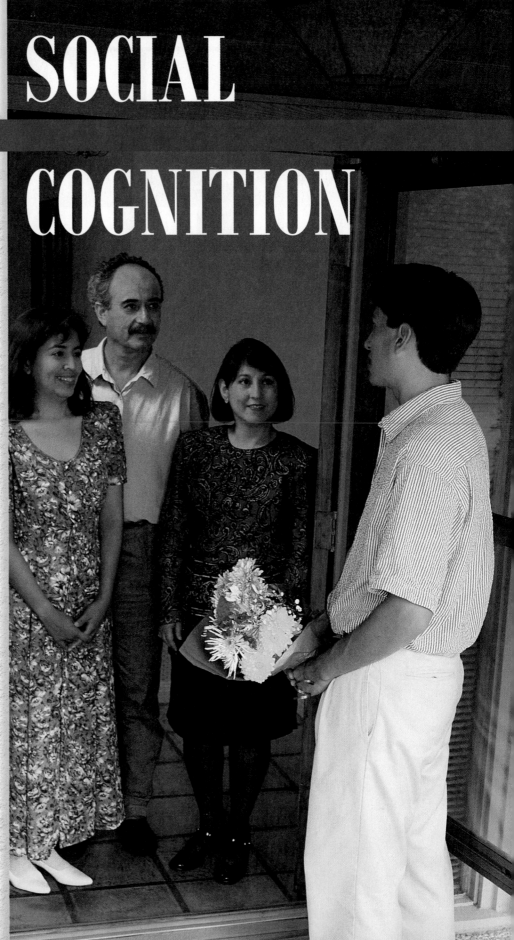

Chapter 20

SOCIAL COGNITION

Read to Discover

1 What are attitudes, and how do they develop?

2 How does persuasion affect people's attitudes and behavior?

3 What are the causes of prejudice, and how can it be overcome?

4 What factors influence our perceptions of other people, and how do people use various forms of nonverbal communication?

5 What role does attraction play in friendships and love relationships?

A DAY IN THE LIFE

On Saturday morning Marc was in a complete panic when he called Linda at home. That night, Marc was to have dinner with Linda's entire family—grandparents and all—and he was really nervous.

"Why are you so nervous?" Linda asked with a smile. "You know how much my parents like you."

"I know," Marc said, "but have you forgotten their attitude toward me at first? They didn't like me very much. I finally convinced your parents that I'm a good guy—now I have to go through the same thing with your grandparents."

"Marc, my parents first met you when we were six years old. When we started dating this year, they only remembered you from when we were little kids. Now that they know you better, they really like you," Linda tried to assure him.

"But what about your grandparents?" Marc said. "I really want them to like me the first time I meet them. What if I still come across as that same clumsy kid?"

"You'll be fine," Linda said. "Just relax, and I'll see you at six o'clock. I have to go now—I promised Hannah I'd help her out this afternoon."

"Okay," Marc sighed. Somehow Linda had managed to calm his fears. "What are you and Hannah doing today?" he asked. For the first time all morning, he was able to think about something other than the upcoming dinner.

"Remember how that representative from the performing arts foundation offered her a scholarship? Well, she has to pass an interview before they'll give her the scholarship, and I promised her that I'd help her prepare for it," Linda said.

"What are you going to help her with?" Marc asked.

"Well, she's been practicing the types of things she wants to say in the interview, and she wants to try them out on me first. She also wants me to help her decide what she should wear for the interview," Linda explained.

"Oh no!" Marc suddenly exclaimed in panic.

"What's wrong?" Linda asked.

"What am I going to wear to dinner tonight?"

Linda just laughed. "Really, Marc, I think you're taking this first impression thing a little too seriously."

- attitude
- cognitive evaluation
- cognitive anchor
- persuasion
- central route
- peripheral route
- two-sided argument
- emotional appeal
- sales resistance
- prejudice
- discrimination
- scapegoat
- social perception
- primacy effect
- recency effect
- attribution theory
- actor-observer bias
- fundamental attribution error
- self-serving bias
- attraction
- matching hypothesis
- reciprocity
- triangular model of love
- intimacy
- passion
- commitment

· · ·

Both Marc and Hannah want to make a good impression on other people. Their concern about how other people see them is one of the major aspects of the field of social psychology referred to as social cognition, which is the subject of this chapter.

Social cognition refers to the way people think and act in social situations. It is concerned not only with first impressions but also with attitudes, persuasion, attraction, and love. These and other aspects of social cognition are the focus of this chapter.

HOLT

Psychology Video Program

Watch the video to explore the role of male physical beauty among a group of West African nomads.

SECTION 1

Attitudes

Attitudes are beliefs and feelings about objects, people, and events that can affect how people behave in certain situations. A person's attitude about strangers, for example, can influence how that person feels and behaves around people he or she does not know. If a person believes that strangers are dangerous, that person is likely to feel afraid around strangers and may try to avoid situations where he or she is likely to meet new people. On the other hand, if a person believes that strangers are people just like him or her, that person is more likely to feel open to strangers and try to know them better.

Attitudes are a major aspect of social cognition. In fact, our attitudes may be the primary motivator for how we behave and how we view the world.

Attitudes are such an important aspect of our psychological lives because they foster strong emotions, such as love or hate (Petty et al., 1997). Attitudes can also vary greatly. A person belonging to a particular cultural group may have attitudes that have been shaped by the traditional physical environment of that group.

Under certain circumstances, a person's attitudes can change. They tend to remain stable, however, unless that person is strongly encouraged to change them. This section examines several aspects of attitudes—how they develop, how they affect behavior, and how behavior affects them.

How Attitudes Develop

People often have attitudes about things they have never experienced directly. People may be opposed to war or capital punishment, for example, even though they have no personal experience of either event. Where do such attitudes come from?

Attitudes develop in a variety of ways. Conditioning, observational learning, cognitive evaluation, and the use of cognitive anchors all play roles in the development of attitudes.

Conditioning Learning through conditioning plays an important role in acquiring attitudes. Children are often reinforced for saying and doing things that are consistent with the attitudes held by their parents, teachers, and other authority figures. For example, parents who believe that it is important to share with others may praise, or reinforce, a child who shares a toy with a friend. Through such conditioning, the child acquires an attitude about the importance of sharing.

Observational Learning People also acquire attitudes by observing other people. For example, teens may observe that classmates who dress, talk, or act in certain ways seem to be admired by their peers. These teens may adopt the same ways of dressing, talking, or acting because they have learned through observation that doing so might lead to acceptance and approval.

People who act with kindness and generosity toward others—such as the teens pictured here—may come to like other people better.

Cognitive Evaluation People often evaluate evidence and form beliefs on the basis of their evaluations. This process, which is known as **cognitive evaluation**, also plays a role in the development of attitudes. People evaluate evidence that comes from many sources. Part of the process of cognitive evaluation is learning to examine data carefully. For example, when looking at statistics provided in a news story, a viewer should consider issues such as whether the statistics were gathered properly, and what audience is being targeted by the story. A news story providing statistics indicating that seat belt use provides little protection in a car accident should be viewed skeptically.

People are especially likely to evaluate evidence if they think they will have to justify their attitudes to other people (Tetlock, 1983). For example, a teen who wants a part-time job after school may evaluate the evidence about working if he knows he will have to justify it to his parents. He may ask friends who have part-time jobs how they handle the extra responsibility and still do their schoolwork.

A DAY IN THE LIFE Cognitive evaluation was involved in Linda's parents' change in attitude toward Marc. At first, Linda's parents did not especially like Marc, an attitude that was based on their knowledge of him as a child who misbehaved. Once they came to know the teenage Marc, however, they formed a more positive attitude toward him.

Cognitive Anchors A person's earliest attitudes tend to serve as **cognitive anchors**, or persistent beliefs that shape the ways in which he or she sees the world and interprets events. Cognitive anchors tend to keep a person's attitudes from changing. Attitudes that emerge later in life may be rejected if they differ greatly from a person's cognitive anchors (Petty et al., 1999; Wood, 2000).

Attitudes and Behavior

The definition of *attitudes* suggests that people's behaviors are always consistent with their attitudes. However, the link between attitudes and behavior is not always strong (Eagly & Chaiken, 1993). In fact, people often behave in ways that contradict their attitudes. For example, many people know that smoking cigarettes and drinking alcohol excessively are harmful to their health, yet they still smoke and drink excessively. Likewise, most people realize that it is dangerous and illegal to drink and drive, yet some do it just the same (Stacy et al., 1994).

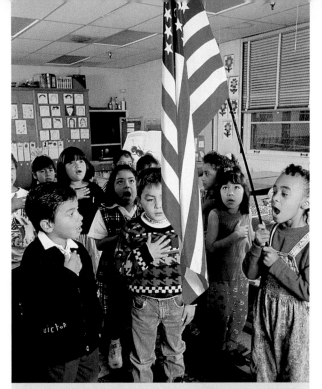

These children are learning an attitude of patriotism, which may serve as a cognitive anchor later in life.

When Behavior Follows Attitudes People are more likely to behave in accordance with their attitudes if the attitudes are specifically tied to the behaviors. For example, someone who believes that aerobic exercise is necessary to prevent heart disease is more likely to exercise regularly than someone who believes that only a healthy lifestyle is important for good health. Similarly, strong attitudes are better predictors of behavior than weak attitudes (Petty et al., 1997). Students who believe strongly in the value of hard work, for example, may be more likely to study than students who believe less strongly in the benefits of hard work.

People are also more likely to behave in accordance with their attitudes when they have a vested interest, or a personal stake, in the outcome of a behavior (Crano, 1997). People are more likely to go to the polls and vote on an issue, for example, if the issue affects them directly. That is one reason why issues such as tax reform often have high voter turnouts.

Attitudes are more likely to guide behavior when people are aware of them, particularly if the attitudes are put into words and spoken (Fazio, 1990; Krosnick, 1989). Verbalizing and repeating an attitude makes it come to mind quickly, and attitudes that come to mind quickly are more likely to influence how people act (Fazio, 1990). People are also more likely to be aware of attitudes that affect them emotionally (Wu & Shaffer, 1987). Someone who loves animals is likely to be aware of his attitude about animal rights, for example. Likewise, someone who is angered by destruction of the environment is likely to be aware of her attitudes about recycling and conservation.

When Attitudes Follow Behavior   Most of the time attitudes come first and behavior follows (Petty et al., 1997, 1999). However, sometimes the reverse is true. In some situations, attitudes follow behavior.

Attitudes are especially likely to follow behavior when people are encouraged to behave in ways that go against their attitudes. In such situations, people may suffer cognitive dissonance, an uncomfortable feeling of tension that may accompany a contradiction between attitudes and behaviors (Festinger, 1957). In order to reduce the tension they feel, people may try to justify their behavior and gradually change their attitudes to fit their acts.

As an example, in one experiment, people were asked to argue in favor of something they did not believe in. Doing so made them feel very uncomfortable, and they eventually modified their

attitudes to bring them more in line with their arguments (Cialdini, 1993).

 TRUTH OR fiction ■REVISITED■   *It is not true that people's attitudes are always consistent with their behavior. People can also change their attitudes to make them consistent with their behavior.*

Although the patterns may change, one thing is certain—attitudes and behavior influence each other. As Figure 20.1 shows, people tend to act as they believe, but they may also come to believe as they act.

SECTION 1 REVIEW   go. hrw .com **Homework Practice Online**   Keyword: SY7 HP20

1. What do psychologists mean by *attitude,* and how do attitudes develop?
2. Why should people be cautious when using statistics from news stories or information from other sources?
3. **Critical Thinking**   *Drawing Inferences and Conclusions*   In what ways do people adjust their behavior to fit various situations?

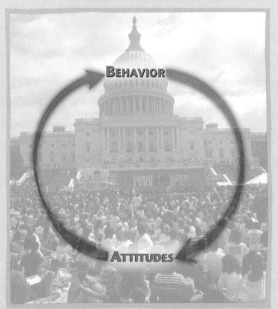

The Relationship Between Attitudes and Behavior

BEHAVIOR

ATTITUDES

FIGURE 20.1   *Behavior usually follows attitudes, but attitudes can follow behavior when people behave in ways that go against their attitudes.*

Persuasion

Attitudes tend to remain constant unless people are strongly motivated to change them. People may change their attitudes because they are persuaded to do so. **Persuasion** is a direct attempt to influence other people's attitudes or views. Parents, for example, may try to persuade their children to adopt the same values that they hold. Children, on the other hand, may try to persuade their parents to allow them more freedoms and privileges.

A DAY IN THE LIFE   Both Marc and Hannah want to persuade others to have a favorable impression of them. Both are hoping to influence people by the way they will dress for two important occasions— Hannah's interview with the performing arts foundation and Marc's first meeting with Linda's grandparents.

Methods of Persuasion

There are two basic ways to persuade people: via the central route and via the peripheral route (Petty et al., 1997). The most persuasive messages use both routes.

The **central route** uses evidence and logical arguments to persuade people (Eagly & Chaiken, 1993). Advertisements might point out the superior quality of a product or a service—the superior taste and nutritional content of a breakfast cereal, for example. Similarly, a parent might use statistics on bicycle accidents and injuries to persuade a child to wear a safety helmet.

The **peripheral route** is indirect. It attempts to associate objects, people, or events with positive or negative cues. For example, an advertisement for athletic shoes might feature a famous athlete. A public service announcement for staying in school might feature an admired actor. The aim is to influence people to associate their positive feelings for the famous individual with the product or the message that is being endorsed.

In the central route, the message itself is most important. In the peripheral route, other factors, including the messenger, the situation, and the nature of the audience, are also important. Each of these aspects of persuasion is considered in turn.

*Politicians try to persuade people to vote for them. Yet it is not always clear which route is being used—the central route or the peripheral route. **Which route do you think politicians use most often?***

The Message

Research shows that repeated exposure to a stimulus eventually results in a more favorable attitude toward that stimulus. For example, studies have found that people respond more favorably to abstract art (Heingartner & Hall, 1974) or classical music (Smith & Dorfman, 1975) after being repeatedly exposed to it.

Advertisers, political candidates, and others who want to persuade people use repetition to encourage people to adopt a favorable attitude toward their product or ideas. Many television commercials are repeated over and over so that potential consumers will react favorably to the products—and buy them—when they see these items in the store. One might think that such repetition would offend or annoy viewers (and to some extent it does), but research suggests that commercials are more effective when they are repeated regularly (Haugtvedt et al., 1994). Similarly, political candidates who appear regularly in television commercials tend to receive more votes than candidates who appear less often in commercials (Grush, 1980).

TRUTH OR fiction ▪ REVISITED ▪ *It is not true that showing television commercials over and over reduces their effectiveness.* In fact, studies have shown that the more often a commercial is repeated, the more likely it is to be persuasive.

In addition to being presented frequently, the persuasive message can be presented in ways that are especially effective. Two-sided arguments tend to be more effective than one-sided arguments, especially when the audience is uncertain about its position on the issue (Jacks & Devine, 2000). Emotional appeals are also very effective.

Two-Sided Arguments   One of the most persuasive types of messages is the **two-sided argument**, in which people present not only their side of the argument but also the opposition's side. The purpose is to discredit the opposition's views. For example, a cereal advertiser admits that its brand of cereal is not as sweet as competing brands and then explains how the less sweet taste is evidence that the product is more nutritious. Admitting weaknesses in this way also makes the message seem more honest (Bridgwater, 1982).

Emotional Appeals Another effective way to present a persuasive message is to appeal to the audience's emotions. **Emotional appeals** persuade by arousing such feelings as loyalty, desire, or fear rather than by convincing through evidence and logic. Thus, an emotional appeal is a peripheral route in persuasion.

Arousing fear is a particularly effective method of persuasion. Smokers are more likely to be convinced to quit smoking, for example, when they are presented with frightening photos of blackened lungs rather than dry, unemotional statistics on lung cancer. In general, appeals based on fear tend to be most effective when they are strong, when the audience believes them, and when the audience believes it can avoid the danger by changing its behavior (Eagly & Chaiken, 1993).

Advertisements such as this one are meant to appeal to the emotions of the audience rather than to convince them through logic.

The Messenger

Some people are more persuasive than others. Research (Hennigan et al., 1982; Mackie et al., 1990; Wilder, 1990) shows that people are persuasive if they are

- experts. This makes the audience more likely to follow their advice.

- trustworthy. This makes the audience more likely to believe what they say.

- physically attractive. This makes the audience more likely to pay attention to them.

- similar to their audience in ethnicity, age, and other physical characteristics. People are more likely to imitate others who appear similar to themselves.

Messengers who stand to gain from their persuasive efforts are less likely than others to be effective. For example, if the president of a company says his or her company's product is the best one on the market, people are generally less likely to be persuaded by his or her arguments.

The Situation

When a person is in a good mood, he or she is less likely to evaluate messages carefully (Petty et al., 1991; Schwarz et al., 1991). As a result, people tend to be more receptive to persuasion when they are feeling good. Thus, putting people in a good mood—with a compliment, for example—tends to boost the acceptance of persuasive messages.

The Audience

Most messages are aimed at a specific audience. A political candidate is trying to reach the voters in his or her district, for example. Differences in age, sex, and other characteristics of the intended audience influence how the message should be delivered to be most persuasive. Emotional appeals may work better with children, for example, whereas logic may be more effective with adults (Kunkel & Roberts, 1991).

Saying No to Persuasive Messages

Some people are less easily persuaded than others. For example, some people have developed an attitude called **sales resistance**. People possessing sales resistance have no trouble turning down requests to buy products or services. Other people have little or no sales resistance. They find it difficult to refuse a sales pitch or other types of requests.

Research suggests that two personality factors may be involved in sales resistance—self-esteem and social anxiety (Rhodes & Wood, 1992; Santee & Maslach, 1982). People who find it easy to refuse requests tend to have high self-esteem and low social anxiety. They believe in themselves, stand up for what they want, and are not overly concerned about what other people think of them.

People who find it difficult to say no, on the other hand, are likely to have lower self-esteem and greater social anxiety. They may worry what sales-people will think of them, for example, or be concerned that the people requesting donations will be insulted if they refused to give. Such people may also believe they should help others rather than act self-centered (Schwartz & Gottman, 1976).

People with low self-esteem and high social anxiety are likely to be easily persuaded in situations other than sales and donations. For example, they may be more easily persuaded to engage in activities that go against their attitudes, beliefs, and values, such as using alcohol or other drugs.

SECTION 2 REVIEW

After a Muslim terrorist group attacked the United States on September 11, 2001, some Americans became prejudiced against all Muslims, even though most Muslims strongly oppose terrorism. Here, American Muslims call for an end to hate-motivated violence.

Homework Practice Online
Keyword: SY7 HP20

1. In what ways does persuasion affect people's attitudes and behavior?

2. What characteristics would you expect to find in an individual with sales resistance?

3. **Critical Thinking** *Categorizing* List the different types of advertising, and give examples of ways an advertiser might use persuasion to sell a car.

SECTION 3

Prejudice

A type of attitude that causes a great deal of harm is prejudice. **Prejudice**—a generalized attitude toward a specific group of people—literally means "prejudgment." People who are prejudiced judge other people on the basis of their group membership rather than as individuals. People who are prejudiced may decide, for example, that one person is deceitful because he or she belongs to a particular ethnic group or that another person is highly intelligent because that individual belongs to another ethnic group. Prejudicial attitudes such as these are based on stereotypes.

Stereotypes

Stereotypes are unchanging, oversimplified, and usually distorted beliefs about groups of people. People tend to develop or adopt stereotypes as a way to organize information about their social world (Azar, 2002; Langlois et al., 2000). Stereotypes make it easier for people to interpret the behavior of others, even though the interpretations

are often wrong. For example, if we expect an older man to be sexist because a sexist attitude is part of our stereotype of older males, then we are more likely to interpret his words and deeds as sexist.

Another reason people tend to develop stereotypes is because they assume that those who are different from themselves are similar to each other in many ways (Mussweiler & Bodenhausen, 2002). Traits seen in some members of a group are incorrectly assumed to characterize all members of the group. An Asian American may think, for example, that all European Americans or all African Americans have similar personality traits, behavior patterns, or attitudes.

Stereotypes are harmful because they ignore people's individual natures and assign traits to them on the basis of the groups to which they belong. One of the many problems with stereotyping is that the traits assigned are usually negative. However, stereotypes can also include positive traits—such as the belief that members of a particular group are hard workers.

Stereotypes limit possibilities by discouraging the expression of the full range of an individual's talents, interests, and feelings. Even positive stereotypes can be harmful because they may put pressure on people to live up to unrealistic expectations.

Discrimination

Prejudice often leads to negative behavior in the form of discrimination. **Discrimination** refers to the unfair treatment of individuals because they are members of a particular group. For example, people may be denied jobs, housing, voting privileges, or other rights because of their skin color, sex, or religion. Victims of discrimination may begin to see themselves as inferior. Thus, they are likely to have low self-esteem (Bohon et al., 1993). People with low self-esteem tend to have low expectations for themselves, thus reducing their chances for success.

Causes of Prejudice

Why are some people prejudiced and others are not? Psychologists and other researchers have studied the origins of prejudice and have found many potential causes.

Exaggerating Differences   One reason some people are prejudiced is that they exaggerate how different others are from themselves. People tend to prefer (as friends and acquaintances) those who are similar to themselves and who share their attitudes. People who differ in one or several ways—in skin color or religion, for example—are often assumed to have attitudes and customs that are more different than they really are.

Justifying Economic Status   People also tend to develop prejudice against those who are not in the same economic group. Those in higher socioeconomic groups often justify their own economic superiority by assuming that people who have a lower economic status are inferior to them. They may believe that people who are worse off than themselves work less hard or are less motivated to succeed. Such beliefs may be used as an excuse for—and thus help maintain—existing injustices.

Social Learning   Children, like adults, acquire many attitudes from other people. They are especially likely to acquire the attitudes of their parents. Children tend to imitate their parents, and parents often reinforce their children when they do. In this way, parents who are prejudiced often pass along their prejudicial attitudes to their children.

Victimization   Sometimes people who are the victims of prejudice feel empathy for others who are discriminated against. However, this is not always the case. In fact, some victims of prejudice try to gain a sense of power and pride by asserting their superiority over people that are even worse off than themselves (Van Brunt, 1994). Thus, victimization may lead to further prejudice.

Scapegoating   A **scapegoat** is an individual or group that is blamed for the problems of others because the real cause of the problems is either too complex, too powerful, or too remote to be confronted. The term *scapegoating* refers to aggression against the group that has been made the target.

The scapegoat group is likely to have certain characteristics that make it a safe and highly visible target. Typically, scapegoats are people who are too weak to defend themselves or who choose not to return the attack. They are also likely to stand out because of their differences from majority groups.

Probably the best-known and most extreme example of scapegoating is the victimization of European Jews in the 1930s and 1940s. Nazi dictator Adolf Hitler blamed Jewish people for Germany's serious economic troubles. Under Hitler's leadership, millions of Jews were killed.

Intergroup contact can reduce feelings of prejudice by giving people the opportunity to work together and come to know each other as individuals.

CASE STUDIES
AND OTHER TRUE STORIES

Being Black in America

W. E. B. Du Bois was one of the most influential educators, writers, and social leaders in American history. A child of mixed European and African ancestry, he was born in Massachusetts in 1868, just five years after President Abraham Lincoln issued the Emancipation Proclamation.

After earning a Ph.D. from Harvard University, he became active in the movement to gain equality for African Americans and became a prominent member of the National Association for the Advancement of Colored People (NAACP). He died in 1963 at the height of the civil rights movement—a movement he helped to foster and one that inspired millions of Americans to call for equality and freedom.

In 1903 Du Bois published a classic work titled *The Souls of Black Folk.* The book is partly autobiographical, and in the following excerpt, Du Bois reveals how he felt when he first learned, as a schoolboy, that he was "different from the others" and "shut out from their world." The incident may seem trivial, but it had a profound effect on him for the rest of his life.

W. E. B. Du Bois

> It is in the early days of rollicking boyhood that the revelation first bursts upon one, all in a day, as it were. I remember well when the shadow swept across me. I was a little thing, away up in the hills of New England. . . . In a wee wooden schoolhouse, something put it into the boys' and girls' heads to buy gorgeous visiting-cards—ten cents a package—and exchange. The exchange was merry, till one girl, a tall newcomer, refused my card. . . . Then it dawned upon me with a certain suddenness that I was different from the others; or like, mayhap, in heart and life and longing, but shut out from their world by

a vast veil. I had thereafter no desire to tear down that veil, to creep through; I held all beyond it in common contempt, and lived above it in a region of blue sky and great wandering shadows. That sky was bluest when I could beat my mates at examination-time, or beat them at a foot-race. . . . Alas, with the years all this fine contempt began how to fade; for the words I longed for, and all their dazzling opportunities, were theirs, not mine. But they should not keep these prizes, I said; some, all, I would wrest from them. Just how I would do it I could never decide: by reading law, by healing the sick, by telling the wonderful tales that swam in my head—some way. With other black boys the strife was not so fiercely sunny: their youth shrank into tasteless sycophancy [fawning], or into silent hatred of the pale world about them and mocking distrust of everything white; or wasted itself in a bitter cry, Why did God make me an outcast and a stranger in mine own house?

The U.S. government has passed many laws against discrimination, and considerable progress in race relations has been achieved since Du Bois published *The Souls of Black Folk.* However, attitudes of racial prejudice still exist. The NAACP and other groups continue to work to eliminate discrimination in American society.

THINKING CRITICALLY

1. **Summarizing** According to Du Bois, how did racial prejudice affect some other African American boys?
2. **Drawing Inferences and Conclusions** What do you think Du Bois meant when he said he was "shut out from their world by a vast veil"?

Overcoming Prejudice

Although prejudice is difficult to overcome, it can be done. Increased contact among members of different groups is one of the best ways for people to develop less prejudicial attitudes. For example, when people work together to achieve common goals, they are likely to learn about one another as individuals, and this may weaken the stereotypes.

On an individual level, one can reduce prejudice by speaking up when other people act or talk in ways that reflect prejudicial attitudes. Individuals can also set an example of tolerance and understanding for others by their own words and actions.

Finally, prejudicial attitudes do not have to lead to discriminatory behavior. A person who is prejudiced can make a conscious effort to treat other people courteously and fairly, regardless of the groups to which they belong. This, in turn, may help reduce the person's own prejudicial attitudes.

SECTION 3 REVIEW

go.hrw.com **Homework Practice Online**
Keyword: SY7 HP20

1. Explain the difference between prejudice and discrimination.
2. Identify several causes of prejudice.
3. **Critical Thinking** *Summarizing* Identify three ways people can help reduce prejudice in their communities.

SECTION 4
Social Perception

Social perception refers to the ways in which people perceive one another. Social perception affects the attitudes people form toward others. For example, Marc believed that if he made a negative first impression on Linda's grandparents, it would be difficult to change their opinion of him later. He assumed that first impressions have a lasting effect on people's attitudes toward others. As you will see in this section, Marc was right.

Primacy and Recency Effects

People often wear their best clothes to job interviews. Likewise, defense attorneys encourage their clients to be well dressed when they are in the courtroom and within view of the jury. The reason? People think that their first impressions of other people are accurate (Gleitman et al., 1997), and first impressions are often based on how a person looks. The tendency for people to form opinions of others on the basis of first impressions is called the **primacy effect**.

First impressions are important because they may have lasting effects on our relationships with others. If our first impression of a new acquaintance is negative because the person appears to be self-centered, for example, then we are unlikely to want to know the person better. However, if our first impression is positive—the person seems friendly and interesting—then we are more likely to want to develop a relationship with that person.

How people interpret the future behavior of others is also influenced by their first impressions. For example, someone who impresses us as intelligent and well educated is more likely to be taken seriously in future encounters than someone who comes across as superficial and silly.

TRUTH
OR
fiction
■ R E V I S I T E D ■

It is true that our first impressions of other people tend to have lasting effects on our relationships with them. This is because people often interpret another person's future behavior in light of their first impressions.

The **recency effect** occurs when people change their opinions of others on the basis of recent interactions instead of holding on to their first impressions. This is what happened with Linda's parents and Marc. Linda's parents' first impression of him was of a rude and misbehaving six-year-old. After they got to know Marc as a teen, however, they saw him in a more positive light and changed their attitude toward him.

Attribution Theory

People often explain the behavior of others differently from the way in which they explain their own behavior. According to **attribution theory**, people tend to explain behavior in terms of either dispositional, or personality, factors or in terms of situational, or external, factors. For example, suppose you meet someone at a party who seems reluctant

PSYCHOLOGY
IN THE WORLD TODAY

What Can Be Done About Prejudice?

Prejudice is not just an abstract concept that affects people other than ourselves. Prejudice dwells within us. In fact, people are often unaware of their own prejudices because such attitudes tend to be deep-seated. Thus, overcoming prejudice can be difficult. What can you do to help reduce prejudice?

Speak Out Against Prejudice   Even people who do not have feelings of prejudice themselves often do little to counter the prejudice of others. They may say nothing when they hear another person make a sexist joke or an ethnic slur. They may do nothing when their club or other organization denies admission to people of other racial or religious groups.

By saying and doing nothing when they encounter prejudice, people appear to be condoning, or excusing, the prejudicial words or actions. Therefore, it is important to speak out against prejudice as well as to show an attitude of tolerance in one's own words and actions.

Break Down Stereotypes   Prejudice is based on stereotypes. Thus, one of the best ways to combat prejudice is to break down stereotypes. The more contact we have with people of other races, ethnic groups, or religions, the more aware we become that these groups are made up of individuals who are not only different from one another but also similar to ourselves in many ways. Through intergroup contact, we are likely to learn that people of the same skin color, for example, differ from one another in a variety of ways, including language, values, abilities, religious beliefs, and interests.

Intergroup contact is especially effective at breaking down stereotypes and reducing prejudicial attitudes when individuals work cooperatively to achieve common goals. Playing together on the same sports team, working together on a class project, or working side by side on the school yearbook are examples of cooperative efforts that can foster increased understanding and tolerance of others.

If individuals share similar backgrounds, intergroup contact is even more effective at breaking down stereotypes and reducing prejudice. People who have the same socioeconomic background, religious beliefs, or level of education, for example, are more likely to have the same values. Shared values, in turn, promote liking and openness toward others.

Intergroup contact is generally more effective when it is informal. Informal contacts, such as sitting together in the school cafeteria or hanging out together at the mall, encourage people to get to know one another as individuals. In contrast, more formal contacts, such as participating in the same class debate or attending the same religious service, allow people to maintain their distance from one another.

Brief contacts are also less likely to produce lasting changes in stereotypes and prejudicial attitudes than contacts that last longer periods of time. Chatting with a stranger on a bus, for example, is not likely to bring about a permanent change in attitudes toward the group that the stranger represents. However, working in chemistry lab throughout the school year with a lab partner who belongs to a different group may better break down stereotypes and reduce prejudice in society.

Combat Discrimination   Even when people's attitudes of prejudice cannot be changed, it is still possible to combat discrimination. Discrimination on the basis of sex, religion, race, or disability is against the law. Thus, people who are discriminated against can seek legal remedies to stop the discrimination.

Think About It

Analyzing Information Give examples of ways not mentioned in the feature that students might work together in or out of school to break down their own stereotypes and reduce their prejudices toward others.

The same man is shown in both of these photographs, but he looks very different in each. If you were the taxi driver, whom would you be more likely to pick up? How does this relate to the concept of social perception?

to talk to other people. You may assume that this person is either shy or conceited. This would be a dispositional attribution. On the other hand, you may assume that this person is usually friendly but simply does not know anyone at the party. This would be a situational attribution.

Actor-Observer Bias   For the most part, people tend to attribute the behavior of others to dispositional, or internal, factors and to attribute their own behavior to situational, or external, factors. This tendency is called the **actor-observer bias** (Jellison & Green, 1981). Actor-observer bias occurs because we tend to judge others only by the behavior we witness, and people's behavior may not always be a true reflection of their personalities.

Suppose you observe a stranger acting in a rude manner. If this is your only encounter with the person, you are likely to assume that the stranger has a rude disposition—that is, that he or she is a rude person. In most other situations, however, the same person might behave in a very polite fashion. Observing the stranger in most other situations, then, would lead to the assumption that he or she has a polite, respectful disposition. This may in fact be the case. The person might have acted rudely only because of the circumstances. For example, perhaps the person was provoked.

Fundamental Attribution Error   The tendency to overestimate the effect of dispositional causes for another person's behavior, and to underestimate the effect of situational causes, is referred to as the **fundamental attribution error**. It is a common mistake that affects many of our interactions with other people. To further understand this concept, look at the photographs on page 471. If you observed this teenager in only one situation you might assume that she was either an extremely helpful person or a very rude person. That is, you might commit a fundamental attribution error and overlook or misinterpret the true causes of her behavior.

Self-Serving Bias   People are more likely to attribute their own successes to dispositional, or personality, factors. They are also more likely to attribute their failures to situational factors (Campbell & Sedihides, 1999; Duval & Silvia, 2002). This is called a **self-serving bias**. The self-serving bias allows individuals to place the blame for their failures on circumstances outside their control. At the same time, however, it enables them to take full credit for their successes.

If Hannah's scholarship interview is a success, for example, she may attribute it to the fact that she is talented and motivated. If, on the other hand, the interview goes badly, she may attribute it to circumstances beyond her control—perhaps she had a headache that day, or the interviewer was in a bad mood.

Nonverbal Communication

It is not only what people say and do but how they say and do it that influences our perceptions of them. Forms of nonverbal, or unspoken, communication include facial expressions, gestures, posture, and the distance we keep from others. These and other forms of "body langauge" affect our perceptions of people, largely because they often indicate feelings. Feelings of sympathy or anger, for example, may be inferred from a concerned look or frown.

Some nonverbal forms of communication are learned early. Even young children can "read" a tone of voice, a facial expression, or other forms of nonverbal communication. Thus, before they understand all the words their parents are speaking, they can tell from nonverbal communication how their parents are feeling (Saarni, 1990).

Without necessarily being aware of it, people use nonverbal communication to send messages to other people (Patterson, 1991). They may even use nonverbal communication to mask their true feelings (DePaulo, 1992). For example, a parent who wishes to hide his fear or worry from his child might use nonverbal forms of communication, such as smiles and a relaxed bearing, to convince the child that all is well.

Physical Contact   Touching is one way in which people communicate nonverbally. However, not all people use physical contact to communicate with others. For example, American women are more likely than American men to touch the people with whom they are interacting (Stier & Hall, 1984). There is also considerable cultural variation in the use of touch to communicate with others.

Touching can be an effective means of communication. In one experiment, college students who had filled out several personality questionnaires were asked by the experimenter to stay and help in another study. Students who were touched during the request were more likely to help in the subsequent study (Powell et al., 1994). In another study, waitresses received larger tips when they touched customers on the hand or shoulder while making change (Crusco & Wetzel, 1984).

A study in a nursing home found that the ways in which people respond to touch depend on many factors. In the study, whether touching was responded to favorably or unfavorably depended on the status of the staff member doing the touching, the type of touch, and the part of the body that was touched. Touching was not appreciated when it was inappropriate or forceful (Hollinger & Buschmann, 1993).

Eye Contact   People can learn a great deal about the feelings of others from eye contact. When someone who is talking looks directly into the eyes of the

How do you think first impressions of this teen might vary from one situation to another?

Source: BLONDIE reprinted with special permission of King Features Syndicate.

listener, for example, the talker is usually telling the truth. Avoidance of eye contact, on the other hand, may indicate that the talker is lying. This is why a message is more believable and persuasive when the messenger makes eye contact with the audience.

One type of eye contact is gazing, or looking at someone with a steady, intent look that conveys eagerness or attention. Gazing usually is interpreted as a sign of liking or friendliness, and it may greatly influence relationships (Kleinke, 1986).

Another type of eye contact is staring, or looking fixedly with wide-open eyes. Staring is usually interpreted as a sign of anger. Being the object of staring makes most people uncomfortable, and they may try to avoid the stare. For example, one study found that drivers who were stared at by other drivers at an intersection crossed the intersection faster when the light changed (Ellsworth et al., 1972).

Whether or not they are aware of it, most people send unspoken messages that can greatly influence how other people see them. Thus, becoming more aware of nonverbal communication can increase our understanding of others.

SECTION 4 REVIEW

1. List several factors that influence perceptions of other people.

2. Define *fundamental attribution error.*

3. **Critical Thinking** *Analyzing Information* Think about a recent interaction you had with another person. What forms of nonverbal communication did you, or the other person, use to convey thoughts or feelings?

Interpersonal Attraction

Attraction is a kind of attitude—an attitude of liking. Attraction to another person often leads to friendship or love. Factors that attract us to particular people as potential friends or partners include physical appearance, similarity to ourselves, and evidence that our attraction is returned.

Physical Appearance

Physical appearance tends to influence our choice of friends and partners. What qualities make someone physically attractive? There is no single answer. Some people find blond hair most attractive; others may prefer black hair. Some people may find a slim body build most attractive, while others may prefer a more muscular build. Clearly, people's ideas of attractiveness differ.

Universals of Beauty Although there is variation among people in the types of traits they consider attractive, some aspects of attractiveness appear to be widely shared or even universal. For example, a smiling person is generally perceived to be more attractive than a person who is frowning (Reis et al., 1990).

Studies have also found that certain types of facial features are attractive to most people. In one study, both British and Japanese people were asked to identify the types of features they found most attractive in women. People from both cultures identified large eyes, high cheekbones, and narrow jaws as the most attractive types of facial features (Perrett et al., 1994).

Another study investigated the kinds of faces that infants find most attractive (Langlois, 1994). This was judged by the amount of time the infants spent looking at the faces of strangers—the longer the gaze, the greater the presumed attraction. As early as the age of two months, infants in the study seemed to prefer faces that were also rated by adults as most attractive. This evidence suggests that we do not "learn" what is attractive by being socialized in a particular culture. Other research, however, indicates that people do learn what features are considered attractive.

Differences in Body Shape Preference

Although preferences for certain facial features may be universal, preferences for body shape vary greatly (Etcoff, 1994). There is, in fact, a great deal of variation in people's standard for attractiveness of body shape—both in the shape we prefer in others and the shape we perceive ourselves as having.

This was demonstrated in a study of college men and women (Fallon & Rozin, 1985). The men in the study tended to believe their own body shape closely approached the "ideal" shape that women find attractive. However, the women tended to believe that they were heavier than the "ideal" shape men find attractive.

The results of this study are important. They suggest that females are more likely than males to incorrectly think they are too heavy to be attractive. Not surprisingly, women are more likely than men to go on weight-loss diets, and they have far higher rates of eating disorders. (See Chapter 11.)

Evidence suggests that in the United States, many men prefer their partners to be shorter than themselves, whereas many women prefer their partners to be taller (Goode, 2000; Hensley, 1994). On the job as well as in relationships, tallness tends to be perceived as an asset for men, whereas height in women tends to have less impact on their jobs (Pierce, 1996; Wade et al., 2000).

This is not to say, however, that physical appearance will determine an individual's ability to succeed on the job or in relationships. The initial attraction one feels for another person may be based on the person's physical appearance. However, other traits usually become more important as people get to know one another better. Traits such as honesty, loyalty, warmth, and sensitivity tend to be more important than physical appearance in forming and maintaining long-term relationships.

Similarity and Reciprocity

You may be familiar with the saying "Birds of a feather flock together." This saying suggests that we are usually attracted to people who are like us. On the other hand, another popular saying asserts "Opposites attract." Which of these two contradictory statements is true? Generally speaking, the answer is that we are more attracted to people who are like us.

Similarity in Physical Attractiveness

According to the **matching hypothesis**, people tend to choose as friends and partners those who are similar to themselves in attractiveness (Feingold, 1988b). One reason for this may be the fear of rejection—the belief that someone more attractive will not be interested in them (Bernstein et al., 1983).

Although conceptions of beauty vary from culture to culture, studies have shown that certain aspects of attractiveness appear to be widely shared or even universal.

People are more likely to form relationships with people who are similar to themselves than with those who differ in terms of level of attractiveness, age, and level of education.

Similarity in Other Characteristics People's friends and partners also tend to be similar to them in race, ethnicity, age, level of education, and religion (Michael et al., 1994). One reason we choose friends and partners with backgrounds that are similar to our own is that we tend to live among people who are similar to ourselves. Thus, these are the people we are most likely to meet, to know, to date, and possibly to marry (Michael et al., 1994).

Another reason people tend to choose friends and partners with similar backgrounds is that such people often have similar attitudes as well—and people tend to be attracted to others with attitudes similar to their own. In fact, similarity of attitudes is a key contributor to attraction in both friendships and romantic relationships (Cappella & Palmer, 1990; Laumann et al., 1994). Attitudes toward religion and children tend to be the most important factors in people's attraction to potential partners (Singh & Ho, 2000; Watson et al., 2000).

TRUTH **OR** **fiction** ■ R E V I S I T E D ■ *It is not true that when it comes to choosing a partner or friend, "opposites attract."* People are more likely to choose as partners—and also as friends—people who are similar to themselves in many ways.

Reciprocity When we have feelings of attraction or affection for another person, we want that person to return those feelings. **Reciprocity** is the mutual exchange of feelings or attitudes. It applies to situations in which the person we like likes us back. In other words, our feelings are returned, or reciprocated. Like similarity, reciprocity is a powerful contributor to feelings of attraction (Sprecher, 1998).

Reciprocity of feelings is a major factor in forming romantic relationships, but it may also apply to casual encounters. Research shows that people are more open, warm, and helpful when they are talking with strangers who seem to like them (Clark et al., 1989; Curtis & Miller, 1986).

Friendship

Friends are people for whom one has affection, respect, and trust. Most people value friends because of the rewards that friendship offers. For example, friends are concerned about one another and help and support one another when they can. As friendships develop, people may evaluate, consciously or unconsciously, how well the relationship is providing the rewards they seek in the friendship.

The people we choose as friends tend to be people with whom we have frequent contact—a next-door neighbor or a student who sits beside us in class. The people we find attractive and the people who approve of us are the people we are likely to choose as friends. In addition, they are likely to be similar to us in important ways, such as in attitudes, in values, and often in their selection of other friends (Gonzales et al., 1983).

Love

The word *love* is used in everyday life in numerous ways. Love refers to the feelings of attachment that exist between children and their parents. Love also refers to feelings of patriotism for one's country or to feelings of passion about strongly held values such as freedom. Most commonly, however, love refers to the feelings of mutual attraction, affection, and attachment shared by people who are "in love."

To better understand the relationships of people in love, psychologist Robert Sternberg (1988) developed the **triangular model of love**, shown in Figure 20.2. As defined in the figure, Sternberg identifies seven types of love relationships, each of which is characterized by at least one of three components: intimacy, passion, or commitment.

Intimacy refers to closeness and caring. It is reflected by mutual concern and by the sharing of

The Triangular Model of Love

Liking
Intimacy Alone
(true friendships without passion
or long-term commitment)

Intimacy

Romantic Love
Intimacy + Passion
(lovers physically and emotionally attracted to each other but
without commitment, as in a
summer romance)

Companionate Love
Intimacy + Commitment
(long-term committed friendship such as a marriage in
which the passion has faded)

Consummate Love
Intimacy + Passion + Commitment
(a complete love consisting of all three
components—an ideal difficult to attain)

Passion

Commitment

Infatuation
Passion Alone
(passionate, obsessive
love at first sight without
intimacy or commitment)

Fatuous Love
Passion + Commitment
(commitment based on passion
but without time for intimacy to
develop; shallow relationship
such as a whirlwind courtship)

Empty Love
Commitment Alone
(decision to love each
other without intimacy
or passion)

FIGURE 20.2 *Robert Sternberg believes that love rela-
tionships are characterized by at least one of three* *components: intimacy, passion, or commitment.
Consummate love combines all three components.*

feelings and resources. **Passion** refers to feelings of romantic and sexual attraction. In addition to verbal expressions of love, passion is reflected by many types of nonverbal communication, such as gazing, hugging, and kissing. **Commitment** refers to a couple's recognition that they are "in love" and want to be together, "for better or for worse." According to Sternberg (1988), consummate (or complete) love is an ideal that is difficult to attain and that is characterized by all three components.

Most couples start out with feelings of physical attraction that may develop into passion. If they are compatible, their intimacy and passion may grow. Eventually, they may decide to make a commitment to each other. Thus, from dating, to a steady relationship, to marriage, love changes as our relationships endure, deepen, and become a more important part of our lives.

SECTION 5 REVIEW

go.
hrw
.com

**Homework
Practice
Online**

Keyword: SY7 HP20

1. How does physical attractiveness influence one's
choice of friends and partners?

2. Why are most people attracted to people who
are similar to themselves?

3. **Critical Thinking** *Evaluating* If you were
to create a triangular model of friendship similar to the triangular model of love shown in
Figure 20.2, what components of friendship
would you think should make up the three
corners of the triangle?

Writing a Summary

Using standard grammar, spelling, sentence structure, and punctuation, summarize the information in this chapter. Consider:

- how attitudes develop, and how persuasion affects attitudes and behavior
- the causes of prejudice, and factors that influence perceptions of people
- the role of attraction in friendships and romantic relationships

Identifying People and Ideas

Identify the following terms or people and use them in appropriate sentences.

1. attitude
2. cognitive evaluation
3. central route
4. sales resistance
5. scapegoat
6. social perception
7. primacy effect
8. attribution theory
9. fundamental attribution error
10. commitment

Understanding Main Ideas

SECTION 1 (pp. 460–462)
1. Summarize the relationship between attitudes and behavior.
2. What are cognitive anchors?

SECTION 2 (pp. 462–465)
3. Why are two-sided arguments generally more persuasive than one-sided arguments?

SECTION 3 (pp. 465–468)
4. What is the relationship between prejudice and stereotyping?

SECTION 4 (pp. 468–472)
5. What is an example of actor-observer bias?

SECTION 5 (pp. 472–475)
6. What is reciprocity?

Thinking Critically

1. **Making Generalizations and Predictions** What are several ways that advertising slogans might be effective in reinforcing or changing people's attitudes about a product or service?

2. **Analyzing Information** Using a central route and then a peripheral route, give examples of how you might persuade a friend to join you in a walk-a-thon for a good cause.

3. **Drawing Inferences and Conclusions** Why might interpreting events with a self-serving bias boost a person's self-esteem?

4. **Supporting a Point of View** Do you think that the saying "Beauty is in the eye of the beholder" is true? Explain your answer.

Writing About Psychology

1. **Summarizing** Go to the library to learn more about how a cultural group's perspectives can be affected by the group's traditional physical environment. Then create a visual that outlines what you have learned. Be sure to include captions for your visual.

2. **Evaluating** Over the next few days, collect examples of nonverbal communication you observe in other people. For each example, write a brief description of the feelings that were expressed. Also note whether the feelings were consistent with the people's words and whether it was the spoken or the unspoken message that seemed to make a greater impact on the recipient of the message. Share what you have learned from your observations in a brief report. Use the graphic organizer below to help you write your report.

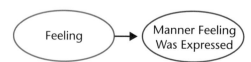

Feeling → Manner Feeling Was Expressed

Interpreting Graphs

Study the bar graph below. Then use the information in the graph to help you answer the questions that follow.

Personality Stereotypes

Judged Probability vs Personality Traits (Independence, Competitiveness, Emotionality) — Men, Women

Source: Deaux et al., *Social Cognition*, 1985

1. Which of the following best reflects the information in the graph?

   a. People tend to believe that men are more emotional than women.

   b. People tend to believe that men are more likely to be competitive than women.

   c. People tend to believe that women are more likely to be independent than men.

   d. People tend to believe that women are more likely to be competitive than men.

2. How might a psychologist use this information when studying how people perceive other people?

Analyzing Primary Sources

Read the following excerpt, which discusses how children's interaction with other people affects how often the children smile. Then answer the questions that follow.

"Experience will do more than direct the smile; it will also determine its frequency. Experiments have shown that infants who receive no social stimulation after smiling, such as an adult's approving gaze, will begin smiling less often, somewhat in the manner of rats that stop their bar-pressing after the rewards cease. And infants raised in environments with inadequate social stimulation, such as foundling homes, will smile much less at 8 months or a year than will infants raised in middle-class homes. Nonetheless, the appearance of a reliable social smile by about 3 months of age is affected very little by learning. Maturation initiates, after which experience can differentiate."

3. What does the author mean by "maturation initiates, after which experience can differentiate"?

   a. A child's experiences have little effect on whether he or she smiles often.

   b. Whether a child smiles often is dictated by heredity.

   c. Most children learn a social smile as infants, but how often they smile later in life is affected by their experiences.

   d. Little is known about why some children smile more often than others.

4. What does the quote suggest about how experience might affect the way a person interacts with others?

PSYCHOLOGY PROJECTS

Cooperative Learning

Research in Psychology With a partner, watch several television commercials for a variety of products. Discuss the ways in which the advertisers try to sell their products. Do they take a central or a peripheral route? Whom do they use for a messenger? What, if anything, makes the messenger persuasive? With your partner, decide which two ads you think are likely to be the most effective for their intended audience. Describe the ads to the rest of the class and explain why you think they are effective.

internet connect

Internet Activity: go.hrw.com
KEYWORD: SY7 CH20

Choose an activity on social cognition to:

- create an annotated display on attitudes and behavior.
- design an advertisement employing methods of persuasion.
- create a theoretical profile analyzing prejudice and bias.

Chapter 21

21

SOCIAL INTERACTION

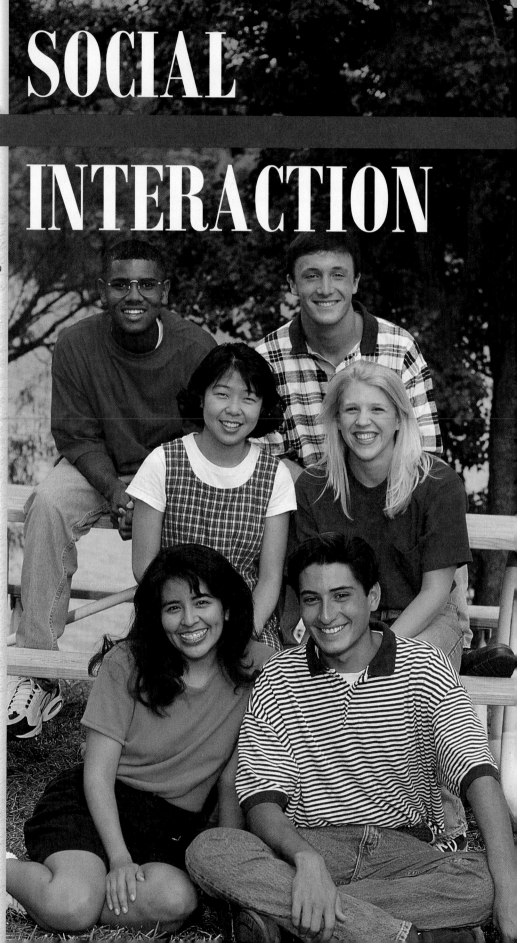

Read to Discover

1 How can membership in a group influence individual behavior?

2 What factors lead people to conform to social norms?

3 Why do most people tend to obey authority figures?

4 What are the various views on the causes of aggressive behavior?

5 What is altruism, and what are the factors that promote and the factors that inhibit altruistic behavior?

A DAY IN THE LIFE

"I can't believe we are graduating in four days," Janet said excitedly.

Janet and Linda were still setting up the picnic table when Marc, Hannah, Todd, and Dan arrived. They had decided to meet for a picnic lunch, and all they were able to talk about was memories of high school and the fact that it was almost over.

"Todd, remember when we first met?" Linda asked. "We were in introductory biology together. You really helped me a lot in that class—not to mention the fact that you always kept me laughing."

"I remember," Todd said. "I had just moved here, and you introduced me to your friends."

"I'd forgotten all about that," Dan replied. "Marc and I were at Janet's track meet that day."

"Hey, I made it to district finals that day," Janet reminded them.

"Of course you did," Hannah chimed in. "The track meet was at home, and all your friends were cheering you on."

They all sat quietly for a while, eating their lunches and thinking about their futures, their pasts, and their friends. Suddenly, Todd started laughing. "Do you remember the time we went to the amusement park, and we all decided to take the shortcut back to the gate? We ended up missing our bus home."

"Wait a minute, Todd!" Hannah exclaimed. "If I remember correctly, you were the one who insisted on that 'shortcut.' We just went along with you."

"Hey, it seemed like a good idea. Besides, it's not my fault that you all listened to me," Todd joked.

"Listening to you isn't always a bad idea," Dan said. "If it weren't for you, I would have fought that guy at the basketball game. Remember that? He bumped into me by accident, but I thought he shoved me on purpose. You were the only person who could calm me down."

"Who knows what any of us would be doing if we didn't have each other," Hannah added. "I'm excited about college, but I'm going to miss seeing all of you every day."

Key Terms

- social facilitation
- evaluation apprehension
- social loafing
- diffusion of responsibility
- risky shift
- social decision schemes
- majority-wins scheme
- truth-wins scheme
- two-thirds-majority scheme
- first-shift scheme
- group polarization
- authoritarian leaders
- democratic leaders
- laissez-faire leaders
- conform
- social norms
- explicit norms
- implicit norms
- foot-in-the-door effect
- catharsis
- altruism
- bystander effect

Todd often influenced his friends—to take a shortcut and to avoid a fight, for example—because they respected his opinions. Having an audience helped Janet run faster and play better. These are just two examples of social influence, or the way other people affect what we say and do. Other people can also influence us by giving us orders or pressuring us to adapt to their standards of behavior.

People behave differently when they are around other people than they do when they are by themselves. How people behave toward others depends on many factors. Sometimes people behave aggressively toward others; sometimes they help others. In this chapter, you will learn more about all of these aspects of social interaction.

HOLT

Psychology Video Program

Watch the video to explore social interaction and control in cults.

Read the following statements about psychology. Do you think they are true or false? You will learn whether each statement is true or false as you read the chapter.

- People tend to take greater risks as part of a group than they would if they were acting alone.
- When there is no right or wrong choice, people often go along with the majority.
- Most people try to act as individuals and not simply "go along with the crowd."
- People seldom obey orders to do things that conflict with their own attitudes.
- It is human nature to be aggressive.
- People are more likely to help someone in trouble when no one else is present to help.

SECTION 1

Group Behavior

Competing on their home court with fans cheering them on usually motivates players to play harder. *What concept of social psychology does this illustrate?*

How people behave as part of a group often differs from how they behave as individuals. People may try harder, take greater risks, or make different decisions when they are with others than they would if they were alone. The ways in which groups affect individual behavior are discussed in this section.

Social Facilitation

Social facilitation refers to the concept that people often perform better when other people are watching than they do when they are alone. In other words, the presence of other people seems to facilitate and encourage one's performance. Hannah, for example, was not at all surprised that Janet had done so well at the track meet. She had witnessed before that Janet competed harder when her friends cheered her on.

Social facilitation is not limited to people. Psychologist Robert Zajonc (1980) found that dogs and cats—and even cockroaches—do things faster when they are in a group than when they are alone. These suggest that social facilitation may be a basic animal response. Zajonc believes that animals, including humans, respond in this way because the presence of others increases their level of excitement.

Evaluation apprehension, or the concern about the opinion of others, is another reason that the presence of other people may improve an individual's performance (Mullen et al., 1997; Sanna & Shotland, 1990). Evaluation apprehension may motivate people to try harder so that others will think more highly of them.

Social Loafing

Being a member of a group does not always improve one's performance. When people are working together toward a common goal rather than working on individual tasks, they may "slack off" and not try as hard. This behavior is referred to as **social loafing**. Social loafing is especially likely to occur when people see that other members of the group are not pulling their share of the load.

Social loafing may occur because of **diffusion of responsibility**—the tendency for people to feel less responsible for accomplishing a task when the effort is shared among members of a group. As part of a group, individuals are likely to feel less accountable for their actions. Therefore, they are less likely to worry about what others think of them because they have less evaluation apprehension. They may even feel that their contribution to the group's effort is not very important (Shepperd, 1993). When Todd said, "it's not my fault that you all listened to me [about the shortcut]," he was diffusing, or spreading out, his own responsibility for an unwise decision to the other members of the group.

Risky Shift

A related social phenomenon is the **risky shift**—the tendency for people to take greater risks when they are part of a group than they would as individuals acting on their own. People may feel more powerful (or less vulnerable) as part of a group. This is because the responsibilty for a particular situation or action is shared with the other group members (Kamalanabhan et al., 2000; Myers, 1996; Smith and Mackie, 1995). The risky shift may help explain such events as prison riots and mob attacks.

It is true that people tend to take greater risks as part of a group than they would if they were acting alone. This is because individuals can share responsibility for a decision.

Group Decision Making

Many important decisions are made by groups rather than by individuals. Committees, for example, are often appointed to study and make decisions about specific issues. Juries decide on the guilt or innocence of people accused of crimes. Similarly, a group of friends may make a joint decision about which movie to see. These are examples of group decision making.

Because many decisions are made by groups, psychologists have studied how being part of a group affects the decision-making process. They have identified a number of **social decision schemes**, or rules that govern group decision making (Gigone & Hastie, 1997; Stasser, 1999). These include the majority-wins scheme, the truth-wins scheme, the two-thirds-majority scheme, and the first-shift scheme.

Majority-Wins Scheme   In the **majority-wins scheme**, the group agrees to a decision that was initially supported by a majority of group members. For example, a group of five friends might be trying to decide what to do on the weekend—say, whether to go to a movie or to a video arcade. At first, three of the five friends might opt for the movie and the other two friends for the arcade. However, after discussing the two choices, all five friends might agree to go to the movie, the option that was initially supported by the majority.

The majority-wins scheme applies most often to situations in which there are no right or wrong choices. In the example just given, both the movie and the arcade were acceptable options—neither one was right or wrong. Rather, the preference of the majority guided the decisions of the others.

It is true that when there is no right or wrong choice, people often go along with the majority. This is called the majority-wins scheme of group decision making.

Truth-Wins Scheme   Often, the members of a group come to realize that one option is better than others after they learn more about the different choices available. This is referred to as the **truth-wins scheme**. Suppose that in the example just given, the five friends learn that the movie they hoped to see has been canceled and that another movie is being shown, one that interests them less. After gathering and sharing the information, the group might decide to go to the arcade instead, a decision that is based on a clearly better choice between their two options.

Two-Thirds–Majority Scheme   Some groups concur with a decision after two thirds of their members come to an agreement about the correct choice. This is called the **two-thirds-majority scheme**. It often applies to decisions made by juries. When two thirds of a jury initially vote for conviction, the remaining third may go along with the decision of the others.

First-Shift Scheme   The **first-shift scheme** applies to groups that are deadlocked, or split fifty-fifty, about a decision. If just one person changes his or her mind, or shifts from one side to the other, others may follow and shift to the opposite side as well. For example, a jury might be deadlocked, with half believing the defendant is guilty and half believing the defendant is innocent. Those jurors who initially thought the defendant was guilty might follow the lead of the first juror who changes his or her vote from guilty to not guilty, even in the absence of additional information about the case.

Polarization

Members of a group usually share similar attitudes. Indeed, shared attitudes are often what attracts people to particular groups in the first place. For example, teens who are concerned about cruelty to animals might join an organization that has the goal of ending laboratory experimentation on animal subjects. Teens who are not as concerned about animal rights, on the other hand, are unlikely to join such a group.

The shared attitudes that group members hold are likely to grow stronger over time. This strengthening of a group's shared attitudes is called **group polarization**. It occurs as group members discuss and act upon the attitudes they share.

Polarization can be positive or negative. If group members are prejudiced against people of other races or religions, for example, then polarization is likely to increase their prejudice. If, on the other hand, group members are tolerant of people who are different, then polarization may make them even more so (Myers & Bishop, 1970; Zuber et al., 1992). Such polarization in group attitudes is illustrated in Figure 21.1.

Group Leadership

All groups, regardless of their nature, have leaders who serve several important functions in their groups. Leaders help group members identify the group's goals and establish and implement plans for reaching them. Leaders may also offer emotional support to group members.

Some leaders are appointed by outsiders; others are chosen by a vote of group members. The president of an organization might be elected by a vote of group members, for example. The president, in turn, might appoint a member of the group to head a committee to study a particular issue or complete a particular task.

Organizations such as businesses, schools, and the military usually have clear chains of command, or leadership. Group members know to whom they report and whose directions to follow.

FIGURE 21.1 *A group's shared attitudes tend to grow stronger with discussion. In one study involving high school students, a discussion of racial issues increased prejudice in the high-prejudice group and decreased it in the low-prejudice group.*

Source: "Discussion Effects on Racial Attitudes" (1970) by D. G. Myers and G. D. Bishop, *Science, 169,* 778–779.

CASE STUDIES

AND OTHER TRUE STORIES

Dr. Martin Luther King Jr. and Nonviolent Action

People are usually influenced by the views of the majority. In some cases, however, the opinion of a single individual has influenced the behavior of the majority, and that minority influence has changed the course of history.

Researchers have investigated factors that enable a minority to influence the majority. They have found that the most influential individuals are those who hold steadfastly to their views and never waver, in words or actions, from what they believe. One of the best examples of such unyielding commitment is provided by Reverend Martin Luther King Jr. His belief in nonviolent action shaped the course of the civil rights movement throughout the 1960s and beyond.

King believed that the only way African Americans could achieve racial equality in the United States was through nonviolent action. Even as a boy, King reacted to racial insults and violence with nonviolence. When a school bully attacked him, he did not fight back. When a white woman in a store slapped him, he said nothing (Osborne, 1968).

King's extraordinary leadership qualities and his strong belief in nonviolent action changed the course of the civil rights movement. In 1955, inspired by Rosa Parks, King led a boycott of Montgomery, Alabama, city buses that eventually resulted in an integrated bus system there and in nearly every other city in the South as well.

King continued to lead nonviolent protests against racial inequality in the United States. He led lunch-counter sit-ins to desegregate eating facilities and organized prayer vigils to focus the nation's attention on the need to desegregate public parks and rest rooms. But he is probably best known for the 1963 March on Washington.

Dr. Martin Luther King Jr. (left)

During this historic event, more than 200,000 people gathered at the Lincoln Memorial in Washington, D.C., to hear King deliver his famous speech, "I Have a Dream."

At these and other events King remained steadfast in his belief in nonviolence. Despite repeated arrests and physical violence against himself and his family, King never wavered in his belief that nonviolence was the best way to solve racial inequality.

King was feared and attacked by some white people because his methods were so effective. He was also criticized by African Americans who saw nonviolence as weakness. When one civil rights activist was shot soon after the start of a freedom march, some members of the movement questioned the wisdom of King's nonviolent approach. King, however, patiently urged his followers to remain true to the nonviolence movement. He was persuasive, and the march continued peacefully.

King's influence on the civil rights movement was profound. Nonviolence continually proved to be the most effective means of change. In 1964 Martin Luther King Jr. received the Nobel Peace Prize for his struggle to achieve racial equality through peaceful means. By 1965, because of his influence, civil rights organizations across the country had adopted nonviolent action as their primary method of addressing racial inequality.

THINKING CRITICALLY

1. **Summarizing** What types of nonviolent protests did King and others use to oppose segregation and racial inequality?
2. **Drawing Inferences and Conclusions** Why do you think nonviolent action is so effective in bringing about change?

Informal groups, such as groups of friends, may not have official leaders. However, some members are likely to have more influence over the group than others. This was true of Todd and his circle of friends. Todd tended to be the leader of the group and to influence the others because of his intelligence and leadership abilities. He influenced his friends to take a shortcut at the amusement park, for example, and he persuaded Dan not to fight.

Like Todd, group leaders often have certain personality traits and social skills that enable them to influence the decisions and behavior of others. For example, leaders tend to be more self-confident, outgoing, and intelligent than other group members (Smith & Mackie, 1995). Despite these similarities, leaders may differ in how they operate. In other words, they may have different styles of leadership. Leaders may be authoritarian, democratic, or laissez-faire.

Authoritarian Leaders   **Authoritarian leaders** exert absolute control over all decisions for the group. They tell other group members what to do and demand that group members obey their orders. Military leaders, for example, are usually authoritarian. They give orders to those of lesser rank and expect their orders to be carried out immediately and without question.

Democratic Leaders   Although military leaders tend to be authoritarian toward those below them in the chain of command, they are more democratic when they are planning strategies with other officers. **Democratic leaders** encourage group members to express and discuss their ideas and to make their own decisions. Such leaders may try to build a consensus—that is, to encourage unanimous agreement on a decision. Alternatively, they may request that group members take a vote and follow the decision of the majority.

Laissez-Faire Leaders   The term *laissez-faire* is French for "to let (people) do (as they choose)." Like democratic leaders, **laissez-faire leaders** encourage group members to express and explore their own ideas. However, laissez-faire leaders tend to take a less active role in the decision-making process. They tend to stand back from the group and allow group members to move in whatever direction they wish, even if the group seems to be making false starts or poor choices.

Comparing Leadership Styles   No one style of leadership is best for every group or situation. In times of crisis, authoritarian leaders may be more effective because they can make decisions quickly and know that those decisions will be carried out promptly. This is one reason nations often prefer authoritarian leaders when they are having serious problems.

In other situations, democratic or laissez-faire leaders may be more effective. Their styles of leadership allow group members to express themselves and grow as individuals. Such leadership may be important when the group is searching for new ways to solve a problem or when trying to help group members meet challenges in their lives.

<table>
<tr><td>**SECTION 1 REVIEW**</td><td> **Homework Practice Online**
Keyword: SY7 HP21</td></tr>
</table>

1. Explain the difference between social facilitation and social loafing.

2. List four social decision schemes.

3. **Critical Thinking**   *Drawing Inferences and Conclusions*   Give an example of a group or situation that might benefit from a laissez-faire style of leadership. Explain your choice.

Conformity

The least direct social influence on behavior is the pressure to **conform**, or to modify one's attitudes and behavior to make them consistent with those of other people. People who conform bring their behavior in line with that of a group. The group may be a formal organization, such as a school club, or a loose collection of people, such as several friends who always hang out together. Linda, Marc, Todd, and the others in their circle of friends are an example of such a group.

Importance of Groups

Being accepted by a group can be important because groups help people satisfy many needs. Groups can fulfill an individual's needs for belonging, affection, and attention. Meeting such needs is one reason why many teens join clubs at school, sports teams, academic clubs, and other social organizations.

Social norms vary from one group to another. People of different ages and occupations tend to have different standards of dress, for example. **How might this be an example of both explicit and implicit norms?**

Groups are also important because they offer support to individuals when they are facing difficult problems. People who are grieving the loss of a loved one, for example, may benefit by joining a support group. (See Chapter 19.) Groups may also help people accomplish things they could not accomplish on their own. For instance, workers may join together to form a labor union in order to fight for better working conditions or higher wages.

Social Norms

Belonging to a group usually means following, or conforming to, the group's social norms. **Social norms** are the standards of behavior that people share. They serve as guidelines for what people should and should not do or say in a given situation. For example, social norms tell people what to eat, what to wear, and when and where to make a joke.

Social norms can be explicit or implicit. **Explicit norms** are spoken or written rules. Examples include traffic rules and school dress codes. **Implicit norms** are unspoken, unwritten rules. Examples include modes of dress or ways of greeting that are unique to a particular group. Although implicit norms are unstated, they nonetheless guide people's words and actions.

Social norms can be useful or harmful. They are useful if they help promote the safety and well-being of individuals or groups. Bathing regularly and not talking in a theater during a movie are examples of useful social norms. Social norms are harmful when they promote risky behavior. Smoking cigarettes—a norm in some groups—is an example of harmful social norms.

Asch's Studies of Conformity

To what extent will people conform to social norms? Psychologist Solomon Asch (1955) addressed this question in a series of well-known experiments. Asch wanted to determine whether people would go along with group opinion even when the group opinion differed from their own.

Procedure   Asch asked participants in the study to look at three lines of varying length and to compare them with a standard line, as shown in Figure 21.2 on page 486. The participants were asked to indicate which of the three lines was the same length as the standard line. Each participant was tested in a group of several other people. However, the other group members were really Asch's associates, who were simply posing as study participants.

For the first few comparisons, all of Asch's associates gave the correct answer. However, for many of the remaining comparisons, all of the associates gave the same *wrong* answer. For example, they might have said that line 1 was the same length as the standard line.

Results   When Asch's associates gave an answer that was obviously wrong, many study participants conformed to the group opinion and gave the same wrong answer. About three fourths of study participants went along with group opinion at least once, one third went along with the group at least half the time, and one fourth went along with the group virtually all the time. Study participants who conformed to group opinion later admitted that they knew the answers they gave were incorrect, but they went along with the group so as not to appear different from the others.

TRUTH
OR
fiction
■ REVISITED ■

It is not true that most people try to act as individuals and not just "go along with the crowd." Asch's studies of conformity revealed that most people conform to those around them so as not to appear different.

Why Do People Conform?

"Going along with the crowd" is probably at least as common in everyday life as it was in Asch's experiments. Most people avoid talking, acting, or dressing differently from other members of the groups to which they belong. Why is conformity so common? Several factors may contribute to the tendency to

Asch's Conformity Experiment

| 1 | 2 | 3 |

Standard line   **Comparison lines**

FIGURE 21.2 *In this example from Asch's studies, line 2 is clearly the same length as the standard line.*

conform to social norms (Bond & Smith, 1996; Myers, 1996; Smith & Mackie, 1995).

Cultural Influences Some cultures are collectivistic, which means that they place greater emphasis on the group than on its individual members. In many Asian cultures, for example, the person is seen primarily as part of the family and society rather than as an individual. (See Chapter 14.) In such cultures, individuals show a greater tendency to conform to the group, and they may feel extremely uncomfortable if they are singled out as different from the others in the group.

Need for Acceptance Some people conform to social norms in order to be liked and accepted by others. This need to conform stems from the belief that people who dress, talk, or act differently from other people stand out from the crowd and thus draw negative attention to themselves. In actuality, however, this is not always true.

People who depend the most on the acceptance and approval of others tend to be those with low self-esteem and high social anxiety (Singh & Sharma, 1989). They may value being liked more than they value being right. They may also be very self-conscious about standing out from others, fearing that others will ridicule or reject them if they appear different.

Other Factors Several other factors contribute to the tendency to conform to social norms. For example, the chances of conforming to a group's norms increase as the group grows in size—at least up to about eight members. Further increases in size (past eight members) seem to have little effect on the tendency to conform.

Individuals are more likely to conform to the group when all other members of the group are unanimous in their words and actions. However, if even one person disagrees with the rest of the group, others in the group also are less likely to conform.

SECTION 2 REVIEW

go.
hrw
.com

Homework Practice Online

Keyword: SY7 HP21

1. What is the difference between explicit norms and implicit norms?

2. What factors influence people to conform to social norms?

3. **Critical Thinking** *Summarizing* How did Asch show that people tend to conform to the opinions of others?

SECTION 3
Obedience

One of the most obvious and direct social influences on people's attitudes and behavior is the power of people in positions of authority. Parents often order their children to clean their own rooms or do their homework. Judges often order law-breakers to pay fines or perform community service. Most children obey their parents, teachers, and other adults. Most adults obey police officers, judges, and other authority figures. Such obedience is necessary to protect the safety and well-being of the community and its people.

Throughout history, however, many people have also obeyed orders to commit immoral acts, such as killing innocent people. In the 1900s alone, Turks killed Armenians, Nazis killed Jews in Europe, and Serbs killed Muslims in Bosnia. In each case, those who did the killing justified their acts by saying they were "just following orders."

Milgram's Studies of Obedience

Are people who commit immoral acts unusual or abnormal? Or would most people be obedient in a similar situation? Yale University psychologist Stanley Milgram, whose own parents were killed by the Nazis during World War II, investigated this question in a series of studies conducted in the 1960s and 1970s. The purpose of Milgram's research was to determine whether the average person would obey the commands of authority figures.

Procedure In the first phase of his research, Milgram (1963) placed advertisements in local newspapers, seeking male volunteers to participate in a study of learning. In response, 40 men, ranging in age from 20 to 50, volunteered for the study. The volunteers represented a wide range of educational levels—from people who had not completed elementary school to others who had earned graduate degrees. Study participants also represented a variety of occupations, including teachers, engineers, laborers, and salespeople.

Instead of revealing the true nature of the study, Milgram told participants that its purpose was to investigate the effects that punishment has on memory. Some participants, Milgram explained, would be "teachers," and others would be "learners." In reality, all the volunteers who answered the advertisement

Scenes such as this one may come to mind when we hear the phrase "obedience to authority," but obedience characterizes many of our interactions in daily life. **Can you think of other examples of obedience?**

were assigned to the teacher group, whereas those in the learner group were Milgram's associates.

Study participants were told that learners were expected to learn word pairs that would be read to them from a list. After the learners had heard the entire list, the teachers read the words one at a time. Each learner was then asked to provide the word that was paired with the word read by the teacher. If a learner made the correct choice, nothing happened, and teacher and learner went on to the next test item. However, if a learner made an incorrect choice, the teacher was to deliver an electric shock. With each mistake a learner made, the teacher was to increase the amount of voltage.

As shown in the middle photograph in the series on page 488, learners were strapped into chairs and electrodes were attached to their wrists. The teachers sat at a console in an adjacent room. On the console were levers labeled with the voltage they controlled (from 15 to 450 volts) and the seriousness of the shocks they delivered (from slight to severe). Although the teachers were led to believe that the learners received shocks for each incorrect answer, the equipment did not really deliver shocks, and the learners were never hurt or put at risk in any way.

Teachers were first given a sample shock of 45 volts so that they would have some idea of what learners supposedly would be experiencing. A shock of 45 volts is not harmful, but it was unpleasant enough to convince teachers that high-voltage shocks would be painful, even dangerous. Teachers

SOCIAL INTERACTION **487**

The machine and the procedure used in Stanley Milgram's classic study on obedience are pictured here. The bottom photograph in the series shows one of the few participants who refused to continue with the experiment.

Source: © 1965 by Stanley Milgram. From the film *Obedience*. Distributed by New York University Film Division and the Pennsylvania State University, PCR.

were told that they could quit at any time. However, if they hesitated to deliver a shock or to go on with the experiment, they were urged by repeated commands from the researcher to continue. The researcher also offered reassurances that the shocks, although painful, would cause no permanent damage.

Results As learners made errors, teachers delivered greater and greater voltage in each shock. At 300 volts, learners pounded on the other side of the wall, even screamed in make-believe pain. Yet 35 of the 40 participants continued with the experiment. Nine participants refused to continue somewhere between the 300-volt and the 450-volt level. However, the rest, almost two thirds of the participants, obeyed instructions to give shocks throughout the entire range of voltage, up to 450 volts, even though these participants later said that they had been afraid of harming the people receiving the shocks (Milgram, 1971).

Were the people who volunteered for Milgram's study abnormally insensitive, even cruel? Apparently not. They showed signs of great distress as the shocks they delivered increased in voltage. They sweated, bit their lips, trembled, stuttered, groaned, and dug their fingernails into their palms. Some even had fits of nervous laughter. Many also told the researcher that they wanted to stop. Nonetheless, most continued to deliver shocks of increasing voltage to the learners in the study.

Milgram repeated the experiment with other participants, including women and college students, and in other settings, including a storefront on a city street. In each phase of the research, at least half the participants obeyed the researcher and administered the entire series of electric shocks.

TRUTH
OR
fiction
■ REVISITED ■

It is not true that people seldom obey orders to do things that conflict with their own attitudes. Milgram's studies of obedience showed that the majority of people will obey such orders, even though doing so may cause them great emotional distress.

Why Do People Obey?

Why did the participants in Milgram's studies obey the researcher? What causes people, in general, to obey? Several causes have been identified.

Socialization One reason people tend to be obedient is that they have been socialized from childhood to obey authority figures, such as parents, teachers, and police officers. Study participants saw the researchers in Milgram's studies as authority figures, so they obeyed orders to give shocks to the learners. To do otherwise would have conflicted with deeply held attitudes about correct behavior (Blass, 1991).

Foot-in-the-Door Effect Another reason people tend to be obedient to authority figures is the **foot-in-the-door effect**. This behavior is the tendency for people to give in to major demands once they have given in to minor ones (Burger, 1999). The foot-in-the-door effect is an example of how people may gradually change their attitudes to justify their behavior. (See Chapter 20.)

After participants in Milgram's studies had delivered small shocks to learners, it was easier for them to deliver increasingly larger shocks. In a similar way, soldiers become accustomed to obeying commands concerning relatively unimportant matters, such as how to dress, when and where to eat, and how to perform routine drills. Later on, they are more likely to obey commands relating to much more important matters that may involve risking their lives or taking the lives of other people.

Confusion About Attitudes People who are aware of their attitudes are more likely to behave in accordance with those attitudes (Fazio, 1990; Krosnick, 1989). As people become disturbed by what is happening around them—by the learners' screams and wall pounding in Milgram's studies, for example—they are likely to become less aware of, or at least more confused about, their own beliefs. Thus, they may be more likely to behave in ways that are in conflict with their attitudes.

Buffers When people are buffered, or protected, from observing the consequences of their actions, they are more likely to follow orders, even immoral ones. In the first phase of Milgram's research, for example, teachers and learners were placed in sep-

Obedience—even to immoral commands, as in Milgram's studies—may be an offshoot of the socially desirable respect for authority figures that most people learn in childhood.

arate rooms. Thus, the teachers could not see how their actions were affecting others. In later phases of the research, teachers and learners were placed in the same room so that the teachers could see the pain they were inflicting on the learners. Without the buffer of a wall to separate them from the people they thought they were hurting, compliance with the researcher's demands dropped from 65 percent to about 40 percent (Miller, 1986).

Today many soldiers are similarly buffered from their enemies. Their only contact with opposing forces may be a blip on a radar screen. Attacking their enemies may involve little more than pressing a button that launches a missile. The results of Milgram's studies suggest that obeying orders to kill enemies in this way may be easier than obeying orders to kill other human beings at close range.

SECTION 3 REVIEW

Homework Practice Online
Keyword: SY7 HP21

1. What did Milgram's studies reveal about obedience to authority?

2. Identify some of the reasons that explain why people tend to obey the orders of those in authority.

3. **Critical Thinking** *Analyzing Information* Give examples of situations in which obedience to authority is considered socially acceptable.

Aggression

Aggression refers to words or actions that are meant to hurt other people. It is a serious and widespread social problem. For example, murder is the second-leading cause of death in the United States among young people between the ages of 15 and 24 (Centers for Disease Control, 2000), and more than a million children each year are victims of abuse. Children not only suffer from the results of aggression; they seem to be fascinated by it. For example, children are drawn to video games in which they can manipulate figures to kill or torture others.

Why are people aggressive? Several reasons have been suggested. They include biological, psychoanalytic, cognitive, learning, and sociocultural views.

Biological View

The brain and hormones appear to be involved in aggression. In response to certain stimuli, many lower animals react with instinctive aggression. For example, the male robin responds aggressively to the red breast of another robin. A brain structure (the hypothalamus) appears to be involved in

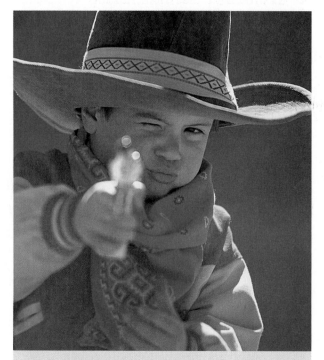

Children's games often involve make-believe aggression.

this instinctive reaction: Electrical stimulation of part of the hypothalamus triggers aggressive behavior in many kinds of animals. However, humans have more complex brains, and other parts of the brain apparently dampen possible aggressive instincts.

The male sex hormone testosterone is also involved in aggression. Testosterone appears to be connected with the tendencies to try to dominate and control other people. Men have higher testosterone levels than women do and are also usually more aggressive than women, particularly in contacts with male strangers (Pope et al., 2000). Studies show, for example, that aggressive 9- to 11-year-old boys are likely to have higher testosterone levels than less aggressive age-mates (Chance et al., 2000). Also, members of "wild" college fraternities have higher testosterone levels, on average, than members of "well-behaved" fraternities (Dabbs et al., 1996). Testosterone levels also vary with the occasion: men's testosterone levels tend to be higher when they are winning—whether at football or chess (Bernhardt et al., 1998).

Throughout the animal kingdom, more aggressive individuals are more likely to survive and transmit their genes to future generations. Aggression may be "natural" in people as in other species, but intelligence is also a key to survival in the case of humans. The capacity to outwit other species may be more important to human survival than aggressiveness. Now that people have organized themselves into societies in which many acts of aggression is outlawed or confined to sports, intelligence and organizational skills may be more important than aggressiveness to human survival.

TRUTH OR fiction ■ REVISITED ■ *It is not true that it is human nature to be aggressive.* While aggression may be a part of the biological makeup of our species, it is unlikely that all aggressive behavior is caused by genetic or biological factors.

Psychoanalytic View

Sigmund Freud believed that aggressive urges are unavoidable reactions to the frustrations of daily life. According to this view, it is normal for people to have urges to hurt other people who do not meet their wishes or demands. Such urges tend to be repressed, however, because people fear hurting others (especially their parents) and, in turn, being rejected by them.

Freud also believed that repressed aggressive urges are likely to find other outlets. The urges might be expressed indirectly—for example, by the aggressive individual destroying other people's possessions or disobeying their orders. Alternatively, the urges might be expressed directly but toward strangers later in life.

Freud believed that the best way to reduce the tension caused by repressed aggressive urges and to prevent harmful aggression toward other people is to allow, or even encourage, less harmful expressions of aggression. For example, verbal aggression in the form of sarcasm or the expression of angry feelings might vent some of the aggressive feelings in the unconscious without causing bodily harm to other people. So might cheering on one's team or watching aggressive sports such as boxing or wrestling. Psychologists refer to such venting of aggressive impulses as **catharsis**.

Does catharsis really act as a safety valve, reducing feelings of tension and lowering the chances of harmful aggression toward others? Some studies have found that catharsis does seem to play this role (Doob & Wood, 1972). Other studies, however, have found that "letting off steam," either verbally or by watching aggressive sports, seems to encourage people to be more, not less, aggressive (Bushman et al., 1999). Thus, it is unclear whether catharsis increases or decreases aggressive behavior.

Cognitive View

Cognitive psychologists believe that people's behavior, including aggressive behavior, is not influenced by inherited tendencies or repressed urges. Instead, they maintain that aggressive behavior is influenced by people's values, the ways in which they perceive events, and the choices they make. According to this view, people choose to act aggressively because they believe that aggression is justified and necessary—either in general or in particular situations (Feshbach, 1994).

Some cognitive psychologists have suggested that frustration and suffering trigger feelings of anger and that these feelings in turn cause people to act aggressively (Rule et al., 1987). However, they also argue that people do not act aggressively automatically and without thought. Rather, people decide whether they will act aggressively on the basis of such factors as their previous experiences

These sports fans are obviously excited by the soccer match they are watching. **Is watching the aggressive play of a sports team a harmless way to vent aggressive urges, or does it encourage aggression?**

with aggression and their interpretation of other people's behavior (Berkowitz, 1994).

How people interpret the behavior of others may be especially important in this regard. Some people tend to interpret other people's behavior as intentionally insulting or cruel, even when it is not (Akhtar & Bradley, 1991; Crick & Dodge, 1994; Dodge et al., 1990). This interpretation may stir up feelings of anger that in turn lead to aggression (Lochman, 1992; Lochman & Dodge, 1994). That is what happened to Dan. When someone accidentally bumped into him at a basketball game, he thought he had been shoved on purpose. It made him so angry that he almost started a fight.

Learning Views

Learning theorists believe that people learn to repeat behaviors that are reinforced. Thus, when aggressive behavior is reinforced, people learn to behave aggressively.

One reason that aggression may be reinforced is that it helps people to get their own way. For example, teens who bully other people may be able to control others with force or threats of force. Although other people may stay out of their way, bullies are also likely to be rejected as friends by most of their peers. Thus, it is questionable whether such behavior is really reinforced.

However, there is little question that other types of aggressive behavior are reinforced. In many sports, aggression helps players win games. Winning, in turn, gains them the admiration of fans and often, at least in professional sports, large paychecks.

Learning theorists also believe that people learn many behaviors by observing others. People observe aggressive behavior on television, in the movies, and in video games (Anderson & Dill, 2000; Huesmann & Miller, 1994; Yohota & Thompson, 2000). Many people also observe aggressive behavior in their own homes and neighborhoods. Thus, most people have ample opportunity to observe aggression and learn from their observations.

The role that television violence plays in teaching children aggressive behavior has received a considerable amount of attention. This is because most children spend a great deal of time watching television—more time, in fact, than they spend in school. Evidence suggests that by the time the average child reaches middle school, he or she has viewed more than 8,000 murders and 100,000 other acts of violence on television (Huston et al., 1992).

Most experts agree that watching violence on television leads people to act more aggressively (Holland, 2000). Figure 21.3 shows some of the data that support this conclusion. It shows how the seriousness of criminal acts committed by age 30 corresponds to the amount of television watched before age 8.

Watching violence on television may influence people to become more aggressive because television may reinforce an individual's ideas about violence and thus lessen his or her inhibitions against aggression. Children may also learn to imitate the acts of violence they see on television.

Sociocultural View

Sociocultural theorists argue that some cultures encourage independence and competitiveness and that this, in turn, promotes aggression. The United

Television Viewing and Aggression

Seriousness of criminal acts by age 30

males

females

Low Medium High   Low Medium High

Frequency of television viewing

* The seriousness of crimes refers to a score assigned to each crime by the New York State Criminal Justice Division in which each type of offense is assigned a specific score (Rossi et al., 1974).

FIGURE 21.3 *This graph illustrates the results of a study that measured the seriousness of criminal acts by age 30 as a function of the frequency of television viewing at age 8.*

Huesmann, L. R., Eron, L. D., Dubow, E. F., & Seebauer, E. (1988). Television Viewing Habits in Childhood and Adult Aggression. *Child Development.*

States is a good example. Most Americans place a high value on individual rights and freedoms. They also emphasize competition. When so much importance is attached to the individual, getting along with others becomes less important. When one person is strongly encouraged to win over others, hostility and aggression may result.

Other cultures place greater value on the welfare of the group and encourage people to cooperate. This may reduce levels of aggression. Children in cultures such as Thailand and Jamaica, for example, where courtesy, respect, and cooperation are encouraged, tend to be less aggressive than children in the United States (Tharp, 1991).

SECTION 4 REVIEW

go.hrw.com
Homework Practice Online
Keyword: SY7 HP21

1. What is the biological view of aggressive behavior?

2. According to learning theorists, how do children learn aggressive behavior?

3. **Critical Thinking** *Evaluating* Why is it important to understand the causes of aggression?

PSYCHOLOGY

CONFORMITY AND INDIVIDUAL CHOICE

How far will an individual deviate from his or her own beliefs to conform to the beliefs and actions of the majority? Could the power of social conformity influence an average man to commit murder? In the most extreme cases, the answer seems to be yes.

The following excerpts are from American historian Christopher R. Browning's book *Ordinary Men: Reserve Police Battalion 101 and the Final Solution in Poland* (1992). The book is a reconstruction of the events and motives that led 500 middle-aged, middle-class German men of Reserve Police Battalion 101 to launch a reign of terror against Jews in Poland in July 1942. By November 1943, these ordinary civilians had brutally killed at least 85,000 Jewish people.

It is important to note that the commanding officer, Major Trapp, explicitly offered to excuse any man who did not want to participate in the impending mass murder. Trapp's offer thrust responsibility onto each man individually. Unlike regular soldiers, these policemen bore the burden of choice. They were not "just following orders." The pressure to conform to their peers' expectations, however, was paramount.

> Only the very exceptional remained indifferent to taunts of 'weakling' from their comrades and could live with the fact that they were considered to be 'no man.'. . . Killing was seen as a collective obligation, so not killing was asocial vis-à-vis one's comrades. Those who did not shoot risked isolation [and] rejection . . . —a very uncomfortable prospect within the framework of a tight-knit unit stationed abroad among a hostile population, so that the individual had virtually nowhere else to turn for support and social contact. (pp.184–185)

Browning notes that no member of Reserve Police Battalion 101 was physically harmed or officially punished for refusing to shoot. Instead, outright refusal—total nonconformity—brought other, more subtle, consequences.

> There is the threat of isolation. . . . Stepping out could have been seen as a moral reproach of one's comrades: the nonshooter was potentially indicating that he was 'too good' to do such things. . . . Most nonshooters intuitively tried to diffuse the criticism of their comrades. . . . They pleaded not that they were 'too good' but rather that they were 'too weak' to kill. (p.185)

> . . . most of those who did not shoot only reaffirmed the 'macho' values of the majority—according to which it was a positive quality to be 'tough' enough to kill unarmed, noncombatant men, women, and children—and tried not to rupture the bonds of comradeship that constituted their social world.

> What, then, is one to conclude? . . . The reserve policemen faced choices, and most of them committed terrible deeds. But those who killed cannot be absolved by the notion that anyone in the same situation would have done as they did. For even among them, some refused to kill and others stopped killing. (p.188)

> Yet 80 to 90 percent of the men proceeded to kill, though all of them—at least initially—were horrified and disgusted by what they were doing. To break ranks and step out, to adopt overtly nonconformist behavior, was simply beyond most of the men. It was easier for them to shoot. (p.184)

> . . . Within virtually every social collective, the peer group exerts tremendous pressures on behavior and sets moral norms. If the men of Reserve Police Battalion 101 could become killers under such circumstances, what group of men cannot? (p.189)

Think About It

Analyzing Information What factors might have led more men to refuse to conform to the murderous actions of the rest of the group?

Altruism

Altruism is an unselfish concern for the welfare of other people. Altruistic people sacrifice their own well-being to help others in need. For example, an altruistic person might jump into the water to save someone who is drowning, even though doing so could put the would-be rescuer's own life in danger.

Explaining Altruism

Evolutionary psychologists believe that altruism, like aggression, is linked to genetics (Guisinger & Blatt, 1994; Rushton, 1989). Although altruistic behavior benefits other people, evolutionary psychologists believe it can also help people pass on their genes to future generations. At least it can do so if the altruistic behavior is directed toward relatives—that is, toward people who have many of the same genes as the altruist.

By helping their relatives survive and reproduce, evolutionary psychologists argue, early humans indirectly passed on their own genes to the next generation. In this way, genes for altruism have come to be part of the human gene pool. Thus, according to the evolutionary view, humans are altruistic by nature (Simon, 1990).

The evolutionary explanation of altruism has been criticized for many of the same reasons that the evolutionary explanation of aggression has been criticized: no clear-cut genetic basis for altruistic behavior has been found, and the tendency to act altruistically varies too widely to be under genetic control. The evolutionary view of altruism has also been criticized for failing to explain why people act altruistically toward those who are not related to themselves.

Factors Promoting Altruism

Research has shown that several factors influence whether a person will help others in particular situations. One factor is the person's state of mind. Many studies have found that people are more likely to help others when they are in a good mood (Berkowitz, 1987; Manucia et al., 1984). Being in a good mood seems to make people feel more generous and eager to help others (Carlson et al., 1988). It also may make people feel more powerful and thus better able to provide aid to those in need (Cunningham et al., 1990).

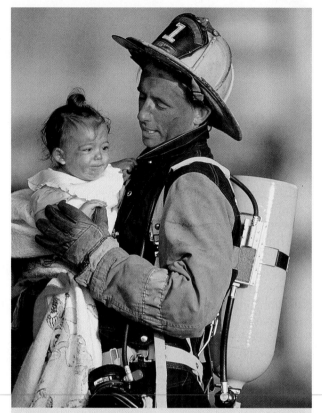

Altruism is just part of the job for the firefighter pictured here. **Can you think of other professions that require altruistic behavior?**

People who have problems themselves may also be more likely to act altruistically, perhaps because their own problems make them sensitive to the troubles of others (Thompson et al., 1980). People who are empathic—that is, able to put themselves in another's place—may be more likely to be altruistic for the same reason (Darley, 1993).

Being competent to help others seems to increase the chances that people will act altruistically. For example, registered nurses are more likely than people with no medical training to come to the aid of accident victims (Cramer et al., 1988). Similarly, police officers, who are trained to intervene in violent and dangerous situations, are more likely than the average person to help people in trouble. Being a good student himself, Todd felt competent to help others with their schoolwork and did so for Linda when they first met in biology class.

People with a strong need for approval also may be more likely to act altruistically. By doing so, they hope to gain the approval of others. In addition, a sense of personal responsibility may increase the chances of altruistic behavior (Maruyama et al., 1982). Teachers and camp counselors, for example, are responsible for those in their care, and they are more likely to act altruistically toward them than others are.

Factors Inhibiting Altruism

There are also several factors that seem to make people reluctant to help others in distress. In some cases, people may not be aware that another person is in trouble. In fact, the less sure they are that another person needs help, the less likely they are to offer assistance (Shotland & Heinold, 1985).

Some people may fail to act altruistically because they think there is nothing they can do to help. Others may be afraid of making a social blunder and being ridiculed (Pantin & Carver, 1982). For example, someone who sees an individual with a disability struggling with a door may fear offending the person by offering help. Finally, people may fail to act altruistically, particularly in dangerous situations, because they fear injuring themselves in the attempt.

Bystander Effect

The chances of people helping someone in need also depend on how many other people are present to help. Research has shown that people are less likely to give aid when other bystanders are present. This is called the **bystander effect**.

A classic experiment by psychologists John Darley and Bibb Latané (1968) is one of many studies that have documented the bystander effect. In one phase of the study, participants were placed in separate cubicles and asked to talk with one another over an intercom. One of the participants was actually an associate of the researchers. When his turn came to talk, he called for help and then made sounds that suggested he was having an epileptic seizure.

Some study participants had been led to believe that they alone could hear the person having the seizure. Others had been led to believe that from one to four other participants could hear him as well. About 85 percent of participants who thought that no one else could hear the person came to his aid. However, when participants thought that others could also hear the individual in trouble, fewer of them tried to help. In fact, the more people who were presumed to be able to hear him, the less likely participants were to become involved. Only 31

percent of participants made an effort to help when they thought that four other people could hear the person in need.

It seems that diffusion of responsibility limits altruistic behavior. When people are members of a group, they are likely to stand back and wait for others to help the person in need. However, when others are not around, they are more likely to act altruistically.

SECTION 5 REVIEW

go.hrw.com
Homework Practice Online
Keyword: SY7 HP21

1. Define *altruism*.
2. What factors promote altruistic behavior? What factors inhibit it?
3. **Critical Thinking** *Categorizing* Describe two situations, one in which bystanders are likely to help a person in trouble and one in which bystanders are less likely to help. Explain your answer.

Whether we act altruistically to help others in need depends on many factors, including the presence of other bystanders who could also offer assistance.

Writing a Summary

Using standard grammar, spelling, sentence structure, and punctuation, summarize the information in this chapter. Consider:
- social norms, obedience to authority figures, and the ways group membership can influence individual behavior
- aggressive and altruistic behavior

Identifying People and Ideas

Identify the following terms or people and use them in appropriate sentences.

1. social facilitation
2. evaluation apprehension
3. social loafing
4. risky shift
5. majority-wins schemes
6. group polarization
7. social norms
8. implicit norms
9. catharsis
10. altruism

Understanding Main Ideas

SECTION 1 (pp. 480–84)
1. What is the relationship between diffusion of responsibility and the risky shift?

SECTION 2 (pp. 484–86)
2. How do explicit and implicit social norms differ?

SECTION 3 (pp. 487–89)
3. What is the difference between obedience and conformity?

SECTION 4 (pp. 490–92)
4. Why do some psychologists believe that catharsis can help prevent aggression?

SECTION 5 (pp. 494–95)
5. What is the bystander effect?

Thinking Critically

1. **Analyzing Information** How would an evolutionary psychologist and a learning theorist explain the tendency for people to obey authority figures?

2. **Evaluating** In what ways might a group of teens trying to raise money for a high school club come to a decision using the truth-wins social decision scheme?

3. **Comparing and Contrasting** How are the explanations of aggression provided by evolutionary psychologists and psychoanalysts similar and different?

4. **Drawing Inferences and Conclusions** How is the bystander effect related to evaluation apprehension?

Writing About Psychology

1. **Summarizing** Request permission to attend a meeting of a school or community organization. During the meeting, take notes on how the group's leader conducts the meeting. Afterward, review your notes and decide what style of leadership was used. How might the meeting have been conducted if another style of leadership had been used instead? Write a brief summary of what you have learned.

2. **Analyzing Information** Read more about the evolutionary explanation for human aggression or altruism. What types of evidence and arguments are used to back the claims that the behavior helps individuals survive, reproduce, and contribute their genes to the next generation? What evidence and arguments have been presented to refute the claims? Describe the evidence that supports and refutes the claims in a short written report. Conclude the report with a statement of your own position on the subject. Use the graphic organizer below to help you write your report.

Supports	Refutes

Interpreting Graphs

Study the graph below. Then use the information in the graph to help you answer the questions that follow.

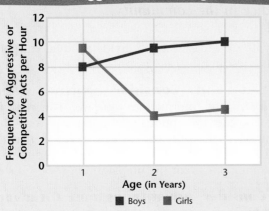

Gender and Aggression in Young Children

Source: Maccoby, *The Two Sexes*, 1998

1. Which of the following statements best reflects the information presented in the graph?

   a. Aggression is an inherited trait.

   b. Aggression is a learned trait.

   c. As they grow older, girls remain as aggressive as boys.

   d. As they grow older, boys become more aggressive than girls.

2. What information would you request from the psychologist to learn more about this study and its usefulness?

Analyzing Primary Sources

Read the following excerpt, in which Thomas J. Socha and Diana M. Socha consider problems that arise during group communication among young children. Then answer the questions that follow.

"There are a number of interactional problems that prevent dialogue from occurring, which teachers and group facilitators need to consider. First, one child may dominate a group discussion with his or her voice, ideas, or behavior. . . . Second, the uncooperative child, the child who does not want to do his or her part, may be ignored by a group. . . . Third, turn taking was problematic in the discussions until a "no interrupting" rule was put in place. . . . Finally . . . it will be difficult for a teacher or group facilitator to resist participating. . . . Our analysis shows that children rely immediately on an adult for a solution and use that adult's authority to "fix" the problem, instead of learning communication strategies to manage it themselves."

3. Which of the following statements best reflects the arguments presented in the excerpt?

   a. Children are as capable of managing group communications as adults are.

   b. Children cannot function in groups.

   c. Adults will always lead children's groups, whether they intend to or not.

   d. Children's groups work best when some adult assistance is available.

4. What responsibilities and difficulties do adults face when they work with groups of children?

PSYCHOLOGY PROJECTS

Linking to Community

Applying Psychology With several other classmates, work together to create a skit that shows how teens in the community are pressured to conform to their peers. As you work on the skit, help develop a supportive climate within the group. After presenting the skit, ask the class to identify the ways in which characters in the skit conformed to group norms. Help your group lead the class in a discussion of what might have happened if the individuals had decided not to conform.

🖥 internet connect

Internet Activity: go.hrw.com
KEYWORD: SY7 PS21

Choose an activity on social interaction to:
- create a skit illustrating characteristics of group behavior.
- create a pamphlet that describes and explains conformity.
- profile one of the theories that attempts to explain aggression.

PSYCHOLOGY IN ACTION

YOU SOLVE THE PROBLEM . . .

How can students reduce prejudice in the community?

Complete the following activity in small groups. Imagine that your group is preparing a presentation about ways to reduce prejudice. Prepare a poster outlining the best way to accomplish this task.

1. Gather Information. Use your textbook and other resources to find information that might influence your plan of action. Remember that your poster must include adequate information to convince your classmates that your proposed method will be effective in dealing with prejudice. This information might include charts, graphs, or other visuals. You may want to divide up different parts of the research among group members.

2. List and Consider Options. After reviewing the information you have gathered, list and consider the options you might use. Your final solution to the problem may be easier to reach if you consider all options. Be sure to record your possible options for the preparation of your poster.

3. Consider Advantages and Disadvantages. Now consider the advantages and disadvantages of taking each option. Your group should ask itself questions such as,

- Which course of action will have the best chance of being seen or heard by members of our community?
- What segments of the community are being targeted by this project?

Once you have considered the advantages and disadvantages, record them as notes for use in preparing your poster.

4. Choose and Implement a Solution. After considering the advantages and disadvantages, you should choose a solution. Then plan and create your poster for that solution. Be sure to make your poster very clear.

5. Evaluate the Effectiveness of the Solution. Once you have prepared your poster, write a paragraph evaluating the effectiveness of your group's recommendation. When you are ready, decide which group members will present the poster. Then take your report to the rest of the class. Good luck!

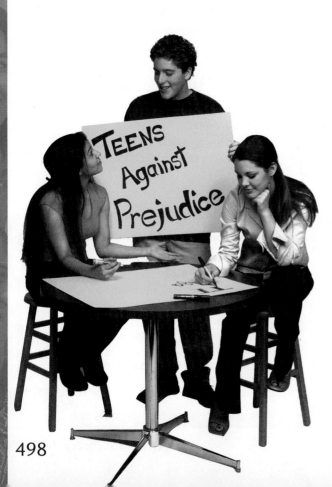

HOLT
PSYCHOLOGY:
PRINCIPLES IN PRACTICE

REFERENCE SECTION

CAREERS IN PSYCHOLOGY

Overview

A career in psychology is bound to be fascinating, for the fundamental subject matter is, after all, us. That so many people decide to study human behavior, in all its diversity, should come as no surprise. The range of specializations and kinds of jobs available within the broad area of psychology are so varied that there may well be a career in psychology to suit almost everyone's interests.

But how can you start narrowing the field for yourself? What educational training and personality characteristics are required for each psychology-related career? How do you decide on a specialization and actually become a psychologist?

Career opportunities in the field abound on every educational level. If you are most interested in relating to people directly, and helping them deal with serious mental or emotional problems in therapy, perhaps you will consider becoming a clinical psychologist. This is the area that most people think of when they hear the word *psychologist*. Many clinical psychologists specialize in treating one or more specific problems, such as substance abuse, eating disorders, or phobias. Others specialize in group treatment settings, working as family therapists or couples therapists, for instance. But clinical psychology is just one of numerous possibilities.

Other careers in psychology do not necessarily involve working directly with people or doing therapy at all. If you enjoy working in a laboratory and conducting basic scientific research, you may be attracted to the exacting field of experimental psychology. Some fields offer a combination of research- and people-oriented work. As an industrial or organizational psychologist, for example, you might apply psychological techniques to work-oriented issues in a business environment.

The first step to pursuing a career in psychology is usually a four-year university degree, consisting of specific core courses. In addition, today's student is well-advised to take a course in computer science, which is mandatory for conducting research.

Not all careers related to psychology require graduate study. Options in psychological careers with a four-year bachelor's degree (B.A. or B.S.) alone do exist, although they tend to be somewhat limited in scope. Examples include working as an aide or a social worker in a mental hospital, hospice, nursing home, residential treatment center for disturbed youth, or

government agency. These same settings, among others, offer psychology-related careers in administration, human resources, and customer service.

Most careers in psychology, however, now require at least a master of arts or master of science degree (M.A. or M.S.), and often a doctoral degree (Ph.D. or Ed.Psy.). It takes about two years of study in a graduate program to earn a master's degree, and about four to six years above that to earn a doctoral degree.

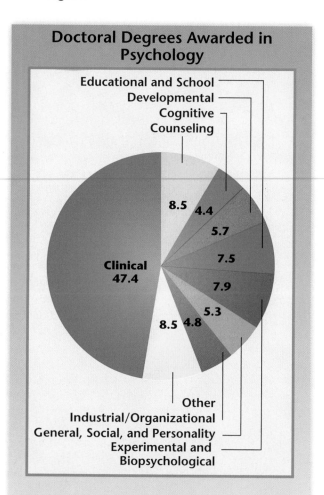

Doctoral Degrees Awarded in Psychology

Educational and School
Developmental
Cognitive
Counseling

8.5 4.4

5.7

7.5

Clinical
47.4

7.9

5.3

8.5 4.8

Other
Industrial/Organizational
General, Social, and Personality
Experimental and
Biopsychological

Career opportunities in the field of psychology are both numerous and diverse. Preparation for these careers generally begins with a doctoral degree. This graph illustrates the percentage of doctoral degrees awarded in the various areas of psychological specialization.

Source: Kyle, T. M. & Williams, S. (2000 May); 1998–1999 APA Survey of Graduate Departments of Psychology, Tables 13A & 13B.

Clinical psychologists are trained to diagnose and treat individuals with various psychological disorders such as this woman suffering from depression—as well as other social and adjustment problems.

For careers in educational, social, experimental, clinical, or counseling psychology, a doctoral degree is highly recommended. However, many people take some time off after receiving their undergraduate degree to gain valuable experience in laboratory or clinical work instead of plunging into years and years of schooling. In fact, if you intend to become a school or educational psychologist, your state may require that you first gain a few years of teaching experience.

Whatever career you ultimately select, it should be rewarding for you, personally. Rewarding opportunities in psychology exist on all levels.

Clinical Psychologist

About half of all graduate degrees in psychology are awarded in the demanding field of clinical psychology. In this sense, clinical psychology is the most popular branch of psychology. Some clinical psychologists work with individuals who suffer from severe psychological disorders, while others prefer to limit their practices to treating people with less

severe behavioral or adjustment problems. In the course of their work, clinical psychologists may deal with such diverse problems as severe depression and other psychological disorders, juvenile delinquency, drug abuse, marital problems, or eating disorders.

People often confuse clinical psychologists with psychiatrists. The distinction is a significant one, however. In treating their patients, clinical psychologists conduct interviews, practice methods of psychotherapy, and administer and interpret psychological tests. They are not, however, able to prescribe medication or administer other kinds of biological therapy. Psychiatrists, on the other hand, are medical doctors who specialize in the treatment of psychological disorders. By law, only psychiatrists have the right and responsibility to prescribe medication to their clients.

Many clinical psychologists with doctoral degrees maintain a private practice, where they see clients who voluntarily come to them for treatment. Others, however, work in veteran's hospitals, mental health clinics, schools for the mentally retarded, or correctional institutions, where they are generally assigned to a specific number of patients.

Many clinical psychologists teach—primarily in colleges, universities, or medical schools—where they pass on their experience and knowledge to others, rather than apply their skills directly. Still others conduct workshops on specific topics, and engage in the training of business professionals or other psychologists. Those with literary talents often write scholarly or popular books and articles.

Clinical psychologists may be self-employed, or hired by government, business, schools, universities, hospitals, prisons, or nonprofit organizations, as consultants or full-time employees. The field is extremely flexible, thus it is also becoming more competitive, as is admission to strong graduate programs. Clinical psychologists also must be licensed by the state in which they live and work.

Counseling Psychologist

Like clinical psychologists, counseling psychologists work with people experiencing distress. Counseling psychologists, however, tend to treat people who are confronted with stressful or highly emotional situations, rather than people who have more severe mental disorders. For example, a couple having marital difficulties might go to a counseling psychologist in the hopes of avoiding a divorce. The suicide of a family member may prompt a person to seek out a counseling psychologist's support and perspective for a few months.

People with a chronic physical disease or a catastrophic illness often look to counselors for help in coping with difficulties of various magnitudes that feel overwhelming. It may be that a high school student feels anxious because she believes that her parents expect too much of her, for instance, or that a formerly happy young man experiences depression after a job loss.

Differences between clinical and counseling psychologists are growing fainter. Both the work itself and the educational requirements in most graduate schools, are nearly identical. Also, the same types of employers that hire clinical psychologists are likely to hire counseling psychologists of the same educational level for the same positions. The final choice to become a clinical or a counseling psychologist ultimately may be determined by the specific graduate program that you find most appealing.

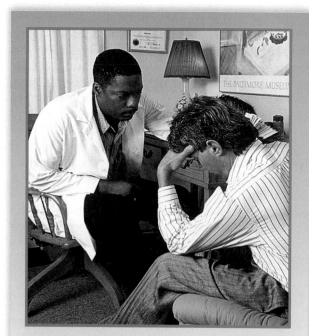

Counseling psychologists tend to work with patients who are faced with stressful or emotional situations. They help people to confront and overcome their fears or other disturbing emotions.

Both clinical and counseling psychologists use the techniques and theories with which they personally agree. They must be careful, however, not to impose their views on their clients. Both types of psychologists may use psychological assessments or tests to evaluate their clients. Graduate programs in counseling psychology, however, tend not to emphasize research as much as programs that train clinical psychologists.

Subspecialties in Counseling Psychology

Career counselors (also known as vocational counselors) administer interest-inventory and other psychological tests to help people make appropriate and gratifying career choices. They may work with university students, with adult career-changers, or in private businesses or corporations. Career counselors may lead workshops on job-searching skills, facilitate discussion and support groups, and sometimes work with motivated clients on a one-on-one basis. Some career counselors also function as intermediaries between industry and colleges, helping to place new graduates in jobs, or directing them to other resources. This career attracts outgoing people who love helping others and who thrive in a relatively fast-paced, upbeat environment that addresses a rather limited range of problems in a practical manner.

Rehabilitation counselors work with physically challenged individuals, helping them adapt to their disabilities and become self-sufficient and self-supporting. They work with people of all ages, whether handicapped after an accident, an illness, or from birth. Their primary job is a tough one: helping people face the hard reality of having physical limitations while remaining realistic, yet hopeful, about the client's potential.

Rehabilitation (or occupational) counselors help prepare clients for jobs that they are capable of doing. In some cases, they also arrange for additional training. Part of their job may entail soliciting potential employers for their clients while also acting as morale boosters in an individual's physical and emotional rehabilitative process.

A master's degree in rehabilitative counseling (often offered within university departments of education or health/kinesthesiology) is recommended, but a bachelor's degree in psychology, especially when combined with volunteer experience, may be an acceptable substitute. This can be an extremely rewarding career, though also a frustrating one, as in the case of any career that requires frequent contact with bureaucratic agencies. Rehabilitation counselors must demonstrate persistence, dedication, patience, and stamina.

Teachers of special education face similar tasks and issues as rehabilitation counselors (or therapists, as they are sometimes known). The objective of both special education teachers and rehabilitation counselors is the same: helping people with disabilities achieve their full potential.

School counselors (or school psychologists) work with students, teachers, and administrators to make the school the best possible environment for learning. One of their primary tasks is to help students who are having problems that interfere with learning. These problems may involve peers, families, teachers, coursework, or a combination of these and other factors. Such counselors must be observant and knowledgeable enough to identify and diagnose a student's problems, devise possible solutions, and make recommendations regarding a student's placement in special education or gifted classes.

Like other counseling psychologists, school counselors make use of a range of intelligence, interest, and psychological tests. A routine part of the job is administering and scoring standardized tests. More importantly, the school psychologist interprets these test results. This interpretation is then used to identify and address the special needs of individual students.

In some cases, school psychologists are also called in to resolve conflicts, either between students and teachers, students and parents, or students and other students. The psychologist will generally listen to both sides of the dispute and try to resolve the conflict with an amicable compromise.

Some states require school counselors to obtain teaching credentials and gain practical experience in the classroom. Training for school counselors usually takes place through a college's department of education, not necessarily within the psychology department. If you are tactful yet assertive, and flourish in the challenging school environment, this rewarding career may be high on your list of considerations.

Educational Psychologist

Should classrooms consist of only students of the same age, or should students be grouped according to skill levels, regardless of age? Should a school district revise its curriculum and teaching methods to meet the changing needs of students? How can computers facilitate learning in the classroom?

Educational psychologists study how people learn. They perform research—both in and out of the classroom—geared to facilitating the learning process and improving education as a whole. Although educational psychologists typically work for school districts, they are frequently employed by universities, where they engage in research and assist in training teachers and school counselors.

Unlike school psychologists, educational psychologists are more involved with theoretical issues that affect learning rather than with individual students. Their research often involves measuring a group's abilities and achievements by administering, and sometimes creating, standardized tests. Educational psychologists then use the results of these tests to help place students in specific programs and to develop curricula in schools.

Educational psychologists may focus on several other issues. They may, for example, study the psychological factors that affect a student's test-taking

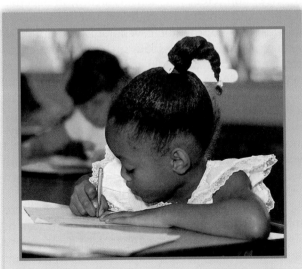

The primary tasks of a school counselor are to administer, score, and interpret the results of standardized tests.

Educational psychologists do not generally work with individual students. They do, however, develop curriculum standards and teaching methods. Thus, indirectly, they have a profound effect on the individual student's education.

ability or school performance in general. They may research the effects that cultural and gender differences have on learning.

Educational psychologists also analyze the range of instructional methods available to teachers in the classroom. Then they use their research discoveries to expand or refine these instructional options.

Work for educational psychologists is not necessarily limited to the academic environment, however. Large corporations and government agencies often hire educational psychologists to devise staff training programs.

A bachelor's degree in psychology is the first step in the long, complex process of becoming an educational psychologist. Candidates are urged to gain teaching experience on the elementary, middle school, or high school levels before pursuing a doctoral program within a university's education or psychology department. Since the work of educational psychologists involves evaluating and interpreting research data, the training requires proficiency in mathematics, statistics, and computer science.

Depending on the graduate program, the final degree earned will be a Doctor of Education (Ed.D.) or a Doctor of Philosophy (Ph.D.). Although educational psychology is a difficult profession to break into, it is an attractive career for those who wish to influence the course of the educational system itself.

Developmental Psychologist

At what age do children develop the ability to think abstractly? Does isolation reduce short-term memory in elderly people? Why do infants need more sleep than older children? If questions related to stages of life intrigue you, perhaps you would want to become a developmental psychologist.

Developmental psychologists study the behavioral changes that occur at various stages in a person's life. In the past, developmental psychology was limited to the study of changes in the developmental stages of children. For this reason, it was called *child psychology.* Recently, however, researchers have become aware that people experience complex and interconnected physical, psychological, intellectual, and social changes throughout the entire life span.

Among the contemporary issues developmental psychologists are concerned with is the question of how our ability to perform certain tasks changes throughout our lifetime. Developmental psychologists also investigate language acquisition, changes in perception, creativity, sensory acuity, intellectual abilities, and emotions at different stages of life.

Most developmental psychologists focus on a certain period in the life span, such as infancy, childhood, adolescence, middle age, or old age. This last category, called *gerontology,* promises to be particularly important in the future, as the country's population ages and life spans increase.

Another topic of interest to developmental psychologists includes the changing roles of men and women in society. They study the impact of gender stereotyping and the implications of that stereotyping on a child's development.

Developmental psychologists usually work for universities, teaching and conducting research. Many combine academic careers with a secondary career in writing, as a natural outgrowth of their interests. Some developmental psychologists also work in clinical settings such as hospitals, prisons, nursing homes, schools, group homes, nursery schools, or hospices.

Developmental psychologists no longer limit their research to children. The field has expanded to address the behavioral changes that occur throughout the life span.

As our society changes, new and exciting issues will be raised. Developmental psychologists are likely to lead the way in answering these questions. The more we learn, the more we will understand about human development and behavior.

Social Psychologist

How do individuals behave in social and group situations? Do boys and girls play differently, and if so, why? Do people's styles of interacting change in the workplace?

Social psychologists study the effects of group membership on individual behavior. Their primary focus is, generally, how behavior in social situations affects individuals. However, social psychologists tend to focus on external influences and environments. They focus on such issues as attitudes, influence, and social cognition and interaction.

Social psychologists are often confused with social workers. Both focus on social behavior. Social workers, however, are more involved with individuals. Their work is more practical and less research oriented than the work of the social psychologist.

There is also a distinct overlap with the field of anthropology. Anthropologists also study social behavior, but they are more concerned with the social customs, rituals, and interactions of various groups of people.

Finally, social psychology is also closely related to sociology. There is, however, a distinct difference between the two. Social psychologists focus on the effects of group membership on the behavior of an individual person. Sociologists, on the other hand, are more concerned with the group as a whole—its structure and characteristics.

Some issues that social psychologists explore may involve gender studies, conformity, or peer

Social psychologists study the effects of group membership on individual behavior. They may be interested to study how this aggressive crowd as a whole affects the thoughts and behavior of any single individual in the crowd.

pressure. They may study more specific issues as well—such as the effects of prejudice and discrimination on self-esteem.

Many social psychologists prefer to conduct their research in a naturalistic environment rather than in a laboratory. In a naturalistic observation they have less control of the variables in the study, but the results are based on real-life factors.

Preparation for this multi-dimensional career is by no means uniform. Social psychologists usually first obtain a bachelor's degree in psychology, anthropology, or sociology. A doctoral degree in social psychology or anthropology offers the most flexibility and career advancement in research.

Many social psychologists are employed in research facilities or in universities. They may work in industry, where they can study consumer spending habits. They may work for the newspaper where they write articles on the causes and possible prevention of riots. The options in this field are vast and rewarding. People who enjoy observing others, gathering and synthesizing information, and being associated with academic settings are most likely to be happy in this stimulating field.

Experimental Psychologist

Why do people need sleep? What biological processes contribute to the feelings of happiness and sadness? Where in the brain does the ability to recognize faces reside?

Generally considered the most scientific of psychological disciplines, experimental psychologists conduct research into the basic biological processes related to behavior, thoughts, and emotions. They follow a set of strictly controlled scientific procedures to learn about the relationship between two or more variables. Their research usually emphasizes physiological studies of the nervous system, the brain itself, and the basic processes of thinking, feeling, remembering, and perceiving external stimuli.

Experimental psychologists lay the groundwork for more practical kinds of psychological research and counseling. This basic research, which may seem to have no practical value at the time it is conducted, has led other researchers to develop useful techniques for reducing stress, increasing motivation, enhancing memory, and encouraging longer attention spans, for example.

Experimental psychologists often work with animals. They try, however, to ensure that the animals are handled in a humane manner.

Experimental psychologists do not necessarily try to apply the knowledge they acquire. That is, they do not try to use their research to solve practical problems. They generally leave the actual application of research findings to psychologists from other fields.

In conducting their research, experimental psychologists often work with animals. They may compare the behavior of one species with that of another. In many cases, experimental psychologists use primates because their behavior is so similar to that of humans. The use of animals in research procedures is a matter of continual ethical debate. The benefits from using them, however, generally outweigh the potential harms. Also, experimental psychologists are careful to ensure that the animals receive humane treatment.

Temperament may be one of the most important factors when considering a career in experimental psychology because it takes a certain type of person to think in these process-oriented terms. Like those in other basic research fields, experimental psychologists tend to be highly detail-oriented, patient individuals who easily become absorbed in their work, and do not require regular, close contact with other people. They tend to be independent, abstract thinkers who prefer working in laboratory settings. A doctoral degree is mandatory for the most engrossing work in experimental psychology. Candidates must have strong preparation in the hard sciences, with a concentration on courses in neuroanatomy, physiology, biology and molecular biology, and genetics. Undergraduates often major in psychology, but a degree in any biological science, accompanied with appropriate courses in psychology, is usually an acceptable start.

Most graduate programs prefer candidates who have already demonstrated some competency in research and laboratory skills before entering the doctoral program. If a career in experimental psychology appeals to you, it would be wise to gain some exposure to research science as an undergraduate, or even while still in high school.

Industrial/Organizational Psychologist

What color package most attracts the eyes of shoppers? How can a company arrange cubicles to maximize space without isolating employees from each other? How would a department lay-off affect the company's morale, as a whole?

Psychology enters the workplace with industrial, or organizational, psychologists. Organizational psychologists are usually employed by business or government to figure out ways of increasing productivity, improving working conditions, and saving money in the process. Organizational psychologists generally consult with various divisions of one or more companies.

Organizational psychologists are often consulted by the marketing divisions of companies. Here, they conduct surveys and focus groups to help marketing divisions determine their advertising campaigns based on the psychological profile of their intended audience. They may also be called upon by the human resource department to create a new series of questions for interviewers, or to suggest ways to improve employee morale. They may also be called upon by the administrative department to assess the company's time-management program.

The more the workplace changes, the more need there will be for organizational/industrial psychologists to smooth things out. And so far, there is no sign that the workplace will cease changing.

Like counselors, organizational/industrial psychologists assume the titles indicated by the specific work they perform. If working for an oil company or a conservation organization, they may be called *environmental psychologists.* If they work for an advertising firm, perhaps they will be called *consumer psychologists.* Working for a hospital, a health-care organization, or a government health agency on issues of preventive health and health promotion awareness, they may be called *health psychologists.*

As is the case throughout the psychological profession, a master's degree is usually the basic educational requirement for more challenging positions, with doctorates becoming more prevalent. Although industrial/organizational psychology is one of the less visible careers in psychology, it is one of the most far-reaching in terms of the work's impact on the public. The career choices available to those individuals qualified for industrial/organizational psychology are quite extensive. There are no fewer choices than there are types of industries. Industrial/Organizational psychology, thus, offers some of the most varied of career opportunities. The field is most appealing to people who have a knack for spotting trends, are relatively outgoing, and who get along well with a variety of individuals and groups.

An organizational/industrial psychologist may be interested in studying how stressful work environments—such as that experienced by surgeons— affect a person's psychological health.

Aaronson, B. S. (1972). Color perception and effect. *American Journal of Clinical Hypnosis, 14,* 38–43.

Abeles, N. (1997). Memory problems in later life. *APA Monitor, 28*(6), 2.

Aber, J. L., & Allen, J. P. (1987). Effects of maltreatment of young children on young children's socioemotional development: An attachment theory perspective. *Developmental Psychology, 23,* 406–414.

Abramson, L. Y., Seligman, M. E. P., & Teasdale, J. D. (1978). Learned helplessness in humans: Critique and reformulation. *Journal of Abnormal Psychology, 87,* 49–74.

Abramson, M. Y., Metalsky, G. I., & Alloy, L. B. (1989). Hopelessness-depression: A theory-based subtype of depression. *Psychological Review, 9,* 358–372.

Ackerman, G. L. (1993). A congressional view of youth suicide. *American Psychologist, 48,* 183–184.

Adams, D. M., Overholser, J. C., & Spirito, A. (1992, August). *Life stress related to adolescent suicide attempts.* Paper presented at the meeting of the American Psychological Association, Washington, DC.

Ader, D. N., & Johnson, S. B. (1994). Sample description, reporting, and analysis of sex in psychological research: A look at APA and APA division journals in 1990. *American Psychologist, 49,* 216–218.

Ader, R. (1993). Conditioned responses. In B. Moyers (Ed.), *Healing and the mind.* New York: Doubleday.

Adler, A. (1927). *Understanding human nature.* Greenwich, CT: Fawcett.

Adler, T. (1993a). Shy, bold temperament? It's mostly in the genes. *APA Monitor, 24*(1), 7–8.

Agras, W. S., & Kirkley, B. G. (1986). Bulimia: Theories of etiology. In K. D. Brownell & J. P. Foreyt (Eds.), *Handbook of eating disorders.* New York: Basic Books.

Ainsworth, M. D. S. (1973). The development of infant-mother attachment. In B. Caldwell & H. Ricciuti (Eds.), *Review of child development research* (Vol. 3). Chicago: University of Chicago Press.

Ainsworth, M. D. S. (1979). Infant-mother attachment. *American Psychologist, 34,* 932–937.

Ainsworth, M. D. S., & Bowlby, J. (1991). An ethological approach to personality development. *American Psychologist, 46,* 333–341.

Ainsworth, M. D. S., Blehar, M. L., Waters, E., & Wall, S. (1978). *Patterns of attachment.* Hillsdale, NJ: Erlbaum.

Akhtar, N., & Bradley, E. J. (1991). Social information processing deficits of aggressive children: Present findings and implications for social skills training. *Clinical Psychology Review, 11,* 621–644.

Alexander, C. N., et al. (1996). Trial of stress reduction for hypertension in older African Americans: II. Sex and risk Subgroup analysis. *Hypertension, 28,* 228–237.

Allen, J., Blanton, P., Johnson-Greene, D., Murphy-Farmer, C., et al. (1992). Need for achievement and performance on measures of behavioral fluency. *Psychological Reports, 71,* 471–478.

Allen, L. (1993, August). Integrating a sociocultural perspective into the psychology curriculum. G. Stanley Hall lecture presented to the American Psychological Association, Toronto, Canada.

Allison, D. B., et al. (1999). Annual deaths attributable to obesity in the United States. *Journal of the American Medical Association online, 282*(16).

Allison, J., Blatt, S. J., & Zimet, C. N. (1988). *The interpretation of psychological tests.* Washington, DC: Hemisphere.

Allison, K. W., Crawford, I., Echemendia, R., Robinson, L. V., & Knepp, D. (1994). Human diveristy and professional competence. *American Psychologist, 49,* 792–796.

Alloy, L. B. (1988). *Cognitive processes in depression.* New York: Guilford Press.

Alloy, L. B., & Clements, C. M. (1992). Illusion of control: Invulnerability to negative affect and depressive symptoms after laboratory and natural stressors. *Journal of Abnormal Psychology, 101,* 234–245.

Allport, G. (1937). *Personality: A psychological interpretation.* New York: Holt, Rinehart and Winston.

Allport, G. (1961). *Pattern and growth in personality.* New York: Holt, Rinehart and Winston.

Allport, G. (1965). *Letters from Jenny.* New York: Harcourt Brace Jovanovich.

Allport, G. (1966). Traits revisited. *American Psychologist, 21,* 1–10.

Allport, G., & Odbert, H. S. (1936). Trait names: A psycho-lexical study. *Psychological Monographs, 47*(211), 1–171.

Allread, R. A. (1990). Gender differences in spelling achievement in grades 1 through 6. *Journal of Educational Research, 83,* 187–193.

Alsaker, F. D. (1992). Pubertal timing, overweight, and psychological adjustment. *Journal of Early Adolescence, 12,* 396–419.

Amaro, H. (1995). Love, sex, and power: Considering women's realities in HIV prevention. *American Psychologist, 50,* 437–447.

Amato, P. R., & Keith, B. (1991). Parental divorce and the well–being of children: A meta-analysis. *Psychological Bulletin, 110,* 26–46.

American Association of University Women. (1992). *How schools shortchange women: The A.A.U.W. report.* Washington, DC: A.A.U.W. Educational Foundation.

American Heart Association online (2000a). *2000 Heart and stroke statistical update.* http://www.americanheart.org.

American Lung Association (2000). *Smoking fact sheet,* http://www.lungusa.org.

American Polygraph Association. (1992). Cited in Bashore, T. R., & Rapp, P. E. (1993). Are there alternatives to traditional polygraph procedures? *Psychological Bulletin, 113,* 3–22.

American Psychiatric Association. (1987). *Diagnostic and Statistical Manual of Mental Disorders* (3rd ed.). Washington DC: Author.

American Psychiatric Association. (1994). *Diagnostic and Statistical Manual of Mental Disorders* (4th ed.). Washington DC: Author.

American Psychological Association. (1990). *The practice of electroconvulsive therapy.* Washington, DC: Author.

American Psychological Association. (1993a). American Psychological Association Commission on Violence and Youth. *American Psychologist, 48,* 89.

American Psychological Association. (1993b). Guidelines for providers of psychological services to ethnic, linguistic, and culturally diverse populations. *American Psychologist, 48,* 45–48.

American Psychological Association. (1994a). *Ethical principles of psychologists and code of conduct.* Washington, DC: Author.

American Psychological Association. (1994b). *Publication manual of the American Psychological Association* (4th ed.). Washington, DC: Author.

Andersen, B. L., Kiecolt–Glaser, J. K., & Glaser, R. (1994). A biobehavioral model of cancer stress and disease course. *American Psychologist, 49,* 389–404.

Anderson, C. A., & Dill, K. E. (2000). Video games and aggressive thoughts, feelings, and behavior in the laboratory and in life. *Journal of Personality and Social Psychology, 78*(4), 772–790.

Andersson, T., & Magnusson, D. (1990). Biological maturation in adolescence and the development of drinking habits and alcohol abuse among young males: A prospective longitudinal study. *Journal of Youth and Adolescence, 19*(1), 33–41.

Andreasen, N. C. (1988). Brain imaging: Applications in psychiatry. *Science, 239,* 1381–1388.

Andreasen, N., Ehrhardt, J., Sayze, V., Alliger, R., Yuh, W., Cohen, G., & Ziebell, S. (1990). Magnetic resonance imaging of the brain in schizophrenia. *Archives of General Psychiatry, 47,* 35–44.

Angell, M. (1993). Privilege and health—What is the connection? *New England Journal of Medicine, 329,* 126–127.

Angier, N. (1994). Factor in female sexuality. *The New York Times,* p. C13.

Annunziata, J., & Jacobson-Kram, P. (1995). *Solving your problems together: Family therapy for the whole family.* Washington, DC: American Psychological Association.

Antoni, M. H. (1987). Neuroendocrine influences in psychoimmunology and neoplasia: A review. *Psychology and Health, 1,* 3–24.

Antoni, M. H., et al. (1991). Cognitive-behavioral stress management intervention buffers distress responses and immunologic changes following notification of HIV-1 seropositivity. *Journal of Consulting and Clinical Psychology, 59,* 906–915.

Antonuccio, D. (1995). Psychotherapy for depression: No stronger medicine. *American Psychologist, 50,* 452–454.

APA Research Office (2000). First-year (full-time) students in doctoral-level departments of psychology by race/ethnicity: 1999–2000. *Graduate Study in Psychology 2000.* Washington, D.C.: American Psychological Association.

Apter, T. (1995). *Secret paths: Women in the new midlife.* New York: Norton.

Archer, R. P., & Cash, T. F. (1985). Physical attractiveness and maladjustment among psychiatric patients. *Journal of Social and Clinical Psychology, 3,* 170–180.

Archer, S. L. (1991). Gender differences in identity development. In J. Brooks-Gunn, R. Lerner, & A. C. Petersen (Eds.), *Encyclopedia of adolescence, II.* New York: Garland.

Archer, S. L. (1992). A feminist's approach to identity research. In G. R. Adams, T. P. Gullotta, & R. Montemayor (Eds.), *Adolescent identity formation.* Newbury Park, CA: Sage.

Archer, S. L., & Waterman, A. S. (1990). Varieties of identity diffusions and foreclosures: An exploration of subcategories of the identity statuses. *Journal of Adolescent Research, 5,* 96–111.

Arlow, J. A. (1989). Psychoanalysis. In R. J. Corsini & D. Wedding (Eds.), *Current psychotherapies* (4th ed., pp. 19–62). Itasca, IL: Peacock.

Armeli, S., Carney. M. A., Tennen, H., Affleck, G., & O'Neil. (2000). Stress and alcohol use: A daily process examination of the stressor-vulnerability model. *Journal of Personality and Social Psychology, 78*(5), 979–994.

Arnold, D. H., Lonigan, C. J., Whitehurst, G. J., & Epstein, J. N. (1994). Accelerating language development through picture book reading: Replication and extension to a videotape training format. *Journal of Educational Psychology, 86,* 235–243.

Asch, S. E. (1955). Opinions and social pressure. *Scientific American, 193,* 31–35.

Atchley, R. C. (1991). *Social forces and aging* (6th ed.). Belmont, CA: Wadsworth.

Atkinson, R. C. (1975). Mnemotechnics in second-language learning. *American Psychologist, 30,* 821–828.

Atkinson, R. L., Atkinson, R. C., Smith, E. E., Bem, D. J., & Nolen-Hoeksema, S. (1996). *Hilgard's introduction to psychology* (12th ed.). Fort Worth, TX: Harcourt Brace Jovanovich.

Attie, I., Brooks-Gunn, J., & Petersen, A. C. (1990). A developmental perspective on eating disorders and eating problems. In M. Lewis & S. M. Miller (Eds.), *Handbook of developmental psychopathology.* New York: Plenum Press.

Audrain, J. E., Klesges, R. C., & Klesges, L. M. (1995). Relationship between obesity status and the metabolic effects of smoking in women. *Health Psychology, 14,* 116–123.

Averill, J. R. (1993). Autonomic response patterns during sadness and mirth. *Psychophysiology, 5,* 399–414.

Ayllon, T., & Haughton, E. (1962). Control of the behavior of schizophrenic patients by food. *Journal of the Experimental Analysis of Behavior, 5,* 343–352.

Azar, B. (1995). Breaking through barriers to creativity. *APA Monitor, 26*(8), 1, 20.

Azar, B. (1996). Scientists examine cancer patients' fears. *APA Monitor, 27*(8), 32.

Azar, B. (1997). It may cause anxiety, but day care can benefit kids. *APA Monitor, 28*(6), 13.

Bachman, J. G., Safron, D. J., Sy, S. R., & Schulenberg, J. E. (2003). Wishing to work: New perspectives on how adolescents' part-time work intensity is linked to educational disengagement, substance use, and other problem behaviours. *International Journal of Behavioral Development, 27*(4), 301–315.

Baddeley, A. D. (1982). *Your memory: A user's guide.* New York: Macmillan.

Baenninger, M. A., & Elenteny, K. (1997). Cited in Azar, B. (1997). Environment can mitigate differences in spatial ability. *APA Monitor, 28*(6), 28.

Bahrick, H. P., Bahrick, P. O., & Wittlinger, R. P. (1975). Fifty years of memory for names and faces: A cross-sectional approach. *Journal of Experimental Psychology: General, 104,* 54–75.

Baker, C. W., Whisman, M. A., & Brownell, K. D. (2000). Studying intergenerational transmission of eating attitudes and behaviors: Methodological and conceptual questions. *Health Psychology, 19*(4), 376–381.

Baker, L. A., DeFries, J. C., & Fulker, D. W. (1983). Longitudinal stability of cognitive ability in the Colorado adoption project. *Child Development, 54,* 290–297.

Baldo, J. V., Delis, D. C., Wilkins, D. P., & Shimamura, A. P. (2004). Is it bigger than a breadbox? Performance of patients with prefrontal lesions on a new executive function test. *Archives of Clinical Neuropsychology, 19*(3), 407–419.

Baldry, A. C. (2003). Bullying in schools and exposure to domestic violence. *Child Abuse & Neglect, 27*(7), 713–732.

Baltes, P. B. (1997). On the incomplete architecture of human ontogeny: Selection, optimization, and compensation as foundation of developmental theory. *American Psychologist, 52,* 366–380.

Baltes, P., & Baltes, M. (1995). Cited in Margoshes, P. (1995). For many, old age is the prime of life. *APA Monitor, 26*(5), 36–37.

Bandura, A. (1991). Human agency: The rhetoric and the reality. *American Psychologist, 46,* 157–162.

Bandura, A., Blanchard, E. B., & Ritter, B. (1969). The relative efficacy of desensitization and modeling approaches for inducing behavioral, affective, and cognitive changes. *Journal of Personality and Social Psychology, 13,* 173–199.

Bandura, A., & McDonald, F. J. (1963). Influence of social reinforcement and the behavior of models in shaping children's moral judgments. *Journal of Abnormal and Social Psychology, 67,* 274–281.

Bandura, A., Ross, S. A., & Ross, D. (1963). Imitation of film-mediated aggressive models. *Journal of Abnormal and Social Psychology, 66,* 3–11.

Bandura, A., Taylor, C. B., Williams, S. I., Medford, I. N., & Barchas, J. D. (1985). Catecholamine secretion as a function of perceived coping self-efficacy. *Journal of Consulting and Clinical Psychology, 53,* 406–414.

Banks, S. M., et al. (1995). The effects of message framing on mammography utilization. *Health Psychology, 14,* 178–184.

Barber, T. X. (2000). A deeper understanding of hypnosis: Its secrets, its nature, its essence. *American Journal of Clinical Hypnosis, 42*(3–4), 208–272.

Bard, P. (1934). The neurohumoral basis of emotional reactions. In C. A. Murchison (Ed.), *Handbook of general experimental psychology.* Worcester, MA: Clark University Press.

Barlow, D. H. (1994). Cited in Howard, K., Barlow, D., Christiensen, A., & Frank, E. (1994). *Evaluating outcomes of psychological interventions: Evaluating the effectiveness of psychotherapy.* Symposium conducted at the meeting of the American Psychological Association, Los Angeles.

Barlow, D. H. (1996). Health care policy, psychotherapy research, and the future of psychotherapy. *American Psychologist, 51,* 1050–1058.

Barlow, D. H., Adler, C. M., Craske, M. G., & Kirshenbaum, S. (1989). "Fear of Panic": An investigation of its role in panic occurrence, phobic avoidance, and treatment outcome. *Behaviour Research and Therapy, 27*(4), 391–396.

Barnes, D. (1987). Biological issues in schizophrenia. *Science, 235,* 430–433.

Barnett, W. S., & Escobar, C. M. (1990). Economic costs and benefits of early intervention. In S. J. Meisels & J. P. Shonkoff (Eds.), *Handbook of early childhood intervention.* New York: Cambridge University Press.

Baron, M., Gruen, R., Ranier, J., Kane, J., & Asnis, L. (1985). A family study of schizophrenia and normal control probands: Implications for the spectrum concept of schizophrenia. *American Journal of Psychiatry, 142,* 447–455.

Baron, R. A., & Richardon, D. R. (1994). *Human aggression* (2nd ed.). New York: Plenum Press.

Barringer, F. (1993, April 25). Polling on sexual issues has its drawbacks. *The New York Times,* p. A23.

Bart, P. (1970). Mother Portnoy's complaints. *Trans-action, 8,* 69–74.

Bartecchi, C. E., MacKenzie, T. D., & Schrier, R. W. (1994). The human cost of tobacco use. *New England Journal of Medicine, 330,* 907–912.

Bartoshuk, L. M. (2000). Psychophysical advances aid the study of genetic variation in taste. *Appetite, 34*(1), 105.

Bashore, T. R., & Rapp, P. E. (1993). Are there alternatives to traditional polygraph procedures? *Psychological Bulletin, 113,* 3–22.

Basic Behavioral Science Task Force of the National Advisory Mental Health Council. (1996b). Basic behavioral science research for mental health: Perception, attention, learning, and memory. *American Psychologist, 51,* 133–142.

Basic Behavioral Science Task Force of the National Advisory Mental Health Council. (1996). Basic behavioral science research for mental health: Sociocultural and environmental practices. *American Psychologist, 51*, 722–731.

Basic Behavioral Science Task Force of the National Advisory Mental Health Council. (1996). Basic behavioral science research for mental health: Vulnerability and resilience. *American Psychologist, 51*, 22–28.

Bateman, D. N. (2000). Triptans and migraine. *The Lancet, 355*, 860–861.

Batson, C. D., et al. (1989). Negative state relief and the empathy-altruism hypothesis. *Journal of Personality and Social Psychology, 56*, 922–933.

Baumeister, R. F., Stillwell, A. M., & Heatherton, T. F. (1994). Guilt: An interpersonal approach. *Psychologial Bulletin, 115*, 243–267.

Baumgardner, A. H., Heppner, P. P., & Arkin, R. M. (1986). Role of causal attribution in personal problem solving. *Journal of Personality and Social Psychology, 50*, 636–643.

Baumrind, D. (1989). Rearing competent children. In W. Damon (Ed.), *Child development today and tomorrow*. San Francisco: Jossey-Bass.

Baumrind, D. (1991a). The influence of parenting style on adolescent competence and substance abuse. *Journal of Early Adolescence, 11*, 56–95.

Baumrind, D. (1991b). Parenting styles and adolescent development. In J. Brooks-Gunn, R. Lerner, & A. C. Petersen, (Eds.), *Encyclopedia of adolescence, II*. New York: Garland.

Baumrind, D. (1993). The average expectable environment is not good enough. A response to Scarr. *Child Development, 64*, 129–1317.

Beck, A. T. (1963). Thinking and depression: I. Idiosyncratic content and cognitive distortions. *Archives of General Psychiatry, 9*, 324–333.

Beck, A. T. (1976). *Cognitive therapy and the emotional disorders*. New York: International Universities Press.

Beck, A. T. (1991). Cognitive therapy: A 30-year retrospective. *American Psychologist, 46*, 368–375.

Beck, A. T. (1993). Cognitive therapy: Past, present, and future. *Journal of Consulting and Clinical Psychology, 61*, 194–198.

Beck, A. T., & Freeman, A. (1990). *Cognitive therapy of personality disorders*. New York: Guilford Press.

Bekoff, M. (2002). *Minding animals: Awareness, emotions, and heart*. New York: Oxford University Press.

Beller, M., & Gafni, N. (2000). Can item format (multiple choice vs. open-ended) account for gender differences in mathematics achievement? *Sex Roles, 42*(1–2), 1–21.

Belsky, J. (1990). Developmental risks associated with infant day care. I. S. Cherazi (Ed.), *Psychosocial issues in day care* (pp. 37–68). New York: American Psychiatric Press.

Belsky, J. (1993). Etiology of child maltreatment: A developmental-ecological analysis. *Psychological Bulletin, 114*, 413–434.

Belsky, J., Fish, M., & Isabella, R. (1991). Continuity and discontinuity in infant negative and positive emotionality: Family attachments and attachment consequences. *Developmental Psychology, 27*, 421–431.

Bem, D. J., & Honorton, C. (1994). Does psi exist? Replicable evidence for an anomalous process of information transfer. *Psychological Bulletin, 115*, 4–18.

Bem, S. L. (1993). *The lenses of gender*. New Haven, CT: Yale University Press.

Bennett, J. C. (1991). The irrationality of the catharsis theory of aggression as justification for educators' support of interscholastic football. *Perceptual and Motor Skills, 72*, 415–418.

Benson, F. (1995). Cited in Margoshes, P. (1995). For many, old age is the prime of life. *APA Monitor, 26*(5), 36–37.

Benson, H., Manzetta, B. R., & Rosner, B. (1973). Decreased systolic blood pressure in hypertensive subjects who practiced meditation. *Journal of Clinical Investigation, 52*, 8.

Berger, B. D. (1993). Drinking to cope with stress: The effect of self-efficacy and alcohol expectancy on alcohol consumption. *Dissertation Abstracts International, 53*, 12–B. (6539)

Berger, K. S. (1994). *The developing person through the life span* (3rd ed.). New York: Worth.

Berkman, L. F., & Breslow, L. (1983). *Health and ways of living: The Alameda County study*. New York: Oxford University Press.

Berkowitz, L. (1987). Mood, self-awareness, and willingness to help. *Journal of Personality and Social Psychology, 52*, 721–729.

Berkowitz, L. (1994). Is something missing? Some observations prompted by the cognitive-neoassociationist view of anger and emotional aggression. In L. R. Huesmann (Ed.), *Aggressive behavior: current perspectives*. New York: Plenum Press.

Berman, A. L., & Jobes, D. A. (1991). *Adolescent suicide: Assessment and intervention*. Washington, DC: American Psychological Association.

Berman, M., Gladue, B., & Taylor, S. (1993). The effects of hormones, type A behavior pattern, and provocation on aggression in men. *Motivation and Emotion, 17*, 125–138.

Bernal, M. E., & Castro, F. G. (1994). Are clinical psychologists prepared for service and research with ethnic minorities? *American Psychologist, 49*, 797–805.

Bernardin, H. J., Cooke, D. K., & Villanova, P. (2000). Conscientiousness and agreeableness as predictors of rating leniency. *Journal of Applied Psychology, 85*(2) 232–236.

Berndt, T. J., & Perry, T. B. (1990). Distinctive features and effects of early adolescent friendships. In R. Montemayor, G. R. Adams, & T. P. Gullotta (Eds.), *From childhood to adolescence: A transitional period?* Newbury Park, CA: Sage.

Berne, E. (1976). *Beyond games and scripts.* New York: Grove Press.

Bernhardt, P. C., Dabbs, J. M., Jr., Fielden, J. A., & Lutter, C. D. (1998). Testosterone changes during vicarious experiences of winning and losing among fans at sporting events. *Physiology & Behavior, 65*(1) 59–62.

Bernstein, W. M., Stephenson, B. O., Snyder, M. L., & Wicklund, R. A. (1983). Causal ambiguity and heterosexual affiliation. *Journal of Experimental Social Psychology, 19,* 78–92.

Bersoff, D. (1994). Cited in DeAngelis, T. (1994). Experts see little impact from insanity plea ruling. *APA Monitor, 25*(6), 28.

Berzonsky, M. C., Kuk, L. S., & Storer, C. J. (1993, March). *Identity development, autonomy, and personal effectiveness.* Paper presented at the meeting of the Society for Research in Child Development, New Orleans, LA.

Bettencourt, B. A., Brewer, M. B., Croak, M. R., & Miller, N. (1992). Cooperation and the reduction of intergroup bias: The role of reward structure and social orientation. *Journal of Experimental Social Psychology, 28,* 301–319.

Beutler, L. E. (1991). Have all won and must all have prizes? *Journal of Consulting and Clinical Psychology, 59,* 226–232.

Bevan, W., & Kessel, F. (1994). Plain truths and home cooking: Thoughts on the making and remaking of psychology. *American Psychologist, 49,* 505–509.

Bexton, W. H., Heron, W., & Scott, T. H. (1954). Effects of decreased variation in the sensory environment. *Canadian Journal of Psychology, 8,* 70–76.

Billings, D. W., Folkman, S., Acree, M., & Moskowitz, J. T. (2000). Coping and physical health during caregiving: The roles of positive and negative affect. *Journal of Personality and Social Psychology, 79*(1), 131–142.

Birks, Y., & Roger, D. (2000). Identifying components of type-A behaviour: "Toxic" and "non-toxic" achieving. *Personality & Individual Differences, 28*(6), 1093–1105.

Bjorkqvist, K., Lagerspetz, K. M., & Kaukiainen, A. (1992). Do girls manipulate and boys fight? Developmental trends in regard to direct and indirect aggression. *Aggressive Behavior, 18,* 117–127.

Blakeslee, S. (1992, January 7). Scientists unraveling chemistry of dreams. *The New York Times,* pp. C1, C10.

Blanchard, E. B. (1992a). Psychological treatment of benign headache disorders. *Journal of Consulting and Clinical Psychology, 60,* 537–551.

Blanchard, E. B. (1992b). Introduction to the special issue on behavioral medicine: An update for the 1990s. *Journal of Consulting and Clinical Psychology, 60,* 491–492.

Blanchard, E. B., et al. (1990a). A controlled evaluation of thermal biofeedback and thermal feedback combined with cognitive therapy in the treatment of vascular headache. *Journal of Consulting and Clinical Psychology, 58,* 216–224.

Blanchard, E. B., et al. (1990b). Placebo-controlled evaluation of abbreviated progressive muscle relaxation and of relaxation combined with cognitive therapy in the treatment of tension headache. *Journal of Consulting and Clinical Psychology, 58,* 210–215.

Blanchard, E. B., et al. (1991). The role of regular home practice in the relaxation treatment of tension headache. *Journal of Consulting and Clinical Psychology, 59,* 467–470.

Blanck, P. D., Bellack, A. S., Rosnow, R. L., Rotheram-Borus, M. J., & Schooler, N. R. (1992). Scientific rewards and conflicts in ethical choices in human subjects research. *American Psychologist, 47,* 959–965.

Blass, T. (1991). Understanding behavior in the Milgram obedience experiment: The roles of personality, situations, and their interactions. *Journal of Personality and Social Psychology, 60,* 398–413.

Bloom, B. L. (1992). Computer assisted psychological intervention: A review and commentary. *Clinical Psychology Review, 12,* 169–197.

Blum, R. W., Harmon, B., Harris, L., Bergeisen, L., & Resnick, M. D. (1992). American Indian-Alaska native youth health. *Journal of the American Medical Association, 267,* 1637–1644.

Boccia, M., & Campos, J. J. (1989). Maternal emotional signals, social referencing, and infants' reactions to strangers. In N. Eisenberg (Ed.), *Empathy and related emotional responses.* New Directions for Child Development, no. 44. San Francisco: Jossey-Bass.

Bodenhausen, G. V. (1988). Stereotypic biases in social decision making and memory. *Journal of Personality and Social Psychology, 55,* 726–737.

Bohon, L. M., Singer, R. D., & Santos, S. J. (1993). The effects of real-world status and manipulated status on the self-esteem and social competition of Anglo-Americans and Mexican-Americans. *Hispanic Journal of Behavioral Sciences, 15,* 63–79.

Bond, R., & Smith, P. B. (1996). Culture and conformity: A meta-analysis of studies using Asch's line judgment task. *Psychological Bulletin, 119,* 111–137.

Bonin, M. F., McCreary, D. R., & Sadava, S. W. (2000). Problem drinking behavior in two community-based samples of adults: Influence of gender, coping, loneliness, and depression. *Psychology of Addictive Behaviors, 14*(2), 151–161.

Bordo, S. (1993). *Unbearable weight: Feminism, Western culture, and the body.* Berkeley: University of California Press.

Borkovec, T. D., & Costello, E. (1993). Efficacy of applied relaxation and cognitive-behavioral therapy in the treatment of generalized anxiety disorder. *Journal of Consulting and Clinical Psychology, 61,* 611–619.

Bouchard, C. (1991). Is weight fluctuation a risk factor? *New England Journal of Medicine, 324,* 1887–1889.

Bouchard, T. J., Jr., & Loehlin, J. C. (2001). Genes, evolution, and personality. *Behavior Genetics, 31*(3), 243–273.

Bouchard, T. J., Jr., Lykken, D. T., McGue, M., Segal, N. L., & Tellegren, A. (1990). Sources of human psychological differences: The Minnesota study of twins reared apart. *Science, 250,* 223–228.

Bower, G. H. (1981). Mood and memory. *American Psychologist, 36,* 129–148.

Bowers, K. S., & Woody, E. Z. (1996). Hypnotic amnesia and the paradox of intentional forgetting. *Journal of Abnormal Psychology, 105,* 381–390.

Bowers, T. G., & Clum, G. Z. (1988). Relative contribution of specific and nonspecific treatment effects: Meta-analysis of placebo-controlled behavior therapy research. *Psychological Bulletin, 103,* 315–323.

Bowman, M. L. (1989). Testing individual differences in ancient China. *American Psychologist, 44,* 576–578.

Boyd, J. H., & Weissman, M. M. (1984). Epidemiology of affective disorders: A reexamination and future directions. *Archives of General Psychiatry, 38,* 1039–1045.

Boyd, J. H., Weissman, M. M., Thompson, W. D., & Myers, J. K. (1982). Screening for depression in a community sample: Understanding the discrepancies between depression syndrome and diagnostic scales. *Archives of General Psychiatry, 39,* 1195–1200.

Bradley, R. H., et al. (1989). Home environment and cognitive development in the first three years of life: A collaborative study involving six sites and three ethnic groups in North America. *Developmental Psychology, 25,* 217–235.

Bradshaw, J. L., Nettleton, N. C., & Taylor, M. J. (1981). Right hemisphere language and cognitive deficit in sinistrals. *Neuropsychologia, 19,* 113–132.

Brain-link camera gives blind a limited view. (2000, January 18). *The New York Times online.*

Brandstätter, H., & Farthofer, A. (2003). Influence of part-time work on university students' academic performance. *Zeitschrift für Arbeits-und Organisationspsychologie, 47*(3), 134–145.

Bray, R. M., & Sugarman, R. (1980). Social facilitation among interaction groups: Evidence for the evaluation-apprehension hypothesis. *Personality and Social Psychology Bulletin, 6,* 137–142.

Breckler, S. J., & Wiggins, E. C. (1989). Affect versus evaluation in the structure of attitudes. *Journal of Experimental Social Psychology, 25,* 253–271.

Brenner, J. (1992). Cited in Williams, L. (1992, February 6). Woman's image in a mirror: Who defines what she sees? *The New Times,* pp. A1, B7.

Bridges, K. (1932). Emotional development in early infancy. *Child Development, 3,* 324–341.

Bridgewater, C. A. (1982). What candor can do. *Psychology Today, 16*(5), 16.

Brigham, J. C. (1980). Limiting conditions of the "physical attractiveness stereotype": Attributions about divorce. *Journal of Research in Personality, 14,* 365–375.

Bril, B. (1986). Motor development and cultural attitudes. In H. T. A. Whiting & M. G. Wade (Eds.), *Themes in motor development.* Dordrecht, Netherlands: Martinus Nijhoff.

Broberg, A. G., Wessels, H., Lamb, M. E., & Hwang, C. P. (1997). Effects of day care on the development of cognitive abilities in 8-year-olds: A longitudinal study. *Developmental Psychology, 33*(1), 62–69.

Brody, J. E. (1990, January 19). High cholesterol poses heart risk in older men. *The New York Times,* p. A19.

Brody, J. E. (1992a, January 8). Migraines and the estrogen connection. *The New York Times,* p. C12.

Brody, J. E. (1992b, June 16). Suicide myths cloud efforts to save children. *The New York Times,* pp. A1, B7.

Brody, J. E. (1992c, December 30). How weight loss changes risk. *The New York Times,* p. C6.

Brody, J. E. (1994, March 16). Cancer pain is beatable, but too few know it. *The New York Times,* p. C12.

Brody, J. E. (1995a). Cited in DeAngelis, T. (1995). Eat well, keep fit, and let go of stress. *APA Monitor, 26*(10), 20.

Brody, J. E. (1995b, August 30). Hormone replacement therapy for men: When does it help? *The New York Times,* p. C8.

Brook, J. S., Whiteman, M. M., & Finch, S. (1993). Childhood aggression, adolescent delinquency, and drug use: A longitudinal study. *Journal of Genetic Psychology, 153,* 369–383.

Brooks-Gunn, J., & Furstenberg, F. F. (1989). Adolescent sexual behavior. *American Psychologist, 44,* 249–257.

Broverman, I. K., Vogel, S. R., Broverman, D. M., Clarkson, F. E., & Rosenkrantz, P. S. (1972). Sex-role stereotypes: A current appraisal. *Journal of Social Issues, 28,* 59–78.

Brown, B. B., Mounts, N., Lamborn, S. D., & Steinberg, L. (1993). Parenting practices and peer group affiliation in adolescence. *Child Development, 64,* 467–482.

Brown, D. E. (1991). *Human universals.* Philadelphia: Temple University Press.

Brownell, K. D. (1993). Whether obesity should be treated. *Health Psychology, 12,* 339–341.

Brownell, K. D., & Rodin, J. (1994). The dieting maelstrom: Is it possible and advisable to lose weight? *American Psychologist, 49,* 781–791.

Brownell, K. D., & Wadden, T. A. (1992). Obesity: Understanding a serious, prevalent, and refactory disorder. *Journal of Consulting and Clinical Psychology, 60,* 505–517.

Browning, C. (1992). *Ordinary men: Reserve Police Battalion 101 and the Final Solution in Poland.* New York: HarperCollins.

Buchanan, C. M., Eccles, J. S., & Becker, J. B. (1992). Are adolescents the victims of raging hormones? Evidence for activational effects of hormones on moods and behavior at adolescence. *Psychological Bulletin, 111,* 62–107.

Buchanan, R. W., Pearlson, G., & Tamminga, C. A. (2004). Prefrontal cortex, structural analysis: Segmenting the prefrontal cortex. *American Journal of Psychiatry, 161*(11), 1978.

Budzynski, T. H., & Stoyra, J. M. (1984). Biofeedback methods in the treatment of anxiety and stress. In R. I. Woolfolk & P. M. Lehrer (Eds.), *Principles and practice of stress management*. New York: Guilford Press.

Burger, J. M. (1999). The foot-in-the-door compliance procedure: A multiple-process analysis and review. *Personality & Social Psychology Review, 3*(4), 303–325.

Burish, T. G., Carey, M. P., Krozely, M. G., & Greco, F. A. (1987). Conditioned side effects induced by cancer chemotherapy: Prevention through behavioral treatment. *Journal of Consulting and Clinical Psychology, 55,* 42–48.

Burkett, S. (1980). Religiosity, beliefs and normative standards and adolescent drinking. *Journal of Studies on Alcohol, 41,* 662–671.

Burman, B., & Margolin, G. (1992). Analysis of the association between marital relationships and health problems: An interactional perspective. *Psychological Bulletin, 112,* 39–63.

Burns, G. L., & Farina, A. (1987). Physical attractiveness and self-perception of mental disorder. *Journal of Abnormal Psychology, 96,* 161–163.

Burnstein, E., & Schul, Y. (1982). The informational basis of social judgments: Operations in forming an impression of another person. *Journal of Experimental Social Psychology, 18,* 217–234.

Bushman, B. J., Baumeister, R. F., & Stack, A. D. (1999). Catharsis, aggression, and persuasive influence: Self-fulfilling or self-defeating prophecies? *Journal of Personality & Social Psychology, 76*(3), 367–376.

Buss, D. M. (1989). Sex differences in human mate preferences: Evolutionary hypotheses tested in 37 cultures. *Behavioral and Brain Sciences, 12,* 1–49.

Buss, D. M. (1992). Is there a universal human nature? *Contemporary Psychology, 37,* 1262–1263.

Buss, D. M. (1994). *The evolution of desire: Strategies of human mating.* New York: Basic Books.

Buss, D. M. (1995). Psychological sex differences: Origins through sexual selection. *American Psychologist, 50,* 164–168.

Buss, D. M. (1999). Adaptive individual differences revisited. *Journal of Personality, 67*(2), 259–264.

Buss, D. M., & Barnes, M. (1986). Preferences in human mate selection. *Journal of Personality and Social Psychology, 50,* 559–570.

Butler, J. C. (2000). Personality and emotional correlates of right-wing authoritarianism. *Social Behavior & Personality, 28*(1), 1–14.

Butterfield, F. (1992, January 1). Studies find a family link to criminality. *The New York Times,* pp. A1, A8.

Byrnes, J., & Takahira, S. (1993). Explaining gender differences on SAT-math items. *Developmental Psychology, 29,* 805–810.

Caldwell, C. B., & Gotteman, I. I. (1990). Schizophrenics kill themselves too: A review of the risk factors for suicide. *Schizophrenia Bulletin, 16,* 571–589.

Califano, J. A. (1995). The wrong way to stay slim. *New England Journal of Medicine, 333,* 1214–1216.

Camarena, P. M. (1991). Conformity in adolescence. In R. M. Lerner, A. C. Petersen, & J. Brooks-Gunn (Eds.), *Encyclopedia of adolescence.* New York: Garland.

Campbell, W. K., & Sedikides, C. (1999). Self-threat magnifies the self-serving bias: A meta-analytic integration. *Review of General Psychology, 3*(1), 23–43.

Campos, J. J. (2000). Cited in Azar, B. (2000). What's in a face? *Monitor on Psychology, 31*(1), 44–45.

Campos, J. J., Langer, A., & Krowitz, A. (1970). Cardiac responses on the visual cliff in prelocomotor infants. *Science, 170,* 196–197.

Cannon, W. B. (1927). The James-Lange theory of emotions: A critical examination and an alternative theory. *American Journal of Psychology, 39,* 106–124.

Cannon, W. B. (1939). *The wisdom of the body.* New York: Norton.

Cappella, J. N., & Palmer, M. T. (1990). Attitude similarity, relational history, and attraction: The mediating effects of kinesic and vocal behaviors. *Communication Monographs, 5,* 161–183.

Carey, G. (1992). Twin imitation for antisocial behavior: Implications for genetic and family environment research. *Journal of Abnormal Psychology, 101,* 18–25.

Carlson, J. G., & Hatfield, E. (1992). *Psychology of emotion.* Fort Worth, TX: Harcourt Brace Jovanovich.

Carlson, M., Charlin, V., & Miller, N. (1988). Positive mood and helping behavior: A test of six hypotheses. *Journal of Personality and Social Psychology, 55,* 211–229.

Carmichael, L. L., Hogan, H. O., & Walter, A. A. (1932). An experimental study of the effect of language on the reproduction of visually perceived form. *Journal of Experimental Psychology, 15,* 73–86.

Carrère, S., Buehlman, K. T., Gottman, J. M., Coan, J. A., & Ruckstuhl, L. (2000). Predicting marital stability and divorce in newlywed couples. *Journal of Family Psychology, 14*(1), 42–58.

Carroll, K. M., Rounsaville, B. J., & Nich, C. (1994). Blind man's bluff: Effectiveness and significance of psychotherapy and pharmacotherapy blinding procedures in a clinical trial. *Journal of Consulting and Clinical Psychology, 62,* 276–280.

Carson, R. C. (1989). Personality. *Annual Review of Psychology, 40,* 227–248.

Carstensen, L. (1995). Cited in Margoshes, P. (1995). For many, old age is the prime of life. *APA Monitor, 26*(5), 36–37.

Caspi, A., Lynam, D., Moffitt, T. E., & Silva, P. A. (1993). Unraveling girls' delinquency: Biological, dispositional, and contextual contributions to adolescent misbehavior. *Developmental Psychology, 29,* 19–30.

Cassidy, J. (1988). Child-mother attachment and the self in six-year-olds. *Child Development, 39*(1), 121–134.

Castelli, W. (1994). Cited in Brody, J. E. (1994, February 8). Scientist at work—William Castelli: Preaching the gospel of healthy hearts. *The New York Times,* pp. C1, C10.

Cattell, R. (1965). *The scientific analysis of personality.* Baltimore: Penguin Books.

Caulfield, M., et al. (1994). Linkage of the angiotensinogen gene to essential hypertension. *New England Journal of Medicine, 330,* 1629–1633.

Cavaliere, F. (1996). Bilingual schools face big political challenges. *APA Monitor, 27*(2), 36.

Cavanaugh, J. C., & Green, E. E. (1990). I believe, therefore I can: Self-efficacy beliefs in memory aging. In E. A. Lovelace (Ed.), *Aging and cognition: Mental processes, self-awareness, and interventions.* North-Holland, Elsevier.

Ceci, S. J., & Bruck, M. (1993). Suggestibility of the child witness. *Psychological Bulletin, 113,* 403–439.

Cellar, D. F., Nelson, Z. C., & Yorke, C. M. (2000). The five-factor model and driving behavior: Personality and involvement in vehicular accidents. *Psychological Reports, 86*(2) 454–456.

Centers for Disease Control and Prevention. (1993). Infant mortality—United States, 1990. *Morbidity and Mortality Weekly Report, 42,* 161–165.

Centers for Disease Control and Prevention. (1993, October). *HIV/AIDS surveillance: Third quarter edition. U.S. AIDS cases reported through September 1993.* Atlanta, GA: U.S. Department of Health and Human Services.

Centers for Disease Control and Prevention. (2000, June 9). Youth risk behavior surveillance—United States, 1999. *Morbidity and Mortality Weekly Report, 49*(SS05); 1–96.

Chadwick, P. D. J., & Lowe, C. F. (1990). Measurement and modification of delusional beliefs. *Journal of Consulting and Clinical Psychology, 58,* 225–232.

Chafee, M. V., & Goldman-Rakic, P. S. (2000). Inactivation of parietal and prefrontal cortex reveals interdependence of neural activity during memory-guided saccades. *Journal of Neurophysiology, 83*(3), 1550–1566.

Chance, S. E., Brown, R. T., Dabbs, J. M., Jr., & Casey, R. (2000). Testosterone, intelligence and behavior disorders in young boys. *Personality & Individual Differences, 28*(3) 437–445.

Chase, J., Jessor, R., & Donovan, J. (1980). Psychological correlates of marijuana use and drinking in a national sample of adolescents. *American Journal of Public Health, 70,* 604–612.

Chassin, L., Presson, C. C., Pitts, S. C., & Sherman, S. J. (2000). The natural history of cigarette smoking from adolescence to adulthood in a Midwestern community sample: Multiple trajectories and their psychological correlates. *Health Psychology, 19,* 223–231.

Cherlin, J. (1992). *Marriage, divorce, remarriage: Social trends in the United States.* Cambridge, MA: Harvard University Press.

Chira, S. (1992, February 12). Bias against girls found rife in schools, with lasting damage. *The New York Times,* pp. A1, A23.

Chomsky, N. (1980). Rules and representations. *Behavioral and Brain Sciences, 3,* 1–16.

Chomsky, N. (1991). Linguistics and cognitive science: Problems and mysteries. In A. Kasher (Ed.), *The Chomskyan turn.* Cambridge, MA: Blackwell.

Cialdini, R. B. (1993). *Influence: Science and practice* (3rd ed.). New York: HarperCollins.

Cialdini, R. B. (2000). Cited in McKinley, J. C., Jr. (2000, August 11). It isn't just a game: Clues to avid rooting. *The New York Times online.*

Cicchetti, D., & Olson, K. (1990). The developmental psychopathology of child maltreatment. In M. Lewis & S. M. Miller (Eds.), *Handbook of developmental psychopathology* (pp. 261–279). New York: Plenum Press.

Ciesielski, K., Beech, H., & Gordon, P. (1981). Some electrophysical observations in obessional states. *British Journal of Psychiatry, 138,* 479–484.

Clark, K. B. (1955/1988). *Prejudice and your child.* Middletown, CT: Wesleyan University Press.

Clark, K. B., & Clark, M. P. (1947). Racial identification and preference in Negro children. In T. M. Newcomb & E. L. Hartley (Eds.), *Readings in Social Psychology.* New York: Holt, Rinehart and Winston.

Clark, M. S., Mills, J. R., & Corcoran, D. M. (1989). Keeping track of needs and inputs of friends and strangers. *Personality and Social Psychology Bulletin, 15,* 533–542.

Clark, R., Anderson, N. B., Clark, V. R., & Williams, D. R. (1999). Racism as a stressor for African Americans. *American Psychologist, 54*(10), 805–816.

Clarke-Stewart, K. A. (1989). Infant day care: Maligned or malignant? *American Psychologist, 44,* 266–273.

Clarke-Stewart, K. A. (1991). A home is not a school: The effects of child care on children's development. *Journal of Social Issues, 47,* 105–123.

Clarke-Stewart, K. A., Vandell, D. L., McCartney, K., Owen, M. T., & Booth, C. (2000). Effects of parental separation and divorce on very young children. *Journal of Family Psychology, 14*(2), 304–326.

Coe, C. (1993). Cited in Adler, T. (1993). Men and women affected by stress, but differently. *APA Monitor, 24*(7), 8–9.

Cohen, D., et al. (2000). Absence of cognitive impairment at long-term follow-up in adolescents treated with ECT for severe mood disorder. *American Journal of Psychiatry, 157,* 460–462.

Cohen, L. A. (1987, November). Diet and cancer. *Scientific American,* pp. 42–48, 53–54.

Cohen, S., Tyrrell, D. A. J., & Smith, A. P. (1993). Negative life events, perceived stress, negative affect, and susceptibility to the common cold. *Journal of Personality and Social Psychology, 64,* 131–140.

Cohen, S., & Williamson, G. M. (1991). Stress and infectious disease in humans. *Psychological Bulletin, 109,* 5–24.

Coleman, J., Butcher, J., & Carson, R. (1984). *Abnormal psychology and modern life* (7th ed.). Glenview, IL: Scott, Foresman.

Coleman, L. (1990). Cited in Goleman, G. (1990, August 2). The quiet comeback of electroshock therapy. *The New York Times,* p. B5.

Collaer, M. L., & Hines, M. (1995). Human behavioral sex differences: A role for gonadal hormones during early development? *Psychological Bulletin, 118,* 55–107.

Collier, G. (1994). *Social origins of mental ability.* New York: Wiley.

Collins, J. F. (2000). Biracial Japanese American identity: An evolving process. *Cultural Diversity & Ethnic Minority Psychology, 6*(2), 115–133.

Collins, W. A. (1990). Parent-child relationships in the transition of adolescence: Continuity and change in ineraction, affect, and cognition. In R. Montemayor, G. R. Adams, & T. P. Gullotta (Eds.), *From childhood to adolescence: A transitional period.* Newbury Park, CA: Sage.

Collins, W. A., & Russell, G. (1991). Mother-child and father-child relationships in middle childhood and adolescence: A developmental analysis. *Developmental Review, 11,* 99–136.

Colvin, M. K., Funnell, M. G., & Gazzaniga, M. S. (2005). Numerical processing in the two hemispheres: Studies of a split–brain patient. *Brain & Cognition, 57*(1), 43–52.

Comas-Diaz, L. (1994, February). Race and gender in psychotherapy with women of color. *Winter roundtable on cross-cultural counseling and psychotherapy: Race and gender.* New York: Teachers College, Columbia University.

Condon, J. W., & Crano, W. D. (1988). Inferred evaluation and the relation between attitude similarity and interpersonal attraction. *Journal of Personality and Social Psychology, 54,* 789–797.

Conger, J. J. (1978). Adolescence: A time for becoming. In M. Lamb (Ed.), *Social and personality development.* New York: Holt, Rinehart and Winston.

Coolidge, F. L., DenBoer, J. W., & Segal, D. L. (2004). Personality and neuropsychological correlates of bullying behavior. *Personality & Individual Differences, 36*(7), 1559–1569.

Cools, J., Schotte, D. E., & McNally, R. J. (1992). Emotional arousal and overeating in restrained eaters. *Journal of Abnormal Psychology, 101,* 348-351.

Coon, H., Fulker, D. W., DeFries, J. C., & Plomin, R. (1990). Home environment and cognitive ability of 7-year-old children in the Colorado Adoption Project: Genetic and environmental etiologies. *Developmental Psychology, 26,* 459-468.

Cooper, J. R., Bloom, F. E., & Roth, R. H. (1991). *The biochemical basis of neuropharmacology.* New York: Oxford University Press.

Corballis, P. M., Funnell, M. G., & Gazzaniga, M. S. (2002). Hemispheric asymmetries for simple visual judgments in the split brain. *Neuropsychologia, 40*(4), 401-410.

Corkin, S., et al. (1985). Analyses of global memory impairments of different etiologies. In D. S. Olton, E. Gamzu, & S. Corkin (Eds.), *Memory dysfunction.* New York: New York Academy of Sciences.

Cotman, C. W. (2000, July). Amyloid toxicity. Paper presented to the World Alzheimer Congress 2000, Washington, DC.

Cousins, N. (1979). *Anatomy of an illness as perceived by the patient: Reflections on helaing and regeneration.* New York: Norton.

Cox, B. J., Borger, S. C., Asmundson, G. J. G., & Taylor, S. (2000). Hypochondriasis: Dimensions of hypochondriasis and the five-factor model of personality. *Personality & Individual Differences, 29*(1), 99-108.

Cox, M. J., Owen, M. T., Henderson, V. K., & Margand, N. A. (1992). Prediction of infant-father and infant-mother attachment. *Developmental Psychology, 28,* 474-483.

Cox, W. M., & Alm, R. (2005, February 28). Scientists are made, not born. *The New York Times Magazine.*

Coyne, J. C., & Downey, G. (1991). Social factors and psychopathology: Stress, social support, and coping processes. *Annual Review of Psychology, 42,* 401-425.

Craighead, L. W., & Agras, W. S. (1991). Mechanisms of action in cognitive-behavioral and pharmacological interventions for obesity and bulimia nervosa. *Journal of Consulting and Clinical Psychology, 59,* 115-125.

Crain, W. C. (1992). *Theories of development: Concepts and applications* (3rd ed.). Englewood Cliffs, NJ: Prentice-Hall.

Cramer, R. E., McMaster, M. R., Bartell, P. A., & Dragna, M. (1988). Subject competence and minimization of the bystander effect. *Journal of Applied Social Psychology, 18,* 1133-1148.

Crano, W. D. (1997). Vested interest, symbolic politics, and attitude-behavior consistency. *Journal of Personality and Social Psychology, 72*(3), 485-491.

Crews, D. (1994). Animal sexuality. *Scientific American, 270*(1), 108-114.

Crick, N. R., & Dodge, K. A. (1994). A review and reformulation of social information-processing mechanisms in children's social adjustment. *Psychological Bulletin, 115,* 74-101.

Crosby, F. J., & Jaskar, K. L. (1993). Women and men at home and at work: Realities and illusions. In S. Oskamp & M. Costanzo (Eds.), *Gender issues in contemporary society.* Newbury Park, CA: Sage.

Cross, W. (1991). *Shades of identity.* Philadelphia: Temple University Press.

BOOKSHELF

Cross, W. E., Parham, T. A., & Helms, J. E. (1991). The states of Black identity development: Nigrescence models. In R. Jones (Ed.), *Black psychology* (3rd ed., pp. 319–338). Hampton, VA: Cobb & Henry.

Crowe, R. A. (1990). Astrology and the scientific method. *Psychological Reports, 67,* 163–191.

Crusco, A. H., & Wetzel, C. G. (1984). The Midas touch: The effects of interpersonal touch on restaurant tipping. *Personality and Social Psychology Bulletin, 10,* 512–517.

Cummings, J. L. (1995, June 10). Dementia: the failing brain. *Lancet,* p. 772.

Cunningham, M. R., Shaffer, D. R., Barbee, A. P., Wolff, P. L., & Kelley, D. J. (1990). Separate processes in the relation of elation and depression to helping: Social versus personal concerns. *Journal of Experimental Social Psychology, 26,* 13–33.

Curb, J. D., & Marcus, E. B. (1991). Body fat and obesity in Japanese Americans. *American Journal of Clinical Nutrition, 53,* 1552S–1555S.

Curfman, G. D. (1993a). The health benefits of exercise: A critical reappraisal. *New England Journal of Medicine, 328,* 574–576.

Curfman, G. D. (1993b). Is exercise beneficial—or hazardous—to your heart? *New England Journal of Medicine, 329,* 1730–1731.

Curtis, R. C., & Miller, K. (1986). Believing another likes or dislikes you: Behavior making the beliefs come true. *Journal of Personality and Social Psychology, 51,* 284–290.

Dabbs, J. M., Jr., Chang, E-L., Strong, R. A., & Milun, R. (1998). Spatial ability, navigation strategy, and geographic knowledge among men and women. *Evolution & Human Behavior, 19*(2) 89–98.

Dabbs, J. M., Jr., Hargrove, M. F., & Heusel, C. (1996). Testosterone differences among college fraternities: Well-behaved vs rambunctious. *Personality & Individual Differences, 20*(2), 157–161.

Damaged gene is linked to lung cancer. (1996, April 6). *The New York Times,* p. A24.

Damasio, H., & Damasio, A. (1992, September). Brain and language. *Scientific American,* pp. 89–95.

Darwin, C. (1872). *The expression of the emotions in man and animals.* London: J. Murray.

Davey, L. F. (1993, March). *Developmental implications of shared and divergent perceptions in the parent-adolescent relationship.* Paper presented at the biennial meeting of the Society for Research in Child Development, New Orleans, LA.

Davidson, E. S., Yasuna, A., & Tower, A. (1979). The effects of television cartoons on sex-role stereotyping in young girls. *Child Development, 50,* 597–600.

Davidson, J. E. (1986). The role of insight in giftedness. In R. J. Sternberg & J. E. Davidson (Eds.), *Conceptions of giftedness.* New York: Cambridge University Press.

Davies, P. T., & Cummings, E. M. (1994). Marital conflict and child adjustment. *Psychological Bulletin, 116,* 387–411.

Davis, J. H. (1975). The design processes of 6– and 12–person mock juries assigned unanimous and two-thirds majority rules. *Journal of Personality and Social Psychology, 32,* 1–14.

Davis, J. H., Tindale, R. S., Nagao, D. H., Hinsz, V. B., & Robertson, B. (1984). Order effects in multiple decisions by groups: A demonstration with mock juries and trial procedures. *Journal of Personality and Social Psychology, 47,* 1003–1012.

Davison, G., & Neale, J. (1990). *Abnormal psychology* (5th ed.). New York: Wiley.

Dawes, R. M. (1999). Two methods for studying the incremental validity of a Rorschach variable. Psychological Assessment, 11(3), 297–302.

De Houwer, J., Thomas, S., & Baeyens, F. (2001). Associative learning of likes and dislikes: A review of 25 years of research on human evaluative conditioning. *Psychological Bulletin, 127*(6), 853–869.

DeAngelis, T. (1993a). It's baaack: TV violence, concern for kid viewers. *APA Monitor, 24*(8), 16.

DeAngelis, T. (1993b). Law helps American Indians enter field. *APA Monitor, 24*(3), 26–27.

DeAngelis, T. (1995). Mental health care is elusive for Hispanic. *APA Monitor, 26*(7), 49.

DeAngelis, T. (1997). Abused children have more conflicts with friends. *APA Monitor, 28*(6), 32.

Deaux, K., & Lewis, L. L. (1983). Assessment of gender stereotypes: Methodology and components. *Psychological Documents, 13*(25, Ms. No. 2583).

DeFries, J. C., Plomin, R., & LaBudam, M. C. (1987). Genetic stability of cognitive development from childhood to adulthood. *Developmental Psychology, 23,* 4–12.

DeGree, C. E., & Snyder, C. R. (1995). Adler's psychology (of use) today: Personal history of traumatic life events as a self-handicapping strategy. *Journal of Personality and Social Psychology, 48,* 1512–1519.

DeKovic, M., & Janssens, J. (1992). Parents' child-rearing style and child's sociometric status. *Developmental Psychology, 28,* 925–932.

Delgado, J. M. R. (1969). *Physical control of the mind.* New York: Harper & Row.

Delhanty, D. L., et al. (1996). Time course of natural killer cell activity and lymphocyte proliferation in response to two acute stressors in healthy men. *Health Psychology, 15,* 48–55.

Denmark, F. L. (1998). Women and psychology: An international perspective. *American Psychologist, 53*(4), 465–473.

DePaulo, B. M. (1992). Nonverbal behavior and self-presentation. *Psychological Bulletin, 111,* 203–243.

Desmond, A. M. (1994). Adolescent pregnancy in the United States: Not a minority issue. *Health Care for Women International, 15*(4), 325–331.

Deutsch, M., & Collins, M. (1951). *Interracial housing: A psychological evaluation of a social experiment.* Minneapolis: University of Minnesota Press.

Devine, P. G. (1989). Stereotypes and prejudice: Their automatic and controlled components. *Journal of Personality and Social Psychology, 56,* 5–18.

DeWit, D. J., et al. (2000). Age at first alcohol use: A risk factor for the development of alcohol disorders. *American Journal of Psychiatry, 157,* 745–750.

Diaz, R. M. (1985). Bilingual cognitive development: Addressing three gaps in current research. *Child Development, 56,* 1376–1388.

Digman, J. M., & Inouye, J. (1986). Specification of the five robust factors of personality. *Journal of Personality and Social Psychology, 50,* 116–123.

DiLalla, D. L., Carey, G., Gottesman, I. I., & Bouchard, T. J., Jr. (1996). Heritability of MMPI personality indicators of psychopathology in twins reared apart. *Journal of Abnormal Psychology, 105,* 491–499.

DiLalla, L. F., & Gottesman, I. I. (1991). Biological and genetic contributors to violence: Widom's untold tale. *Psychological Bulletin, 109,* 125–129.

Dill, C. A., Gilden, E. R., Hill, P. C., & Hanselka, L. L. (1982). Federal human subjects regulations: A methodological artifact. *Personality and Social Psychology Bulletin, 8,* 417–425.

Dindia, K., & Allen, M. (1992). Sex differences in self-disclosure: A meta-analysis. *Psychological Bulletin, 112,* 106–124.

Dix, T. (1991). The affective organization of parenting: Adaptive and maladaptive processes. *Psychological Bulletin, 110,* 3–25.

Doctors tie male mentality to shorter life span. (1995, June 14). *The New York Times,* p. C14.

Dodge, K. A., Price, J. M., Bachorowski, J., & Newman, J. P. (1990). Hostile attributional biases in severely aggressive adolescents. *Journal of Abnormal Psychology, 99,* 385–392.

Dogil, G., et al. (2002). The speaking brain: A tutorial introduction to fMRI experiments in the production of speech, prosody and syntax. *Journal of Neurolinguistics, 15*(1), 59–90.

Doob, A. N., & Wood, L. (1972). Catharsis and aggression: The effects of annoyance and retaliation on aggressive behavior. *Journal of Personality and Social Psychology, 22,* 236–245.

Dovidio, J. H., Evans, N., & Tyler, R. B. (1986). Racial stereotypes: The contents of their cognitive representations. *Journal of Experimental Social Psychology, 22,* 22–37.

Draguns, J. G. (1988). Personality and culture: Are they relevant for the enhancement of quality of mental life? In P. R. Dasen, J. W. Berry, & N. Sartorius (Eds.), *Health and cross-cultural psychology: Toward applications.* Newberry Park, CA: Sage.

Drapkin, R. G., Wing, R. R., & Shiffman, S. (1995). Responses to hypothetical high risk situations: Do they predict weight loss in a behavioral treatment program or the context of dietary lapses? *Health Psychology, 14,* 427–434.

Du Bois, W. E. B. (1903/1990). *Souls of black folk.* New York: Random House.

Dubbert, P. M. (1992). Exercise in behavioral medicine. *Journal of Consulting and Clinical Psychology, 60,* 613–618.

Duberstein, P. R., et al. (2000). Personality traits and suicidal behavior and ideation in depressed inpatients 50 years of age and older. *Journals of Gerontology: Series B: Psychological Sciences & Social Sciences, 55B*(1), P18–P26.

DuBois, D. L., & Hirsh, B. J. (1990). School and neighborhood friendship patterns of Blacks and Whites in adolescence. *Child Development, 61,* 524–536.

Duckitt, J. (1992). Psychology and prejudice: A historical analysis and integrative framework. *American Psychologist, 47,* 1182–1193.

Duffy, V. B., Peterson, J. M., & Bartoshuk, L. M. (2004). Associations between taste genetics, oral sensation and alcohol intake. *Physiology & Behavior, 82*(2–3), 435–445.

Dumas, J. E., & LaFreniere, P. J. (1993). Mother-child relationships as a support of support or stress: A comparison of competent, average, aggressive, and anxious dyads. *Child Development, 64.*

Duncan, J., et al. (2000). A neural basis for general intelligence. *Science, 289*(5478), 457–460.

Duncker, K. (1945). On problem solving. *Psychological Monographs,* 58. (Whole No. 270)

Dunphy, D. C. (1963). The social structure of urban adolescent peer groups. *Sociometry, 26,* 230–246.

Duval, T. S., & Silvia, P. J. (2002). Self-awareness, probability of improvement, and the self-serving bias. *Journal of Personality & Social Psychology, 82*(1), 49–61.

Dweck, C. S. (1990). Toward a theory of goals: Their role in motivation in personality. In R. A. Dienstbier (Ed.), *Nebraska symposium on motivation, 38.* Lincoln: University of Nebraska Press.

Eagly, A. H. (1987). *Sex differences in social behavior: A social-role interpretation.* Hillsdale, NJ: Erlbaum.

Eagly, A. H., & Chaiken, S. (1993). *The psychology of attitudes.* Fort Worth, TX: Harcourt Brace Jovanovich.

Eagly, A. H., & Steffen, V. J. (1986). Gender and aggressive behavior: A meta-analytic review of the social psychological literature. *Psychological Bulletin, 100,* 309–330.

Eagly, A. H., & Wood, W. (1991). Explaining sex differences in social behavior: A meta-analytic perspective. *Personality and Social Psychology Bulletin, 17,* 306–315.

Eagly, A. H., & Wood, W. (1999). The origins of sex differences in human behavior: Evolved dispositions versus social roles. *American Psychologist, 54*(6), 408–423.

Eagly, A. H., Ashmore, R. D., Makhijani, M. G., & Longo, L. C. (1991). What is beautiful is good, but . . . : A meta-analytic review of research on the physical attractiveness stereotype. *Psychological Bulletin, 110,* 109–128.

Ebbinghaus, H. (1913/1885). *Memory: A contribution to experimental psychology* (H. A. Roger & C. E. Bussenius, Trans.). New York: Columbia University Press.

Eccles, J. S. (1993). *Parents as gender-role socializers during middle childhood and adolescence.* Paper presented at the meeting of the Society for Research on Child Development, New Orleans, LA.

Eccles, J. S., Wigfield, A., Harold, R. D., & Blumenfeld, P. (1993). Age and gender differences in children's self- and task perceptions during elementary school. *Child Development, 64,* 830–847.

Egeland, B., Jacobvitz, D., & Sroufe, L. A. (1988). Breaking the cycle of abuse. *Child Development, 59,* 1080–1088.

Egeth, H. E. (1993). What do we *not* know about eyewitness identification? *American Psychologist, 48,* 577–580.

Eggers, D. (2000, May 7). Intimacies. *The New York Times magazine,* pp. 76–77.

Eisenberg, N., Wolchik, S. A., Hernandez, R., & Pasternack, J. F. (1985). Parental socialization of young children's play: A short-term longitudinal study. *Child Development, 56,* 1506–1513.

Ekman, P. (1980). *The face of man.* New York: Garland.

Ekman, P. (1982). *Emotion and the human face* (2nd. ed.). New York: Cambridge University Press.

Ekman, P. (1992). Are there basic emotions? *Psychological Review, 99,* 550–553.

Ekman, P. (1993). Facial expression and emotion. *American Psychologist, 48,* 384–392.

Ekman, P. (1994). Strong evidence for universals in facial expression. *Psychological Bulletin, 115,* 268–287.

Ekman, P., & Friesen, W. (1984). *Unmasking the face* (2nd ed.). Palo Alto, CA: Consulting Psychologists Press.

Ekman, P., et al. (1995). Universals and cultural differences in the judgments of facial expressions of emotion. *Journal of Personality and Social Psychology, 14,* 109–145.

Ekvall, S. W. (Ed.). (1993). *Pediatric nutrition in chronic diseases and developmental disorders: Prevention, assessment, and treatment.* New York: Oxford University Press.

Elias, M. J., & Zins, J. E. (2003). Bullying, other forms of peer harassment, and victimization in the schools: Issues for school psychology research and practice. *Journal of Applied School Psychology, 19*(2), 1–5.

Ellis, A. (1977). The basic clinical theory of rational-emotive therapy. In A. Ellis & R. Grieger (Eds.), *Handbook of rational-emotive therapy.* New York: Springer.

Ellis, A. (1984). Rational-emotive therapy. In R. J. Corsini (Ed.), *Current psychotherapies.* Itasca, IL: Peacock.

Ellis, A. (1993). Reflections on rational-emotive therapy. *Journal of Consulting and Clinical Pscyhology, 61,* 199–201.

Ellis, A. (1995). Thinking processes involved in irrational beliefs and their disturbed consequences. *Journal of Cognitive Psychotherapy: An International Quarterly, 9*(2), 105–116.

Ellis, A., & Dryden, W. (1987). *The practice of rational emotional therapy.* New York: Springer-Verlag.

Ellis, A., & Dryden, W. (1996). *The practice of rational emotive behavior therapy.* New York: Springer.

Ellis, E. M. (2000). *Divorce wars: Interventions with families in conflict.* Washington, D.C.: American Psychological Association.

Ellsworth, P. C., Carlsmith, J. M., & Henson, A. (1972). The stare as a stimulus to flight in human subjects. *Journal of Personality and Social Psychology, 21,* 302–311.

Emde, R. (1993). Cited in Adler, T. (1993). Shy, bold temperament? It's mostly in the genes. *APA Monitor, 24*(1), 7, 8.

Engels, G. I., Garnefski, N., & Diekstra, R. F. W. (1993). Efficacy of rational-emotive therapy: A quantitative analysis. *Journal of Consulting and Clinical Psychology, 61,* 1083–1090.

Epstein, L. H., et al. (1995). Effects of decreasing sedentary behavior and increasing activity on weight change in obese children. *Health Psychology, 14,* 109–115.

Erel, O., & Burman, B. (1995). Interrelatedness of marital relations and parent-child relations: A meta-analytic review. *Psychological Bulletin, 118,* 108–132.

Erel, O., Oberman, Y., & Yirmiya, N. (2000). Maternal versus nonmaternal care and seven domains of children's development. *Psychological Bulletin, 126*(5), 727–747.

Erikson, E. H. (1950). *Childhood and society* (1st ed.). New York: Norton.

Erikson, E. H. (1963). *Childhood and society* (2nd ed.). New York: Norton.

Erikson, E. H. (1968). *Identity: Youth and crisis.* New York: Norton.

Eron, L. D. (1993). Cited in DeAngelis, T. (1993a). It's baaack: TV violence, concern for kid viewers. *APA Monitor, 24*(8), 16.

Errington, D., & Gewertz, D. (1987). *Cultural alternatives and a feminist anthropology: An analysis of culturally constructed gender interest in Papua, New Guinea.* New York: Cambridge University Press.

Ertem, I. O., Leventhal, J. M., & Dobbs, S. (2000). Intergenerational continuity of child physical abuse: how good is the evidence? *Lancet, 356,* 814–819.

Esterling, B. A., Antoni, M. H., Kumar, M., & Schneiderman, N. (1993). Defensiveness, trait anxiety, and Epstein-Barr viral capsid antigen antibody titers in healthy college students. *Health Psychology, 12,* 132–139.

Etaugh, C., & Rathus, S. A. (1995). *The world of children.* Fort Worth, TX: Harcourt Brace Jovanovich.

Etcoff, N. L. (1994). Cited in Brody, J. E. (1994, March 21). Notions of beauty transcend culture, new study suggests. *The New York Times,* p. A14.

Eysenck, H. J. (1953). *The structure of human personality.* London: Meuthen.

Facts on File. (1994, October 20), p. 772.

Fagot, B. I. (1978). The influence of sex of child on parental reactions to toddler children. *Child Development, 49,* 459–465.

Fagot, B. I., Hagan, R., Leinbach, M. D., & Kronsberg, S. (1985). Differential reactions to assertive and communicative acts of toddler boys and girls. *Child Development, 56,* 1499–1505.

Fallon, A. E., & Rozin, P. (1985). Sex differences in perceptions of desirable body shape. *Journal of Abnormal Psychology, 94,* 102–105.

Fantz, R. L. (1961). The origin of form perception. *Scientific American, 204*(5), 66–72.

Farina, A., Burns, G. L., Austad, C., Bugglin, C. S., & Fischer, E. H. (1986). The role of physical attractiveness in the readjustment of discharged psychiatric patients. *Journal of Abnormal Psychology, 95,* 139–143.

Farley, F. (1993). Cited in Michaelson, R. (1993). Farley calls for more money for health, behavior research. *APA Monitor, 24*(4), 3.

Farrell, A. D., Camplair, P. S., & McCullough, L. (1987). Identification of target complaints by computer interview: Evaluation of the Computerized Assessment System for Psychotherapy Evaluation and Research. *Journal of Consulting and Clinical Psychology, 55,* 691–700.

Fazio, R. H. (1990). Multiple processes by which attitudes guide behavior: The MODE model as an integrative framework. In M. P. Zanna (Ed.), *Advances in experimental social psychology.* San Diego, CA: Academic Press.

Feingold, A. (1988). Matching for attractiveness in romantic partners and same-sex friends: A meta-analysis and theoretical critique. *Psychological Bulletin, 104,* 226–235.

Feingold, A. (1992). Gender differences in mate selection preferences. *Psychological Bulletin, 112,* 125–139.

Feingold, A. (1992a). Gender differences in mate selection preferences: A test of the parental investment model. *Psychological Bulletin, 112,* 125–139.

Feingold, A. (1992b). Good-looking people are not what we think. *Psychological Bulletin, 111,* 304–341.

Feingold, A. (1992c). Sex differences in the effects of similarity and physical attractiveness on opposite-sex attraction. *Basic and Applied Social Psychology, 12,* 357–367.

Feingold, A. (1994). Gender differences in personality: A meta-analysis. *Psychological Bulletin, 116,* 429–456.

Feiring, C. (1993, March). *Developing concepts of romance from 15 to 18 years.* Paper presented at the meeting of the Society for Research in Child Development, New Orleans, LA.

Feshbach, S. (1994). Nationalism, patriotism, and aggression: A clarification of functional differences. In L. R. Huesmann (Ed.), *Aggressive behavior: Current perspectives.* New York: Plenum Press.

Festinger, L. (1957). *A theory of cognitive dissonance.* Stanford, CA: Stanford University Press.

Festinger, L., & Carlsmith, J. M. (1959). Cognitive consequences of forced compliance. *Journal of Abnormal and Social Psychology, 58,* 203–210.

Field, T. M. (1991). Young children's adaptations to repeated separations from their mothers. *Child Development, 62,* 539–547.

Field, T. M., Schanberg, S. M., Scafidi, F., Bauer, C. R., Vega-Lahr, N., Garcia, R., Nystrom, J., & Kuhn, C. M. (1986). Tactile/kinesthetic stimulation effects on preterm neonates. *Pediatrics, 77,* 654–658.

Finkelhor, D., & Dziuba-Leatherman, J. (1994). Victimization of children. *American Psychologist, 49,* 173–183.

Finn, P. R., Sharkansky, E. J., Brandt, K. M., & Turcotte, N. (2000). The effects of familial risk, personality, and expectancies on alcohol use and abuse. *Journal of Abnormal Psychology, 109*(1), 122–133.

Fischer, K. W., Shavber, P. R., & Carochan, P. (1990). How emotions develop and how they organize development. *Cognition and Emotion, 4,* 81–127.

Fisher, C. B., & Fyrberg, D. (1994). Participant partners: College students weigh the costs and benefits of deceptive research. *American Psychologist, 49,* 417–427.

Fisher, H. E. (1992). *Anatomy of love: The natural history of monogamy, adultery and divorce.* New York: Norton.

Fisher-Thompson, D. (1990). Adult sex typing of children's toys. *Sex Roles, 23,* 291–303.

Fiske, S. T. (1989). *Interdependence and stereotyping: From the laboratory to the Supreme Court (and back).* Paper presented to the meeting of the American Psychological Association, New Orleans, LA.

Fiske, S. T. (1993). Controlling other people: The impact of power on stereotyping. *American Psychologist, 48,* 621–628.

Fiske, S. T., & Taylor, S. E. (1984). *Social cognition.* Reading, MA: Addison-Wesley.

Fitzgibbon, M. L., Stolley, M. R., & Kirschenbaum, D. S. (1993). Obese people who seek treatment have different characteristics than those who do not seek treatment. *Health Psychology, 12,* 342–345.

Flack, W. F., Jr., Laird, J. D., & Cavallaro, L. A. (1999). Separate and combined effects of facial expressions and bodily postures on emotional feelings. *European Journal of Social Psychology, 29*(2–3), 203–217.

Flannery, D. J., Rowe, D. C., & Gulley, B. L. (1993). Impact of pubertal status, timing, and age on adolescent sexual experience and delinquency. *Journal of Adolescent Research, 8,* 21–40.

Flavell, J. H., Miller, P. H., & Miller, S. A. (1993). *Cognitive development* (3rd ed.). Englewood Cliffs, NJ: Prentice-Hall.

Flegal, K. M., Carroll, M. D., Ogden, C. L., & Johnson, C. L. (2002). Prevalence and trends in obesity among US adults, 1999–2000. Journal of the American Medical Association, 288(14), 1723–1727.

Fling, S., Smith, L., Rodriguez, T., Thornton, D., et al. (1992). Video games, aggression, and self-esteem: A survey. *Social Behavior & Personality, 20,* 39–45.

Fogel, D. B. (2000, July). Paper presented at the 2000 Congress on Evolutionary Computation, San Diego.

Folkman, S., & Moskowitz, J. T. (2000). The context matters. *Personality & Social Psychology Bulletin, 26*(2), 150–151.

Folkman, S., & Moskowitz, J. T. (2000a). Positive affect and the other side of coping. *American Psychologist, 55*(6), 647–654.

Foster-Clark, F. S., & Blyth, D. A. (1991). Peer relations and influences. In R. M. Lerner, A. C. Petersen, & J. Brooks-Gunn (Eds.), *Encyclopedia of adolescence.* New York: Garland.

Fowler, W., Ogston, K., Roberts–Fiati, G., & Swenson, A. (1993, February). *The long term development of giftedness and high competencies in children enriched in language during infancy.* Paper presented at the Esther Katz Rosen Symposium on the Psychological Development of Gifted Children, University of Kansas.

Frangione, B. (2000, July). Amyloid and dementia: To be or not to be. Paper presented to the World Alzheimer Congress 2000, Washington, DC.

Frankenberg, W., Dodds. J., Archer, P., Shapiro, H., & Bresnick, B. (1992). The Denver II: A major revision and restandardization of the Denver Developmental Screening Test. *Pediatrics, 89,* 91–97.

Franzoi, S. L., & Herzog, M. E. (1987). Judging physical attractiveness: What body aspects do we use? *Personality and Social Psychology Bulletin, 13,* 19–33.

Freud, S. (1933/1964). New introductory lectures. In J. Strachey (Ed. and Trans.), *The standard edition of the complete psychological works of Sigmund Freud* (Vol. 22). London: Hogarth.

Freud, S. (1936). *The problem of anxiety.* New York: Norton.

Freud, S. (1952). *A general introduction to psychoanalysis.* New York: Washington Square Press. (Original work published 1920)

Frey, M. C., & Detterman, D. K. (2004). Scholastic assessment or g? The relationship between the scholastic assessment test and general cognitive ability. *Psychological Science, 15*(6), 373–378.

Friedman, M. A., & Brownell, K. D. (1995). Psychological correlates of obesity: Moving to the next research generation. *Psychological Bulletin, 117,* 3–20.

Friedman, M., & Ulmer, D. (1984). *Treating type A behavior and your heart.* New York: Fawcett Crest.

Frodi, A. M., Macauley, J., & Thome, P. R. (1977). Are women always less aggressive than men? A review of the experimental literature. *Psychologicla Bulletin, 84,* 634–660.

Fromm-Reichmann, F. (1948). Notes on the development of treatment of schizophrenics by psychoanalytic psychotherapy. *Psychiatry, 11,* 263–273.

Furedy, J. J. (1990, July). *Experimental psychophysiology and pseudoscientific polygraphy: Conceptual concerns and practical problems.* Symposium at the 5th International Congress of Psychophysiology, Budapest, Hungary.

Furman, W., & Buhrmester, D. (1992). Age and sex differences in perceptions of networks of personal relationships. *Child Development, 63,* 103–115.

Gais, S., & Born, J. (2004). Declarative memory consolidation: Mechanisms acting during human sleep. *Learning & Memory, 11*(6), 679–685.

Galambos, N. L. (1992). Parent-adolescent relations. *Current Directions in Psychological Science, 1,* 146–149.

Galambos, N. L., & Almeida, D. M. (1992). Does parent-adolescent conflict increase in early adolescence? *Journal of Marriage and the Family, 54,* 737–747.

Galambos, N. L., & Turner, P. K. (1999). Parent and adolescent temperaments and the quality of parent-adolescent relations. *Merrill-Palmer Quarterly, 45*(3), 493–511.

Galanter, E. (1962). Contemporary psychophysics. In R. Brown et al. (Eds.), *New directions in psychology.* New York: Holt, Rinehart and Winston.

Galassi, J. P. (1988). Four cognitive-behavioral approaches: Additional considerations. *Counseling Psychologist, 16*(1), 102–105.

Gallagher, A. M., et al.(2000). Gender differences in advanced mathematical problem solving. *Journal of Experimental Child Psychology, 75*(3), 165–190.

Gallagher, R. (1996). Cited in Murray, B. (1996). College youth haunted by increased pressures. *APA Monitor, 26*(4), 47.

Gallucci, W. T., et al. (1993). Sex differences in sensitivity of the hypothalamic-pituitary-adrenal axis. *Health Psychology, 12,* 420–425.

Gardner, B., & Garnder, G. (1980). Object permanence in child and chimpanzee. *Animal Learning and Behavior, 8*(1), 3–9.

Gardner, H. (1983). *Frames of mind: The theory of multiple intelligences.* New York: Basic Books.

Gardner, H. (1993). *Creating minds: An anatomy of creativity seen through the lives of Freud, Einstein, Picasso, Stravinsky, Eliot, Graham and Gandhi.* New York: Basic Books.

Gardner, H. (1995, November). Reflections on multiple intelligences: Myths and messages. *Phi Delta Kappan, 77,* 200–208.

Gardner, H., & Hatch, T. (1989). Multiple intelligences go to school: Educational implications of the theory of multiple intelligences. *Educational Researcher, 18*(8), 4–10.

Garfinkel, R. (1995). Cited in Margoshes, P. (1995). For many, old age is the prime of life. *APA Monitor, 26*(5), 36–37.

Garland, A. F., & Zigler, E. (1993). Adolescent suicide prevention. *American Psychologist, 48,* 169–182.

Gauthier, J., Côte, G., & French, D. (1994). The role of home practice in the thermal biofeedback treatment of migraine headache. *Journal of Consulting and Clinical Psychology, 62,* 180–184.

Gazzinga, M. S. (1992). *Nature's mind.* New York: Basic Books.

Geen, R. G., Stonner, D., & Shope, G. L. (1975). The facilitation of aggression by aggression: Evidence against the catharsis hypothesis. *Journal of Personality and Social Psychology, 31,* 721–726.

Gelernter, D. (1994). *The muse in the machine: Computerizing the poetry of human thought.* New York: Free Press.

Gentry, J., & Eron, L. D. (1993). American Psychological Association Commission on Violence and Youth. *American Psychologist, 48,* 89.

Geschwind, N. (1979, September). Specializations of the human brain. *Scientific American,* pp. 180–199.

Gibbs, J. T. (1992). Negotiating ethnic identity: Issues for Black-White biracial adolescents. In M. P. P. Root (Ed.), *Racially mixed people in America.* Newbury Park, CA: Sage.

Gibson, M., & Ogbu, J. (Eds.). (1991). *Minority status and schooling: A comparative study of immigrant and involuntary minorities.* New York: Garland.

Gick, M. L., & Holyoak, K. J. (1980). Analogical problem solving. *Cognitive Psychology, 12,* 306–355.

Gigerenzer, G., Hoffrage, U., & Kleinböting, H. (1991). Probabilistic mental models: A Brunswikian theory of confidence. *Psychological Review, 98,* 506–528.

Gigone, D., & Hastie, R. (1997). Proper analysis of the accuracy of group judgments. *Psychological Bulletin, 121,* 149–167.

Gilbert, S. J. (1981). Another look at the Milgram obedience studies: The role of the gradated series of shocks. *Personality and Social Psychology Bulletin, 7,* 690–695.

Gilligan, C. (1982). *In a different voice.* Cambridge, MA: Harvard University Press.

Gilligan, C., Lyons, P., & Hanmer, T. J. (Eds.). (1990). *Making connections.* Cambridge, MA: Harvard University Press.

Gilligan, C., Rogers, A. G., & Tolman, D. L. (Eds.). (1991). *Women, girls, and psychotherapy.* New York: Haworth Press.

Gilligan, C., Ward, J. V., & Taylor, J. M. (1989). *Mapping the moral domain: A contribution of women's thinking to psychological theory and education.* Cambridge, MA: Harvard University Press.

Gillin, J. C. (1991). The long and short of sleeping pills. *New England Journal of Medicine, 324,* 1735–1736.

Gillis, J. S., & Avis, W. E. (1980). The male-taller norm in mate selection. *Personality and Social Psychology Bulletin, 6,* 396–401.

Gingerich, W. J. (1990). Expert systems: New tools for professional decision-making. *Computers in Human Services, 6,* 219–230.

Ginsburg, G., & Bronstein, P. (1993). Family factors related to children's intrinsic/extrinsic motivational orientation and academic performance. *Child Development, 64,* 1461–1474.

Glaser, R., et al. (1991). Stress-related activation of Epstein-Barr virus. *Brain, Behavior, and Immunity, 5,* 219–232.

Glaser, R., et al. (1993). Stress and the memory T-cell response to the Epstein-Barr virus. *Health Psychology, 12,* 435–442.

Gleason, J. B., & Ratner, N. B. (1993). Language development in children. In J. B. Gleason & N. B. Ratner (Eds.), *Psycholinguistics.* Fort Worth, TX: Harcourt Brace Jovanovich.

Gleaves, D. H., Williamson, D. A., & Barker, S. E. (1993). Confirmatory factor analysis of a multidimensional model of bulimia nervosa. *Journal of Abnormal Psychology, 102,* 173–176.

Gleitman, H., Rozin, P., & Sabini, J. (1997). Solomon E. Asch (1907–1996). *American Psychologist, 52,* 984–985.

Godden, D. R., & Baddeley, A. D. (1975). Context-dependent memory in two natural environments: On land and underwater. *British Journal of Psychology, 66,* 325–331.

Goldberg, L. R. (1993). The structure of phenotypic personality traits. *American Psychologist, 48,* 26–34.

Goldfried, M. R., & Padawer, W. (1982). Curent status and future directions in psychotherapy. In M. R. Goldfried (Ed.), *Converging themes in psychotherapy: Trends in psychodynamic, humanistic, and behavioral practice.* New York: Springer.

Goldman, K. (1993, June 1). Jordan & Co. play ball on Madison Avenue. *The Wall Street Journal,* p. B9.

Goldsmith, H. H. (1993). Cited in Adler, T. (1993a). Shy, bold temperament? It's mostly in the genes. *APA Monitor, 24*(1), 7–8.

Goldstein, M., Baker, B., & Jamison, K. (1986). *Abnormal Psychology* (2nd ed.). Boston: Little, Brown.

Goleman, D. (1995a, March 28). The brain manages happiness and sadness in different centers. *The New York Times,* pp. C1, C9.

Goleman, D. (1995b, May 2). Biologists find site of working memory. *The New York Times,* pp. C1, C9.

Goleman, D. (1995c, December 5). Making room on the couch for culture. *The New York Times,* pp. B5, B10.

Goleman, D. J. (1995d). *Emotional intelligence.* New York: Bantam Books.

Golombok, S., & Fivesh, R. (1994). *Gender development.* New York: Cambridge University Press.

Gonzales, M. H., et al. (1983). Interactional approach to interpersonal attraction. *Journal of Personality and Social Psychology, 44,* 1192–1197.

Goode, E. (2000, June 25). Thinner: The male battle with anorexia. *The New York Times,* p. MH8.

Goodnow, J. J., & Bowes, J. M. (1994). *Men, women, and household work.* Melbourne: Oxford University Press.

Goodwin, F. K., & Jamison, K. R. (1990). *Manic-depressive illness.* New York: Oxford University Press.

Gorman, J., Liebowitz, M., Fyer, A., & Stein, J. (1989). A neuroanatomical hypothesis for panic disorder. *The American Journal of Psychiatry, 146,* 148–161.

Gotlib, I. H., Lewinsohn, P. M., Seeley, J. R., Rohde, P., & Redner, J. E. (1993). Negative cognitions and attributional style in depressed adolescents: An examination of stability and specificity. *Journal of Abnormal Psychology, 102,* 607–615.

Gottesman, I., & Shields, J. (1982). *Schizophrenia: The epigenetic puzzle.* Cambridge, MA: Cambridge University Press.

Gottfried, A. E., Fleming, J. S., & Gottfried, A. W. (1994). Role of parental motivational practices in children's academic intrinsic motivation and achievement. *Journal of Educational Psychology, 86,* 104–113.

Gottman, J. M., Coan, J., Carrère, S. & Swanson, C. (1998). Predicting marital happiness and stability from newlywed interactions. *Journal of Marriage and the Family, 60,* 5–22.

Graber, J. A., Lewinsohn, P. M., Seeley, J. R., & Brooks-Gunn, J. (1997). Is psychopathology associated with the timing of pubertal development? *Journal of the American Academy of Child & Adolescent Psychiatry, 36*(12), 1768–1776.

Graf, P. (1990). Life-span changes in implicit and explicit memory. *Bulletin of the Psychonomic Society, 28,* 353–358.

Green, S. K., Buchanan, D. R., & Heuer, S. K. (1984). Winners, losers, and choosers: A field investigation of dating initiation. *Personality and Social Psychology Bulletin, 10,* 502–511.

Greenberg, P. D. (1987). Tumor immunology. In D. P. Stites et al. (Eds.), *Basic and clinical immunology* (6th ed.). Norwalk, CT: Appleton & Lange.

Greene, A. L., & Grimsley, M. D. (1990). Age and gender differences in adolescents' preferences for parental advice: Mum's the word. *Journal of Adolescent Research, 5,* 396–413.

Greene, A. S., & Saxe, L. (1990). *Tall tales told to teachers.* Unpublished manuscript, Brandeis University.

Greene, B. A. (1992). Still here: A perspective on psychotherapy with African American women. In J. Chrisler & D. Howard (Eds.), *New directions in feminist psychology.* New York: Springer.

Greene, B. A. (1993). African American women. In L. Comas-Diaz & B. A. Greene (Eds.), *Women of color and mental health.* New York: Guilford Press.

Greeno, C. G., & Wing, R. R. (1994). Stress-induced eating. *Psychological Bulletin, 115,* 444–464.

Gregory, N. (2004). Crime and the family: Like grandfather, like father, like son? *British Journal of Forensic Practice, 6*(4), 32–36.

Grey, J., Feldon, J., Rawlins, J., Hemsley, D., & Smith, A. (1991). The neuropsychology of schizophrenia. *Behavioral and Brain Sciences, 14,* 1–84.

Griffin, E., & Sparks, G. G. (1990). Friends forever: A longitudinal exploration of intimacy in same-sex friends and platonic pairs. *Journal of Social and Personal Relationships, 7,* 29–46.

Griffin, R. S., & Gross, A. M. (2004). Childhood bullying: Current empirical findings and future directions for research. *Aggression & Violent Behavior, 9*(4), 379–400.

Grimshaw, G. M., Bryden, M. P., & Finegan, J. K. (1995). Relations between prenatal testosterone and cerebral lateralization in children. *Neuropsychology, 9*(1), 68–79.

Grogger, J., & Bronars, S. (1993). The socioeconomic consequences of teenage childbearing: Findings from a natural experiment. *Family Planning Perspectives, 25,* 156–161.

Grön, G., Wunderlich, A. P., Spitzer, M., Tomczak, R. & Riepe, M. W. (2000). Brain activation during human navigation: gender-different neural networks as substrate of performance. *Nature Neuroscience, 3*(4), 404–408.

Gruder, C. L., et al. (1993). Effects of social support and relapse prevention training as adjuncts to a televised smoking-cessation intervention. *Journal of Consulting and Clinical Psychology, 61,* 113–120.

Grush, J. E. (1980). The impact of candidate expenditures, regionality, and prior outcomes on the 1976 Democratic presidential primaries. *Journal of Personality and Social Psychology, 38,* 337–347.

Grych, J. H., & Fincham, F. D. (1993). Children's appraisals of marital conflict. *Child Development, 64,* 215–230.

Guilford, J. P. (1967). *The nature of human intelligence.* New York: McGraw-Hill.

Guisinger, S., & Blatt, S. J. (1994). Individuality and relatedness: Evolution of a fundamental dialectic. *American Psychologist, 49,* 104–111.

Gulevich, G., Dement, W., & Johnson, L. (1966). Psychiatric and EEG observations on a case of prolonged (264 hours) wakefulness. *Archives of General Psychiatry, 15,* 29–35.

Gurrera, R. J., Nestor, P. G., & O'Donnell, B. F. (2000). Personality traits in schizophrenia: Comparison with a community sample. *Journal of Nervous & Mental Disease, 188*(1), 31–35.

Haaf, R. A., Smith, P. H., & Smitley, S. (1983). Infant response to facelike patterns under fixed trial and infant–control procedures. *Child Development, 54,* 172–177.

Haaga, D. A. F., & Davison, G. C. (1993). An appraisal of rational-emotive therapy. *Journal of Consulting and Clinical Psychology, 61,* 215–220.

Haaland, K. Y. (1992). Introduction to the special section on the emotional concomitants of brain damage. *Journal of Consulting and Clinical Psychology, 50,* 327–328.

Haan, M. N. (2000, July). Cognitive decline is not normal in aging. Paper presented to the World Alzheimer Congress 2000, Washington, DC.

Haber, R. N. (1980). Eidetic images are not just imaginary. *Psychology Today, 14*(11), 72–82.

Hall, J. A. (1978). Gender effects in decoding nonverbal cures. *Psychological Bulletin, 85,* 845–875.

Hall, J. A. (1984). *Nonverbal sex differences: Communication accuracy and expressive style.* Baltimore, MD: Johns Hopkins University Press.

Halpern, D. F. (1992). *Sex differences in cognitive abilities* (2nd ed.). Hillsdale, NJ: Erlbaum.

Halpern, D. F. (1997). Sex differences in intelligence: Implications for education. *American Psychologist, 52,* 1091–1102.

Halpern, D. F., & LaMay, M. L. (2000). The smarter sex: A critical review of sex differences in intelligence. *Educational Psychology Review, 12*(2), 229–246.

Hamby, S. L., & Finkelhor, D. (2000). The victimization of children: Recommendations for assessment and instrument development. *Journal of the American Academy of Child & Adolescent Psychiatry, 39*(7) 829–840.

Harkins, S. (1987). Social loafing and social facilitation. *Journal of Experimental Social Psychology, 23,* 1–18.

Harlow, H. F. (1959). Love in infant monkeys. *Scientific American, 200,* 68–86.

Harlow, H. F., & Zimmermann, R. R. (1959). Affectional responses in the infant monkey. *Science, 130,* 421–432.

Harlow, H. F., Harlow, M. K., & Meyer, D. R. (1950). Learning motivated by a manipulation drive. *Journal of Experimental Psychology, 40,* 228–234.

Harris, L., & Associates (1995). Cited in Mom the provider. (1995, May 14). *The New York Times,* p. A14.

Harter, S. (1990a). Issues in the assessment of the self-concept of children and adolescents. In A. LaGrea (Ed.), *Through the eyes of a child.* Boston: Allyn & Bacon.

Hartup, W. W. (1993). Adolescents and their friends. In B. Laursen (Ed.), Close friendships in adolescence. *New Directions in Child Development,* no. 60. San Francisco: Jossey-Bass.

Hashima, P. Y., & Finkelhor, D. (1999). Violent victimization of youth versus adults in the National Crime Victimization Survey. *Journal of Interpersonal Violence, 14*(8), 799–820.

Hasselhorn, M. (1992). Task dependency and the role of typicality and metamemory in the development of an organizational strategy. *Child Development, 63,* 202–214.

Hassinger, H. J., Semenchuk, E. M., & O'Brien, W. H. (1999). Appraisal and coping responses to pain and stress in migraine headache sufferers. *Journal of Behavioral Medicine, 22*(4), 327–340.

Haugtvedt, C. P., Schumann, D. W., Schneier, W. L., & Warren, W. L. (1994). Advertising repetition and variation strategies: Implications for understanding attitude strength. *Journal of Consumer Research, 21,* 176–189.

Hauser-Cram, P., Pierson, D. E., Walker, D. K., & Tivnan, T. (1991). *Early education in the public schools.* San Francisco: Josey-Bass.

Hawkins, J. D., Catalano, R. F., & Miller, J. Y. (1992). Risk and protective factors for alcohol and other drug problems in adolescence and early adulthood: Implications for substance abuse prevention. *Psychological Bulletin, 112,* 64–105.

Hayes, K. J., & Hayes, C. (1951). The intellectual development of a home-raised chimpanzee. *Proceedings of the American Philosophical Society, 95,* 105–109.

Hayes, P. (1993). Cited in Chartrand, S. (1993, July 18). A split in thinking among keepers of artificial intelligence. *The New York Times,* p. E6.

Hayflick, L. (1977). The cellular basis for biological aging. In C. E. Finch & L. Hayflick (Eds.), *Handbook of the biology of aging.* New York: Van Nostrand Reinhold.

Hayflick, L. (1994). *How and why we age.* New York: Ballantine Books.

Hays, K. F. (1995). Putting sport psychology into (your) practice. *Professional Psychology: Research and Practice, 26,* 33–40.

Heatherton, T. F., Mahamedi, F., Striepe, M., Field, A. E., & Keel, P. (1997). A 10–year longitudinal study of body weight, dieting, and eating disorder symptoms. *Journal of Abnormal Psychology, 106,* 117–125.

Heckler, M. (1985). The fight against Alzheimer's disease. *American Psychologist, 40,* 1240–1244.

Heider, F. (1958). *The psychology of interpersonal relations.* New York: Wiley.

Heingartner, A., & Hall, J. V. (1974). Affective consequences in adults and children of repeated exposure to auditory stimuli. *Journal of Personality and Social Psychology, 29,* 719–723.

Helmes, E., & Reddon, J. R. (1993). A perspective on developments in assessing psychopathology: A critical review of the MMPI and MMPI-2. *Psychological Bulletin, 113,* 453–471.

Helms, J. E. (1992). Why is there no study of cultural equivalence of standardized cognitive ability testing? *American Psychologist, 47,* 1083–1101.

Helson, R. (1993). In K. D. Hulbert & D. T. Schuster (Eds.), *Women's lives through time* (pp. 190–210). San Francisco: Jossey-Bass.

Helson, R., & Moane, G. (1987). Personality change in women from college to midlife. *Journal of Personality and Social Psychology, 53,* 176–186.

Helson, R., Stewart, A. J. & Ostrove, J. (1995). Identity in three cohorts of midlife women. *Journal of Personality and Social Psychology, 69,* 544–557.

Hendrick, C. D., Wells, K. S., & Faletti, M. V. (1982). Social and emotional effects of geographical relocation on elderly retirees. *Journal of Personality and Social Psychology, 42,* 951–962.

BOOKSHELF

Hennigan, K. M., Cook, T. D., & Gruder, C. L. (1982). Cognitive tuning set, source credibility, and the temporal persistence of attitude change. *Journal of Personality and Social Psychology, 42,* 412–425.

Hensley, W. E. (1994). Height as a basis for interpersonal attraction. *Adolescence, 29*(114), 469–474.

Hepworth, J. T., & West, S. G. (1988). Lynchings and the economy: A time-series reanalysis of Hovland and Sears (1940). *Journal of Personality and Social Psychology, 55,* 239–247.

Herbert, T. B., & Cohen, S. (1993). Depression and immunity: A meta-analytic review. *Psychological Bulletin, 113,* 472–486.

Herek, G. M. (1993). Sexual orientation and military service: A social science perspective. *American Psychologist, 48,* 538–549.

Hergenhahn, B. R. (2005). *An introduction to the history of psychology,* 5th ed. Belmont, CA: Wadsworth Publishing Company.

Herman-Giddens, M. E., et al. (1999). Underascertainment of child abuse mortality in the United States. *Journal of the American Medical Association, 282,* 463–467.

Herrmann, D. J. (1991). *Super memory.* Emmaus, PA: Rodale Press.

Hershenson, R. (2000, August 6). Debating the Mozart theory. *The New York Times magazine online.*

Herzog, D. B., Keller, M. B., & Lavori, P. W. (1988). Outcome in anorexia and bulimia nervosa: A review of the literature. *Journal of Nervous and Mental Disease, 176,* 131–143.

Heston, L. L. (1966). Psychiatric disorders in foster home reared children of schizophrenic mothers. *British Journal of Psychiatry, 112,* 819–825.

Hetland, L. (2000). Cited in Hershenson, R. (2000, August 6). Debating the Mozart theory. *The New York Times magazine online.*

Hewstone, M., & Hamberger, J. (2000). Perceived variability and stereotype change. *Journal of Experimental Social Psychology, 36*(2), 103–124.

Hiller, J. B., Rosenthal, R., Bornstein, R. F., Berry, D. T. R., & Brunell-Neuleib, S. (1999). A comparative meta-analysis of Rorschach and MMPI validity. Psychological Assessment, 11(3), 278–296.

Hinshaw, S. P. (1992). Externalizing behavior problems and academic underachievement in childhood and adolescence: Causal relationships and underlying mechanisms. *Psychological Bulletin, 111,* 127–155.

Hirschfeld, R. M. A., & Goodwin, F. K. (1988). Mood disorders. In J. A. Talbott, R. E. Hales, & S. C. Yudofsky (Eds.), *Textbook of psychiatry.* Washington, DC: American Psychiatric Press.

Hobfoll, S. E., Ritter, C., Lavin, J., Hulsizer, M. R., & Cameron, R. P. (1995). Depression prevalence and incidence among inner-city pregnant and postpartum women. *Journal of Consulting and Clinical Psychology, 63,* 445–453.

Hoffman, C., & Hurst, N. (1990). Gender stereotypes: Perception or rationalization? *Journal of Personality and Social Psychology, 58,* 197–208.

Hogrebe, M. C., Nist, S. L., & Newman, I. (1985). Are there gender differences in reading achievement? An investigation using the high school and beyond data. *Journal of Educational Psychology, 77,* 716–724.

Holahan, C. J., & Moos, R. H. (1990). Life stressors, resistance factors, and psychological health: An extension of the stress-resistance paradigm. *Journal of Personality and Social Psychology, 58,* 909–917.

Holahan, C. J., Moos, R. H., Holahan, C. K., & Brennan, P. L. (1995). Social support, coping, and depressive symptoms in a late-middle-aged sample of patients reporting cardiac illness. *Health Psychology, 14,* 152–163.

Holden, C. (1980). Identical twins reared apart. *Science, 207,* 1323–1325.

Holden, G. W., & Ritchie, K. L. (1991). Linking extreme marital discord, child rearing, and child behavior problems. *Child Development, 62,* 311–327.

Holland, J. J. (2000, July 25). Groups link media to child violence. The Associated Press online.

Hollinger, L. M., & Buschmann, M. B. (1993). Factors influencing the perception of touch by elderly nursing home residents and their health caregivers. *International Journal of Nursing Studies, 30,* 445–461.

Hollmann, F. W., & Mulder, T. J. (2000, January 13). Census Bureau projects doubling of nation's population by 2100 U.S. Census Bureau: Public Information Office.

Hollon, S. D., Shelton, R. C., & Loosen, P. T. (1991). Cognitive therapy and pharmacotherapy for depression. *Journal of Consulting and Clinical Psychology, 59,* 88–99.

Holloway, J. H. (2004). Part-time work and student achievement. Alexandria VA: Association for Supervision and Curriculum Development.

Holmbeck, G. N., & Hill, J. P. (1991). Conflictive engagement, positive affect, and menarche in families with seventh-grade girls. *Child Development, 62,* 1030–1048.

Holmes, S. A. (1996, October 5). U.S. reports drop in rate of births to unwed women. *The New York Times,* pp. A1, A9.

Holmes, T. H., & Rahe, R. H. (1967). The social readjustment scale. *Journal of Psychosomatic Research, 11,* 213–218.

Honan, W. H. (1966, April 11). Male professors keep 30% lead in pay over women, study says. *The New York Times,* p. B9.

Honorton, C., et al. (1990). Psi communication in the Ganzfield: Experiments with an automated testing system and a comparison with a meta-analysis of earlier studies. *Journal of Parapsychology, 54,* 99–139.

Honts, C. R., Hodes, R. L., & Raskin, D. C. (1985). Effects of physical countermeasures on the physiological detection of deception. *Journal of Applied Psychology, 70*(1), 177–187.

Honts, C., Hodes, R., & Raskin, D. (1985). *Journal of Applied Psychology, 70*(1).

Hopper, J. L., & Seeman, E. (1994). The bone density of female twins discordant for tobacco use. *New England Journal of Medicine, 330,* 387–392.

Horgan, O., & MacLachlan, M. (2004). Psychosocial adjustment to lower-limb amputation: A review. *Disability & Rehabilitation: An International Multidisciplinary Journal, 26*(14–15), 837–850.

Horn, J. M. (1983). The Texas adoption project: Adopted children and their intellectual resemblance to biological and adoptive parents. *Child Development, 54,* 268–275.

Horney, K. (1937). *The neurotic personality of our time.* New York: Norton.

House, J. S., Robbins, C., & Metzner, H. L. (1982). The association of social relationships and activities with mortality: Prospective evidence from the Tecumseh Community Health Study. *American Journal of Epidemiology, 116,* 123–140.

Hovey, J. D. (2000). Acculturative stress, depression, and suicidal ideation in Mexican immigrants. *Cultural Diversity and Ethnic Minority Psychology, 6*(2), 134–151.

Howard, J. A., Blumstein, P., & Schwartz, P. (1987). Social or evolutionary theories: Some observations on preferences in mate selection. *Journal of Personality and Social Psychology, 53,* 194–200.

Hudson, J. (1993). Cited in Goleman, D. J. (1993, April 6). Studying the secrets of childhood memory. *The New York Times,* pp. C1, C11.

Huesmann, L. R. (1993). Cited in DeAngelis, T. (1993a). It's baaack: TV violence, concern for kid viewers. *APA Monitor, 24*(8), 16.

Huesmann, L. R., & Miller, L. S. (1994). Long-term effects of repeated exposure to media violence in childhood. In L. R. Huesmann (Ed.), *Aggressive behavior: Current perspectives.* New York: Plenum Press.

Hultquist, C. M., et al. (1995). The effect of smoking and light activity on metabolism in men. *Health Psychology, 14,* 124–131.

Humphrey, L. L. (1986). Family dynamics in bulimia. In S. C. Feinstein et al. (Eds.), *Adolescent psychiatry.* Chicago: University of Chicago Press.

Hunsley, J., & Bailey, J. M. (1999). The clinical utility of the Rorschach: Unfulfilled promises and an uncertain future. *Psychological Assessment, 11*(3), 266–277.

Hunter, S. C., & Boyle, J. M. E. (2004). Appraisal and coping strategy use in victims of school bullying. *British Journal of Educational Psychology, 74*(1), 83–107.

Hussong, A. M., & Chassin, L. (1993, March). *The stress-negative affect model of adolescent alcohol use: Disaggregating negative affect.* Paper presented at the meeting of the Society for Research in Child Development, New Orleans, LA.

Hyde, J. S., & Linn, M. C. (1988). Gender differences in verbal ability: A meta-analysis. *Psychological Bulletin, 104,* 53–69.

Hyde, J. S., & Plant, E. A. (1995). Magnitude of psychological gender differences: Another side to the story. *American Psychologist, 50,* 159–161.

Hyde, J. S., Fennema, E., & Lamon, S. J. (1990). Gender differences in mathematics performance: A meta-analysis. *Psychological Bulletin, 107,* 139–155.

Hyman, R. (1994). Anomaly or artifact? Comments on Bem and Honorton. *Psychological Bulletin, 115,* 19–24.

Iacono, W. G., & Lykken, D. T. (1997). The validity of the lie detector: Two surveys of scientific opinion. *Journal of Applied Psychology, 82*(3), 426–433.

Ironson, G. (1993). Cited in Adler, T. (1993). Men and women affected by stress, but differently. *APA Monitor, 24*(7), 8–9.

Isen, A. M., & Means, B. (1983). The influence of positive affect on decision-making strategy. *Social Cognition, 2,* 28–31.

Isen, A. M., Daubman, K. A., & Gorgoglione, J. M. (1987). The influence of positive affect on cognitive organization: Implications for education. In R. E. Snow & M. J. Farr (Eds.), *Aptitude, learning, and instruction* (Vol. 3, pp. 143–164). Hillsdale, NJ: Erlbaum.

Izard, C. E. (1984). Emotion-cognition relationships and human development. In C. E. Izard, J. Kagan, & R. B. Zajonc (Eds.), *Emotions, cognition, and behavior.* New York: Cambridge University Press.

Izard, C. E. (1989). The structure and function of emotions: Implications for cognition, motivation, and personality. In I. S. Cohen (Ed.), *The G. Stanley Hall Lecture Series* (Vol. 9, pp. 37–73). Washington, DC: American Psychological Association.

Izard, C. E. (1990). Facial expression and the regulation of emotions. *Journal of Personality and Social Psychology, 58,* 487–498.

Izard, C. E. (1994). Basic emotions, relations among emotions, and emotion-cognition relations. *Psychological Bulletin, 115,* 561–565.

Jacklin, C. N., DiPietro, J. A., & Maccoby, E. E. (1984). Sex-typing behavior and sex-typing pressure in child-parent interaction. *Archives of Sexual Behavior, 13,* 413–425.

Jacklin, C. N., Maccoby, E. E., & Dick, A. E. (1973). Barrier behavior and toy preference: Sex differences (and their absence) in the year-old child. *Child Development, 44,* 196–200.

Jacks, J. Z., & Devine, P. G. (2000). Attitude importance, forewarning of message content, and resistance to persuasion. *Basic & Applied Social Psychology, 22*(1) 19–29.

Jackson, J. F. (1993). Human behavioral genetics, Scarr's theory, and her views on interventions: A critical review and commentary on their implications for African American children. *Child Development, 64,* 1318–1332.

Jacobson, N. S., & Addis, M. E. (1993). Research on couples and couples therapy: What do we know? Where are we going? *Journal of Consulting and Clinical Psychology, 61,* 85–93.

Jacobson, N. S., & Hollon, S. D. (1996). Cognitive-behavior therapy versus pharmocotherapy: Now that the jury's returned its verdict, it's time to present the rest of the evidence. *Journal of Consulting and Clinical Psychology, 64,* 74–80.

Jacobson, N. S., et al. (1985). Efficacy of ECT: A meta-analysis. *American Journal of Psychiatry, 142,* 297–302.

Jacox, A., Carr, D. B., & Payne, R. (1994). New clinical-practice guidelines for the management of pain in patients with cancer. *New England Journal of Medicine, 330,* 651–655.

James, W. (1890). *The principles of psychology* (Vols. 1 and 2). New York: Henry Holt and Company.

James, W. (1902/1958). *Varieties of religious experience.* New York: Mentor Books.

Janicak, P. G., et al. (1985). Efficacy of ECT: A meta-analysis. *American Journal of Psychiatry, 142,* 297–302.

Janos, P. M. (1987). A fifty-year follow-up of Terman's youngest college students and IQ-matched agemates. *Gifted Child Quarterly, 31,* 55–58.

Janowitz, H. D., & Grossman, M. I. (1949). Effects of variations in nutritive density on intake of food in cats and dogs. *American Journal of Physiology, 158,* 184–193.

Jeffery, R. W., et al. (2000). Long-term maintenance of weight loss: Current status. *Health Psychology, 19*(Suppl 1), 5–16.

Jellison, J. M., & Green, J. (1981). A self-presentation approach to the fundamental attribution error: The norm of internality. *Journal of Personality and Social Psychology, 40,* 643–649.

Jenkins, C. D. (1988). Epidemiology of cardiovascular diseases. *Journal of Consulting and Clinical Psychology, 56,* 324–332.

Johnson, B. T., & Eagly, A. H. (1989). Effects of involvement on persuasion: A meta-analysis. *Psychological Bulletin, 106,* 290–314.

Johnson, D. J. (1992). Developmental pathways: Toward an ecological theoretical formulation of race identity in Black-White biracial children. In M. P. P. Root (Ed.), *Racially mixed people in America.* Newbury Park, CA: Sage.

Johnson, E. J., & Tversky, A. (1983). Affect, generalization, and the perception of risk. *Journal of Personality and Social Psychology, 45,* 20–31.

Johnson, W., Emde, R. N., Pannabecker, B., Stenberg, C., & Davis, M. (1982). Maternal perception of infant emotion from birth to 18 months. *Infant Behavior and Development, 5,* 313–322.

Johnston, L. D., O'Malley, P. M., & Bachman, J. G. (2000). *The Monitoring the Future National survey results on adolescent drug use: Overview of key findings, 1999* (NIH Publication No. 00–4690). Rockville, MD: National Institute on Drug Abuse, c. 56 pp.

Johnston, L. D., O'Malley, P. M., & Bachman, J. G. (1995, December). The Monitoring the Future Study. The University of Michigan Institute for Social Research; National Institute on Drug Abuse, 5600 Fishers Lane, Rockville, MD 20957; USDHHS, Public Health Service, National Institutes of Health.

Johnstone, E., Owens, D., Bydder, G., Colter, N., Crow, T., & Frith, C. (1989). The spectrum of structural brain changes in schizophrenia: Age of onset as a predictor of cognitive and clinical impairments and their cerebral correlates. *Psychological Medicine, 19,* 91–103.

Joiner, T. E., Heatherton, T. F., Rudd, M. D., & Schmidt, N. B. (1997). Perfectionism, perceived weight status, and bulimic symptoms. *Journal of Abnormal Psychology, 106,* 145–153.

Jones, E. E. (1990). *Interpersonal perception.* New York: W. H. Freeman.

Jones, J. L., & Leary, M. R. (1994). Effects of appearance-based admonitions against sun exposure on tanning intentions in young adults. *Health Psychology, 13,* 86–90.

Jones, M. C. (1924). Elimination of children's fears. *Journal of Experimental Psychology, 7,* 381–390.

Jones, S. R. G. (1992). Was there a Hawthorne Effect? *American Journal of Sociology, 98,* 451–468.

Jonsdottir, I. H., Hellstrand, K., Thoren, P., & Hoffman, P. (2000). Enhancement of natural immunity seen after voluntary exercise in rats. Role of central opioid receptors. *Life Sciences, 66*(13), 1231–1239.

Jordan, J. V., Kaplan, A. G., Miller, J. B., Stiver, L. P., & Stiver, J. L. (Eds.). (1991). *Women's growth in connection.* New York: Guilford Press.

Judd, C. M., & Park, B. (1988). Out-group homogeneity: Judgments of variability at the individual and group levels. *Journal of Personality and Social Psychology, 54,* 778–788.

Jung, C. G. (1917/1966). *The collected works of C. G. Jung No. 7: Two essays on analytical psychology.* Princeton, NJ: Princeton University Press.

Jung, C. J. (1936/1968). *The collected works of C. G. Jung No. 9, Pt. 1: The archetypes and the collective unconcious.* Princeton, NJ: Princeton University Press.

Kahlbaugh, P., & Haviland, J. M. (1991). Formal operational thinking and identity. In R. M. Lerner, A. C. Petersen, & J. Brooks-Gunn (Eds.), *Encyclopedia of adolescence.* New York: Garland.

Kallgren, C. A., Reno, R. R., & Cialdini, R. B. (2000). A focus theory of normative conduct: When norms do and do not affect behavior. *Personality & Social Psychology Bulletin, 26*(8), 1002–1012.

Kamphaus, R. W., Petoskey, M. D., & Rowe, E. W. (2000). Current trends in psychological testing of children. *Professional Psychology: Research and Practice, 31*(2), 155–164.

Kandil, O., & Borysenko, M. (1987). Decline of natural killer cell target binding and lytic activity in mice exposed to rotation stress. *Health Psychology, 6,* 89–99.

Kane, J. M. (1996). Schizophrenia. *New England Journal of Medicine, 334,* 34–41.

Kanner, A. D., Coyne, J. C., Schaefer, C., & Lazarus, R. S. (1981). Comparison of two modes of stress measurement: Daily hassles and uplifts versus major life events. *Journal of Behavioral Medicine, 4,* 1–39.

Kantrowitz, B. (1992, August 3). Teenagers and AIDS. *Newsweek,* 45–50.

Kaplan, H., & Hill, K. (1985). Hunting ability and reproductive success among male Ache foragers: Preliminary results. *Current Anthropology, 26*(1), 131–133.

Kaplan, M., Lazoff, M., Kelly, K., Lukin, R., & Garver, D. (1990). Enlargements of cerebral third ventricle in psychotic patients with delayed response to neuroleptics. *Biological Psychiatry, 27,* 205–214.

Kaplan, S. J. (1991). Physical abuse and neglect. In M. Lewis (Ed.), *Child and adolescent psychiatry: A comprehensive textbook* (pp. 1010–1019). Baltimore, MD: Williams & Wilkins.

Karney, B. R., & Bradbury, T. N. (1995). The longitudinal course of marital quality and stability: A review of theory, method, and research. *Psychological Bulletin, 118,* 3–34.

Katzman, M., Wolchik, S., & Braver, S. (1984). The prevalence of frequent binge eating and bulimia in nonclinical sample. *International Journal of Eating Disorders, 3,* 53–62.

Katzman, R. (2000, July). Epidemiology of Alzheimer's disease. Paper presented to the World Alzheimer Congress 2000, Washington, DC.

Kaufman, J., & Zigler, E. (1989). The intergenerational transmission of child abuse. In D. Cichetti & V. Carlson (Eds.), *Child maltreatment: Theory and research on the causes and consequences of child abuse and neglect* (pp. 129–150). Cambridge, England: Cambridge University Press.

Kaye, W. H.; Klump, K. L., Frank, G. K. W., & Strober, M. (2000). Anorexia and bulimia nervosa. *Annual Review of Medicine, 51,* 299–313.

Kazdin, A. E. (1993). Adolescent mental health: Prevention and treatment programs. *American Pscyhologist, 48,* 127–141.

Keesey, R. E. (1986). A set-point theory of obesity. In K. D. Brownell & J. P. Foreyt (Eds.), *Handbook of eating disorders: Physiology, psychology, and treatment of obesity, anorexia, and bulimia.* New York: Basic Books.

Keil, J., et al. (1993). Mortality rates and risk factors for coronary disease in Black as compared with White men and women. *New England Journal of Medicine, 329,* 73–78.

Keller, H., & Boigs, R. (1991). The development of exploratory behavior. In M. E. Lamb & H. Keller (Eds.), *Infant development: Perspectives from German-speaking countries* (pp. 275–297). Hillsdale, NJ: Erlbaum.

Keller, M. B., et al. (2000). A Comparison of nefazodone, the cognitive behavioral-analysis system of psychotherapy, and their combination for the treatment of chronic depression. *The New England Journal of Medicine, 342*(20), 1462–1470.

Kellerman, J., Lewis, J., & Laird, J. D. (1989). Looking and loving: The effects of mutual gaze on feelings of romantic love. *Journal of Research in Personality, 23,* 145–161.

Kellner, R. (1990). Somatization: Theories and research. *Journal of Nervous and Mental Disease, 178,* 150–160.

Kemeny, M. E. (1993). Emotions and the immune system. In B. Moyers (Ed.), *Healing and the mind.* New York: Doubleday.

Kemeny, M. E., Weiner, H., Taylor, S. E., Schneider, S., Visscher, B., & Fahey, J. L. (1994). Repeated bereavement, depressed mood, and immune parameters in HIV seropositive and seronegative gay men. *Health Psychology, 13,* 14–24.

Kemper, P., & Murtaugh, C. M. (1991). Lifetime use of nursing home care. *New England Journal of Medicine, 324,* 595–600.

Kendler, K., Gruenberg, A., & Tsuang, M. (1985). Psychiatric illness in first-degree relatives of schizophrenics and surgical control patients: A family study using DSM-III criteria. *Archives of General Psychiatry, 42,* 770–779.

Kerr, N. L., & Bruun, S. E. (1983). Dispensability of member effort and group motivation losses: Free-rider effects. *Journal of Personality and Social Psychology, 44,* 78–94.

Kerr, N. L., & MacCoun, R. J. (1985). The effects of jury size and polling method on the process and product of jury deliberation. *Journal of Personality and Social Psychology, 48,* 349–363.

Kershner, J. R., & Ledger, G. (1985). Effect of sex, intelligence, and style of thinking on creativity: A comparison of gifted and average IQ children. *Journal of Personality and Social Psychology, 48,* 1033–1040.

Kevorkian found not guilty. (1996, March 8). Reuters. America Online.

Khanna, R., & Rathee, R. (1992). Altruism, mood, and help to drug addicts. Special Series I: Alcohol and drug use. *Journal of Personality and Clinical Studies, 8,* 23–26.

Kihlstrom, J. F., Glisky, M. L., & Angiulo, M. J. (1994). Dissociative tendencies and dissociative disorders. *Journal of Abnormal Psychology, 103,* 117–124.

Kilborn, P. T. (1995, March 16). Women and minorities still face "glass ceilings." *The New York Times,* p. A22.

Kimble, D. P. (1992). *Biological psychology* (2nd ed.). Fort Worth, TX: Harcourt Brace Jovanovich.

Kimble, G. A. (1994). A frame of reference for psychology. *American Psychologist, 49,* 510–519.

Kinnunen, T., Zamansky, H. S., & Block, M. L. (1994). Is the hypnotized patient lying? *Journal of Abnormal Psychology, 103,* 184–191.

Kirchler, E., Pombeni, M. L., & Palmonari, A. (1991). Sweet sixteen . . . : Adolescents' problems and the peer group as a source of support. *European Journal of Psychology of Education, 6,* 393–410.

Kleinke, C. L. (1977). Compliance to requests made by gazing and touching experimenters in field settings. *Journal of Experimental Social Psychology, 13,* 218–223.

Kleinke, C. L. (1986). Gaze and eye contact: A research review. *Psychological Review, 100,* 78–100.

Kleinmuntz, B., & Szucko, J. J. (1984). Lie detection in ancient and modern times: A call for contemporary scientific study. *American Psychologist, 39,* 766–776.

Knafo, A., Iervolino, A. C., & Plomin, R. (2005). Masculine girls and feminine boys: Genetic and environmental contributions to atypical gender development in early childhood. *Journal of Personality & Social Psychology, 88*(2), 400–412.

Kneip, R. C., et al. (1993). Self- and spouse ratings of anger and hostility as predictors of coronary heart disease. *Health Psychology, 12,* 301–307.

Knight, G. P., Fabes, R. A., & Higgins, D. A. (1996). Concerns about drawing causal inferences from meta-analyses: An example in the study of gender differences in aggression. *Psychological Bulletin, 119,* 410–421.

Kobasa, S. C. O., Maddi, S. R., Puccetti, M. C., & Zola, M. A. (1994). Effectiveness of hardiness, exercise, and social support as resources against illness. In A. Steptoe & J. Wardle (Eds.), *Psychosocial processes and health* (pp. 247–260). Cambridge, England: Cambridge University Press.

Kobasa, S. C., Maddi, S. R., & Kahn, S. (1982). Hardiness and health: A prospective study. *Journal of Personality and Social Psychology, 42,* 168–177.

Kohlberg, L. (1963). Moral development and identification. In H. W. Stevenson (Ed.), *Yearbook of the national survey for the study of education: 1. Child psychology.* Chicago: University of Chicago Press.

Kohlberg, L. (1969). *Stages in the development of moral thought and action.* New York: Holt, Rinehart and Winston.

Kohout, J., & Williams, S. (1999). Far more psychology degrees are going to women. *APA Monitor online, 30*(10).

Kolata, G. (2000, January 18). True secret of fad diets: It's calories. *The New York Times,* p. F7.

Kolb, B., & Taylor, L. (1981). Affective behavior in patients with localized cortical excisions: Role of lesion site and side, *Science, 214,* 89–91.

Kolko, D. J., & Richard-Figueroa, J. L. (1985). Effects of video games on the adverse corollaries of chemotherapy in pediatric oncology patients: A single-case analysis. *Journal of Consulting and Clinical Psychology, 53,* 223–228.

Kooijman, C. M., et al. (2000). Phantom pain and phantom sensations in upper limb amputees: An epidemiological study. *Pain, 87*(1), 33–41.

Kopera-Frye, K., Ager, J., Saltz, E., Poindexter, J., & Lee, S. (1993, March). *Predictors of adolescent delinquency.* Paper presented at the meeting of the Society for Research in Child Development, New Orleans, LA.

Kornblum, W. (1994). *Sociology in a changing world* (3rd ed.). Fort Worth, TX: Harcourt Brace Jovanovich.

Krosnick, J. A. (1989). Attitude importance and attitude accessibility. *Personality and Social Psychology Bulletin, 15,* 297–308.

Krueger, R. F., Schmutte, P. S., Caspi, A., Moffitt, T. E., Campbell, K., & Silva, P. A. (1993, May). *Delinquency affect and constraint: Personality and illegal behavior in late adolescence.* Paper presented at the meeting of the Midwestern Psychological Association, Chicago.

Kübler-Ross, E. (1969). *On death and dying.* New York: Macmillan.

Kuczaj, S. A., II. (1982). On the nature of syntactic development. In S. A. Kuczaj, II (Ed.), *Language development, Vol. 1.: Syntax and semantics.* Hillsdale, NJ: Erlbaum.

Kuczmarski, R. J. (1992). Prevalence of overweight and weight gain in the United States. *American Journal of Clinical Nutrition, 55*(Suppl.), 495S–502S.

Kuhn, D., et al. (1978). Sex-role concepts of two- and three-year-olds. *Child Development, 49,* 445–451.

Kunkel, D., & Roberts, D. (1991). Young minds and marketplace values: Issues in children's television advertising. *Journal of Social Issues, 47,* 57–72.

Kurzweil, R. (2000, June 19). Will my PC be smarter than I am? *Time magazine,* pp. 82–83.

Kutner, L. (1993, February 4). For both boys and girls, early or late puberty can lead to social or emotional problems. *The New York Times,* p. B6.

Kyle, T. M., & Williams, S. (2000, May). Results of the 1998–1999 APA survey of graduate departments of psychology, Tables 13A & 13B. APA Research Office. Washington, D.C.: American Psychological Association.

LaFramboise, T. (1994). Cited in DeAngelis, T. (1994). History, culture affect treatment for Indians. *APA Monitor, 27*(10), 36.

Lagerspetz, K. M., Bjorkqvist, K., & Peltonen, T. (1988). Is indirect aggression typical of females? Gender differences in aggressiveness in 11- to 12-year-old children. *Aggressive Behavior, 14,* 403–414.

Laitinen-Krispijn, S., Van der Ende, J., Hazebroek-Kampschreur, A. A. J. M., & Verhulst, F. C. (1999). Pubertal maturation and the development of behavioural and emotional problems in early adolescence. *Acta Psychiatrica Scandinavica, 99*(1), 16–25.

Lakka, T. A., et al. (1994). Relation of leisure-time physical activity and cardiorespiratory fitness to the risk of acute myocardial infarction in men. *New England Journal of Medicine, 330,* 1549–1554.

Lamb, L. E. (1993). Aging: the cross-linking link. *Muscle and Fitness, 54*(4), 166–167.

Lamb, M. E. (1977). Father-infant and mother-infant interaction in the first year of life. *Child Development, 48,* 167–181.

Lamb, M. E., Sternberg, K. J., & Prodomidis, M. (1992). Nonmaternal care and the security of infant-mother attachment: A reanalysis of the data. *Infant Behavior and Development, 15,* 71–83.

Lambert, W. E. (1990). Persistent issues in bilingualism. In B. Harley et al. (Eds.), *The development of second language proficiency.* Cambridge, England: Cambridge University Press.

Lambert, W. E., Genesee, F., Holobow, N., & Chartrand, L. (1991). *Bilingual education for majority English-speaking children.* Montreal: McGill University.

Lancaster, T., Stead, L., Silagy, C., & Sowden, A. (2000). Regular review: Effectiveness of interventions to help people stop smoking: Findings from the Cochrane Library. *British Medical Journal, 321,* 355–358.

Lang, E. V., et al. (2000). Adjunctive non-pharmacological analgesia for invasive medical procedures: a randomised trial. *The Lancet, 355,* 1486–1490.

Langlois, J. H. (1994). Cited in Brody, J. E. (1994, March 21). Notions of beauty transcend culture, new study suggests. *The New York Times,* p. A14.

Langlois, J. H., & Downs, C. (1980). Mothers, fathers and peers as socialization agents of sex-typed play behavior in young children. *Child Development, 51,* 1217–1247.

Langlois, J. H., et al. (2000). Maxims or myths of beauty? A meta-analytic and theoretical review. *Psychological Bulletin, 126*(3), 390–423.

LaPerriere, A. R., et al. (1991). Aerobic exercise training in an AIDS risk group. *International Journal of Sports Medicine, 12,* S53–S57.

Larson, R., & Richards, M. H. (1991). Daily companionship in late childhood and early adolescence: Changing development contexts. *Child Development, 62,* 284–300.

Laufer, A., & Harel, Y. (2003). Correlation between school perception and pupil involvement in bullying, physical fights and weapon carrying. *Megamot, 42*(3), 437–459.

Laumann, E. O., Gagnon, J. H., Michael, R. T., & Michaels, S. (1994). *The social organization of sexuality: Sexual practices in the United States.* Chicago: University of Chicago Press.

Lavie, P., & Herer, P., & Hoffstein, H. (2000). Obstructive sleep apnoea syndrome as a risk factor for hypertension: population study. *British Medical Journal, 320,* 479–482.

Lawton, C. A., & Morrin, K. A. (1999). Gender differences in pointing accuracy in computer-simulated 3D mazes. *Sex Roles, 40*(1–2), 73–92.

Lazarus, A. A. (1990). If this be research . . . *American Psychologist, 45,* 670–671.

Lazarus, R. S. (1991). Cognition and motivation in emotion. *American Psychologist, 46,* 352–367.

Lazarus, R. S., DeLongis, A., Folkman, S., & Gruen, R. (1985). Stress and adaptational outcomes: The problem of confounded measures. *American Psychologist, 40,* 770–779.

Leary, W. E. (1991, October 22). Black hypertension may reflect other ills. *The New York Times,* p. C3.

Leary, W. E. (1995, May 2). Billions suffering needlessly, study says. *The New York Times,* p. C5.

LeDoux, J. E. (1994, June). Emotion, memory, and the brain. *Scientific American,* pp. 50–57.

Lefcourt, H. M., & Martin, R. A. (1986). *Humor and life stress: Antidote to adversity.* New York: Springer-Verlag.

Leff, J., & Vaughn, C. (1985). *Expressed emotion in families.* New York: Guilford Press.

Lehrman, S. (1995, January). Can the clock be slowed? *Harvard Health Letter, 20*(3), 1–3.

Leibel, R. L., Rosenbaum, M., & Hirsch, J. (1995). Changes in energy expenditure resulting from altered body weight. *New England Journal of Medicine, 332,* 621–628.

Leippe, M. R. (1985). The influence of eye-witness non-identifications on mock-jurors' judgments of a court case. *Journal of Applied Social Psychology, 15,* 656–672.

Lenneberg, E. H. (1967). *Biological foundations of language.* New York: Wiley.

Leon, G. R., & Dinklage, D. (1989). Obesity and anorexia nervosa. In T. H. Ollendick & M. Hersen (Eds.), *Handbook of child psychopathology* (2nd ed., pp. 247–263). New York: Plenum Press.

Leslie, C. (1993, August 2). Girls will be girls. *Newsweek,* p. 44.

Lesnik-Oberstein, M., & Cohen, L. (1984). Cognitive style, sensation seeking, and assortive mating. *Journal of Personality and Social Psychology, 46,* 57–66.

Levinson, D. J. (1996). *The seasons of a woman's life.* New York: Knopf.

Levinson, D. J., Darrow, C. N., Klein, E. B., Levinson, M. H., & McKee, B. (1978). *The seasons of a man's life.* New York: Knopf.

Levy, D., et al. (2000). Evidence for a gene influencing blood pressure on chromosome 17 : Genome scan linkage results for longitudinal blood pressure phenotypes in subjects from the Framingham Heart Study. *Hypertension, 36,* 477–483.

Levy, R., & Goldman-Rakic, P. S. (1999). Association of storage and processing functions in the dorsolateral prefrontal cortex of the nonhuman primate. *Journal of Neuroscience, 19*(12), 5149–5158.

Levy, S. M., Herberman, R. B., Maluish, A. M., Schlien, B., & Lippman, M. (1985). Prognostic risk assessment in the primary breast cancer by behavioral and immunological parameters. *Health Psychology, 4,* 99–113.

Lewin, T. (1995, December 7). Parents poll shows higher incidence of child abuse. *The New York Times,* p. B16.

Lewin, T. (1995, September 18). Women are becoming equal providers. *The New York Times,* p. A27.

Lewinsohn, P. M., et al. (1994). Adolescent psychopathology: II. Psychosocial risk factors for depression. *Journal of Abnormal Psychology, 103,* 302–315.

Lewis-Fernández, R. & Kleinman, A. (1994). Culture, personality, and psychopathology. *Journal of Abnormal Psychology, 103,* 67–71.

Lichtenstein, E., & Glasgow, R. E. (1992). Smoking cessation: What have we learned in the past decade? *Journal of Consulting and Clinical Psychology, 60,* 518–527.

Lichtenstein, P., et al. (2000). Environmental and heritable factors in the causation of cancer: Analyses of cohorts of twins from Sweden, Denmark, and Finland. *New England Journal of Medicine, 343*(2), 78–85.

Liebert, R. M., Sprafkin, J. N., & Davidson, E. S. (1989). *The early window: Effects of television on children and youth* (3rd ed.). New York, Pergamon Press.

Liebert, R., & Spiegler, M. (1982). *Personality: Strategies and issues.* Homewood, IL: Dorsey Press.

Lillqvist, O., & Lindeman, M. (1998). Belief in astrology as a strategy for self-verification and coping with negative life-events. *European Psychologist, 3*(3), 202–208.

Lindpaintner, K. (1995). Finding an obesity gene-A tale of mice and man. *New England Journal of Medicine, 332,* 679–680.

Lindsay, R. C. L., Lim, R., Marando, L., & Culley, D. (1986). Mock-juror evaluations of eyewitness testimony: A test of metamemory hypotheses. *Journal of Applied Social Psychology, 16,* 447–459.

Linn, M. C., & Petersen, A. C. (1986). A meta-analysis of gender differences in spatial ability: Implications for mathematics and science achievement. In J. S. Hyde & M. C. Linn (Eds.), *The psychology of gender: Advances through meta-analysis* (pp. 67–101). Baltimore, MD: Johns Hopkins University Press.

Linville, P. W., Fischer, G. W., & Salovey, P. (1989). Perceived distribution of the characteristics of in-group and out-group members. *Journal of Personality and Social Psychology, 57,* 165–188.

Lips, H. (1993). *Sex and gender: An introduction* (2nd ed.). Mountain View, CA: Mayfield.

Lipsey, M. W., & Wilson, D. B. (1993). The efficacy of psychological, educational, and behavioral treatment: Confirmation from meta-analysis. *American Psychologist, 48,* 1181–1209.

Lisanby, S. H., et al. (2000). The effects of electroconvulsive therapy on memory of autobiographical and public events. *Archives of General Psychiatry, 57*(6), 581–590.

Livson, N., & Peskin, H. (1972). Pre- and postpubertal personality and adult psychological functioning. *Seminars in Psychiatry, 4*(4), 343–353.

Lochman, J. E. (1992). Cognitive-behavioral intervention with aggressive boys: Three-year follow-up and preventive effects. *Journal of Consulting and Clinical Psychology, 60,* 426–432.

Lochman, J. E., & Dodge, K. A. (1994). Social-cognitive processes of severely violent, moderately aggressive, and nonagressive boys. *Journal of Consulting and Clinical Psychology, 62,* 366–374.

Loehlin, J. C., Willerman, L., & Horn, J. M. (1988). Human behavior genetics. *Annual Review of Psychology, 39,* 101–133.

Loftus, E. F. (1983). Silence is not golden. *American Psychologist, 38,* 564–572.

Loftus, E. F. (1993). Psychologists in the eyewitness world. *American Psychologist, 48,* 550–552.

Loftus, E. F. (1994). Conference on memory, Harvard Medical School. Cited in D. Goleman (1994, May 31). Miscoding is seen as the root of false memories. *The New York Times,* pp. C1, C8.

Loftus, E. F. (2004). Memories of things unseen. *Current Directions in Psychological Science, 13*(4) 145–147.

Loftus, E. F., & Loftus, G. R. (1980). On the permanence of stored information in the brain. *American Psychologist, 35,* 409–420.

Loftus, E. F., & Palmer, J. C. (1974). Reconstruction of automobile destruction: An example of interaction between language and memory. *Journal of Verbal Learning and Verbal Behavior, 13,* 585–589.

Longer, healthier, better. (1997, March 9). *The New York Times Magazine,* pp. 44–45.

Lore, R. K., & Schultz, L. A. (1993). Control of human aggression: A comparative perspective. *American Psychologist, 48,* 16–25.

Lorenz, K. (1937). The companion in the bird's world. *Auk, 54,* 245–273.

Lowe, M. R., and others. (1996). Restraint, dieting, and the continuum model of bulimia nervosa. *Journal of Abnormal Psychology, 105,* 508–517.

Lown, J., & Dolan, E. (1988). Financial challenges in remarriage. *Lifestyles: Family and Economic Issues, 9,* 73–88.

Lubell, S. (2004, February 19). On the therapists's couch, a jolt of virtual reality. *The New York Times online.*

Lubinski, D., & Benbow, C. P. (2000). States of excellence. *American Psychologist, 55,* 137–150.

Luchins, A. S., & Luchins, E. H. (1959). *Rigidity of behavior.* Eugene: University of Oregon Press.

Ludwick-Rosenthal, R., & Neufeld, R. W. J. (1993). Preparation for undergoing an invasive medical procedure: Interacting effects of information and coping style. *Journal of Consulting and Clinical Psychology, 61,* 156–164.

Lundeberg, M. A., Fox, P. W., & Puncochar, J. (1994). Highly confident but wrong: Gender differences and similarities in confidence of judgments. *Journal of Educational Psychology, 86,* 114–121.

Lykken, D., & Tellegen, A. (1996). Happiness is a stochastic phenomenon. *Psychological Science, 7*(3), 186–189.

Lyons-Ruth, K., Alpern, L., & Repacholi, B. (1993). Disorganized infant attachment classification and maternal psychosocial problems as predictors of hostile-aggressive behavior in the preschool classroom. *Child Development, 64,* 575–585.

Maccoby, E. E. (1990). Gender and relationships. *American Psychologist, 45,* 513–520.

Maccoby, E. E., & Jacklin, C. N. (1974). *The psychology of sex differences.* Stanford, CA: Stanford University Press.

Maccoby, E., & Martin, J. A. (1983). Socialization in the context of the family: Parent-child interaction. In E. M. Hetherington (Ed.), *Handbook of child psychology* (Vol. 4). New York: Wiley.

MacDonald, K. (1992). Warmth as a developmental construct: An evolutionary analysis. *Child Development, 63,* 753–773.

Maciejewski, P. K., Prigerson, H. G., & Mazure, C. M. (2000). Self-efficacy as a mediator between stressful life events and depressive symptoms: Differences based on history of prior depression. *British Journal of Psychiatry, 176,* 373–378.

Mackert, B., et al. (2003). The eloquence of silent cortex: Analysis of afferent input to deafferented cortex in arm amputees. *Neuroreport: For Rapid Communication of Neuroscience Research, 14*(3), 409–412.

Mackie, D. M., Worth, L. T., & Asuncion, A. G. (1990). Processing of persuasive in-group messages. *Journal of Personality and Social Psychology, 58,* 812–822.

Maier, N. R. F. (1931). Reasoning in human beings: II. The solution of a problem and its appearance in consciousness. *Journal of Comparative Psychology, 12,* 181–194.

Malina, R. M. (1978). Adolescent growth and maturation: Selected aspects of current research. *Yearbook of Physical Anthropology, 21,* 63–94.

Malinosky-Rummell, R., & Hansen, D. H. (1993). Long-term consequences of childhood physical abuse. *Psychological Bulletin, 114,* 68–79.

Manke, B. (1993, March). *Dimensions of intimacy during adolescence: Correlates and antecedents.* Paper presented at the meeting of the Society for Research in Child Development, New Orleans, LA.

Manson, J. E., et al. (1995). Body weight and mortality among women. *New England Journal of Medicine, 333,* 677–685.

Manucia, G. K., Baumann, D. J., & Cialdini, R. B. (1984). Mood influences on helping: Direct effects or side effects? *Journal of Personality and Social Psychology, 46,* 357–364.

March, J., Johnston, H., & Greist, J. (1989). Obsessive-compulsive disorder. *American Family Practice, 39,* 175–182.

Marcia, J. E. (1966). Development and validation of ego identity status. *Journal of Personality and Social Psychology, 3,* 551–558.

Marcia, J. E. (1991). Identity and self-development. In R. M. Lerner, A. C. Petersen, & J. Brooks-Gunn (Eds.), *Encyclopedia of adolescence.* New York: Garland.

Marcia, J. E., Waterman, A. S., Matteson, D. R., Archer, S. L., & Orlofsky, J. L. (1993). *Ego identity: A handbook for psychosocial research.* New York: Springer-Verlag.

Marenberg, M. E., et al. (1994). Genetic susceptibility to death from coronary heart disease in women. *New England Journal of Medicine, 330,* 1041–1046.

Margoshes, P. (1995). For many, old age is the prime of life. *APA Monitor, 26*(5), 36–37.

Margules, D. L., & Olds, J. (1962). Identical "feeding" and "rewarding" systems in the lateral hypothalmus of rats. *Science, 135,* 374–375.

Marital Status and Living Arrangements. (1998, March). Current Population Survey data. U. S. Bureau of the Census, Current Population Reports, Series P20–514.

Markel, H. (2000, July 25). Anorexia can strike boys, too. *The New York Times online.*

Markman, H. J., Renick, M. J., Floyd, F. J., Stanley, S. M., & Clements, M. (1993). Preventing marital distress through communication and conflict management training: A 4- and 5-year follow-up. *Journal of Consulting and Clinical Psychology, 61,* 70–77.

Marks, C. (1984). *World artists,* 1950–1980 (pp. 664–675). New York: H. W. Wilson.

Markstrom-Adams, C. (1992). A consideration of intervening factors in adolescent identity formation. In G. R. Adams, T. P. Gullotta, & R. Montemayor (Eds.), *Adolescent identity formation.* Newbury Park, CA: Sage.

Markus, H., & Kitayama, S. (1991). Culture and the self: Implications for cognition, emotion, and motivation. *Psychological Review, 98*(2), 224–253.

Marler, P. (1991). The instinct for vocal learning: Songbirds. In S. E. Brauth, W. S. Hall, & R. J. Dooling (Eds.), *Plasticity of development* (pp. 107–125). Cambridge, MA: MIT Press.

Marriott, M. (1991, June 5). Beyond "yuck" for girls in science. *The New York Times,* p. A26.

Marsh, H. W., Craven, R. G., & Debus, R. (1991). Self-concepts of young children 5 to 8 years of age: Measurement and multidimensional structure. *Journal of Educational Psychology, 83,* 377–392.

Martin, C. L. (1987). A ratio measure of sex stereotyping. *Journal of Personality and Social Psychology, 52,* 489–499.

Martin, C. L., & Halverson, C. F., Jr. (1981). A schematic processing model of sex typing and stereotyping in children. *Child Development, 54,* 1119–1134.

Martin, R. A., & Lefcourt, H. M. (1983). Sense of humor as a moderator of the relation between stressors and moods. *Journal of Personality and Social Psychology, 45,* 1313–1324.

Maruyama, G., Fraser, S. C., & Miller, N. (1982). Personal responsibility and altruism in children. *Journal of Personality and Social Psychology, 42,* 658–664.

Maslow, A. H. (1970). *Motivation and personality* (2nd ed.). New York: Harper & Row.

Matarazzo, J. D. (1990). Psychological assessment versus psychological testing. *American Psychologist, 45,* 999–1017.

Matarazzo, J. D. (1993). Cited in Michaelson, R. (1993). Behavior gets big billing in medical schools today. *APA Monitor, 24*(8), 56.

Matlin, M. (1996). *The psychology of women* (3rd ed.). Fort Worth, TX: Harcourt Brace Jovanovich.

Matlin, M. W. (1999). *The psychology of women* (4th ed.). Fort Worth: Harcourt College Publishers.

Matthews, K., and others. (1997). Women's Health Initiative. *American Psychologist, 52,* 101–116.

Maultsby, M. C. (1971). Systematic written homework in psychotherapy. *Psychotherapy, Theory, Research, and Practice, 8,* 195–198.

Maybury-Lewis, D. (1992). *Millennium: Tribal wisdom and the modern world.* New York: Viking.

McCall, R. B. (1977). Children's IQs as predictors of adult educational and occupational status. *Science, 297,* 482–483.

McCarley, R. W. (1992). Cited in Blakeslee, S. (1992, January 7). Scientists unraveling chemistry of dreams. *The New York Times,* pp. C1, C10.

McCarthy, K. (1993). Research on women's health doesn't show whole picture. *APA Monitor, 24*(7), 14–15.

McClave, E. Z. (2000). Linguistic functions of head movements in the context of speech. *Journal of Pragmatics, 32*(7), 855–878.

McClelland, D. C. (1965). Achievement and entrepreneurship: A longitudinal study. *Journal of Personality and Social Psychology, 1,* 389–392.

McCourt, K., et al. (1999). Authoritarianism revisited: Genetic and environmental influences examined in twins reared apart and together. *Personality & Individual Differences, 27*(5), 985–1014.

McCrae, R. R., & Costa, P. T., Jr. (1997). Personality trait structure as a human universal. *American Psychologist, 52,* 509–516.

McCrae, R. R., Costa, P. T., Jr., et al. (2000). Nature over nurture: Temperament, personality, and life span development. *Journal of Personality & Social Psychology, 78*(1), 173–186.

McDermott, D. (1997, May 14). Yes, computers *can* think. *The New York Times,* p. A21.

McDougall, W. (1908). *An introduction to social psychology.* London: Meuthen.

McGowan, R. J., & Johnson, D. K. (1984). The mother-child relationship and other antecedents of childhood intelligence: A casual analysis. *Child Development, 55,* 810–820.

McIntosh, H. (1996). Solitude provides an emotional tune-up. *APA Monitor, 26*(3), 1, 10.

McLeod, J. D., Kessler, R. C., & Landis, K. R. (1992). Speed of recovery from major depressive episodes in a community sample of married men and women. *Journal of Abnormal Psychology, 101,* 277–286.

Mead, M. (1935). *Sex and temperament in three primitive societies.* New York: Dell.

Meehan, P. J., Lamb, J. A., Saltzman, L. E., & O'Carroll, P. W. (1992). Attempted suicide among young adults: Progress toward a meaningful estimate of prevalence. *American Journal of Psychiatry, 149,* 41–44.

Meichenbaum, D. (1993). Changing conceptions of cognitive behavior modification: Retrospect and prospect. *Journal of Consulting and Clinical Psychology, 61,* 202–204.

Melle, I., & Friis, S. (1991). Psychosocial treatment of schizophrenia. *Nordisk Psykiatrisk Tidsskrift, 45,* 97–108.

Metalsky, G. I., Joiner, T. E., Jr., Hardin, T. S., & Abramson, L. Y. (1993). Depressive reactions to failure in naturalistic setting: A test of the hopelessness and self–esteem theories of depression. *Journal of Abnormal Psychology, 102,* 101–109.

Mevkens, F. L. (1990). Coming of age—The chemoprevention of cancer. *New England Journal of Medicine, 323,* 825–827.

Meyer, G. J. (2000). Incremental validity of the Rorschach Prognostic Rating scale over the MMPI Ego Strength Scale and IQ. *Journal of Personality Assessment, 74*(3), 356–370.

Michael, R. T., Gagnon, J. H., Laumann, E. O., & Kolata, G. (1994). *Sex in America: A definitive survey.* Boston: Little, Brown.

Michaelson, R. (1993). Tug-of-war is developing over defining retardation. *APA Monitor, 24*(5), 34–35.

Michels, R., & Marzuk, P. M. (1993). Progress in psychiatry: II. *New England Journal of Medicine, 329,* 628–638.

Mikesell, R. H., Lusterman, D., & McDaniel, S. (Eds.). (1995). *Family psychology and systems therapy.* Washington, DC: American Psychological Association.

Milgram, S. (1963). Behavioral study of obedience. *Journal of Abnormal and Social Psychology, 67,* 371–378.

Miller, A. (1992, June 29). Baby makers, Inc. *Newsweek,* pp. 38–39.

Miller, B. C., McCoy, J. K, & Olson, T. D. (1986). Dating age and stage as correlates of adolescent sexual attitudes and behavior. *Journal of Adolescent Research, 1,* 361–371.

Miller, G. A. (1956). The magical number seven, plus or minus two: Some limits on our capacity for processing information. *Psychological Review, 63,* 81–97.

Miller, J. L. (1992). Trouble in mind. *Scientific American, 267*(3), 180.

Miller, N. B., Cowan, P. A., Cowan, C. P., Hetherington, E. M., & Clingempeel, W. G. (1993). Externalizing in preschoolers and early adolescents: A cross-study replication of a family model. *Developmental Psychology, 29,* 3–18.

Miller, N. E. (1995). Clinical-experimental interactions in the development of neuroscience. *American Psychologist, 50,* 901–911.

Millon, T. (1981). *Disorders of personality.* New York: Wiley.

Mineka, S. (1991, August). Paper presented to the annual meeting of the American Psychological Association, San Francisco, CA. Cited in Turkington, C. (1991). Evolutionary memories may have phobia role. *APA Monitor, 22*(11), 14.

Mintz, L. B., Bartels, K. M., & Rideout, C. A. (1995). Training in counseling ethnic minorities and race-based availability of graduate school resources. *Professional Psychology: Research in Practice, 26,* 316–321.

Mitchell, J. E., & Eckert, E. D. (1987). Scope and significance of eating disorders. *Journal of Consulting and Clinical Psychology, 55,* 628–634.

Moffet, M. (1990). The dance of the electric honeybee. *National Geographic, 177,* 134–140.

Mokdad, A. H., et al. (2000). The continuing epidemic of obesity in the United States. *Journal of the American Medical Association online, 284*(13).

Moldin, S. O. (1994). Indicators of liability to schizophrenia: Perspectives from genetic epidemiology. *Schizophrenia Bulletin, 20*(1), 169–184.

Moliterno, D. J., et al. (1994). Coronary-artery vasoconstriction induced by cocaine, cigarette smoking, or both. *New England Journal of Medicine, 330,* 454–459.

Mom, Dad, I want a job. (1993, May 17). *U.S. News & World Report,* pp. 68–72.

Money, J. (1987). Sin, sickness or status—Homosexual gender identity and psychoneuroendocrinology. *American Psychologist, 42,* 384–399.

Money, J. (1994). The concept of gender identity disorder in childhood and adolescence after 39 years. *Journal of Sex and Marital Therapy, 20*(3), 163–177.

Montemayor, R., & Flannery, D. J. (1991). Parent-adolescent relations in middle and late adolescence. In R. M. Lerner, A. C. Petersen, & J. Brooks-Gunn (Eds.), *Encyclopedia of adolescence.* New York: Garland.

Montgomery, G. H., DuHamel, K. N., & Redd, W. H. (2000). A meta-analysis of hypnotically induced analgesia: How effective is hypnosis? *International Journal of Clinical & Experimental Hypnosis, 48*(2), 138–153.

Moore, K. A., & Stief, T. M. (1992). Changes in marriage and fertility behavior: Behavior versus attitudes of young adults. *Youth and Society, 22,* 362–386.

Morrison, A. M., & Von Glinow, M. A. (1990). Women and minorities in management. *American Psychologist, 45,* 200–209.

Mortimer, J. T., & Johnson, M. K. (1998). Adolescents' part-time work and educational achievement. In Borman, K., & Schneider, B. (Eds.). *The adolescent years: Social influences and educational challenges: Ninety-seventh yearbook of the National Society for the Study of Education, Part I.* (pp. 183–206). Chicago: The National Society for the Study of Education.

Mott, M. (2005, January 4). Did animals sense tsunami was coming? *National Geographic News online.*

Moyer, K. E. (1983). The physiology of motivation: Aggression as a model. In C. J. Scheier & A. M. Rogers (Eds.), *G. Stanley Hall Lecture Series* (Vol. 3). Washington, DC: American Psychological Association.

Mullen, B., Bryant, B., & Driskell, J. E. (1997). Presence of others and arousal: An integration. *Group Dynamics, 1*(1), 52–64.

Mulvihill, K. (2000, March 14). Many miss out on migraine remedies. *The New York Times online.*

Muñoz, R. F., Hollon, S. D., McGarth, E., Rehm, L. P., & VandenBos, G. R. (1994). On the AHCPR Depression in Primary Care guidelines: Further consideration for practitioners. *American Psychologist, 49,* 42–61.

Munro, G. D., & Munro, J. E. (2000). Using daily horoscopes to demonstrate expectancy confirmation. *Teaching of Psychology, 27*(2), 114–116.

Murray, B. (1996). College youth haunted by increased pressures. *APA Monitor, 26*(4), 47.

Mussweiler, T., & Bodenhausen, G. V. (2002). I know you are, but what am I? Self-evaluative consequences of judging in-group and out-group members. *Journal of Personality & Social Psychology, 82*(1), 19–32.

Must, A., et al. (1999). The disease burden associated with overweight and obesity. *Journal of the American Medical Association online, 282*(16).

Myers, D. G. (1996). *Social psychology* (5th ed.). New York: McGraw-Hill.

Myers, D. G., & Bishop, G. D. (1970). Discussion effects on racial attitudes. *Science, 169,* 778–779.

Myers, J. K., Weissman, M. M., Tischler, G. L., Holzer, C. E., Leaf, P. J., Orvaschel, H. A., Anthony, J. C., Boyd, J. H., Burke, J. D., Kramer, M., & Stoltzman, R. (1984). Six-month prevalence of psychiatric disorders in three communities: 1980–1982. *Archives of General Psychiatry, 41,* 959–967.

Nansel, T. R., Haynie, D. L., & Simons-Morton, B. G. (2003). The association of bullying and victimization with middle school adjustment. *Journal of Applied School Psychology, 19*(2), 45–61.

Nantais, K. M., & Schellenberg, E. G. (1999). The Mozart effect: An artifact of preference. *Psychological Science, 10*(4), 370–373.

National Center for Health Statistics (1982). *Monthly Vital Statistics Report, Advance Report of Final Natality Statistics, 33*(6), supplement.

National Institute of Child Health and Human Development. (1996). Infant child care and attachment security: Results of the NICHD study of early child care. Cited in Chira, D. J. (1996, April 21). Study says babies in child care keep secure bonds to mothers. *The New York Times,* pp. C10, C32.

National Institute of Mental Health. (1985). *Electroconvulsive therapy: Consensus Development Conference statement.* Bethesda, MD: U.S. Department of Health and Human Services.

Neher, A. (1991). Maslow's theory of motivation: A critique. *Journal of Humanistic Psychology, 31,* 89–112.

Neisser, U. (1993). Cited in Goleman, D. J. (1993, April 6). Studying the secrets of childhood memory. *The New York Times,* pp. C1, C11.

Neisser, U., et al. (1996). Intelligence: Knowns and unknowns. *American Psychologist, 51*(2), 77–101.

Nevid, J. S. (1984). Sex differences in factors of romantic attraction. *Sex Roles, 11,* 401–411.

Nevid, J. S., Rathus, S. A., & Greene, B. A. (1997). *Abnormal psychology in a changing world* (3rd ed.). Englewood Cliffs, NJ: Prentice-Hall.

Newcomb, M. D., & Bentler, P. M. (1992, August). *Substance abuse and gender: Accounting for the differences.* Paper presented at the meeting of the American Psychological Association, Washington, DC.

Newcomb, T. M. (1981). Heiderian balance as a group phenomenon. *Journal of Personality and Social Psychology, 40,* 862–867.

Nides, M. A., et al. (1995). Predictors of initial smoking cessation and relapse through the first 2 years of the lung health study. *Journal of Consulting and Clinical Psychology, 63,* 60–69.

Nigg, J. T., & Goldsmith, H. H. (1994). Genetics of personality disorders: Perspectives from personality and psychopathology research. *Psychological Bulletin, 115,* 346–380.

Noller, P., & Callan, V. J. (1990). Adolescents' perceptions of the nature of their communication with parents. *Journal of Youth and Adolescence, 19,* 349–362.

Norton, A., & Moorman, J. (1987). Current trends in marriage and divorce among American women. *Journal of Marriage and the Family, 49,* 3–14.

Novacek, J., Raskin, R., & Hogan, R. (1991). Why do adolescents use drugs? Age, sex, and user differences. *Journal of Youth and Adolescence, 20,* 475–492.

O'Connor, T. G., Caspi, A., DeFries, J. C., & Plomin, R. (2000). Are associations between parental divorce and children's adjustment genetically mediated? An adoption study. *Developmental Psychology, 36*(4), 429–437.

Ogbu, J. U. (1993). Differences in cultural frame of reference. *International Journal of Behavioral Development, 16,* 483–506.

Oldenburg, D. (2005, January 9). Animals' "reported sixth sense" is explored. *The Washington Post online.*

Olds, J. (1969) The central nervous system and the reinforcement of behavior. *American Psychologist, 24,* 114–132.

O'Leary, A. (1990). Stress, emotion, and human immune function. *Psychological Bulletin, 108,* 363–382.

Olson, S. L., Bates, J. E., & Kaskie, B. (1992). Caregiver-infant interaction antecedents of children's school-age cognitive ability. *Merrill-Palmer Quarterly, 38,* 309–330.

Olweus, D. (1986). Aggression and hormones: Behavioral relationship with testosterone and adrenaline. In D. Olweus, J. Block, & M. Radke-Yarrow (Eds.), *Development of antisocial and prosocial behavior* (pp. 51–72). New York: Academic Press.

Orive, R. (1988). Social projective and social comparison of opinion. *Journal of Personality and Social Psychology, 54,* 953–964.

Osborne, C. (Ed.). (1968). *I have a dream: The story of Martin Luther King in text and pictures.* New York: Time-Life Books.

Osofsky, J. D., Osofsky, H. J., & Diamond, M. O. (1988). The transition to parenthood: Special tasks and risk factors for adolescent parents. In G. Y. Michaels & W. A. Goldberg (Eds.), *The transition to parenthood: Current theory and research.* New York: Cambridge University Press.

Otani, H., et al. (2005). Remembering a nuclear accident in Japan: Did it trigger flashbulb memories? *Memory, 13*(1), 6–20.

Padgham, J. J., & Blyth, D. A. (1991). Dating during adolescence. In R. M. Lerner, A. C. Petersen, & J. Brooks-Gunn (Eds.), *Encyclopedia of adolescence.* New York: Garland.

Paffenbarger, R. S., Jr., et al. (1993). The association of changes in physical-activity level and other lifestyle characteristics with mortality among men. *New England Journal of Medicine, 328,* 538–545.

Paikoff, R. L., & Collins, A. C. (1991). Editor's notes: Shared views in the family during adolescence. In R. L. Paikoff & A. C. Collins (Eds.), New Directions for Child Development, no. 51. San Francisco: Josey-Bass.

Pantiel, M. (1995, September). Should your teenager work? *Better Homes and Gardens,* p. 226.

Pantin, H. M., & Carver, C. S. (1982). Induced competence and the bystander effect. *Journal of Applied Social Psychology, 12,* 100–111.

Papini, D. R., & Roggman, L. A. (1992). Adolescent perceived attachment to parents in relation to competence, depression, and anxiety: A longitudinal study. *Journal of Early Adolecence, 12,* 420–440.

Papousek, M., Papousek, H., & Symmes, D. (1991). The meanings of melodies in motherese in tone and stress languages. *Infant Behavior and Development, 14,* 415–440.

Park, J., & Banaji, M. R. (2000). Mood and heuristics: The influence of happy and sad states on sensitivity and bias in stereotyping. *Journal of Personality & Social Psychology, 78*(6), 1005–1023.

Parker, J. G., & Herrera, C. (1996). Interpersonal processes in friendship: A comparison of abused and nonabused children's experience. *Developmental Psychology, 32,* 1025–1038.

Patterson, D. R. (2004). Treating pain with hypnosis. *Current Directions in Psychological Science, 13*(6), 252–255.

Patterson, M. L. (1991). Functions of nonverbal behavior in interpersonal interaction. In R. S. Feldman & B. Rime (Eds.), *Fundamentals of nonverbal behavior.* Cambridge, England: Cambridge University Press.

Patterson, S. J., Sochting, I., & Marcia, J. E. (1992). The inner space and beyond: Women and identity. In G. R. Adams, T. P. Gullotta, & R. Montemayor (Eds.), *Adolescent identity formation.* Newbury Park, CA: Sage.

Pearlman, C. (1994, January). Pets can be great friends: Research shows animal owners have less stress and live longer lives. *Safety & Health,* pp. 80–81.

Pena, N., & Bricklin, M. (1990). The future of fitness. *Prevention, 42*(1), 41–43.

Penfield, W. (1969). Consciousness, memory, and man's conditioned reflexes. In K. H. Pribram (Ed.), *On the biology of learning.* New York: Harcourt Brace Jovanovich.

Penn, N. E., Kar, S., Kramer, J., Skinner, J., & Zambrana, R. E. (1995). Panel IV. Ethnic minorities, health care systems, and behavior. *Health Psychology, 14,* 641–648.

Penninx, B. W. et al. (1998). Chronically depressed mood and cancer risk in older persons. *Journal of the National Cancer Institute, 90,* 1888–1893.

Peppard, P. E., Young, T., Palta, M., & Skatrud, J. (2000). Prospective study of the association between sleep-disordered breathing and hypertension. *The New England Journal of Medicine online, 342*(19).

Pereira, B., Mendonça, D., Neto, C., Valente, L., & Smith, P. K. (2004). Bullying in Portuguese schools. *School Psychology International, 25*(2), 241–254.

Perils of part-time work for teens. (1991, March 30). *Science News,* p. 205.

Perrett, D. I. (1994). Cited in Brody, J. E. (1994, March 21). Notions of beauty transcend culture, new study suggests. *The New York Times,* p. A14.

Perry, C. L. (1991). Programs for smoking prevention with early adolescents. In R. M. Lerner, A. C. Petersen, & J. Brooks-Gunn (Eds.), *Encyclopedia of adolescence.* New York: Garland.

Perry, D. G., & Bussey, K. (1979). The social learning theory of sex differences: Imitation is alive and well. *Journal of Personality and Social Psychology, 37,* 1699–1712.

Petersen, A. C. (1987, September). Those gangly years. *Psychology Today,* pp. 28–34.

Peterson, C., & Seligman, M. E. P. (1985). The learned helplessness model of depression: Current status of theory and research. In E. E. Beckham & W. R. Leber (Eds.), *Handbook of depression* (pp. 914–939). Homewood, IL: Dorsey.

Peterson, L. R., & Peterson, M. J. (1959). Short-term retention of individual verbal items. *Journal of Experimental Psychology, 58,* 193–198.

Pettingale, K. W., et al. (1985). Mental attitudes to cancer: An additional prognostic factor. *Lancet, 1,* 750.

Petty, R. E., & Cacioppo, J. T. (1986). The elaboration-likelihood model of persuasion. In L. Berkowitz (Ed.), *Advances in experimental social psychology* (Vol. 19). New York: Academic Press.

Petty, R. E., Fleming, M. A., & White, P. H. (1999). Stigmatized sources and persuasion: Prejudice as a determinant of argument scrutiny. *Journal of Personality & Social Psychology, 76*(1), 19–34.

Petty, R. E., Gleicher, F., & Baker, S. M. (1991). Multiple roles for affect in persuasion. In J. Forgas (Ed.), *Emotion and social judgments.* London: Pergamon Press.

Petty, R. E., Wegener, D. T., & Fabrigar, L. R. (1997). Attitudes and attitude change. *Annual Review of Psychology, 48,* 609–647.

Phinney, J. S. (2000). Identity formation across cultures: The interaction of personal, societal, and historical change. *Human Development, 43*(1), 27–31.

Phinney, J. S., & Devich-Navarro, M. (1997). Variations in bicultural identification among African American and Mexican American adolescents. *Journal of Research on Adolescence, 7*(1), 3–32.

Phinney, J. S., & Rosenthal, D. A. (1992). Ethnic identity in adolescence. In G. R. Adams, T. P. Gullotta, & R. Montemayor (Eds.), *Adolescent identity formation.* Newbury Park, CA: Sage.

Phinney, J. S., Chavira, V., & Williamson, L. (1992). Acculturation attitudes and self-esteem among high school and college students. *Youth and society, 23*(3), 299–312.

Piaget, J. (1932). *The moral judgment of the child.* New York: Harcourt Brace Jovanovich.

Pierce, C. A. (1996). Body height and romantic attraction: A meta-analytic test of the male-taller norm. *Social Behavior & Personality, 24*(2), 143–149.

Pike, K. M., & Rodin, J. (1991). Mothers, daughters, and disordered eating. *Journal of Abnormal Psychology, 100,* 198–204.

Pinker, S. (1990). Language acquisition. In D. N. Osherson & H. Lasnik (Eds.), *An invitation to cognitive science: Language* (Vol. 1). Cambridge, MA: MIT Press.

Pinker, S. (1994a, June 19). Building a better brain. *The New York Times Book Review,* pp. 13–14.

Pinker, S. (1994b). *The language instinct: How the mind creates language.* New York: William Morrow.

Pinnell, C. M., & Covino, N. A. (2000). Empirical findings on the use of hypnosis in medicine: A critical review. *International Journal of Clinical & Experimental Hypnosis, 48*(2), 170–194.

Plant, E. A., Hyde, J. S., Keltner, D., & Devine, P. G. (2000). The gender stereotyping of emotions. *Psychology of Women Quarterly, 24*(1) 81–92.

Plomin, R. (1989). Enviornment and genes: Determinants of behavior. *American Psychologist, 44,* 105–111.

Plomin, R., & McGuffin, P. (2003). Psychopathology in the postgenomic era. *Annual Review of Psychology, 54,* 205–228.

Plutchik, R. (1984). A general psychoevolutionary theory. In K. Scherer & P. Ekman (Eds.), *Approaches to emotion.* Hillsdale, NJ: Erlbaum.

Pombeni, M. L., Kirchler, E., & Palmonari, A. (1990). Identification with peers as a strategy to muddle through the troubles of the adolescent years. *Journal of Adolescence, 13,* 351–369.

Pomerantz, E. M., Frey, K., Greulich, F., & Ruble, D. N. (1993, March). *Explaining the decrease in perceived competence: Grade and gender differences in perceptions of ability as stable.* Paper presented at the meeting of the Society for Research in Child Development. New Orleans, LA.

Pope, H.G., Kouri, E. M., & Hudson, J. I. (2000). Effects of supraphysiologic doses of testosterone on mood and aggression in normal men: a randomized controlled trial. *Archives of General Psychiatry, 57,* 133–140.

Pope-Davis, D. B., Reynolds, A. L., Dings, J. G., & Nielson, D. (1995). Examining multicultural counseling competencies of graduate students in psychology. *Professional Psychology: Research and Practice, 26,* 322–329.

Posner, M. I. (1988). Structures and functions of selective attention. In T. Boll & B. Bryant (Eds.), *Clinical neuropsychology and brain function* (pp. 169–202). Washington, DC: American Psychological Association.

Posner, M. I., & Raichle, M. E. (1994). *Images of mind.* New York: W. H. Freeman.

Powell, J. L., Meil, W., Patterson, M. L., Chouinard, E. F., et al. (1994). Effects of timing of touch on compliance to a request. *Journal of Social Behavior and Personality, 9,* 153–162.

Powers, R. (2000, May 7). American dreaming. *The New York Times magazine,* pp. 66–67.

Price, L. H., & Heninger, G. R. (1994). Lithium in the treatment of mood disorders. *New England Journal of Medicine, 331,* 591–598.

Prochaska, J. O., & Norcross, J. C. (1999). *Systems of psychotherapy* (4th ed.). Pacific Grove, CA: Brooks/Cole.

Putallaz, M., & Heflin, A. H. (1990). Parent-child interaction. In S. R. Asher & J. D. Coie (Eds.), *Peer rejection in childhood.* New York: Cambridge University Press.

Putnam, F., Guroff, J., Silberman, E., Barban, L., & Post, R. (1986). The clinical phenomenology of multiple personality disorder: Review of 100 recent cases. *Journal of Clinical Psychiatry, 47,* 285–293.

Quattrone, G. A. (1982). Overattribution and unit formation: When behavior engulfs the person. *Journal of Personality and Social Psychology, 42,* 593–607.

Quinn, S. (1987). *A mind of her own: The life of Karen Horney.* New York: Summit Books.

Raichle, M. E. (1994). Visualizing the mind. *Scientific American, 270*(4), 58–64.

Rakowski, W. (1995). Cited in Margoshes, P. (1995). For many, old age is the prime of life. *APA Monitor, 26*(5), 36–37.

Rapoport, J. (1989a, March). The biology of obsessions and compulsions. *Scientific American,* pp. 83–89.

Rapoport, J. L. (1989b). *The boy who couldn't stop washing.* New York: Penguin Books USA.

Rappaport, N. B., McAnulty, D. P., & Brantley, P. J. (1988). Exploration of the type A behavior pattern in chronic headache sufferers. *Journal of Consulting and Clinical Psychology, 56,* 621–623.

Rathus, J. H., & Sanderson, W. C. (1999). *Marital distress: Cognitive behavioral interventions for couples.* Northvale, NJ: Jason Aronson.

Rathus, S. A. (2006). *Childhood and adolescence: Voyages in development,* 2d. Ed. Belmont, CA: Wadsworth Publishing Company.

Rathus, S. A., Nevid, J. S., & Fichner-Rathus, L. (1997). *Human sexuality in a world of diversity* (3rd ed.). Boston: Allyn & Bacon.

Rauscher, F. H. (1998). Response to Katie Overy's paper, "Can music really 'improve' the mind?" *Psychology of Music, 26*(2), 197–199.

Rauscher, F. H., & Shaw, G. L. (1998). Key components of the Mozart effect. *Perceptual & Motor Skills, 86*(3), 835–841.

Raynor, J. (1970). Relationships between achievement-related motives, future orientation, and academic performance. *Journal of Personality and Social Psychology, 15,* 28–33.

Redd, W. H., et al. (1987). Cognitive/attentional distraction in the control of conditioned nausea in pediatric cancer patients receiving chemotherapy. *Journal of Consulting and Clinical Psychology, 55,* 391–395.

Regier, D. A., Narrow, W. E., Rae, D. S. Manderscheid, R. W., Locke, B. Z., & Goodwin, F. K. (1993). The de facto U.S. mental and addictive disorders service system: Epidemiologic catchment area prospective 1-year prevalence rates of disorders and services. *Archives of General Psychiatry, 50,* 85–94.

Reinke, B. J., Holmes, D. S., & Harris, R. L. (1985). The timing of psychosocial changes in women's lives. *Journal of Personality and Social Psychology, 48,* 1353–1364.

Reis, H. T., et al. (1990). What is smiling is beautiful and good. *European Journal of Social Psychology, 20,* 259–267.

Reisman, J. M. (1990). Intimacy in same-sex friendships. *Sex Roles, 23,* 65–72.

Remafedi, G. (1990). Study group report on impact of television portrayals of gender roles on youth. *Journal of Adolescent Health Care, 11*(1), 59–61.

Renzulli, J. S. (1986). The three ring conception of giftedness: A developmental model for creative productivity. In R. J. Sternberg & J. E. Davidson (Eds.), *Conceptions of giftedness.* New York: Cambridge University Press.

Rhodes, N., & Wood, W. (1992). Self-esteem and intelligence affect influenceability: The mediating role of message reception. *Psychological Bulletin, 111,* 156–171.

Ribeiro, S., & Nicolelis, M. A. L. (2004). Reverberation, storage, and postsynaptic propagation of memories during sleep. *Learning & Memory, 11*(6), 686–696.

Richards, J. C., Hof, A., & Alvarenga, M. (2000). Serum lipids and their relationships with hostility and angry affect and behaviors in men. *Health Psychology, 19*(4) 393–398.

Richter, S., & Barbara, H. (2003). Bullying behavior: Current issues, research, and interventions. *Journal of Developmental & Behavioral Pediatrics, 24*(5), 382–383.

Rickard, T. C., et al., (2000). The calculating brain: An fMRI study. *Neuropsychologia, 38*(3), 325–335.

Riley, V. (1981). Psychoneuroendocrine influences on immuno-competence and neoplasia. *Science, 212,* 1100–1109.

Rinn, W. E. (1991). Neuropsychology of facial expression. In R. S. Feldman & B. Rime (Eds.), *Fundamentals of nonverbal behavior.* Cambridge, England: Cambridge University Press.

Ritvo, E. R., Freeman, B. J., Mason-Brothers, A., Mo, A., & Ritvo, A. M. (1985). Concordance for the syndrome of autism in 40 pairs of afflicted twins. *American Journal of Psychiatry, 142,* 74–77.

Robbins, C., & Ehri, L. C. (1994). Reading storybooks to kindergartners helps them to learn new vocabulary words. *Journal of Educational Psychology, 86,* 54–64.

Robins, C. J., & Hayes, A. M. (1993). An appraisal of cognitive therapy. *Journal of Consulting and Clinical Psychology, 61,* 205–214.

Robins, L. (1987). The epidemiology of antisocial personality. In J. Cavenar (Ed.), *Psychiatry.* Philadelphia: Lippincott.

Robinson, N. M. (1992, August). *Development and variation: The challenge of nurturing gifted young children.* Paper presented at the meeting of the American Psychological Association, Washington, DC.

Robinson, P. (1993). *Freud and his critics.* Berkeley: University of California Press.

Roche, A. F. (1979). Structural trends in stature, weight, and maturation. In A. F. Roche (Ed.), Secular trends in growth, maturation, and development of children. *Monographs of the Society for Research in Child Development, 44,* 3–27.

Rogers, C. (1961). *On becoming a person: A therapist's view of psychotherapy.* Boston: Houghton Mifflin.

Rogers, C. (1963). The actualizing tendency in relation to "motives" and to consciousness. In M. R. Jones (Ed.), *Nebraska Symposium on Motivation* (pp. 1–24). Lincoln: University of Nebraska Press.

Rogers, C. (1974). In retrospect: 46 years. *American Psychologist, 29,* 115–123.

Rogers, C. (1977). *On personal power: Inner strength and its revolutionary impact.* New York: Delacorte.

Rogers, C. (1986). Client-centered therapy. In I. Kutash & A. Wolf (Eds.), *Psychotherapist's casebook.* San Francisco: Jossey-Bass.

Rogers, C. R. (1951). *Client-centered therapy.* Boston: Houghton Mifflin.

Rose, R. J. (1995). Genes and human behavior. *Annual Review of Psychology, 46,* 625–654.

Rosenberg, J., Perlstadt, H., & Phillips, W. R. (1993). Now that we are here: Discrimination, disparagement, and harassment at work and the experience of women lawyers. *Gender & Society, 7,* 415–433.

Rosenthal, E. (1993, July 20). Listening to the emotional needs of cancer patients. *The New York Times,* pp. C1, C7.

Roskies, E., et al. (1986). The Montreal Type A Intervention Project: Major findings. *Health Psychology, 5,* 45–69.

Ross, A. (1987). *Personality: The scientific study of complex human behavior.* New York: Holt, Rinehart and Winston.

Ross, J. L., Roeltgen, D., Feuillan, P., Kushner, H., & Cutler, W. B. (2000). Use of estrogen in young girls with Turner syndrome: Effects on memory. *Neurology, 54*(1), 164–170.

Rothbart, M. K., & Ahadi, S. A. (1994). Temperament and the development of personality. *Journal of Abnormal Psychology, 103,* 55–66.

Rowatt, W. C., Cunningham, M. R., & Druen, P. B. (1999). Lying to get a date: The effect of facial physical attractiveness on the willingness to deceive prospective dating partners. *Journal of Social & Personal Relationships, 16*(2) 209–223.

Rubinstein, S., & Caballero, B. (2000). Is Miss America an undernourished role model? *Journal of the American Medical Association online, 283*(12).

Ruble, D. N., & Ruble, T. L. (1982). Sex stereotypes. In A. G. Miller (Ed.), *In the eye of the beholder: Contemporary issues in stereotyping.* New York: Praeger.

Rule, B. G., Taylor, B. R., & Dobbs, A. R. (1987). Priming effects of heat on aggressive thoughts. *Social cognition, 5,* 131–143.

Rymer, R. (1993). *Genie: An abused child's flight from silence.* New York: HarperCollins.

Saarni, C. (1990). Emotional competence: How emotions and relationships become integrated. In R. Thompson (Ed.), *Nebraska Symposium on Motivation: Vol. 36. Socioemotional development.* Lincoln: University of Nebraska Press.

Saccuzzo, D. (1994, August). *Coping with the complexities of contemporary psychological testing: Negotiating shifting sands.* G. Stanley Hall Lecture presented at the meeting of the American Psychological Association, Los Angeles.

Sadker, M., & Sadker, D. (1994). *How America's schools cheat girls.* New York: Scribners.

Salgado de Snyder, V. N., Cervantes, R. C., & Padilla, A. M. (1990). Gender and ethnic differences in psychosocial stress and generalized distress among Hispanics. *Sex roles, 22,* 441–453.

Salovey, P., Rothman, A. J., Detweiler, J. B., & Steward, W. T. (2000). Emotional states and physical health. *American Psychologist, 55,* 110–121.

Sanders, G. S. (1984). Effects of context cues on eyewitness identification responses. *Journal of Applied Social Psychology, 14,* 386–397.

Sanders, G. S., & Chiu, W. (1988). Eyewitness errors in free recall of actions. *Journal of Applied Social Psychology, 18,* 1241–1259.

Sandman, C., & Crinella, F. (1995). Cited in Margoshes, P. (1995). For many, old age is the prime of life. *APA Monitor, 26*(5), 36–37.

Sangrador, J. L., & Yela, C. (2000). "What is beautiful is loved": Physical attractiveness in love relationships in a representative sample. *Social Behavior & Personality, 28*(3) 207–218.

Sanna, L. J., & Shotland, R. L. (1990). Valence of anticipated evaluation and social facilitation. *Journal of Experimental Social Psychology, 26,* 82–92.

Sansone, R. A., & Levitt, J. L. (2005). Borderline personality and eating disorders. *Eating Disorders: The Journal of Treatment & Prevention, 13*(1), 71–83.

Santee, R. T., & Maslach, C. (1982). To agree or not to agree: Personal dissent amid social pressure to conform. *Journal of Personality and Social Psychology, 42,* 690–700.

Sarwer, D. B. & Wadden, T. A. (1999). The treatment of obesity: What's new, what's recommended. *Journal of Women's Health & Gender-Based Medicine, 8*(4), 483–493.

Sattler, J. M. (1988). *Assessment of children.* San Diego, CA: Jerome M. Sattler.

Savage-Rumbaugh, E. S., Murphy, J., Sevcik, R. A., Brakke, K. E., Williams, S. L., & Rumbaugh, D. M., with commentary by Bates, E. (1993). Language comprehension in ape and child. *Monographs of the Society for Research in Child Development, 58*(233), 1–254.

Savin-Williams, R. C., & Berndt, T. (1990). Friendship and peer relations. In S. S. Feldman & G. R. Elliott (Eds.), *At the threshold: The developing adolescent.* Cambridge, MA: Harvard University Press.

Saxe, L. (1991a). Lying. *American Psychologist, 46,* 409–415.

Saxe, L. (1991b). Science and the CQT polygraph: A theoretical critique. *Integration of Physiological and Behavioral Sciences, 26,* 223–231.

Saxe, L., & Ben-Shakhar, G. (1999). Admissibility of polygraph tests: The application of scientific standards post-Daubert. *Psychology, Public Policy, & Law, 5*(1), 203–223.

Scarr, S., & Weinberg, R. A. (1983). The Minnesota adoption studies: Genetic differences and malleability. *Child Development, 54,* 260–267.

Schachter, S. (1959). *The psychology of affiliation.* Stanford, CA: Stanford University Press.

Schachter, S., & Singer, J. E. (1962). Cognitive, social, and physiological determinants of emotional state. *Psychological Review, 69,* 379–399.

Schacter, D. L. (1992). Understanding implicit memory: A cognitive neuroscience approach. *American Psychologist, 47*(4), 559–569.

Schafer, R. B., & Keith, P. M. (1990). Matching by weight in married couples: A life cycle perspective. *Journal of Social Psychology, 130,* 657–664.

Schaie, K. W. (1993). The Seattle longitudinal studies of adult intelligence. *Current Directions, 2,* 171–175.

Schaie, K. W. (1994). The course of adult intellectual development. *American Psychologist, 49,* 304–313.

Schaie, K. W., & Willis, S. L. (1991). Adult personality and psychomotor performance. Cross-sectional and longitudinal analyses. *Journal of Gerontology: Psychological Sciences, 46,* 275–284.

Schau, C. G., Kahn, L., Diepold, J. H., & Cherry, F. (1980). The relationship to parental expectations and preschool children's verbal sex-typing to their sex-typed toy play behavior. *Child Development, 51,* 607–609.

Schellenberg, E. G. (2000). Cited in Hershenson, R. (2000, August 6). Debating the Mozart theory. *The New York Times magazine online.*

Schenk, D. (2000, July). *A possible vaccine for Alzheimer's disease.* Paper presented to the World Alzheimer Congress 2000, Washington, DC.

Schiffman, S. S. (2000). Taste quality and neural coding: Implications from psychophysics and neurophysiology. *Physiology and Behavior, 69*(1–2), 147–159.

Schiffman, S. S., et al. (2003). Effect of repeated presentation on sweetness intensity of binary and ternary mixtures of sweeteners. *Chemical Senses, 28*(3), 219–229.

Schneider, R. H., et al. (1995). A randomized controlled trial of stress reduction for hypertension in older African Americans. *Hypertension, 26*, 820.

Schneider, W., & Bjorklund, D. (1992). Expertise, aptitude, and strategic remembering. *Child Development, 63*, 461–473.

Schwartz, R. M., & Gottman, J. M. (1976). Toward a task analysis of assertive behavior. *Journal of Consulting and Clinical Psychology, 44*, 910–920.

Schwarz, N., & Clore, G. L. (1983). Mood, misattribution, and judgments of well-being: Informative and directive functions of affective states. *Journal of Personality and Social Psychology, 45*, 513–523.

Schwarz, N., Bless, H., & Bohner, G. (1991). Mood and persuasion: Affective states influence the processing of persuasive communications. In M. Zanna (Ed.), *Advances in experimental social psychology* (Vol. 24). New York: Academic Press.

Schweinhart, L. J., & Weikart, D. P. (Eds.). (1993). *Significant benefits: The High/Scope Perry Preschool Study through age 27.* Ypsilanti, MI: High/Scope Press.

Segal, N. (1993). Twin, sibling, and adoption methods. *American Psychologist, 48*, 943–956.

Segall, M. H., Campbell, D. T., & Herskovits, M. J. (1966). *The influence of culture on visual perception.* New York: Bobbs-Merrill.

Selfe, L. (1978). Cited in Bootzin, R. R., & Acocella, J. R. (1984). *Abnormal pscyhology: Current perspectives* (4th ed.). New York: Random House.

Seligman, M. E. P. (1975). *Helplessness: On depression, development, and death.* New York: W. H. Freeman.

Seligman, M. E. P. (1996, August). *Predicting and preventing depression.* Master lecture presented to the meeting of the *American Psychological Association,* Toronto.

Selkoe, D. J. (1992). Aging brain, aging mind. *Scientific American, 267*(3), 134–142.

Selye, H. (1976). *The stress of life* (rev. ed.). New York: McGraw-Hill.

Seppa, N. (1997). Children's TV remains steeped in violence. *APA Monitor, 28*(6), 36.

Shader, R. I., & Greenblatt, D. J. (1993). Drug therapy: Use of benzodiazepines in anxiety disorders. *New England Journal of Medicine, 328*, 1398–1405.

Shadish, W. R., Matt, G. E., Navarro, A. M., & Phillips, G. (2000). The effects of psychological therapies under clinically representative conditions: A meta-analysis. *Psychological Bulletin, 126*(4), 512–529.

Shah, M., & Jeffery, R. W. (1991). Is obesity due to overeating and inactivity or to a defective metabolic rate? A review. *Annals of Behavioral Medicine, 13*, 73–81.

Shavitt, S. (1990). The role of attitude objects in attitude functions. *Journal of Experimental Social Psychology, 26*, 124–148.

Shayley, A. Y., et al. (2000). Auditory startle response in trauma survivors with posttraumatic stress disorder: A prospective study. *American Journal of Psychiatry, 157*, 255–261.

Sheehy, G. (1976). *Passages: Predictable crises of adult life.* New York: Dutton.

Sheehy, G. (1995). *New passages: Mapping your life across time.* New York: Random House.

Shenal, B. V., & Harrison, D. W. (2003). Investigation of the laterality of hostility, cardiovascular regulation, and auditory recognition. *International Journal of Neuroscience, 113*(2), 205–222.

Shepherd, J., et al. (1995). Prevention of coronary heart disease with pravastatin in men with hypercholesterolemia. *New England Journal of Medicine, 333*, 1301–1307.

Sheppard, J. A., & Strathman, A. J. (1989). Attractiveness and height: The role of stature in dating preference, frequency of dating, and perceptions of attractiveness. *Personality and Social Psychology Bulletin, 15*, 617–627.

Shepperd, J. A. (1993). Productivity loss in performance groups. *Psychological Bulletin, 113*, 67–81.

Sherman, J. W., & Frost, L. A. (2000). On the encoding of stereotype-relevant information under cognitive load. *Personality & Social Psychology Bulletin, 26*(1), 26–34.

Shneidman, E. S. (Ed.). (1984). *Death: Current perspectives* (3rd ed.) Mountain View, CA: Mayfield.

Shoham-Salomon, V. (1991). Introduction to special section on client-therapy interaction research. *Journal of Consulting and Clinical Psychology, 59*, 203–204.

Shotland, R. L., & Heinold, W. D. (1985). Bystander response to arterial bleeding: Helping skills, the decision-making process, and differentiating the helping response. *Journal of Personality and Social Psychology, 49*, 347–356.

Shusterman, G., & Saxe, L. (1990). *Deception in romantic relationships.* Unpublished manuscript.

Siegal, M. (1987). Are sons and daughters treated more differently by fathers than by mothers? *Developmental Review, 7*, 183–209.

Siegel, L. J., & Senna, J. J. (1994). *Juvenile delinquency: Theory, practice and law.* St. Paul, MN: West.

Silver, E., Cirincione, C., & Steadman, H. J. (1994, February). *Law and Human Behavior.* Cited in DeAngelis, T. (1994). Public's view of insanity plea quite inaccurate, study finds. *APA Monitor, 25*(6), 28.

Silverstein, L. B. (1991). Transforming the debate about child care and maternal employment. *American Psychologist, 46*, 1025–1032.

Simmons, R. G., & Blyth, D. A. (1987). *Moving into adolescence: The impact of pubertal change and school context.* New York: Aldine de Gruyter.

Simon, H. A. (1990). A mechanism for social selection and successful altruism. *Science, 250,* 1665–1668.

Simons, A. D., Gordon, J. S., Monroe, S. M., & Thase, M. E. (1995). Toward an integration of psychologic, social, and biologic factors in depression: Effects on outcome and course of cognitive therapy. *Journal of Consulting and Clinical Psychology, 63,* 369–377.

Simons, R. K., Whitbeck, L. B., Conger, R. D., & Chyi-In, W. (1991). Intergenerational transmission of harsh parenting. *Developmental Psychology, 27,* 159–171.

Simonton, D. (1988). Age and outstanding achievement: What do we know after a century of research? *Psychological Bulletin, 104,* 251–267.

Simonton, D. K. (2000). Creativity: Cognitive, personal, developmental, and social aspects. *American Psychologist, 55,* 151–158.

Singh, R. B., & Sharma, S. K. (1989). Anxiety and conformity behavior. *Indian Journal of Current Psychological Research, 42,* 98–102.

Singh, R., & Ho, S. Y. (2000). Attitudes and attraction: A new test of the attraction, repulsion and similarity-dissimilarity asymmetry hypotheses. *British Journal of Social Psychology, 39*(2), 197–211.

Skinner, B. F. (1938/1966). *The behavior of organisms.* New York: Appleton Century Crofts.

Skinner, B. F. (1948). *Walden Two.* New York: Macmillan.

Skinner, B. F. (1961). Teaching machines. *Scientific American, 205,* 90–102.

Skinner, B. F. (1971). *Beyond Freedom and Dignity.* New York: Knopf.

Skinner, B. F. (1987). Whatever happened to psychology as the science of behavior? *American Psychologist, 42,* 780–786.

Sleek, S. (1995a). Group therapy: Tapping the power of teamwork. *APA Monitor, 26*(7), 1, 38–39.

Sleek, S. (1995b). Rallying the troops inside our bodies. *APA Monitor, 26*(12), 1, 24–25.

Sleek, S. (1996). Side effects undermine drug compliance. *APA Monitor, 26*(3), 32.

Sleepers suffer WTC nightmares. (2001, November 22). *The Associated Press.*

Slobin, D. I. (1983, April). *Crosslinguistic evidence of basic child grammar.* Paper presented at the biennial meeting of the Society for Research in Child Development, Detroit, MI.

Smetana, J. G., Killen, M., & Turiel, E. (1991). Children's reasoning about interpersonal and moral conflicts. *Child Development, 62,* 629–644.

Smetana, J. G., Yau, J., Restrepo, A., & Braeges, J. L. (1991). Conflict and adaptation in adolescence: Adolescent–parent conflict. In M. E. Colten & S. Gore (Eds.), *Adolescent stress: Causes and consequences.* New York: Aldine de Gruyter.

Smetana, J., & Gaines, C. (1999). Adolescent-parent conflict in middle-class African American families. *Child Development, 70*(6), 1447–1463.

Smiley, J. (2000, May 7). The good life. *The New York Times magazine,* pp. 58–59.

Smith, E. R., & Mackie, D. M. (1995). *Social psychology.* New York: Worth.

Smith, G. F., & Dorfman, D. (1975). The effect of stimulus uncertainty on the relationship between frequency of exposure and liking. *Journal of Personality and Social Psychology, 31,* 150–155.

Smith, M. L., & Glass, G. V. (1977). Meta-analysis of psychotherapy outcome studies. *American Psychologist, 32,* 752–760.

Smith, P. K., & Daglish, L. (1977). Sex differences in parent and infant behavior in the home. *Child Development, 48,* 1250–1254.

Smith, P. K., Boulton, M. J., & Cowie, H. (1993). The impact of cooperative group work on ethnic relations in middle school. *Social Psychology International, 14,* 21–42.

Smith, R. E., Smoll, F. L., & Ptacek, J. T. (1990). Conjunctive moderator variables in vulnerability and resiliency research: Life stress, social support and coping skills, and adolescent sport injuries. *Journal of Personality and Social Psychology, 58,* 360–370.

Smith, S. M., Glenberg, A. M., & Bjork, R. A. (1978). Environmental context and human memory. *Memory and Cognition, 6,* 342–355.

Snow, C. E., (1993). Bilingualism and second language acquisition. In J. Berko-Gleason & N. B. Ratner (Eds.), *Psycholinguistics.* Fort Worth, TX: Harcourt Brace Jovanovich.

Snow, R. E. (1991). Aptitude-treatment interaction as a framework for research on individual differences in psychotherapy. *Journal of Consulting and Clinical Psychology, 59,* 205–216.

Snyder, M., & DeBono, G. (1989). Understanding the functions of attitudes. In A. R. Pratkanis et al. (Eds.), *Attitude structure and function.* Hillsdale, NJ: Erlbaum.

Snyderman, M., & Rothman, S. (1987). Survey of expert opinion on intelligence and aptitude testing. *American Psychologist, 43,* 137–144.

Snyderman, M., & Rothman, S. (1990). *The I.Q. controversy.* New Brunswick, NJ: Transaction.

Solomon, R. L. (1980). The opponent-process theory of acquired motivation: The costs of pleasure and the benefits of pain. *American Psychologist, 35,* 691–712.

Solomon, R., & Corbitt, J. (1974). An opponent-process theory of motivation. *Psychological Review, 81,* 119–145.

Sorenson, S. B., & Rutter, C. M. (1991). Transgenerational patterns of suicide attempt. *Journal of Consulting and Clinical Psychology, 59,* 861–866.

Sorrentino, R. M., et al. (1988). Uncertainty orientation and persuasion. *Journal of Personality and Social Psychology, 55,* 371–375.

Southern, T., & Jones, E. D. (1991). *The academic acceleration of gifted children.* New York: Teachers College Press.

Spanos, N. O. (1994). Multiple identity enactments and multiple personality disorder: A sociocultural perspective. *Psychological Bulletin, 116*(1), 143–165.

Spencer, M. B., & Markstrom-Adams, C. (1990). Identity processes among racial and ethnic minority children in America. *Child Development, 61,* 290–310.

Spencer, M. B., Dornbusch, S. M., & Mont-Reynaud, R. (1990). Challenges in studying minority youth. In S. S. Feldman & G. R. Elliott (Eds.), *At the threshold: The developing adolescent.* Cambridge, MA: Harvard University Press.

Spinhoven, P., Labbe, M. R., & Rombouts, R. (1993). Feasibility of computerized psychological testing with psychiatric outpatients. *Journal of Clinical Psychology, 49,* 440–447.

Spitzer, R. L., Gibbon, M., Skodol, A. E., Williams, J. B. W., & First, M. B. (1989). *DSM-III-R casebook.* Washington, DC: American Psychiatric Press.

Spreat, S., & Behar, D. (1994). Trends in the residential (inpatient) treatment of individuals with a dual diagnosis. *Journal of Consulting and Clinical Psychology, 61,* 43–48.

Sprecher, S. (1998). Insiders' perspectives on reasons for attraction to a close other. *Social Psychology Quarterly, 61*(4) 287–300.

Sprecher, S., Sullivan, Q., & Hatfield, E. (1994). Mate selection preferences. *Journal of Personality and Social Psychology, 66*(6), 1074–1080.Azar, B. (2002). At the frontier of science. *Monitor on Psychology online, 33*(1).

Squire, L. R. (1993). Memory and the hippocampus. *Psychological Review, 99,* 195–231.

Squire, L. R. (1996, August). Memory systems of the brain. Master lecture presented to the meeting of the American Psychological Association, Toronto.

Squire, L. R., Cohen, N. J., & Nadel, L. (1984). The medical temporal region and memory consolidations: A new hypothesis. In H. Weingartner & E. Parker (Eds.), *Memory consolidation.* Hillsdale, NJ: Erlbaum.

Stacy, A. W., Bentler, P. M., & Flay, B. R. (1994). Attitudes and health behavior in diverse populations: Drunk driving, alcohol use, binge eating, marijuana use, and cigarette use. *Health Psychology, 13,* 73–85.

Stampfer, M. J., Hu, F. B., Manson, J. E., Rimm, E. B., & Willett, W. C. (2000). Primary prevention of coronary heart disease in women through diet and lifestyle. *New England Journal of Medicine, 343*(1), 16–22.

Stasser, G. (1999). A primer of social decision scheme theory: Models of group influence, competitive model-testing, and prospective modeling. *Organizational Behavior & Human Decision Processes, 80*(1), 3–20.

Stasser, G., Taylor, L. A., & Hanna, C. (1989). Information sampling in structured and unstructured discussion of three- and six-person groups. *Journal of Personality and Social Psychology, 57,* 67–78.

Steinberg, L. (1991). Parent-adolescent relations. In R. M. Lerner, A. C. Petersen, & J. Brooks-Gunn (Eds.), *Encyclopedia of adolescence.* New York: Garland.

Steinberg, L., Lamborn, S. F., Dornbusch, S. M., & Darling, N. (1992). Impact of parenting practices on adolescent achievement: Authoritative parenting, school involvement, and encouragement to succeed. *Child Development, 63,* 1266–1281.

Steinbrook, R. (1992). The polygraph test—A flawed diagnostic method. *New England Journal of Medicine, 327,* 122–123.

Steinhauer, J. (1995, July 6). No marriage, no apologies. *The New York Times,* pp. C1, C7.

Stericker, A., & LeVesconte, S. (1982). Effect of brief training on sex-related differences in visual-spatial skill. *Journal of Personality and Social Psychology, 43,* 1018–1029.

Sternberg, R. J. (1988). Triangulating love. In R. J. Sternberg & M. J. Barnes (Eds.), *The psychology of love.* New Haven, CT: Yale University Press.

Sternberg, R. J. (1990). Wisdom and its relations to intelligence and creativity. In R. J. Sternberg (Ed.), *Wisdom: Its nature, origins, and development.* New York: Cambridge University Press.

Sternberg, R. J. (1995). *In search of the human mind.* Fort Worth, TX: Harcourt Brace Jovanovich.

Sternberg, R. J. (1996). Love stories. *Personal Relationships, 3,* 59–79.

Sternberg, R. J. (1997). The concept of intelligence and its role in lifelong learning and success. *American Psychologist, 52,* 1030–1037.

Sternberg, R. J. (1997). What does it mean to be smart? *Educational Leadership, 54,* 20–24.

Sternberg, R. J. (2001). What is the common thread of creativity? *American Psychologist, 56*(4), 360–362.

Sternberg, R. J., & Lubart, T. I. (1995). *Defying the crowd: Cultivating creativity in a culture of conformity.* New York: Free Press.

Sternberg, R. J., & Lubart, T. I. (1996). Investing in creativity. *American Psychologist, 51,* 677–688.

Sternberg, R. J., & Williams, W. M. (1997). Does the Graduate Record Examination predict meaningful success in the graduate training of psychologists? *American Psychologist, 52,* 630–641.

Sternberg, R. J., Lautrey, J., & Lubart, T. I. (2003). Models of intelligence: International perspectives. Washington, D.C.: *American Psychological Association.*

Sternberg, R. J., Wagner, R. K., Williams, W. M., & Horvath, J. A. (1995). Testing common sense. *American Psychologist, 50,* 912–927.

Stewart, A. J., & Ostrove, J. M. (1998). Women's personality in middle age: Gender, history, and midcourse corrections. *American Psychologist, 53*(11), 1185–1194.

Stewart, M. W., Knight, R. G., Palmer, D. G., & Highton, J. (1994). Differential relationships between stress and disease activity for immunologically distinct subgroups of people with rheumatoid arthritis. *Journal of Abnormal Psychology, 103,* 251–258.

Stier, D. S., & Hall, J. A. (1984). Gender differences in touch: An empirical and theoretical review. *Journal of Personality and Social Psychology, 47,* 440–459.

Stock, R. (1995, June 1). Wrongheaded views persist about the old. *The New York Times,* p. C8.

Stone, N. M. (1993). Parental abuse as a precursor to childhood onset depression and suicidality. *Child Psychiatry and Human Development, 24,* 13–24.

Strober, M., et al. (2000). Controlled family study of anorexia nervosa and bulimia nervosa: Evidence of shared liability and transmission of partial syndromes. *American Journal of Psychiatry, 157,* 393–401.

Strughold, H. (1924). On the density and thresholds in the areas of pain on the epidermis in the various regions of the body. *Z. Biol, 80,* (in German), 367–380.

Strupp, H. H. (1992). The future of psychodynamic psychotherapy. *Psychotherapy, 29,* 21–27.

Study finds smaller pay gap for male and female doctors. (1996, April 11). *The New York Times,* p. B9.

Stunkard, A. J., & Sørensen, T. I. A. (1993). Obesity and socioeconomic status—A complex relation. *New England Journal of Medicine, 329,* 1036–1037.

Stunkard, A. J., Harris, J. R., Pedersen, N. L., & McLearn, G. E. (1990). A separated twin study of the body mass index. *New England Journal of Medicine, 322,* 1483–1487.

Suarez, E. C., Harlan, E., Peoples, M. C., & Williams, R. B., Jr. (1993). Cardiovascular and emotional responses in women: The role of hostility and harassment. *Health Psychology, 12,* 459–468.

Suddath, R., Casanova, M., Goldberg, T., Daniel, D., Kelsoe, J., & Weinberger, D. (1989). Temporal lobe pathology in schizophrenia: A quantitative magnetic resonance imaging study. *American Journal of Psychiatry, 146,* 464–472.

Sullivan, J. M. (2000) Cellular and molecular mechanisms underlying learning and memory impairments produced by cannabinoids. *Learning & Memory, 7*(3), 132–139.

Suls, J., Wan, C. K., & Costa, P. T., Jr. (1995). Relationship of trait anger to resting high blood pressure: A meta-analysis. *Health Psychology, 14,* 444–456.

Sundberg, N. D. (1990). *Assessment of persons* (2nd ed.). Englewood Cliffs, NJ: Prentice-Hall.

Swearer, S. M., & Cary, P. T. (2003). Perceptions and attitudes toward bullying in middle school youth: A developmental examination across the bully/victim continuum. *Journal of Applied School Psychology, 19*(2), 63–79.

Swedo, S., Rapoport, J., Chelow, D., Leonard, H., Ayoub, E., Hosier, D., & Wald, E. (1989). High prevalence of obsessive-compulsive symptoms in patients with Sydenham's chorea. *American Journal of Psychiatry, 146,* 246–249.

Swendsen, J. D., et al. (2000). Mood and alcohol consumption: An experience sampling test of the self-medication hypothesis. *Journal of Abnormal Psychology, 109*(2), 198–204.

Tahka, S., Wood, M., & Loewenthal, K. (1981). Age changes in the ability to replicate foreign pronunciation and intonation. *Language and Speech, 24,* 363–372.

Tanfer, K. (1987). Patterns of premarital cohabitation among never married women. *Journal of Marriage and the Family, 49,* 483–497.

Tannen, D. (1990). *You just don't understand.* New York: Ballantine Books.

Tanner, J. M. (1978). *Fetus into man: Physical growth from conception to maturity* (p. 118). Cambridge, MA: Harvard University Press.

Tanner, J. M. (1991). Adolescent growth spurt. In R. M. Lerner, A. C. Petersen, & J. Brooks-Gunn (Eds.), *Encyclopedia of adolescence.* New York: Garland.

Tanzi, R. E. (1995). A promising animal model of Alzheimer's disease. *New England Journal of Medicine, 332,* 1512–1513.

Taylor, I., & Taylor, M. M. (1990). *Psycholinguistics: Learning and using language.* Englewood Cliffs, NJ: Prentice-Hall.

Taylor, S. E. (1990). Health psychology: The science and the field. *American Psychologist, 45,* 40–50.

Teachout, T. (2000, April 2). For more artists, a fine old age. *The New York Times online.*

Tennen, H. & Affleck, G. (2000). The perception of personal control: Sufficiently important to warrant careful scrutiny. *Personality & Social Psychology Bulletin, 26*(2), 152–156.

Teri, L., & Wagner, A. (1992). Alzheimer's disease and depression. *Journal of Consulting and Clinical Psychology, 60,* 379–391.

Terry, D. (2000, July 16). Getting under my skin. *The New York Times online.*

Tetlock, P. E. (1983). Accountability and complexity of thought. *Journal of Personality and Social Psychology, 45,* 74–83.

Tharp, R. G. (1991). Cultural diversity and treatment of children. *Journal of Consulting and Clinical Psychology, 59,* 799–812.

Thase, M. E., & Kupfer, D. J. (1996). Recent developments in the pharmacotherapy of mood disorders. *Journal of Consulting and Clinical Psychology, 64,* 646–659.

Thom, A., Sartory, G., & Jöhren, P. (2000). Comparison between one-session psychological treatment and benzodiazepine in dental phobia. *Journal of Consulting and Clinical Psychology, 68*(3), 378–387.

Thompson, C. P., Anderson, L. P., & Bakeman, R. A. (2000). Effects of racial socialization and racial identity on acculturative stress in African American college students. *Cultural Diversity and Ethnic Minority Psychology, 6*(2), 196–210.

Thompson, R. A. (1991a). Attachment theory and research. In M. Lewis (Ed.), *Child and adolescent psychiatry: A comprehensive textbook.* Baltimore, MD: Williams & Wilkins.

Thompson, R. A. (1991b). Infant daycare: Concerns, controversies, choices. In J. V. Lerner & N. L. Galambos (Eds.), *Employed mothers and their children* (pp. 9–36). New York: Garland.

Thompson, R. A., & Limber, S. P. (1990). "Social anxiety" in infancy: Stranger and separation reaction. In H. Leitenberg (Ed.), *Handbook of social and evaluation anxiety.* New York: Plenum Press.

Thompson, W. C., Cowan, C. L., & Rosenhan, D. L. (1980). Focus of attention mediates the impact of negative affect on altruism. *Journal of Personality and Social Psychology, 38,* 291–300.

Thoresen, C., & Powell, L. H. (1992). Type A behavior pattern: New perspectives on theory, assessment, and intervention. *Journal of Consulting and Clinical Psychology, 60,* 595–604.

Tkachuk, G. A. & Martin, G. L. (1999). Exercise therapy for patients with psychiatric disorders: Research and clinical implications. *Professional Psychology: Research and Practice, 30*(3), 275–282.

Togersen, S. (1983). Genetic factors in anxiety disorders. *Archives of General Psychiatry, 40,* 1085–1089.

Tolman, E. C., & Honzik, C. H. (1930). Introduction and removal of reward, and maze performance in rats. *University of California Publications in Psychology, 4,* 257–275.

Tomes, H. (1995). Minorities' access to care is top priority. *APA Monitor, 26*(7), 52.

Triandis, H. C. (1990). Cross-cultural studies of individualism and collectivisim. In J. J. Berman (Ed.), *Nebraska symposium on motivation, 1989. Cross-cultural perspectives.* Lincoln: University of Nebraska Press.

Triandis, H. C. (1994). *Culture and social behavior.* New York: McGraw-Hill.

Trickett, P. K., Aber, J. L., Carlson, V., & Cicchetti, D. (1991). Relationship of socioeconomic status to etiology and developmental sequence of physical child abuse. *Developmental Psychology, 27,* 148–158.

Turnbull, C. (1961). Some observations regarding the experiences and behavior of the Bambuti Pygmies. *American Journal of Psychology, 74,* 301–308.

Turner, S., Beidel, D., & Nathan, R. (1985). Biological factors in obsessive-compulsive disorders. *Psychological Bulletin, 97,* 430–450.

U.S. Bureau of the Census. (2000). *Statistical abstract of the United States* (120th ed.). Washington, D.C.: U.S. Government Printing Office.

Uchino, B. N., Cacioppo, J. T., & Kiecolt-Glaser, J. K. (1996). The relationship between social support and physiological processes. *Psychological Bulletin, 119,* 488–531.

United States Bureau of the Census. (1993). *Statistical abstract of the United States* (113th ed.). Washington, DC: U.S. Government Printing Office.

United States Bureau of the Census. (1995). *Statistical abstract of the United States* (115th ed.). Washington, DC: U.S. Government Printing Office.

United States Bureau of the Census. (annual). *Current population reports.* Washington, DC: U.S. Government Printing Office.

United States National Center for Health Statistics. (annual). *Vital statistics of the United States and Monthly vital statistics reports.*

United States Public Health Service (1967). *Vital statistics of the United States, 1900–1967.*

USBC (U.S. Bureau of the Census). (1998). *Statistical abstract of the United States* (118th ed.). Washington, DC: U.S. Government Printing Office.

Vaillant, G. E. (1994). Ego mechanisms of defense and personality psychopathology. *Journal of Abnormal Psychology, 103,* 44–50.

Valenstein, E. S. (1986). *Great and desperate cures: The rise and decline of psychosurgery and other radical treatments for mental illness.* New York: Basic Books.

Van Brunt, L. (1994, March 27). About men: Whites without money. *The New York Times Magazine,* p. 38.

Van der Pligt, J., & Eiser, J. R. (1983). Actors' and observers' attributions, self-serving bias, and positivity bias. *European Journal of Social Psychology, 13,* 95–104.

van Hiel, A., Kossowska, M., & Mervielde, I. (2000). The relationship between Openness to Experience and political ideology. *Personality & Individual Differences, 28*(4) 741–751.

Vandell, D. L., & Corasaniti, M. A. (1990). Child care and the family: Complex contributors to child development. In K. McCartney (Ed.), *New Directions for Child Development,* no. 49, pp. 23–37. San Francisco: Josey-Bass.

Vernberg, E. M., La Greca, A. M., Silverman, W. K., & Prinstein, M. J. (1996). Prediction of posttraumatic stress symptoms in children after Hurricane Andrew. *Journal of Abnormal Psychology, 105,* 237–248.

Vik, P. W., Carrello, P., Tate, S. R., & Field, C. (2000). Progression of consequences among heavy-drinking college students. *Psychology of Addictive Behaviors, 14*(2), 91–101.

Villa, K. K., & Abeles, N. (2000). Broad spectrum intervention and the remediation of prospective memory declines in the able elderly. *Aging & Mental Health, 4*(1), 21–29.

Visitainer, M. A., Volpicelli, J. R., & Seligman, M. E. P. (1982). Tumor rejection in rats after inescapable or escapable shock. *Science, 216,* 437–439.

Vitousek, K., & Manke, F. (1994). Personality variables and disorders in anorexia nervosa and bulimia nervosa. *Journal of Abnormal Psychology, 103,* 137–147.

Voyer, D., Voyer, S., & Bryden, M. P. (1995). Magnitude of sex differences in spatial abilities: A meta-analysis and consideration of critical variables. *Psychological Bulletin, 117,* 250–270.

Wachtel, P. L. (1994). Cyclical processes in personality and psychopathology. Journal of Abnormal Psycholog*y, 103,* 51–54.

Wadden, T. A., et al. (1997). Exercise in the treatment of obesity. *Journal of Consulting and Clinical Psychology, 65,* 269–277.

Wade, T. D., Bulik, C. M., Neale, M., & Kendler, K. S. (2000). Anorexia nervosa and major depression: Shared genetic and environmental risk factors. *American Journal of Psychiatry, 157*(3), 469–471.

Wagner, R. K. (1997). Intelligence, training, and employment. (1997). *American Psychologist, 52,* 1059–1069.

Walk, R. D., & Gibson, E. J. (1961). A comparative and analytical study of visual depth perception. *Psychology Monographs, 75,* 15. (Whole No. 519)

Wallerstein, J. S., & Blakeslee, S. (1989). *Second chances: Women and children a decade after divorce.* New York: Ticknor & Fields.

Walsh, M. R. (1993, August). *Teaching the psychology of women and gender for undergraduate and graduate faculty.* Workshop of the Psychology of Women Institute presented at the meeting of the American Psychological Association, Toronto.

Walsh, W. B., & Betz, N. E. (1990). *Tests and assessment* (2nd ed.). Englewood Cliffs, NJ: Prentice-Hall.

Wan, W. W. N., Luk, C., & Lai, J. C. L. (2000). Personality correlates of loving styles among Chinese students in Hong Kong. *Personality & Individual Differences, 29*(1) 169–175.

Wang, X., et al. (2000). Longitudinal study of earthquake-related PTSD in a randomly selected community sample in North China. *American Journal of Psychiatry, 157,* 1260–1266.

Wann, D. L., & Waddill, P. J. (2003). Predicting sport fan motivation using anatomical sex and gender role orientation. *North American Journal of Psychology, 5*(3), 485–498.

Wann, D. L., Royalty, J., & Roberts, A. (2000). The self-presentation of sports fans: Investigating the importance of team identification and self-esteem. *Journal of Sport Behavior, 23*(2), 198–206.

Waterman, A. S. (1992). Identity as an aspect of optimal psychological functioning. In G. R. Adams, T. P. Gullotta, & R. Montemayor (Eds.), *Adolescent identity formulation.* Newbury Park, CA: Sage.

Watkins, C. E., Jr., Campbell, V. L., Nieberding, R., & Hallmark, R. (1995). Contemporary practice of psychological assessment by clinical psychologists. *Professional Psychology: Research and Practice, 26,* 54–60.

Watson, D., Hubbard, B., & Wiese, D. (2000). Self-other agreement in personality and affectivity: The role of acquaintanceship, trait visibility, and assumed similarity. *Journal of Personality & Social Psychology, 78*(3), 546–558.

Watson, J. B. (1924). *Behaviorism.* New York: Norton.

Weiner, R. D. (2000). Retrograde amnesia with electroconvulsive therapy. *Archives of General Psychiatry online, 57*(6).

Weiss, J. M (1982, August). *A model for the neurochemical study of depression.* Paper presented at the meeting of the American Psychological Association, Washington, DC.

Welch, K. M. A. (1993). Drug therapy of migraine. *New England Journal of Medicine, 329,* 1476–1483.

Wells, G. L. (1993). What do we know about eyewitness identification? *American Psychologist, 48,* 553–571.

Wells, G. L., et al. (2000). From the lab to the police station: A successful application of eyewitness research. *American Psychologist, 55*(6), 581–598.

Wentzel, K. R. (1994). Relations of social goal pursuit to social acceptance, classroom behavior, and perceived social support. *Journal of Educational Psychology, 86,* 173–182.

Westerman, M. A. (1990). Coordination of maternal directives with preschoolers' behavior in compliance-problem and healthy dyads. *Developmental Psychology, 26,* 621–630.

Wetzler, S. E., & Sweeney, J. A. (1986). Childhood amnesia. In D. C. Rubin (Ed.), *Autobiographical memory.* New York: Cambridge University Press.

Whisman, M. A., Miller, I. W., Norman, W. H., & Keitner, G. I. (1991). Cognitive therapy with depressed inpatients: Specific effects on dysfunctional cognitions. *Journal of Consulting and Clinical Psychology, 61,* 261–269.

White, S. D., & DeBlassie, R. R. (1992). Adolescent sexual behavior. *Adolescence, 27,* 183–191.

Whitehead, W. E. (1994). Assessing the effects of stress on physical symptoms. *Health Psychology, 13,* 99–102.

Widiger, T. A., & Costa, P. T., Jr. (1994). Personality and personality disorders. *Journal of Abnormal Psychology, 103,* 78–91.

Wiggins, J. G., Jr. (1994). Would you want your child to be a psychologist? *American Psychologist, 49,* 485–492.

Wilcox, V. L., Kasl, S. V., & Berkman, L. F. (1994). Social support and physical disability in older people after hospitalization. *Health Psychology, 13,* 170–179.

Wilder, D. A. (1986). Social categorization: Implications for creation and reduction of intergroup bias. In L. Berkowitz (Ed.), *Advances in experimental social psychology.* New York: Academic Press.

Wilder, D. A. (1990). Some determinants of the persuasive power of in-groups and out-groups: Organization of information and attribution of independence. *Journal of Personality and Social Psychology, 59,* 1202–1213.

Wilgoren, J. (2000, March 15). Effort to curb binge drinking in college falls short. *The New York Times,* p. A16.

Wilkie, D. M., Mumby, D. G., Needham, G., & Smeele, M. (1992). Sustained arm visiting by nondeprived, nonrewarded rats in a radial maze. *Bulletin of the Psychonomic Society, 30,* 314–316.

Willett, W. C., et al. (1990). Relation of meat, fat, and fiber intake to the risk of colon cancer in a prospective study among women. *New England Journal of Medicine, 323,* 1664–1672.

Williams, J. E., & Best, D. L. (1994). Cross-cultural views of women and men. In W. J. Lonner & R. Malpass (Eds.), *Psychology and culture.* Boston: Allyn & Bacon.

Williams, L. (1992, February 6). Woman's image in a mirror: Who defines what she sees? *The New York Times,* pp. A1, B7.

Williams, S. M., et al. (2000). Combinations of variations in multiple genes are associated with hypertension. *Hypertension, 36,* 2–6.

Williamson, D. A., Cubic, B. A., & Gleaves, D. H. (1993). Equivalence of body image disturbances in anorexia and bulimia nervosa. *Journal of Abnormal Psychology, 102,* 177–180.

Willoughby, T., Wood, E., & Khan, M. (1994). Isolating variables that impact on or detract from the effectiveness of elaboration strategies. *Journal of Educational Research, 86,* 279–289.

Wills, T. A., Gibbons, F. X., Gerrard, M., & Brody, G. H. (2000). Protection and vulnerability processes relevant for early onset of substance use: A test among African American children. *Health Psychology, 19,* 253–263.

Wills, T. A., McNamara, G., Vaccaro, D., & Hirky, A. E. (1996). Escalated substance abuse: A longitudinal grouping analysis from early to middle adolescence. *Journal of Abnormal Psychology, 195,* 166–180.

Wilson, E. O. (1975). *Sociobiology: The new synthesis.* Cambridge, MA: Harvard University Press.

Wilson, G. T. (1993). Cited in O'Neill, M. (1993, September 29). Diet sabotage: The new battle of the sexes. *The New York Times,* pp. C1, C6.

Winner, E. (2000). The origins and ends of giftedness. *American Psychologist, 55,* 159–169.

Wintre, M. G., & Sugar, L. A. (2000). Relationships with parents, personality, and the university transition. *Journal of College Student Development, 41*(2), 202–214.

Winzelberg, A. J., et al. (2000). Effectiveness of an Internet-based program for reducing risk factors for eating disorders. *Journal of Consulting and Clinical Psychology, 68,* 346–350.

Witelson, S. F. (1991). Neural sexual mosaicism: Sexual differentiation of the human temporo-parietal region for functional asymmetry. *Psychoneuroendocrinology, 16,* 131–153.

Wolf, N. (1991). *The beauty myth: How images of beauty are used against women.* New York: William Morrow.

Wolock, I., & Horowitz, B. (1984). Child maltreatment as a social problem: The neglect of neglect. *American Journal of Orthopsychiatry, 54,* 530–545.

Woloshyn, V. E., Paivio, A., & Pressley, M. (1994). Use of elaborative interrogation to help students acquire information consistent with prior knowledge and information inconsistent with prior knowledge. *Journal of Educational Psychology, 86,* 78–89.

Wolpe, J. (1990). *The practice of behavior therapy* (4th ed.). New York: Pergamon Press.

Wolpe, J., & Lazarus, A. A. (1966). *Behavior therapy techniques: A guide to the treatment of neurosis.* Elmsford, NY: Pergamon Press.

Wong, D., Wagner, H., Tune, L., Dannals, R., Pealson, G., Links, J., Tamminga, C., Broussolle, E., Ravert, H., Wilson, A., Tuong, J., Malat, J., Williams, J., O'Tuama, L., Snyder, S., Kuhar, M., & Gjedde, A. (1986). Positron emission tomography reveals elevated D2 dopamine receptors in drug-naive schizophrenics. *Science, 234,* 1558–1563.

Wood, J. M., & Bootzin, R. R. (1990). The prevalence of nightmares and their independence from anxiety. *Journal of Abnormal Psychology, 99,* 64–68.

Wood, J. M., Bootzin, R. R., Rosenhan, D., Nolen-Hoeksema, S., & Jourden, F. (1992). Effects of the 1989 San Francisco earthquake on frequency and content of nightmares. *Journal of Abnormal Psychology, 101,* 219–224.

Wood, P. D., et al. (1991). The effects on plasma lipoproteins of a prudent weight-reducing diet, with or without exercise, in overweight men and women. *New England Journal of Medicine, 325,* 461–466.

Wood, W. (2000). Attitude change: Persuasion and social influence. *Annual Review of Psychology, 51,* 539–570.

Wood, W., & Eagly, A. H. (2000). Once again, the origins of sex differences. *American Psychologist, 55*(9), 1062–1063.

Wood, W., Wong, F. Y., & Chachere, J. G. (1991). Effects of media violence on viewers' aggression in unconstrained social interaction. *Psychological Bulletin, 109,* 371–383.

World Health Organization. (2003). *Training in the management of severe malnutrition.* World Health Organization Department of Nutrition for Health and Development. Geneva.

World Health Organization. (2004, March 3). *Alleviating protein-energy malnutrition.*

Wren, C. S. (1996, February 20). Marijuana use by youths continues to rise. *The New York Times,* p. A11.

Wu, C., & Shaffer, C. R. (1987). Susceptibility to persuasive appeals as a function of source credibility and prior experience with the attitude object. *Journal of Personality and Social Psychology, 52,* 677–688.

WuDunn, S. (1995, July 9). Many Japanese women are resisting servility. *The New York Times,* p. A10.

Yaffe, K., et al. (2000). Cognitive decline in women in relation to non-protein-bound oestradiol concentrations. *Lancet, 356,* 708–712.

Yoder, J. D., & Kahn, A. S. (1993). Working toward an inclusive psychology of women. *American Psychologist, 48,* 846–850.

Yokota, F., & Thompson, K. M. (2000). Violence in G-rated animated films. *Journal of the American Medical Association, 283,* 2716–2720.

Youngblade, L. M., & Belsky, J. (1992). Parent-child antecedents of 5-year-olds' close friendships: A longitudinal analysis. *Developmental Psychology, 28,* 700–713.

Youniss, J., & Haynie, D. L. (1992). Friendship in adolescence. *Developmental and Behavioral Pediatrics, 13,* 59–66.

Yutrzenka, B. A. (1995). Making a case for training in ethnic and cultural diversity in increasing treatment efficacy. *Journal of Consulting and Clinical Psychology, 63,* 197–206.

Zajonc, R. B. (1965). Social facilitation. *Science, 149,* 269–275.

Zajonc, R. B. (1980). Compresence. In P. Paulus (Ed.), *The psychology of group influence.* Hillsdale, NJ: Erlbaum.

Zajonc, R. B. (1984). On the primacy of affect. *American Psychologist, 39,* 117–123.

Zigler, E. (1995). *Modernizing early childhood intervention to better serve children and families in poverty.* Master lecture delivered at the meeting of the American Psychological Association, New York.

Zigler, E., Taussig, C., & Black, K. (1992). Early childhood intervention: A promising preventative for juvenile delinquency. *American Psychologist, 47,* 997–1006.

Zimbardo, P. G., LaBerge, S., & Butler, L. D. (1993). Psychophysiological consequences of unexplained arousal: A posthypnotic suggestion paradigm. *Journal of Abnormal Psychology, 102,* 466–473.

Zipfel, S., et al. (2000). Long-term prognosis in anorexia nervosa: Lessons from a 21-year follow-up study. *The Lancet, 355*(9205), 721–722.

Ziv, T. A., & Lo, B. (1995). Denial of care to illegal immigrants —Proposition 187 in California. *New England Journal of Medicine, 332,* 1095–1098.

Zuber, J. A., Crott, H. W., & Werner, J. (1992). Choice shift and group polarization: An analysis of the status of arguments and social decision schemes. *Journal of Personality and Social Psychology, 62,* 50–61.

ETHICAL PRINCIPLES
OF PSYCHOLOGISTS AND CODE OF CONDUCT

PREAMBLE

Psychologists are committed to increasing scientific and professional knowledge of behavior and people's understanding of themselves and others and to the use of such knowledge to improve the condition of individuals, organizations, and society. Psychologists respect and protect civil and human rights and the central importance of freedom of inquiry and expression in research, teaching, and publication. They strive to help the public in developing informed judgments and choices concerning human behavior. In doing so, they perform many roles, such as researcher, educator, diagnostician, therapist, supervisor, consultant, administrator, social interventionist, and expert witness. This Ethics Code provides a common set of principles and standards upon which psychologists build their professional and scientific work.

This Ethics Code is intended to provide specific standards to cover most situations encountered by psychologists. It has as its goals the welfare and protection of the individuals and groups with whom psychologists work and the education of members, students, and the public regarding ethical standards of the discipline.

The development of a dynamic set of ethical standards for psychologists' work-related conduct requires a personal commitment and lifelong effort to act ethically; to encourage ethical behavior by students, supervisees, employees, and colleagues; and to consult with others concerning ethical problems.

GENERAL PRINCIPLES

This section consists of General Principles. General Principles, as opposed to Ethical Standards, are aspirational in nature. Their intent is to guide and inspire psychologists toward the very highest ethical ideals of the profession. General Principles, in contrast to Ethical Standards, do not represent obligations and should not form the basis for imposing sanctions. Relying upon General Principles for either of these reasons distorts both their meaning and purpose.

PRINCIPLE A: BENEFICENCE AND NONMALEFICENCE

Psychologists strive to benefit those with whom they work and take care to do no harm. In their professional actions, psychologists seek to safeguard the welfare and rights of those with whom they interact professionally and other affected persons, and the welfare of animal subjects of research. When conflicts occur among psychologists' obligations or concerns, they attempt to resolve these conflicts in a responsible fashion that avoids or minimizes harm. Because psychologists' scientific and professional judgments and actions may affect the lives of others, they are alert to and guard against personal, financial, social, organizational, or political factors that might lead to misuse of their influence. Psychologists strive to be aware of the possible effect of their own physical and mental health on their ability to help those with whom they work.

PRINCIPLE B: FIDELITY AND RESPONSIBILITY

Psychologists establish relationships of trust with those with whom they work. They are aware of their professional and scientific responsibilities to society and to the specific communities in which they work. Psychologists uphold professional standards of conduct, clarify their professional roles and obligations, accept appropriate responsibility for their behavior, and seek to manage conflicts of interest that could lead to exploitation or harm. Psychologists consult with, refer to, or cooperate with other professionals and institutions to the extent needed to serve the best interests of those with whom they work. They are concerned about the ethical compliance of their colleagues' scientific and professional conduct. Psychologists strive to contribute a portion of their professional time for little or no compensation or personal advantage.

PRINCIPLE C: INTEGRITY

Psychologists seek to promote accuracy, honesty, and truthfulness in the science, teaching, and practice of psychology. In these activities psychologists do not steal, cheat, or engage in fraud, subterfuge, or intentional misrepresentation of fact. Psychologists strive to keep their promises and to avoid unwise or unclear commitments. In situations in which deception may be ethically justifiable to maximize benefits and minimize harm, psychologists have a serious obligation to consider the need for, the possible consequences of, and their responsibility to correct any resulting mistrust or other harmful effects that arise from the use of such techniques.

PRINCIPLE D: JUSTICE

Psychologists recognize that fairness and justice entitle all persons to access to and benefit from the contributions of psychology and to equal quality in the processes, procedures, and services being conducted by psychologists. Psychologists exercise reasonable judgment and take precautions to ensure that their potential biases, the boundaries of their competence, and the limitations of their expertise do not lead to or condone unjust practices.

PRINCIPLE E: RESPECT FOR PEOPLE'S RIGHTS AND DIGNITY

Psychologists respect the dignity and worth of all people, and the rights of individuals to privacy, confidentiality, and self-determination. Psychologists are aware that special safeguards may be necessary to protect the rights and welfare of persons or communities whose vulnerabilities impair autonomous decision making. Psychologists are aware of and respect cultural, individual, and role differences, including those based on age, gender, gender identity, race, ethnicity, culture, national origin, religion, sexual orientation, disability, language, and socioeconomic status and consider these factors when working with members of such groups. Psychologists try to eliminate the effect on their work of biases based on those factors, and they do not knowingly participate in or condone activities of others based upon such prejudices.

ETHICAL STANDARDS

1. Resolving Ethical Issues

1.01 Misuse of Psychologists' Work

If psychologists learn of misuse or misrepresentation of their work, they take reasonable steps to correct or minimize the misuse or misrepresentation.

1.02 Conflicts Between Ethics and Law, Regulations, or Other Governing Legal Authority

If psychologists' ethical responsibilities conflict with law, regulations, or other governing legal authority, psychologists make known their commitment to the Ethics Code and take steps to resolve the conflict. If the conflict is unresolvable via such means, psychologists may adhere to the requirements of the law, regulations, or other governing legal authority.

1.03 Conflicts Between Ethics and Organizational Demands

If the demands of an organization with which psychologists are affiliated or for whom they are working conflict with this Ethics Code, psychologists clarify the nature of the conflict, make known their commitment to the Ethics Code, and to the extent feasible, resolve the conflict in a way that permits adherence to the Ethics Code.

1.04 Informal Resolution of Ethical Violations

When psychologists believe that there may have been an ethical violation by another psychologist, they attempt to resolve the issue by bringing it to the attention of that individual, if an informal resolution appears appropriate and the intervention does not violate any confidentiality rights that may be involved. (See also Standards 1.02, Conflicts Between Ethics and Law, Regulations, or Other Governing Legal Authority, and 1.03, Conflicts Between Ethics and Organizational Demands.)

1.05 Reporting Ethical Violations

If an apparent ethical violation has substantially harmed or is likely to substantially harm a person or organization and is not appropriate for informal resolution under Standard 1.04, Informal Resolution of Ethical Violations, or is not resolved properly in that fashion, psychologists take further action appropriate to the situation. Such action might include referral to state or national committees on professional ethics, to state licensing boards, or to the appropriate institutional authorities. This standard does not apply when an intervention would violate confidentiality rights or when psychologists have been retained to review the work of another psychologist whose professional conduct is in question. (See also Standard 1.02, Conflicts Between Ethics and Law, Regulations, or Other Governing Legal Authority.)

1.06 Cooperating With Ethics Committees

Psychologists cooperate in ethics investigations, proceedings, and resulting requirements of the APA or any affiliated state psychological association to which they belong. In doing so, they address any confidentiality issues. Failure to cooperate is itself an ethics violation. However, making a request for deferment of adjudication of an ethics complaint pending the outcome of litigation does not alone constitute noncooperation.

1.07 Improper Complaints

Psychologists do not file or encourage the filing of ethics complaints that are made with reckless disregard for or willful ignorance of facts that would disprove the allegation.

1.08 Unfair Discrimination Against Complainants and Respondents

Psychologists do not deny persons employment, advancement, admissions to academic or other programs, tenure, or promotion, based solely upon their having made or their being the subject of an ethics complaint. This does not preclude taking action based upon the outcome of such proceedings or considering other appropriate information.

2. COMPETENCE

2.01 Boundaries of Competence

(a) Psychologists provide services, teach, and conduct research with populations and in areas only within the boundaries of their competence, based on their education, training, supervised experience, consultation, study, or professional experience.

(b) Where scientific or professional knowledge in the discipline of psychology establishes that an understanding of factors associated with age, gender, gender identity, race, ethnicity, culture, national origin, religion, sexual orientation, disability, language, or socioeconomic status is essential for effective implementation of their services or research, psychologists have or obtain the training, experience, consultation, or supervision necessary to ensure the competence of their services, or they make appropriate referrals, except as provided in Standard 2.02, Providing Services in Emergencies.

(c) Psychologists planning to provide services, teach, or conduct research involving populations, areas, techniques, or technologies new to them undertake relevant education, training, supervised experience, consultation, or study.

(d) When psychologists are asked to provide services to individuals for whom appropriate mental health services are not available and for which psychologists have not obtained the competence necessary, psychologists with closely related prior training or experience may provide such services in order to ensure that services are not denied if they make a reasonable effort to obtain the competence required by using relevant research, training, consultation, or study.

(e) In those emerging areas in which generally recognized standards for preparatory training do not yet exist, psychologists nevertheless take reasonable steps to ensure the competence of their work and to protect clients/patients, students, supervisees, research participants, organizational clients, and others from harm.

(f) When assuming forensic roles, psychologists are or become reasonably familiar with the judicial or administrative rules governing their roles.

2.02 Providing Services in Emergencies

In emergencies, when psychologists provide services to individuals for whom other mental health services are not available and for which psychologists have not obtained the necessary training, psychologists may provide such services in order to ensure that services are not denied. The services are discontinued as soon as the emergency has ended or appropriate services are available.

2.03 Maintaining Competence

Psychologists undertake ongoing efforts to develop and maintain their competence.

2.04 Bases for Scientific and Professional Judgments

Psychologists' work is based upon established scientific and professional knowledge of the discipline. (See also Standards 2.01e, Boundaries of Competence, and 10.01b, Informed Consent to Therapy.)

2.05 Delegation of Work to Others

Psychologists who delegate work to employees, supervisees, or research or teaching assistants or who use the services of others, such as interpreters, take reasonable steps to (1) avoid delegating such work to persons who have a multiple relationship with those being served that would likely lead to exploitation or loss of objectivity; (2) authorize only those responsibilities that such persons can be expected to perform competently on the basis of their education, training, or experience, either independently or with the level of supervision being provided; and (3) see that such persons perform these services competently. (See also Standards 2.02, Providing Services in Emergencies; 3.05, Multiple Relationships; 4.01, Maintaining Confidentiality; 9.01, Bases for Assessments; 9.02, Use of Assessments; 9.03, Informed Consent in Assessments; and 9.07, Assessment by Unqualified Persons.)

2.06 Personal Problems and Conflicts

(a) Psychologists refrain from initiating an activity when they know or should know that there is a substantial likelihood that their personal problems will prevent them from performing their work-related activities in a competent manner.

(b) When psychologists become aware of personal problems that may interfere with their performing work-related duties adequately, they take appropriate measures, such as obtaining professional consultation or assistance, and determine whether they should limit, suspend, or terminate their work-related duties. (See also Standard 10.10, Terminating Therapy.)

3. HUMAN RELATIONS

3.01 Unfair Discrimination

In their work-related activities, psychologists do not engage in unfair discrimination based on age, gender, gender identity, race, ethnicity, culture, national origin, religion, sexual orientation, disability, socioeconomic status, or any basis proscribed by law.

3.02 Sexual Harassment

Psychologists do not engage in sexual harassment. Sexual harassment is sexual solicitation, physical advances, or verbal or nonverbal conduct that is sexual in nature, that occurs in connection with the psychologist's activities or roles as a psychologist, and that either (1) is unwelcome, is offensive, or creates a hostile workplace or educational environment, and the psychologist knows or is told this or (2) is sufficiently severe or intense to be abusive to a reasonable person in the context. Sexual harassment can consist of a single intense or severe act or of multiple persistent or pervasive acts. (See also Standard 1.08, Unfair Discrimination Against Complainants and Respondents.)

3.03 Other Harassment

Psychologists do not knowingly engage in behavior that is harassing or demeaning to persons with whom they interact in their work based on factors such as those persons' age, gender, gender identity, race, ethnicity, culture, national origin, religion, sexual orientation, disability, language, or socioeconomic status.

3.04 Avoiding Harm

Psychologists take reasonable steps to avoid harming their clients/patients, students, supervisees, research participants, organizational clients, and others with whom they work, and to minimize harm where it is foreseeable and unavoidable.

3.05 Multiple Relationships

(a) A multiple relationship occurs when a psychologist is in a professional role with a person and (1) at the same time is in another role with the same person, (2) at the same time is in a relationship with a person closely associated with or related to the person with whom the psychologist has the professional relationship, or (3) promises to enter into another relationship in the future with the person or a person closely associated with or related to the person.

A psychologist refrains from entering into a multiple relationship if the multiple relationship could reasonably be expected to impair the psychologist's objectivity, competence, or effectiveness in performing his or her functions as a psychologist, or otherwise risks exploitation or harm to the person with whom the professional relationship exists.

Multiple relationships that would not reasonably be expected to cause impairment or risk exploitation or harm are not unethical.

(b) If a psychologist finds that, due to unforeseen factors, a potentially harmful multiple relationship has arisen, the psychologist takes reasonable steps to resolve it with due regard for the best interests of the affected person and maximal compliance with the Ethics Code.

(c) When psychologists are required by law, institutional policy, or extraordinary circumstances to serve in more than one role in judicial or administrative proceedings, at the outset they clarify role expectations and the extent of confidentiality and thereafter as changes occur. (See also Standards 3.04, Avoiding Harm, and 3.07, Third-Party Requests for Services.)

3.06 Conflict of Interest

Psychologists refrain from taking on a professional role when personal, scientific, professional, legal, financial, or other interests or relationships could reasonably be expected to (1) impair their objectivity, competence, or effectiveness in performing their functions as psychologists or (2) expose the person or organization with whom the professional relationship exists to harm or exploitation.

3.07 Third-Party Requests for Services

When psychologists agree to provide services to a person or entity at the request of a third party, psychologists attempt to clarify at the outset of the service the nature of the relationship with all individuals or organizations involved. This clarification includes the role of the psychologist (e.g., therapist, consultant, diagnostician, or expert witness), an identification of who is the client, the probable uses of the services provided or the information obtained, and the fact that there may be limits to confidentiality. (See also Standards 3.05, Multiple Relationships, and 4.02, Discussing the Limits of Confidentiality.)

3.08 Exploitative Relationships

Psychologists do not exploit persons over whom they have supervisory, evaluative, or other authority such as clients/patients, students, supervisees, research participants, and employees. (See also Standards 3.05, Multiple Relationships; 6.04, Fees and Financial Arrangements; 6.05, Barter With Clients/Patients; 7.07, Sexual Relationships With Students and Supervisees; 10.05, Sexual Intimacies With Current Therapy Clients/Patients; 10.06, Sexual Intimacies With Relatives or Significant Others of Current Therapy Clients/Patients; 10.07, Therapy With Former Sexual Partners; and 10.08, Sexual Intimacies With Former Therapy Clients/Patients.)

3.09 Cooperation With Other Professionals

When indicated and professionally appropriate, psychologists cooperate with other professionals in order to serve their clients/patients effectively and appropriately. (See also Standard 4.05, Disclosures.)

3.10 Informed Consent

(a) When psychologists conduct research or provide assessment, therapy, counseling, or consulting services in person or via electronic transmission or other forms of communication, they obtain the informed consent of the individual or individuals using language that is reasonably understandable to that person or persons except when conducting such activities without consent is mandated by law or governmental regulation or as otherwise provided in this Ethics Code. (See also Standards 8.02, Informed Consent to Research; 9.03, Informed Consent in Assessments; and 10.01, Informed Consent to Therapy.)

(b) For persons who are legally incapable of giving informed consent, psychologists nevertheless (1) provide an appropriate explanation, (2) seek the individual's assent, (3) consider such persons' preferences and best interests, and (4) obtain appropriate permission from a legally authorized person, if such substitute consent is permitted or required by law. When consent by a legally authorized person is not permitted or required by law, psychologists take reasonable steps to protect the individual's rights and welfare.

(c) When psychological services are court ordered or otherwise mandated, psychologists inform the individual of the nature of the anticipated services, including whether the services are court ordered or mandated and any limits of confidentiality, before proceeding.

(d) Psychologists appropriately document written or oral consent, permission, and assent. (See also Standards 8.02, Informed Consent to Research; 9.03, Informed Consent in Assessments; and 10.01, Informed Consent to Therapy.)

3.11 Psychological Services Delivered To or Through Organizations

(a) Psychologists delivering services to or through organizations provide information beforehand to clients and when appropriate those directly affected by the services about (1) the nature and objectives of the services, (2) the intended recipients, (3) which of the individuals are clients, (4) the relationship the psychologist will have with each person and the organization, (5) the probable uses of services provided and information obtained, (6) who will have access to the information, and (7) limits of confidentiality. As soon as feasible, they provide information about the results and conclusions of such services to appropriate persons.

(b) If psychologists will be precluded by law or by organizational roles from providing such information to particular individuals or groups, they so inform those individuals or groups at the outset of the service.

3.12 Interruption of Psychological Services

Unless otherwise covered by contract, psychologists make reasonable efforts to plan for facilitating services in the event that psychological services are interrupted by factors such as the psychologist's illness, death, unavailability, relocation, or retirement or by the client's/patient's relocation or financial limitations. (See also Standard 6.02c, Maintenance, Dissemination, and Disposal of Confidential Records of Professional and Scientific Work.)

4. PRIVACY AND CONFIDENTIALITY

4.01 Maintaining Confidentiality

Psychologists have a primary obligation and take reasonable precautions to protect confidential information obtained through or stored in any medium, recognizing that the extent and limits of confidentiality may be regulated by law or established by institutional rules or professional or scientific relationship. (See also Standard 2.05, Delegation of Work to Others.)

4.02 Discussing the Limits of Confidentiality

(a) Psychologists discuss with persons (including, to the extent feasible, persons who are legally incapable of giving informed consent and their legal representatives) and organizations with whom they establish a scientific or professional relationship (1) the relevant limits of confidentiality and (2) the foreseeable uses of the information generated through their psychological activities. (See also Standard 3.10, Informed Consent.)

(b) Unless it is not feasible or is contraindicated, the discussion of confidentiality occurs at the outset of the relationship and thereafter as new circumstances may warrant.

(c) Psychologists who offer services, products, or information via electronic transmission inform clients/patients of the risks to privacy and limits of confidentiality.

4.03 Recording

Before recording the voices or images of individuals to whom they provide services, psychologists obtain permission from all such persons or their legal representatives. (See also Standards 8.03, Informed Consent for Recording Voices and Images in Research; 8.05, Dispensing With Informed Consent for Research; and 8.07, Deception in Research.)

4.04 Minimizing Intrusions on Privacy

(a) Psychologists include in written and oral reports and consultations, only information germane to the purpose for which the communication is made.

(b) Psychologists discuss confidential information obtained in their work only for appropriate scientific or professional purposes and only with persons clearly concerned with such matters.

4.05 Disclosures

(a) Psychologists may disclose confidential information with the appropriate consent of the organizational client, the individual client/patient, or another legally authorized person on behalf of the client/patient unless prohibited by law.

(b) Psychologists disclose confidential information without the consent of the individual only as mandated by law, or where permitted by law for a valid purpose such as to (1) provide needed professional services; (2) obtain appropriate professional consultations; (3) protect the client/patient, psychologist, or others from harm; or (4) obtain payment for services from a client/patient, in which instance disclosure is limited to the minimum that is necessary to achieve the purpose. (See also Standard 6.04e, Fees and Financial Arrangements.)

4.06 Consultations

When consulting with colleagues, (1) psychologists do not disclose confidential information that reasonably could lead to the identification of a client/patient, research participant, or other person or organization with whom they have a confidential relationship unless they have obtained the prior consent of the person or organization or the disclosure cannot be avoided, and (2) they disclose information only to the extent necessary to achieve the purposes of the consultation. (See also Standard 4.01, Maintaining Confidentiality.)

4.07 Use of Confidential Information for Didactic or Other Purposes

Psychologists do not disclose in their writings, lectures, or other public media, confidential, personally identifiable information concerning their clients/patients, students, research participants, organizational clients, or other recipients of their services that they obtained during the course of their work, unless (1) they take reasonable steps to disguise the person or organization, (2) the person or organization has consented in writing, or (3) there is legal authorization for doing so.

5. ADVERTISING AND OTHER PUBLIC STATEMENTS

5.01 Avoidance of False or Deceptive Statements

(a) Public statements include but are not limited to paid or unpaid advertising, product endorsements, grant applications, licensing applications, other credentialing applications, brochures, printed matter, directory listings, personal resumes or curricula vitae, or comments for use in media such as print or electronic transmission, statements in legal proceedings, lectures and public oral presentations, and published materials. Psychologists do not knowingly make public statements that are false, deceptive, or fraudulent concerning their research, practice, or other work activities or those of persons or organizations with which they are affiliated.

(b) Psychologists do not make false, deceptive, or fraudulent statements concerning (1) their training, experience, or competence; (2) their academic degrees; (3) their credentials; (4) their institutional or association affiliations; (5) their services; (6) the scientific or clinical basis for, or results or degree of success of, their services; (7) their fees; or (8) their publications or research findings.

(c) Psychologists claim degrees as credentials for their health services only if those degrees (1) were earned from a regionally accredited educational institution or (2) were the basis for psychology licensure by the state in which they practice.

5.02 Statements by Others

(a) Psychologists who engage others to create or place public statements that promote their professional practice, products, or activities retain professional responsibility for such statements.

(b) Psychologists do not compensate employees of press, radio, television, or other communication media in return for publicity in a news item. (See also Standard 1.01, Misuse of Psychologists' Work.)

(c) A paid advertisement relating to psychologists' activities must be identified or clearly recognizable as such.

5.03 Descriptions of Workshops and Non-Degree-Granting Educational Programs

To the degree to which they exercise control, psychologists responsible for announcements, catalogs, brochures, or advertisements describing workshops, seminars, or other non-degree-granting educational programs ensure that they accurately describe the audience for which the program is intended, the educational objectives, the presenters, and the fees involved.

5.04 Media Presentations

When psychologists provide public advice or comment via print, internet, or other electronic transmission, they take precautions to ensure that statements (1) are based on their professional knowledge, training, or experience in accord with appropriate psychological literature and practice; (2) are otherwise consistent with this Ethics Code; and (3) do not indicate that a professional relationship has been established with the recipient. (See also Standard 2.04, Bases for Scientific and Professional Judgments.)

5.05 Testimonials

Psychologists do not solicit testimonials from current therapy clients/patients or other persons who because of their particular circumstances are vulnerable to undue influence.

5.06 In-Person Solicitation

Psychologists do not engage, directly or through agents, in uninvited in-person solicitation of business from actual or potential therapy clients/patients or other persons who because of their particular circumstances are vulnerable to undue influence. However, this prohibition does not preclude (1) attempting to implement appropriate collateral contacts for the purpose of benefiting an already engaged therapy client/patient or (2) providing disaster or community outreach services.

6. RECORD KEEPING AND FEES

6.01 Documentation of Professional and Scientific Work and Maintenance of Records

Psychologists create, and to the extent the records are under their control, maintain, disseminate, store, retain, and dispose of records and data relating to their professional and scientific work in order to (1) facilitate provision of services later by them or by other professionals, (2) allow for replication of research design and analyses, (3) meet institutional requirements, (4) ensure accuracy of billing and payments, and (5) ensure compliance

with law. (See also Standard 4.01, Maintaining Confidentiality.)

6.02 Maintenance, Dissemination, and Disposal of Confidential Records of Professional and Scientific Work

(a) Psychologists maintain confidentiality in creating, storing, accessing, transferring, and disposing of records under their control, whether these are written, automated, or in any other medium. (See also Standards 4.01, Maintaining Confidentiality, and 6.01, Documentation of Professional and Scientific Work and Maintenance of Records.)

(b) If confidential information concerning recipients of psychological services is entered into databases or systems of records available to persons whose access has not been consented to by the recipient, psychologists use coding or other techniques to avoid the inclusion of personal identifiers.

(c) Psychologists make plans in advance to facilitate the appropriate transfer and to protect the confidentiality of records and data in the event of psychologists' withdrawal from positions or practice. (See also Standards 3.12, Interruption of Psychological Services, and 10.09, Interruption of Therapy.)

6.03 Withholding Records for Nonpayment

Psychologists may not withhold records under their control that are requested and needed for a client's/patient's emergency treatment solely because payment has not been received.

6.04 Fees and Financial Arrangements

(a) As early as is feasible in a professional or scientific relationship, psychologists and recipients of psychological services reach an agreement specifying compensation and billing arrangements.

(b) Psychologists' fee practices are consistent with law.

(c) Psychologists do not misrepresent their fees.

(d) If limitations to services can be anticipated because of limitations in financing, this is discussed with the recipient of services as early as is feasible. (See also Standards 10.09, Interruption of Therapy, and 10.10, Terminating Therapy.)

(e) If the recipient of services does not pay for services as agreed, and if psychologists intend to use collection agencies or legal measures to collect the fees, psychologists first inform the person that such measures will be taken and provide that person an opportunity to make prompt payment. (See also Standards 4.05, Disclosures; 6.03, Withholding Records for Nonpayment; and 10.01, Informed Consent to Therapy.)

6.05 Barter With Clients/Patients

Barter is the acceptance of goods, services, or other nonmonetary remuneration from clients/patients in return for psychological services. Psychologists may barter only if (1) it is not clinically contraindicated, and (2) the resulting arrangement is not exploitative. (See also Standards 3.05, Multiple Relationships, and 6.04, Fees and Financial Arrangements.)

6.06 Accuracy in Reports to Payors and Funding Sources

In their reports to payors for services or sources of research funding, psychologists take reasonable steps to ensure the accurate reporting of the nature of the service provided or research conducted, the fees, charges, or payments, and where applicable, the identity of the provider, the findings, and the diagnosis. (See also Standards 4.01, Maintaining Confidentiality; 4.04, Minimizing Intrusions on Privacy; and 4.05, Disclosures.)

6.07 Referrals and Fees

When psychologists pay, receive payment from, or divide fees with another professional, other than in an employer-employee relationship, the payment to each is based on the services pro-

ETHICS

vided (clinical, consultative, administrative, or other) and is not based on the referral itself. (See also Standard 3.09, Cooperation With Other Professionals.)

7. EDUCATION AND TRAINING

7.01 Design of Education and Training Programs

Psychologists responsible for education and training programs take reasonable steps to ensure that the programs are designed to provide the appropriate knowledge and proper experiences, and to meet the requirements for licensure, certification, or other goals for which claims are made by the program. (See also Standard 5.03, Descriptions of Workshops and Non-Degree-Granting Educational Programs.)

7.02 Descriptions of Education and Training Programs

Psychologists responsible for education and training programs take reasonable steps to ensure that there is a current and accurate description of the program content (including participation in required course- or program-related counseling, psychotherapy, experiential groups, consulting projects, or community service), training goals and objectives, stipends and benefits, and requirements that must be met for satisfactory completion of the program. This information must be made readily available to all interested parties.

7.03 Accuracy in Teaching

(a) Psychologists take reasonable steps to ensure that course syllabi are accurate regarding the subject matter to be covered, bases for evaluating progress, and the nature of course experiences. This standard does not preclude an instructor from modifying course content or requirements when the instructor considers it pedagogically necessary or desirable, so long as students are made aware of these modifications in a manner that enables them to fulfill course requirements. (See also Standard 5.01, Avoidance of False or Deceptive Statements.)

(b) When engaged in teaching or training, psychologists present psychological information accurately. (See also Standard 2.03, Maintaining Competence.)

7.04 Student Disclosure of Personal Information

Psychologists do not require students or supervisees to disclose personal information in course- or program-related activities, either orally or in writing, regarding sexual history, history of abuse and neglect, psychological treatment, and relationships with parents, peers, and spouses or significant others except if (1) the program or training facility has clearly identified this requirement in its admissions and program materials or (2) the information is necessary to evaluate or obtain assistance for students whose personal problems could reasonably be judged to be preventing them from performing their training- or professionally related activities in a competent manner or posing a threat to the students or others.

7.05 Mandatory Individual or Group Therapy

(a) When individual or group therapy is a program or course requirement, psychologists responsible for that program allow students in undergraduate and graduate programs the option of selecting such therapy from practitioners unaffiliated with the program. (See also Standard 7.02, Descriptions of Education and Training Programs.)

(b) Faculty who are or are likely to be responsible for evaluating students' academic performance do not themselves provide that therapy. (See also Standard 3.05, Multiple Relationships.)

7.06 Assessing Student and Supervisee Performance

(a) In academic and supervisory relationships, psychologists establish a timely and specific process for providing feedback to students and supervisees. Information regarding the process is provided to the student at the beginning of supervision.

(b) Psychologists evaluate students and supervisees on the basis of their actual performance on relevant and established program requirements.

7.07 Sexual Relationships With Students and Supervisees

Psychologists do not engage in sexual relationships with students or supervisees who are in their department, agency, or training center or over whom psychologists have or are likely to have evaluative authority. (See also Standard 3.05, Multiple Relationships.)

8. RESEARCH AND PUBLICATION

8.01 Institutional Approval

When institutional approval is required, psychologists provide accurate information about their research proposals and obtain approval prior to conducting the research. They conduct the research in accordance with the approved research protocol.

8.02 Informed Consent to Research

(a) When obtaining informed consent as required in Standard 3.10, Informed Consent, psychologists inform participants about (1) the purpose of the research, expected duration, and procedures; (2) their right to decline to participate and to withdraw from the research once participation has begun; (3) the foreseeable consequences of declining or withdrawing; (4) reasonably foreseeable factors that may be expected to influence their willingness to participate such as potential risks, discomfort, or adverse effects; (5) any prospective research benefits; (6) limits of confidentiality; (7) incentives for participation; and (8) whom to contact for questions about the research and research participants' rights. They provide opportunity for the prospective participants to ask questions and receive answers. (See also Standards 8.03, Informed Consent for Recording Voices and Images in Research; 8.05, Dispensing With Informed Consent for Research; and 8.07, Deception in Research.)

(b) Psychologists conducting intervention research involving the use of experimental treatments clarify to participants at the outset of the research (1) the experimental nature of the treatment; (2) the services that will or will not be available to the control group(s) if appropriate; (3) the means by which assignment to treatment and control groups will be made; (4) available treatment alternatives if an individual does not wish to participate in the research or wishes to withdraw once a study has begun; and (5) compensation for or monetary costs of participating including, if appropriate, whether reimbursement from the participant or a third-party payor will be sought. (See also Standard 8.02a, Informed Consent to Research.)

8.03 Informed Consent for Recording Voices and Images in Research

Psychologists obtain informed consent from research participants prior to recording their voices or images for data collection unless (1) the research consists solely of naturalistic observations in public places, and it is not anticipated that the recording will be used in a manner that could cause personal identification or harm, or (2) the research design includes deception, and consent for the use of the recording is obtained during debriefing. (See also Standard 8.07, Deception in Research.)

8.04 Client/Patient, Student, and Subordinate Research Participants

(a) When psychologists conduct research with clients/patients, students, or subordinates as participants, psychologists take steps to protect the prospective participants from adverse consequences of declining or withdrawing from participation.

(b) When research participation is a course requirement or an opportunity for extra credit, the prospective participant is given the choice of equitable alternative activities.

8.05 Dispensing With Informed Consent for Research

Psychologists may dispense with informed consent only (1) where research would not reasonably be assumed to create distress or harm and involves (a) the study of normal educational practices, curricula, or classroom management methods conducted in educational settings; (b) only anonymous questionnaires, naturalistic observations, or archival research for which disclosure of responses would not place participants at risk of criminal or civil liability or damage their financial standing, employability, or reputation, and confidentiality is protected; or (c) the study of factors related to job or organization effectiveness conducted in organizational settings for which there is no risk to participants' employability, and confidentiality is protected or (2) where otherwise permitted by law or federal or institutional regulations.

8.06 Offering Inducements for Research Participation

(a) Psychologists make reasonable efforts to avoid offering excessive or inappropriate financial or other inducements for research participation when such inducements are likely to coerce participation.

(b) When offering professional services as an inducement for research participation, psychologists clarify the nature of the services, as well as the risks, obligations, and limitations. (See also Standard 6.05, Barter With Clients/Patients.)

8.07 Deception in Research

(a) Psychologists do not conduct a study involving deception unless they have determined that the use of deceptive techniques is justified by the study's significant prospective scientific, educational, or applied value and that effective nondeceptive alternative procedures are not feasible.

(b) Psychologists do not deceive prospective participants about research that is reasonably expected to cause physical pain or severe emotional distress.

(c) Psychologists explain any deception that is an integral feature of the design and conduct of an experiment to participants as early as is feasible, preferably at the conclusion of their participation, but no later than at the conclusion of the data collection, and permit participants to withdraw their data. (See also Standard 8.08, Debriefing.)

8.08 Debriefing

(a) Psychologists provide a prompt opportunity for participants to obtain appropriate information about the nature, results, and conclusions of the research, and they take reasonable steps to correct any misconceptions that participants may have of which the psychologists are aware.

(b) If scientific or humane values justify delaying or withholding this information, psychologists take reasonable measures to reduce the risk of harm.

(c) When psychologists become aware that research procedures have harmed a participant, they take reasonable steps to minimize the harm.

8.09 Humane Care and Use of Animals in Research

(a) Psychologists acquire, care for, use, and dispose of animals in compliance with current federal, state, and local laws and regulations, and with professional standards.

(b) Psychologists trained in research methods and experienced in the care of laboratory animals supervise all procedures involving animals and are responsible for ensuring appropriate consideration of their comfort, health, and humane treatment.

(c) Psychologists ensure that all individuals under their supervision who are using animals have received instruction in research methods and in the care, maintenance, and handling of the species being used, to the extent appropriate to their role. (See also Standard 2.05, Delegation of Work to Others.)

(d) Psychologists make reasonable efforts to minimize the discomfort, infection, illness, and pain of animal subjects.

(e) Psychologists use a procedure subjecting animals to pain, stress, or privation only when an alternative procedure is unavailable and the goal is justified by its prospective scientific, educational, or applied value.

(f) Psychologists perform surgical procedures under appropriate anesthesia and follow techniques to avoid infection and minimize pain during and after surgery.

(g) When it is appropriate that an animal's life be terminated, psychologists proceed rapidly, with an effort to minimize pain and in accordance with accepted procedures.

8.10 Reporting Research Results

(a) Psychologists do not fabricate data. (See also Standard 5.01a, Avoidance of False or Deceptive Statements.)

(b) If psychologists discover significant errors in their published data, they take reasonable steps to correct such errors in a correction, retraction, erratum, or other appropriate publication means.

8.11 Plagiarism

Psychologists do not present portions of another's work or data as their own, even if the other work or data source is cited occasionally.

8.12 Publication Credit

(a) Psychologists take responsibility and credit, including authorship credit, only for work they have actually performed or to which they have substantially contributed. (See also Standard 8.12b, Publication Credit.)

(b) Principal authorship and other publication credits accurately reflect the relative scientific or professional contributions of the individuals involved, regardless of their relative status. Mere possession of an institutional position, such as department chair, does not justify authorship credit. Minor contributions to the research or to the writing for publications are acknowledged appropriately, such as in footnotes or in an introductory statement.

(c) Except under exceptional circumstances, a student is listed as principal author on any multiple-authored article that is substantially based on the student's doctoral dissertation. Faculty advisors discuss publication credit with students as early as feasible and throughout the research and publication process as appropriate. (See also Standard 8.12b, Publication Credit.)

8.13 Duplicate Publication of Data

Psychologists do not publish, as original data, data that have been previously published. This does not preclude republishing

ETHICS

data when they are accompanied by proper acknowledgment.

8.14 Sharing Research Data for Verification

(a) After research results are published, psychologists do not withhold the data on which their conclusions are based from other competent professionals who seek to verify the substantive claims through reanalysis and who intend to use such data only for that purpose, provided that the confidentiality of the participants can be protected and unless legal rights concerning proprietary data preclude their release. This does not preclude psychologists from requiring that such individuals or groups be responsible for costs associated with the provision of such information.

(b) Psychologists who request data from other psychologists to verify the substantive claims through reanalysis may use shared data only for the declared purpose. Requesting psychologists obtain prior written agreement for all other uses of the data.

8.15 Reviewers

Psychologists who review material submitted for presentation, publication, grant, or research proposal review respect the confidentiality of and the proprietary rights in such information of those who submitted it.

9. ASSESSMENT

9.01 Bases for Assessments

(a) Psychologists base the opinions contained in their recommendations, reports, and diagnostic or evaluative statements, including forensic testimony, on information and techniques sufficient to substantiate their findings. (See also Standard 2.04, Bases for Scientific and Professional Judgments.)

(b) Except as noted in 9.01c, psychologists provide opinions of the psychological characteristics of individuals only after they have conducted an examination of the individuals adequate to support their statements or conclusions. When, despite reasonable efforts, such an examination is not practical, psychologists document the efforts they made and the result of those efforts, clarify the probable impact of their limited information on the reliability and validity of their opinions, and appropriately limit the nature and extent of their conclusions or recommendations. (See also Standards 2.01, Boundaries of Competence, and 9.06, Interpreting Assessment Results.)

(c) When psychologists conduct a record review or provide consultation or supervision and an individual examination is not warranted or necessary for the opinion, psychologists explain this and the sources of information on which they based their conclusions and recommendations.

9.02 Use of Assessments

(a) Psychologists administer, adapt, score, interpret, or use assessment techniques, interviews, tests, or instruments in a manner and for purposes that are appropriate in light of the research on or evidence of the usefulness and proper application of the techniques.

(b) Psychologists use assessment instruments whose validity and reliability have been established for use with members of the population tested. When such validity or reliability has not been established, psychologists describe the strengths and limitations of test results and interpretation.

(c) Psychologists use assessment methods that are appropriate to an individual's language preference and competence, unless the use of an alternative language is relevant to the assessment issues.

9.03 Informed Consent in Assessments

(a) Psychologists obtain informed consent for assessments, evaluations, or diagnostic services, as described in Standard 3.10, Informed Consent, except when (1) testing is mandated by law or governmental regulations; (2) informed consent is implied because testing is conducted as a routine educational, institutional, or organizational activity (e.g., when participants voluntarily agree to assessment when applying for a job); or (3) one purpose of the testing is to evaluate decisional capacity. Informed consent includes an explanation of the nature and purpose of the assessment, fees, involvement of third parties, and limits of confidentiality and sufficient opportunity for the client/patient to ask questions and receive answers.

(b) Psychologists inform persons with questionable capacity to consent or for whom testing is mandated by law or governmental regulations about the nature and purpose of the proposed assessment services, using language that is reasonably understandable to the person being assessed.

(c) Psychologists using the services of an interpreter obtain informed consent from the client/patient to use that interpreter, ensure that confidentiality of test results and test security are maintained, and include in their recommendations, reports, and diagnostic or evaluative statements, including forensic testimony, discussion of any limitations on the data obtained. (See also Standards 2.05, Delegation of Work to Others; 4.01, Maintaining Confidentiality; 9.01, Bases for Assessments; 9.06, Interpreting Assessment Results; and 9.07, Assessment by Unqualified Persons.)

9.04 Release of Test Data

(a) The term test data refers to raw and scaled scores, client/patient responses to test questions or stimuli, and psychologists' notes and recordings concerning client/patient statements and behavior during an examination. Those portions of test materials that include client/patient responses are included in the definition of test data. Pursuant to a client/patient release, psychologists provide test data to the client/patient or other persons identified in the release. Psychologists may refrain from releasing test data to protect a client/patient or others from substantial harm or misuse or misrepresentation of the data or the test, recognizing that in many instances release of confidential information under these circumstances is regulated by law. (See also Standard 9.11, Maintaining Test Security.)

(b) In the absence of a client/patient release, psychologists provide test data only as required by law or court order.

9.05 Test Construction

Psychologists who develop tests and other assessment techniques use appropriate psychometric procedures and current scientific or professional knowledge for test design, standardization, validation, reduction or elimination of bias, and recommendations for use.

9.06 Interpreting Assessment Results

When interpreting assessment results, including automated interpretations, psychologists take into account the purpose of the assessment as well as the various test factors, test-taking abilities, and other characteristics of the person being assessed, such as situational, personal, linguistic, and cultural differences, that might affect psychologists' judgments or reduce the accuracy of their interpretations. They indicate any significant limitations of their interpretations. (See also Standards 2.01b and c,

Boundaries of Competence, and 3.01, Unfair Discrimination.)

9.07 Assessment by Unqualified Persons

Psychologists do not promote the use of psychological assessment techniques by unqualified persons, except when such use is conducted for training purposes with appropriate supervision. (See also Standard 2.05, Delegation of Work to Others.)

9.08 Obsolete Tests and Outdated Test Results

(a) Psychologists do not base their assessment or intervention decisions or recommendations on data or test results that are outdated for the current purpose.

(b) Psychologists do not base such decisions or recommendations on tests and measures that are obsolete and not useful for the current purpose.

9.09 Test Scoring and Interpretation Services

(a) Psychologists who offer assessment or scoring services to other professionals accurately describe the purpose, norms, validity, reliability, and applications of the procedures and any special qualifications applicable to their use.

(b) Psychologists select scoring and interpretation services (including automated services) on the basis of evidence of the validity of the program and procedures as well as on other appropriate considerations. (See also Standard 2.01b and c, Boundaries of Competence.)

(c) Psychologists retain responsibility for the appropriate application, interpretation, and use of assessment instruments, whether they score and interpret such tests themselves or use automated or other services.

9.10 Explaining Assessment Results

Regardless of whether the scoring and interpretation are done by psychologists, by employees or assistants, or by automated or other outside services, psychologists take reasonable steps to ensure that explanations of results are given to the individual or designated representative unless the nature of the relationship precludes provision of an explanation of results (such as in some organizational consulting, preemployment or security screenings, and forensic evaluations), and this fact has been clearly explained to the person being assessed in advance.

9.11. Maintaining Test Security

The term test materials refers to manuals, instruments, protocols, and test questions or stimuli and does not include test data as defined in Standard 9.04, Release of Test Data. Psychologists make reasonable efforts to maintain the integrity and security of test materials and other assessment techniques consistent with law and contractual obligations, and in a manner that permits adherence to this Ethics Code.

10. THERAPY

10.01 Informed Consent to Therapy

(a) When obtaining informed consent to therapy as required in Standard 3.10, Informed Consent, psychologists inform clients/patients as early as is feasible in the therapeutic relationship about the nature and anticipated course of therapy, fees, involvement of third parties, and limits of confidentiality and provide sufficient opportunity for the client/patient to ask questions and receive answers. (See also Standards 4.02, Discussing the Limits of Confidentiality, and 6.04, Fees and Financial Arrangements.)

(b) When obtaining informed consent for treatment for which generally recognized techniques and procedures have not been established, psychologists inform their clients/patients of the developing nature of the treatment, the potential risks involved, alternative treatments that may be available, and the voluntary nature of their participation. (See also Standards 2.01e, Boundaries of Competence, and 3.10, Informed Consent.)

(c) When the therapist is a trainee and the legal responsibility for the treatment provided resides with the supervisor, the client/patient, as part of the informed consent procedure, is informed that the therapist is in training and is being supervised and is given the name of the supervisor.

10.02 Therapy Involving Couples or Families

(a) When psychologists agree to provide services to several persons who have a relationship (such as spouses, significant others, or parents and children), they take reasonable steps to clarify at the outset (1) which of the individuals are clients/patients and (2) the relationship the psychologist will have with each person. This clarification includes the psychologist's role and the probable uses of the services provided or the information obtained. (See also Standard 4.02, Discussing the Limits of Confidentiality.)

(b) If it becomes apparent that psychologists may be called on to perform potentially conflicting roles (such as family therapist and then witness for one party in divorce proceedings), psychologists take reasonable steps to clarify and modify, or withdraw from, roles appropriately. (See also Standard 3.05c, Multiple Relationships.)

10.03 Group Therapy

When psychologists provide services to several persons in a group setting, they describe at the outset the roles and responsibilities of all parties and the limits of confidentiality.

10.04 Providing Therapy to Those Served by Others

In deciding whether to offer or provide services to those already receiving mental health services elsewhere, psychologists carefully consider the treatment issues and the potential client's/patient's welfare. Psychologists discuss these issues with the client/patient or another legally authorized person on behalf of the client/patient in order to minimize the risk of confusion and conflict, consult with the other service providers when appropriate, and proceed with caution and sensitivity to the therapeutic issues.

10.05 Sexual Intimacies With Current Therapy Clients/Patients

Psychologists do not engage in sexual intimacies with current therapy clients/patients.

10.06 Sexual Intimacies With Relatives or Significant Others of Current Therapy Clients/Patients

Psychologists do not engage in sexual intimacies with individuals they know to be close relatives, guardians, or significant others of current clients/patients. Psychologists do not terminate therapy to circumvent this standard.

10.07 Therapy With Former Sexual Partners

Psychologists do not accept as therapy clients/patients persons with whom they have engaged in sexual intimacies.

10.08 Sexual Intimacies With Former Therapy Clients/Patients

(a) Psychologists do not engage in sexual intimacies with former clients/patients for at least two years after cessation or termination of therapy.

(b) Psychologists do not engage in sexual intimacies with former clients/patients even after a two-year interval except in the most unusual circumstances. Psychologists who engage in such activity after the two years following cessation or termination of therapy and of having no sexual contact with the former client/patient bear the burden of demonstrating that there has been no exploitation, in light of all relevant factors, including (1) the amount of time that has passed since therapy terminated; (2) the nature, duration, and intensity of the therapy; (3) the circumstances of termination; (4) the client's/patient's personal history; (5) the client's/patient's current mental status; (6) the likelihood of adverse impact on the client/patient; and (7) any statements or actions made by the therapist during the course of therapy suggesting or inviting the possibility of a posttermination sexual or romantic relationship with the client/patient. (See also Standard 3.05, Multiple Relationships.)

10.09 Interruption of Therapy

When entering into employment or contractual relationships, psychologists make reasonable efforts to provide for orderly and appropriate resolution of responsibility for client/patient care in the event that the employment or contractual relationship ends, with paramount consideration given to the welfare of the client/patient. (See also Standard 3.12, Interruption of Psychological Services.)

10.10 Terminating Therapy

(a) Psychologists terminate therapy when it becomes reasonably clear that the client/patient no longer needs the service, is not likely to benefit, or is being harmed by continued service.

(b) Psychologists may terminate therapy when threatened or otherwise endangered by the client/patient or another person with whom the client/patient has a relationship.

(c) Except where precluded by the actions of clients/patients or third-party payors, prior to termination psychologists provide pretermination counseling and suggest alternative service providers as appropriate.

ETHICS

GLOSSARY

Glossary

This glossary contains terms you need to understand as you study psychology. After each term there is a brief definition or explanation of the term as it is used in *Holt Psychology: Principles in Practice.* The page number refers to the page on which the term is introduced in the textbook.

Phonetic Respelling and Pronunciation Guide

Many of the key terms in this textbook have been respelled to help you pronounce them. The letter combinations used in the respellings throughout the narrative are explained in the following phonetic respelling and pronunciation guide. The guide is adapted from *Merriam-Webster's Tenth New Collegiate Dictionary, Merriam-Webster's New Geographical Dictionary,* and *Merriam-Webster's New Biographical Dictionary.*

MARK	AS IN	RESPELLING	EXAMPLE
a	alphabet	a	*AL-fuh-bet
ā	Asia	ay	AY-zhuh
ä	cart, top	ah	KAHRT, TAHP
e	let, ten	e	LET, TEN
ē	even, leaf	ee	EE-vuhn, LEEF
i	it, tip, British	i	IT, TIP, BRIT-ish
ī	site, buy, Ohio	y	SYT, BY, oh-HY-oh
	iris	eye	EYE-ris
k	card	k	KAHRD
ō	over, rainbow	oh	oh-vuhr, RAYN-boh
ù	book, wood	ooh	BOOHK, WOOHD
ò	all, orchid	aw	AWL, AWR-kid
òi	foil, coin	oy	FOYL, KOYN
aù	out	ow	OWT
ə	cup, butter	uh	KUHP, BUHT-uhr
ü	rule, food	oo	ROOL, FOOD
yü	few	yoo	FYOO
zh	vision	zh	VIZH-uhn

*A syllable printed in small capital letters receives heavier emphasis than the other syllable(s) in a word.

absolute threshold   the smallest amount of a particular stimulus that can be detected, **78**

accommodation   the process of adjusting existing ways of thinking to encompass new information, ideas, or objects, **241**

acculturation   the process of adapting to a new or different culture, **339**

achievement   knowledge and skills gained from experience and education, **206**

achievement motivation   the desire to persevere with work and to avoid distraction in order to reach personal goals, **308**

achievement test   test that measures the amount of knowledge one has in specific academic areas, **347**

active coping   a response to a stressor that reduces stress by changing the situation to eliminate or lessen the negative effects of the stressor, **403**

active listening   empathic listening in which the listener acknowledges, restates, and clarifies the speaker's thoughts and concerns, **444**

actor-observer bias   the tendency to attribute one's own behavior to situational factors but to attribute the behavior of others to dispositional factors, **470**

addiction   a compulsive need for and use of a habit-forming substance, **116**

adolescent growth spurt a sudden, brief burst of physical growth during which adolescents typically make great gains in height and weight, **252**

affiliation the desire to join with others and to be a part of something larger than oneself, **310**

afterimage the visual sensation that occurs after the original stimulus has been removed, **84**

agoraphobia a fear of crowded, public places, **416**

algorithm a problem-solving strategy that eventually leads to a solution; usually involves trying random solutions to a problem in a systematic way, **179**

altered state of consciousness a type of consciousness other than normal waking consciousness, **106**

altruism unselfish regard for the welfare of others, **494**

Alzheimer's disease an irreversible, progressive brain disorder characterized by the deterioration of memory, language, and eventually, physical functioning, **287**

amphetamine a type of stimulant often used to stay awake or to reduce appetite, **118**

anchoring heuristic the process of making decisions based on certain ideas or standards held by the decision maker, **193**

anorexia nervosa an eating disorder characterized by extreme weight loss due to self-starvation, **265**

anterograde amnesia the inability to form new memories because of brain trauma, **170**

antianxiety drug a type of medication that relieves anxiety disorders and panic disorders by depressing the activity of the central nervous system, **451**

antidepressant drug a type of medication used to treat major depression by increasing the amount of one or both of the neurotransmitters noradrenaline and serotonin, **452**

antipsychotic drug a type of medication used to reduce agitation, delusions, and hallucinations by blocking the activity of dopamine in the brain; also called a major tranquilizer, **452**

anxiety a psychological state characterized by tension and apprehension, foreboding, and dread, **415**

approach-approach conflict a type of conflict involving a choice between two positive but mutually exclusive options, **388**

approach-avoidance conflict a type of conflict involving a single goal that has both positive and negative aspects, **390**

aptitude test a test that is designed to predict a person's future performance or capacity to learn, **348**

archetypes original models from which later forms develop; in Jung's personality theory, archetypes are primitive images or concepts that reside in the collective unconscious, **330**

assimilation the process by which new information is placed into pre-existing categories, **241**

association areas areas of the cerebral cortex that are involved in such mental operations as thinking, memory, learning, and problem solving, **63**

associationism a learned connection between two ideas or events, **12**

attachment an active and intense emotional relationship between two people that endures over time, **234**

attitude an enduring belief about people, places, or objects that evokes certain feelings and influences behavior, **460**

attraction in social psychology, an attitude of liking (positive attraction) or disliking (negative attraction), **472**

attribution theory the suggestion that there is a tendency to explain a person's behavior in terms of the situation or the person's personality, **468**

auditory nerve the cranial nerve that carries sound from the cochlea of the inner ear to the brain, **86**

authoritarian a leadership or parenting style that stresses unquestioning obedience, **237**

authoritarian leader a leader who makes decisions for the group and tells other group members what to do, **484**

authoritative a leadership or parenting style based on recognized authority or knowledge and characterized by mutual respect, **237**

autonomic nervous system the subdivision of the peripheral nervous system that regulates body functions, such as respiration and digestion, **58**

availability heuristic the tendency to make decisions on the basis of information that is available in one's immediate consciousness, **193**

aversive conditioning a type of counterconditioning that links an unpleasant state with an unwanted behavior in an attempt to eliminate the behavior, **449**

avoidance-avoidance conflict a type of conflict involving a choice between two negative or undesirable options, **390**

axon a long tubelike structure attached to a neuron that transmits impulses away from the neuron cell body, **55**

axon terminals small fibers branching out from an axon, **55**

𝕭

balance theory the view that people have a need to organize their perceptions, opinions, and beliefs in a manner that is in harmony with those of the people around them, **309**

basic research research that is conducted for its own sake, that is, without seeking a solution to a specific problem, **10**

behavior observable and measurable actions of people and animals, **4**

behaviorism   the school of psychology, founded by John Watson, that defines psychology as the scientific study of observable behavior, **14**

behavior-rating scales   systematic means of recording the frequency with which certain behaviors occur, **344**

bereaved   suffering from the death of a loved one, **293**

bias   a predisposition to a certain point of view, **33**

binocular cues   visual cues for depth that require the use of both eyes, **96**

biofeedback   a system for monitoring and feeding back information about certain biological processes, such as blood pressure, **112**

biological perspective   the psychological perspective that stresses the influence of biology on behavior, **18**

bipolar disorder   a disorder in which a person's mood inappropriately alternates between extremes of elation and depression, **423**

blind spot   the part of the retina that contains no photoreceptors, **83**

bulimia nervosa   an eating disorder in which enormous quantities of food are consumed and then purged by means of laxatives or self-induced vomiting, **265**

bystander effect   the tendency for a person to be less likely to give aid if other bystanders are present, **495**

C

case study   an in-depth study of a single person or group to reveal some universal principle, **35**

catatonic stupor   an immobile, expressionless, coma-like state associated with schizophrenia, **426**

catharsis   in psychology, the release of aggressive energy through action or fantasy, **491**

cell body   the part of a neuron that produces the energy needed for the activity of the cell, **55**

cellular damage theories   the view that aging occurs because body cells lose the capacity to reproduce and maintain themselves as a result of damage, **285**

central nervous system   the part of the nervous system that consists of the brain and spinal cord, **54**

central route   a method of persuasion that uses evidence and logical arguments to influence people, **463**

cerebellum   the area of the brain that is responsible for voluntary movement and balance, **60**

cerebral cortex   the wrinkled, convoluted surface of the brain; the body's control and information-processing center, **61**

cerebrum   the large mass of the forebrain, consisting of two hemispheres, **61**

childhood   the stage of life that follows infancy and spans the period from the second birthday to the beginning of adolescence, **231**

chromosome   a microscopic threadlike structure in the nucleus of every living cell; it contains genes, the basic units of heredity, **70**

chunking   a mental process for organizing information into meaningful units, or "chunks," **162**

circadian rhythm   a regular sequence of biological processes, such as temperature and sleep, that occurs every 24 hours, **106**

classical conditioning   a type of learning in which a neutral stimulus comes to elicit an unconditioned response when that neutral stimulus is repeatedly paired with a stimulus that normally causes an unconditioned response, **128**

clique   a small, exclusive group of people, **258**

closure   the tendency to perceive a complete or whole figure despite gaps in sensory information, **93**

cochlea   the fluid-filled structure of the inner ear that transmits sound impulses to the auditory nerve, **86**

cognitive activities   private, unobservable mental processes such as sensation, perception, thought, and problem solving, **4**

cognitive anchors   early attitudes and persistent beliefs that shape how people see and interpret the world, **461**

cognitive consistency   the state in which a person's thoughts and behaviors match his or her beliefs and the expectations of others, **309**

cognitive-dissonance theory   the theory that suggests that people make attitudinal changes to reduce the tension that occurs when their thoughts and attitudes are inconsistent with their actions, **310**

cognitive evaluation   the process whereby the formation of beliefs or attitudes and motivation of behaviors is based on one's evaluation of evidence, **461**

cognitive perspective   the viewpoint that stresses that thought processes largely determine behavior, **18**

cognitive restructuring   a coping method whereby one changes one's thoughts in particular situations, **359**

collective unconscious   Jung's concept of a shared, inherited body of memory that all humans have, **330**

commitment   a pledge or promise, **475**

common fate   the tendency to perceive objects that are moving together as belonging together, **94**

complementary   the colors across from each other on the color circle, **84**

compulsion   an apparently irresistible urge to repeat an act or engage in ritualistic behavior, **416**

concept   a mental structure used to categorize objects, people, or events that share similar characteristics, **178**

concrete-operational stage   according to Piaget, the stage of cognitive development during which children acquire the ability to think logically, **243**

conditional positive regard an expression of esteem given only when an individual has exhibited suitable behavior, **240**

conditioned response a learned response to a previously neutral stimulus, **130**

conditioned stimulus a previously neutral stimulus that, because of pairing with an unconditioned stimulus, now causes a conditioned response, **130**

conditioning a type of learning that involves stimulus-response connections, in which the response is conditional on the stimulus, **128**

conductive deafness hearing loss caused by damage to the middle ear, thus interfering with the transmission of sound waves to the cochlea, **87**

confirmation bias the tendency to look for information that confirms one's preconceived notions, **190**

conform to change one's attitudes or behavior in accordance with generally accepted standards, **484**

congruence agreement; in psychology, consistency between one's self-concept and one's experience, **335**

consciousness awareness of oneself and one's environment, **103**

conservation according to Piaget, the principle that the properties of substances remain the same despite changes in their shape or arrangement, **242**

construct a concept or idea, which is assumed to be real but cannot be seen or measured directly, **26**

contact comfort the satisfaction obtained from pleasant, soft stimulation, **234**

context-dependent memories information that is more easily retrieved in the context in which it was encoded and stored, **159**

continuity the perceptual tendency to group stimuli into continuous patterns, **94**

continuous reinforcement the reinforcement of a desired response every time it occurs, **139**

control group in an experiment, the group that does not receive the treatment, **41**

controlled experiment an experiment that uses both a control group and an experimental group to determine whether the independent variable influences behavior and, if so, how it does so, **41**

conventional moral reasoning the level of moral development at which a person makes judgments based on conventional standards of right and wrong, **246**

convergent thinking thinking that is limited to available facts, **187**

corpus callosum the nerve fibers that connect the left and right hemispheres of the cerebral cortex, **61**

correlation the relationship between variables, **39**

counterconditioning a therapy procedure based on classical conditioning that replaces a negative response to a stimulus with a positive response, **135**

creativity the ability to invent new solutions to problems or to create original or ingenious materials, **216**

critical period a stage or point in development during which a person or animal is best suited to learn a particular skill or behavior, **229**

cross-linking a possible cause of aging in which proteins within a cell bind together, toughening body tissues and eventually leading to the breakdown of various bodily processes, **286**

cross-sectional method a method of research that looks at different age groups at the same time in order to understand changes that occur during the life span, **36**

crowd large groups of people who share attitudes and a group identity, **258**

culture-bound syndrome clusters of symptoms that define or describe an illness in a particular culture, **411**

decay disintegration; in psychology, the fading away of memory, **169**

deductive reasoning a form of thinking in which conclusions are inferred from premises; the conclusions are true if the premises are true, **189**

defense mechanisms psychological distortions used to remain psychologically stable or in balance, **326**

defensive coping a response to a stressor that temporarily reduces stress but may be harmful in the long run because it neither changes the situation nor removes the stressor, **403**

delusion an erroneous belief, as of persecution or grandeur, that may accompany certain psychotic disorders, **120**

dementia a serious loss of cognitive function, **286**

democratic leader a leader who encourages group members to express and discuss their ideas and to make their own decisions, **484**

dendrites the branchlike extensions of a neuron that receive impulses and conduct them toward the cell, **55**

denial a defense mechanism in which the individual refuses to admit that a problem exists, **327**

dependent variable in an experiment, the factor that is being measured and that may change in response to manipulations of the independent variable, **41**

depersonalization a dissociative disorder characterized by persistent feelings that one is unreal or is detached from one's own experiences or body, **421**

depressant a drug that reduces neural activity and slows body functions, **117**

depression a psychological disorder characterized by extreme sadness, an inability to concentrate, and feelings of helplessness and dejection, **423**

detoxification   the removal of a poisonous or otherwise harmful substance, such as alcohol or other drugs, from the body, **121**

developmental psychology   the branch of psychology that studies the physical, cognitive, and social changes that occur throughout the life cycle, **228**

difference reduction   a problem-solving method that involves reducing the difference between the present situation and the desired one, **182**

difference threshold   the minimum difference that an individual can detect between two stimuli, **78**

diffusion of responsibility   the sharing of responsibility for a decision or behavior among the members of a group, **480**

discrimination   (1) in classical conditioning, the ability to distinguish the conditioned stimulus from other stimuli that are similar, **133**; (2) unfair treatment of a person or group based on prejudice, **465**

displacement   the defense mechanism that shifts negative impulses toward a more acceptable object or person, **326**

dissociation   a split in consciousness, **420**

distress   stress that is damaging or negative, **386**

divergent thinking   a thought process that attempts to generate multiple solutions to a problem, **187**

double-blind study   an experiment in which neither the participant nor the researcher knows whether the participant has received the treatment or the placebo, **43**

dream analysis   a technique used by psychoanalysts to interpret the content of patients' dreams, **441**

drives   conditions of arousal or tension within an organism that motivate the organism; usually associated with a need, **300**

E

echoic memory   the sensory register in which traces of sounds are held and may be retrieved within several seconds, **161**

ego   in psychoanalytic theory, the personality component that is conscious and that controls behavior, **325**

egocentrism   in Piaget's theory, the inability of the preoperational child to understand another's point of view, **243**

ego integrity   according to Erikson, a strong sense of identity during late adulthood that is characterized by the wisdom to accept the fact that life is limited, **288**

eidetic imagery   the maintenance of a very detailed visual memory over several months, **161**

elaborative rehearsal   a memory device that creates a meaningful link between new information and the information already known, **157**

electroconvulsive therapy   a radical treatment for psychological disorders that involves passing an electric current through the brain of an anesthetized patient, **452**

emotions   states of feeling that involve physical arousal, expressive behaviors, and conscious experience, **311**

emotional appeal   a type of persuasive communication that influences behavior on the basis of feelings rather than on an analysis of the issues, **464**

empty-nest syndrome   a sense of depression and a loss of purpose that some parents experience when the youngest child leaves home, **282**

encoding   the translation of information into a form that can be stored in memory, **156**

encounter group   a structured group that aims to foster self-awareness by focusing on how group members relate to one another in a setting that encourages frank expression of feelings, **440**

endocrine system   the glands that secrete hormones into the bloodstream, **67**

episodic memory   a memory of a specific experienced event, **154**

ethics   rules and standards for proper and responsible behavior, **44**

ethnic group   a group united by cultural heritage, race, language, or common history, **21**

eustress   stress that is positive or motivating, **386**

euthanasia   the act of killing or enabling the death of a hopelessly sick or injured individual in a relatively painless way; also called mercy killing, **292**

evaluation apprehension   concern that others are judging one's performance, **480**

evolutionary perspective   the theory focusing on the evolution of behavior and mental processes, **18**

experiment   a controlled scientific procedure to determine whether certain variables manipulated by the researcher have an effect on other variables, **40**

experimental group   in a study, the participants who receive the treatment, **41**

explicit memory   a memory of specific information, **155**

explicit norms   spoken or written rules of social behavior, such as traffic rules, **485**

extinction   in classical conditioning, the disappearance of a conditioned response when an unconditioned stimulus no longer follows a conditioned stimulus, **131**

extrinsic rewards   something external given in response to the attainment of a goal, such as good grades, **309**

GLOSSARY

extrovert a person who tends to be active and self-expressive and to gain energy from interaction with others, **322**

F

first-shift scheme situation in which one person changes his or her mind to break a deadlock, **481**

flashbulb memories clear memories of emotionally significant moments or events, **154**

flooding based on the principles of classical conditioning, a fear-reduction technique that involves exposing the individual to a harmless stimulus until fear responses to that stimulus are extinguished, **133**

foot-in-the-door effect the tendency for people to comply with a large request after they have agreed to smaller requests, **489**

forced-choice format a method of presenting test questions that requires a respondent to select one of several possible answers, **349**

formal-operational stage according to Piaget, the stage of cognitive development during which people begin to think logically about abstract concepts, **244**

framing effect the influence of wording, or the way in which information is presented, on decision making, **194**

free association in psychoanalysis, the uncensored uttering of all thoughts that come to mind, **441**

free radical an unstable molecule present in the human body that is thought by some scientists to be a cause of aging, **285**

functional fixedness a barrier to problem solving that involves the tendency to think of objects only in terms of their common uses, **187**

functionalism the school of psychology, founded by William James, that emphasizes the purposes of behavior and mental processes, **13**

fundamental attribution error a bias in social perception characterized by the tendency to assume that others generally act on the basis of their dispositions, even when there is evidence suggesting the importance of their situations, **470**

G

gate theory the suggestion that only a certain amount of information can be processed by the nervous system at a given time, **91**

gender classifications of sex, based on mostly nonbiological traits such as physical structure and appearance, **364**

gender roles the differing sets of behaviors that a culture considers appropriate for males or females, **364**

gender schema the set of traits and behaviors by which a child learns to classify male and female gender roles and by which the child models and measures his or her own relation to those roles, **376**

gender stereotypes oversimplified generalizations about the characteristics of males and females, **365**

gender typing the process by which people learn to conform to gender roles, **372**

genes the basic building blocks of heredity, **70**

general adaptation syndrome (GAS) the three-stage sequence of behavior in response to stress, consisting of an alarm reaction, a resistance stage, and an exhaustion stage, **395**

generalization the tendency to respond in the same way to stimuli that have similar characteristics, **132**

generativity according to Erikson, the ability to create, originate, and produce throughout adulthood, **280**

Gestalt psychology the school of psychology that emphasizes the tendency to organize perceptions into meaningful wholes, **16**

gifted a term used to describe children with IQ scores above 130 or children with outstanding talent for performing at much higher levels than others of the same age and background, **216**

group polarization the strengthening of a group's shared attitudes over time, **482**

H

hallucination a false sensory perception that occurs in the absence of any actual stimulus, **120**

hallucinogen a psychedelic drug, such as LSD, that distorts perceptions and evokes sensory images in the absence of actual sensory input, **120**

heredity the genetic transmission of traits from one generation to the next, **69**

heritability the proportion of variation among individuals that can be attributed to genes, **219**

heuristic a strategy for making judgments and solving problems, **181**

homeostasis an internal balance or equilibrium that is achieved through adjustments of the nervous system, **301**

hormones chemicals produced by the endocrine glands that regulate specific body functions, **67**

hospice a type of care for terminally ill patients; an organization that provides such care, **292**

humanistic perspective the psychological view that assumes the existence of the self and emphasizes the importance of self-awareness and the freedom to make choices, **19**

humanistic therapy a treatment method based on the assumption that most people are basically good and have a natural tendency to strive for self-actualization, **444**

hypnosis   a condition in which people appear to be highly suggestible and to behave as if they are in a trance, **113**

hypothalamus   the neural structure located below the thalamus that controls temperature, hunger, thirst, and various aspects of emotion, **61**

hypothesis   a prediction or assumption about behavior that is tested through scientific research, **26**

iconic memory   the sensory register that briefly holds mental images of visual stimuli, **161**

id   in psychoanalytic theory, the reservoir of unconscious psychic energy that strives to satisfy basic sexual and aggressive drives, **325**

identification   in psychoanalytic theory, the process by which children adopt the values of their parents, **328**

identity achievement   a stage in identity development in which a person has committed to an occupational direction and made decisions about important life questions, **262**

identity crisis   a period of inner conflict during which one examines one's values and makes decisions about one's life direction, **260**

identity diffusion   the constant search for meaning and identity without committing oneself to a set of personal beliefs or an occupational path, **262**

identity foreclosure   the act of making a commitment based on other's values in order to avoid an identity crisis, **262**

identity moratorium   a period of time in the development of identity in which a person delays making a decision about important issues but actively explores various alternatives, **262**

identity status   according to Marcia, one of four reaction patterns or processes in the development of identity during adolescence, **262**

imbalance   a state in which people who have strong feelings about each other disagree on a major issue, **310**

implicit memory   a memory that consists of the skills and procedures one has learned, **155**

implicit norms   unspoken, unwritten standards of behavior for a group of people, **485**

imprinting   the process by which animals form strong attachments during a critical period very early in life, **235**

incubation effect   the tendency to arrive at a solution after a period of time away from the problem, **185**

independent variable   the factor that is manipulated by the researcher to determine its effect on another variable, **41**

inductive reasoning   a form of thinking that involves using individual cases or particular facts to reach a general conclusion, **190**

infancy   in humans, the stage of life from birth to age two, **231**

infantile amnesia   the inability to remember events that occurred during one's early years (before age three), **169**

inferiority complex   according to Adler, feelings of inadequacy and insecurity that serve as a central source of motivation, **330**

informed consent   an agreement by an individual to participate in research after receiving information about the purpose of the study and the nature of the treatment, **46**

insomnia   a sleep disorder characterized by recurring problems in falling asleep or staying asleep, **110**

instincts   complex, unlearned behaviors that are present throughout a species, **300**

intelligence   the capacity to learn from experience, solve problems, and adapt to a changing environment, **206**

intelligence quotient   the ratio of mental age to chronological age multiplied by 100; the average performance for a given age is assigned a score of 100, **212**

interference   the process that occurs when new information appears in short-term memory and replaces what was already there, **163**

intimacy   feelings of closeness and concern for another person, **474**

intoxication   a state of drunkenness characterized by impaired coordination and judgment, **117**

intrinsic rewards   internal rewards, such as self-satisfaction, that are given in response to the attainment of a goal, **309**

introspection   an examination of one's own thoughts and feelings, **12**

introvert   a person who tends to be more interested in his or her own thoughts and feelings than in what is going on around him or her, **322**

juvenile delinquency   a violation of the law committed by a child or adolescent, **268**

K

kinesthesis   the sense that provides information about the position and movement of individual body parts, **92**

L

laboratory observation   the study of behavior in a controlled situation, **37**

laissez-faire leader   a leader who stands back from decision making and allows group members to explore and express their own ideas, **484**

language the communication of ideas through sounds and symbols that are arranged according to the rules of grammar, **195**

language acquisition device according to Chomsky, the inborn ability of humans to acquire language, **199**

latent content according to Freud, the hidden meaning of a dream, **441**

latent learning learning that occurs but remains hidden until there is a need to use it, **145**

lateralization the development, prior to birth, of the tendencies of the brain's left and right hemispheres to specialize in certain functions, **372**

learning goals achievements that are motivated by the desire to enhance one's knowledge and skills, **309**

learning perspective the psychological point of view that emphasizes the effects of experience on behavior, **20**

lens the transparent structure of the eye that focuses light on the retina, **81**

limbic system a group of neural structures at the base of the cerebral hemispheres that is associated with emotion and motivation, **61**

lithium a chemical used to treat the mood swings of bipolar disorder, **452**

living wills legal documents in which the signer requests to be allowed to die rather than be kept alive by artificial means if disabled beyond a reasonable expectation of recovery, **293**

longitudinal method a type of research in which the same people are studied over a long time period, **36**

long-term memory the type or stage of memory capable of large and relatively permanent storage, **163**

𝓜

maintenance rehearsal the repetition of new information in an attempt to keep from forgetting it, **157**

majority-wins scheme in group decision making, an agreement initially supported by a majority of the group members and then agreed to by all, **481**

mania a mood characterized by extreme elation and hyperactivity, **424**

manifest content according to Freud, the apparent and remembered content of a dream, **441**

matching hypothesis the view that people tend to choose other people similar to themselves in attractiveness and attitudes in the formation of interpersonal relationships, **473**

maturation developmental changes that occur as a result of automatic, genetically determined signals, **229**

means-end analysis a heuristic device in which a solution to a problem is found by evaluating the difference between the current situation and the goal, **183**

meditation a systematic narrowing of attention that slows the metabolism and helps produce feelings of relaxation, **112**

medulla a structure at the base of the brain stem that controls vital functions such as heartbeat and breathing, **59**

memory the processes by which information is encoded, stored, and retrieved, **154**

menarche a female's first menstrual period, **254**

menopause the cessation of menstruation; also, the biological changes that a woman experiences during the years of her declining ability to reproduce, **283**

mental age the level of intellectual functioning, which is compared to chronological age to give an IQ, **211**

mental retardation intellectual functioning that is below average, as indicated by an intelligence score at or below 70, **215**

mental set the tendency to approach a new problem in a way that has been successful in the past, **186**

midlife crisis a turning point experienced by many people between ages 45 to 65, when they realize that life may be half over and they feel trapped in meaningless life roles, **281**

midlife transition a period in middle adulthood when a person's perspective on his or her life may change significantly, **280**

migraine headache a headache characterized by sudden onset and severe throbbing pain on one side of the head, **399**

modeling the process of learning behavior through the observation and imitation of others, **374**

monocular cues cues for distance that may be available to either eye alone, **95**

morpheme the smallest meaningful unit of language, such as a prefix or suffix, **195**

motive a need or desire that energizes and directs behavior, **300**

multiple approach-avoidance conflict a conflict involving a choice between two or more options, each of which has both positive and negative aspects, **390**

myelin a white, fatty substance that insulates axons and enables rapid transmission of neural impulses, **55**

𝓝

narcolepsy an uncommon sleep disorder characterized by brief attacks of REM sleep, often at inopportune moments, **112**

narcotic a type of drug that dulls the senses, relieves pain, and induces sleep; the term is usually reserved for those drugs derived from the opium poppy plant, **117**

naturalistic observation the study of behavior in naturally occurring situations without manipulation or control on the part of the observer, **36**

need the biological or psychological requirements for the well-being of an organism, **300**

negative correlation an unpleasant stimulus between two variables in which one variable increases as the other variable decreases, **39**

negative reinforcer an unpleasant stimulus that increases the frequency of behavior when it is removed, **137**

neuron a nerve cell; the basic building block of the nervous system, **54**

neurotransmitter a chemical messenger that carries impulses across the synaptic gaps between neurons, **56**

night terror a sleep disorder characterized by high arousal and apparent terror; unlike nightmares, night terrors are seldom remembered, **111**

nonbalance in balance theory, a condition in which people who dislike each other or have no feeling for each other feel indifferent if they disagree, **310**

nonconscious descriptive of bodily processes, such as the growing of hair, of which we are not aware, **105**

nondirective therapy a type of therapy in which the client rather than the therapist is encouraged to take the lead, **444**

norm an established standard of performance or behavior, **347**

norm group a group of test takers whose scores establish the norm for a particular test, **347**

nurturance loving care and attention, **368**

obese a condition characterized by excessive body fat, **304**

objective test a test that has a group of standardized test items and specific answers that are considered to be correct, **350**

object permanence the awareness that people and objects continue to exist even when they cannot be perceived, **242**

observational learning learning by observing and imitating the behavior of others, **146**

obsession a recurring thought or image that seems to be beyond control, **416**

olfactory nerve the nerve that transmits information about odors from olfactory receptors to the brain, **89**

open-ended format a testing format that is open to the respondent's interpretations, often used with projective tests, **352**

operant conditioning learning that is strengthened when behavior is followed by positive reinforcement, **135**

opponent-process theory according to Solomon, the idea that an intense emotion often is followed by its opposite, **314**

overregularization the formation of plurals and the past tense of irregular nouns and verbs according to rules of grammar that apply to regular nouns and verbs; characteristic of the speech of young children, **199**

panic attack an episode of intense dread in which a person experiences terror or frightening sensations such as chest pain, rapid heartbeat, or choking, **416**

partial reinforcement a type of conditioned learning in which only some of the responses are reinforced, **140**

passion a feeling of romantic or sexual attraction, **475**

patriarchy a social organization marked by the supremacy of males in the clan or family, **276**

perception the process of organizing and interpreting sensory information, **78**

performance goals achievements motivated by a concrete, external reward, **308**

peripheral nervous system the neurons that connect the central nervous system to the rest of the body, including the muscles and glands, **54**

peripheral route a method of persuasion characterized by an emphasis on factors other than the message itself, **463**

personality the pattern of feelings, thoughts, and behavior that sets people apart from one another, **321**

person-centered therapy a humanistic therapy, developed by Carl Rogers, in which the therapist creates an accepting, empathic environment to facilitate the client's growth, **444**

persuasion the attempt to influence people's attitudes and choices through argument, entreaty, or explanation, **462**

phobia an excessive, irrational fear out of proportion to the actual danger, **415**

phoneme the basic sound unit in spoken language, **195**

photoreceptors neurons that respond to light, **83**

placebo an inert substance used in controlled experiments to test the effectiveness of another substance, **42**

pons a brain structure located at the top of the brain stem that is involved in respiration, movement, and sleep, **59**

positive correlation a relationship between variables in which one variable increases as the other variable also increases, **39**

positive reinforcers encouraging stimuli that increase the frequency of a behavior when they are presented, **137**

postconventional moral reasoning according to Kohlberg, a level of moral development during which moral judgments are derived from a person's own moral standards, **246**

posthypnotic suggestion instructions given to a person under hypnosis that are supposed to be carried out after the hypnosis session has ended, **116**

post-traumatic stress disorder a disorder that follows a distressing event outside the range of normal human experience and is characterized by intense fear, avoidance of stimuli associated with the event, and reliving of the event, **417**

preconscious descriptive of information that is not conscious but is retrievable into conscious awareness, **105**

preconventional moral reasoning according to Kohlberg, a level of moral development in which moral judgments are based on fear of punishment or desire for pleasure, **246**

prefrontal lobotomy a radical form of psychosurgery in which a section of the frontal lobe of the brain is severed or destroyed, **453**

prejudice an unjustifiable, and usually negative, attitude toward a person or group, **465**

premise a statement or assertion that serves as the basis for an argument, **189**

preoperational stage in Piaget's theory, the stage during which a child learns to use language but does not yet think logically, **242**

primacy effect (1) the tendency to recall the initial item or items in a series, **162**; (2) the tendency to form opinions of others based on first impressions, **468**

primary reinforcers stimuli, such as food or warmth, that have reinforcement value without learning, **137**

primary sex characteristics the organs that make sexual reproduction possible, such as the ovaries and testes, **253**

principle a rule or law, **6**

programmed theories the view that aging is the result of genetics, **285**

projection in psychoanalytic theory, the defense mechanism by which people attribute their own unacceptable impulses to others, **327**

projective test a psychological test that presents ambiguous stimuli designed to elicit a response that reflects the test taker's feelings, interests, and biases, **352**

prototype an original model on which others in the same category are patterned, **179**

proximity the perceptual tendency to group together visual and auditory events that are near each other, **93**

psychoanalysis the school of psychology, founded by Sigmund Freud, that emphasizes the importance of unconscious motives and conflicts as determinants of human behavior, **17**

psychoanalytic perspective the perspective that stresses the influences of unconscious forces on human behavior, **19**

psychodynamic thinking the theory that most of what fills an individual's mind is unconscious and consists of conflicting impulses, urges, and wishes, **17**

psychological constructs theoretical entities, or concepts, that enable one to discuss something that cannot be seen, touched, or measured directly, **4**

psychological disorder a pattern of behavior or a mental process that causes serious personal suffering or interferes with a person's ability to cope with everyday life, **410**

psychology the scientific study of behavior and mental processes, **4**

psychosurgery biological treatments in which specific areas or structures of the brain are removed or destroyed to change behavior, **453**

psychotherapy the application of psychological principles and techniques to influence a person's thoughts, feelings, or behaviors in an attempt to help that person overcome psychological disorders or adjust to problems in living, **436**

puberty the period of sexual maturation; the onset of one's ability to reproduce, **253**

pupil the opening in the center of the eye that adjusts to allow light to enter, **81**

R

random sample a survey population, selected by chance, which fairly represents the general population, **31**

rapid-eye-movement sleep a stage of sleep characterized by rapid eye movements and linked to dreaming; also called REM sleep, **108**

rational-emotive behavior therapy a confrontational cognitive therapy, developed by Albert Ellis, that challenges people to change false assumptions that lead to incorrect and unrealistic thinking, **447**

rationalization in psychoanalytic theory, the defense mechanism by which an individual finds justifications for unacceptable thoughts, impulses, or behaviors, **326**

reaction formation in psychoanalytic theory, a defense mechanism by which the ego unconsciously switches unacceptable impulses into their opposites, **327**

reasoning the process of drawing logical conclusions from facts and arguments, **189**

recall retrieval of learned information, **168**

recency effect (1) the tendency to recall the last item in a series, **162**; (2) the tendency for people to change their opinions of others based on recent interactions, **468**

GLOSSARY

reciprocity in interpersonal relationships, the tendency to return feelings and attitudes that are expressed about us, **474**

recognition a memory process in which one identifies objects or events that have previously been encountered, **167**

reflex an automatic, unlearned response to a sensory stimulus, **230**

regression in psychoanalytic theory, a defense mechanism by which an individual retreats to an earlier stage of development when faced with anxiety, **327**

reinforcement a stimulus or event that follows a response and increases the frequency of that response, **136**

relearning learning material a second time, usually in less time than it was originally learned, **169**

reliability the extent to which a test yields consistent results, **214**

replicate to repeat a research study, usually with different participants and in different situations, to confirm the results of the original study, **28**

representativeness heuristic the process of making decisions about a sample according to the population that the sample appears to represent, **192**

repression in psychoanalytic theory, the defense mechanism that removes anxiety-arousing thoughts, feelings, and memories from one's consciousness, **326**

resistance in psychoanalysis, a blocking from consciousness of issues that might cause anxiety, **441**

response an observable reaction to a stimulus, **128**

reticular activating system the part of the brain that is involved in attention, sleep, and arousal, **60**

retina the light-sensitive inner surface of the eye that contains the rods, cones, and neurons that process visual stimuli, **81**

retinal disparity a binocular cue for perceiving depth based on the difference between the two images of an object that the retina receives as the object moves closer or farther away, **96**

retrieval the process of recalling information from memory storage, **158**

retrograde amnesia the failure to remember events that occurred prior to physical trauma because of the effects of the trauma, **170**

risky shift the tendency to make riskier decisions as a member of a group than as an individual acting alone, **481**

S

sales resistance the ability to refuse a request or sales pitch, **464**

sample a representative segment of a target population, **31**

scapegoat a person or group unfairly blamed for the problems of others; to blame a person or group unfairly, **466**

schedule of reinforcement a timetable for when and how often reinforcement for a particular behavior occurs, **139**

schema an idea or mental framework that helps one organize and interpret information, **164**

schizophrenia a group of severe psychotic disorders characterized by distortions in thinking, perception, emotion, and behavior, **426**

secondary reinforcers stimuli that increase the probability of a response because of their association with a primary reinforcer, **137**

secondary sex characteristics sexual characteristics that are not involved in reproduction, such as the growth of facial hair in males and the rounding of hips and breasts in females, **253**

selective attention the focusing of attention on a particular stimulus, **104**

self-actualization according to Maslow, the self-motivated striving to reach one's potential, **302**

self-concept one's view of oneself as an individual, **335**

self-efficacy expectation a person's beliefs that he or she can bring about desired changes or goals through his or her own efforts, **393**

self-esteem the value or worth that people attach to themselves, **240**

self-help group a type of therapy group in which members share a common problem, such as alcoholism, **440**

self-report an interview or questionnaire in which a person reports his or her attitudes, feelings, and behaviors, **344**

self-serving bias the tendency to view one's successes as stemming from internal factors and one's failures as stemming from external factors, **470**

semantic memory a memory of general knowledge and information that can be recalled, **154**

semantics the study of meaning in language; the relationship between language and the objects depicted by the language, **196**

senile dementia a decrease in mental ability that sometimes occurs after the age of 65, **286**

sensation the stimulation of sensory receptors and the transmission of sensory information to the brain, **78**

sensorimotor stage according to Piaget, the stage during which infants know the world mostly in terms of their sensory impressions and motor activities, **242**

sensorineural deafness deafness that results from damage to the auditory nerve, **87**

sensory adaptation   the process by which an organism becomes more sensitive to stimuli that are low in magnitude and less sensitive to stimuli that are constant, **80**

sensory deprivation   a state in which there is little or no sensory stimulation, **307**

sensory memory   the immediate, initial recording of sensory information in the memory system, **160**

separation anxiety   distress that is sometimes experienced by infants when they are separated from their primary caregivers, **234**

shaping   in operant conditioning, a procedure in which reinforcement guides behavior toward closer approximations of the desired goal, **142**

short-term memory   memory that holds information briefly before it is stored or forgotten, **161**

signal-detection theory   the idea that distinguishing sensory stimuli takes into account not only the strength of the stimuli but also such elements as setting and one's physical state, mood, and attitudes, **79**

similarity   the perceptual tendency to group together elements that seem alike, **94**

simple phobia   an anxiety disorder characterized by a persistent, irrational fear of a specific object or situation, **415**

single-blind study   a study in which the participants are unaware of whether they are in the control group or the experimental group, **43**

sleep apnea   a sleep disorder in which breathing is interrupted, **111**

social decision scheme   rules for predicting the final outcome of group decision making, **481**

social facilitation   improved performance of tasks because of the presence of others, **480**

socialization   the guidance of people, especially children, into socially desirable behavior by means of verbal messages, the systematic use of rewards and punishments, and other teaching methods, **333**

social-learning theory   the theory that suggests that people have the ability to change their environments or to create new ones, **20**

social loafing   the tendency for people to exert less effort toward completing a task when they are part of a group than when they are performing the task alone, **480**

social norm   explicit and implicit rules that reflect social expectations and influence the ways in which people behave in social situations, **485**

social perception   the ways in which people form and modify their impressions of others, **468**

social phobia   an irrational fear of social situations in which one might be exposed to the close scrutiny of others, **416**

sociocultural perspective   in psychology, the perspective that focuses on the roles of ethnicity, gender, culture, and socioeconomic status in personality formation, behavior, and mental processes, **21**

somatic nervous system   the division of the peripheral nervous system that connects the central nervous system with sensory receptors, muscles, and the skin, **57**

somatization   the expression of psychological distress through physical symptoms, **421**

spinal cord   a column of nerves within the spine that transmit messages to and from the brain, **57**

spontaneous recovery   the reappearance of an extinguished conditioned response after some time has passed, **132**

standard deviation   a measure of the distance of every score to the mean, **44**

standardized tests   tests for which norms are based on the performance of a range of individuals, **344**

state-dependent memories   memories in which information is more easily retrieved when one is in the same physiological or emotional state as when the memory was originally encoded or learned, **160**

status offenses   actions that are illegal when committed by a minor, such as consuming alcohol, **269**

stimulant   a drug that increases neural activity and speeds up body functions, **118**

stimulus   a feature in the environment that is detected by an organism or that leads to a change in behavior, **128**

stimulus motives   desires for increased stimulation, **306**

storage   the maintenance of encoded information over time, **157**

stranger anxiety   the fear of strangers that infants commonly display, **234**

stratified sample   a sample drawn in such a way that known subgroups within a population are represented in proportion to their numbers in the general population, **31**

stress   the physical and mental strain a person experiences in association with demands to adapt to a challenging situation, **386**

stressor   an event or circumstance that produces stress, **386**

stroboscopic motion   a visual illusion in which the perception of motion is generated by the presentation of a series of stationary images in rapid succession, **95**

structuralism   the school of psychology, founded by Wilhelm Wundt, that maintains that conscious experience breaks down into objective sensations and subjective feelings, **13**

sublimation   in psychoanalytic theory, the defense mechanism by which people channel their socially unacceptable impulses into more acceptable activities, **327**

successive approximations   in operant conditioning, a series of behaviors that gradually become more similar to a desired behavior, **450**

superego   according to Freud, the part of personality that represents the individual's internalized ideals and provides standards for judgment, **326**

survey   a research technique for acquiring data about the attitudes or behaviors of a group of people, usually by asking questions of a representative, random sample, **29**

symbol   an object or an act that stands for something else, **178**

synapse   the junction between the axon terminals of the sending neuron and the dendrites of the receiving neuron, **55**

syntax   the ways in which words and phrases are arranged into grammatical sentences, **195**

systematic desensitization   a type of counterconditioning, used to treat phobias, in which a pleasant, relaxed state is associated with gradually increasing anxiety-triggering stimuli, **133**

𝑻

target population   the total group to be studied or described and from whom samples may be drawn, **31**

taste aversion   a type of classical conditioning in which a previously desirable or neutral food comes to be perceived as repugnant because it is associated with negative stimulation, **130**

test-retest reliability   a method for determining the reliability of a test by comparing a test taker's scores on the same test taken on separate occasions, **214**

thalamus   the structure of the brain that relays messages from the sense organs to the cerebral cortex, **61**

theory   a set of assumptions about why something is the way it is and happens the way it does, **6**

thinking   mental activity that involves understanding, manipulating, and communicating information, **178**

tip-of-the-tongue phenomenon   the belief that a piece of information is stored in our memory although we cannot retrieve it easily, **160**

token economy   a controlled environment in which people's desired behaviors are reinforced with tokens that may be exchanged for privileges or other rewards, **450**

trait   an aspect of personality that is considered to be reasonably consistent, **322**

transference   in psychoanalysis, the patient's transfer of emotions associated with other relationships to the therapist, **442**

transformed score   a score that has been changed from a raw score in a systematic way, **212**

triangular model of love   according to Sternberg, the components of love, which include passion, intimacy, and commitment, **474**

truth-wins scheme   in group decision making, an agreement reached when members realize that one option is clearly better than the others, **481**

two-sided argument   a method of discrediting an opponent by presenting his or her argument and then refuting it, **463**

two-thirds–majority scheme   in group decision making, an agreement that is supported by two thirds of the members, **481**

𝒰

unconditional positive regard   a consistent expression of esteem for the basic value of a person, **240**

unconditioned response   in classical conditioning, an unlearned response, **130**

unconditioned stimulus   in classical conditioning, a stimulus that elicits an unlearned, naturally occurring response, **130**

unconscious   according to Freud, a reservoir of mostly unacceptable thoughts, wishes, feelings, and memories of which we are unaware but which influences our behavior, **105**

𝒱

validity   the extent to which a test measures what it is suppose to measure, **214**

validity scale   a group of test items that suggest whether or not the test taker is answering honestly, **345**

variables   factors that are measured or controlled in a scientific study, **41**

vestibular sense   the sense that provides information about the position of the body, **92**

visual acuity   keenness or sharpness of vision, **83**

vocational interest inventories   tests that are used to help people make decisions about career options, **348**

volunteer bias   the concept that people who volunteer to participate in research studies often differ from those who do not volunteer, **33**

INDEX

INDEX

INDEX

For permission to reprint copyrighted material, grateful acknowledgment is made to the following sources:

American Psychiatric Association: "Some Culture-Bound Syndromes," "Categories of Psychological Disorders in the *DSM-IV*," "Two Examples of Somatoform Disorders," "Types of Mood Disorders and Their Characteristics," "Characteristics of Schizophrenia and Other Psychotic Disorders," and "Personality Disorders and Their Characteristics," adapted from the *Diagnostic and Statistical Manual of Mental Disorders, Fourth Edition, Text Revision.* Copyright © 2000 by the American Psychiatric Association.

American Psychological Association: "Ethical Principles of Psychologists and Code of Conduct" from *American Psychologist,* vol. 47, pp. 1597–1611, 1992. Copyright © 1992 by the American Psychological Association. Revised Fall 2002. For current standards, see http://www.apa.org/ethics.

Mathilda B. Canter and the American Psychological Association: From "Ethical Principles" from *Ethics for Psychologists: A Commentary on the APA Ethics Code* by Mathilda B. Canter, Bruce E. Bennett, Stanley E. Jones, and Thomas F. Nagy. Copyright © 1994 by the American Psychological Association.

R.N. Emde and the American Psychological Association: "Cardiac and behavioral inter-relationships in the reactions of infants to strangers" by J. J. Campos, R. N. Emde, T. Gaensbauer, and C. Henderson from *Developmental Psychology II,* 1975, p. 594. Copyright © 1975 by the American Psychological Association.

Jason Aronson Inc.: From *Cognitive Hypnotherapy* by E. Thomas Dowd, Ph.D., ABPP. Copyright © 2000 by Jason Aronson Inc.

Thomas J. Bouchard, Jr. and American Association for the Advancement of Science: From "Sources of Human Psychological Differences: The Minnesota Study of Twins Reared Apart" by Thomas J. Bouchard, Jr., David T. Lykken, Matthew McGue, Nancy L. Segal, and Auke Tellegen from *Science,* vol. 250, October 1990. Copyright © 1990 by American Association for the Advancement of Science.

Brooks/Cole, an imprint of the Wadsworth Group, a division of Thomas Learning, Fax 800 730-2215: "Figure 2.1 (behavior of young baboons and adults)" from *Human Behavior: A Systems Approach,* 1st Edition by V. Ellingstad and N. Heimstra. Copyright © 1974 by Brooks/Cole.

Butterworth-Heinemann Ltd.: From "From Crisis to Coping: Theories and Helping Practices" by J. Gibson-Cline, M. Dikaiou, and M. Haritos-Fatouras with B. Shafrir and G. Ondis from *Adolescence: From Crisis to Coping: A Thirteen Nation Study,* edited by Janice Gibson-Cline. Copyright © 1996 by Butterworth-Heineman Ltd.

Cambridge University Press: Figure 2.1 from *Language, Memory, and Aging,* edited by Leah L. Light and Deborah M. Burke. Copyright © 1988 by Cambridge University Press. From "Love Stories" by Robert J. Sternberg from *Personal Relationships,* vol. 3, 1996. Copyright © 1996 by Cambridge University Press.

Doubleday, a division of Random House, Inc.: From "The Psychotherapists" from *The Story of Psychology* by Morton Hunt. Copyright © 1993 by Morton Hunt.

Lawrence Erlbaum Associates, Inc.: From "Children's Task-Group Communication: Did We Learn It All in Kindergarten?" by Thomas J. Socha and Diana M. Socha from *Group Communication in Context: Studies of Natural Groups,* edited by Lawrence R. Frey. Copyright © 1994 by Lawrence Erlbaum Associates, Inc.

The Free Press, a division of Simon & Schuster, Inc.: From "Adolescence and Stress" by Anne C. Petersen and Ralph Spiga, and "Figure 8-3: Summary relationship between test anxiety and problem-solving performance" from *Handbook of Stress: Theoretical and Clinical Aspects,* edited by Leo Goldberger and Shlomo Breznitz. Copyright © 1982 by The Free Press.

HarperCollins Publishers, Inc.: From *Ordinary Men: Reserve Police Battalion 101 and the Final Solution in Poland* by Christopher R. Browning. Copyright © 1992, 1998 by Christopher R. Browning.

Harvard University Press: poem 632 "The Brain is wider than the sky" from *The Poems of Emily Dickinson,* edited by Thomas H. Johnson. Copyright © 1951, 1955, 1979 by the President and Fellows of Harvard College. Published by The Belknap Press of Harvard University Press, Cambridge, Mass. From "Divergence in Childhood" from *The Two Sexes: Growing Up Apart, Coming Together* by Eleanor E. Maccoby. Copyright © 1998 by The President and Fellows of Harvard College.

Alfred A. Knopf, a division of Random House, Inc.: From *Beyond Freedom and Dignity* by B. F. Skinner. Copyright © 1971 by B. F. Skinner.

Pearson Education, Inc.: From "Self-Actualizing People: A Study of Psychological Health" from *Motivation and Personality* by Abraham H. Maslow. Copyright © 1954 by Harper & Row Publishers, Inc.; copyright © 1970 by Abraham H. Maslow.

Princeton University Press: From "Understanding 'Intelligence'" from *Inequality by Design: Cracking the Bell Curve Myth* by Claude S. Fischer et al. Copyright © 1996 by Princeton University Press.

Psychology Today: From "The Enigmatic Smile" by M. Konner from *Psychology Today,* pp. 42-44, 46, March 1987, as reprinted in *Psychology 88/89: Annual Editions.* Copyright © 1987 by Sussex Publishers, Inc.

Routledge: From Introduction: "Through the Looking Glass" from *Worlds of Sense: Exploring the Senses in History and Across Cultures* by Constance Classen. Copyright © 1993 by Constance Classen.

B. F. Skinner Foundation: From *Walden Two* by B. F. Skinner. Copyright © 1948, 1976 by B. F. Skinner.

Simon & Schuster, Inc.: From "Third Stage: Bargaining" from *On Death and Dying* by Elisabeth Kübler-Ross, M.D. Copyright © 1969 by Elisabeth Kübler-Ross.

University of Nebraska Press: From "The Actualizing Tendency in Relation to 'Motives' and to Consciousness" by Carl R. Rogers. Reprinted from 1963 *Nebraska Symposium on Motivation.* Copyright © 1963 and renewed © 1993 by the University of Nebraska Press.

Sources Cited:

From "Autobiographical Memory" by Martin A. Conway from *Memory,* edited by Elizabeth Ligon Bjork and Robert A. Bjork. Published by Academic Press, Inc., San Diego, CA, 1996.

"Figure 2.1 Physical Duration" from *The Unity of the Senses: Interrelations Among the Modalities* by Lawrence E. Marks. Published by Academic Press, Inc., San Diego, CA, 1978.

From "Plasticity of sensorimotor development in the human infant" from *The Causes of Behavior II,* edited by J. F. Rosenblith and W. Allinsmith. Published by Allyn and Bacon, Inc., Boston, MA, 1966.

From "Pathways to Change and Development: The Life of a School Psychologist" by Stephen Poland from *Career Paths in Psychology: Where Your Degree Can Take You,* edited by Robert J. Sternberg. Published by the American Psychological Association, Washington, D.C., 1997.

From "Problem Solving" by Alan Lesgold from *The Psychology of Human Thought,* edited by Robert J. Sternberg and Edward E. Smith. Published by Cambridge University Press, New York, 1988.

From "Individual Psychology" by Alfred Adler from *Psychologies of 1930,* edited by Carl Murchison. Published by Clark University Press, Worcester, MA, 1930.

From *Psychological Testing in Cultural Contexts* by Theodora M. Abel. Published by College & University Press Services, Inc., New Haven, CT, 1973.

Bar graph (Identical and fraternal twins as best friends) from *Entwined Lives: Twins and What They Tell Us About Human Behavior* by Nancy L. Segal, Ph.D. Published by Dutton, New York, 1999.

From *Lectures on Conditioned Reflexes* by Ivan Pavlov. Published by International Publishers, New York, 1928.

From "Historical Antecedents" from *Disorders of Personality: DSM-IV™ and Beyond* by Theodore Millon with Roger Davis. Published by John Wiley & Sons, Inc., New York, 1996.

PHOTOGRAPHY

All photos, unless otherwise noted, by Sam Dudgeon or Victoria Smith/Holt Rinehart Winston.

Abbreviated as follows: (t) top; (b) bottom; (l) left; (r) right; (c) center, (bckgd) background, (bdr) border.

Author/Copyright Page: Page ii(tl), Ken Karp/HRW.

Table of Contents: Page iv (bl), Cleo/PhotoEdit/PictureQuest; iv (cl), Archive Photos/Getty Images; v (bl), Mehmet Biber/Photo Researchers, Inc.; v (cl), Diane Schuimo/Photographs; vi (bl), H.S. Terrace/Animals Animals/Earth Scenes; vi (cl), Ian Shaw / Tony Stone Images; vi (tl), Mitch Kezar/Tony Stone Images; vii (bl), Richard Hutching/PhotoEdit; vii (c), SuperStock; vii (tl), L. Kesterson/Sygma; viii (bl), SuperStock; viii (cr), John Henley/The Stock Market; viii (tl), Zigy Kalunzy / Tony Stone Images; ix (bl), Elizabeth Zuckerman/ PhotoEdit; ix (cl), Bob Daemmrich/Bob Daemmrich Photography; ix (tl), Giraudon/Art Resource; x (bl), Bruce Ayres/Tony Stone Images; x (cl), Derek Bayes/Tony Stone Images; x (tl), Michael Newman/ PhotoEdit; xi (cl), Hulton Archive/Getty Images; xi (tl), Michael Newman/PhotoEdit; xii(tl), Frank Siteman/Tony Stone Images; xxii(tl), Jim Pickerell/Tony Stone; xxii(bl), Bruce Ayres/Tony Stone; xxiii (tr), ©Art Montes DeOcal/ Getty Images/FPG International.

Skills Handbook: Page S4 (tl), Warren Anatomical Museum, Harvard Medical School; S17 (br), Tom McCarthy/PhotoEdit; S17 (c), David Phillips/HRW.

Unit One: Page 1(c), Cleo/PhotoEdit/PictureQuest.

Chapter One: Page 5(t), Bob Daemmrich/Bob Daemmrich Photography; 6(b), Yoav Levy/PhotoTake; 7 (c), Ghislain & Marie David de Lossy/Getty Images/The Image Bank; 9(t), Paul Meredeth/Tony Stone Images; 11(t), Bob Daemmrich/Bob Daemmrich Photography; 12(b), Archive Photos; 13(t), Corbis- The Bettmann Archive; 13(b), Corbis—The Bettmann Archive; 14(c), Archive Photos; 15(c), AP/Wide World Photos; 16(t), Corbis-The Bettmann Archive; 16(b), L.L.T. Rhodes/Animals Animals/Earth Scenes; 17(b), NY Public Library Prints Division; 19(t), Yoav Levy/PhotoTake; 21(t), Bob Daemmrich/Bob Daemmrich Photography; **Chapter Two:** Page 28(t), SuperStock; 30(b), Jeff Greeenberg/Photo Edit; 32(c), Mark Scott/FPG International; 35(t), Jim Pickerell/Tony Stone Images; 37(t), David Macdonald/Animals Animals/Earth Scenes; 39(bckgd),Russell Dian/ HRW; 42(b), Michael Newman/PhotoEdit; 47(t), Michael Schwarz/The Image Works;

Unit Two: Page 51(bl), Chris Cheadle/Tony Stone Images;

Chapter Three: Page 56(t), Brad Mangin/Duomo; 56(b), SuperStock; 58(t), Richard Hutchings/PhotoEdit; 64(tl), Roon Chapple/FPG International; 64(tr), SuperStock; 65(c), Warren Anatomical Museum, Harvard Medical School; 66(bl), Jim Pickerell/Tony Stone Images; 66(br), Charles Thatcher/Tony Stone Images; 67(t), Jan Halaska/Tony Stone Images; 69(t), Charles Thatcher/Tony Stone Images; 70(b), Mugshots/The Stock Market; 72(t), Cosmo Condina/Tony Stone Images; **Chapter Four:** Page 80(t), Peter A. Simon/PhotoTake; 82 (br), © Darren Whiteside/ Reuters/Corbis; 85(t), Diane Schuimo/Fundamental Photographs; 87(b), Kurt Viavant/Sipa Press; 88(t), Bob Daemmrich/Bob Daemmrich Photography; 92(t), William R. Sallaz/Duomo; 95(t), Kim Taylor/Bruce Coleman, Inc.; **Chapter Five:** Page 105(t), Bob Daemmrich/The Image Works; 107(t), Richard Haynes/ HRW; 109(t), Banque d'Images, ADAGP/Art Resource, NY, © ARS, NY, *Les Valeurs Personnelles,* oil on canvas; 111(t), Jane Meddaugh/David Frazier Photolibrary; 112(b), Bill Wassman/The Stock Market; 115(t), The Bettmann Archive; 117(t), Culver Pictures, Inc.; 119(c), Mehmet Biber/Photo Researchers, Inc.; 120 (tl), courtesy of National Clearinghouse for Alcohol and Drug Information; 121(t), M. Siluk/The Image Works;

Unit Three: Page 125(br), Robert A. Propper/Leo de Wys, Inc.;

Chapter Six: Page 128(b), ©1992 Molkenthin/The Stock Marke; 131(b), Ed Degginger/Animals Animals/Earth Scenes; 133(t), James Hackett/Leo de Wys, Inc.; 134(c), Tom McCarthy/The Stock Market; 139 (br), Will Hart/PhotoEdit; 140(bc), © F64/Getty Images; 141(t), SuperStock; 143 (c), Michael L. Abramson/TimePix; 144(t), Mitch Kezar/Tony Stone Images, Inc.; 145(b), Will & Deni McIntyre/Photo Researchers, Inc.; 146(b), Dion Ogust/The Image Works; 149(t), Jose L. Pelaez/The Stock Market; 149(t), Jose L. Pelaez/The Stock Market; **Chapter Seven:** Page 155 (tr), Thomas E. Franklin/The Record (Bergen County, NJ)/ CORBIS/ SABA; 156(t), Ian Shaw/Tony Stone Images; 158(t), H. Kaiser/Leo de Wys, Inc.; 161(b), Micahel Krasowitz/FPG International; 165(c), John Neubauer/PhotoEdit; **Chapter Eight:** Page 178(t), Copyright © 1996 by the American Psychological Association. Reprinted with permission.; 179(t), Charles Gupton/Tony Stone Images; 182(b), Amy Etra/PhotoEdit; 183(t), Bob Daemmrich/The Image Works; 185(tl), SuperStock; 185(tc), SuperStock; 185(tr), SuperStock; 188(b), Bruce Ayres/Tony Stone Images; 192(b), SuperStock; 193 (tr), Chris Trotman/ Duomo/CORBIS; 194(b), Jon Riley/Tony Stone Images; 196(b), Joe Carini/The Image Works; 197(b), Universal Press; 198(b), Chip Henderson/Tony Stone Images; 199(b), Craig Newbauer/Peter Arnold; 200(c), H.S. Terrace/Animals Animals/Earth Scenes; 201 (bl), Michael Newman/PhotoEdit; **Chapter Nine:** Page 206(br), © John Nordell/The Christian Science Monitor via Getty Images; 207(t), Bob Daemmrich/Bob Daemmrich Photography; 207(b), AP/Wide World Photos; 208(tr), © Miep van Damm/Masterfile; 209(c), L. Kesterson/Sygma; 210(t), David Frazier/David R. Frazier Photolibrary; 212(t), © 100 Images Ltd; 216(t), Bob Daemmrich/Bob Daemmrich Photography; 216(b), Dick Luria/FPG International; 217(c), Corbis-The Bettmann Archive; 218(t), Scala/Art Resource, NY; 219(t), David Young Wolff/Tony Stone Images; 220(b), N. Rowan/The Image Works; 221(t), Bob Daemmrich/Bob Daemmrich Photography;

Unit Four: Page 225(b), Dan Bosler/Tony Stone Images;

Chapter Ten: Page 228(b), SuperStock; 230(b), Laura Dwight/Peter Arnold, Inc.; 232(t), Super Stock; 233(t), Mark Richards/PhotoEdit; 234(b), Tim Brown/Tony Stone Images; 235(t), Martin Rogers/Tony Stone Images; 235(b), Nina Leen, Life Magazine © Time, Inc.; 238(br), © Zave Smith/CORBIS; 240(t), Ariel Skelley/The Stock Market; 241(c), Archive PhotosLine: Archive Photos/A.F.P.; 242(t), Michael Newman/ PhotoEdit; 245(tc), © Gideon Mendel/CORBIS; **Chapter Eleven:** Page 254(t), Richard Hutchings/ PhotoEdit; 255(c), Mark Richards/PhotoEdit; 258(t), © Laura Dwight/PhotoEdit; 259(t), © Bob Daemmrich/Bob Daemmrich Photography; 260(b), © Bob Daemmrich/Tony Stone Images; 264(t), © Ellen Ozier/Reuters/ Corbis; 266(t), © Bob Daemmrich/Bob Daemmrich Photography; 267(t), © Tom McCarthy/PhotoEdit; 268(t), © Rhoda Sidney/ PhotoEdit; 269(t), © Michael Newman/PhotoEdit; **Chapter Twelve:** Page 275(t), SuperStock; 276(t), Paul Rees/Tony Stone Images; 278(t), M. Greenlar/The Image Works; 279(b), Michael Newman/ PhotoEdit; 281(t), SuperStock; 282(t), United Media; 282(b), Michael Newman/PhotoEdit; 284(bckgd), HRW; 284 (bl), © Walter Hodges/Getty Images/Stone; 285(t), Zigy Kaluzny/ Tony Stone Images; 286 (tl), Walter Hodges/CORBIS; 288(t), SuperStock; 290(t), Tom McCarthy/Photo Edit; 292(t), SuperStock; 293(t), Leslye Borden/PhotoEdit;

Unit Five: Page 297(b), Super Stock;

Chapter Thirteen: Page 298(r) HRW/Michelle Bridwell; 301(t), SuperStock; 303(t), Eric R. Berndt/Unicorn Stock Photos; 304(t), Picture taken by J.A.F. Stevenson, a collaborator on the original study, but first published by Neal E. Miller in an article summarizing a number of studies from his laboratory.; 306(t), © Mark Richards/CORBIS; 307(b), Super Stock; 308(tl), Harlow Primate Laboratory, University of Wisconsin (Madison); 308(tr), James McLoughlin/FPG; 309(b), John Henley/The Stock Market; 311(b), Bob Daemmrich/Bob Daemmrich Photography; 314(t), SuperStock; 315(bl), M. Eastcott/The Image Works; 315(br), Michael Goldman/FPG; 315(bcl), David Frazier/David Frazier Photolibrary; 315(bcr), Comstock; **Chapter Fourteen:** Page 25(t),Reuters/Corbis-Bettmann; 327(b), Lawrence Migdale/Tony Stone Images; 328(br), © Ralph Barrera/The Austin American-Statesman; 329(t), Giraudon/Art Resource, NY; 330(tl), John Neubauer/PhotoEdit; 330(tr), Ben Simmons/The Stock Market; 334(t), SuperStock; 335(b), Rhoda Sidney/The Image Works; 337(b), Charles Gupton/ The Stock Market; **Chapter Fifteen:** Page 345(t), Bonnie Kamin/ PhotoEdit; 346(c), Super Stock; 347(t), Martha M Bride/Unicorn Stock Photos; 348(t), Laura Elliott/Comstock; 349(cl), SuperStock; 349(cr), Thomas Ives/The Stock Market; 349(bl), Bob Daemmrich/ Bob Daemmrich Photography; 349(br), Ted Horowitz/The Stock Market; 350(t), SuperStock; 352(b), Bob Daemmrich/Bob Daemmrich Photography; 355(t), Robert Brenner/PhotoEdit; 357(t), Comstock; 358(b), Bob Daemmrich/Bob Daemmrich Photography; 359(t), SuperStock; **Chapter Sixteen:** Page 365(tl), SuperStock; 365(tc), SuperStock; 365(tr), Tony Freeman/PhotoEdit; 366(b), Tony Freeman/PhotoEdit; 368(t), Tony Freeman/PhotoEdit; 370(tl), John Giffin/Image Works; 370(tcl), Fujifotos/The Image Works; 370/371(tcr), Super Stock; 371(tr), SuperStock; 373(br), © PictureQuest; 374(t), Tony Freeman/Photo Edit; 376(b), Elizabeth Zuckerman/PhotoEdit; 378(t), SuperStock; 378(b), D. Young-Wolff/Photo Edit; 379(t), Margret Mead Papers, Manuscript Divion, Library of Congress;

Unit Six: Page 383(br), Super Stock;

Chapter Seventeen: Page 387(b), Joes Pelaez/The Stock Market; 388(t), Michael Newman/PhotoEdit; 392(t), Jose L. Pelaez/The Stock Market; 392(b), The Stock Market; 393(t), Bob Daemmrich; 394(t), David Young-Wolff/PhotoEdit; 395(t), SuperStock; 397(t), Tony Freeman/PhotoEdit; 398(b), SuperStock; 400(c), Christian Michaels/ FPG; 403(bl), Michael Newman/PhotoEdit/PhotoEdit; 405(t), Michael Newman/PhotoEdit; **Chapter Eighteen:** Page 410(t), Art Montes DeOcal/FPG; 412(c), UPI/Corbis-Bettmann; 416(t), Luis Rosendo/FPG; 417(b), Bob Dammrich/Image Works; 418 (tc), AP/ Wide World Photos; 426(b), Derek Bayes/Tony Stone; 427 (tr), Benelux Press/Getty Images/FPG International; 428(t), Monkmeyer/ Grunnitus; 431(t), Ron Chapple/FPG; **Chapter Nineteen:** Page 436(t), Zigy Kaluzny/Tony Stone; 439(t), David Harry Stewart/Tony Stone; 440(t), F. Pedrick/The Image Works; 442(t), Bruce Ayres/Tony Stone; 443(c), © Brand X/Imagestate; 445(c) HRW/Michelle Bridwell; 448(t), Peter Steiner/The Stock Market; 449(t), Michael Newman/Photo Edit; 449(c), Michael Newman/Photo Edit; 449(b), Michael New man/Photo Edit; 453(t), Will & Deni McIntyre/Tony Stone;

Unit Seven: Page 457(br), composite, David Young-Wolff/ Photo Edit, © 1996 Daivd Eisenberg/Development Center for Appropriate Technology/Habitat for Humanity; **Chapter Twenty:** Page 460(b), Myrleen Ferguson/Photo Edit; 461(t), Michael Newman/Photo Edit; 462(b), Paul Conklin/Photo Edit; 463(b), Stock Market; 463 (bl), Phil Sandlin/AP/Wide World Photos; 464(t), Courtesy American Lung Association; 465(t), © AP Photo/Kenneth Lambert; 466(b), Michael Newman/Photo Edit; 467(c), Archive Photos; 473(bl), Art Wolfe/Tony Stone; 473(br), Bob Daemmrich/ HRW; 473(bcl), Bill Wassman/The Stock Market; 473(bcr), Zviki-Eshet/The Stock Market; 474(t), Tony Freeman/Photo Edit; **Chapter Twenty-One:** Page 480(t),Chuck Savage/The Stock Market; 483(c), Archive Photos; 485(tl), Eastcott/The Image Bank; 485(tc), Stock Market ©1994 Latin Stock/Carlos Goldin/Stock Market; 485(tr), David Young Wolff/Tony Stone Images; 487(t), Anthony Edgeworth/Stock Market; 488(t)(c)(b), From the film OBEDIENCE, © 1965 by Stanley Milgram, and distributed by PennState Media Sales. Permission granted by Alexandra Milgram; 489(b), R Hutchings/Photo Edit; 490(b), Leanna Rathkelly/Tony Stone Images; 491(t), Glyn Kirk/Tony Stone; 494(t), Frank Siteman/Tony Stone; 495(b), Michael Newman/Photo Edit;

Careers: Page R3(t), SuperStock; R4(b), Michael Newman/Photo Edit; R5(b), Martha M. Bride/Unicorn Stock Photos; R6(t), Comstock; R7(t), Ariel Skelley/The Stock Market; R7(b), Glyn Kirk/ Tony Stone; R8(t), Michael Schwarz/The Image Works; R9(b), SuperStock

ACKNOWLEDGMENTS